July 25, 1989

For Tracy Gary —

as woman, in Emma Goldman's spirit, with a vision, and tenacity to find alternative ways to find alternative ways, and in the system, strengthening women, and in trying to create a more equitable world.

Enjoy the book, and Emma's sad, but transcendent story of trying to match her intimate life with her social vision.

And thank you for extending yourself to the Emma Goldman Papers —

with admiration for your work, and respect,

Candace Falk

At the Woman's Building
San Francisco.

77

LOVE, ANARCHY, AND
EMMA GOLDMAN

LOVE, ANARCHY, AND
EMMA
GOLDMAN

Candace Falk

HOLT, RINEHART AND WINSTON
NEW YORK

Published by Holt, Rinehart and Winston,
383 Madison Avenue, New York, New York 10017.
Published simultaneously in Canada by Holt, Rinehart and
Winston of Canada, Limited.

Library of Congress Cataloging in Publication Data
Falk, Candace.
Love, anarchy, and Emma Goldman.
Bibliography: p.
Includes index.
1. Goldman, Emma, 1869—1940.   2. Anarchism and
anarchists—United States—Biography.   3. Feminists—
United States—Biography.   4. Women and socialism—
United States—Biography.   5. Free love—Biography.
I. Title.
HX843.G6F34 1984   335'.83'0924 [B]   83-18405
ISBN 0-03-043626-5

First Edition

Design by Lucy Albanese
Printed in the United States of America
10 9 8 7 6 5 4 3 2 1

ISBN 0-03-043626-5

Grateful acknowledgment is made to the following: the University of Illinois at Chicago Library, Manuscript Collection, for permission to quote extensively from the Ben Lewis Reitman Papers; the Department of Rare Books and Special Collections, the University of Michigan, Ann Arbor, for permission to quote from Emma Goldman letters in the Labadie Collection; Boston University Libraries, Special Collections, for permission to quote from correspondence with Almeda Sperry and Ben Lewis Reitman; the Schlesinger Library, Radcliffe College, for permission to quote from letters in the Emma Goldman collection; the Tamiment Library at New York University for permission to quote from their Emma Goldman Papers; the New York Public Library for permission to quote from the Emma Goldman Papers, the Rose Pesotta Papers and the Emma Goldman Scrapbook in the Rare Books and Manuscripts Division, New York Public Library, Astor, Lenox, and Tilden Foundations; Yale University Library for permission to quote from the Harry Weinberger Papers; the Beinecke Rare Book and Manuscript Library, Yale University, for permission to quote from the Hutchins Hapgood Papers; the University of California, Berkeley, Bancroft Library, for permission to quote from a letter from Emma Goldman to Fremont Older; the Sophia Smith Collection, Smith College, for permission to quote from the Henriette Posner Collection and from the Margaret Sanger Collection; The State Historical Society of Wisconsin for permission to quote from the Theodore Herfurth Collection and the Gwyneth K. Roe collection; and the International Institute for Social History in Amsterdam for permission to quote from their extensive collection of Emma Goldman material.

TO SARAH T. CROME, WHOSE ENERGY, INTELLIGENCE, AND HARD WORK FACILITATED THE COMPLETION OF LOVE, ANARCHY, AND EMMA GOLDMAN, *AND IN WHOSE LIFELONG COMMITMENT TO MAKING THE WORLD MORE JUST AND SANE EMMA GOLDMAN'S SPIRIT LIVES ON.*

The real revolutionist—the dreamer, the creative artist, the iconoclast in whatever line—is fated to be
misunderstood, not only by his own kin, but often by
his own comrades. That is the doom of all great spirits:
they are detached from their environment. Theirs is a
lonely life—the life of the transition stage, the hardest
and the most difficult period for the individual as well
as for a people.

—EMMA GOLDMAN,
"Lonely Lives—Hauptmann,"
The Social Significance of the
Modern Drama

CONTENTS

CONTENTS

Photograph sections follow pages 204 and 404.

PREFACE

It all began with my dog, Emma, a beautiful combination Irish setter and golden retriever, with an alternately wild and loving disposition. In 1971, when I rescued Emma from a dog pound on the East Side of Manhattan, almost everyone in the new women's movement was naming things after Emma Goldman—health collectives, dogs, even babies. T-shirts bore her name and face, and paraphrased her: "If I can't dance, it's not my revolution." At a time when the resurgent feminist movement was beginning to assert women's right to untraditional career and family choices, we looked for models, for women who dared to defy convention. Emma Goldman's autobiography became required reading. In this moving account by a woman whose concerns seemed remarkably contemporary, Emma articulated a new vision of the organization of personal life at a time when women were just beginning to see the widespread possibilities of developing skills and claiming a voice in the public sphere, and of breaking out of more traditional domestic roles. *Living My Life* countered the stereotypes of political activists as drab automatons, for in the book Emma told how she had refused to sacrifice her private life to the demands of her public career. Emma became a symbol of courage and passion; her example evoked feelings of hope and expectation in people taking their first steps into political activism.

In the summer of 1975, Lowell, my husband-to-be, and "Red Emma" accompanied me on a drive back to California after a turbulent session of teaching at Sagaris, a short-lived feminist institute in Vermont. We stopped in the Hyde Park area of Chicago, a place familiar from my time at the university. Lowell, Emma, and I walked around the neighborhood, dropping by a guitar shop where an old friend, John Bowen, worked, repairing instruments. We admonished Emma to stay outside, but in a few minutes, true to her nature, she followed us in.

Instead of being annoyed, my friend at the guitar shop knelt to pet her. "What a great dog," he said. "What's her name?" "Emma," I replied, "Red Emma Goldman." He scratched his own head, while scratching Emma's. In a slow voice he said, "Emma Goldman . . . I think I saw some letters of hers in the back room of the shop about five years ago. I remember thinking that they must be worth saving, so I put them on a top shelf so they wouldn't get flooded out when the winter snow and rain leak in."

He disappeared into the storeroom of the shop while Lowell, Emma, and I went next door to get some ice cream. After a ten-minute search, he came running after us, shouting, "I found them!" Sure enough, there was an old shoebox holding hundreds of yellowed letters. Although the return address on the envelopes indicated that they were from "E Goldman," all the letters were signed "Mommy." As we read through them, deciphering her huge scrawl, we saw that these were passionate love letters to Ben Reitman, whom I knew to have been her lover and manager from 1908 to 1917. Although the spirit of the letters reflected the passionate Emma I had imagined, there was also a tone of depression, even of resignation, that I had never associated with this freedom fighter. My friend offered to part with the letters long enough for us to photocopy them. Delighted, we went to the university, stacked up our nickels at an old coin-operated machine, and carefully placed each page on the screen. Near the end of the pile, we came across a letter to Ben written just before Emma began her autobiography. Apparently, he had loaned her these letters to refresh her memory about their relationship. Emma had planned to hire a secretary to transcribe them, but she could not bring herself to let anyone else see them. "It is like tearing off my clothes to let them see the mad outpouring of my tortured spirit, the frantic struggle for my love, the all absorbing devotion each letter breathes, I can't do it!"

We stopped copying the letters, and resolved to keep Emma's secret. Back in California, where I was doing doctoral work at the University of California at Santa Cruz, I put the photocopies on my shelf, to remain for a year. The originals were returned to their shelf in the guitar shop.

The focus of my academic work had been political theory, in particular the works of the new feminist writers as they departed from more traditional political theories. Emma Goldman may have been part of the inspiration for my work, but she was by no means the center of it. I did not want to expose Emma to public scrutiny, but I continued to wonder how the issues raised in her private letters related to her public life. I began to read more about her, partly in an effort to reconcile my prior image with the aspect of her private life that had been revealed to me.

In 1976, a year after I found the letters, a call came from the owner of the guitar shop. He had found the letters, it turned out, in a trunk while cleaning the attic of a neighbor's house, which had at one time belonged to Ben Reitman. A library was interested in buying the letters, but when the guitar-shop owner asked me to outbid, I declined, convinced by the manuscript archivist that the letters ought to be with Emma's other papers—in a library archive, preserved for history. However, once I was informed by the librarian that other unpublished letters of the same genre were public—not hidden away, as Emma had wanted them to be during her lifetime—I began to feel bolder about my interest in piecing together the history of her romance. I was also confident that my respect for Emma Goldman would enable me to tell the story of her private life in a sensitive manner that might cast new light on her inspiring but elusive political vision.

Finding the letters and trying to understand what they meant in the context of Emma Goldman's life changed the course of my own life. With the encouragement of one of my professors, Herbert Marcuse, I undertook what became a consuming quest to reconcile my prior image of the public Emma Goldman with this new, private person.

No single source could answer my questions about Emma. There was a path-breaking biography by Richard Drinnon, *Rebel in Paradise,* but it did not delve deeply into the relationship between Emma and Ben. For several years, like a detective, I went from library to library, across the United States to Washington, New York, Chicago, Boston, then on to Amsterdam, retracing Emma's steps through thousands of her letters, articles she had written, and newspaper accounts of her activities.

The simple act of writing a letter had always been Emma's way to ground her experience, mute her sense of isolation, provide herself with an opportunity to articulate the ideals that had won her public acclaim and to transpose those ideals into her personal life. A close friend, the anarchist historian Max Nettlau, once remarked to Emma: "In letters happily, though tip top up to date otherwise, you are eighteenth century, doing honour to the good old art of letter writing, which the wire and telephone have strangled, and this is a good thing, as a thoughtful way of communication by letters is an intellectual act of value of its own, which rapid talk cannot replace." And so Emma often wrote ten letters in a day; what has been preserved of her correspondence is scattered in libraries and personal collections all over the world.

Gradually, as I traveled from archive to archive, I began to discern the patterns in Emma's life organized around the issues of love and anarchy. The intense emotion and bravado of both her personal and her public life made the task of searching out and reading thousands of letters compelling. Although my search was thorough, no doubt there are other letters, other lovers yet to be discovered.

I even persuaded my husband to visit old anarchist friends of Emma Goldman's, in exile in Cuernavaca, on our honeymoon in 1977. (They insisted that we were still "companions," no matter how the state now saw us.) At first Mollie Steimer and Senya Fleshine flinched at the thought of exposing the intimate part of Emma's life. They were horrified that I would name a dog Emma—"Red Emma," no less, when the anarchist color was black! They interrogated me to determine my sincerity, and my politics. Mollie Steimer summed up her thoughts in a letter to me:

Now, to the point. When you and your companion spoke about your plan to sort of analyze EG's relations with Ben Reitman in book form, I inwardly resented this idea. After all, love life—sex relations between human beings is a very PERSONAL EXPERI-ENCE! None of us liked Ben and [we] wondered "how can Emma care for him?" But he was a handsome devil and was successful with women—EG knew all his faults yet loved him very much.

I feared that the disclosure of her letters to BR will bring about futile discussions—or, rather, adverse reactions on the part of the reader. But, to judge from your letter, you are a sincere, interesting and sympathetic woman who (I hope) will do justice to Emma. Besides, as we both know, she DID DISENTANGLE herself from Ben in spite of all her suffering!

Here, she proved once again her strength of character that she was, is and always will be: THE GREAT EXAMPLE! She loved deeply, passionately, but would not sacrifice her dignity. Another thing. Emma never asked for equal rights. She ACTED AS AN EQUAL. She had convictions and stood by them even at the loss of her personal happiness.

When I had passed the test, Mollie admitted to me that she and Senya had counseled Emma not to use her letters to Ben or dwell on the torment of her years with him in her autobiography, believing that it would divert attention from the anarchist cause. Evidently, after the autobiography was published, Mollie and Emma still fought over Mollie's criticism that Emma paid too much attention to her romances and personal feelings, and not enough to anarchism.

The dozens of quotes that I had brought to Mollie, in which Emma referred to the inevitability of her letters' being published posthumously, may have helped convince her that the letters should be made public. In fact, after Emma's death, her lawyer, Harry Weinberger, had begun to "look for a Ph.D. student" to write a biography of the relationship between Emma and Ben. Emma was conscious of herself as a historical figure, even in her most intimate correspondence. She, herself, had dated every letter and even placed some of the most personal ones in the International Institute for Social History in Amsterdam.

The research and writing of the book took six years. When I was almost finished, I found myself unable to bear the thought of writing the end of Emma's life. From all evidence, her despair and bitterness had grown with age, and I myself felt increasingly depressed. Then one Sunday morning the telephone rang. A man introduced himself as Arthur Bortolotti. "I was a friend of Emma Goldman's. Just before she died she saved my life. I heard that you were working on a project to collect and order her papers so that they will be available to the public for history. I want to help you out."

The National Historical Publications and Records Commission of the National Archives in Washington had heard about my collection of Goldman documents and had asked me to edit the Emma Goldman Papers as part of what I like to think of as their "Founding Mothers' Program," adding their own government documents. Since collecting her papers had become my job in writing the book, I welcomed the National Archive's help in that search. But this man's telephone call breathed fresh life into the task of organizing Emma's literary legacy and helped me finish my book. The good that Emma Goldman had done survived her. Arthur Bortolotti's loyalty to Emma, forty-two years after her death, as well as the dozens of accounts of her inspirational effect on others, is testimony enough to her lasting greatness.

AUTHOR'S NOTE

To facilitate the reading of Emma Goldman and Ben Reitman's letters, I have taken the liberty of spelling out abbreviations and correcting their erratic spelling and grammatical idiosyncrasies, the results of rudimentary education in Ben's case and Emma's self-taught and floridly romantic written English.

SOMETHING TO HIDE

In 1927, at the age of fifty-eight, Emma Goldman began to write the story of her life. This was eight years after her deportation from the United States. For two decades before her banishment, Emma Goldman had been known as the "Anarchist Queen." Thousands of people flocked to hear her fiery speeches, to share her vision of what life could be if only we lived out the best of our humanity. She had advocated free love at a time when conventional marriage was the only norm and birth control when even literature on the subject was banned. She had fought for free speech when that right was often violated in practice and had agitated for the eight-hour workday when twelve hours was standard.

Emma defined anarchism as "the philosophy of a new social order based on liberty unrestricted by man-made law; the theory that all forms of government rest on violence, and are therefore wrong and harmful, as well as unnecessary." In her autobiography she wrote, "I want freedom, the right to self-expression, everybody's right to beautiful, radiant things." All her life Emma struggled to change the social order. In 1917, when she voiced her position against involuntary conscription, she lost her freedom to live in America, her chosen home. She spent eighteen months in prison for her beliefs, her citizenship was revoked, and she, along with hundreds of others, was deported to the Soviet Union. Ironically, this return to her birthplace, and to the land of a young revolution, did not feel like a homecoming. After two years there, Emma spoke out, denouncing the denial of freedom that had succeeded the heroic idealism of the Russian Revolution. Exiled, wandering from country to country, Emma was now condemned by both the left and the right, and barred from engaging in political activity. Wherever she went, Emma felt constrained and often depressed.

By 1927, she felt that her usefulness was at an end. Like "the real revolutionist—the dreamer, the artist, the iconoclast" she had described in her criticism of Gerhart Hauptmann's play *Lonely Lives*, Emma began to feel ever more detached from her environment. She had provided the inspiration for many others to reject a cruel and unjust world. She had insisted that the ability to imagine a life of freedom was a necessary step toward a new order. But she herself was preoccupied with memories and doubts about whether her place in history was secure, uncertain that her vision would ever become a reality. She began to retreat emotionally from the frustrations of her life as an exile into the glories of her past in America.

In planning her book, she relied on her thousands of letters to chart her turbulent political career. She had always found letters easier to write than books or lectures, particularly because "I know they will not be published while I am alive." For this woman who lived alone most of her life, letters meant camaraderie at any time of the day or night. In her correspondence, Emma had written as frankly about her sexual feelings as she had about her political leanings. She gradually retrieved more of her past, as friends agreed to part, sometimes reluctantly, with the letters she had sent them. She sat in her small Toronto apartment, transported back into her own past. She planned to take her discovered treasures with her to "Bon Esprit," the cottage in St.-Tropez where she would actually write her memoirs.

Emma had resolved that hers would not be a conventional auto-biography: she would not present the public figure without giving an account of her struggle to realize her political ideals in her personal life. But she expressed ambivalence about where to put the emphasis in her work. She felt that she was "woven of many skeins, conflicting in shade and texture," and that to the end of her days she would "be torn between the yearning for a personal life and the need of giving all to [her] ideal."

She wrote to her most constant friend, Alexander Berkman:

> I am writing about the life of Emma Goldman, the public person, not the private individual. I naturally want to let people see what one can do if imbued with an ideal, what one can endure and how one can overcome all difficulties and suffering in life. Will I be able to do that and yet give also the other side, the woman, the personality in quest for the unattainable in a personal sense? That's going to be the rub. But I mean to do it. . . .

When this letter was written, Emma was having an affair with a married man. And she was immersed in reading the letters she had written to the man who had occupied a central role in her public and intimate life during her most productive political years. Those ten stormy years with Ben Reitman, from 1908 to 1917, had been years of raw emotion, in which Emma's most exalted expectations of love were shattered.

The flamboyant, strikingly handsome Reitman had various personas throughout his life as the "King of the Hobos," a crusader for the unemployed, a gynecologist, a sociologist, and a public-relations agent. He had entered Emma Goldman's life in 1908 "with the sweep of a cyclone, only to take [himself] out with the same force." Now, years after their estrangement, he complied with Emma's request to return the hundreds of love letters she had written to him. With the letters came Ben's note: "When you read these over, you will be surprised once you loved me." But for Emma, the letters recalled more than love. Reading them summoned the painful insecurity and despair that had plagued her during most of their relationship. She concluded that it was a part of her past she could not reveal, because she felt too exposed and vulnerable to public censure. In fact, she never managed to write the complete story of that relationship in her autobiography.

Years before, at the height of her passion for Ben, Emma had candidly expressed the ultimate reason for her reluctance to share with the world the story of her relationship with Reitman. "If ever our correspondence should be published, the world would stand aghast that I, Emma Goldman, the strong revolutionist, the daredevil, the one who has defied laws and convention, should have been as helpless as a shipwrecked crew on a foaming ocean."

She understood but felt helpless to resolve the terrible conflict between her experience of constant turmoil and her expectation that this idealized relationship should provide her with a feeling of peace. She feared the overwhelming aspects of her own newly unleashed passion even as she became aware of its pleasure. And she feared the consequences of her dependence on Ben, though she desperately wanted him. Then, when Emma raged with fury at Ben's inconstant behavior, she wished that by an act of will she could reject the darker parts of reality. In one tormented period, Emma wrote to Ben: "I'd rather do without reality if my ideal is forever to be abused, insulted, spat upon, dragged through the mud." Is it any wonder that Emma chose to minimize the significance of her relationship to Ben in a book that attempted to hold up her own life as an inspiring testimonial to the force of her ideal?

It was painful for her to look back at the letters and realize that, within a month of meeting Ben, she had felt so completely overwhelmed by the power of her attraction to him that she had written: "Do you know, lover mine, that it is the first time in my life that love stands over me, like a mighty spectre, and that it has both life and death for me?" Her new lover had awakened in her a sexual vitality that shook her rational sense of herself. Six months into their relationship, Emma confessed in a letter the depth of his impact on her:

> You have opened up the prison gates of my womanhood. And all the passion that was unsatisfied in me for so many years, leaped into a wild reckless storm boundless as the sea? . . . can you then imagine that I could stay away from you? What is love, family ties, the power of association to the wanderer in the desert. His mind is bent on the spring that will quench his thirst. . . . Yet, if I were asked to choose between a world of understanding and the spring that fills my body with fire, I should have to choose the spring. It is life, sunshine, music, untold ecstasy. The Spring, oh ye Gods, that have tortured my body all these years, I will give you my soul only

let me drink, drink from the Spring of my master lover. . . . There. You have the confession of a starved tortured being, my Ben.

It was not just that Ben's sexual attraction threatened to overpower the strong, independent, rational woman, the feared and respected leader that the public Emma Goldman had become; to make matters worse, Ben continued throughout his relationship with Emma to live up to his reputation as a "lady's man." Although Emma was an outspoken advocate of free love and an opponent of marriage, she had to admit that Ben's frequent escapades "tear at my very vitals, . . . turn me into something foreign to myself." Once, after discovering that Ben had gone almost immediately from her to another woman, she wrote:

All is blank before me, all is dark and dreary, nothing is left behind. Oh, Ben, Ben! Fate is hard and cruel—38½ years I walked through life with a burning and insatiable longing in my heart for the unknown. I could reason then, oh so clearly on all human subjects, on every secret string of the human heart. The miracle came, in a most radiant glorious color. It enveloped me, took possession of me, crept into my soul and body and robbed me of all reason. It's but 24 hours ago, the miracle lifted me to a dazzling light, with the world all puny and insignificant at my feet. Now all is dark, I cannot see, nothing is left of life. Oh, Ben, Ben, Ben! I am so chilled and pained, I am struggling the bitterest struggle of my life and if I succeed, I fear I shall never be able to see you again. Yet, if I fail, I shall stand condemned before the bar of my own reason—

Grasping for some way to contain her jealous rage, Emma cast herself in the role of the abused but forgiving mother, and Ben as the wayward son. This revealing metaphor became a leitmotif of their relationship.

Almost in the same breath, Emma could forget her pain and disappointment to thank Ben effusively for his love: "Ben dear, I shall always carry it with me and when the moment comes that I shall have to forfeit my life for my ideas, . . . [these last] moments will illuminate my soul and I shall feel, I have not lived in vain, no, I have not lived in vain!"

Emma consoled herself with the knowledge that she was not the only woman with political ideas to have experienced deep ambivalence about the costs of personal involvement with a man. Nor was she the only such woman to have felt powerless and submissive when everything she stood for indicated she should feel otherwise. Emma knew of the anguish Mary Wollstonecraft, the author of the pathbreaking work *A Vindication of the Rights of Women*, experienced in her relationship with the unfaithful Gilbert Imlay. In 1911, while their relationship was still young, Emma wrote to Ben: "Mary Wollstonecraft, the most daring woman of her time, freest and boldest exponent of liberty, of free love, the slave of her passion for Imlay. How could anyone forgive such weakness? Thus I reasoned many years ago. Today? Emma Goldman, the Wollstonecraft of the 20th century, even like her great sister is weak and dependent, clinging to the man, no matter how worthless and faithless he is. What an irony of fate."

In addition to any embarrassment she may have felt at the disparity between her life and her ideals, there were other considerations that counseled against full disclosure. Not the least of these was her hope that the publication of *Living My Life*, despite its message of unrelenting and unrepentant opposition to the existing order in the United States, might somehow help her to regain her citizenship. Feverishly at work in Toronto, just miles across the unyielding border, she was driven by a desire to secure her place in history, but also by memories that left her longing "for America like a woman for a man." Even more than her advocacy of the overthrow of the state, frank discussion of her unconventional sexual life might bar her return forever.

She also feared that a book written without any self-censorship might not be accepted for publication, or, perhaps worse, would be viewed as sensational, obscuring everything that she had to say. She wrote to her friend Hutchins Hapgood

About my proposed memoirs. You say it could be a great work if it were "absolutely truthful." Who do you think would publish an absolutely truthful work? I do not think there is any publisher who would or could undertake it—possibly in France, but certainly not in the United States. And as I would want my memoirs to reach a large public it will probably not be possible to write as frankly as I would like to about some of my intimate experiences, but I do want to make it as frank as I can without killing the chances of ever having it see the light of day. The fact is I am not sure that even at best my memoirs will be accepted for publication. I certainly don't intend to make it a sensational sex story. I want the events of my life to stand out in bold relief from the social background in America and the various events that helped to make me what I am: a sort of conjunction between my own inner struggle and the social struggles outside. I am not sure that this is what will appeal to American publishers. They prefer something hot from the flesh to represent the thrillers of the pathologically curious reading public. I don't think I can give that.

To Frank Harris, author of a sexually explicit autobiography, Emma wrote, "Besides, in my case I should want to reach not the few who are interested merely in the sex part of an autobiography, but the many who while appreciating the importance of sex in a vivid life, realize that it is but one part of the many elements that help to make a complex life. . . ."

Finally, to Ben himself, Emma wrote insisting that he promise not to publish or write about their correspondence. "Letters should only be published as letters and after the death of the writer—not that I am ashamed of anything I might have written. But love letters are written to a lover, not for every Tom, Dick, and Harry. I feel sure you will comply with my request *never to use my letters in your story*."

Ben reluctantly agreed, claiming that he would never have published her letters in a way that would hurt or embarrass her: "The worst I would do would be to try and shine in a little of your reflected glory." But even though Emma promised never to use his letters, Ben knew that her book would have to include some account of his role in her life. Recalling somewhat sheepishly the pain he had caused her, Ben wished Emma well and hoped for a kind portrayal:

Again, let me hold your hand and stroke your beautiful hair, and look into your wonderful blue eyes and say, "lover and friend and

7

teacher, with all my heart, I wish you well," I want you to write a great book. I feel certain that in spite of all my neglect and weaknesses and brutality, your love of justice, your sense of honesty, your willingness to give the other fellow fair play will entitle me to a page in your book. I hope you can say of me what I will say of you in my book, "that the ten years with you were not only the best ten years of my life," but if ever I amount to a damn, if ever I give anything worthwhile to society, it will be because you loved me and worked with me. . . .

Emma could not bring herself to write in such glowing terms of Ben or of their years together. She still felt disappointed about the failure of their relationship, and it was difficult for her to hide her anger at Ben in her autobiography. Yet she allowed that he had played a pivotal role in widening her audience and increasing the circulation of *Mother Earth*, her anarchist magazine. He had dedicated himself almost completely to her work, as few men would have done.

His flamboyance and what Emma called his "primitive" qualities lent themselves to the romantic, almost melodramatic, style of her autobiography. She acknowledged that he had awakened her to the force of her sexual passions, but there were only vague suggestions of his other effects upon her. She would admit merely that his letters were "like a narcotic," which made her heart beat faster but put her brain to sleep. Her account of the years with Ben seems revealing and intimate; indeed, Emma displayed her vulnerabilities to a greater extent than could be expected from even the frankest memoirs. But this apparent openness concealed the self-doubt and weakness Emma had experienced. She settled on a portrayal that emphasized the sharp contrast between Ben's crude nature and her own refined and civilized character. As soon as she recognized that he would never share or even fully comprehend her ideal, she explained, her rejection of him became a natural decision.

In the end, it was easier for Emma to criticize Ben than to face the questions that their relationship raised about the viability of her own dreams and expectations, when translated from abstract political principles into real life.

Emma's early writings, speeches, and lectures centered on a vision of a total, liberating transformation in every realm of human life. Her dreams had not materialized, and the writing of the autobiography was a lonely coming to terms with a long series of disappointments. Her many political defeats, however, had never succeeded in destroying her spirit:

> It was very painful to relive everything, and much more so than the actual living of my life. I was much younger, then, and so cocksure that I would continue, till the end of my days, to serve the ideal I had chosen as my goal. It was different while I was writing my book. All my hopes for activity had been buried, really nothing to look forward to, and the past seemed oceans and miles away. To resurrect it was, indeed, a painful process; but it had to be done to make the story real and vivid. Well, if the book will bring nothing else, it is some comfort to know it impresses the reader. In it, I have been able to let those whose opinion I care about, see me as I was. Perhaps it will also help the young generation to see that no life is worth anything which does not contain a great ideal, and which does not bring forth determination to serve it to the uttermost. That would be a great reward, indeed.

But the autobiography gave expression to only the heroic part of Emma's life. The tension between great ideas and individual limitations tormented Emma. She did not want her letters, which she considered the artifacts of her weaknesses, published in her lifetime, while she was trying to show the world her strengths. But she wanted them published eventually, for she believed that they were critical to an understanding of the woman who stood behind the podium. She deliberately dated and ordered her letters, and addressed herself to her friends, lovers, and comrades, and, perhaps, to those in an unknown future audience, who could hear their own voices in her voice, envision their own struggles in hers.

In 1927, when Emma began to collect the material for the auto-biography that would take her more than three years to complete, it was impossible for her to write a full account of her relationship with Ben and to draw from it implications for her life and politics. She read their

9

letters largely as stinging reminders of a part of her complex past that she planned to leave for others to unravel. During her lifetime, she became increasingly more certain that she did have something intimate to hide.

Emma confided in Sasha (Alexander Berkman): "We all have something to hide. Nor is it cowardice which makes us shrink from turning ourselves inside out. It is more the dread that people do not understand, that what may mean something very vital to you, to them is a thing to be spat upon."

2

THE DAUGHTER OF A DREAM

The years she shared with Ben Reitman were the best years of Emma's life, because she was doing what she valued most. Her skills as a public speaker brought audiences all over the country to hear her scathing critique of the established order and witness her vision of a new world, in which people would realize their capacity for love and integrity, a world without greed and pettiness. In a predominantly male political sphere, such a powerfully eloquent woman was both feared and revered.

Because Emma was portrayed by law-enforcement officials as "the most dangerous woman in America," people were often surprised by the woman herself. Roger Baldwin, founder of the American Civil Liberties Union, remarked in his *Recollections* that hearing one of Emma Goldman's lectures in 1908, when he was a young man, had been a turning point in his intellectual life. At first, he recalled, he had resisted attending a talk by this dangerous woman, who, he had heard, "condoned assassination and violence." But he was taunted into going by a friend's accusation that he was a protected Harvard man who evidently could not bear to listen to the other side.

I was 25 years old, and what I heard in that crowded working-class hall, from a woman who spoke with passion and intelligence, was a challenge to society I had never heard before. Here was a vision of the end of poverty and injustice to be brought about by the free association of those who worked, by the abolition of privilege, and by the organized power of the exploited. Emma Goldman dealt with real issues—poverty, injustice, the lack of opportunity—the problems for which I had been searching to find some solution. . . . I went away from that meeting with the desire to meet and talk with her during her brief stay in St. Louis. An interview was arranged by one of the city's leading dissenters, William Marion Reedy, editor and publisher of *Reedy's Mirror*, a courageous and influential weekly.

William Reedy had become an enthusiastic supporter of Emma's work long before being called upon by Baldwin for an introduction. As a widely respected journalist, he was in a position to counter the caricatures most of the press offered of Emma Goldman as "an ignorant, vulgar, shrieking harridan, with a bomb in one hand and a bottle of vitriol in the other." His own portrayal, in an article entitled "The Daughter of a Dream," began with a Biblical passage: "Where there is no vision, the people perish."

She's a little woman, somewhat stout, with neatly wavy hair, a clear blue eye, a mouth sensitive if not of classic lines. She is not pretty, but when her face lights up with the glow and color of her inner enthusiasm she is remarkably attractive. She has a fine manner, easy without swagger, free without trace of coarseness, and her smile is positively winsome. Conversationally, she is a delight. Her information is broad, her experience comprehensive, her reading in at least three languages almost limitless. She has wit and humor, too, and a compelling sincerity. What does she talk? Art, letters, science, economics, travel, philosophy, men and women. Pictures, poetry, the drama, personalities—the best substance for talk, and all from the standpoint of one who looks forward to the revolution. She has the eye for character and the gift of succinct expression. She is simple and not violent. She is positive without truculence. She is gentle and even at times tender. Her whole personality pulsates with a fervor that is infectious. She is a woman who believes in her cause and feels it with a concentrated intensity. It is the yardstick by which she measures all values. She sees in the world nothing but the material to be remolded into something nearer to her heart's desire. And what is her heart's desire? Freedom—absolute, unconditioned, uninvasive freedom. That is anarchy. Is it ugly or brutal or vicious? It is not. It is an aspiration toward and an effort for the perfection of humanity—"the one far off, divine event to which the whole creation moves." This little woman denies law, but she does not invoke it. She doesn't demand that she be considered respectable. She lives free and is willing to pay the price of misrepresentation, abuse, poverty, persecution. And amid it all she is serene. She is as one sure that she is sane in a mad world. She is like the immortal Don, invincibly inspired with an ideal that the world cannot yet behold with her eyes. There is nothing wrong with Miss Goldman's gospel that I can see, except this: She is about eight thousand years ahead of her age. Her vision is [that] of every truly great-souled man or woman who has ever lived. A dream, you say. But life is death, without the dream. The dream is the reality to which we move.

The woman who inspired this tribute, the daughter of a struggling Russian Jewish merchant, was, as a child, thrust out of a crumbling society into a new world of phenomenal but ruthless progress. Her "dream" was a lifelong yearning for an exalted existence, free of the banality and brutality that scarred the lives of her parents, siblings, and neighbors.

Emma Goldman was born in the Jewish quarter of the small Russian city of Kovno, in modern Lithuania, on June 27, 1869. She was the child of Taube and Abraham Goldman, whose relationship was filled with turmoil. Her mother was a dynamic, intelligent, but embittered woman, according to Emma's account in her autobiography, whose ability to love seemed to have been buried with her first husband. Emma was her mother's third child and her father's first. At Emma's birth, her mother was still in mourning over the death of her first husband, Labe Zodokoff, and awkwardly trying to make the best of her arranged marriage to Abraham Goldman. Emma's arrival promised to revive Taube's spirits by diverting her from the loss of her husband and the recent death of her mother, Chava. But Abraham's overt disappointment that his first child should be a girl left Taube with the task of providing her husband with a son, which she did within the year. So it seems that Emma was the object of considerable, if mixed, attention from both her parents in her first months, only to have it withdrawn in the excitement over the birth of her younger brother. By the time two other brothers were born, Herman in 1873 and Morris in 1875, whatever love her parents had expressed was overshadowed by resentment and obligatory care. How to support the children financially became a continual source of tension.

Emma later interpreted her father's frequent wild and violent fits of anger as an expression of his frustration with her mother's emphatic sexual coldness. She described him as a handsome, dashing character only twenty-two years old when Emma was born, full of vitality but given to fearsome rages. His dissatisfaction and anger were exacerbated by repeated failures in business, and by his humiliation at having invested and lost Taube's oldest daughter's inheritance. He moved the family to the Baltic town of Popelan, where he became an innkeeper and was eventually elected as a petty government official. As a Jew he was easily scapegoated in his role as middleman, and blamed for the drunkenness of the peasants at the inn by the officials and for any transgressions of the peasants toward the officials. Feeling his manhood threatened on all fronts, he retreated to his last stronghold as the stern patriarch. Emma was at once attracted to and deeply frightened by the power of her father's outbursts, sometimes identifying with his rage and at other times feeling repelled by it.

Emma had two older half-sisters, Lena and Helena. Lena was as sharp-tempered as Helena was timid. It was from Helena that Emma drew emotional support, for her mother was generally withdrawn in depression, despite her public persona as a talented spokesperson to government officials on behalf of the Jewish mothers trying to keep their boys out of the Russian army. Taube's health had begun to fail after the birth of her last child, Morris. To add to her mother's unhappiness, her first-born son (one year Emma's junior) died at the age of six. The family's trauma over his death, and Emma's in particular, may account for the suppression of any direct reference to him in the published version of her autobiography.

Emma linked herself to the "good" elements of her family—to Helena and Morris. No doubt the untimely death of a young sibling left a painful mark on children whose understanding of cause and effect was still limited. Emma, in particular, must have felt the most direct rivalry with this boy who fulfilled her father's expectations as she could not. Her sense of loss was probably linked to feelings of guilt for her brother's death, as well as a sense of power that she could have such control over another human being's fate. Emma's mother, still unhappy over the loss of her first husband, must have sunk even deeper into depression at the death of her son. Her sadness and fear of further pain turned into what seemed like cold indifference to her children. She withdrew her affection from all but her youngest son. Emma's father, raging and often physically abusive of his children, especially Emma, lacked the emotional resources to cope with such a devastating blow. Sometimes Emma even daydreamed about being "stricken with some consuming disease," just to soften her father's heart, to keep him from beating her. He had lost his government position only the year before the tragic death, so his financial status was another source of anxiety. From a very early age, Emma knew that she wanted to escape the turmoil of her family—her mother's inaccessibility, her father's rages, her sisters' and brothers' desperate scramble for what little affection was available.

When Emma was eight years old, her father sent her to live with her maternal grandmother in Königsberg, where she would attend school. Emma felt alone without her mother and father, without the calm of the countryside, but was somewhat relieved to be away from her father, who threatened to beat her if she did anything wrong during her stay. The experience, however, turned out to be traumatic: her grandmother unexpectedly and without explanation departed, and Emma was left to the whims of her uncle and aunt.

Emma's uncle took her out of school, forced her to do housework instead, and treated her with outrageous cruelty; one day he kicked her down a flight of steps for refusing to walk several miles to deliver a package for him. It was the physical abuse that prompted two kind women in the downstairs flat to take Emma from him, nurse her back to health, and, with the urging of her mother's sister, wire Emma's father and grandmother to return. When they did, Emma's father actually held her in his arms affectionately, her uncle was banished from Emma's grandmother's house, and before long Emma was back in Popelan. Later the family moved to Königsberg together, then to the capital, St. Petersburg. But no doubt Emma carried the fear of abandonment into the rest of her life, and perhaps associated it with punishment for the death of her younger brother.

Occasional bright moments gave Emma a sense that life had more to offer than her parents' miserable existence. Perhaps most important was the continuity and security of her close and loving relationship with her older half-sister, Helena. Their many moves because of anti-Semitism and Abraham's business failures often involved painful transitions, even downward economic mobility, but at least they expanded Emma's horizons and showed her the varied possibilities of life.

During the time the family lived in Popelan, a peasant named Petrushka, who had been hired to look after the family's cows and sheep, took particular delight in playing with the young Emma. Petrushka's ease in expressing his affection differed markedly from the restraint of the Goldman family and left a lasting impression. When Emma was eleven, her German teacher in Königsberg took an interest in introducing her to European culture and took her to her first opera, *Il Trovatore*. That story of tragic love set to music resonated with Emma's dreams for herself. The convoluted plot involving revenge for an unjust death, the kidnapping of a young man mistakenly believed to have been killed, but who is, in fact, his older brother's rival for the love of a woman who is willing to die for the younger brother's freedom excited the young Emma's imagination, with its echoes of her own fantasies and experiences.

Her formal education was a patchwork of strict Jewish schools, intermingled with some private tutoring. Like other Russian Jews of that time, her parents sought to give their children an education steeped in high German culture and morality. For Emma, the great literature was a source of inspiration while the strict codes of behavior inspired only rebellion. Although she was labeled troublemaker by some of her teachers, the one who took her to the opera recognized and nurtured Emma's intelligence.

Later, when her father moved the family to St. Petersburg, the center of cultural creativity and political ferment in Russia, Emma glimpsed new joys and pleasures. St. Petersburg was rife with tales of heroes and heroines of the early Russian revolutionary movement, among whom were the nihilists and other related rebel groups who had dared to attempt to kill the Czar. Too young to participate in such activities, which contradicted the conservative teachings and traditions of her family, Emma spent every available moment reading. She began to shift her attention from German to Russian classics. Books by Russian authors—Chernyshevsky, Goncharov, and Turgenev—now gave her a feeling for the vigor of the radical circles that had sprouted in the Russian cities in reaction to the growing repressiveness of czarist rule. She found characters in the great novels of prerevolutionary Russia to feed her dreams. The daring and unconventional Vera Pavlovna in Chernyshevsky's novel, *What Is to Be Done?*, inspired Emma to imagine that she might become a woman unencumbered by the restrictions of her sex, who could love freely outside the confines of marriage. Emma, who at the age of thirteen had to leave her studies to go to work sewing shawls, then gloves, in sweat shops to help support the family, dreamed of the cooperative sewing shop Vera Pavlovna had started, freeing herself and her co-workers from dependence on the system under which impoverished workers toiled to amass huge fortunes for the owners.

Inspired by Vera Pavlovna, Emma imagined a world without restraint, in which families would be bound by love and ideals rather than duty and tradition. Even as an adolescent, she resolved not to re-create the frustrated numbness of her own family, but instead to form a family and community based on shared beliefs and shared work. The Russian populists and nihilists sparked her imagination and reinforced her general faith that injustice could be righted by the people. Determined to live a nobler life than her parents, Emma rejected the conventions of the time for an unknown future, which she was sure would be better.

Emma's ability to sustain idealism in the face of poverty and unhappiness was not uncommon within her culture. As a Jew, she had experienced the anti-Semitism that forced her family to move from place to place, searching for security and a sense of belonging while maintaining a belief in ultimate justice, and in the strength of a people without a state to survive adversity. Emma fantasized becoming an avenger like Judith, who cut off the head of Holofernes, a symbol of evil. In the Jewish tradition, it was not unusual for women to play a central social role. Although her own father was a merchant, Jewish men often devoted their lives to religious study while their wives took responsibility for the families' economic survival. Yet Emma chose to believe that her dreams represented a radical break with the past and everything that bound her to the old world.

In fact, the old world itself was changing. The subservient roles women generally played within the authoritarian family, the domination by the father, and the system of arranged marriages were all being undermined. Even the Yiddish stories of Sholem Aleichem, which reflected a small but increasing trend, suggested a sympathetic attitude toward romantic love and toward young women who opposed arranged marriages. When Emma came to feel that living with dignity demanded a total break with the past, she was not alone. For women in this society, even for an adolescent girl, there was a sense that an old world was dying and a new one was struggling to be born. Isolated, with little to guide them, young women took the first tentative steps toward a new kind of social and economic freedom, pulling away from their suffocating roles in the family.

Her reading and the handful of experiences she treasured gave

Emma a vision that contrasted starkly with the future that seemed to await her: factory work, a husband chosen by her father, constant awareness that as a Jew she was an outcast and as a woman a second-class citizen. In retrospect, she began to understand a young boy she had befriended in Königsberg who had eventually been sentenced to death for attempting to put a bomb under the Czar's train. He had thought it better to die for acting on his beliefs than to submit to the injustice of the Czar's rule.

Although Emma could sympathize with such conviction, she was too young and uninitiated politically to participate in the struggle to free Russia from the Czar's domination. Her visions were intensely personal, concerned with finding a conducive environment in which to grow as an individual and a free spirit.

As it did for so many Russian Jews of that pogrom-plagued era, America seemed to offer hope. Lena, Emma's oldest sister, had been the first in the family to go to America. In Emma's mind, everything there was new and open; there she could find love and romance, and perhaps live as Vera Pavlovna had lived. Even her sister Helena, who had been thought of as timid and obedient, was planning an escape to America from the heavy hand of tradition (in the form of her stepfather), which forbade her to marry the non-Jew with whom she had fallen in love. Although she did not marry this man, she was determined to leave home and find her own mate in America. Emma also battled with her father, who labeled her desire to live on her own, away from her parents, proof of her loose character. Then, Abraham responded with anger rather than compassion when Helena found that Emma had been raped by a young friend in a St. Petersburg hotel. He fought to retain his power to arrange a marriage for her, and relaxed his control over his daughters only when Emma threatened to jump into the Neva River. The slight improvement was not enough for his two daughters, who had had enough of brute male force. They decided the time had come to leave. Helena would pay Emma's way.

The sixteen-year-old Emma and twenty-four-year-old Helena set sail for America in late 1885, both temporarily taking on the surname of Emma's mother's wealthy family, Binowitz, as the shipmaster recorded.

After landing at Castle Garden (the clearinghouse for immigrants in New York City), they went to Rochester, where Lena was living. Like most immigrants, Emma and Helena were allowed to enter the United States only after providing proof that they had families waiting for them who would guarantee their welfare. Lena was pregnant when her two sisters arrived; her husband, Samuel Comminsky, earned only $12 a week as a tinsmith. After they had settled into the room they would share, Emma and Helena immediately began to look for work.

Emma had scarcely unpacked her bags when she realized that her life in the New World might turn out to be little better than the one she had fled. Here, too, she was constrained by strict discipline, this time imposed by the relatives who had taken her in. There was even talk of an arranged marriage! She was once again a seamstress, working long hours in a factory. And although the American factory appeared more modern than the one she had left behind, the working conditions were more regimented. In St. Petersburg, there had been camaraderie among the factory women, who talked and sang together while they worked. Here in Rochester, she felt isolated from the other workers. Conversation was strictly forbidden by the stern foremen who stood over the women as they toiled at their machines. Any belief she may have held in Jewish solidarity was also quickly shaken, as she recognized the vast gulf between the wealthy German Jew who owned the factory and the Russian Jewish immigrant workers he exploited as a source of submissive, cheap labor.

After only a few weeks of work, Emma strode fearlessly into the owner's office to complain that $2.50 for a 6-day week of 10½-hour days left her with no extra money to buy a book or even a flower, and with no time for a life outside work. When the owner replied that such tastes were too extravagant for a factory girl, Emma found another job.

It was not long before Emma met a textile worker named Jacob Kershner, a recent Russian Jewish immigrant like herself, who loved to read and dance. He seemed indifferent to accumulating money and, also like Emma, longed to escape factory work. They shared their secret desire to travel, to search for the America of their dreams that had thus far eluded them.

Emma, at seventeen, began to think that marriage to the handsome twenty-one-year-old Kershner would be her ticket to escape the oppressive drudgery of work and the stifling restrictions of family that had followed her to the New World. They became engaged to marry. Her sense of suffocating confinement had grown even worse when, in the late fall of 1886, Emma's parents, driven out of Russia by growing anti-Semitism, were forced to start over in Rochester. Jacob became a boarder in a household that included, besides Emma's parents, her sister Helena and her two brothers. Emma decided to shorten her engagement and marry Jacob, to carve out her own life, again away from her parents.

On her wedding night in February 1887, however, Emma was faced with a new kind of loneliness and isolation, when she and Jacob failed to consummate their marriage. At first, Emma attributed their difficulty to Kershner's nervousness, but it soon became apparent that the problem was more serious. Kershner was, in fact, impotent. A shocking disappointment to Emma, the revelation left Kershner so humiliated that he fell into a deep depression. His interest in books and dancing, which had provided their common ground, suddenly evaporated, and he retreated into long hours of cardplaying with male companions. And while he squandered his own time and what little money they had in such diversions, he was madly jealous of Emma's friends and the time she spent away from him.

The couple sometimes fought openly, but mostly smoldered in dissatisfaction. Having quit her job to stay home and be a proper wife, Emma felt isolated and unhappy. The proximity of her mother and father at the very time when she was discovering Kershner's impotence plunged Emma back into troubling memories of some childhood experiences that had clouded her attitudes toward sexuality. Her mother had been quick to exhibit disapproval when she discovered Emma masturbating. Later, when Emma had informed her mother that her first menstrual cycle had begun, instead of receiving maternal comfort and reassurance she was greeted with a slap in the face—a folk tradition intended to warn of the painful aspects of child-bearing. Her mother said sternly, "This is necessary for a girl, when she becomes a woman, as a protection against disgrace."

And there were frightening childhood memories of her father, the man to whom she had turned for love and affirmation of her developing sexual identity, only to meet with his stern remoteness and sporadic outbursts of violent anger.

In Rochester, Emma understood for the first time that the delight she had experienced as a little girl playfully wrestling with the peasant Petrushka had been pleasurable sexual sensations, feelings foreign to the erratic, loveless, stifling atmosphere of her parents' relationship. Her marriage had failed to exorcise her brutal introduction to intercourse as a young teenager.

Looking back on these disturbing experiences, Emma would remark late in life that she had "always felt between two fires in the presence of men. Their lure remained strong, but it was always mingled with violent revulsion. I could not bear to have them touch me." But now Emma could see only that the door was closing on her dreams of searching together with her young husband for a radiant world of freedom and fulfillment. Kershner, no longer the soulmate she had hoped for, was retreating further into himself, his cardplaying a symbol for Emma of the boredom and emptiness that threatened her no matter where she turned.

She felt more alone in her marriage than she had ever felt in the confines of her own family: at least she had been able to hope to leave there someday, but here she was expected to endure her misery. Divorce was rare in her traditional Jewish community, a step taken only when desperation overcame the fear of disapproval and rejection by family and neighbors that was sure to follow. Emma at first sought to sublimate her misery, but not as Kershner had done with his cards. Emma became possessed by the political fires that were raging around her.

It was 1887, and the newspapers were filled with sensational accounts of the Chicago conspiracy and murder trial of a group of eight anarchist revolutionaries and labor organizers who were bearing the brunt of a campaign to suppress labor radicalism. On May 4, 1886, in what came to be known around the world as the Haymarket Affair, one Chicago policeman had been killed and scores of citizens injured by a bomb blast on the fourth day of a massive general strike in support of workers' demands for the eight-hour day and five-day work week. The eight defendants, speakers at the rally, were charged with the death but were, in reality, tried for their political beliefs. In a trial that Illinois Governor John P. Altgeld would describe a few years later as a mockery of justice, the men were convicted on the strength of an extremely flimsy case, and all but one were sentenced to hang.

Emma was deeply moved by the impassioned orations delivered by the condemned men at their sentencing. When four of them were executed on November 11, 1887, after pardon pleas to Altgeld's predecessor had failed, she was outraged.

It was the individualist strain of the anarchist movement that attracted Emma. She heard in the words of the Haymarket martyrs their courage in standing as individuals against injustice and living out their ideals even if it meant facing death, and their belief that such individual acts played an important role in inspiring others. She was excited to think that their deaths might awaken new life and political consciousness in the world. Emma listened to their call to action.

The words of one of the executed anarchists, August Spies, rang in her ears: "If you think that by hanging us you can stamp out the labor movement—the movement from which the downtrodden millions who toil and live in want and misery—the wage slaves—expect salvation—if this is your opinion, then hang us! Here you will tread upon a spark, but there and there, and behind you and in front of you, and everywhere, flames will blaze up."

Distracted from her troubles with Kershner, she found herself indignant at the complacency and ignorance of the people around her who failed to appreciate the significance of Haymarket. At one point her rage became so uncontrollable that she threw a glass of water at a relative who was visiting her mother, for blaspheming the martyrs. This new intensity within her, which had been catalyzed by the woman's cold conservatism, both frightened and thrilled her.

Swept out of her depression by anger and the inspiration of the Haymarket martyrs, Emma began to feel justified in her desire to leave Kershner. Within two years, not yet twenty years old, Emma gathered the courage to announce that she was divorcing him. Determined to make a complete break from both Kershner and the narrowness of her family, she left Rochester and moved to New Haven. Escape from the pain of her own situation to a new place, which offered the promise of a more inspired life and refuge from her past, was to become a lifelong pattern. As it had for the American pioneers, so it was for Emma that the frontier offered more promise than staying to fight oppression at the local source. Her newfound political fervor gave her an arena of power and a way to direct the anger and pain within herself toward socially useful work.

In New Haven, she found a job in a corset factory whose workers enjoyed fairly good conditions as a result of union-organizing victories. She met a group of young Russian immigrants who gathered frequently after work to argue the burning questions of socialism and anarchism. No matter how exhausted she might be after work, Emma forced herself to attend the evening meetings, for she had at last found kindred spirits there, people striving to realize their vision of a new society. Although she was more attracted to the purity of anarchism than the more conflict-laden socialism, the general level of political discussion about both theories thrilled her. But the strain of long hours in the factory during the day and political meetings at night took its toll, and her emotional and physical exhaustion worsened. What had begun as just a cough turned into tuberculosis, and the pains in her feet and legs developed into a severe case of varicose veins. Most enervating were her excruciating menstrual cramps.

Within two months, she gravitated back to her sister Helena, now married to Jacob Hochstein and the mother of a young child. Helena's poverty and Emma's weak physical state opened the way for Kershner's reappearance: when Kershner begged her to return, threatening to commit suicide if she did not, Emma, badly in need of care herself, was unable to resist. With the exception of Helena, who had never liked Kershner, her family was relieved that their daughter had reformed after her act of youthful rebellion. Emma actually remarried him.

But any hopes she had of a new start were quickly dashed; as soon as Emma and Kershner were reunited, their destructive patterns began again. There was a bracing finality to this return to Kershner and her past. Emma had to face rationally what she had felt viscerally before—that she must start anew or perish in misery. She secretly took a course in dressmaking to add to her means of self-support.

When Emma determined to leave Kershner for the second time, though, the cost was great. She was spurned by the Jewish community of Rochester. She developed an intimate but turbulent friendship with a young man named Bernstein, which helped her pry herself away from Kershner. Her parents, who had disapproved of her original divorce, now disowned her for what seemed to them her utter disregard of her responsibility to them and to her own future security. Their lack of sympathy hurt deeply.

With no one to turn to for support except Helena, Emma eventually packed up her sewing machine and took a bus to New York City. Years later, she would sum up her feelings about her four years in Rochester, 1885 to 1889, in a few biting lines: "Rochester, N.Y., the city of my inauguration into the beauties of American factory life; the place where I first learned the brazenness of American liberty. Rochester, where I was made to suffer the narrow American provincialism, with its busy-body guardianship of every soul unlike its own. Here, too, it was that I understood the mockery of the legalized sanctity of the home. Rochester also, where I first beheld the light of liberty, of independence."

The diversity and anonymity of New York was a relief to her after the narrow conformity of the Rochester Jewish community. On the morning of her arrival, August 15, 1889, New York was sweltering under a heat wave, but even the heat was welcome, seeming to purge her of her past. Her first move was a mistake: she went to an aunt and uncle who owned a photo gallery, but their chilly welcome dampened the excitement of her arrival. Leaving her belongings, she excused herself to go look for a man named Hillel Solotaroff, whom she had heard lecture in New Haven. Once she found him, by sheer luck and determination, they went almost directly to the famous meeting place of the Lower East Side radicals, Sach's Cafe on Suffolk Street. Sach's rang with animated political conversations in Russian and Yiddish, and the smell of Eastern European Jewish cooking took her back to her girlhood.

Emma felt at once that she was in her element. She had long dreamed of meeting the people whose work and thoughts she had heard of at the meetings in New Haven; now she had made her way to the very center of labor activism for the Jewish immigrant. At Sach's, she was drawn immediately to one particularly energetic man. Alexander, or "Sasha," Berkman, a cigar maker and shirt packer during the day, an anarchist activist at night, had come to New York from Vilna, Russia, just the previous year, in 1888. He talked to Emma with kindness and wit and seemed, like her, to be searching for a soulmate. He was known for his admonishment—"If we eat grass, it's better than dirt, but we must never begin to think of ourselves as cattle."

Sasha invited Emma to go with him that very night to a talk by Johann Most, a golden-tongued though facially deformed anarchist from Germany. Most, a former member of the Reichstag and of the German Social Democratic Party, had been an editor of the *Berliner Freie Presse*, and had written a popular summary of Marx's *Das Kapital*. Expelled from Germany, he emigrated to London, where he published *Die Freiheit*, whose editorial policies leaned heavily toward anarchism. Sach's was Emma's fantasy of life in America come true.

Solotaroff had already introduced Emma to two sisters, Anna and Helen Minkin, who were looking for a boarder in their family's home. Emma was delighted to have the opportunity to be independent of her aunt and the stifling effect of family obligation. That night, after they all attended Most's lecture, Emma slept at Anna and Helen's house. Although the Minkin home was not peaceful, and Emma eventually moved out to avoid another difficult father, it provided her with the initial roots she needed to establish herself in New York. At first she worked in a corset factory, and then found a silk-waist factory that would allow her to take sewing home. This meant she could escape factory discipline and have the flexibility to attend anarchist activities. It was the anarchists in New York who offered the most appealing and colorful approach to life and politics in this new phase of Emma's life.

She eventually moved to a room by herself on Suffolk Street, not far from Sach's Cafe, where she could sew all day without disturbing others and where the dissonance of family life did not intrude on her new experiences. Moving did not faze Emma, who had begun to draw a sense of stability from her political work. Her enthusiasm for anarchism was bolstered by the interest shown in her by the Minkin sisters, and by important anarchists like Alexander Berkman and Johann Most.

Emma found herself the object of attention from both men. Most began to escort her to the city's cultural events. When Emma recounted, in great detail, the story of her first, elevating exposure to opera, *Il Trovatore*, Most was impressed by her facility with language and her capacity to express her feelings. He had an ear for the dramatic, having dreamed of becoming an actor himself. Emma was touched by the tragedy of his lifelong struggle to compensate for his outward grotesqueness with the inner beauty of the cause. They even found relief in sharing the dismal stories of their childhoods, whose themes resonated with those of Verdi's opera. Most decided to train this attractive and impressionable girl in the art of public speaking. She was thrilled to think that such a great speaker saw potential talent in her. Eager to learn from her new idol and teacher, she was entranced with the possibility that she, too, might inspire audiences with the cause of anarchism.

Their alliance was mutually fulfilling as long as Emma remained Most's follower. As she struggled to develop her own ideas, however, his attention waned. Slowly Emma realized that even in anarchist circles, many male activists who professed commitment to absolute freedom for the individual and rejected inequality and hierarchies enjoyed and exploited their dominance over women. She risked offending the "great Most" by asserting her independence from his controlling pedantry. Although eventually he apologized for his behavior, claiming that he was misdirecting his love for her, Emma never forgot how quickly he had turned her into a sexual object, ignoring her ideas, and how tense he had become when he was around Sasha.

Sasha, on the other hand, with his warm and sincere manner, seemed more willing to support Emma's newfound sense of herself. Rather than trying to mold the young Emma, Sasha was fascinated with her strength of character and with the originality of her ideas. As their friendship grew, they discovered more and more in common. Sasha, too, had been inspired by Chernyshevsky's *What Is to Be Done?* during his early days in Russia. While Emma had identified strongly with Vera, Sasha's imagination had been stirred by Rakhmetov, the character who gives up everything—home, sweetheart, children, and security—to serve his ideal. After a meeting in which Most delivered an extraordinarily moving speech calling for vengeance against the terrible injustices of the Haymarket Affair, Emma and Sasha returned to Emma's small apartment and made love. They began to think about living together, all their youthful fantasies coming into play.

Within that first year in New York, Emma, Sasha, and Sasha's cousin "Fedya" (Modest Stein), a young artist, and for a brief while Helen Minkin, who worked in a corset factory, moved into a four-room apartment on Forty-second Street, forming what they thought of as a small commune. The personalities of Sasha and Fedya formed two poles in this little system, with Emma in between. Fedya's love of flowers and color balanced Sasha's asceticism. Although Fedya at times thought of Sasha as a fanatic with no sense of beauty, they lived compatibly together and enjoyed the warmth generated by this new "chosen family" they had created with Emma. For the first time in her life, Emma felt really loved and genuinely happy.

At one point, Fedya and Sasha almost came to blows over what Sasha called Fedya's incurable bourgeois tendencies. When Fedya had spent the cooperative's money to buy himself a blue-and-white-striped silk jersey, Sasha got so angry that he left the apartment in a rage and stayed away for several days. During that time, Emma felt drawn to Fedya. She appreciated his aesthetic sensibilities, and she could relax with him, because he never expected her to live up to the cause. His flexibility contrasted strongly with Sasha's severity. But when Fedya had Emma pose nude for him, he became overwhelmed with physical desire. While she was putting her clothes back on, she heard him weeping in the next room. She confronted him, and he confessed that he had come to love her. His fear of hurting Sasha and his efforts to repress his feelings for Emma left him so frustrated that he was seriously considering moving out. Emma realized that she, too, had fallen in love, and they decided to tell Sasha, to test their belief that love was not exclusive or subject to feelings of possession. But they did not have the courage to tell him immediately, probably suspecting that his abrupt departure was at least in part triggered by his awareness of the growing sexual attraction between Emma and Fedya. Many years later, Sasha commented on his reaction to Emma and Fedya's relationship in a letter to Emma written in response to an early draft of her autobiography:

> Also your intimacy with F. you picture wrong. Both in re time as well as in character. You describe it as if I knew nothing about it; and that when you were ready to tell me, it was not necessary. Gives the impression that we were no more intimate then. As a matter of fact, I once went to get something, and when I returned I knocked on the door, because for some reason it was locked. F. came out and told me that you had "a spell" such as you used to take in those days, and that he was trying "to quieten" you. Of course I understood, though I said nothing. I was no more communicative at 20 than at 58. F. asked me to return in about 15 minutes or so. I remained an hour and I remember that when I returned then, F. again told me that he had not succeeded in quieting you yet, and I went away again.

Sasha came back anxious to prove to Emma that his reaction to Fedya's purchase had nothing to do with a lack of appreciation for beauty. He explained that he loved life and beautiful things but he was willing to give them up for the cause. Sasha continued to do everything he could to support Emma's work. When Most asked her to go out on the road for her first speaking tour, by ironic coincidence originating in Rochester, Sasha splurged to give Emma an American Beauty rose as her train was about to pull away from the station.

Within the next few months, however, Sasha had moved out of the flat. He and Anna Minkin developed a physical attachment to each other. He had become more disapproving of what he considered to be Emma's blatant exhibitionist tendencies—her insistence that she could dance at union-organizing socials as wildly as anyone else. And he may have been jealous of Fedya and the other men who were attracted to Emma, although he never admitted it.

It was during this time, when Emma was daily asserting her independence and beginning to feel the power of her own sexuality, that she made the conscious decision not to bear children. She was incapacitated for weeks with extraordinarily painful menstrual cramps and the symptoms of undiagnosed endometriosis. The doctors who treated her, again and again, attributed her difficulties to an inverted womb, which was a catch-all diagnosis of the time for women's menstrual and fertility problems. Her friend Dr. Hillel Solotaroff took her to a physician who told her that Emma could never bear children with this condition. The same doctor (incorrectly) suggested that an operation could cure her monthly pain and make it possible for her to conceive a child. But Emma decided to forgo the operation and "overcome the strongest and most primitive craving of a woman—the desire for a child," attributing this decision to the memory of her own brutal childhood, her awareness of the numbers of unwanted and impoverished children in the world, and her newfound dedication to the cause. She "would pay the price . . . endure the suffering," as the martyrs had done, and find an outlet for her "mother-need in the love of *all* children." She turned her physical ailment to her advantage, using it as natural birth control. During her recuperation period, she balanced her conscious decision not to have a child with the confirmation of her sexuality that had taken place when she and Fedya became lovers. Emma believed that her affair did not conflict with her love for Sasha or her dedication to the cause. In fact, she felt that her decision not to have an operation was proof enough of her willingness to sacrifice for the cause.

When Emma finally told Sasha about her intimate relationship with Fedya, he outwardly responded with generosity and respect. He acknowledged, but fought against, his feelings of jealousy, which he believed were only a remnant of his bourgeois background. Sasha's devotion was rooted in his friendship with Fedya, his intimacy with Emma, and his political camaraderie with them both. He believed that he could overcome any possessive feelings in the name of revolution.

That night, Sasha, Fedya, and Emma made a formal pact "to dedicate themselves to the cause in some supreme deed and to die together if necessary." Their vow to commit "a great deed" was in the grand tradition of the Russian revolutionaries, who expressed rebellion in symbolic, often violent actions, in a country where opportunities to speak out were scarce and the level of political education was low. The message was in the dramatic effect of the act. Sasha, Fedya, and Emma believed that they were following the noble traditions of their Russian heroines and heroes, both fictional characters like Vera Pavlovna and Rakhmetov and the male and female revolutionaries who had died seeking to free the Russian masses from the rule of the Czar. For Emma this pact guaranteed that her life would be elevated "above the common herd," to become meaningful at last. By this time, Helen Minkin had moved back with her sister, and Emma had moved to an apartment on Thirteenth Street with the two men.

Their loose *ménage à trois* reinforced by this solemn pledge, the three young idealists felt they could meet any challenge with the strength of their commitment and the knowledge that they were not alone. Fedya preferred to remain in the background, to express his dedication to his friends and to the cause through his art rather than through direct propaganda. Yet he was determined to live with Emma and Sasha as part of a communal economic, as well as political, unit. With the resistance movement against the growing repression of the Russian Czar clearly in need of support, Sasha and Emma contemplated a return to Russia. In consultation with Most, they decided that although Emma might have a future as a speaker in America, Sasha could better serve the Russian Revolution. They thought Sasha could learn some necessary printing skills in New Haven. Emma did not want to be away from him, so she followed to form the cooperative dress shop of her dreams, with Anna and Helen Minkin. But lack of business or money forced Emma and Helen to go to work in a corset factory, while Anna stayed home sewing. Emma did all the cutting and fitting of the dresses for Anna and all the cooking for the household. Together they organized political and cultural events that turned out to be quite popular with the progressive circles of New Haven. Fedya, although still committed to communal living, preferred to return to New York where he could earn a stable income. Anna returned to New York, too, suffering from consumption. Helen, who had fallen in love with Most during his speaking tour in Manhattan, followed him to New York. After that, Emma and Helen became estranged, as did Sasha and Most, over veiled issues of love and jealousy. Within months, Emma and Sasha's business ventures proved complete failures, and they rejoined Fedya in New York and rented an apartment with him on Forsythe Street. There they waited for the response to a confidential appeal Most had sent to trustworthy comrades for funds to return to Russia.

On May 1, 1891, Most was arrested for a speech he had given urging workers to arm themselves. May Day had been proclaimed by an International Socialist Congress in 1889 to be a worldwide holiday to honor labor. Emma and Sasha came to Most's support, burying their differences, but they could not prevent the courts from sentencing him to the penitentiary. In the meantime, Fedya asked Emma to join him in Springfield, Massachusetts, where he had found well-paid photography work. Emma, seizing the opportunity to leave the city and the long hours of piece-work sewing with which she and Sasha supported themselves, went first. Once Sasha had joined them, the three attempted to start a photography business in Worcester. The studio failed, but their next idea, opening an ice-cream parlor, met with success. The comrades enjoyed their new venture, which promised to provide them with the minimal economic security they needed to continue their political work, and even some extra cash to send in support of the revolutionaries in Russia. The smell of Emma's coffee filled the shop, and before long it became a popular local haunt, even though some children of the town were forbidden to buy ice cream—never mind that it was a penny or two cheaper than in other shops—because word had gotten out that Emma and Sasha lived together out of wedlock.

Just as the new business was becoming established, however, a national political event intruded on their lives, presenting a challenge that the young comrades could not ignore. On July 6, 1892, the workers at the Carnegie Steel plant in Homestead, Pennsylvania, after going on strike to protest the company's refusal to negotiate wage increases, had been replaced by scabs, locked out of their company houses, and threatened with violence. Henry Clay Frick, chairman of the board of Carnegie Steel, had then called in three hundred Pinkerton guards to keep the factory open; their presence predictably led to violence, in which three Pinkertons and ten workers were killed. Sasha, in particular, felt determined to avenge the lives of the ten workers. He decided to assassinate Frick.

The twenty-two-year-old Berkman began to prepare for this act. He and Emma closed their ice-cream parlor and focused all their attention on developing his plan. They traveled to New York together, but Sasha refused even the company of Emma and Fedya on his trip to Pittsburgh. Emma was given the task of explaining his act to the people once it had been accomplished. And so, without the support or approval of any organized movement, Emma and Sasha planned an individual act of violence against the capitalist oppressors that they hoped would be immediately understood by the workers as justifiable retaliation. This was the moment to test their dedication to the cause, even if it meant sacrificing their own lives.

At first Sasha attempted to make a bomb; when he failed, he left for Pittsburgh with a little money and the hope of purchasing a gun and a respectable suit of clothing that would give him access to Frick's office, as a representative of the fictitious Simon Bachman employment agency. Sasha said good-bye to Emma, convinced that his act would arouse the working class to action.

After he had left for Pittsburgh, the lonely Emma racked her brain for a scheme with which to finance their plot, to help her lover avenge the working people with his sacrifice for their ideals. Emma rejected one idea after another; then her audacity came into play. When all else fails, a woman can sell her body, she figured. Certainly, in the service of the cause, she would not be degrading herself. Dressed in what she thought was the appropriate attire, Emma waited on a street corner for a sign of recognition. When at last a man in a suit came her way, giving her a knowing look and an invitation, she followed him to a wine house on Union Square; suddenly she realized she had been there before, with Most, and so she led him to another saloon, at Thirteenth and Third Avenue. As they talked, it became apparent to him that Emma was a novice, nervously trying to act out the toughness of this unaccustomed role. He ended up telling her she was not meant to be a streetwalker, giving her some money, and sending her away without asking for her favors. Ultimately, Emma had to write to her sister Helena for the rest of the money, feigning illness.

Berkman stayed with friends in Allegheny, Pennsylvania, then registered in a hotel room near the steel mills as "Bakhmetov" (a variation on his boyhood hero, Rachmetov). On July 23, 1892, in Homestead, Berkman succeeded in forcing his way into Frick's office, whereupon he fired three bullets, knocking the steel baron to the floor with serious but nonfatal wounds. He then lurched forward in an attempt to finish Frick off with a knife. Ironically, some workers who had been doing repairs in Frick's office came to his defense, along with Frick's assistant, beating the dazed Berkman into unconsciousness. Not only had Sasha missed his chance to deal a death blow to a symbol of capitalist oppression, but the workers, instead of supporting his valiant effort to free them, had actually protected their common enemy against him! At the station house, Berkman concealed a dynamite capsule in his mouth, but it was confiscated immediately. Instead of a martyr's death, he was to have fourteen years behind bars in which to contemplate these moments, and his act would be a subject of debate in the movement for years to come.

Emma assumed that Sasha's act would be a signal to workers across the country to take the power to which their toil rightfully entitled them by seizing the factories. Instead, the failed attempt triggered a new wave of repression against dissidents and further divided the workers' movement into factions battling over tactics.

Seeking to link Emma to the crime, the police raided her empty apartment. Two days after the raid, the landlord evicted her from her flat. Close friends who had known nothing about Sasha's act were charged with complicity. Emma moved in with a friend, who ultimately was too scared to hide her. She tried living in her grandmother's crowded apartment. She sat in cafés, or rode the subways, feeling that she had nowhere to go. Within weeks, Emma changed her name to E. G. Smith and impulsively registered in a boardinghouse, only to discover that it was a house of prostitution. Ironically, it was a fine place to earn a living sewing dresses for the women. While she felt united with the other women in hiding from the law, she soon felt compelled to move on to avoid discovery, as publicity about "Red Emma's" complicity in the Frick shooting increased. She next sought refuge in a lodging place for Czech revolutionaries.

The tension between hope and reality mounted for the young Emma. She and Sasha had lived out their Russian anarchist dreams in the context of twentieth-century America. The failure of the Frick *attentat*, or terrorist act, made the chasm between them and the New World clear. They were unrealistic about the effectiveness of any one such act, particularly because Frick was not a political figure, and the general political awareness was too low to make the meaning of their attempted assassination comprehensible.

With her closest comrade in prison, Emma felt that perhaps she, too, should have gone to jail, given her involvement in the crime. Since she was still free, she felt at first overwhelmed with guilt for her freedom and compelled to live for Berkman, to rededicate her life to the realization of their dreams for the revolution. But gradually she began to wonder whether their act had been too hasty, whether it had made enough of a contribution to the workers' movement to justify Sasha's spending more than a decade behind bars. Although she staunchly supported him in public, privately Emma's doubts grew. She began to form ideas independent of Sasha's about how best to serve the cause of anarchism.

Six months after the *attentat*, at a weekly meeting organized to elicit support for the commutation of Sasha's prison sentence, Emma found herself annoyed by and drawn to a tall blond man who had the nervous habit of incessantly swinging his leg and fidgeting with matches. She flirtatiously grabbed the matches from him, commenting that "children should not play with fire." The forty-year-old man was quick to respond to the young Emma: "All right, grandmother, but you should know that I am a revolutionist; I love fire. Don't you?" "In the right place," Emma replied, and then admonished him for swinging his leg, which she said made her, and others, nervous. Her playfulness turned to embarrassment when he told her it was a nervous habit he had picked up during his ten years in prison. She identified his experience with Sasha's and was eager to know him.

Ed Brady had just arrived from Austria, where he had recently completed a prison term for the publication of illegal anarchist literature. Here was a comrade in the struggle who could also satisfy Emma's craving for a taste of the elevated world of culture. Brady introduced her to literary classics—Goethe, Shakespeare, Rousseau, Voltaire. He taught her French, and together they read Molière, Racine, and Corneille. He even taught her Austrian and French cooking. Soon their comradeship deepened into love. They began to frequent the local anarchist saloon, Justus Schwab's, where they could debate and enjoy the conversation of the New York literati. Emma worked ten hours a day at her sewing machine, then studied under Ed's tutelage and relaxed into his embraces at night.

The emotional pressures, however, of balancing her work, her concern for Sasha, and her new relationship with Ed Brady were too great for her, and once again her body succumbed to tuberculosis. Her illness was so debilitating that she returned to Rochester, where she rested in a small garden-side room in a home far away from the turmoil of her life in Manhattan and nearby, but not too close, to her family. There, with the help of a young nurse, she began to recuperate. Before she had fully recovered, however, Emma decided that she would go back to New York to work for the unemployed, that political activity would cure her, not isolation in Rochester. Ed Brady greeted her with open arms but tried to discourage her from political work until she got well. Although Emma craved his attention, she resented his presumption of power over her.

Before long, despite the atmosphere of political repression and guilt by association that had surrounded her since Sasha's *attentat*, she dared to re-emerge to give public talks. In 1893, at a rally in Union Square in New York, Emma marched with the women's and girl's contingent of unemployed during a mass demonstration, carrying a red banner, and dared to tell workers to "demonstrate before the palaces of the rich; demand work. If they do not give you work, demand bread. If they deny you both, take bread. It is your sacred right." Not surprisingly, the next day, as she was about to give a talk to the unemployed of Philadelphia, Emma was arrested and extradited to New York. She was charged with "inciting a riot and . . . disbelief in God and government." Emma's friend and contemporary in the anarchist movement, Voltairine de Cleyre, remarked on the fear elicited by Emma's declaration of the power of people to assert their basic rights to economic survival.

> There is no doubt but that power is latently in you; there is no doubt it can be developed; there is no doubt the authorities know this, and fear it, and are ready to exert as much force as is necessary to repress any signs of its development. And this is the explanation of Emma Goldman's imprisonment. The authorities do not fear you as you are; they only fear what you may become. The dangerous thing was "the voice crying in the wilderness," foretelling the power which was to come after it. You should have seen how they feared it in Philadelphia. They got out a whole platoon of police and detectives, and executed a military manoeuvre to catch the woman who had been running around under their noses for three days. And when she walked up to them, then they surrounded and captured her, and guarded the city hall where they kept her over night, and put a detective in the next cell to make notes. Why so much fear? Did they shrink from the stab of the dressmaker's needle? Or did they dread some stronger weapon? . . . *The spirit which animates Emma Goldman is the only one which will emancipate the slave from his slavery, the tyrant from his tyranny—the spirit which is willing to dare and suffer.*

When the police saw that Emma had weakened physically, they thought that she might agree to make a deal to keep herself out of jail. One of her interrogators offered to pay Emma for informing the police about New York radical activities. Outraged, she called him "a miserable cur . . . a Judas." "I'll take prison for life, but no one will ever buy me!" she shouted.

For this affront, combined with her Union Square pronouncement, she was sentenced to one year at Blackwell's Prison. Despite her punishment, however, she triumphed in the wide newspaper coverage of her eloquent courtroom defense.

In prison, Emma was put in charge of a sewing shop, but refused to act as foreman over the other women. Her defiance won her the admiration of her fellow inmates. A bout of rheumatism put her in the prison infirmary, where upon her recovery the visiting physician assigned her to be the head nurse, even though she was completely untrained. Emma began to enjoy her work, to appreciate the riches in friends, attention, and a sense of purpose she had in prison life. She felt, too, that she and Sasha were still kindred spirits, both sacrificing for the cause, their lives temporarily constrained but unreservedly dedicated to creating the conditions for a free future.

When Emma was released from prison in 1894, a grand reception was held for her in New York at the Thalia Theatre on the Upper West Side. She re-entered the political world to find a strong community. Emma Goldman realized that she had become a national celebrity, and had begun to emerge from the predominantly Yiddish-speaking left.

Under the wing of intellectuals and such celebrated members of the avant-garde literary circles as Ambrose Bierce, James Huneker, Sadakichi Hartmann, and John Swinton, Emma was introduced to the roots of indigenous American radicalism. Gradually she gave up her idea that no "idealists" had been born in this country and resolved to address a wider audience. She made new friends, among them a woman named Emma Lee who had been in prison and was currently devoting herself to prison reform.

Emma's relationship with Ed Brady solidified in their decision to find an apartment and live together, but Ed did not seem at all pleased with Emma's independence. He longed to have her to himself; she claimed her own room, however, and had more visitors than he could handle. He dreamed of having a child with her; she asserted that no absorption in the development of one human life would ever shift her attention from her duties to the larger needs of the people. He wanted her to stay at home; instead she found a job in her new prison-acquired profession—nursing. And when he had to give up his job because of poor health Emma started up an ice-cream parlor in Brownsville, with him and another friend. The failure of that venture left Emma convinced that in order to earn the money for them both, she had to obtain her credentials as a nurse. And it was Ed who insisted, despite Emma's early feeling that he did not want her to be independent, that she go to Vienna to study nursing and midwifery in the Allgemeines Krankenhaus. Fedya paid Emma's passage and even sent her $25 a month while she was there. Ed, who was willing to endure yet another year of separation from Emma, sent her off to his beloved Austria to learn a skill and finally to experience the culture and charm of his favorite city.

Emma was twenty-six when she went to Vienna, in August 1895. She also went to London and surrounding towns for a speaking tour. In London, she met some of the great European radical figures of the time: Peter Kropotkin and Enrico Malatesta, the anarchist theorists; and Louise Michel, the heroine of the Paris Commune.

From Kropotkin, Emma took her belief that modern technology, and not a pure rejection of the capitalist world, could be the basis for a communism of abundance. The basis of his vision was an assumption of communal solidarity and cooperation, which he called mutual aid. Kropotkin's sense of revolution as a natural process was more appealing to Emma than the prospect of untamed destruction. It affirmed her sense that while others might regard anarchists as standing outside of history, they were actually in step with history *as it should be*. She was merely hastening the inevitable; political and social education would minimize the destruction and violence that total, immediate change might incur.

But she also embraced the realism of the militant Malatesta. Malatesta was a spokesman for "direct action." He did not want the anarchists to emancipate the people, but the people to emancipate themselves: "In our opinion, all action which is directed towards the destruction of economic and political oppression; which serves to raise the moral and intellectual level of the people; which gives them an awareness of their individual rights and their power, and persuades them to act on their own behalf is a good thing. . . ." Acts of violence and sabotage by small groups or individuals were considered necessary for building the consciousness of the people. Emma accepted the logic of this, but did not make it the focus of her work or activities. She emphasized education first.

During her stay in Vienna, she heard about the work of Sigmund Freud, which confirmed her belief in the centrality of sexual repression and its effects on human thought and action. Emma studied hard enough to earn degrees in midwifery and in nursing, but what had really excited her in Vienna was the culture and the ideas to which she was introduced.

She returned to New York richer in spirit, to a new apartment, which represented Ed's relatively new affluence in the album business. An elegant dinner party of friends greeted her, accompanied by a welcome-home letter from Sasha. He had been released from brutal isolation, where he had been straitjacketed in his own excrement. Now he had access to the prison library and could interact with other inmates. Unfortunately, the most recent plea for a shortening of his sentence had been denied.

Instead of practicing nursing or midwifery, Emma became more deeply involved in the movement, and less involved with Ed. Her days and nights were filled with meetings, much to the disappointment of her lover, who had waited so faithfully for her. Ed's business pressures had undermined his own political activism, and even Fedya was no longer committed to political action, having finally been accepted into the affluent artists' circles of New York. One night, Ed began to rave that Emma was drifting away from him. He gave her an ultimatum: she must choose between him and her political work. He did not want to share her with "anybody or anything." When Emma did not respond to his anger, he walked out of the apartment and resolved never to return.

In the weeks that followed, Emma mourned her loss of Ed. Although she had been preoccupied, she still depended on the stability of his love. She tried to forget him and began to do the work she had trained for as a nurse-midwife. But after the high drama of a birth she would feel empty and depressed about the children born unwanted into poverty. After two weeks, she broke down and wrote to Ed. He ran back to her, and so she tried to reduce her political activities in favor of building a stronger home life with him. Although Emma claimed that she thrived on adversity and "could find expression only in the clashing of wills," her turbulent relationship with Ed began to weaken her. She developed nervous physical symptoms; her self-confidence declined as she felt his growing disapproval of her. For a little while her unstable physical condition, caused by what the doctors called her inverted womb, brought her closer to Ed, who relished taking care of her. He began to realize, though, that he couldn't keep her as a caged bird; when she was well she went on tour again. And once she was in the public eye, he could not restrain his old resentment. As soon as Emma returned from two weeks on the road, she and Ed were at each other again. By the time she left for the next leg of her tour, Emma had begun to see the end of their relationship as inevitable.

Ed wrote to Emma claiming that he had learned to be content with less of her, now that he realized that his sweetheart was married to public life. He even welcomed Emma's suggestion that her youngest brother come to live with them to pursue his medical studies away from Rochester. Making the best of the situation, he agreed, thinking he might enjoy some company while Emma was off on tour. Emma herself began to think of continuing her education and studying medicine, and Ed considered that he might eventually be able to finance such ambitious plans for her.

But while Emma toured the Midwest and the West, she found herself attracted to other men in the anarchist movement. She enjoyed her freedom to follow her impulses, and resented any reminder that Ed was waiting impatiently for her. She continued to write to him, and even did some business for him, marketing one of his inventions at stationery stores across the country. But, when Emma returned, they hardly spoke. She welcomed the chance to do support work for a textile strike in Somerset, New Jersey, as a way of legitimizing her distance from him. When her political work escalated into organizing a mass rally, Emma even hoped secretly that she would be arrested to escape the turmoil she felt with Ed. For his part, Ed resolved to try once more—particularly at this point, when Emma faced danger—to salvage their relationship.

A few weeks after Emma's return from New Jersey, Ed developed pneumonia and needed Emma to nurse him. One evening after Ed had started to feel better, Emma left him with Fedya to attend a meeting, then returned to find Ed asleep alone. Deeply frightened the next morning, when he did not wake up, Emma realized that he had taken morphine in an apparent attempt to kill himself. But he had only taken enough to scare Emma, to cure her of her "mania for meetings," he told her some time after his full recovery. The shock of Ed's desperate act, and Emma's realization that the cause and all their shared ideas meant only "meetings" and "separations" to him, was the ultimate death blow to their seven-year relationship. Knowing that she could never be the available wife that he longed for, Emma, after much distress, walked out of the home that he had made for her.

Her first plan was to attend an anarchist conference in Europe with her Midwestern admirer, Max Baginsky. But free love turned his fancy to yet another young woman, and so Emma set off on a public-speaking tour in the United States, essentially alone.

Emma's spirits were lifted when two wealthy friends of another anarchist admirer, the recently deceased Robert Reitzel, offered to send her to medical school in Switzerland, so that she could have a profession to support her political work. Both successful businessmen, Herman Miller and Carl Stone were motivated as much by sympathy with Emma's political views as by a benevolent impulse to help a promising young idealist acquire respectable skills with which to serve humanity. In the interim, Emma succumbed to Ed's insistence that she return, this time, to a strictly platonic living arrangement with him in their old apartment. But one night before she left for Europe, unable to stand what seemed to him her studied neglect of him, he got so angry he broke his most valuable vases and even tore apart Fedya's nude sketch of Emma.

Within weeks of Emma's departure, Ed was living with another woman and Emma's brother moved out.

Back in Europe, in 1899, Emma found herself resisting the regimentation of medical school, and gravitating toward politics and romance. She met a Czech revolutionist named Hippolyte Havel, whom she found fascinating, despite his possessiveness. Havel had once been admitted to an insane asylum on the grounds that only a lunatic could disbelieve in government. It was Professor Krafft-Ebing who had him released, asserting that he was "saner than all of us." The colorful Havel would often expound on the theme by standing on a street corner with just the frame of an umbrella over his head until a crowd would gather to hear him proclaim that he was "no more ridiculous than this society you live in." During their brief affair, Emma ran off with him to Paris, leaving medical school behind.

The harsh discipline of medical school was only one of the factors that convinced Emma to leave—indeed, the life of a medical student, though arduous, contained more privileges than her former life. Perhaps, in part, she was acting on a deliberate desire not to be respectable, a refusal of possibilities that would have taken her away from the Bohemian political ranks that had come to represent home to her. Her rationale was provided by Kropotkin, who convinced her that she would do more good as a doctor of society's social ills. When she ran off, however, her benefactors of course withdrew their support.

In Paris Emma attended a small Malthusian Congress, dedicated to the controversial cause of disseminating information about contraception and birth control. Emma did not have to face this issue as most women did, because of her "inverted womb," which made conception practically impossible. Yet she felt that the contraception campaign was consistent with many of her own political beliefs. Contraception, she recognized, could have a revolutionary effect on the development of sexual freedom. Through her experiences as a midwife, Emma had witnessed the contrast between a child born in love, free choice, and economic security and the unwanted child born into poverty.

When Emma returned to New York on December 7, 1900, she felt she had at last found a calling that brought together her many talents and interests. By combining her work as midwife with her interest in birth control, Emma could make a direct contribution to the liberation of women, while performing the supportive functions of a devoted mother. She could return to the speaker's platform to advocate contraception, proclaiming that a revolution in sexual values was now possible, striking simultaneously at the restraints placed on personal freedom by the government and by societal convention. At the same time, she could channel her maternal desires into her work as a nurse and midwife, sharing in the intense moment of birthing, experiencing the acute connection between life and death, without the day-to-day work of caring for a child. This preference for living from one "exalted moment" to another echoed through much of her life, from one public platform to another.

The personal situations of Emma's old friends had changed in her absence. She found that Ed was not only married but actually the father of a young child. They managed to see each other on occasion—without his wife and child. And, nine years into his prison term, she was granted permission to visit Sasha. He had become thinner and paler, his body weakened from the year of solitary confinement that had followed an abortive jailbreak. His eyes revealed the tortures of prison life and haunted Emma's return.

Months passed, and Emma slowly re-established herself in New York, beginning to find new strength in her independence; then, on September 7, 1901, came a newspaper headline, echoing others throughout the country: ASSASSIN OF PRESIDENT MCKINLEY AN ANARCHIST, CONFESSES TO HAVING BEEN INCITED BY EMMA GOLDMAN. WOMAN ANARCHIST WANTED.

Leon Czolgosz, a twenty-eight-year-old factory worker and farmhand, called himself an anarchist. He did not believe in governments, rulers, voting, religion, or marriage. On September 6, in Buffalo, New York, he shot and killed the President of the United States. The year before, he told police, he had heard a speech given by Emma Goldman, and from this it was inferred that "Red Emma" was responsible for his act.

The police began a nationwide search for Emma. She disguised herself and left St. Louis, where she was on tour, for Chicago, where she could arrange a better hideout. The local police managed to track her down in the home of an old friend, the wealthy son of a prominent preacher. For a while she pretended to be a Swedish servant, but could not sustain the charade. Emma was interrogated and temporarily jailed. Ed found out about Emma's arrest and wired to assure her that she would have the backing of his firm: "We stand by you to the last." Buffalo officials tried to extradite her, and failed; Emma was set free.

After that, Emma defended Czolgosz, more ardently than anyone else, arguing that the anarchists should not abandon him even if his act was misguided, but all her efforts could not prevent him from being sent to the electric chair.

The irony of Emma's implication in Czolgosz's crime was that she no longer believed in the efficacy of such individual acts of violence. "Acts of violence, except as demonstrations of a sensitive human soul, have proven utterly useless," she wrote. Even so, she sympathized with the state of mind that would prompt someone to commit such a political act, and she vowed never to abandon the memory of Czolgosz's despairing gesture. She dedicated a speech to "those men who close the chapter of their lives with a violent outbreak against our system." In her essay and lecture "The Psychology of Political Violence," Emma quoted Scandinavian playwright Björnstjerne Björnson on those anarchists who saw themselves in the role of "modern martyrs who pay for their faith with blood, and who welcome death with a smile because they believe, as truly as Christ did, that their martyrdom will redeem humanity." Emma placed

> the guilt of those homicides . . . upon every man and woman who intentionally or by cold indifference helps to keep up social conditions that drive human beings to despair. The man who flings his whole life into the attempt, at the cost of his own life, to protest against the wrongs of his fellow men, is a saint compared to the active and passive upholders of cruelty and injustice, even if his protest destroys other lives besides his own. Let him who is without sin in society cast the first stone at such a one.

She joined the argument that such people are not driven by the teachings of anarchism, which valued human life above all else, but by the tremendous pressure of conditions that made their lives unbearable.

> High strung, like a violin string, they weep and moan for life, so relentless, so cruel, so terribly inhuman. In a desperate moment the string breaks. Untuned ears hear nothing but discord. But those

who feel the agonized cry understand its harmony; they hear in it the fulfillment of the most compelling moment of human nature. Such is the psychology of political violence.

The nation's response to Czolgosz's act was a wave of repression against anarchists, which led to the passage of stringent anti-anarchist immigration laws two years later. In nineteenth-century Russia, such tactics might have inspired people to revolt. In the United States, acts of individual violence tended to alienate rather than inspire people. Given the country's more fluid social structure, advocates of change in the United States had more options and could adopt a broader spectrum of attitudes and strategies for social reform and revolution.

Perhaps the strength of Emma's response to Czolgosz came from her memories of planning Frick's assassination with Berkman. Forced to re-evaluate her own past, she now realized that the revolutionary tactics appropriate to Russia could not be transposed to the very different conditions of the United States. Though she still thought the assassination attempts had been justified, she now concluded that they had been serious tactical mistakes. The public had not reached the requisite level of awareness to appreciate the meaning of such political violence.

But the press did not grasp the nuances of Emma's changed ideology, and seized on the chance for another sensational attack on anarchists. The *New York World* of September 14, 1901, described Emma, who was only thirty-two years old, as "a wrinkled, ugly Russian woman" who "would kill all rulers." It was she "who inspired McKinley's assassination," working in secret, plotting with "slayers who are singled out from her body of anarchists. . . . She has been in more than one plot to kill."

During the next several years Emma had to narrow her wide circle of friends and associates: everyone who knew her was questioned. Her father lost many customers at his furniture store and was even asked to leave his synagogue in Rochester. She continued to practice midwifery, but relied on her niece, Stella Comminsky, to act as an intermediary while she stayed away from the public platform. Stella shopped and performed all public functions for Emma, who had to stay in the background.

Stella, the daughter of Emma's oldest sister, Lena, had long been in awe of her great "Tante Emma" and was glad to have the opportunity to help her. Emma had always been drawn to her young niece, identifying with Stella as an adventurous spirit in a stifling family. In turn, Emma's fugitive status gave Stella new freedom and expanded her life experiences.

Emma even resorted to an underground identity as "E. G. Smith" in order to obtain housing during this difficult period. Although Ed offered her their old apartment, she had too much pride to accept, and she thought she could rescue some of their longtime affection by asserting her distance from him. But a more compelling reason for Emma to secure some privacy from Ed was the romantic feeling she had recently developed for a nineteen-year-old friend of her younger brother.

Emma could not sustain her underground life, or contain her impulse to give public talks. Before long she was on the road, speaking to raise money for a coal miners' strike and for the victims of prerevolutionary Russian atrocities. There seemed to be an opening in the clouds that had hovered over her since her implication in Czolgosz's *attentat*. Ed even insisted, just before Christmas, on knowing her measurements so that he could outfit her in high style for the New Year. The festivity ended, however, when the police arrested her at a train station and took her in for questioning, just because she was Emma Goldman. They released her eventually, but the mood in the country had clearly become more repressive.

In 1903, Congress passed the anti-anarchist immigration law, which prohibited entry into the United States of any person who did not believe in organized government. After years of warnings by radicals that such threats to the free expression of opposition political views must be combatted, liberals finally began to take the issue seriously. In an effort to draw attention to their cause, members of liberal intellectual groups sought Emma out as a well-known spokesperson for free expression who could teach them what anarchism really was. Emma enjoyed her exposure to the middle-class liberal intelligentsia, and the easing of her financial worries as well. Nursing and speaking became her means of support once again; she even had the time and peace of mind to read and enjoy living alone.

The coming years were to see radicals' first efforts to invoke the protection of the First Amendment, previously dormant. On many occasions, organizations would defy the wrath of local authorities by inviting Emma Goldman to speak, acting as often out of a desire to assert Emma's right to speak her mind, however heretical, as from any agreement with what she had to say.

One day, Ed came to her in great distress. He had become involved with a woman he later married on the rebound from Emma, he claimed, as a way to assuage his anger and resentment at her rejection. After weeks of immersion in drink and sex, he had found himself actually disliking his girl friend. When he had tried to break up with her, she had cried and pleaded with him to stay with her, even pretending she was pregnant. His conscience had prompted him to marry her. Later, when his wife actually did become pregnant and then presented him with a child, the mellowing experience of fatherhood kept him with her, but in his heart he still longed to be near Emma. He felt that the constant arguments between him and his wife were harming his child, and he resolved to take his daughter away with him. Still holding on to his dream of creating a family with Emma, now he asked her to go to Vienna with him and his child. Emma refused, on the grounds that it would be unfair to his wife, waxing poetic on the helplessness of motherhood rather than facing her own lack of interest in rekindling things with Ed or in mothering his child.

In April, two months before Ed's intended trip, while he was drinking at a saloon near a Long Island Railroad station, he tried to walk to the bathroom and fell, hitting his head against the bar. Some strangers in the bar sent him home in a taxi. He had been supposed to meet a friend hours earlier, and the friend was still waiting when the cab pulled up to Ed's door. But by the time the friend could carry Ed upstairs and call for a doctor, Ed had had a heart attack and could not be revived; the self-abnegating, inwardly raging Ed had died. Emma preferred to see his death as a senseless waste, the pathetic consequence of his drinking and his unhappy marriage, not wishing to consider what contribution the constant push-pull quality of their relationship might have made. His wife, however, banned Emma from the funeral and became hysterical when Emma managed to steal a last look at him in his coffin, before the funeral service. Each woman blamed the other for the tragic end to his life.

Emma kept up her work as a nurse and in fighting the anti-anarchist law. As successive landlords grew uncomfortable about having a notorious anarchist in their house, Emma had to move from place to place. For a while she lived with her brother and another young anarchist, Albert Zibelin; then, in 1904, she rented part of a flat at the recently built 210 East Thirteenth Street from her friends Alexander Horr and his wife. Horr had a particular fondness for Emma. This apartment was to be her most stable base for the next ten years.

Within the first year, Emma's niece Stella, who had always longed for an escape from Rochester, returned to New York to live and work near her Tante Emma. Stella became secretary to a judge. At night, she and Emma did political work, primarily in raising people's awareness of the revolutionary situation in Russia. When Emma's nursing became too taxing, a manicurist she knew suggested that she open a "Vienna scalp and facial" massage parlor, a skill Emma had acquired while she was studying nursing in Vienna, which might support her anarchist work in fewer hours and with less emotional stress. Encouraged by her friends, Emma set up a small office at Seventeenth Street and Broadway, which proved quite successful.

Then, while taking a brief vacation with Stella on Hunter's Island, in the Bronx's Pelham Bay Park, Emma learned that the Pavel Orleneff Theatre Troupe from Russia had been evicted from their living quarters in New York and were now penniless. Emma got a friend to borrow enough money to bring the whole troupe to Hunter's Island to camp out with her and Stella.

Emma had long been intrigued by the emergence of a progressive, inspirational Russian theater, seeing in it a possible alternative to direct agitation and propaganda. Pavel Orleneff appreciated Emma's talents, too, and after several weeks on the island asked her whether she would consider working as the translator and manager of his theater troupe. He agreed that she would have to assume an alias. As "Miss Smith," Emma took the job.

The relationship was a mutually beneficial and rewarding one. For Orleneff and his leading lady, Alla Nazimova, Emma's skill and dedication in promoting them and anchoring their work in a little theater on East Third Street was indispensable. For Emma, working in Orleneff's behalf made it possible to combine her love of art and her dedication to politics. She found the theater, as she had hoped, an ideal vehicle for conveying a message of freedom without suffering the repression that had become an increasingly inevitable result of more direct political expression. Orleneff's production of Chirikov's *The Chosen People* was a protest against Russian pogroms. His dramatic interpretation of *Crime and Punishment* displayed the spirit of the Russian people in a positive light at a time when anti-Russian feeling was rife. Hundreds of Americans came and shared the magic of his performances even though they did not understand the Russian language.

The experience with Orleneff and Nazimova later became the cornerstone of Emma's book *The Social Significance of the Modern Drama*, in which she described the theater as the medium that "mirrors the complex struggle of life," and is "at once the reflex and the inspiration of mankind in its eternal seeking for things higher and better." She saw modern dramatic art as "the dynamite which undermines superstition, shakes the social pillars and prepares men and women for the reconstruction."

Although Orleneff's troupe was not always financially successful, Emma's resourcefulness kept them afloat through all sorts of adversity. When it was time for Orleneff to return to Russia, he and his troupe expressed their gratitude to Emma, who had never received a salary, by giving a special benefit performance of Ibsen's *Ghosts* to raise money to help realize Emma's dream of starting a new political magazine. The magazine would provide Emma with a platform from which to disseminate anarchist ideas on politics, social science, and literature. She could make it the focus of her political work and use it as a vehicle for a return to the speaker's podium, where she felt her greatest strength and satisfaction lay.

Emma planned to christen her magazine *The Open Road* until she found there was already a publication with that name. Instead she named it *Mother Earth*, evoking an image of regenerative natural powers that could prepare the ground for the growth of a new, anarchist world. The name also expressed Emma's own powerful maternal urges, which now had no other structured outlet since the demands of starting the new magazine forced her to drop all her other work, nursing, midwifery, and even her massage parlor.

This change in her career came at a point when, at the age of thirty-five, she was passing beyond what were then considered the child-bearing years. But now, she told herself, she would give birth to the magazine, nurse it through its infancy, and nurture it to maturity. Frequent allusions in *Mother Earth* to the magazine as "a child born of love" made it clear that this was a substitute for the baby she would never have. It was also at this time that Emma's intimacy with her brother's young friend Dan, which had been going on for some time, ended abruptly, in the misunderstandings inevitable given their thirteen-year age difference. The magazine gave her a sense of fulfillment that counterbalanced her loss.

Mother Earth, launched in March 1906, was to stand out as an anarchist alternative to the more theoretical and socialist-oriented popular periodical, *The Masses*. Her magazine would bring political messages formulated by the playwrights and poets of the time to a less intellectual and more radical audience than that of *The Masses*. Stamped by Emma's unique combination of politics and art, it quickly became a leading forum for discussion of anarchist ideas and the controversial issues of the time. It reported on anarchist activity throughout the world, and chronicled Emma's own activities and thoughts. An unusually large number of its pages were devoted to political poetry and drama criticism. It was meant to be inspirational and included little criticism of the movement. The first issue of *Mother Earth* sold three thousand copies within a week; another thousand copies were printed to fill orders.

Although running the magazine amounted to a constant battle for economic survival, Emma would never sacrifice her principles in the quest for broader circulation. Dedicating the October 1906 issue to the memory of Leon Czolgosz, for example, cost the magazine many early subscribers. But somehow the struggling monthly survived.

On May 18, 1906, while Emma was organizing and preparing the magazine, Alexander Berkman was released. The brutality of those fourteen years in prison had left deep scars, both on Sasha's spirit and on his body. Emma was overwhelmed by sadness, and Sasha by a profound depression. Despite their former closeness, they seemed to each other like strangers who had known each other only in a dream. They still felt deep love and devotion for one another, but the differences in their lives over those fourteen years had created a great distance between them. Emma had become more sophisticated and had pursued diverse interests, from midwifery to *Mother Earth*.

Berkman's confinement, on the other hand, had given him a distorted sense of the wider world. He had spent the time absorbing the harsh lessons of the prison underworld, struggling to survive in a penal system that debilitated rather than reformed. He emerged from prison to find a dramatically changed world, while his own identity as a zealous left-wing militant had remained essentially unchanged. Smothered by what he experienced as Emma's overprotectiveness, at the point of suicide many times, Sasha struggled with the conflicts of his emotional re-entry for nearly two years.

In October 1906, not six months after Sasha's release, Emma thought that it was time for him to go on a speaking tour, to re-introduce himself to the anarchist circles and share what he had learned in prison. The idea appealed to him at first, but once he was actually out of New York on tour, he found himself in a constant state of agitation. No audience or reception seemed welcoming or massive enough for him to regain his sense of worth, and he was subject to a frenzied compulsion to find total privacy, in reaction against the lack of privacy he had suffered in prison. One night he actually went running through the streets looking for a place to be alone.

Becoming obsessed with the desire to end his life, he bought a revolver and traveled to Buffalo, where he knew no one. But in Buffalo he felt suddenly drawn to go back to New York City, and there he wandered the streets for days. Finally Sasha checked into a room on the Bowery. He was on the verge of killing himself several times, but for his urge to see Emma once again. When he sent word to her from a telegraph station,

Emma came to him, terrified by his desperation. She had organized a search party, sure that he was already dead.

Emma promised Sasha that she would protect him from the crowds of people who habitually frequented her apartment. Only Stella, Max Baginsky, and a young anarchist friend named Becky Edelson would be allowed to visit. Emma tried to give Sasha the quiet and protection that he craved after his release but was too distraught and disoriented to ask for.

Meanwhile, Emma continued her activities outside of their apartment. After three young anarchists were arrested at a meeting to discuss Czolgosz and his act, Emma was asked to speak at a meeting to protest their arrest. Ten minutes into the speech of one of the young anarchists, who had been bailed out, the police broke in and began to abuse the people at the meeting physically. One policeman struck Emma on the back and arrested her, though she was bailed out, pending an indictment for her offense under New York's new Criminal Anarchy Act, and eventually the charges were dropped. The tactics against anarchists were, by necessity, becoming more subtle, but no less persistent: raids of anarchist social events, for instance, and harassment of hall-keepers who rented space to the anarchists. The one positive side effect of Emma's arrest and the general zeal with which she and her friends were now hounded by the police was that Sasha mobilized himself to fight for them. This work pulled him out of the aimlessness that had followed his release from prison.

But his period of activity and hope did not last long. Depression returned, this time focused on his resentment of his economic dependence on Emma. Emma convinced a friend to lend Sasha money to set up a printshop. But this short-lived project brought him back face to face with his own inability to cope with a changed world—and with a much less pliable or impressionable Emma. He was critical of her and probably felt rejected by this woman of the world who had occupied a central role in his dreams of intimacy throughout his confinement. Although she inwardly craved his affection, Emma acted more maternal to him than intimate while his spirit was so broken, and her attitude probably played into his insecurities. As an anarchist, Sasha felt that he could express only respect for Emma's sexual freedom, not his own disappointment. Instead, he managed to find legitimate political reasons to undermine her in every other way. Emma escaped his constant criticism by planning a cross-country speaking tour in behalf of *Mother Earth*, which would mean leaving the major editing, writing, and organizational work to Sasha. Although Sasha would have preferred having his own weekly paper, geared more directly to workers, he agreed to help Emma.

During her tour, Emma wished that she and Sasha could rekindle their feelings of sexual communion. All of her public greatness, the positive but double-edged newspaper coverage (such as "Noted Anarchist Is Tame"), meant nothing to her without his love, she wrote him. She felt bound to Sasha as she had never been to anyone before or since their involvement. But they had made idols of each other while they were apart, and now, faced with reality, they were in constant battle. On tour, Emma re-created her image of an intimate relationship with her old comrade and lover:

My greatness adds nothing to my life or the wealth of my nature. If I am proud of anything, it is that I have learned to appreciate real true value in human nature, that I have learned the power of love. Everything else means naught to me. 12,000 people applauded, waved hats and handkerchiefs, screamed and yelled last night, when I finished, yet I saw them not. I only saw one face, one soul being far away from me and yet so close, I could almost feel his warmth. And my soul cried out for the being all night. Do you know who it is, can you guess it? . . . Let me bring the joy of life, . . . the ecstasy of love.

But when Emma returned, Sasha was still depressed and angry. His criticisms struck her as naïvely purist and unjustifiably extreme. Although at first he seemed competent to do his work on the magazine, he could not transfer this ability to his personal relationship with Emma. Disappointed by the summer, she left once again, this time to attend an International Anarchist Conference in Amsterdam.

Emma traveled to Holland with her old comrade and casual lover, Max Baginsky. The trip banished the emptiness she had felt. She enjoyed the discussions about the pros and cons of organizations fostering individual freedom, and the international ambience of the conference. She went on to Paris, where Stella had been living since early 1907 and working as a stenographer for the American Consulate in Paris. They had a wonderful time frequenting cafés and visiting old comrades, including Peter Kropotkin. But her carefree time ended abruptly when she and Max went on to London and were informed that the United States government was planning to stop Emma's re-entry on the basis of its anti-anarchist law. After being shadowed by Scotland Yard, Emma and Max skillfully dodged their surveillance and made their way to Liverpool, from which they sailed to Montreal and then on to New York.

When she returned, *Mother Earth* was in complete disorder, finances were worse than they had ever been, and Sasha, besides being harsh with and critical of Emma, had become sexually involved with Becky Edelson, who was only fifteen. Emma rationalized Sasha's attraction to someone so young by noting that his life had stopped during the fourteen years he spent in prison. But inwardly, Emma felt hurt that he was no longer attracted to her.

The illusion of their continued love affair had long since worn thin, but Sasha's affair made the fact that it was an illusion clear to Emma. Although she did manage to salvage some of the warmth and camaraderie of her relationship with Sasha, the inner calm she had felt during their long separation—the omnipotent assurance of being unconditionally loved by her brave hero behind bars—was shaken by this withdrawal of both sexual affection and political approval. She had had many lovers during his imprisonment, but she had thought that her ambivalence toward them might in part be the result of her loyalty to Sasha, her profound hope that together they could act out their dreams of love and anarchism upon his release. Besides Ed Brady, Johann Most and Robert Reitzel had both died in the last few years as well. Now, although Sasha was alive, all hope of a romantic reconciliation with him was dead, too. Emma continued to work for her ideal, but inwardly she felt more alone and less hopeful than she had felt since that hot summer day in 1889 when she left Rochester to come to New York.

3

LOVE, LIKE A MIGHTY SPECTRE

Yes, I am a woman, indeed too much of it. That's my tragedy. The great abyss between my woman nature and the nature of the relentless revolutionist is too great to allow much happiness in my life. But then who can boast of happiness?

By the time she wrote these words, in a 1907 letter to the anarchist historian Max Nettlau, Emma felt that her personal fate was already sealed. Now that intimacy with Sasha was no longer even a fantasy, her past seemed like a string of tragic love affairs. She resigned herself to the prospect of a life in which the satisfaction she took in her growing public reputation and political effectiveness would coexist with the sense of failure and lack of fulfillment she experienced in her private life. The contrast struck her most acutely during her promotion tours for *Mother Earth*. In city after city, depression and loneliness would engulf her the moment she stepped from the platform after addressing a large crowd. The exhilaration of these moments in the public spotlight was followed by long nights in hotel rooms, or even sometimes in the local jail. Her soul-stirring speeches had earned her the title "High Priestess of Anarchism," and for the time being Emma was willing to endure the primarily solitary existence that seemed to be its price: lurking in her consciousness of herself as a public woman was the fear that if indeed she did find love, it might mean the loss of her work, even of her personality.

Thus, when Emma charged into Chicago on March 5, 1908, she anticipated finding, at best, gratification from a warmly receptive audience, not from a lover. The police were in an especially ugly mood, determined to stop Emma from speaking anywhere in the city. They had not yet recovered from the shock of the massive march of the unemployed on January 23, 1907, in which they suspected the involvement of local anarchists. Then, just two days before Emma's scheduled arrival, a Russian immigrant who had been clubbed by the police during the demonstration made an attempt on the life of Police Chief Shippy. Shippy escaped injury, but Lazarus Averbuch, his assailant, was shot and killed by the police chief's son. The police and press, who had been in a panic at the prospect of an alliance between the anarchists and the restless masses of unemployed workers, quickly labeled Averbuch an anarchist, although no one in the anarchist ranks knew much about him.

The *Chicago Daily Tribune* of March 3, 1908, in a seven-column front-page story, described the would-be killer as

> an insane type, a disciple of Emma Goldman, "Queen of the Reds," and probably a marcher in the recent parade of the unemployed which had "Dr." Ben L. Reitman at its head. He was inspired to his murderous attack upon the Chief of Police partly by the rebuff which the marchers had received that day at the hands of the police and partly by the announcement of the police department that Miss Goldman would not be allowed to speak on anarchy at German Hod Carriers hall next Friday.

In an accompanying front-page article, the *Tribune*, fully aware of Emma Goldman's imminent arrival, reported the right-wing reaction. They seized on the assassination attempt as proof of the need for legislation that would "make it impossible for the assassin to fire his bullet from under the cloak of 'reason' and 'personal rights.'" Their editorial urged adoption of a measure modeled after recent New York State legislation "which prohibits, under heavy penalties, the making of anarchist speeches or circulation of anarchist literature."

The resurgence of anti-anarchist repression was not restricted to Chicago. On the same day that the *Tribune* article appeared, the U.S. Secretary of Commerce and Labor issued an order to all immigration officials seeking their cooperation in an effort to rid the country of "all alien anarchists and criminals falling within the law relating to deportation."

Emma's arrival in Chicago—the city that had been the scene of the Haymarket Affair—was greeted with venomous newspaper articles. BOLD PRIESTESS OF REDS APPEARS, trumpeted the headline in the *Chicago Daily Tribune* of March 6; EMMA GOLDMAN ARRIVES IN CHICAGO WITH SNEERS FOR THE POLICE AND PRAISE FOR AVERBUCH. WILL NOT KEEP PEACE, DETERMINED TO PREACH ANARCHY IN PUBLIC. Always ready for a fight, Emma told reporters that it was ludicrous to assume that Averbuch was an anarchist just because he had tried to kill the police chief. She also implied that the police might have staged the events, to justify the killing of Averbuch as self-defense. She made known her intention to attend Averbuch's funeral, which was to be held at the same cemetery in which the Haymarket martyrs had been buried.

Emma searched without success for a lecture hall: landlords heeded police warnings that they were prepared to raid any hall that would provide a stage for Emma, and her plans to use the Masonic Temple fell through when the lease of the sponsoring organization was suddenly canceled. Although Emma had planned to deliver a number of speeches and lectures in different locations in Chicago, she began to fear that she would not be able to speak at all. Efforts by local anarchist comrades to outwit the police by making secret arrangements for a hall were getting nowhere. Gradually she became so worn down that she literally collapsed in exhaustion. A doctor in the anarchist movement cared for Emma in her house. The office of this local anarchist, Dr.

Becky Yampolsky, became Emma's temporary base of operations. Dr. Ben Lewis Reitman, a leader of the recent march of the unemployed, appeared one day at Dr. Yampolsky's. Reitman, an offbeat local celebrity who had earned the title of "Hobo King," had come to offer the "Red Queen" the use of his Hobo Hall. It was a meeting of outcast royalty.

Emma had been curious to meet Reitman ever since reading newspaper accounts of the beating he had been given by the Chicago police during the march of the unemployed. She was intrigued by this figure who had one foot in the respectable medical world and the other in the underworld of pimps, prostitutes, hobos, and other outcasts. Although Ben had no formal ties to anarchist circles, Emma had recognized, in the accounts of his role in the march, a fellow crusader for justice. She did not know that he had been recruited by the socialists to participate in the march, only becoming a leader by default when others backed out in fear of police violence. Ben's scars and daring ways fed Emma's wishful assumption that he was a long-term leftist political activist as well. She found herself drawn to Reitman immediately, and revived from her weakened physical and mental state. She later recalled their meeting in her autobiography:

> He arrived in the afternoon, an exotic picturesque figure with a large black cowboy hat, flowing silk ties, and huge cane . . . a tall man with a finely shaped head covered with a mass of black curly hair, which evidently had not been washed for some time. His eyes were brown, large and dreamy. His lips, disclosing beautiful teeth when he smiled, were full and passionate. He looked a handsome brute. His hands, narrow and white, exerted a peculiar fascination. His finger nails, like his hair, seemed to be on strike against soap and brush. I could not take my eyes off his hands. A strange charm seemed to emanate from them.

As they met repeatedly over the next few days to discuss how to transform the shabby headquarters of his Brotherhood Welfare Association into a fit place for Emma to speak, each sensed in the other a boldness and willingness to take chances. Their conversation remained focused on ways Reitman might be able to help overcome Emma's immediate political frustrations, but they were both distracted by a growing sexual attraction:

> From the moment he had first entered Yampolsky's office, I had been profoundly stirred by him. Our being much together since had strengthened his physical appeal for me. I was aware that he also had been aroused; he had shown it in every look, and one day he had suddenly seized me in an effort to embrace me. I had resented his presumption, though his touch had thrilled me. In the quiet of the night, alone with my thoughts, I became aware of a growing passion for the wild-looking handsome creature, whose hands exerted such a fascination.

Emma remembered their first encounter as one of earthy excitement. For Reitman, it was the glimpse of what seemed a more elevated life that held the strongest fascination: "Prior to meeting Emma Goldman and her associates I thought there was only one force in the world to make men good and improve conditions, and that was religion. After I became acquainted with Emma Goldman, anarchism and social philosophies, religion had a new meaning for me."

Reitman was a Chicago gynecologist who pioneered in the treatment and prevention of venereal disease. He had been dubbed "King of the Hobos" for his earlier work as an organizer of the Hobo College, which provided an educational and political base for the migrant workers. He was born on New Year's Day 1879 in St. Paul, Minnesota. In 1907, Ben described himself in an essay as "an American by birth, a Jew by parentage, a Baptist by adoption, single by good fortune, a physician and teacher by profession, cosmopolitan by choice, a Socialist by inclination, a rascal by nature, a celebrity by accident, a tramp by 20 years experience, and a Tramp Reformer by inspiration."

He is best known for his book *Sister of the Road: The Autobiography of Box Car Bertha*, which chronicles the life of a woman on the road, surviving marginally among the hobo clans of that era. His insight into social marginality came from his own experiences growing up in a predominantly Irish and Black red-light district of Chicago. When he was a small boy, his father deserted him, his mother, Ida, and brother, Lew. Eventually his brother, who identified more with his father, left home, too. Ben became the favored son and his mother's mainstay. Poverty had forced him to rummage through trash for scrap metal he could sell to the junk man for ready cash, and to run errands to saloons for prostitutes and pimps in return for free lunches. His mother did odd jobs, and may have even been a prostitute herself. Ben remembered her as having many "husbands" during these years. He played in railroad yards and explored empty boxcars, where he met hobos who told him about their adventures tramping from city to city. The young boy found these tales of vagabondage so alluring that he quit school before he was eleven, and ran away to become a hobo himself. His wanderlust was also a means of breaking, at least temporarily, his strong and sometimes terrifying tie to his mother. On the road he was influenced by railroad-chapel ministers who inspired him to believe in a religion based on the idea of love and service to humanity. When he was seventeen, he went to sea as a fireman, and was sent to Antwerp, London, Marseilles, the Black Sea, Egypt, Africa, India, Persia, and Arabia. He had even enlisted in the army, then decided that his own orders were the only ones he meant to obey, and he promptly deserted.

Returning to Chicago as his home base, he took many odd jobs, one of which, as a janitor in Chicago's Polyclinic Laboratory, led him into the world of medicine. It seems that he stopped his mopping so many times to listen to the lecture of a visiting Viennese doctor that when the doctor was late to his new class, Ben was able to put on a white jacket and successfully deliver an identical medical discourse, masquerading as the absent professor. The medical-school officials were both outraged and amazed by Ben's prank. Professor Leo Loeb, a pathologist at the College of Physicians and Surgeons, was impressed by Ben's zeal and ability despite his lack of education, and urged him to become a medical student, even paid his tuition. But after Reitman had successfully gone through medical school and established a private practice, he still found himself with the old hobo itch, and would periodically close his office to climb aboard a boxcar. He tramped through Europe, then returned only to set off for the West, where he encountered the San Francisco earthquake of 1906. He rode the rails through the Southwest and served for a time as doctor to a railroad construction gang in Mexico.

As he was returning from his expeditions, he stopped off in St. Louis to see friends who were involved in the Brotherhood Welfare Association. More commonly known as the Hobo College, the association was a center for informal education, political organizing, and social services for people traveling from town to town on the rails, a place where a hobo was sure to find a friend and a roof over his or her head. The college functioned as a political pressure group to reform vagrancy laws, improve municipal lodging houses, demand pay for work done in jail, and in general improve the lot of the itinerant laborer. Ben became convinced that he should open a Chicago branch of the college. On May 20, 1907, in a flamboyant attempt to bring the plight of the hobo to national attention, Ben invited all social outcasts in Chicago from "the county jail, the hospitals, lodges, missions and barrelhouses . . . from Hinky Dink's saloon" to a "Hobo banquet" at one of Chicago's finest hotels, the Windsor-Clifton. The event was described in a book about these *Knights of the Road*: "Although Reitman declared the banquet a success, he lamented that reporters who covered the event saw only the hoopla and not the pathos. From the gutter bums to the boys who had only recently run away from home, the crowd could have told the writers a hundred poignant tales. But Reitman's serious purpose in gathering the men together was lost in stories the following day about hundreds of Weary Willies messing good hotel carpets."

Both the "hobo banquet" and the "march of the unemployed" had put Reitman at the center of local political controversy. Yet he probably did not appreciate the consequences of his decision to help Emma: his offer of the Hobo Hall was a decisive step for Ben into the tumultuous world of American radicals.

Ben's initial offer was frustrated when the fire department suddenly proclaimed his hall unsafe for more than nine people. Ben and Emma were still determined to go ahead with the event; but when the evening came, they found the Hobo Hall's entrance blocked by the police. The *Chicago Daily Tribune* gave front-page coverage to this latest successful police effort to prevent Emma from speaking: "Nearly 200 anarchists, socialists and others with an appetite for highly spiced intellectual food assembled last night in front of a vacant store building at 892 Dearborn Street to hear another of Emma Goldman's lectures, but it failed to come off. . . . Forty or fifty policemen, with Inspector Wheeler in charge, told the crowd to go away. 'I offered to put in a new floor,' said Reitman, 'and to take the doors off their hinges, but the police didn't seem to want any meeting held.'"

Generally, Emma's speaking tours were widely attended by audiences from a broad political and social spectrum. In those days, evening lectures were a common form of entertainment as well as enlightenment. Emma spoke in lecture halls and sometimes even in barrooms, to the intelligentsia as well as uneducated workers, with responses ranging from wild enthusiasm to disrespectful howling. The strength of Emma's personality and the provocative nature of her talks guaranteed an interesting evening, although she tended to be more genteel with her upper-class audiences and more brazen in addressing the working class. Anarchist clubs, free-speech groups, and labor organizations generally arranged for her lectures and accommodations. After her talks there would be time for socializing and the chance to lionize Emma.

Emma's mere presence in the audience of a Chicago Anthropological Society meeting, the night after the police broke up her own meeting, warranted detective infiltration and another front-page article in the Daily Tribune, which noted that "Miss Goldman with pinkish cheeks and sparkling eyes that her rimless glasses could not hide, was looking her prettiest. She had on a black silk dress with the neat white lawn cuffs escalloped on the edge."

There were so many plainclothes officers present that the anthropologist presiding over the evening's proceedings, irritated by the disruption they caused at the back of the room, invited them to sit down and make themselves comfortable, adding, "There's plenty of room up front, gentlemen." Shortly after a detective sat down beside her, Emma left the hall with Ben—followed by the two detectives who had been assigned to shadow them.

Determined to work with Ben to find a place to speak, Emma included him in a secret meeting, called by the anarchists who had helped to arrange her visit, to make plans for an unpublicized appearance at an anarchist cultural event, for the Literary Society at Workman's Hall. But when the event was under way and Emma arrived on stage to deliver her speech, "Anarchy as It Really Is," she was met by police, who literally pushed her out the door.

As Ben described it, "Captain Mahoney, a great, big, pig-faced Irishman, weighing about two hundred and fifty pounds, rushed to the stage and without the slightest provocation dragged Miss Goldman from the platform, and pulled and hauled her through the hall like a sack of flour, cursing and shoving her all the way. . . ."

Her extensive experience at handling such harassment was evident in her response; rather than succumbing to the fear and confusion of the situation, Emma made an unexpected request of her audience: "The police are here to cause another Haymarket riot. Don't give them a chance. Walk out quietly and you will help our cause a thousand times more." The audience responded with symbolic defiance, singing a revolutionary song as they filed out. The following day, the newspapers derided the police for having inadvertently played into the hands of the anarchists by drawing added attention to Emma Goldman in their effort to deny her the right to speak. The *Daily Tribune* of March 17, 1908, reported the conversation between the police captain and Emma, which concluded with this exchange: "'Thought you'd come here to make trouble, eh?' the Captain continued. 'Behave yourself,' said Miss Goldman sharply. 'Talk like a man, even if you are a policeman.'"

Every well-known anarchist in town was present, the article continued, "with the single exception of Lucy Parsons, with whom Emma Goldman is not on the best of terms": the fact that Emma sold and promoted Frank Harris's book *The Bomb*, which exposed the personal lives of the Haymarket martyrs, enraged Lucy. Lucy, who was devoted to the cause of the workers, accused Emma of compromising her politics by addressing large middle-class audiences. Emma had always resented the way in which Lucy Parsons, widow of the martyr Albert Parsons, traded on her husband's heroism. To Emma, Lucy was another case of a woman taking her identity from her husband. Emma thought Lucy should prove herself through her own political activity, as Emma herself had done. And no doubt there was an undercurrent of competitiveness between the two women. Emma generally preferred center stage.

> Ben Reitman, dressed as a tramp, with a cloth cap pulled down over his eyes and with an unshaven face, arrived at the hall a little after 9 o'clock as the advance guard of Miss Goldman who was secreted even then behind the wings, though no one knew when she was smuggled in. Reitman, at the latter end of the program, delivered a recitation himself, "Celestine of Camp Royal." . . . Dr. Reitman, who was arrested by the police when he tried to lead a parade of the unemployed, and dislikes trouble, disappeared in the confusion following the suppression of Miss Goldman. Later he turned up at the Yampolsky flat and told reporters that "Assistant Chief Schuettler failed to keep good faith with us. He promised that if we got a hall and it complied with the building ordinances, Miss Goldman would be permitted to speak. It just shows that the police do not keep their word."

Besides providing this radical civics lesson for Reitman, the widely reported suppression of Emma's speech sparked the formation of a chapter of the Free Speech Society in Chicago and drew curious crowds to Emma's subsequent lectures in other parts of the country.

But for the anarchists who planned the meeting, there was still the question of who had leaked the information about Emma's surprise appearance. Although he had been kicked and dragged down the steps by the police, suspicion fell on the one newcomer, the outsider who had offered his assistance—Dr. Ben L. Reitman. Reitman's conspicuous absence from the follow-up meeting, held to assess the day's events, fueled suspicions. Emma was indignant when she heard the accusations and made excuses for Reitman's failure to attend, but she went home "clinging to [her] faith in the man, yet fearing that he might be at fault."

Recalling later how Ben had assured her the next day that he had no idea who had notified the press and the authorities, she wrote, "Whatever doubts I had had the night before melted like ice at the first rays of the sun. It seemed impossible that anyone with such a frank face could be capable of treachery or deliberate lies." But Emma was exhausted from the whole ordeal, and so distraught and confused about Ben, that she again collapsed and had to postpone her next talk in Milwaukee. Newspapers as far away as San Jose reported EMMA GOLDMAN SUFFERS RELAPSE:

> Emma Goldman, anarchist, suffered a physical and mental collapse last night, and was taken to the home of a physician. Her sudden collapse was attributed to her strenuous efforts during the last few days to secure a hall in which to speak in defiance of the police.
>
> During the last two days Miss Goldman has displayed symptoms of nervousness and mental depression, portending an early breakdown. She has been busy on her lecture, "What Anarchy Really Means," which she intended to deliver in Milwaukee tonight.

A few days later, Emma felt well enough to leave for her next lecture appearance, in Milwaukee, with firmer faith in Ben's integrity and with relief that what had begun as a turbulent trip had ended in relative peace. Asserting the fallacy of the myth that "anyone can lift himself from the gutter to the presidential chair," she lectured in Milwaukee to at least a thousand people; such large audiences were not unusual when Emma had recently received a lot of attention in the press. Yet even the success of her meeting could not assuage the loneliness she felt once again. Despite the warmth of her comrades in Milwaukee, "a great longing possessed me, an irresistible craving for the touch of the man who had so attracted me in Chicago. I wired for him to come, but once he was there, I fought desperately against an inner barrier I could neither explain nor overcome."

When Emma completed her lecture series in Milwaukee, before continuing on to Minneapolis, she and Reitman returned to Chicago, free for the time being to get to know each other without the constant pressures of lectures and meetings. Emma had no plans to do further speaking in Chicago, but her sense of playful abandon inspired her to call the police chief when she arrived to say, "This is Emma Goldman, I just wanted you to know I am back." "Thank you for calling up," he replied. "We heard you were back."

Emma was fascinated by Ben's taste for adventure and his colorful tales of a past so different from her own. He seemed the embodiment of characters she remembered from the novels of Dostoevsky and Gorki. "I craved life and love, I yearned to be in the arms of the man who came from a world so unlike mine. . . . I was caught in the torrent of an elemental passion I had never dreamed any man could rouse in me. I responded shamelessly to its primitive call, its naked beauty, its ecstatic joy."

This unreserved joy changed back to doubt, just as Emma was preparing to leave town for another speaking engagement. At a farewell dinner at Chicago's Bismarck Cafe, Emma's party was seated across the room from a police captain who, to Emma's horror, greeted Reitman with the cordiality of an old friend. She was stunned. "Ben Reitman, whose embrace had filled me with a mad delight, chumming with detectives! . . . Was it Reitman who had informed them? Was it possible? And I had given myself to the man!"

Emma left town confused and angry. When she arrived in Milwaukee, a wire from Ben was waiting for her. Why had she left so abruptly? Emma could not bring herself to reply. That afternoon, she received another telegram from Ben: "I love you, I want you. Please let me come." Emma wired a curt response: she did not want love from any friend of a police captain! Emma reached her next destination, Winnipeg, to find the long letters of a man desperate to exonerate himself. Ben's explanation of his connection to the police captain was convincing enough. His respectability as a doctor was useful to the tramps, hobos, and prostitutes in trouble who often needed a spokesperson to deal with the authorities. "It was never anything else," Ben pleaded; "please believe me and let me prove it to you."

When Emma returned to Minneapolis, she found more letters pleading to let Ben come to her. During the day she managed to keep thoughts of Ben away, by focusing on the political tasks of her trip, but at night

I dreamed that Ben was bending over me, his face close to mine, his hands on my chest. Flames were shooting from his finger tips and slowly enveloping my body. I strained towards them, craving to be consumed by their fire. When I awoke, my heart kept whispering to my rebellious brain that a great passion often inspired high thoughts and fine deeds. Why should I not be able to inspire Ben, to carry him with me to the world of my social ideals? I wired: "Come," and spent twelve hours between sickening doubt and mad desire to believe in the man. It could not be that my instinct should be so misleading, I reiterated to myself—that anyone worthless could so irresistibly appeal to me. Whatever might have been at stake, I had to believe in him with an all embracing faith.

Once reunited with Ben, Emma found her doubts swiftly allayed by his repeated assurances of devotion. But there was work to be done— Minneapolis was just another stop on a long-planned tour that was to take her across the Midwest and on to the West Coast—though neither of the lovers could bear the thought of being separated for months.

Determined to find a way to remain with her, Ben offered to become her aide on the road. He would prove his devotion by putting himself in a place few men were willing to occupy—behind the scenes, as a supporter of the woman he loved. He would arrange meetings, sell literature, and perform any other task, large or small, that would help Emma in her work, anything to be near her. Emma, excited by the prospect of Ben's company on her lonely trek across the country, quickly agreed.

Their destination was California. As the train pulled away from the station, Emma experienced a simultaneous feeling of freedom and security that she had never felt before. But she also had nagging doubts that this new alliance would not work. Ben was of another world, unsophisticated politically, unwilling to be guided by political principles, socially clumsy, and probably unwelcome in her circles. How could she justify the power "this primitive creature" had over her? And surely their strong wills would collide. Yet her deep longing for constant companionship and her passionate attraction to Ben stilled her doubts.

This first of their tours together lived up to Emma's highest expectations. She and Ben were, she thought, effective revolutionaries during the day, and passionate lovers at night. She felt a new exuberance that carried her through the demanding schedule of travel, speaking, press interviews, and encounters with the police that had become a way of life. True to his word, Ben quickly became an effective promoter and assistant. His bold skill at creating a spectacle to attract audiences brought increasing numbers of people to each appearance. Yet Emma disliked the lack of privacy that accompanied celebrity status, and referred to herself as "public property." Given that her talks dealt with controversial ideas about sexuality, she needed to maintain some propriety in her personal life, so as not to make herself any more threatening to the general public than she already was. In a letter written to Ben while he was doing advance work for Emma's tour in October 1908, she outlined the complicated steps they were taking to make the public think Ben was just her "manager":

> I want you to rent a decent furnished room and tell the people you are expecting your wife there. I will go to a hotel, at least I will register there, see reporters there, etc., under my own name. But when I arrive you must take me to your room, that we can celebrate our reunion in freedom and beauty, a reunion that only such love as ours makes worthwhile. Of course, we will be able to carry out this plan only if no one but you knows when I come; also, the room you will get must be in a different section of the city from where the hotels are. Don't you think that is a good plan, sweetheart?

Despite her complaints about Ben's tendency to crave publicity, she had to admit that, judging by the sheer numbers of their listeners, they were proving an effective team. Subscriptions to *Mother Earth*, which increased steadily as Emma and Ben's lives became more entwined, provided another indication of Ben's contribution. Emma thrived in her new love, and was also pleased to note a change in Ben's political views and values. Deeply influenced by the power of her convictions, Ben gradually shifted from his belief in the centrality of divine inspiration toward a new, equally fervent, vision of anarchism.

Because he had worked with unemployed hobos and prostitutes, Ben thought himself familiar with the underside of American society and its strained relations with the authorities. Now, through Emma, he was exposed to new levels of official harassment. From the minute Emma and Ben entered San Francisco in late April 1908, they were surrounded and followed by police and detectives. In fact, uninvited detective "escorts" boarded their train 100 miles outside the city and rode into town with them. Their arrival was greeted gleefully by the local press, happy to have a story combining sensational fears of political violence with illicit love, exotic characters, and intrigue. Although their public relationship as speaker and road manager was quite professional, and hotel-room arrangements always decorous, the mere fact of their traveling together and speaking of free love raised some eyebrows. The headline in the *San Francisco Examiner* read: EMMA GOLDMAN IS ST. FRANCIS GUEST, ANARCHIST ARRIVES FROM SACRAMENTO WITH "KING OF TRAMPS" AND DETECTIVES. The intense surveillance, unusual even for a notorious anarchist, stemmed from a rumor that "Red Emma" had come to blow up the American fleet in the harbor. Emma assured a reporter that she would much prefer dumping the entire navy and army into the Bay to wasting a bomb. She described with pleasure the effect of the dedicated efforts of the upholders of law and order to frustrate her plans:

> Meetings were veritable encampments. For blocks the streets were lined with police in autos, on horseback, and on foot. Inside the hall were heavy police guards, the platform surrounded by officers. Naturally this array of uniformed men advertised our meetings far beyond our expectations. Our hall had a seating capacity of 5 thousand and it proved too small for crowds that clamoured for admittance. . . . It was all due to the stupendous farce staged by the authorities at huge expense to San Francisco taxpayers.

Everywhere they went, Chief Biggy, Acting Captain of Detectives Ryan, and a dozen plainclothes detectives "flitted hither and thither in her vicinity, attempting to catch the conversation" carried on by Goldman, "King Reitman," and their host, Alexander Horr, a local anarchist who himself was once enamored of Emma and had provided her with a home in New York at 210 East Thirteenth Street.

Because of such media and police attention, Emma's audiences were often swollen by people who did not consider themselves radicals but came to hear her out of curiosity. One of Emma's most popular talks was on "Patriotism." Her nostalgic account of the past was directed to audiences who, across a broad spectrum of political beliefs, felt the dehumanizing effects of industrialization, particularly of weapons manufacture. Ben, along with thousands of listeners, was challenged and inspired by Emma's lecture to rethink what love of country meant in the context of America in the early 1900s. Emma attacked the notion that turning the places of one's carefree childhood memories into "factory, mill or mine, while deafening sounds of machinery have replaced the music of the birds," meant progress. "Nor can we hear the tales of great deeds, for the stories our mothers tell today are but those of sorrow and grief." She would continue with these rousing words: "What then is patriotism? 'Patriotism,' sir, 'is the last resort of scoundrels,' said Dr. Johnson. Leo Tolstoy, the greatest anti-patriot of our times, defined patriotism as the principle that justifies the training of wholesale murderers; a trade that requires better equipment for the exercise of man-killing than the making of such necessities as shoes, clothing and houses; and a trade that guarantees better returns and greater glory than that of the honest workingman."

One San Francisco audience broke out in uncontrollable applause when, after hearing this talk, a soldier rushed up to Emma on the platform, shook her hand, and, according to Emma, said, "Thank you, Miss Goldman." Audience pandemonium followed. The military seemed to have been successfully undermined, and hats flew into the air in celebration. Later Emma learned that the young soldier, William Buwalda, had been followed back to his army post by police spies and court-martialed simply for having attended her meeting and for shaking hands with her. An exemplary soldier for fifteen years, Buwalda was stripped of his rank and sentenced to five years in the military prison on Alcatraz Island.

The military version of Buwalda's arrest emphasized the impropriety of his attending in uniform a public meeting where Emma branded the army and navy as "tools of legalized murder." Buwalda claimed that he went merely to practice his newly learned stenography skills. He testified that "as he passed the speaker, she smiled and extended her hand, which he took and said, 'How do you do, Miss Goldman?'" The sentence was so harsh, and public reaction so strongly in favor of Buwalda, that even President Theodore Roosevelt wrote a personal letter to the Judge Advocate General of the army about the case, urging a dishonorable discharge and a six-month sentence.

The military finally decided to release Buwalda, but this was not to be made public until "affairs in the Harbor of San Francisco have settled down to a normal basis." Following the waterfront strikes and the earthquake of 1906, the military were attempting to rebuild the harbor and restore "order." Buwalda's release would not take place for at least another six months, and to the public, who knew nothing of the planned pardon, it seemed as though the powers that had imprisoned him were deaf to all the loud protests.

Emma did not learn of Buwalda's arrest until she arrived in Portland, Oregon, for her next series of appearances. She ended each of her orations with an impassioned plea for people to come to the support of this victimized soldier. The response was positive, and from Emma's perspective it seemed that all strata of society were struck by this outrageous government action: "lawyers, judges, doctors, men of letters, society women, and factory girls came to learn the truth about the ideas they had been taught to fear and to hate." Emma was so determined to rally public support to free Buwalda that even the Socialist Party newspaper acknowledged that she deserved "all praise for doing probably more than any other woman in the whole world for the emancipation of the human race for LIBERTY."

Emma's speeches were generally well received by her Oregon audiences, especially the workers who came to hear her talk on "The Relationship of Anarchism to Trade-Unionism." The conservative press, however, seized on every opportunity to discredit her. Emma met these efforts with characteristic sarcasm, telling a reporter covering one of her speeches, "Do not be alarmed, I have no dynamite in my pocket and so far as I know there is not so much as a firecracker in the house."

Emma experienced relatively little police harassment in Portland, where the strategy of the officials seemed to be reflected in an editorial that appeared in the city's major newspaper, *The Oregonian*: "It is a mistake to attempt to restrain her or to deny her right of free speech. Let her go on. But let us have no false pretense or humbug about 'anarchism' as distinguished from 'anarchy'; and let us learn from observation of her and her associates a lesson in self-restraint and let us continue to see in them pretty much everything that a good citizen ought not to be."

The Pacific Northwest marked the end of Emma's four-month tour. For three of those months, Ben had been a companion, but by June it was time for her to return to New York to attend to *Mother Earth* and for Ben to return to Chicago for the summer—he would stay with his mother before rejoining Emma in New York. Emma had become so accustomed to Ben's presence and support that even the thought of separation was painful.

For a man known for his sense of adventure and independence, Ben was unusually close to his mother. As a child, he had behaved alternately as a protective, devoted son and a bad boy who periodically ran away from home. The pattern had persisted throughout his adult life. He had been briefly married once, even fathered a child whom he eventually abandoned. Emma saw the strong power Ben's mother had over him as one of many tensions in his personality that could erupt at any time in their relationship, and she figured it had contributed to the instability of his other relationships with women. In his letters that summer, Ben acknowledged his competing attractions to the two women in his life by addressing Emma, who was ten years his senior, as "his blue-eyed Mommy." Emma resigned herself to her dual role as mother and lover, and waited for Ben's return.

Although she may have been fearing that passion was fleeting, after all, and that her vision of a life founded upon intense, sustained intimacy was once again to be crushed, Emma was nevertheless unwilling to reconsider her ideal. Instead, she joined the competition, even tried to claim a mother's right to Ben's time by signing her letters to him as "Mummy Reitman" while he was staying with his mother in Chicago. Emma played out her role as "his blue-eyed Mommy" with all of its incestuous titillation. Just as it did for Ben, this fantasy helped Emma to reconcile the disparity between the fleeting relationship with a passionate lover she seemed to be having, and the most stable relationship in the world which she craved—that of mother and child.

> I have a great deep mother instinct for you, baby mine; that instinct has been the great redeeming feature in our relation. It has helped me on more than one occasion to overlook your boyish irresponsible pranks. But my maternal love for you is only one part of my being, the other 99 parts consist of the woman, the intense, passionate savage woman, whom you have given life as no one else ever has. I think therein lies the key to our misery and also to our great bliss, rare as it may be.

Casting herself in the role of Ben's "Mommy" also helped Emma to contain her jealous rage over her strong suspicion that his pull back to Chicago was not exclusively to his mother. She was sure that there were other women waiting for him in the town where he had achieved notoriety as a "womanizer." Intuitive suspicions about Ben's "extra-relational" activities seeped into her letters. The same woman who affirmed in her coast-to-coast lecture tours that "whether love last but one brief span of time or for eternity, it is the only creative, inspiring, elevating basis for a new race, a new world," found herself now in the depths of the uninspiring emotions of jealousy and self-doubt. She feared that, in her absence, Ben would find a new lover. "Hobo, I am raving, I am feverish, I am ill with anxiety. I don't think you love me. Maybe while I suffer, you are with someone else. Oh, I shall commit violence. I must stop, I must pull myself together. It will be hell to wait for an answer to this letter."

On another, deeper, level, Emma's adoption of the role of mommy evinced her secret wish to supplant Ben's mother. She gave morbid expression to this desire in retelling the Yiddish legend of the son who complied with his mistress's request that he prove his love for her by tearing out his mother's heart and bringing it to her. Emma included the story in a June 1908 letter to Reitman during a brief separation that preceded by only a few days his planned return to Chicago to spend the summer with his mother. The immediate source of Emma's distress was one of Ben's impulsive affairs:

> Have I ever told you the legend of a mother's love? A man had a cruel heartless mistress, who would forever tease him with her lack of faith in his love. He wanted her to believe in him. So he said one day, "Is there anything I can do to prove my love?" "Yes, go and bring me your mother's heart." The man adored his mother, she had always been so kind and good to him. But his passion was great, so he killed his mother, tore out her heart and rushed with it to his mistress. On the way he stumbled and fell. And his mother's heart said to him, "my precious child, have you hurt yourself?" It's that side of my nature, Ben dear, that stretches out to you, that would like to embrace you and soothe you. The mother calls to you, my boy, my precious boy!!
>
> But the woman, the woman that lay asleep for 38½ years and that you have awakened into frantic, savage, hungry life, recoils from you, feels outraged because you have thrust her aside for a moment's fancy, because you have outraged her sacred shrine, that tent, oh God, where passion held its glorious maddening feast. Oh, it is horrible, horrible!
>
> But what is the use of grieving when the mother that bore you knew it all before me—

There was an unmistakable tension in her rendition of the tale that suggests an identification with the "cruel heartless mistress, who would forever tease him with her lack of faith in his love," and betrays an unexpressed wish that he would "kill" his real mother and devote himself to Emma. This jealous lover did not want to compete with other young women, certainly, but especially not with a mother who still claimed the attention of her devoted son. The pathos, hostility, and melodrama of this mother-son story permeated Emma's relationship with Ben.

Emma hoped that her parable would influence Ben and protect him against his old, restless ways. "Darling, darling, will you follow the old trail? No! no! I can not believe it, I will not. May my great love and devotion protect you, baby mine darling mine."

As if her worries about Ben's mother and other women were not enough, Emma was plagued again by doubts about the depth of her *political* union with Ben. Why was she so attached to this "intellectually crude" and "socially naive" creature who "like so many other liberal Americans . . . was a reformer of surface evils, without any idea of the sources from which they spring"? Yet his childlike qualities were a welcome relief from the seriousness of the cause. On a more profound level, as well, Ben answered the need Emma had long felt for someone who could love her sexually and still share her work, however incompletely; for although Emma enjoyed the respect and attention paid to a public figure, she was relatively isolated in this period, even among her comrades.

Yet her need for Ben as paramour began to overshadow her need for Ben as political helpmate, to the point where Emma questioned her own political commitment. Suddenly, the fiercely independent Emma Goldman found herself in the grip of the sort of intense love affair of her dreams, only to discover that it was causing an upset in the balance between political fervor and personal passion. Before meeting Ben, she had thought of her involvement in the anarchist cause as her primary relationship. There had been sexual affairs, but, with the possible exception of her relationship with Alexander Berkman, they had all been subordinated to her work, in which she found rewards that she thought a single relationship could not offer. But she had never experienced the longing and emptiness she now felt when she was without Ben. Her commitment to the political work that had become the core of her existence was now shaken by "this worthless Hobo."

Emma chose to soft-pedal this uncertainty in her account of this period in her autobiography, perhaps fearing that she would fail those who looked to her as a model when taking their first steps toward political activism. Admitting only that Ben had assumed an essential place in her life, one that made her more effective as a political activist, she did not reveal that he had, for a time, called her very commitment to political life into question. Her letters to Ben that first summer were full of the torment of a woman who could not envision these two powerful forces—love and anarchism—coexisting peacefully in her life.

Emma recognized in Ben's "primitive spirit" a cause of her own pain as well as pleasure—his lust for her was part of his lust for women in general. She began to see more clearly that his appealing vagabond air carried with it a lack of responsibility to those he loved. His sensual energy renewed her youth and yet reminded her of the ten-year gap between them. Emma, the advocate of "free love," could not accept the apparent fact that Ben could shift his loyalties as easily as he could change beds. She expected her love for Ben to be elevated above "the common herd." She felt helplessly monogamous, though it seemed that Ben did not expect sexual fidelity. Despite her frequent lectures attacking the institution of marriage, she sometimes referred to herself as Ben's "unhappy wife."

Amid this turbulence, Emma and Ben wrote letters each night of their separation, attempting to put their passion into words. Often Emma would be exhausted after a long night of work on *Mother Earth*: "Good night, or, rather, good morning, dear. It's 5 A.M. Even if I am tired and weary and love hungry for my no account lover, I should show him [Willie] some things if he were here. Come close and see two actually big M[ountains] and a little bright-eyed t[reasure] b[ox]. Your mommy."

They created a private erotic language of code letters and words that barely masked the sexual content of their correspondence. Skirting the laws prohibiting "obscenity in the mails," they relished the defiance of their euphemisms and abbreviations. From the few times that they dared spell out their code, it can be deciphered. Her treasure box longed for his Willie, and she longed to have his face between her joy Mountains—Mt. Blanc and Mt. Jura. She wanted to suck the head of his "fountain of life," which "stood over" her "like a mighty spectre." Both lovers reveled in an orally focused sex that particularly emphasized clitoral-area stimulation. She wrote, "I press you to my body close with my hot burning legs. I embrace your precious head." There was very little openness about sexuality in that period, and certainly little affirmation or even general knowledge of women's sexual needs. It was assumed that sexuality was a male prerogative. Females submitted to sex;

if they were lucky, they might enjoy it. Birth-control information was outlawed, though a movement was developing to spread word of it in Europe and the United States. Emma's espousal of free love was a direct challenge to the prevailing attitudes toward love and sexuality, and Reitman's gynecological knowledge made him a fund of information few others possessed. Emma wrote that he had robbed her of her reason, she "would devour you, yes, I would put my teeth into your flesh and make you groan like a wounded animal. You are an animal and you have awakened lust in me." Often their letters excited them so much that they had to "take a bath" to control the passion aroused in writing and reading them.

Away from the orderly life she led in New York City, at her country retreat for anarchists 3.5 miles from Ossining, New York, Emma let her passions surface. The "farm," as she called it, had been given to her by Bolton Hall, the libertarian single-taxer, when she had been pestered by landlords in New York. Max Baginsky and his wife and child had lived there for a while, but now it served as a country home for anarchist friends of Emma's. She lured Ben with the promise of a surprise erotic treat that would surpass his introduction of feathers into their sexual play:

The day seems unbearable if I do not talk to you. I would prefer to do something else to you, to run a red hot velvety t over W and the bushes, so Hobo would go mad with joy and ecstasy. . . . I don't know what's got into me, but never once in these two years did I want you so much, nor W. Oh for one S——at that beautiful head of his or for one drink from that fountain of life. How I would press my lips to the fountain and drink, drink, every drop. Really, Hobo, I am crazy with T-b. longing, I never knew myself to be that way. Just wait, you will see what I prepared for you, the surprise of your life. India, China and Japan are nothing, your feathers are nothing, you'll see. But one condition I must make, no whiskers, no, the t-b cannot stand for that. Besides, the new symphony she has prepared requires a smooth instrument. Lover, Hobo you have never really loved me enough, nor the t-b, nor the m, no, you have not. But I know how to induce you, and if I could draw, you would see, but this way you wait until Oh let it be soon, please, please, come right on. I want you. So you do not care how many are on my back, but I care. I want to be free, completely, absolutely, so that I can give myself to you. If only you were here and I could talk to you, or, still better, demonstrate my real art, you would never again leave Mommy.

I hope to hear from you tomorrow when I can expect you. Our reunion shall be the most wonderful we have ever had. You will never again separate from the t-b or them, never, never. Come let me whisper to you. The t-b sends you the flower.

Mummy Reitman

The passion of their relationship was actually heightened by the physical distance between them, with the steady stream of letters extending the moments they had together. Frequent telephone calls were out of their reach financially, and in some ways too ephemeral for these lovers who took each other's letters to bed—and read them again and again. For Emma, the letters created the illusion of stability; when doubts of infidelity slipped into her mind, she could read one of Ben's letters and feel reassured. Letters made her feel she could create and control their love affair. They dreamed that one day they would go far away together, to immerse themselves in their passion. Emma and Ben even fantasized a trip to Australia, away from the crowds and the critical eyes of her comrades. There they could travel and indulge their passions without reserve or threat of separation.

In the wake of their great plans for escape, just before the Labor Day 1908 meeting at Cooper Union, Emma received a tormented letter from Ben. He had been reading a psychological study called *The Power of a Lie* that propounded the view that a lie could permeate one's life and take control over one's entire psyche. The book impressed itself on Ben so deeply that he felt compelled to reveal to Emma secrets he feared would destroy their mutual respect. He had lied to her from the first day of their meeting. It had, in fact, been he who told a reporter about Emma's planned surprise appearance that day in March when the

Chicago police unexpectedly prevented her from speaking. In his exuberance for publicity he had naïvely overlooked the likelihood of cooperation between newspapers and police. Nor had he been attending to his work with the hobos during the organizers' follow-up meeting that night, as he had told her; he was with a woman he had met at the disrupted event. In fact, in every town during their tour together, Ben had "romanced" women who had come to hear Emma speak. This had taken some ingenuity, given the tight schedule of their tours, but when Emma was being interviewed by newspapers or meeting with other political activists who did not accept him, he had found his own forum elsewhere with women. Although he claimed that these brief sexual liaisons meant nothing to him compared with his profound love for Emma, they nevertheless represented a compulsion he felt he could not control. Even the financial records that he kept for *Mother Earth* were falsified, because from the very beginning he had stolen money for his own support and for his mother, who was alone and dependent on him in Chicago. In sum, he had lied every day of their relationship, and now he begged for permission to begin again.

Emma, the crusader for those impoverished by a capitalist system, could rationalize his stealing, even though it was reprehensible, but how could he squander and debase her love, when love was the most precious resource in the world? Of course she had had inklings of Ben's unfaithfulness before; she had watched "his bedroom eyes" flash across crowded rooms and even knew about one of his affairs. But his flirtations had seemed a harmless expression of his charm. Now Emma felt completely betrayed and confused. How could she have been so blind?

No matter how Emma stretched her capacity for forgiveness, she still found "that to understand a thing does not always help one." She conveyed her jealous rage, writing Ben that his "promiscuity tears my very vitals, fills me with gall and horror and twists my being into something foreign to myself." She demanded that he explain what his love for her meant to him. Somewhat inconsistently, Emma said that she could imagine giving one's love freely, but not when it was as powerful as the love she felt for Ben. His "blue-eyed Mommy" felt more like an abandoned daughter:

The moon standing witness to the Glory of that embrace . . . Yet while you were still aglow with the divine fire you expressed a desire to go to another. And a few hours later, after you had walked with your greatest love, your "first born," you went with another in the same place, that had been made sacred by your love for Mommy. What then is your love if it did not loom out as a beacon light, that would make it impossible for you to follow a moment's fancy? I am unable to answer that question. Yet I know that I never had and never will have a moment's peace until I have answered that question. This too I know, that I shall not be able to work with you, to go to Australia or anywhere else, until I have answered that question.

Do not think I am reproaching you, please do not. I exact nothing, want nothing, that you cannot freely give. Only I cannot partake of a gift if I do not know just what that gift means to the giver.

One thing of all the things that you have said to me yesterday rings in my ear, "You understand that I love you." Yes I do, but what I do not understand is what this love means to you. Has it been a force strong enough to make you strong? Has it caused you to forgo pleasures, to overcome desires and fancies, that were not of any import? Would that love make you endure hardships, face dangers, or prompt you to make great efforts? So far it has done nothing of the sort. You wanted to work hard, to raise means for our trip to Australia. But when it gave you pains to stay away from me, you gave up your decision, without the slightest effort. You longed for me, more than for anything else in the world, yet while you were so intensely longing, while you wrote the most passionate letter, *you went with another woman*. True, it was in a moment of despair and you were half drunk as you said and Mommy was far away. Surely that is some reason, though not weighty enough to show what your love for me really means.

Then you came to me, you had me, as no other man ever had me. Love, Passion, Devotion, Companionship, everything. Yet within four days, you were drawn to another. . . . It's not the woman that troubles me, but the question of your love that I am to understand. What is it? It was not hunger or despair. Mommy was near, Mommy whose quivering body you held close to you in a sublime embrace. . . . And this uncertainty has so unnerved me, especially since the blow of yesterday, I cannot find peace or rest. I cannot stay on the farm, the sight of the place that was my love's place of worship and that has been turned into a dumping ground, is more than I can endure. I am going to the City, though I hope for nothing there. Oh, Ben, Ben, give me peace, give me rest. Tell me, what does your love mean to you?

Ben's promiscuity rapidly became the central issue in their relationship. Although Emma's espousal of the ideal of free love kept her from condemning his behavior on political grounds, her letters revealed a tortured effort to reconcile her bitter disappointment and anger with her ideology. She tried to deny her jealousy, but it gnawed at her. In the midst of her work in the *Mother Earth* office she still had uncontrollable cravings to see Ben.

Ben continued to live in a rented room in New York, and he waited for Emma to take him back, avoiding the *Mother Earth* office until she did. Emma was still living with several of the people on the magazine in the small apartment at 210 East Thirteenth Street that was affectionately called the "home of lost dogs," and "the Inn for wounded souls," because of the numbers of people who used it as their home away from home, as a place of nonstop political and social activity, good food, and conversation. Even local gamblers often used it as a place to hide their paraphernalia, because they knew that the police would look for bombs, not gambling chips, in her apartment. There Emma kept up a front of combined gaiety and seriousness of purpose. In her letters of this period, she searched for an understanding of what kept her and Ben together despite his lies. Emma said she believed in sexual variety, but since meeting Ben she had longed for no other man:

But 210 always makes me rational. You see, dreamy precious-eyed lover of mine, 210 knows little of that torrent you have awakened. It is the E.G., the serious agitator with a thousand responsibilities clinging to her skirt, that is best known at 210. . . . Dearest, I wish I could still be an arch-varietist. I fear that is gone, for now at any rate, maybe forever. Do you think that one who has heard the roar of the ocean, seen the maddening struggle of the waves, who has been carried up to snow-peaked mountains; in short, do you believe that one who has known all the madness of a wild, barbarian primitive love, can reconcile one's self to any relationship under civilization? I believe you have unfitted me for that, hobo mine. . . .

Emma's hopes for escaping her pain seemed to depend on going to another place with Ben to try to re-establish trust. She seized again on the idea of going to Australia, where she had been invited some time before Ben's confession to make a lecture tour. She had even sent advance literature there in preparation for her trip. She would regret leaving her work on *Mother Earth* and her old friends and comrades, but saving her relationship with Ben seemed to require such a drastic move.

Emma needed to get away from the judgmental glances of the *Mother Earth* circle. Even her dearest friend, Sasha, refused to see the relationship as anything more than a temporary infatuation. Perhaps Sasha resented the striking contrast between his own relationship to Emma, so bound to the seriousness of their politics, and Emma's passion for Ben. Perhaps he felt sexually overshadowed, though he and Emma had not been lovers for years. Sasha said nothing to Ben while Ben was visiting the farm at Ossining, but privately scolded Emma for being involved with a man who had "no rebel spirit" and "didn't belong in our movement." Emma was angry with what she saw as Berkman's hypocrisy, chiding him for claiming sympathy with underdogs and the less sophisti-cated yet expressing revulsion on closer contact with them. But she was also hurt, and saw that her friends' efforts to treat Ben with kindness were only forced gestures done out of deference to her. Ben was aware of the condescension of her political comrades.

To most of Emma's associates, the Reitman-Goldman relationship remained a mystery. Roger Baldwin described Ben as "a terrible man, overbearing, arrogant, possessive and dismally disagreeable ... never faithful to Emma, for a minute.... [He had] no sense of humor, he could never see himself.... He dominated her ... she needed it, then [he] acted as her manager and boss—and I think she liked it—I don't like it myself.... Ben was a very vulgar man.... He was in love with her, always taking care of her, I think she liked to have a guardian."

Senya Fleshine, who worked in close quarters with Reitman as a photographer and layout person in the *Mother Earth* office, disliked him intensely. He believed that Emma's attachment to Reitman could be explained only by his ability to satisfy her sexually. While Fleshine and her other friends and admirers remained loyal to her, they had contempt for this newcomer whose vulgarity and opportunism were offensive to their sense of pure dedication to the cause. Ben made crude jokes in proper circles, religious allusions among atheists—anything to shock. On one trip to Portland, Oregon, while staying at a respectable home, he even came to the breakfast table in the nude. He and Emma were promptly asked to leave. But Emma, the individualist, remained stead-fast. She was a loner even among her comrades and felt that she did not receive enough from them to warrant following their judgment. In fact, her attraction to Ben in the face of her friends' disapproval contained an element of spite that intensified her and Ben's relationship. But when Emma took Ben to an Artists Guild meeting in St. Louis, he was such a total embarrassment that she never brought him again.

Also, dearest, you have certainly failed to grasp my meaning if you thought I care what the comrades think of you. That I should want the world to see your worth, dearest, that I should want people to believe in you and respect you, is I think but natural. I love you, you are my very life, why should I not want the World to see how beautiful, how honest, how truly wonderful you can be? Don't you want the World to know and appreciate your Mommie? And does it not hurt you when Mommie is not appreciated? Of course, why then be surprised if I want my comrades to appreciate you? But as to their opinion, my Ben, I have never cared for that. If I did, I would not stand so isolated in the battle. Just think of it, there are thousands of Anarchists in this country. What do they do for M[other] E[arth]? Nothing, absolutely nothing. Why? Because, I have always gone my own way, lived my own life. No, I do not care what the comrades think of you. In fact I love you so intensely because they think ill of you. I know that there is great worth in my Ben, that's why he is not liked by some of my comrades.

Emma defended her love for Reitman and emphatically praised him for his positive qualities, but he began to feel less and less secure in the theoretically sophisticated world of political activism he had entered. No matter how hard Emma tried to restore his confidence, Ben felt that in her world he was the buffoon, the outsider who would never be accepted on his own merits, a "tag-along-wife" of the great speaker, Emma Goldman. Emma believed that Ben's insecurity and her doubts had paralyzed their relationship. Australia was their only hope.

Still, Emma faced new fears. In Australia, she would be leaving many problems behind, but Ben, the real source of all the difficulty, would be going with her. She feared she would be even more dependent on her impulsive mate than she had been during their American travels, so that his promiscuous habits, should they continue, might be even more devastating. Her letters began to focus on convincing Ben that he must reform his ways before he could rejoin her on her current tour or accompany her to Australia:

I have tried hard, so very hard, to ask myself, "Why this to me?" Have I deserved such a shock from Ben? Have I not given him my love, my heart's blood, my thoughts, everything, everything? Why then this awful shock? But I can find no answer, there is no answer for obsessions, is there? As far as my own sorrow or suffering is concerned, I have long made up my mind that your obsession will bring me more than one human being can endure. Yet my love was strong enough to endure even that. But as far as my work is concerned, I cannot and will not let your impulses stand in the way. I am undertaking a colossal task, a tour for nearly a year into distant lands, and I can not run the risk of one of your obsessions to come along and frustrate everything. You have just thrown every-thing overboard, you have refused to act in the capacity you have yourself chosen and gladly so. A letter, a word, an opinion of mine was enough for you to do such a thing. Now, supposing this happens when we are in Australia, when I am helpless, what then? Now, Ben dear, I cannot risk that, really not. I therefore ask you, as tenderly yet decisively as I can put on paper, to reason before you act. Impulses are beautiful, dear, but when it is a vital question, a cause one has had at heart for 20 years, one cannot allow an impulse to destroy it all. It's all right for an impulse to pierce a human heart, to make it bleed and twitch, as your impulses have done more than once. That's what the heart is here for, Mommie's heart is here for. But ideas are more important, dear. Don't you think so? . . . Consider only if you can work with me no matter what differences may come up between us, if you can work and if you feel yourself strong enough to carry out what you undertake until the last. I would rather expect a decisive no, at this moment, than a weak yes that you will break when the obsession comes, in the middle of the tour or when we are in Australia. You are right, dear, why should you reform? Really no reason for it. Except possibly the power of love, which, you have told me, has changed your entire life. No other reason, I am sure.

If the past 7 months have given you nothing, at least [they] should have strengthened your character or made your life worth-while. They have given me a whole World, a beautiful World of all the exquisiteness that a great love can give. I thank you for it, Ben dear. I shall always carry it with me and when the moment comes that I shall have to forfeit my life for my ideas, the World of the last 7 months will illuminate my soul and I shall feel I have not lived in vain, no, I have not lived in vain!

Your Mommie

Their attempt to decide whether to go to Australia, and how to deal with their new frankness about Ben's promiscuity, bred inevitable misunderstandings, which would remain uncorrected for weeks because their resolution depended on the mail. Being misunderstood hurt Emma, who devoted so much energy to the clear communication of her ideas and feelings. In her characteristic double-edged manner, she sent Ben the *Mother Earth* budget, noting that, even though it was not financially wise, she still wanted him to join her as manager on her tour to Australia for a year. Emma apparently wanted him to see the connection in her mind between love and sacrifice, but Ben took this as a way of telling him not to come. When Ben wrote her to that effect, Emma became agitated:

> I know the ecstasy, the inexpressible delight your love can give, but I also know that while my body and soul will feast on the nectar of life, my mind will sit at the palace of your love, famished for the want of understanding, and it will receive nothing. Yes, laugh, laugh and cry at the same time. What on Earth is the matter? Surely I can write English. Surely you can read English. How then is it possible that you should so misconstrue and misunderstand my letter? How is it possible that you should draw such false, such erroneous conclusions. Then too, you have known me 7 months, you have seen me almost daily, have I ever lied to you, have I ever used excuses, or covered up my desires? How, then, can you think that I have used *ME* as a pretext ... [against] our love, our companionship? ... When?
>
> Good night, Hobo mine. Your Mommie has never felt more lonely, more alone, in all her life than tonight. If these lines tell you all, then wire me. I hope they will. Your Mommie.

Misunderstandings followed by forgiveness and reconciliation continued:

> My own, my very own,
> Your lines of the 29th Special was like balm to my bleeding soul. All was dark and gloomy, not a sign of light, or an avenue of escape from the terrible agony of doubt. Oh, I did not doubt your love, indeed not. But I have such fear of your obsessions and I dreaded

that the recent one may take you away to a point where you could not return. As I said, the sky looked grey and sinister and a cold icy hand of death clutched at my heart. Oh, Ben, I could not go through such days again. Then came your Special today, and everything was dispersed. Life has again taken a new aspect. Do you know, lover mine, that it is the first time in my life that love stands over me, like a mighty spectre, and that it has both life and death for me. . . . If you would only realize that you are to me not only the greatest and most sublime gift of the Gods, as a lover, but that I want you to be my Comrade, my friend, my soul companion with whom I can exchange every thought, gloomy or cheerful, every doubt, every hope. . . . Ben, shall I be able to do that in the future? The past speaks against it, and yet, and yet I shall not give up hope, I cannot.

They both knew that their reunion in New York would be tarnished by the awkwardness of Ben's position among her intellectual anarchist friends. Feeling insecure, Ben was sure to play the clown again, accentuating his alienation with his "American swagger." To add to their tensions, Sasha's coldness to Ben had increased. Emma tried to help both men understand each other, but inwardly she was gravely disappointed: "Yes, Alex has wonderful qualities, but like most of us, grave shortcomings. Only he has made good so long that one does not feel like seeing defects. I too am sorry you did not get to know each other. How strange that men are so narrow to each other, when a woman stands between them."

Ultimately Emma affirmed her faith in Ben. When it was established that he would join her on the October tour as her manager, they planned their reunion: "Just think of it, only 23 days until we meet again. It makes me dizzy to think of all the ecstasy, the madness and joy that is awaiting us."

Emma longed for Ben, even wished that he were with her in New York while she was racing around preparing for the trip. One part of her would have abandoned all her political work for a moment of sexual ecstasy with Ben. It was that uncontrolled aspect of her that she kept secret: "Poor forsaken M——, they have grown small and limp, especially when the fear struck them that they might lose their master trainer. As to the t-b, she has been in absolute despair. She kicked and screamed and protested, she said to H—— with *ME,* with the propaganda, with EG the agitator, the speaker, the writer, 'I want my champion lover, my life bearer, my sunshine, my great savage lover, and the rest can go to H——.'"

Meanwhile, there had been strong indications that the political tour might not fare well, because of many factors they could not control. It was an election year, and Americans were focused on the candidates and the issues in the campaigns. In December, Emma wrote to some friends:

> If I were religious, I should believe that an evil spirit is following me. For I have certainly gone through tortures of the damned since I left N.Y. The first obstacle was the campaign time, when it was even impossible to get people to attend a lecture. Then came police interference in Indianapolis. After that the stupidity of our comrades, who, though years in the movement, have not yet been able to learn the simplest ways of arranging meetings. They either get the dirtiest, most obscure halls and don't advertise at all, or they spend $100 in getting up three meetings. You can imagine that my tour has not been very flourishing under the circumstances. I am two months on the road and all I could do is to keep *ME* going and invest about $100 in literature.

Emma and Ben went ahead with the preparations for their trip to Australia, secretly at first, and then with the knowledge and even the grudging help of their anarchist comrades, who resigned themselves to the idea that Emma was determined to go. Sasha had already begun to take more direct responsibility for *Mother Earth*; Emma and Ben planned to send political reports to the magazine from Australia. Everything was falling into place for a January trip. But by January, her northwest tour with Ben had turned into such a financial disaster that she wrote a friend and donor, "After ten weeks, I am further away from my trip to

Australia than when I started. Even Los Angeles is not so successful as last summer. And I have not much more hope for San Francisco. The worst of it is, I have sent over 600 lb. of literature to Australia. If I do not go, it means having the stuff sent back. Oh, I tell you, the joys of touring are wonderful."

On top of their financial woes, the pair had run into trouble with the police again. Emma wrote to another friend: "So you have read of Reitman's and my arrest in Seattle and Bellingham; also, that we were held up on the Canadian border near Vancouver. All that has incurred expense and loss of several meetings, not to speak of the misery. But as you say, if it were not for my determination, I would indeed have given up the struggle. I assure you, I wanted to do it more than once these last few months. But something in my head and heart urges me, on and on."

Their arrests were classic examples of the arbitrary use of the law. In Seattle, Emma described the charges against Ben as "putting his weight too heavily against the door of the hall, which he had found barred" and against her as "protesting his arrest." Their fine was $1.50, to pay for the broken lock on the door, but the result was that they had no time or hall for speeches in Seattle. Again no hall was open to them in the small town of Everett. In Bellingham, they had barely gotten off the train and checked into a hotel when a pair of local police detectives appeared and told them they were under arrest for conspiring to hold an unlawful assembly. Ben, with characteristic audacity, asked the police please to wait until he and Emma had dined. The detectives graciously agreed; Emma and Ben proceeded to have a long, leisurely meal in an expensive local restaurant while the exasperated detectives waited outside. Emma and Ben faced a bail-bond charge of $4,000, but fortunately two lawyers offered bail and their defense services gratis, without even knowing the couple.

By the time Emma and Ben returned to San Francisco, from which they planned to leave for Australia, they were battle-weary from their months of touring. But plans had long been set for Emma to deliver a series of eight speeches in San Francisco, and, tired as she was, she honored her commitment. She was inspired to learn that William Buwalda, the soldier who had been court-martialed for shaking her hand, had just been pardoned by President Roosevelt, after serving ten months in prison. She and Reitman had an emotional reunion with the soldier. It was clear that the public support she had organized for him had been critical to his release. But while the three were on their way to Emma's talk at the Victory Theatre, they were arrested. Buwalda was soon released, with a severe reprimand for associating with "dangerous criminals," but this experience, combined with his earlier imprisonment, prompted a re-evaluation of his attitude toward his country: within four months, Buwalda turned back his Philippine Insurrection badge to the Secretary of War.

Ben and Emma were charged with eight counts of conspiracy to "rout." "Routing" was defined by state law as the assembly of two or more persons at a meeting where measures are advocated that, if actually carried out, would lead to a riot. It was the first time in sixteen years that Emma had been tried in court, although she had been brought before the authorities for questioning many times in the interim. Resigned and desolate, Emma once again wrote to friends for support: "Personally, I do not care what will happen to me. I am pretty tired from the struggle. All my hopes of going to Australia and maintaining ME are gone. I can do nothing here until the trial is over, and of course I cannot leave here. All I can do is to put up a good fight. Unfortunately, it is not NY, where I am better known and where I could get material assistance, as money will be needed in the fight."

No sooner had their bail been dropped, through the clever work of their lawyers, than another indictment charged them with "unlawful assemblage, denouncing as unnecessary all organized governments," and "preaching anarchist doctrines."

The two lovers found themselves behind bars again, this time with $2,000 bail set for each of them. Emma's sadness about imprisonment during her San Francisco tour was no doubt deepened by the news of her father's death. The small prison cell where she awaited a political trial was not an adequate place to mourn. Her father had spent his last years as an invalid, and his coarse temper had mellowed as his body weakened. Emma felt more grief for his wasted, frustrated life than anger for his abuses of her in the past. Inevitably, her feelings of loss carried over from one part of her life to another.

Emma's month-long battle in court resulted in acquittal. Ben even succeeded in persuading the *San Francisco Bulletin* to devote a full page to an interview with Emma on the subject of modern drama. Sensing that the tables had turned in their favor, Emma and Ben postponed their Australian trip until April so that Emma could complete her planned course of lectures. But within two weeks their luck turned once again, when the rainy season began in San Francisco. Emma wrote to her friend and financial backer Louis Meyer, who was among the pool of upper-middle class sympathizers with Emma's work and the anarchist cause who could be counted on for money in an emergency:

> Every gleam of hope is covered with a black sky of disappointment and despair, so that life seems a perfect mockery to me, at times. . . . I wrote you in my last that we have gained a victory over the police, so we have. But it is beyond human power to combat the elements. It has been pouring here for weeks, with the result that every meeting has been a complete failure. You might ask, why we did not discontinue? Did you ever observe the psychology of a gambler? He knows he is losing, that if he goes on, it means complete destruction. But he is driven on by an irresistible force, until he has lost his last shirt. I am such a gambler. My tour was a failure from the beginning. But instead of returning to New York, I kept on gambling and hoping until I have gambled away all my energy together with some of my heart's blood. I knew all along it was insanity, I will not win out, but on I went.

She attributed her ability to cope with the emotional strains of this tour to Ben in the April issue of *Mother Earth*. "More than anything else, the unfaltering optimism, the great zeal and the cheerful Bohemianism of our friend Ben L. Reitman, helped to conquer many obstacles." Even the formerly distant Sasha wrote to compliment Ben on his free-speech fight in San Francisco, adding that he looked forward to renewing their friendship and that he was "glad you count me as one of your best friends."

Hoping to leave their disappointments and losses behind, Emma and Ben once again made preparations for the Australian trip. But just after their farewell party had been arranged, Emma received a shocking telegram from Rochester: WASHINGTON REVOKED KERSHNER'S CITIZEN-SHIP PAPERS, DANGEROUS TO LEAVE COUNTRY.

The only positive by-product of Emma's marriage to Kershner had been that his citizenship papers guaranteed her own citizenship. An investigation of her ex-husband's immigration status, solely for the purpose of identifying possible grounds for legal action against Emma, had revealed that Kershner had been granted citizenship in 1884 on the basis of fraudulent information he had provided regarding his age and the length of time he had been in the country. Inevitably, the government found in the revocation of Kershner's citizenship a way to strike at one of its most outspoken critics. With her citizenship in jeopardy, Emma could not risk leaving the country. She might be denied a return visa to the United States, which, for better or for worse, had become both her home and her political arena. The trip to Australia would have to be postponed. The fact that Kershner's citizenship had been investigated, then revoked, placing Emma's citizenship in jeopardy, confirmed rumors circulating in anarchist circles that the Immigration and Naturalization Service was systematically laying the groundwork for the deportation of foreign-born anarchists, and eventually radicals of many persuasions.

Justice Department communiqués at the time warned the Immigration and Naturalization Service to take "great care not to put the government in a false position," and only act when they could provide an airtight case against the anarchists. So the case against them was being built slowly and carefully.

Emma and Ben, who believed they had already encountered and overcome every conceivable official obstacle to their political work, now found themselves stymied by the Immigration Service's calculated harassment. What would become of their relationship, now that the route by which they hoped to escape their troubles had been cut off?

Instead of Australia, the two lovers headed for Texas on another *Mother Earth* tour—to El Paso, San Antonio, and Houston. This was new territory for them, for they generally determined their itinerary according to the number of long-time anarchist organizations and *Mother Earth* subscribers who were willing to sponsor them, and anarchist circles in the South were only beginning to surface in their support for Emma and the magazine. In addition to the chance Emma took by speaking freely in the South, Emma and Ben risked crossing the Mexican border once, unable to resist the urge to defy the law. They maintained their determination to work and love together, but were acutely aware that their relationship had reached a new and difficult stage. The dreamlike quality of their first tour together had faded. Then it had seemed they were living out the anarchist vision they preached—heeding no authority, responsible only to the comrades in their movement and to the audience of the day. Now they were besieged by quite conventional problems—jealousy, mistrust, and the general criticism of Ben by Emma's comrades.

They chose to set off on a new tour because they could not face the prospect of staying in one place, where all the problems plaguing their relationship might overtake them at once. They would keep moving and working, hoping that they could break through their difficulties to recapture and then sustain the rebellious, seemingly boundless power of their first exalted love for each other.

4

PROMISCUITY AND FREE LOVE

Stung by a series of setbacks, Emma began to see herself as the victim of "a conspiracy of circumstance." The first disappointment had been the generally dismal turnout for her lectures on the fall 1908 cross-country tour. She blamed the lack of interest on the public's preoccupation with the presidential election contest, which was at its height. "Electomania," she termed it with evident disgust, "America's greatest malady, far worse and more destructive than cholera." Next had come the revocation of Kershner's citizenship, forcing the abandonment of the Australian trip and with it her hopes for a new beginning with Ben. The public Emma Goldman was defiant and mocking of the government's efforts to make her a woman without a country. "Poor United States government! Yours is, indeed, a difficult task. . . . You have Emma Goldman's citizenship. But she has the world, and her heritage is the kinship of brave spirits— not a bad bargain." But her use of the third person to refer to herself suggests a desire to distance herself from the precariousness of her situation and the disruption it was causing to both her political and personal plans. Privately, Emma expressed her despair at the prospect of more touring in the United States, followed by a return to New York and the endless work on *Mother Earth*.

To the friends who had helped her through her most recent financial crisis, Sophie and Meyer Shapiro, Emma wrote:

No one will ever know what struggle it has cost me to give up the Australian trip. Of course, I have only postponed it. But it was like pulling teeth. . . . Dear friends, there is no rest for me, so long as *ME* will live. I must lecture the next two months, if I am to keep up the magazine during the Summer. It's like an incurable disease slowly eating your life away. You know it, see it, feel it, but you must go on with it. You might ask, why not give it up? If I only could. But I cannot, at least not just yet.

Amid these difficulties, Emma's dependence on Ben increased, while Ben's tendency toward promiscuity was reactivated. The brief period of monogamy that had followed his grand confession was coming to an end. This pattern of Emma's dependence and Ben's withdrawal was central to their relationship, but they acknowledged it only as a political conflict over their visions of the meaning of free love.

In the winter, Ben returned to Chicago, but as soon as he was separated from Emma, he realized that he had become dependent on being with her. He wrote her a lovesick letter and she replied, "Precious mine, I cannot tell you how my heart aches when I read your cry of agony and loneliness. No, it is not weakness, dear, to want to fly to the one person you love in all the world. I feel as you do, I too feel that I *ought* to pull *myself together,* that *I must* do work. I *must,* I *must,* but a voice in me cries out, no! no!!! There is but one must, that's hobo, hobo, my life's blood, my sunshine, my all."

The warm reception from Sasha and Hippolyte Havel when she arrived home at 210 had done little to ease her loneliness, which filled her letters to Ben:

I love you with the intensity of life itself, as only a woman of my maturity can love. I want you with the savage force that knows no reason, utility or concession. My whole nature is in a perfect uproar against everything and everybody that keeps us apart. How I will continue to live and work away from you, I do not know. All I know is that I will watch, and scheme and plan and not rest, until I have my boy again, until I can be lifted up by him into that World of wild delight and joy.

Money was an obstacle to their reunion. They had planned to save for their Australian trip, but the sparsely attended speaking tour had left them both nearly broke. Ben resolved to set up a medical practice in Chicago, and Emma arranged to lecture in New York. Emma hated Chicago and never considered living there; Ben, who had barely passed his medical exams in Chicago, was not about to risk failure in New York. Unfortunately, Ben's clientele, the hobos, prostitutes, and street people of Chicago, were hardly likely to restore him to solvency. His manner tended to offend middle- and upper-class patients, and his need to have the freedom to travel made it difficult to build a stable practice. Furthermore, though interest in venereal disease was burgeoning, it was not yet recognized as a proper specialty in the medical world. Thus Ben, who like Emma disdained respectability, was financially troubled in part by choice rather than necessity. But they hoped at least to scrape together enough to finance a reunion for part of the summer in New York.

Ben could not find an office in Chicago, however, and soon realized that he had been unrealistic in expecting to establish a profitable medical practice overnight. Instead, he found himself reduced to selling his own blood for money; he contracted an infection that further depleted his finances. In the letter in which Ben wrote Emma about his plight, he also claimed he had not felt loved or petted enough by her. She replied:

Don't you think that's a little cruel of my Hobo to tell his mommy such things? Dearest, I have loved and petted you as much as you would let me. I admit that some of your stunts often upset and hurt me; they always will, dearie. At such a moment I could not give or accept your love. But when you showed the great big beautiful side of your nature, did not my love come to you in all its splendor? Dear, do you think I will feel vexed if you cannot get an office? No, dear heart of mine. . . . Please, please, Ben—why don't you write me when you need money, why did you sell your blood? Good heaven, don't you know, it's my precious blood too?

Ben's money troubles were not the only problems separating them: his pursuit of other women was even more troubling to Emma. Of the many women with whom he was involved in Chicago, Emma eventually knew best Margaret Eleanor Fitzgerald, whom Ben called "Lioness" for her mane of red hair. This young woman, who was devoted to him and his mother, was an attractive combination of Irish and Wisconsin pioneer stock. "Fitzi," as most people called her, had an earnest manner, without political dogmatism or pretense. In the early stages of her relationship with Ben, she had no idea that he and Emma were lovers, or that Ben was promiscuous. She occupied a unique, almost holy place in Ben's life, the one lover with whom he always remained good friends. Intuitively, Emma did not feel quite as jealous of Ben's relationship with Fitzi; it was the countless casual liaisons that once again enraged her. Yet Emma began to reveal that she sometimes enjoyed the pain Ben's promiscuity caused her. Her suffering seemed to provide her with unconscious justification for her enjoyment of their moments of ecstasy without guilt; on the conscious level, it confirmed that their relationship was neither ordinary nor conventional. Emma even admitted that she probably could not survive an untormented relationship:

> As long as I love you and care for you, hobo, I will suffer over many things you do. Yes, I shall always endure great tortures over some of your traits. I am not foolish [enough] to believe or belie myself, that you and I can or will live harmonious and unruffled lives. But with all that I want you, lover dear. It is a weak love indeed that lives only because it has nothing to contend against, when everything is smooth and nice and comfortable. 9 loves out of 10 are of that kind. They die an easy death at the slightest obstacle. Would you be satisfied with such a love, dear, would you? If not, then do not expect Mommy to be happy when her boy has obsessions that pierce her soul. No doubt you cannot help your moods, nor can I help my aversion to some of them. I know, dearest, you want to

make me happy. Dear, if you would so completely satisfy my mind or tastes as you do the t.b., I would think one could not live— besides, the love and passion you give me, dearest, consumes me, so I do not care for anything else. Sweetheart, I do not expect you to be conventional, I am too much opposed to that. But you confound aestheticism with conventions. Something may be repulsive to me, not because it lacks conventionality, but because it lacks grace or cleanliness. You see the difference, dearie?

Emma continued, in another letter to Ben, in an even more melodramatic vein: "I do not believe in the story that love is blind. I hold that a truly great love sees with a thousand eyes. At any rate, my love watches, and when it detects a speck on the beautiful sky of its aspiration it weeps tears of blood."

Although Emma rationalized her attachment to this flawed relationship, and did not stop trying to make Ben understand what she wanted, she and Ben had profoundly different expectations of what commitments and long-term relationships involved. But neither she nor Ben was planning to leave the other. Their work on *Mother Earth* was the structural connection that enabled them to submerge their differences in service to the cause. It was their strongest link to reality and they clung to it, often with the desperation of people who felt themselves lost.

In the spring of 1909, the lovers turned their attention toward a new scheme to enable them to be together: Ben would come to New York to work full-time in the *Mother Earth* office. Emma encouraged him not to worry that others might begin to see him as dependent on *Mother Earth* and on Emma: "They give nothing to the magazine and even less to me, so why should we worry. The only thing that worries me, dear, is that we will probably have very little to live on. Literally nothing comes in for *ME*. My only hope lies in the meetings. If they too fail, we will have a hard summer. But, if I have your love and devotion, we will pull through, I am sure."

Emma wanted Ben near, but vowed to avoid spending too much of her time with him so that the delicious state of longing and desire would linger. Having had Ben's continuous company for months before their separation, she agreed with her friend and comrade Voltairine de Cleyre, the other woman of Emma's public stature in the anarchist movement, who had recently written: "Never allow love to be vulgarized by the common indecencies of continuous close communion. Better be in familiar contempt of your enemy than of the one you love."

Emma had to fight the urge to abandon herself to complete dependence on Ben, while Ben, simultaneously, tried to distance himself from Emma, in part because he felt that his sense of himself as a man was so easily overshadowed by her fame. He was also reluctant to come to New York without any financial security. He wrote to her, "Lover, I cannot come to you until I can pay my own fare and have a few dollars to live on." Emma tried to convince him to ignore his scruples over money matters and allow her to sustain him with her "love," her "devotion," and her "comradeship." But Ben was also subject to the competitive pull of his mother, and bound by his financial responsibility to her. With some ambivalence, Emma wrote to Ben: "I am glad your mother's home is comfortable. I want my own boy to have some comforts, but I want to be the one who gives it to him." With all the uncertainties of her life, Emma longed for a stable home with Ben. When he was away from her, she found the days only "half endurable. . . . I go about, I walk, I do housework, I go to theaters and concerts, only to forget myself."

When it became clear that Ben could find no work outside of arranging Emma's meetings, and their longing for each other had become unbearable, he came to New York. They worked together from the late spring through the early fall of 1909, except for brief trips he made back to Chicago. Together again, they had toured the Northeast. Eleven of their meetings were blocked or disrupted by police, so the focus of Emma's talks quickly shifted to the issue of free speech. In New Haven, the police actually wrote to the United States Attorney General to find out what legal justification they would have for suppressing Emma and Ben's meetings. The reply was not what they wanted to hear: "The bill to deny speech against the government after McKinley's assassination, did not become law." This did not stop the police, however, from preventing the thousands of people who were waiting outside from entering the hall, though they obediently let Emma and Ben in. Emma asked rhetorically in *Mother Earth,* "Is it that these people do not know their rights as guaranteed by the Constitution or is it because they have been police-ridden so long that they have lost the manhood to sustain their rights?"

Once they were back in New York, however, Emma realized that her political fervor still did not stimulate Ben as much as it did her, and that she might have to struggle without him. Depressed by a sense of worthlessness, Ben was feeling the attraction of Chicago. But before he left, he sought to rebuild his self-esteem in characteristic fashion by, as he put it, "entertaining" a new woman. His choosing to consummate the affair in the rented room that he and Emma shared threw Emma into despair. She had an apartment of her own that was the headquarters for *Mother Earth,* but the room Ben had rented for the two of them was her secret *home* and retreat.

By the end of May, Emma feared that her "journey" with Ben had come to an end. It was too difficult to sustain the political activity to which she was committed while she was being tormented by his promiscuity, for every time she discovered he had had another woman, his infidelity colored everything for months. Even the rationale for their separation—that it was time for Ben to establish himself financially—had collapsed. Ben had not found other work and was still dependent on *Mother Earth* for his livelihood. Emma had hoped that Ben would instead support the magazine through his medical practice. She wrote to him with resignation, but also with the self-aggrandizement of moral superiority. Often she stayed up late to write Ben, even when they were in the same city, as they were when she wrote the following:

> It was a hard and thorny journey, but so long as we had faith in our love, we stood the hardships. But faith is gone, Ben, my faith in your love for me and faith in my love for you. I know, I have failed with my love, failed miserably, so what is the use in dragging it on?
>
> I received my first shock when you could not hold out in Chicago, that first time, though you were so sure you would work and get on your feet. For one who has never known weakness it was a shock indeed. But my love said, "Ben loves you and cannot be away from you, that's why he has made no attempt in Chicago." And I listened to love's voice, for it is so good to be loved, you know.
>
> Then you came to N.Y. and you gave me new faith in the power

of my love. You were active, you did try to do things, to write, to work, to be on your own feet. When you left me my love was jubilant, for a time. When I left you, on that memorable day last March, I believed in your determination to practice— Alas, that belief was soon shattered. Your inertia, your lethargy, your absolute indifference since you [have been] in New York has gradually undermined my faith that my love must be an impetus, must give you strength and energy.

And then there is that other thing, the thing so abhorrent, so utterly impossible to endure—your *irresponsible unscrupulous* attitude towards women—your lack of honesty with them, with yourself, with myself. Oh, I know you will ascribe it to jealousy. But it is not. I have told you over and over again, if you really care for a woman, if you love her, no matter how much that may grieve me, I should have strength enough to face it. Or if you were honest in your dealings with women, openly and plainly telling them, "I want you for a sex embrace and no more," that too, I could stand. But your complete lack of justice, of common humanity, of consideration for the rights of another, is simply killing me. You deny leading on these women, but I know that *not one of them,* certainly not Grace, or Lioness or Lilly, or this latest fancy of yours, would consent to be used as a toy, not one of them. Even a prostitute wants to be loved, wants one man at least to have her because of love and passion, and not as a toy. Can't you realize that, Ben? . . .

However, your toys in the past were at least women who can take care of themselves, but what about the last victim? You tell me you do not lead her on; what do you call phoning the shop, making appointments, spending hours at a time with her, except leading her on? Must she not think, and justly so, that if you have singled her out, of all others, you must care for her? She cannot be so stupid as to imagine it is because of your intellectual or spiritual communion with her that you are seeking her. You tell me she is impressionable: more reason for her to assume that you care for her. But you say she is only a child, and you play with her. Oh, Ben, where is your sense of justice, of fairness, that you should play with a human being, no matter of how little importance? Has my love, our love, meant so little that you have not developed a spark of consideration and honesty? . . .

Can you see why I have lost faith in your love and in my love?

Emma felt that her own ego was involved in Ben's affairs. She thought that women trusted him, in part, because he was the lover of Emma Goldman, who was known for her own integrity. "She believes in you," Emma wrote, "because she imagines that the man who is loved by EG can be trusted, must be big, and honest, do you realize that?"

She stopped her letter, intending to finish it later, because she had to prepare a lecture she was to give that evening. She was to address a meeting organized by a nonanarchist leader of a new free-speech club that had been formed in response to the increasing police efforts to block her appearances. One man in particular, Alden Freeman, had taken the risk of inviting a group of people to his home in "lily white and wealthy" East Orange, New Jersey, to hear Emma Goldman speak, since she was denied access to a hall. The town was shocked, but the police could do nothing to prevent such an event on private property.

Emma was enjoying her increasing effectiveness at dodging police restrictions and the new recognition she received from the middle class, even as she was preoccupied with her jealousy and what seemed that night to be the bitter failure of her relationship with Ben. When she returned from her lecture, at 2:00 A.M., she continued her letter to Ben on a different note:

Ben, Ben. How I wish I were like you, carried away by the moment. I, too, would be full of joy that I have made a good speech, was admired by 150 people and treated with deference and enthusiasm. Yet, with all that, I am the most defeated, lonely, wretched spirit in this city tonight. Of what avail is the admiration of the World, if my soul is in pain, if the one human being I love with a maddening, unconquerable passion, outrages all that is fine and big to me. I began my letter with the determination to end our relation but tonight, when I saw you sitting on the stoop and after you left, all my determination was gone. You will never know what life has been to me, most of this year with you. An everlasting reaction against your lack of that which is fine and sacred to me. Nor will you ever know what life will be to me, away from you. The very thought has paralyzed me every time I attempted to break away, just as it has paralyzed me tonight. And yet, can one remain a Christian if one loses faith in Christ? How then am I to continue our relation, a relation that meant life essence to me, when you have killed my faith in your love and in the regenerative power of love? I cannot, Ben, I cannot unless you give me back my faith, unless you make me see that my love has not merely been the impetus of a physical exaltation, but that it has regenerated you, that it has awakened in you a spark of responsibility for the life of other human beings, for their sorrow. Give me back my faith, or let us go different routes. Believe me, I do not scold you, nor do I wish to mold your destiny. I only want you to know that if my love can do nothing to fit you for a new life, new interests, new human valuation, my love is useless and puny and I would rather not give it to you, anymore. Good night, how I wish I would wake no more, unless it were a new morning, great and good, and beautiful as I once believed our love would be

Good night

Mommie

Emma returned repeatedly in the letters of the next few weeks to the theme of her loss of faith in Ben's love and in her own capacity to change Ben. During their brief separation, Emma's letters began to convey resignation:

> I love you, dearest Ben, with all the intensity of my soul. You are in my blood, in my entire system, I could not get you out of myself, even if I tried. . . . You will have your obsessions, as long as you live. *And it has to be that way. . . . You see, dearest,* there was a time when I foolishly flattered myself that I could fill you at the exclusion of any other. . . . I am too miserable over our separation, over the police persecution, over our entire life, to care, at least just now.

Emma's ambivalence continued. She tried to drown her misery "in work, ironing, cleaning, addressing envelopes and what not." But to no avail:

Hobo! Hobo! cried my soul. . . . "Why did you ever enter my life, if you are to be out so much?" Foolish question, is it not? As if we could choose who should be in our lives. You came to me like a stroke of lightning, kindling my soul and body with mad passion, as I have never known before. Ever since you have consumed me, sopped me up into your blood, and when you go away, you leave me weak and nerveless. Yet when you stay, you cause me tortures of Hell. You say you do not want me to enjoy physical contact with others, it's all right for the spiritual relationship. Ben, Ben, can you imagine what I must suffer from your physical obsessions? Can you guess the thousand thoughts and fancies that torture my heart when I think of the day you had that girl in *our room*. Yet, you did not understand, you called me petty. . . . You said I was unreasonable. Oh, dear boy, each one feels his own pain deepest, that's why you do not know how much you have made me suffer As to my physical relationship with others, you need never ask, *I would tell it to you*. I can, however, tell you this right now, that your obsessions and escapades have worn me out, so that this time I no longer feel that great impossibility, as during your absence on the former occasion. I no longer have the mental revulsion at the thought of a relation with anyone else, as I used to have.

Unfortunately, though, I still have that physical revulsion at the very thought of being in another man's arms. My body rebels, the m, the t-b rebels, Oh, you have hypnotized them, you have put them in a trance.

She distracted herself with a grand scheme she and Sasha had concocted to make the fortune that she hoped would put an end to their constant money worries. They planned to commission a bust of Jacob Gordin, a recently deceased Yiddish dramatist, and sell replicas for a profit to his thousands of admirers. The scheme failed, as had all of their get-rich plans, but it served to keep Emma's attention focused outward.

While Emma's political activities continued at their usual high pitch, the two lovers continued their debate. Ben wrote to Emma protesting her accusations, assuring her that he had changed his entire "psychology," even though he had not changed his habits. To Emma, the distinction was ludicrous.

> Unfortunately I am but human, and therefore judge your actions as if my lover were really mature and not the petulant, reckless irresponsible child that he is. . . . Your habits would never have become such a force if not for your psychology. Your psychology is promiscuous, that is, you have no sense of selection, you are attracted by every and any woman and you will have relations with her, if she will only consent. This has become habit with you, because there never has been any other force stronger than your promiscuousness.

> . . . Now, that force has come into your life, your love for me. Such loves have worked miracles with some men, it has cured them of drug habits, drink, gambling, almost anything. What has it cured you of? You love me one year, during that time you have sex relations with at least 10 women, possibly even more. Oh, yes, you will tell me that before you loved me, you had many more. True, but if you have less now, it is not because of your great love for me, but because being together has diminished your opportunities. Also because our relation has naturally diminished your capacity. In short, if you will only be frank with yourself you will find that your love has changed not one particle of your former attractions. . . . Please, dearest, do not imagine I speak of your dependency because I want anything from you. Oh, no, all I want is your love and devotion, not your money. I have never been taken care [of] by any man in all my life and wouldn't be able to stand it, even if you were in a position. When I refer to your dependence, it is only that your love has done nothing. . . . I am not speaking with anger, I am only realizing the greatest tragedy of my life, namely what love has done for other men, it has not done for the *one man in all my life.* . . .

Emma imagined that she had no power over Ben, and saw herself as a victim of his mistreatment. In fact she had a great effect on him, but her early feeling of loneliness was so profound that she always felt like the helpless, unloved child. This psychological state blinded her to how much Ben loved her, and to the influence she exerted on his sense of himself as well as his attitude toward her. She could not see that Ben's contact with and commitment to her had fundamentally changed him.

Ben spent a lot of time in Chicago during the spring and early summer, a fact Emma lamented in her letters. It seemed to her that he had no reason to return to her, with his hobos and his women to keep him company. If he thought he had changed because of his association with Emma, she was sure he was deceiving himself. For her part, however, Emma felt that she had changed completely since meeting Ben:

> My love has indeed changed my psychology, changed my habits, changed even my attitude toward my work. Before I knew you, I cared for other men and was intimate with them. Now, though these men stimulate me, I cannot give way to that stimulation: something more forcible, more elemental, stands between these men and myself, my mad wild love for you. I [have known] you more than a year and not once have I been in anyone's arms save yours. You [have known] me just as long, and you have been in the arms of every woman who wanted you; see the difference.

Emma criticized Ben's personal habits to emphasize how her love had changed her.

> Your method of eating used to turn my stomach and make me uncomfortable for hours. My love for you has overcome that. Your lack of cleanliness used to give me aesthetic convulsions, my love has overcome that. . . . Love has done more; all my life, I was opposed to traveling with anyone, because I hated to take away means intended for the propaganda or *ME*. My love has overcome that to such an extent that now the very thought of traveling without you is impossible.

She was quick to assure Ben that her abstinence was not the result of a lack of sexual energy or desirability, but her words had a defensive ring: "You admit yourself that I am desirable, that I could have many men, worthier men than any of the women who have been in your life, with the exception of Lioness. Why then do I not go to them? Do you suppose they do not stimulate me? They do. Do you think I am less sexed?

"To love me," Emma asserted, "required no sacrifice on your part, dear, nor have you made any." For Emma, sacrifice was proof of love and devotion. Her notions came in part from her Jewish heritage, in which the mother's love was often measured according to her willingness to put her child before herself. But Emma could recognize only her own sacrifice for Ben; she could not see that Ben, too, had disrupted his life and work to be with her. In a sense, Emma did not know exactly what she wanted, but she knew that Ben did not give her the feeling of calm completeness that she imagined perfect love would bring. She was left with her quest for the unattainable, which confirmed her tragic and heroic image of herself.

Given the mores of the time and the intimacy of their relationship, her stated desire for stability and willing fidelity was not outrageous. But as an anarchist, a believer in free love, she was forced to make fine distinctions between liberty and license. She wanted to be open to a transcendent interpretation of free love, and therefore her politics seemed to be the reason for her conflict with Ben. But she could not stop herself from trying to control Ben through guilt, and even warned him in her letters: "There is but one thing that may send you out of my life and that's your disease for women." Emma identified with Karl Marx's daughter, Eleanor Marx Aveling, who committed suicide because her husband "followed up his habits until he drove the woman to desperation." On the surface, Emma assured Ben that she was not threatening to kill herself, merely dramatizing how seriously she felt the strain of his indulgences; inwardly, however, she enjoyed scaring him. In fact, her critical edge provided her with some independence from Ben, for it assured her that she had not become "a complete slave" to this "wild, savage passion."

Emma resisted Ben's suggestion that she "go to it" with another man. "Many people go through life without finding sex exaltation," she wrote to him. "You have given me that and a million things more; how, then, can I be pleased with anything less. I want you, only your ———. I want your body glued to mine, I want you in the t.b., your touch closely gripping my m. . . . Hobo, dear Hobo, I want you so."

Emma planned to make herself so appealing to Ben that it would be impossible for him to "slip" into relationships with another woman. "If you could only see m blanc and juria raise their peaks, us too, they say, we want Hobo. And the tb she simply screams with anxiety. I must stop; if I continue, I shall have to take a bath." And so Emma aroused herself before she said good night to the "master lover" who "so generously" would "give her up to others."

Ben's generosity with "his Mommy's body" was meant to justify his own behavior. Emma paraphrased from Ben's letter, "I see a woman. Immediately some force tells me, here is pleasure," noting that afterward he would recoil in disgust. Emma responded sharply, stating that this represented "the kind of love most men have, small puny parasitic, unwilling to stand the slightest act of devotion, giving nothing, taking all. Surely your love is bigger than that. Besides, though I am not conceited, I am justified in saying that I inspire a greater love." Yet Ben's inability to break this pattern was becoming inescapably evident to Emma. She could no more prevent her revulsion at his promiscuous associations than he could help being stimulated. "If you only knew how I have fought that revulsion, how I have reasoned with it, oh, if you only knew. But *I cannot overcome it, I never will overcome it.* You will not change, and I also know that your tendencies will continue to be a black hideous spot on our great beautiful love. I know that, but I cannot do without you."

Thus, despite their conflicts, Emma looked forward to spending June 27, her fortieth birthday, with "Dr. BLR Lover." Ben had canceled his plan to spend the day with Lioness so that he could be in New York with Emma. As usual, they reveled in their physical passion for each other, and agonized over almost everything else. They enjoyed attending a free-speech protest meeting in Cooper Union on July 2, but had a hard time escaping the shadow of Ben's latest affair.

Emma colluded in her own unhappiness by choosing in Ben a man known for his sexual prowess. And while she identified with his uninhibited sexuality, she was ambivalent about its emotional consequences, and her mistrust, besides being painful, also served to distance her from Ben. Ben therefore received the double message of being appreciated for his unabashed sexuality and scolded for it.

Although their celebration of Emma's birthday in New York was intensely passionate, Emma was confused, no longer sure what their love meant to him. By August she was repeating her old refrain about her insecurity and his promiscuity. Her letters became repetitious. She wrote to him that although "you are light and air, beauty and glory to me," she had been seized by "that creepy, slimy, treacherous thing— doubt." She fought against wondering whether her Ben was "premeditative and mean" or just "wayward and impulsive" in his affairs with other women. And she had moved from feeling disdainful of "that stupid girl" whom Ben had seduced and abandoned to feeling genuinely compassionate: "I sympathize with the girl in her desperate clinging to you." It still seemed inconceivable that she and Ben could have such a "great love" while Ben was causing "misery all around." She countered this contradiction with hope: "We have so much before us, such great and valuable work, our fight, our trip to Australia, and above all, our great great love."

Perhaps her confidence in her passionate connection to Ben sustained her work. Just before their September trip to Vermont and Massachusetts, she wrote, "You are just the manager I want and still more the lover I want." It was not just Ben who excited her, but her own heightened capacity to give and accept sexual pleasure: "Everything I do to give you delight thrills me." She was, as Ben commented to her years later, in love with being in love with Ben. She herself, at least, would live out her part of the vision of what it meant to be deeply and dramatically in love, even if Ben could not.

On October 13, 1909, Emma learned of the death of Francisco Ferrer, a Spanish freethinker who had attempted to wrest the teaching of children from the authoritarian model of education, which was generally under the control of the church, and had begun to establish secular schools to focus on the creativity of the individual and to teach children to think independently. Assumed guilty of fomenting a popular insurrection in Spain, he was arrested and brutally shot by the military in the trenches of Barcelona's Montjuich Fortress. Emma organized a public meeting as a demonstration of protest, with a resolution to continue his work in a modern school movement, but her grief at what had happened to Ferrer got tangled up with feelings about her situation with Ben.

> Through the terrible shock of Ferrer's death, I have forgotten my own useless battle, my own heart's wretchedness. . . . I am broken in spirit and body, I feel weary, just weary. My struggle never seemed more useless, a lone voice against a multitude. My effort to keep our relation on a high plane too has failed. Our relation has grown commonplace and is being dragged through the mire. I do not reproach you, really not, I am only indescribably sad and weary. . . . I fear I am not made for rest, nor am I quite fit for everlasting war.

Emma turned her despair into action; she is now remembered as among those most active in establishing the first Ferrer School of New York, one year after Ferrer's tragic death. She herself felt "ill at ease in the presence of children," other than those she became close to through family and friends. However, the school valued creativity and freethinking above all else, and some of the best minds of the anarchist movement taught there at her behest.

The same psychological mechanism had first thrust Emma into anarchist activity after the death of the Haymarket martyrs. Outrage at blatant injustice, identification with the pain and ecstasy of losing one's life for the "cause," inspired her to take personal responsibility for carrying on the work that the martyrs had started. She herself would make sure that they had not died in vain. Whether or not her work was in part an unconscious response to her own inner turmoil, she did not spread her despair, but shared her vision; in turn, the strength of her vision served to lessen her despair.

Emma could not escape, however, from the incongruities of her own life. She wrote to Ben, "I have no right to speak of Freedom when I myself have become an abject slave in my love." She could not go on extolling the virtues of free love in her "Marriage and Love" lecture without coming to terms with her rejection of Ben's promiscuity. In her lecture on "False Fundamentals of Free Love," she made a sharp distinction between promiscuity and free love. It was painful work, but she needed to clarify to Ben that free love meant something other than indiscriminate sexual relations without deeper commitment. The letters written during her work on this lecture expressed the same themes. She told Ben:

> Your love is all sex, with nothing but indifference left when that is gratified. . . . My love is sex, but it is devotion, care, anxiety, patience, friendship, it is all. How are the two to harmonize? . . . You are always primitive and I am hyper-civilized. Therein lies the chasm, the terrible abyss, therein be the cause of all our misunderstanding. That is also the reason why you have never considered me a complete part of yourself, and why I with all my theoretical notions against too close a relationship have taken you into my life, as a complete part of myself. I know I have about reached the breaking point.

And yet she continued to inspire her audiences with a vision of love rescued from the marketplace of marriage. She tried to reach people who were yearning for love and commitment in their lives, and to expand their vision of the individual's need for love into that of a social need. By making people aware of the conventions that limited their expectations, she was able to connect their inner need for a sense of belonging with their feelings of deprivation at the absence of a larger community. In order to live fully, each person would have to confront societal norms, the hypocrisy and injustices that inhibit freedom. Similarly, by showing the barrenness of the socially approved forms of love, she hoped to inspire people to change the conditions that blocked them from living out their vision of love. Emma recognized in love the weakest link and the strongest link between people. Because everybody wants and needs to be loved, the longing for love makes one feel most vulnerable; even dissatisfaction in one's work life can often be eased with the promise of a more fulfilling, self-contained personal life. Emma's brilliance and originality lay in her ability to bring issues that were ostensibly private into the public sphere.

She was shrewd to begin in the realm of personal life, to hold out a vision of transcendence beyond ordinary love. Her approach affirmed the rights of the individual in a way that everyone could identify with, without retreating from politics. An Emma Goldman lecture on love often moved people to tears, not unlike a wedding sermon, with the added theme of the politicization of love between people who want a bond based on true equality and a love that ennobles.

Her approach was particularly timely in these early years of twentieth-century America, when there was a mood of tension at the rapid transformation of personal life. The residue of Victorianism hampered open discussion of private issues, but at the same time, women had more choices over their lives, for they were less exclusively harnessed to the home and family. The issue of birth control also began to be of vital concern to the urban middle-class family. The social and political consequences of women's new freedoms to limit the size of the family and to participate more fully in the paid work force seemed to threaten the foundation of society. Emma's ability to perceive the deeper issues that such social upheaval raised enabled her to give speeches that set the stage for open discussion of love and sexuality within the family. In some ways it was unimportant whether her views were accepted or that she had no concrete plan of action. Just the opportunity to talk about and argue these issues filled a popular need.

Emma was part of a group of bohemian intellectuals who heralded the age of the New Woman, but her own flair and dramatic presentation of the issues made her a public personality, and she attracted people who were not necessarily anarchists. Her insights into the widespread alienation touched a deep personal chord for all who came in contact with her.

Her lecture on "Marriage and Love" presented her view that marriage inhibits rather than enhances love, that it has been primarily an economic arrangement, "an insurance pact." She cited the high divorce rate and emphasized that marriage was still a patriarchal institution in which women gave up their vitality and freedom to men. Women generally had sacrificed themselves to secure the conventional form of security by minimizing their needs and their work in relation to the needs and work of their husbands.

She also blamed the moral convention of women's virginity before marriage for the sexual tensions that developed in a marriage and often led to divorce. Although it seemed that a woman was protected by the institution of marriage, Emma pointed out, her personality weakened from dependence. (Emma likened marriage to "that other paternal arrangement—capitalism.")

From dismal reality, Emma turned to her vision of a more exalted free love, in which security does not come through a pact of obligation mediated by the state but, rather, comes voluntarily in its most elevating and empowering form:

> Free love? As if love is anything but free: Man has bought brains, but all the millions in the world have failed to buy love. Man has subdued bodies, but all the power on earth has been unable to subdue love. Man has conquered whole nations, but all his armies could not conquer love. Man has chained and fettered the spirit, but he has been utterly helpless before love. High on a throne, with all the splendor and pomp his gold can command, man is yet poor and desolate, if love passes him by. And if it stays, the poorest hovel is radiant with warmth, with life and color. Thus love has the magic power to make of a beggar a king. Yes, love is free; it gives itself unreservedly, abundantly, completely. All the laws on the statutes, all the courts in the universe, cannot tear it from the soil, once love has taken root. If, however, the soil is sterile, how can marriage make it bear fruit? It is like the last desperate struggle of fleeting life against death. . . . In our present pygmy state love is indeed a stranger to most people. Misunderstood and shunned, it rarely takes root; or if it does, it soon withers and dies. Its delicate fiber can not endure the stress and strain of the daily grind. Its soul is too complex to adjust itself to the slimy wool of our social fabric. It weeps and moans and suffers with those who need of it, yet lack the capacity to rise to love's summit. Some day, some day men and women will rise, they will reach the mountain peak, they will meet big and strong and free, ready to receive, to partake, and to bask in the golden rays of love. What fancy, what imagination, what poetic genius can foresee even approximately the potentialities of such a force in the life of men and women. If the world is ever to give birth to true companionship and oneness, not marriage, but love will be the parent.

Emma condemned the institution of marriage for stifling love in a misguided attempt to enforce stability and fidelity, yet found herself "bruised from all the wounds of the lack of stability" with Ben. The growing success of her "Marriage and Love" lecture only emphasized the distance between her vision and reality. She wrote to Ben:

"Marriage and Love" is hateful to me, hateful because my faith in the power of love has been shattered. I used to think it could perform miracles, poor fool that I was. You do not realize, my boy, the shock, the awful shock my love has received. One never survives after such a shock. I may or may not find my way back to you, dear, whichever way will depend on you. One thing is certain—I am beyond the old way. I could not stand for that, really not.

Just a week after they had been in Boston together, Ben again dropped Emma for a moment's fancy. Her "self-respect," her "womanhood," her "humanity had been outraged." She could not concentrate on her work, and she felt herself to be a hypocrite.

It's too bad we did not meet when propaganda meant more to me than everything else in the world, when I had no personal interest in people or things, when I could use everything and everybody for the sake of the Cause. That time is past, much to the disadvantage of my own life. Meetings, free speech, *ME* are nothing to me now, if my love, my life, my peace, my very soul is to be mutilated. Work with you, so long as I had faith in your love, meant the greatest, sweetest joy in life. That may account for my utter abandonment, my utter dissolution to my love for you. That may also account for why I, the woman who has been treated with respect by friend and foe, could crouch on her knees and beg and plead with you. Yes, I teach you to make you see the beauty, the force, the greatness of love—I believe in it no longer, I have no faith in your love, and with it the joy of work with you is gone. I have no right to bring a message to people, when there is no message in my soul.

Emma plunged into depression. "All is dead," she wrote Ben. "Unfortunately, I too shall not die, most people live with dead souls, why not I?"

Within the same week she wrote several letters assessing why she remained in this unsatisfying and anxiety-producing relationship. She was angry about Ben's latest obsession and infuriated that he picked up other women while she was lecturing and being entertained by her hosts. Perhaps, she wrote, Ben gave her all he was capable of giving. Still, she chastised herself for failing to demand more.

Perhaps, if my love for you had not so completely taken hold of me, if it had not swept me off my feet, if it had not excluded everyone and everything, I should have been less exacting. I have never received half the love I gave, but I never missed it particularly. You came into my life with such a terrific force, you gripped my soul, my nerves, my thought, my flesh, until all was blotted out, all else was silenced. Theories, considerations, principles, consistency, friends, nay even pride and self-respect. Only one thing remained, a terrible hunger for your love, an insatiable thirst for it. That explains my clinging, my holding on to you, I who never clung to anyone. That explains my agony when every woman would possess you at the exclusion of myself. Oh, please, don't give me your assurances, I do not believe in them. Did you forget my existence on that night, when you stood out in the rain for ½ [hour] trying to get the woman of your obsession? She spoiled your mood, you wrote. Yes I know, she did not yield, that always spoils your moods.

Emma's despair over their relationship infected her view of the future: she foresaw grim times for herself, politically as well as personally. In the same letter, the melodrama escalated: "Work? success? My work will never be successful again, it will never again amount to anything, the spirit of it was killed. I hate the very thought of meeting[s], it's like prostituting oneself. I cannot keep that up, why should I? *ME?* Nobody wants it. Propaganda? What good does it do? Myself? I can earn more scrubbing floors."

The ecstasy of their first year together had passed. If she could muster enough energy to go on tour again, she would ask Ben to arrange the meetings and do the advance work, as he had done along the way before, because she still believed in his talent as a manager. But this time, she vowed, their collaboration would be on a different basis. Ben would receive a percentage rather than a salary, so that he would not need to ask Emma for any money directly. "We will keep apart as much as possible, outside of our work," she told him. She closed her letter by admonishing Ben to "learn to give occasionally," a point she underlined by asking for the size of his mother's waist so that she could send her a Christmas gift.

Emma continued with her work, lecturing on the positive value of idealism in a talk she titled "The Dream as a Moral Force," but she was plagued with a new pessimism that she kept hidden from the public.

> Life is a hideous nightmare, yet we drag it on and on and find a thousand excuses for it. It is a disgusting business. I am strongly contemplating giving up everything, *ME*, 210, America, and going to Australia, traveling a few years, alone. I can get the money, tomorrow, this minute, if I can only pull up strength and go. I want to do it, as I see in that the only salvation out of my madness. But I have no strength, I have no discussion, I cannot rest or eat or sleep, speaking is torture, nothing brings relief from that awful longing for one human being in all the World. Hobo! Hobo! Hobo! rings in my ear until my head would split. I am mad, sick, worn, I must be strong, I must go away. Mommy.

Again Australia seemed to promise an escape from the forces sapping her spirit. This time, by considering going without Ben, she acknowledged that he was one of those forces. Yet she knew that the government was still searching for a way to revoke her citizenship. If she left the United States now, she might never be able to return. Then, too, she believed that her love for Ben was irreplaceable: "I shall probably never again know such a love, or feel anything for any other man," she wrote him, explaining that she perceived herself as "loving too deeply, too madly, with all the concentrated subtle passion of a woman of my temperament." She ended one letter, "my love for you saps my very blood. It is a mad love, therefore not a normal one. Your sad and lonely, Mommy."

As 1909 drew to a close, Emma was uncertain whether she would find the energy to function on the high political and emotional plane that made her feel that life was worth living. She seemed to surrender to Ben the power to determine her emotional stability. His obsessive affairs felt like repeated assaults on her precarious self-esteem. She kept expecting him to transform himself and longed for an affirmation of his devotion to her that would match her idealized vision of love.

5

ADDICTION TO LOVE

After all, I am right in my belief in the power of love. Two weeks ago today, I was the poorest, most dejected creature on Earth. All life, hope, faith were gone, I was simply stranded. Indeed, I was so terribly poor that I even lacked strength to end it all. . . .

Today, I feel regenerate, reborn, new. What has performed the miracle? Why, love, only love. If I did not love you so fervently so completely, so absolutely, I could not have survived the shock of two weeks ago. I could not feel today, as I do, full of hope and faith. I could not long with all my soul for you. Yes, love is great, is wonderful.

The circular pattern set in motion during their last year, of elation following depression, continued, as did the schedule of their tours and separations. Ben had sent a letter of complete devotion, full of promises to turn over a new leaf, pleas that his intensely emotional lover stay by his side, and hopes for the new year—1910. He did not go so far as to promise to spend his birthday, New Year's Day, with his "blue-eyed Mommy," because he always reserved that day for his actual mother. And Emma did not risk meeting him at the annual Mother Earth New Year's

Ball in New York, because in the previous two years he had followed home the woman of his evening's fancy, leaving Emma to handle all the social duties. "I have a horror [of the] experience at the two Balls you attended. Besides, it is no place for us to meet, after our terrible separation. I want to come to you, soon, dear, that's why I have changed the date to the 9th. . . . With a never dying yet suffering love, Mommy."

The lovers would meet first by themselves, not in the context of a public event, "before the mob." Emma wrote to Ben, in anticipation: "I want to feel my way back to you. . . . Maybe we can still find happiness together, I know I shall not find it without you."

As the rendezvous neared, Ben's letters were fewer and shorter. Emma wrote him that she would never tire of his assurances, and when she did not hear them she began to feel uncertain again. "I may be all wrong in doubting you, but it creeps up again and again like a shadow in the night." Her suspicions led her to remark that even the stationery Ben used seemed like that of a woman he might be courting: "Do you know the phantoms, the horrible spooks and uncertainties that little things conjured before me? . . . I ache all over from lack of sleep and rest."

In fact, she resented Ben's desire to spend his birthday with his mother when she had "hoped to give [him] the greatest gift a woman can give to a man, *herself*, unreservedly, her quivering, passionate complete self."

On Ben's birthday, Emma tried to forget about his absence at a Russian New Year's ball. "I was never so miserable in my life," she wrote to him. At the ball she saw "shadows of the past. I saw those that crowded me out of your life." She went home to stand before Ben's photo, angry and hurt. Then she sat down to write another anguished message to Ben. Perhaps, she wrote, she would cancel her winter lecture tour. She had planned to speak on a wider range of topics, with lectures on Ferrer and the Modern School, women's suffrage, white-slave traffic, the psychology of political violence, the spirit of revolt in modern drama, and her old standby, marriage and love. But doubt had paralyzed her.

Ben replied, "How could you think of giving up the trip? Hobo would die if he could not work with you. There isn't time to tell you that you are my love, my all, and I want you *so* and we must *go on.*"

Easily convinced, Emma agreed to have Ben join her. Within the month, she met him in Chicago. They set off through the Midwest to the West together, dispelling for the moment Emma's feeling of emotional turmoil.

She wrote in *Mother Earth* about the financial cause of her near paralysis. She was faced with the yearly choice of "burying the magazine or invading the country, that is, going on a lecture tour. Feeling deeply with you and not wishing you to go to the expense of wearing mourning, the publisher of this magazine has decided to inflict herself on poor humanity." She continued her report in the January issue of *Mother Earth*, cheering herself on with the fact that although, three years before, she had been dragged off the platform in Chicago and in Detroit, now, after the efforts of the Free Speech Leagues, she had several lectures scheduled for those cities.

Her optimism was premature. In Madison, Wisconsin, just the fact that she spoke on "Marriage and Love" in a building provided by the state for student lectures, and the attendance of several professors at her lecture, threw the town, the state, and the university into an uproar, including threats of dismissing a faculty member who had announced her lecture in his class. At the same time the January issue of *Mother Earth* was suppressed by the Post Office because it contained the text of Emma's widely attended lecture on "White Slave Traffic." It was probably Emma's effort to link a critique of the state and capitalism with the taboo subjects of sex and sex education that led government censors to halt mail distribution of Emma's article. Emma had planned to deliver that lecture on this tour and was determined not to let the laws about what was permissible to send through the mails stop her from speaking. Her lecture was a response to the Mann Act, which made it illegal to transport women across state lines or bring them into the United States for immoral purposes. Red light districts in over thirty cities were closed as a result of its passage. Emma's essay, which took the blame for prostitution away from women (who, she noted, were "not merely white women, but yellow and black women as well"), was considered an outrage against the state. She pinpointed the reasons women became prostitutes: "Exploitation, of course; the merciless Moloch of capitalism that fattens on underpaid labor, thus driving thousands of women and girls into prostitution. With [George Bernard Shaw's] Mrs. Warren, these girls feel, Why waste your life working for a few shillings a week in scullery, eighteen hours a day?" But, beyond the economic cause, she believed,

> a cause much deeper and by far of greater importance is the complete ignorance on sex matters. It is a conceded fact that woman has been reared as a sex commodity, and yet she is kept in absolute ignorance of the meaning and importance of sex. So long as a girl is not to know how to take care of herself, not to know the function of the most important part of her life, we need not be surprised if she becomes an easy prey to prostitution or any other form of a relationship which degrades her to the position of an object for mere sex gratification.

The solution to the prostitution issue was linked to Emma's conception of change through education rather than electoral or reform politics:

> We must rise above our foolish notions of "better than thou," and learn to recognize in the prostitute a product of social conditions. Such a realization will sweep away the attitude of hypocrisy and insure a greater understanding and more humane treatment. As to a thorough eradication of prostitution, nothing can accomplish that save a complete transvaluation of all accepted values—especially the moral ones—coupled with the abolition of industrial slavery.

Audience response to Emma's lecture ranged from moralistic outrage to gratitude. Many prostitutes heard the lecture and told Emma that she had both renewed their faith in themselves and kindled an interest in anarchism.

Although Emma spoke for the dignity of women tarnished by prostitution, and even by marriage, she was never an advocate of the women's suffrage movement. It would be ten years before women won the right to vote, but the suffrage movement was already an important part of left and center political life in the United States, as well as in England. The movement was a logical outgrowth of industrialization with its concomitant increase in the numbers of women in the work force. In the United States, it also stemmed from the abolition movement, for many female abolitionists, once the Civil War had ended, turned their attention to winning the vote. But Emma felt uncomfortable engaging in mainstream political reform. She told one audience, which included Maud Malone, commander of the militant English Flying Squad of Street Suffragettes, that she thought the imprisoned leaders of the English suffrage movement were wasting their time. "Mind you, I'm not opposed to the women having the vote. There is no reason why she shouldn't have just as much chance to make a fool of herself with it as men have made of themselves in the last hundred years. I am here to express my sympathy for the women who are suffering heroic things in England for something they believe in. But the vote is not worth having, that's all."

The suffrage movement's recent tactical decision to narrow its focus solely to the suffrage issue prompted Emma to accuse the movement of being antagonistic to labor, snobbishly middle-class, and moralistic. Emma's comments, of course, alienated most women associated with the movement. Her attacks on their narrow moralism were delivered with her own brand of moralism. Nothing great in history had been won through suffrage, as she saw it. She acknowledged the acerbity of her comments: "Yes, I may be considered an enemy of woman; but if I can help her see the light, I shall not complain." She ended her lecture by asserting that woman should stop wasting her time trying to outdo man.

> Her development, her freedom, her independence, must come from and through herself. First by asserting herself as a personality, and not as a sex commodity. Second by refusing the right to anyone over her body; by refusing to bear children unless she wants them; by refusing to be a servant to God, the State, society, the husband, the family, et cetera, by making her life simpler, but deeper and richer. That is by trying to learn the meaning and substance of life in all its complexities, by freeing herself from the fear of public opinion and public condemnation. Only that, and not the ballot, will set woman free, will make her a force hitherto unknown in

the world, a force for real love, for peace, harmony: a force of divine fire, of life-giving; a creator of free men and women.

Despite her position on the suffrage issue, Emma believed wholeheartedly that "in America women and not men, will prove the most ardent workers for social reconstruction. Already we find in all radical movements women as the most zealous workers. I say this not because I am partial to my sex, but because the middle class and even the professional man has been made an almost complete automaton by our commercial life; he lacks red blood, without which active interest in an ideal is impossible." Women were socialized to be the guardians of emotional life, and tended to connect rather than compartmentalize their inner and outer worlds, which was what men did. Women's traditional role in the home required attentiveness to the emotional and physical needs of her family. Therefore, Emma contended, political commitment in a woman had the potential to be an integrated emotional and intellectual statement.

Emma saw the struggle to live by a consistent set of principles guiding both inner and outer lives, private and public relationships, as essential to the ideal of anarchism. She even gave a lecture on "Life as Art" in which she asserted that "life in all its variety of color, in all its fullness and wealth is art, the highest art."

Emma's efforts to make a consistent whole of her own political and emotional life continued to prove elusive. Despite the success of their lecture tour, she wrote Ben that she "was never more discouraged over [their] relation." On the platform she could transcend the petty problems of daily life, but "the agony that our love has not saved us from the same coarse vulgar scenes of the ordinary herd has completely paralyzed me." Ben evidently tried to console her with a fatalistic expression—"what has to be must be." But Emma could not accept that the turbulent course their relationship had taken was inevitable; she believed that such passivity undermined people's power to create their own lives. Ben and Emma were often polarized in this way, with Ben too quickly accepting whatever happened as if he were not responsible for the consequences of his promiscuity, and Emma too quickly denying her complicity in Ben's behavior and her need alternately to chastise and forgive her "boy." In reaction, she created a separate reality that bypassed her ambivalence.

> If "what has to be must be" why make an effort for the new? Why struggle and face every obstacle? Why write books? Why publish *ME?* Why do the disagreeable thing?
>
> No, I do not believe in this theory, "what has to be must be." It's an excuse for cowards and weaklings. All my life, I have resisted it, fought it, defied it. All my life striven for the ideal, *all my life.* I have refused to accept the cruel hideous reality. It is too late for me to adjust myself to anything that kills my ideal, inch by inch and day by day, *I will not, I cannot.*

Emma's denial of "reality" was a pattern that recurred throughout her life. She expected that a social climate of complete freedom would break down any violent tendencies, greed, or jealousy, both in the society and in each individual. The specific details of this utopia would eventually be worked out by an enlightened population. Attempting to live out her vision, she thought that she could transcend the destructive forces that plagued the world. In her relationship with Ben, she labored under the illusion that she could live and love freely in an unfree society, that she and Ben were "different," and that their commitments to higher values would protect them from succumbing to the temptations and the petty jealousy of "the common herd." When faced with the conscious choice, she wrote to Ben: "I'd rather do without reality if my ideal is forever to be abused, insulted, spat upon, dragged through the mud."

Emma could endure the tumultuousness of her relationship with Ben because she held on to her vision that two people who had been so successful in creating sexual intimacy could not possibly fail to achieve spiritual intimacy.

She countered her personal disappointment with Ben in the pages of *Mother Earth,* by noting that she had not forgotten he was an extraordinarily talented manager: "I think I am not exaggerating when I say that during the last two years I have done better work, have reached more people, certainly more English-speaking people, have disposed of a larger amount of literature, and have helped to make Anarchism more widely known than in many previous tours. The credit for the difference is due chiefly to the zeal, the devotion, and skill of Ben Reitman. I believe in giving even the devil his due."

Her current generosity toward Ben was aroused while he was recovering from plastic surgery he had undergone on his nose. Ben, born a Jew, spent most of his life denying it. A "nose job" may have been his outward statement of what he had already changed inwardly. Whether this operation had some medical justification or was just the result of his vanity is unclear. Emma added a sarcastic comment—"If Ferral can give you a better nose, perhaps he has the power to give you more kindness and thoughtfulness? An operation would be worthwhile, don't you think?"

The balance of that letter was about business, and about Sasha, who had ordered something costly without checking with her first. This action on his part set Emma raging: "But, then, all men love to be the dictators of every situation; they are not so willing to stand the results, though."

Emma needed love from men, even if her lifelong anger kept yielding tension and disappointment. Her closest comrades during this period tended to be male, yet she constantly felt rejected by men. Rationally she understood the irony of having the love and admiration of the men around her while being unable to experience that love because of her absorption with Ben. Ben was well aware of the contradiction in the fact that Emma complained of his "obsessions" with other women though she was always surrounded by other men who loved her. He, too, needed *her* assurances, which she duly gave. She wrote him once that Sasha was "the only being in New York who has a soothing effect on me, like a mother's touch to a sick child," but none could do what Ben did for her:

So you think Max [Baginsky] has my love and confidence, Berkman has my comradeship and devotion, etc., etc. I wish you were right, dear, for my own sake I wish it. Alas, alas, it's all shoved behind me. There is no one, no one, except the one, who is the cruelest, most brutal, most thoughtless creature in the whole World. His name is Ben Reitman, Mommy's own love, Mummy joy and sorrow. No, you do not make me happy, that's true, you are no good to me, that too is true, but I love you, love you, love you!

I said to [Hutch] Hapgood today, if I had to give up everything and everybody in order to go with Ben I would go, he is the most compelling element in my life, even if it means living in Hell.

One explanation for Emma's complete absorption with Ben at this point was her approaching birthday. She wrote to Ben, "on the unfortunate day of my birth," wishing that she could be with him, even though it had only been a week since they were together— "of what avail is reason, intelligence, saneness, freedom, etc., etc., if I am absolutely and completely bound in my love to you?" She waited for a gift or a birthday greeting from Ben, but instead she received a short note. To this she responded with disgust: "Well, your letter came at 9 A.M., a poor puny little scrap of paper, a wretched crumb, while I was famished for your love." No one except Havel and Emma's sister remembered her birthday. Even

Alex, for whom I worked 22 years like a faithful slave, remembered this day only because he saw H[avel]'s flowers. Isn't that enough material for a tragi-comedy? Talk about a fool, there is no one to equal EG, not another woman in the world.

Oh, I do not want to be better, after all, each one has his function to fulfill. Mine is to give, always to give, others' to take. But, God, it hurts, it hurts like hell, I was never more unhappy than this day. . . . I have no pride, no strength, no ambition left. I want you, I want to hold you close to me, I want to touch your body, I want, I want:

I am mad, absolutely mad and miserable. Write Me.

Mommy

"I want" was what the woman who thought that she could mother others and give of herself endlessly felt on this anniversary of her birth. She wanted something in return, as if all her generosity on other days could be reciprocated on this special occasion. She felt she gave in excess the love she had been denied in her early life. And when she did not receive what she felt she would have given to another, she was heartbroken.

After her birthday, however, she continued in the same vein: "My love for you, my Ben, has become the most domineering factor in my life. Its great elemental mysterious force is beating me, wounded and sore, robbing me of all my [well-ordered] ideas and ideals."

Emma considered herself the complete victim of Ben's abusive love of her, not with the perspective of a powerful adult, but through the eyes of a child, who has no power to affect her situation. She described herself as "a trembling leaf exposed to a raging storm."

Ben consoled himself and her by saying that she must fight her depression and throw herself back into her work at 210. But she responded: "You said 210 is in my bones. Poor foolish boy, how little you understand. Why, I am a stranger here, an absolute stranger. My work, my thoughts, my body, my soul, are so melted into yours and with you, I feel at home nowhere away from you. I am absolutely stranded." Her sense of isolation and homelessness even in the most familial situations corresponded to her experience as a child, when she had felt she was an intruding stranger in an already established family. She could be neither the boy of her father's dream, nor the child of her mother's true love.

The weight of her depression about Ben and her fears of the future prompted Ben to complain that Emma's letters "bring no joy." Perhaps he understood that her pain's source preceded their relationship and was deeper than he could ever reach. Feeling inadequate to the task, he withdrew from it. Ben had also been "rejected" early in life, when his father abandoned his mother; no amount of overcompensation in his attachment to his mother could blot that out. Perhaps there was something in Emma's expression of the pain of rejection that he feared in himself and had learned to repress. There was undoubtedly an attraction as well as terror in living around those early feelings again. But, rather than being able to respond with soothing reassurances of his love, Ben felt compelled to maintain some distance from his anxious lover, and from the shadows that had fallen over their relationship.

Ben's withdrawal was devastating. "I am daily knifed, bled, roasted, by the thousand and one things you do," Emma wrote. Finally, she determined that she would give up 210 in the fall. "I must live alone somewhere. If I cannot live with you, I can live even less with others."

It is not surprising that Ben wondered whether or why Emma still loved him, given the intensity of the pain she blamed on him. When he accused her of being cruel to him, leaving him in suspense about her love, she responded: "You foolish boy, has your Mommy ever been one hundred part as cruel as you, as you have to her? I may be harsh with you, but if you would only stop to think [of] all the things you say and do, things that would exasperate a Saint. Oh, baby mine, you are so very blind, how can I make you see?" She was thinking in particular of his "angry cruel voice," quarreling with her on their last day together—"I simply have to run when you begin to shout 'God damn it!'"

Emma had concocted the idea for Ben to take a trip by himself to Europe during the summer, in part to spirit him away from his mother and the lure of other lovers in Chicago. Despite their quarrels, she longed to see Ben on his stopover in New York before his grand trip. Like a mother, she said she wanted the best, the broadest experiences for "her boy," and, yet, as his lover, she actually wanted to have him by her side. The day of his departure brought reminders of her childhood fear of being left behind. She felt that she had learned "that there is a sorrow beyond tears."

> A sorrow so deep and great that one cannot even cry, so awful, so terrible in its effect . . . the anguish Mommy went through during one brief hour. . . . How I wanted to cling to you, to tell you, don't go, don't leave me, I cannot be without you. Yet, there I stood, frozen into stone, paralyzed while you moved further and further away from me, taking my very life blood with you. I dragged myself back to 210 benumbed, bewildered, frightened like a child. I dreaded the loneliness of the flat, still more did I hate the thought of having anyone near me.

When people came to be with her, to talk with her, she felt that they did not perceive "that the light has gone out of my life. . . . Can't they see my soul twitching in mortal agony?"

Lover, my only one, my all, the tragedy of my life is that I cannot live in peace with you. Just think of it, you whom I love with a madness, an abandon, a longing, that excludes everything and everyone else in the World, you who have come into my life like a cyclone, sweeping all ideas, notions, convictions, and consideration aside, taking hold of me as nothing ever has. I cannot live in peace with you. Is that not pathos, is that not the greatest human tragedy? Yet, it is as naught compared to the horror, the blank despair that are mine, without you, away from you.

She experienced Ben's leaving for Europe, although she had helped plan the trip, as an abandonment. "Oh, why did you go away? You cruel, cruel man, I love you." She asked him to write to her of his love, even though she only half believed her "weak, irresponsible, impossible" lover's words. Angrily, she wrote to him: "I will have your love if I have to drink it through your blood, if I have to suck it out of W——, if I have to tear it out of you. It's mine; it's mine; it's mine!"

The "madness," as she called it, of her love for Ben was taking control of her. She felt that her only way out was to work. She would go to the farm to escape her feelings of loss. She even identified with Ben's mother's difficulties with him: "what's the use of grieving when the mother who bore you knew it all before me, that you are mean, cruel, hard, and that you do not even do justice to t.b. Oh, hell, I love you so."

She experienced herself as "the most forlorn human derelict, shipwrecked," and returned to what was for her the central dilemma of their relationship:

How is it possible that one so decided, so energetic, so independent, as I, one who has defied a World and fought so many battles, should have wound herself around a human being without whom life seems absolutely desolate. How has such a process taken place? I cannot find an answer. I only know it is so, that my being is so closely glued to yours, I feel as if all interest, all energy, all desire had gone with you and left me numb and paralyzed. . . . It's terribly weak of me, I know, it's outrageously, unforgivably weak to love you, yet I do, I do, I do.

She stressed their different levels of vulnerability. As she saw it, Ben had the ability to protect himself from the "changing elements of life," whereas she was too easily devastated and only recovered with great difficulty. She viewed this difference as innate: "Fate has been kind to you, it has covered your soul with a good hide, not like Mummy's. Because my poor soul has no skin at all, it is so raw and hurts. I guess that's why I cannot live in my wild man's cave. I love its wildness, its glorious primitiveness, but I bleed and bleed, its roughness tore deep into my flesh. Then again, when I go back to civilization, and do not see my wood sprite, I am more miserable than ever."

Whether she craved the pain, whether that was part of the intensity that she longed for in her relationship, is unclear. But it is clear that she felt she was not getting what she wanted from Ben, and that the emotional price for what she did get was too high. Still, Emma felt herself bound to Ben by a thousand delicate threads, which she could not easily untangle.

At times she wished for a child, to seal their bond. But she generally expressed this wish only in a flirtatious context. When Emma visited Jack London and his pregnant wife, Charmian, she was struck by their domestic attachment to each other, and wrote to Ben about the thoughts their intimacy evoked:

> I think, if you loved me as much as Jack loves her, I too might yearn [for] a child. And yet I might not. I might enjoy the ecstasy of your love so, I'd hate to share it. . . .

> You say in your soul sketch written on the steamer you never thought of wife, children or a home. Do you suppose I ever thought of husband, children and a home. Yet I think so now, I think of more than that because no husband could ever mean what you mean to me. Of a Home, I have never wanted one so much as I do now. But you will never give it to me, because I know you are happier in the cave.

They wrote about the dilemmas they faced living in and out of "the cave."

I knew you are the savage the primitive man of the cave and that you will never be anything else. Yet, I loved you, with a madness and a force that signal only the savagery of a volcano. My repeated attempts to tame the cub were not because I believed it would or could be anything but a lion, but because I could not always endure the exposure of cave life. . . . I have lived in civilization too long, I had paid with my blood for my social consciousness, I had carried the weight of civilized life on my shoulders too long. How can I endure the crack, hard, self-centered, unconcerned, tooth-and-claw atmosphere? And yet I too am savage, a great deal of it, yet I too enjoy the elemental, instinctive force of nature. Whenever that part of me meets with you, there is complete abandon, there is ecstasy undreamed, untold.

Oh, I know your psychology, dearest, I know it only too well. It loves me with all its force and beauty, with all its ferociousness; I must follow it into the cave into the wilderness, and yet it frightens me.

The term "civilization" for Ben and Emma meant the restraints of society and of conscience. Emma's anarchist views on the subject of free love prevented her on a conscious level from feelings of guilt, but Ben was haunted by a sense of guilt about his affairs with married women. In Paris, he was inspired to write an essay entitled "Civilization" in which he portrays himself as a victim of his passions. One wonders whether it was really Emma, not civilization in general, to whom his essay was addressed:

Little black devils dance before me, there is fire in my blood. I cry for water, for a cooling thought, but only breasts, legs and eyes float before me. What an awful thing it is to develop a conscience.

Civilization, damn you, why did you come to me? What have you brought me? Before you took possession of me I was primitive and savage and when passion came to me I set about to satisfy it. I did not stop to think "whose wife is she" or "is the act of satisfying passion fair or moral," but now when my primitiveness is gone and civilization's ideas and standards have been forced upon me, I find that I cannot freely and savagely set about to get a woman. What is this strange influence, Civilization, that makes me stop and think when lust and fire are in my blood.

Civilization! God, how terrible it is! What is life if one cannot respond freely to his passion? If civilization means that a man must stop and think when he desires another man's wife, it is time to do away with it. . . . Why should I think of any woman as a man's wife? I am not responsible for their being married or living together.

Damn you, Civilization! Can't you understand that the fact that a woman stimulates me and responds to me is sufficient justification for me to possess her? Natural passion is greater than all laws, religions, and traditions, I have had men's wives before and my conscience did not bother me. . . .

Go away, Civilization! I want to live. I want to express my life freely, I want to be happy. . . . Our sex life is our private affair. It concerns neither God, man nor Devil. Do you understand, Civilization, I want to be happy, I want to live a natural life. I did not seek this stimulation, it came to me like a summer breeze and though you laugh, grin and taunt me, I shall live life freely and beautifully. . . . Do you mean to tell me that I won't be happy or satisfied if I take my friend's wife? . . . "He would suffer if he knew—and he would know; and my sweetheart will suffer when I tell her." What! Yes, I shall tell my sweetheart.

Oh, Hell!

—BEN L. REITMAN, M.D.
Paris   Sept. 15, 1910.

Ben took the anarchist idea of the absence of restraint being the basis for true freedom and then eroticized its meaning. Although he understood that Emma's vision of free love was quite distinct from promiscuity, he could not, and perhaps did not want to, live up to her principles.

Emma also felt that she was caught between her own definition of the primitive and the civilized world. Her contradictory longing for the security of "husband, children, and a home," while rejecting the forms in which such stability was commonly manifested, kept her from being able to work honestly on a popular revision of her lecture on "Marriage and Love." She wrote to Ben: "Do you know love is beginning to be a mockery to me. When I think of the love my nature has poured forth and how little it was understood, unappreciated, how little it has done for me, and how much less for others, I shiver at the thought of putting it down on paper, my foolish, exalted conception of love which does not exist in reality." When Emma finally forced herself to work seriously on the essay, she decided that, even though she longed for a protracted commitment from a man, the piece she had written against the state sanction of such commitment was her best work. In discussing her recent revisions of it with Ben, she wrote: "The essay on Marriage and Love is the most brilliant, I suppose because I have so little of it. Well, are not all great things merely in the ideal. Thus my ideal of love will die with me, never realized. Perhaps it is well it should be so."

Rarely had Emma been more pessimistic about the prospects for achieving her ideal in society or in her own life. The distance imposed by Ben's trip had thrown her into a complete crisis. She continued, "A nice mess my love for you has made of me. A complete dependent for life's joy on a 'mere man.' I feel like kicking myself all over. Oh, Hobo dear, I am an idiot." She justified her idiocy to herself by claiming to be bound to Ben by a force beyond her control. "Boy, boy, you have hypnotized me. You must have given me a love potion, dearest, you are so much in my blood."

Each day without a letter from Ben left her feeling depressed. She believed that it was his life spirit that gave her the will to struggle and to live, yet Ben felt that he could never truly "possess" Emma. She protested: "No man on Earth ever possessed me more. . . . You either neglect Mommy for other women, or you desert her and go to Europe on 'pleasure trips.' I ought to sue my wayward husband for support." And in a rare moment of humor, the rather plump Emma continued her letter, "Ben, Ben . . . I miss you more than food!" Then she quickly turned on him. "You were angry with Harry [Kelly] when he said, 'Your anarchism begins with your sex organ.' Now you write me that you can not write a warm letter if you are not virile. Does that mean that your love for me does not come from your heart, but your sex organ?"

On his tour of Europe, which began in London, Ben was to meet many of the important anarchists and freethinkers of the Old World. But he was not always received warmly. While Enrico Malatesta, the anarchist who condoned violence, greeted him with open arms, Peter Kropotkin, the anarchist theorist who took a more evolutionary approach to change, emphasizing education, was less cordial, regarding Ben as an emissary from the United States, where his books sold poorly. Emma's attempt to explain the difference in their behavior was revealing of her own views:

> You must not misjudge Kropotkin, dear. He has lived mostly a book life and has little knowledge of the World or people. That's how he managed to retain his idealism, his faith in the people. Then too, he has had a terrible economic struggle, and now that he is old and feeble he must feel the strain terribly. His very complaints of the poor sale of books show how bitterly disappointed he must be in the results of [his] life's activity.
>
> Yes, Malatesta is a dear, he has mixed with life more. His is not such a brain as K's, but his heart is bigger, because he knows human nature better. If you see him again, give him my deepest love and greetings.

On second thought, however, she realized that Kropotkin was angry with her—because of her emphasis on free love and the personal aspects of the anarchist vision—and he must have transferred these feelings to his attitude toward Ben: "One thing more about K. He does not like me, thinks me too 'loose.' I guess I have never made much fuss over him, have gone my own way and developed on independent lines. Like all old teachers, he looks askance at the younger element that leave the old path. That may account for his hostility to you. Anyway, I am glad he became kinder before you left."

Indeed, Emma had left the old path of her anarchist teachers. Having embraced their ideas, she had proceeded to add her own theories and interpretations, particularly in regard to personal life. Kropotkin, who was personally very conventional, and even married a woman who never quite understood why he gave up his title of prince, viewed anarchism as a natural outgrowth of prevailing economic conditions. He

believed that the anarchist revolution was an organic process, a constructive and peaceful displacement of the old system by the new. Emma's
stress on liberating personal life from the social constraints of religious
morality, marriage, and convention was the source of her power and her
following. But, while respected in the world of "great anarchist
thinkers," she was often relegated to the "woman's sphere."

Emma yearned for Ben to be accepted by her world and to share in
the international aspects of the anarchist movement. Yet there was no
denying that Ben was not really an anarchist, and some of his opinions
and behaviors offended even her own sensibilities. She scolded him in
embarrassment for the opinions on violence that he voiced, during his
European trip, to her key friends and comrades and to the public,
standing on soapboxes in London's Hyde Park:

> Hobo my darling. I got two letters from you today, of the 18th,
> 19th and 20th. They made me very unhappy. You said in one of
> them that a Socialist asked you "what are the Anarchists doing
> except talking." I wonder, dear, if you know how well this applies to
> you. Here you go on shouting violence, yet are you ready to commit
> and act? If not, how can you consistently go on urging others and
> endangering their lives? You talk anarchism and claimed to be one
> yet you never for one moment act like an anarchist. You invade a
> private gathering, call the people all kinds of names and yet wonder
> that they are indignant or disgusted with you. Dear Hobo, I do not
> mean to be unkind or to scold you, really not, but only mean to
> show you that you justify the opposition to anarchism. Now, dear,
> will you not remember once and for all that anarchism, if it means
> anything at all, means non-invasion. You can no more force yourself
> and your ideas on a private gathering of people than you can on a
> private flat, at least not as an anarchist. . . . If you can do such a
> thing or justify it, why are you opposed to government. That's
> precisely what government is doing, forcing you to accept its
> invitation. You shout for free speech, but you are astounded if
> people insist upon their freedom to be Socialists, or any other "ist."
> Dear, dear Hobo, I fear you have not learned anything after all, I
> fear that all your reading has not taught you that anarchism

cannot depend on your moods, but that it is a theory based on reason and judgment. You, my dear, do not reason, you merely follow your mood, which invariably leads to disaster for yourself and others. . . .

As to our position on Violence, dear, neither Kropotkin nor Berkman nor I ever denied that conditions drive a man to Violence and that every real revolutionary change necessitates the use of violence. Never in all my life have I denied that in public. As to Alex, dear, he has proven his position better than you and I. What we do insist upon and maintain is that violence is only the last medium of individual and social redress. If no other method is left, violence is not only justifiable, but imperative, not because anarchism teaches it, but because human nature does and must resist repression. Anarchism does teach you to get closer to human nature to understand why acts are committed but it does not teach you to kill and rape. The latter spell government and not freedom. Dear, I have told you that a million times. You have heard me repeating it on the platform many times, yet you yourself go on confounding one thing with another and you are surprised if people resent it. Besides, the question of violence has become an obsession with you. Like all your obsessions, it is based on feeling merely and not on sense and logic. I tell you, Ben, you are playing with fire, you will get yourself into prison for absolutely nothing at all, and the worst of it, you will not serve anarchism. Oh, Hobo, dear boy, I wish you would realize how much harm you are really doing.

Emma continued her lecture on Reitman's simplistic views of violence with a comment on herself:

So long as I resist every convention and law imposed upon me I am a Revolutionist. As to the method I employ, that depends too not on anarchism but the time, place and condition. Intelligent Violence. Why, the very idea of it implies discretion, judgement as to time and place, do you ever exercise it? You go about like a steer smashing blindly everything before you and when people resent it you are surprised!

Finally, Emma recognized the continuity between Ben's political and personal behavior. She believed that his sudden public stance in favor of violence was a response to a whim, perhaps just the chance influence of Malatesta, not a logical progression of their work together; and so strongly opposed to Ben's extreme ideas on violence was she that she used her powers of persuasion to squelch his independence of thought:

> Of course, dear, I realize your right to talk in your own way. But I cannot help being wretched because your way is so childish and irresponsible. I want you to be useful, I want you to do good work, I want you to become a power in the movement. But if you continue following your mood only, I know that you will undo in 5 minutes whatever good you may previously have done in 5 hours, and I suffer, I suffer like Hell.
>
> You will forgive me, dear, but I really do not believe you ought to speak in public until you have thoroughly digested and reasoned out your ideas. . . .
>
> Darling. Do not be angry with mommy. I do not mean to be angry or scolding, but I love you and I want you to be great and big.

Emma continued her summer work of reading and writing, distracting herself from her longing for Ben's return. During this time, she fell and broke her kneecap. In acute pain, with the prospect of an operation followed by five weeks of immobilization, Emma asked Ben to return. Predictably, Ben disappointed her. He sent her love letters, but he himself went on to Paris, and Emma again experienced herself as a helpless victim of his "thoughtless irresponsibility." Nor did she appreciate his jokes about what a pleasant arrangement it must be for her to be forced to lie in bed: "A broken Patella may not mean much in a physical sense but it means a terrible blow to me. I am absolutely helpless and dependent, not to speak of the agony I suffer every minute of the day. More about 'a good deal,' you foolish boy, I cannot get from the bed to a chair, the cast is pulling at my nerves, causing me terrible pain."

Emma's youngest brother, Moe, was at her side, and her friends Sasha Berkman, Hippolyte Havel, Max Baginsky, and Hutch Hapgood sent flowers and fruit. But still she wrote Ben her old refrain: "Human nature is such a foolish thing. Why am I not satisfied with all these friends give, why must I wear myself sick in vain longing to get from you what I can never hope to get. Hobo, my dear Hobo, you will never know the pain and shame of such disappointments as you have caused me, since I know you. The tragedy is that with all that, my love grows stronger and deeper every day."

Their letters soon shifted to a discussion of economic survival. The money that Emma had sent Ben for his return passage had been lost, the magazine was in debt, and Emma again wondered whether to continue work on the magazine at all. This time she thought that the solution might be for Ben to resume his medical practice part-time to support *Mother Earth*. Their discussions about money were never very coherent and were full of half-baked schemes to escape the financial insecurity that underlay every aspect of their lives. That the success of the magazine depended on Ben's ability to promote and support it was an extra complication during this period of their relationship. Emma and Ben did at times hope to live on their love for each other, to escape to Australia at last: "Dearest, I am so glad you want to be with me in peace and harmony. No one can possibly long for it more than Mommy. Think of it, if we could travel as real lovers and go abroad next summer to Australia, around the world, just think of it. It makes me dizzy with delight. Oh, if that could only be. Well, dear, even the hope is comforting."

This dream enabled her to withstand the last weeks of their separation, and to focus on finishing the book, *Anarchism and Other Essays*, that she was to publish through Mother Earth Publishing Company. This work required her to reassess and clarify many of the issues that she brought to audiences: "Anarchism: What It Really Stands For"; "Minorities and Majorities"; "The Psychology of Political Violence"; "Prisons: A Social Crime and Failure"; "Patriotism: A Menace to Liberty"; "Francisco Ferrer and the Modern School"; "The Hypocrisy of Puritanism"; "The Traffic in Women"; "Woman's Suffrage"; "The Tragedy of Woman's Emancipation"; "Marriage and Love"; "The Drama: A Powerful Disseminator of Radical Thought."

Reworking her essays also helped her prepare for the winter lecture tour she would be making with Ben. Though she looked forward to their reunion and shared work, she remained nervous about their "baby," and hoped that "it will be strong and fine."

When Ben returned from his trip, in October, they had a reunion full of enough passion to fuel Emma's hopes that this time the intensity would last; it even helped inspire her to finish the book. Her letters took a more frivolous turn: "First, I must tell you something you know nothing about. I love you, foolishly, devotedly, passionately, what you going to do about it? Secondly, I have two great m—— for you with red-hot peaks, calling for you, a red hot t-b and a whole lot of other wonderful treasures. Third, I have finished the Drama. . . . I really think it is a 'pitcherino,' the largest of all the articles. I think my manager lover will be pleased."

Ben was back in New York, working hard at scheduling meetings for his winter tour with Emma. In the process, he arranged some for himself as well, most notably "An Evening for Outcasts."

Since meeting Emma, Ben had devoted little time to the world of hobos and others on the social and economic margins of society, which had been so much a part of his identity. Perhaps he was spurred to return to his old work by having traveled through Europe alone, enjoying the advantage of Emma's introductions to important anarchist figures without the disadvantage of being in her shadow. Ben's "An Evening for Outcasts" combined the speeches of the most picturesque bohemians and drinking partners in his anarchist world, such as Hutch Hapgood, the American writer fascinated with bohemian life and radical immigrant groups; Sadakichi Hartmann, the offbeat photographer, writer, and painter born of Japanese and German parents; and Hippolyte Havel, the erudite Czech writer and editor who wrote for an Austrian anarchist press and contributed frequently to *Mother Earth*. All of these men were charming—and had had active flirtations with Emma. They were followed by some of the authentic stars of Ben's hobo world, and Ben himself gave a talk on what the world looked like to an outcast. The evening highlighted Ben's talents and typified his sense of himself as "swimming between the land of respect and the criminal and radical islands, across a sea of isolation" through "the gulf of doubt."

Emma recognized Ben's ability as an organizer: "Hobo, dear, you are a wonder. If you were as good a lover as you are a worker, I should go bughouse with joy. But you is a bum lover and a darling worker, see." And when he was feeling confident, as he did after his Chicago evening, and could write letters expressing his overpowering love for Emma, she felt his words "like the rising of the Sun, bathing me in warmth and love . . . when you pour your love as you did the last week and in your dear letter, I am like a flower kissed by the Sun, everything in me begins to bloom, m——, t-b, my whole being. Dear Hobo, not only three years, but the rest of my life, I want to be with you, in love, in work, in everything."

The book would not be ready to send to Ben until December, "with all the love a mother can feel for the father of her child whom she has chosen to 'honor and obey,' in freedom. Darling mine, I don't think any mother can feel for the father of her child as I do for you." She even referred to the cover of the book as their "baby's dress." A telegram to Ben heralded its arrival: "Baby arrived three pm, has beautiful body, hope the soul is also worthwhile specimen, . . . mother still unnerved from strain but busy preparing for last ordeal in New York, roses greeted the newborn and brought cheer to Mommy Mickey." Then, in a letter, she mused that she would "see what a father you make and how tenderly you will look after the poor worn mother."

Emma continued to work hard while she was waiting for Ben to return to New York. In particular, she lectured in support of the victims of a wave of political repression currently plaguing Japan. She wrote in *Mother Earth:*

> Dr. Denjiro Kotoku, his wife, and twenty-four other Socialists and Anarchists . . . were brought before a court specially appointed for the purpose, judged guilty of plotting against the imperial family, and sentenced to death. Denjiro Kotoku is a man who has devoted himself to intellectual pursuits, and has tried to popularize western thought in Japan. His "crime" consists in spreading radical ideas, and in translating the works of Karl Marx, Leo Tolstoy, Peter Kropotkin, and Michael Bakunin. . . . We, the international soldiers of freedom, are not willing to have our friends in Japan fall victims to the reactionary forces.

Between her work for Kotoku and helping to set up several Ferrer Centers, Emma found herself "hoarse as a drunken sailor," sick with a fever, and feeling that the pressure of her political and financial responsibilities was "crushing [her] from all sides." On top of this, she was menstruating with an "excruciating pain in the t-b." She wrote to Ben of the injustice of her sex: "Oh, hobo, hobo, nature is awfully hard on the woman—not a bit of joy without constant agony, while man can have all the glories on Earth without the slightest inconvenience. If I did not love a certain hobo so desperately, I should have cursed your whole d—— sex. But if not for its existence, I would have no hobo and life would be black and cold without him." She perceived herself, at forty-one, to be "just in the age of passion's highest expression," and she threatened to "suspend all meetings and go on an orgy to last a whole week," challenging Ben to keep up with her sexually.

Ben fell sick the next week. "Do you really think my passion can live," Emma wrote him, "when you are ill and depressed? Why, it's all gone, my whole being has turned to ice, I have not a thought left, except the stinging pain that you are ill and far away and I cannot help you."

So soon after her book-baby had been born, when she might have appreciated being at the height of her intellectual powers, she felt reminded once again of what she did not have. Ben's praise of her abilities only seemed to make her more depressed: "But dear, they have never added one wee bit of happiness to my life. I'd much rather be a simple little flower that I might adorn my Hobo's room than a great writer. Equally so would I prefer the glory of love to the glory of fame, which the World will give me when I am dead. Meanwhile I have neither."

She continued with a self-pitying and hostile remark that nevertheless reflected her true feelings about their relationship: "The one I can well forgo but not the other, I really have a great need of love. But I fear I shall never get it except on paper and when separated by 800 miles. There is a tragedy in our relation, dearest, which consists in the fact that you never show your love for me when you are near and that I always doubt your love because I never see it."

Ben evidently defended himself by asserting that when he was with Emma she never let him live his own life. Her reply indicated that he must have been right: "Dearest, have I ever tried to prevent you living your own life. Besides, do you call living one's life when you race around from one place to another?" She continued by undermining his new sense of confidence, and baiting him about his relationship with his mother: "Hobo, dear Hobo, God has not given you consistency in thought or action. In one line you tell me you are your own boss, you can do the things you like to do, you find spiritual companionship with your mother. The next you say your thoughts are centered on me." And yet she ended their quarrel by writing that what he thought did not matter because, regardless, it was she who was bound to him "by a million strings." She had suffered and would continue to suffer "the torture of hell, as [she had] not since [her] early girlhood." She went on to devalue their "love experience," saying that she identified with Hutch Hapgood's bohemian friend who said, "'My love experience makes me sick to my stomach, all I get out of it is some verse.' Well, my love experience with you has made me ill all over and all I get out of it is profound suffering." Everything inside her felt dead except her sexuality, which persisted, perhaps because she was aroused by the drama and misery of their relationship.

At the end of 1910, alone and anticipating the usual pain of being separated from Ben on New Year's Eve so he could spend the next day with his mother, she recognized the weakness in her "habit of love" for Ben. In a moment of clarity she wrote, "I am beginning to think that all this craving for companionship or love or understanding is a weakness, like drink, morphine, gambling, or any other dope." The spokeswoman for the exalted world of the future wrote to Ben about their relationship: "What are all hopes of tomorrow when today is cold and empty." She experienced the past year as "mostly struggle, pain, and soul agony"; she hesitated to hope for more in the next.

One letter written by Ben early in the new year survived the wayward circumstances of history to balance Emma's. He wrote to her on the eve of his departure from Chicago:

My dearest Mommy—

All packed up ready to go. I will be so glad to see you— Oh, it seems as if I will never be unkind or neglectful of you again. Your pathetic letter reminded me that we were strangers. Yes, we were strangers. My great foolish love for you has never made me unfold myself to you. Oh, if I could love you and have you as I really want to. It often seems to me that I will never be able to make you understand me and love me as I want to be loved. To have a home, to have peace and quiet, to have you ... oh will that ever be? ...

"How can I be pregnant when I am not married?" the little girl asked.

How can we be unhappy and worried when we love each other?

Oh, to *understand*. You don't know me. I want to pet and humor you, I want to be a loving sweetheart, but when we are together, business, propaganda, so many things interfere.

You are such a powerful creature it is difficult to be a simple lover to you.

Oh, lover, I come to you full of hope and life, full of burning desire for the big lovely mountains full of mad——for the sweet-tasting treasure box. I come to you full of love for you. I come as your admirer, your lover, your manager.

> Baby, I want you, I love you
> Oh, take, love me, understand me

Take the mountains and treasure box, Will is starved and waits.
> Mommy, I love you,
> Hobo

Emma passed over the love Ben expressed in this letter and responded defensively to his next, especially over the issue of who should provide a home for the two of them. It was one thing for her to be the dominant partner, but in her lonely moments she still longed for a man to give her the protection and security of a home, while Ben still longed to be the child in a home presided over by a "mother":

You hold up the Home your mother has for you as an ideal for me and then proceed in saying "Make me such a home, Mommy, and I will never leave you." Just consider this a moment, dearest, and see how childish this is. Don't [you] think it's time you make something for me. Why [don't] you build a home for me and do what even the poorest man does for the woman he loves, give her some care and devotion. I know you love and admire me, but unfortunately your love has expressed itself so far only on paper.

But Ben still enjoyed playing child to his mother. He gave her all his wages, after which she would give him 75¢ a day for his personal expenses. He would then spend 50¢ of it on cigarettes, the telephone, and carfare, and save the rest. He put himself in a similar position with respect to Emma, depending upon his work as her manager for his financial support. In fact, everyone who worked for the *Mother Earth* office lived marginally, and generally had to ask for a special allowance even to buy underwear. Because of Emma's pivotal public position, she was in the role of "provider" in this organization always on the verge of financial collapse. No matter what else she might long for, she had chosen this life for herself.

Emma and Ben, like others who choose to live unconventionally, were forced into a self-consciousness about their way of life, which was always subject to reassessment and always seemed to require explicit justification. Living freely, outside of a family structure, Ben wondered sometimes about what his relationship with Emma would be like if they actually had a child: "Dear little love, your Hobo is having the first experience of an awakened paternal feeling. This is quite strange for me. This is quite strange considering next month [February 14] little Mae [actually Ben's daughter, Helen, from his first marriage] is 11 and I have much more feeling for Hutch's little girl than I have for her. I wonder if our life would be any different if we had a child."

Ben's paternal feelings were rooted in reality. According to a reminiscence he wrote, there were a few months during which Emma thought she might be pregnant. Despite her general position, that she had chosen to sacrifice her motherhood, her greatest privilege as a woman, to the work of the cause, the visceral feeling that she had already conceived a child brought her longings to the surface. Ben described her devastation: "I've been in jail with her a dozen times, and have seen the mob howling for her blood, and she never lost her poise or her courage. I only saw her weep once, and that was when she learned that she was not pregnant. For several months she had had the hope that we would have a child and she was so happy about it."

If this was in fact true, Emma hid her vulnerability from the public eye, perhaps even from herself. She maintained her stance as a woman who was not interested in having an infant to siphon any of her energy from her work in the larger world.

The two anarchists had set out by train on their winter—1910 to 1911—tour, writing about their meetings in a *Mother Earth* column entitled "On the Trail." Their trail wound up and down the East Coast, then on into the Midwest and the West. Emma noted that in every city their right to free speech was dependent "on the good will and bad taste of police officials." Thus the underlying issue that they raised from city to city, regardless of the "topic" of Emma's lectures, was that of free speech.

A particular town's reaction to Emma's talks was unpredictable. Although there were efforts to harass her, the local police could not always prevent her from talking. In Columbus, Ohio, although the police kept Emma from speaking in the public halls, the militants within the United Mine Workers, who were holding their convention in the city, protested against the police and even against their own union leaders, who had rejected their motion to have her speak to their convention. On their insistence, Emma received a new invitation, subject to approval by the county commissioner. The rank and file seized the opportunity to show their unity and support by marching one thousand strong to Emma's first meeting place, then to the convention hall of the United Mine Workers, where she was allowed to speak. But in other places, such as Pittsburgh, which Emma and Ben believed to be a city modeled after Hell, their meetings were sabotaged by both the police and the socialist opposition.

Their most gratifying success was the change in attitude exemplified by an article about Emma in a St. Louis paper, acknowledging her ideas as serious and deserving of further thought. Her tragic flaw, according to the article, was her "temperament" and lack of patience. Such treatment was in contrast to the usual defamation of her character and ideas.

By the end of their six-month tour, Ben and Emma had visited 18 states and 50 cities. They had held 150 meetings and debates, some with as many as 1,500 in attendance, reaching between 50,000 and 60,000 people; they had traveled about 10,000 miles, and, thanks to Ben's "mesmeric methods," had sold large amounts of literature and had distributed up to 10,000 pieces of literature free of charge. Emma attributed the trip's success to Ben, who did "the drudge work, to prepare the meetings, to look after every detail, to be the real moving tireless, perseverant spirit that would shrink before no difficulty, nor shirk the hardest responsibilities."

Ben, too, reminisced in *Mother Earth* on the anniversary of his third year on the road with Emma, "Our Lady of Sorrow," and commented on the usual responses to her lectures: "The most frequent questions are: Was Czolgosz an Anarchist? What is the Anarchist position in regard to violence? What is the difference between Anarchism and Socialism? Is not drink responsible for a great deal of harm? How can we live without law? Do you practice free love?"

The summer came, the trip was over, and the train that had carried the two lovers across the country together now took Emma back to New York, alone. She wrote to Ben from her berth on the Twentieth Century Limited: "Mommy is in her bed but no Hobo in the upper berth. Dearest lover mine, I wonder if you know how terrible it was to go away and how more terrible is the thought of being without my Hobo weeks and months. I don't believe you know how much I will miss you, my darling own."

She remembered that their last few days together had been the best in the last three years:

Never so tender, so full of sweet attentiveness. Our trip to the park, the boat, the last half hour on the depot. It is all a revelation of the golden possibilities of our love. Oh, Hobo, my darling, why can it not always be so? You are my mate in the true sense of the word, precious. Never in all my life have I known the ecstasy, the sublime madness of sex. In the work too you are so much part of my being, the realization of my wildest hope as to what I might do in propaganda. You are my precious mate and pal yet we do not get along very long. I wonder why. But then, one day like today is worth all the pains of the past, so why bother. . . . Where are you now, what are you doing? My own Hobo, I hope you will not remain long in Chicago, that you will go out somewhere near the lake and have a real genuine summer vacation. And I hope, darling, you will write and prepare something to surprise Mommy. Please do, lover, I am sure you could put in a truly pleasant and profitable Summer and give your mother a little pleasure. Besides, Mommy will live in the hope of the future, when Hobo, browned, strong and vigorous, comes back. . . . Come to me, lover, see the m big and round and white, and the t-b full of precious Jewels. Come take them, they is for you. Let me press my lips to the slender neck of the champagne decanter and drink until mad with joy.

Good night, my best and my most beloved, my Hobo, dearest Hobo

Your Mommy

After the intense months she had spent traveling with Ben, Emma headed into a summer depression, full of the doubts that overpowered her when she was away from him for too long. It was also the time in which she worked in "sweltering New York" on the business of putting out *Mother Earth,* and managing the precarious finances and social relations of the staff. For financial as well as romantic considerations, Emma urged Ben to come to New York in the winter and really put his genius for business into action, or to give up *Mother Earth* forever. But just when it seemed that Ben would come to New York to dedicate himself to the revival of the magazine, Emma began to denigrate *Mother Earth,* even to suggest that they "kill it" in favor of another, more idealized, activity:

It is insanity to continue [*Mother Earth*]. . . . As long as *ME* appears I will be a slave to N.Y. and to those who help with the work and I am tired of both. So long as the magazine continues, all we earn on our tours will be dumped into it and we will return after six months' drudgery, only to swelter and suffer in N.Y. because we cannot afford a holiday. . . . Besides, *ME* is but a minor vehicle for propaganda. Books and pamphlets are infinitely more important, why not rather devote ourselves to that. . . . I fear my baby bastard [which is] born will have to die. I have survived the death of many cherished hopes and ideas. I will survive this too. If only you love me, want me, and will work with me.

Without Ben, Emma felt adrift. Even the magazine was not enough, and once more she regarded herself as a "stranger everywhere": "I feel so lonely, so hungry for an affection that would assert itself in real life. Will it ever come to me? I do not believe it. Miracles do not happen."

Underlying this turmoil was Emma's abstract belief that the struggle, not the outcome, was most important: "After all," she wrote to Ben, "I am like Ibsen. 'It is the struggle for rather than the attainment of liberty which is worth while.' With me it is the struggle for peace and kindness in your love which is the incentive to my being. And even if I fail, I have at least wanted it, with every breath of my life, with every throb of my heart."

Still, Emma could not help herself from screaming "out loud when the dagger is thrust into my soul": once again Ben had succumbed to the romantic temptations of Chicago. It seems that the closer he was to his mother, the more he had to affirm his independence and his sexual identity. Emma preferred to see Chicago itself as wielding a special power over him.

Oh, if you only knew how I feel when I leave you in Chicago. It's like the consciousness that I have left you near something loathsome, something horrible that will find you inevitably. I often wanted to say to you, Do not go to Chicago, oh, please, do not go. But I never got myself to do it, because I know Chicago is to you like whiskey to the drunkard. It is in your blood and you will always return to it, yes, even if your mother were not there.

So long as this will be the case, I fear there will be neither peace nor harmony for us, because that loathsome City with all its strings on you will always, always stand between us.

Emma came to see—even more clearly than before—that it was one thing to preach sexual freedom and another to live it in her own life. She wondered whether she was yearning for the impossible, both

151

historically and personally. She experienced her battles over sexuality and freedom with men as her own failure to achieve her vision of a security based on total freedom and cooperation. At the same time, however, Emma recognized that her failings were not unique, and that many great women had tried without success to free themselves from the demeaning aspects of their relationships with men. Any woman who tried to live outside the confines of the home and family faced her own demons as well as the obstacles of conventional society. Emma felt a special kinship with Mary Wollstonecraft, identifying with her internal battle between weakness in love and strength in politics.

In this context she saw her political life as her "salvation." She even projected her own situation with Ben onto the life of Mary Wollstone-craft. "Perhaps, if Mary could have found a work companion in Imlay she would not have attempted to drown herself, nor would her life [have] been wrecked through that one great passion." Only Ben's loyalty to Emma's work gave her a rationale to continue with him. "You are such a wonderful worker, Hobo, so true and devoted, so completely wrapped up in the work. If not for that side of you, I should have long despaired. Well, let's then work, if our love is such a miserable failure."

Over the summer, she threw herself into supporting the Mexican Revolution as a means of diffusing the pain of her separation from Ben, and of luring him back to work with her in August. In July she confronted Ben with her rendition of the Yiddish expression often hurled at women who hesitate to marry, "The man you will marry hasn't been born yet, and his mother died in childbirth." Emma wrote to Ben, "As to my lover, he is still in the embryo. Will he ever be born into radiant maturity? To strive for it is worth the struggle, because struggle is life."

She embellished the theme of her young lover "in embryo" in subsequent letters. "You see, my boy, I know you much better than you know yourself. I know that you are strong only in one phase, that's our work. In everything else you are as weak as a newborn babe. That's why I never have faith in your resolutions." She warned him not to come to New York during the summer if he was going to misbehave. "You . . . spend your time in the Bowery, grow irritable and inert. I cannot face that again, really I cannot, dear. It makes you impossible as a companion and I am so tired of strife and conflict I simply cannot face them."

She realized that the care that she needed would never come from her "wayward boy." This issue was particularly resonant at the moment because of an old comrade, Ross Winn, who had published the anarchist magazine *Firebrand,* and who now was ill with consumption and too poor to buy medicine. He had always put his best energy into his anarchist political work; his wife had written to Emma begging for help, because she could no longer be the breadwinner and also care for her ailing husband. Emma wrote to Ben, "The whole thing is very terrible to me. Ross Winn gave 20 years to our cause . . . and now he is ill and starving. I suppose that will be my lot too, it is awful." She wanted to believe that the "movement" could be a family, that no one would be isolated, and that political virtue would be rewarded. In fact, the anarchists were more aware of the importance of personal ties than many of the other leftist groups. Still, she longed for immediate physical assurances to allay her fears. "Why are you not here now, my wayward Hobo, I am in need of love and affection, the kind of love that only you can give, though at very rare occasions. One cannot always say the thing one feels, but if you held me close I might be able to get rid of the terrible weight that has been choking me. . . . You have your mother at least, but I have no one."

She continued to write to Ben of her despair and loneliness. If she was still recuperating from the disappointment of not being pregnant, then these feelings of isolation carry a particular poignancy. "I have absolutely no one. I am so completely alienated from the past and those who have been in it, as if no one has ever been in my life. I go about with my sorrow and can find comfort nowhere, until it seems as if I must scream out."

Apparently Ben wrote Emma of his own loneliness and his dependence on her, but Emma could not hear him. "You speak of being dependent on me. Bah! What do you know about it? If your dependence were really a force it would overshadow all else. See how it acts on me. See how it brings me back to you, though I loathe the things you do, though the thought of it makes my flesh creep. That's dependence, dear, a dependence that you know nothing about."

Underlying her depression was Emma's continuing rage at Ben's promiscuity. "Your escapades, your promiscuity, tears my very vital, fills me with gall and horror and twists my whole being into something foreign to myself." She felt that she had been tormented too long and could no longer even feign occasional tolerance: "For three years, Ben dear, I have fought oh so hard against this ever-growing despair, but I know now I shall never never be able to overcome my repulsion every time my faith in you takes root again. Every time I see it sprout and blossom, you shatter it into [a] thousand fragments and leave me chilled to the core." Yet despite her dissatisfaction, she still hoped for "a glorious sweep through the garden of delight" as a way to forget everything.

Emma hid her sadness from the public. Her ideas about free love were so far ahead of her time, and so threatening, that any hint of her own personal failure to live out her vision of an open relationship, or of the fears and regrets she harbored about her own infertility, would have discredited her as well as her ideas. This incongruity was the burden she felt that she had to bear in order to lead people to ultimate freedom.

Emma was faced with having to wait until October to see Ben. He had evidently suggested, as the interim solution to their problems, that she move to Chicago. In horror, she wrote back, "Chicago, indeed, no power on Earth would ever induce me to move to that hideous thing. I want California, or if we do not move, I want to go to Australia, away from old things, from the past, from all the terrible fetters of habit." In the meantime, her life was full of work: "The Mexican cause, Ferrer work, *ME,* not to speak of other sickening burdens."

Ben was not so heartless as one might gather from Emma's letters. After receiving her sad note, he longed to "kiss and massage [your] beautiful tired body. . . . My heart," he wrote, "is full of love for Mommy and I have a maddening desire to get to you." And in fact he hinted at the possibility that he might come the next week to manage the work on the Mexican cause.

Ben's letter was sent to Emma on the farm, but Emma did not receive it immediately; she had delayed her trip because she had become so caught up with work on the magazine in New York. She wrote Ben from the office that she planned to write him a passionate letter the next day from the farm because "I . . . do not want propaganda to be mixed with love"—the love she bore him "regardless of everything." As she continued her letter, she explained new levels of what he meant to her, making profound links between her experience of love and politics: "You are like Anarchism to me. The more I struggle for it the further it grows away from me. The more I struggle for your love, your devotion, the further away it seems from me. Yet struggle I must. For like liberty, you are the highest Goal to me, the most precious treasure."

Emma faced a question that anyone who is committed to change must face: how does one live in the here and now when every day one's best energy is spent criticizing the world as it is and projecting an image of a world of the future? Ben was like anarchism to Emma—a compelling yet ultimately distant force that obsessed her. Her dream gave her the power to inspire people, but the source of her power was also the source of her weakness. Maintaining an intense, idealistic commitment to her vision, she daily experienced the disappointment of the idealist living in an imperfect world. When her relationship with Ben faltered, however, she blamed causes within their control. "It's damnable," she wrote to Ben, "but love and propaganda don't harmonize, do they, lover?"

At the farm, Emma found temporary escape from propaganda and from New York, where she was surrounded by things she hated to do. "Why do I do them? Darling, you say yourself life is not so simple. When once in a net, it is not easy to get out. But out I must. Let's go to Australia when we are through with our tour or let's remain on the Coast, or go to prison. Anything is better than to go back to the net." Again she was consumed with the idea that they could escape their problems.

> Listen, my precious boy, my lover, Ben. We will go away, we will elope, we will give our love a chance, a supreme chance, to express itself in beauty and harmony away from our work. . . . I shall lead you into the secret joys and ecstasies of sex. I shall be your wife, your mate, your co-worker, everything. Only help me get rid of that hideous feeling of doubt. . . . If only I can be with you in Love and beauty the rest can go to Hell. Oh, lover mine, how I would

love to call my friends and bid them farewell, how I would love to tell, I go with my boy, my lover, my all, to find peace and Harmony!! But my lover has never yet been mine, our love has never yet brought us peace and harmony, how then can I call my friends and tell them of my Glory? . . . I feel for your mother, dearest, because I know what it means to be without you. But as a true Jew you must know this, when a man takes unto himself a wife, he must go with her, she is his World. At any rate you are my World, precious boy.

Human nature is a queer thing. I have been with you for three years, I have always wanted you yet never so intensely, so madly as I do now. Sometimes my desires seem uncanny, morbid, but what can I do? I have to force myself into waiting, else I would have sent you a half dozen wires. Never once in these three years did I think of so many details in regard to our reunion, like a young girl to meet her bridegroom, except more subtle, more refined, more maddening. Hobo, if you should disappoint me— *But you will not, you must not.* I expect you Thursday, dearest lover. I shall be ready, as no other woman ever was, for the man of her love. I want to charm you, seduce you, intoxicate you. I only wish I had means, lots of it, so I could prepare a dream of a place for you. So that I could adorn myself in splendor. . . . You shall find your Mommy all different, all new, all radiant. . . . I wanted to have an ideal honeymoon prepared for Hobo. But fate is unkind. I saw a cheap trip to Bermuda advertised. Never realized until I was in the ticket office that it would mean going out of the Country, and of course we could not risk that. Your Mommy is a prisoner of America. It chills my blood.

She understood that what had seemed like just a threat the year before was a reality now: the door had slammed on their dreams of escape. As "a prisoner of America" she could not leave with the assurance of returning. Pockets of light in a dark world, moments of ecstasy in a life of hard work and poverty, were all that Emma could anticipate.

What a terrible force love is and how it does make one a mere tool, absolutely dependent. Or is it only because I am so insatiable? . . . So here we are, the beginning of the road, each pulling in a different direction yet unable to go quite apart. Our only hold must be the few rare moments, rare but sublime. . . . Meanwhile, Hobo dear, I will dream and hope for the miracle to come, since dreams are the only things worth holding on to.

6

TAR AND SAGEBRUSH

Ben had a premonition that something ominous awaited them on their 1912 tour, but he still looked forward to it with the enthusiasm of one convinced he had a world-historic mission to fulfill: "Oh, lover, I am so glad we will tour, really, if I had to stay in Chicago and be respectable I would go mad. I am afraid we will have some little trouble out on the road. I don't know what may happen. I hope something does happen and we can have a real part in the coming revolution."

They had planned an ambitious series of lectures that would include a review of the significant events of 1911: the revolution in China, the war between Italy and Turkey, the Modern School movement, which was the aftermath of Ferrer's brutal execution in Spain, the Mexican Revolution, and the McNamara case, in which two brothers were accused of blowing up the *Los Angeles Times* building. But their real drawing cards were the lectures touching on the larger themes through which current events could be assessed: "Anarchism: The Moving Spirit in the Labor Struggle," "Art and Revolution," "Socialism Caught in the Political Trap," "The Failure of Christianity," "Communism: The Most Practical Basis for Society," and "Sex: The Great Element for Creative

Work." Her lecture on sex countered the Freudian notion that creativity was linked to sexual repression: "the creative spirit is not an antidote to the sex instinct, but a part of its forceful expression. . . . Sex is the source of life. . . . Where sex is missing everything is missing. . . ." Furthermore, "sexual sensibility [is] greater and more enduring in woman than in man." After speaking positively of unconventional sexual practices like homosexuality, which answered the needs and enhanced the love and creativity of many people, she moved on to abortion, child abuse, birth control, divorce—but returned to her basic assertion that since "love is an art, sex love is likewise an art."

She and Ben planned to travel from Ohio to St. Louis to Chicago to Milwaukee, Detroit, Grand Rapids, Ann Arbor, Minneapolis, Omaha, then on to Denver, Los Angeles, and San Diego. In Chicago, Emma debated with Dr. Denslow Lewis, a physician who, although he took the progressive position of encouraging sex education in school, still defended the institution of marriage, on grounds of eugenics, because the state required marriage certificates of health. Emma framed the issue in her usual provocative way: "Resolved, that the institution of marriage is detrimental to the best interests of society." This debate illustrated how Emma set herself against the dominant values of the culture, then argued with liberals more fiercely than with conservatives. She believed that the nuances of her position could be more clearly revealed in this context.

Then, abruptly, the subject of Emma's talks shifted to the day-to-day drama of the strike by more than twenty-five thousand textile workers in Lawrence, Massachusetts, which had been undertaken to protest a wage cut and speed-up. The mill girls' "We want bread and roses too" banner gave the demonstration its popular name, the "Bread and Roses" strike. Now Emma focused her lectures on raising money for the strikers, to support the efforts of Elizabeth Gurley Flynn, the young, dedicated socialist who had worked with the Industrial Workers of the World, and Bill Haywood, the long-time labor leader known affectionately in the ranks as "Big Bill," who took over after two key leaders of the textile strike were arrested. It was also the first time in American labor history that supporters of a strike in other areas took the children of the strikers into their homes and cared for them while their parents were on picket lines and in jail. During this period, Emma felt that "If, then, my work had accomplished nothing else, the help for Lawrence would surely justify the pain the tour entails." She wrote to Ben with some regret, "I wish I were in Lawrence and could help the struggle, I should like that better than preparing theoretical discourses, believe me."

By the time Ben and Emma arrived on the West Coast, in May 1912, quite a different struggle had taken shape. San Diego, a city once known for its openness on the issue of free speech, had recently become a battleground between "vigilantes" and free speech advocates. The vigilantes came from all over the country to "enforce" a new ordinance banning outdoor speeches, aimed at preventing the IWW as well as anarchists from speaking freely. The police and the vigilantes cooperated. On May 7, Joseph Mikolasek, because of his alleged association with an IWW member, was killed in an attack by two policemen—one carrying a gun, the other an ax. The mood in San Diego was so hostile that Mikolasek could not even be buried in town.

Emma helped organize a massive funeral tribute for this victim of right-wing violence. She was determined to go to the scene of the crime to support the victims of terrorism against free speech, but her arrival was greeted by crowds of people shouting, "We want the anarchist murderess." Ben and Emma were rushed up to a hotel room and warned that they could not leave it if they wanted the protection of the law.

No sooner had they settled down than there was a knock on the door and a request that Emma go downstairs to meet with the chief of police, the mayor, and other officials to discuss the arrangements they had made for her "protection" if she would agree to leave town. Although Emma agreed to go downstairs to meet with the officials, she insisted that she had never accepted protection from the police and did not intend to do so now. Her parting shot: "I charge all of you men here with being in league with the vigilantes." But upstairs she found the door to Ben's room locked and no answer from within.

Ben later wrote a dramatic account of what had happened while Emma was being distracted. He was surrounded by seven men, who drew out their revolvers as soon as the door was closed.

"If you utter a sound, or make a move, we'll kill you. . . ."

Then they gathered around me. One man took my right arm, the other the left; a third man grabbed the front of my coat, another the back, and I was taken out into the corridor, down the elevator to the main floor of the hotel, and out into the street past a uniformed policeman and then thrown into an automobile. When the mob saw me in the automobile they set up a howl of delight. . . . I wish I could describe the terror of that twenty mile ride in the beautiful California moonlight. I was in an automobile with six men and a chauffeur, and as soon as we were out of the business district, these Christian gentlemen started cursing, kicking and beating me. Each one seemed to vie with the other to get a blow at me. My long hair was a favorite spot for attack. They took turns pulling it. These Christian patriots put their fingers into my eyes and nose; kicked, pounded, bit me and subjected me to every cruel, diabolical, malicious torture that a God-fearing respectable business man is capable of conceiving. . . . "You won't kiss the American flag, eh? By God, we'll make you; we'll ram it down your throat. . . . Sing the Star Spangled Banner . . . with feeling."

. . . When we reached the county line, some twenty miles out of town [in the town of Escondido], the two automobiles drove to a deserted spot, off the main road, and then they all got out of their machines, and put the two automobiles together, so the lights from the auto lamps made a sickly stage light. Then these fourteen brave defenders of their country formed a ring around me and commanded me to undress. They tore my clothes from me, and in a minute I stood before them naked. . . . At first I refused to kiss the American flag. I was knocked down and compelled to kiss the flag. . . . When I lay naked on the ground, my tormentors kicked and beat me until I was almost insensible. With a lighted cigar they burned I.W.W. on my buttocks; then they poured a can of tar over my head and body, and in the absence of feathers, they rubbed handfuls of sage brush on my body. One very gentle business man, who is active in church work, deliberately attempted to push my cane into my rectum. One unassuming banker twisted my testicles. . . . When these business men were tired of their fun, they gave me my underwear for fear I should meet some women. . . . They also gave me back my vest, in order that I might carry my money, railroad ticket, and watch. The rest of my clothes they stole from me in highwayman fashion. I was ordered to make a speech, and then they commanded me to run the gauntlet. The fourteen vigilantes were lined up, and as I ran past them, each one, in a businesslike manner, gave me a parting blow.

My suffering was terrible, but my greatest pain was anxiety about E.G.

Emma had no idea what had happened to Ben. She knew that she could not call any of her comrades for help, lest they, too, be endangered. Feeling helpless, she paced her room, then dozed off at midnight out of sheer exhaustion, only to be plagued with nightmarish images of Ben "bound and gagged, groping for" her. She woke up with a scream, bathed in sweat, with voices and loud knocking at her door. The house detective informed her that Ben was safe, on a train headed for Los Angeles, and that she would be wise to leave as soon as possible.

"Emma was carried through the basement to the servants entrance, placed in a waiting auto," ran the newspaper account. By 2:45 A.M. she was on the train, barely missing attack by the vigilantes. All the way up the coast she was desperately afraid, searching for Ben at each train stop. When he was not at the Los Angeles station, she was sure he was dead. But she went to the apartment where she and Ben generally stayed in Los Angeles and received an anonymous telephone call informing her that Ben was boarding a train from San Diego and that "his friends should bring a stretcher to the station." Emma went to meet the train in company with the newspaper reporters whom she had informed of Ben's disappearance. She described the scene in her autobiography:

Ben lay in a rear car, all huddled up. He was in blue overalls, his face deathly pale, a terrified look in his eyes. His hat was gone, and his hair was sticky with tar. At the sight of me he cried: "Oh, Mommy, I'm with you at last! Take me away, take me home! . . ." [Later,] [w]hile helping him to undress, I was horrified to see that his body was a mass of bruises covered with blotches of tar. The letters I.W.W. were burned into his flesh. Ben could not speak; only his eyes tried to convey what he had passed through.

The *San Diego Sun* was quick to head-line an article on May 22, 1912: "Reitman Not Tortured Says Reverend Dr. Thorp." And by May 27, Ben was quoted in the same paper warning that he would come back in a month. "I will give them some of their own medicine."

Although Ben continued his tour with Emma up the coast and then back to Denver, giving speeches and organizing support for the victims of repression in San Diego, it was clear even to him that "some of him lived, but most of him died." He felt as though he should have done something different, maybe even risked his life by standing up to the vigilantes, as Emma might have wanted him to. But he had been afraid. Gradually, his buoyancy and exuberance for life returned, but never with the same underlying innocence and faith. He had learned viscerally a lesson about the brutality of the extreme right wing of the "business mob" in America, and about how the police and the press would back them up.

Ben's ordeal was not an isolated incident. This period saw tremendous conflict over the issue of free speech, and anarchists and members of the IWW took the brunt of the sometimes physical attacks. It was a political battle for the right to speak out, to organize unions, and to dissent.

Along with his own experience of defeat, Ben had to face Emma's growing disapproval of the way he handled his feelings in public. In Los Angeles, he had embarrassed her by exposing his branded bottom to an audience that included state officials and liberal supporters. But he could not joke what had happened away. The sense of his own cowardice that permeated his public talks and private letters during this trying period began to diminish Ben in Emma's eyes:

I hope, Hobo dear, that if you ever face another S[an] D[iego] you may not have to herald your action as cowardly, or at least if you feel it to be such, that you will keep it to yourself. It certainly cannot be indifferent to the woman who loves a man, especially the woman who has all her life faced persecution, to hear that man shout from the house tops, he is a coward. It is a million times more painful than [to] have the rest of the World say so.

The San Diego experience had cast a pall on their lives, which was deepened by the news of the death of their friend and comrade Voltairine de Cleyre, a tragic heroine of the anarchist movement. She, like Emma, had been inspired to political action by the Haymarket martyrs. Only thirty-four at her death, Voltairine had given most of her life to writing, speaking, and working to further the anarchist cause. She was a rare combination of propagandist and poet, burdened with a delicate constitution. "After every public appearance, she would be bed-ridden for days, in constant agony from some disease of the nervous system which she developed in early childhood and which continued to grow worse with the years." Voltairine had been an important, though not uncomplicated, figure in both Ben's and Emma's lives.

Ben had always admired Voltairine but thought that she would have been more widely known if she had had the services of a promoter like himself. But Voltairine objected on principle to the extravagant hotels and meals Ben and Emma shared on their tours. Teaching and living among poor immigrants, Voltairine considered spartan living consistent with her beliefs. She had once confided to a friend her fear that under Emma's influence the movement was losing its soul.

While Emma was aware of Voltairine's criticism, she nevertheless felt entitled to occasional luxury: "I do not believe that a Cause which stood for a beautiful ideal, for anarchism, for release and freedom from conventions and prejudice, should demand the denial of life and joy. I insisted that our Cause could not expect me to become a nun and that the movement should not be turned into a cloister. If it meant that, I did not want it."

Voltairine, critical of Emma and those anarchists who addressed their political work to the "bourgeois elements" of society, thought that their activity should be restricted to the working classes—to the "poor, the ignorant, the brutal, the disinherited, the men and women who do the hard and brutalizing work of the world." Emma felt equally commit-ted to the underclass, but asserted that limiting oneself to the masses was "contrary to the spirit of anarchism," which builds "not on classes, but on men and women." She noted that "the pioneers of every new thought rarely come from the ranks of the workers," but "generally emanate from the so-called respectable classes."

As two of the most prominent women in the anarchist movement, Emma and Voltairine were often compared. Not surprisingly, there was an element of jealousy and competitiveness in their relationship. One friend of Emma's remarked that "Emma was jealous of all the pretty women, all the attractive ones, including Voltairine, who came in her path. Yet she was big enough to love them none the less."

In an essay that Emma wrote about Voltairine later in her life, she projected some of her own experience into her discussion by overstating Voltairine's distaste for the Catholic education her father had chosen for her and her subsequent difficulty in relationships with men. Emma thought these problems contributed to a lack of continuity between Voltairine's public and private life: "But the famished soul of Voltairine de Cleyre craved for more than mere admiration which the men had either not the capacity or the grace to give. Each in his own way 'turned on her with a ruthless blow,' and left her desolate, solitary, heart-hungry." Emma used Voltairine's life to exemplify the problems faced by many intellectual women who were resourceful and creative and had the freedom to express themselves, but who could find no men interested in a romantic relationship with such equals:

> Voltairine's emotional defeat is not an exceptional case; it is the tragedy of many intellectual women. Physical attraction always has been, and no doubt always will be, a decisive factor in the love-life of two persons. Sex-relationship among modern people has certainly lost much of its former crudeness and vulgarity. Yet it remains a fact today, as it has been for ages, that men are chiefly attracted not by a woman's brain or talents, but by her physical charm. That does not necessarily imply that they prefer woman to be stupid. It does imply, however, that most men prefer beauty to brains, perhaps because in true male fashion they flatter themselves that they have no need of the former in their own physical make-up and that they have sufficient of the latter not to seek for it in their

wives. At any rate, therein has been the tragedy of many intellectual women.

The irony here is that Voltairine was an American beauty, whereas Emma herself was not considered attractive.

That summer, Emma seemed finally to have attained a certain calm about the distance between herself and Ben, perhaps in part because Ben, still suffering from the emotional aftershocks of the San Diego incident, began to feel more insecure and dependent in his relationship with Emma.

Falling back on old patterns, however, Ben bolstered his self-confidence by indulging his sexual inclinations. He would always come home to his mother, who he believed was the only woman who never faltered in her love and adoration of him. From that vantage, he wrote that he had given up on his fantasy of Emma's building a home for his lovers and their children. He had known that for the last six months Emma kept articulating that she wanted "peace and rest" and was "so tired [of] looking after others." His unwillingness to answer these needs over time infuriated her, and for the first time in many years she began to express sexual interest outside of her relationship with Ben. Ben in turn began to fear that he would soon be replaced.

Emma replied by commenting on how contradictory Ben's messages were: "But you are very strange, you always pretend indifference as to whom I go with and yet you become maddened if there is the slightest reason to believe that I really feel at home with a new man. Such is the mystery of the human soul. . . . You speak of losing me while my soul is crying out for your love."

But Ben continued to feel insecure and inadequate, especially since his recent trauma in San Diego had also affected his sexuality. "Your tender life-giving treasure box demands more than worn out Willie *can* give. But my work and my heart is with *you*. . . . When you desire to become intimate with men—I do not want to know it. I cannot stand it. . . ." At the same time, Ben began to reflect on his own "weaknesses":

God—In a few months to learn 3 terrible truths. 1st that my sex is diminishing, 2nd that I am a coward, and 3rd that I am jealous. I have been thinking about what you said of my attitude about the women in the movement. Mommy, I is old and useless and if you can't love me or let me work with you I must go to the poorhouse or die. It is so terrible to realize one's own weaknesses. But you are so big and brave and strong and must go on and on in spite of any mean man like me or anyone else.

I was thinking of Wagner's Autobiography, when some Musical director came at him and cried, "Wagner, you are a great man, a genius, and you will live but I will die and be forgotten." . . . I have in the first part of this letter admitted defeat that I do care if you "go to it." I am so sorry for my narrowness and weakness, I wanted to leave you free to go the way of your inclination and I mean to always, but Oh the sorrow, the pain, the damnation I suffer when I think My Mountains, my hilly white mountains, has fallen in other hands. It dries up my blood, it takes away life to have the suggestion that others may drink at my fountain of life.

I always want you to feel free, I want no promises of faithfulness from you. I only want you to know that I shall be unhappy if you must love and give my mountains and joy fountains to others. "It is as it is," and I admit defeat. I say what I have said many times, my pure one. Looking back over the years of our relationship I see no bright spots in my life other than in your arms. . . . But I shall do better, I hope, I shall borrow a prayer from the little boy. "Oh, God, make me a good boy, I asked you yesterday and you didn't do it." Come kiss me and forgive me.

In an effort to convince her that she was the only one he truly cared for, Ben then enumerated the women who had haunted Emma over the years:

I want no one but you. There is no one in my life that counts. Lioness is the only one that I keep up any kind of steady correspondence with, and you know just what our relationship is; as to Anna, she is my Mother's friend and never meant anything to me in spite of what her letter may convey.

Parrin is my comrade, whom I never write to except on business. Edith I have not heard from for a year, the same with Bergmann. Gray was a foolish affair which was terrible and I hated myself for it. Baby, I is going to be good and faithful.

Ben's response made Emma feel that perhaps they would finally come to an understanding about the deep pain that his promiscuity had caused her. She felt stronger as he began to weaken, though it is impossible to know whether Emma's new independence was the cause or the result of Ben's insecurity following the San Diego incident. One other wrinkle: Ben had been assaulted in San Diego simply because he was Emma Goldman's manager; perhaps his depression masked anger at her for ignoring his willingness to endure pain and danger for her sake.

But Emma's letters remained preoccupied with "the wound that never heals," Ben's continued promiscuity. She thought of the woman who had come to see him the day Emma and he arrived in Denver, and of others who took him from her in Chicago. When she finally acknowledged Ben's anguish at her new interest in other sexual partners, intimating that this time there was a woman who was pursuing her, she rationalized the news with the thought that this pain might bring them closer to each other: "Hobo mine, the pain you suffered, I have endured 4 years. Do you understand now? I hope you do, dearest, perhaps we will then come closer for the first time in our love life—"

Ben was to meet Emma in New York at the beginning of August. He wrote: "I hold you close. I bite you and pledge you that I want to and will try so hard in my own fool way to make you happy. Life is full of hope and cheer. Tell the Mountains to look out for Hobo is going to eat them and tell the dear treasure box to prepare for great floods. I am yours and I come joyfully to you. Till we meet, Hobo."

He had chosen to meet with Emma, which meant making the difficult decision to be away from his mother: "It is pathetic to see my Mother's sorrow in seeing me pack. Mother is so beautifully devoted to me." But Ben was now determined to devote himself to Emma.

There is little correspondence to chronicle this next period of Emma and Ben's life: they were together, lecturing and working on *Mother Earth*.

What is recorded is Emma's unusual friendship with Almeda

Sperry, a prostitute who was strongly affected by Emma's "White Slave Traffic" lecture. Almeda's admiration for Emma was both political and sexual, and her letters to Emma were full of her desire for sexual intimacy. Something of a radical in the town of New Kensington, Pennsylvania, where she lived while she knew Emma, Almeda had worked to bring lectures on sex to students in a nearby school district, had been involved in union organizing, and occasionally wrote for radical papers. Her letters reveal her insight into the oppression of women, and also her inclination to follow her passions: she was unafraid to assert her lesbian longings for Emma, while acutely aware of her own psychological entrapment with her husband, Fred (whom she described as a "hunk of humanity" who, like herself, "started out wrong in life"). Emma identified with Almeda's physical battles with her husband and repeated some of her account in a letter to Ben:

> How much like our relations. And who should have thought that I, EG, the champion of freedom and beauty in love, would ever get to the point that she would have a violent desire to strike a man. Yes, I came very near striking you that awful day, and it is because I contracted myself by sheer willpower that I had that attack verging on madness. But the things you say to me, Ben dear, are so terrible, so hurtful they set my brain afire and bring out all the venom and violence of my being.
>
> At such a moment, I feel as if your fingers were closing in on the throat of my love, choking, strangling it to death before my very eyes. Then I feel I must run, miles away from you, never to see your face or hear your voice, never to be touched by the same fingers that strangled my beautiful love.
>
> And then the miracle happens, the dominant force of my love reawakens the poor bruised and outraged little flower, wakens it to life again, takes you back into its folds, becomes drunk on your kisses and ecstatic on your embrace, and all the pain and indignities are forgotten until some other hideous moment.

On August 8, 1912, Almeda wrote a frank letter to Emma about her emotional survival as a prostitute, and about the disdain for men that her experiences reinforced. She proclaimed her love for Emma's "untamed parts" and her longing to express that love. Her letters also suggest Almeda's tendencies to seek out, even create, situations that evoked the experience of guilt and the inflicting of pain on her loved one and on herself—she had been a battered child—which emerged in her relationship with her husband and later with Emma.

Aug 8th [1912]

You sweet dear: I just received your letter and am in bed answering it. . . . When a woman makes up her mind to jump the fence that's the only way to go about it—in a matter-of-fact way. She must wear a mental shield over her bosom, else her life would be horrible. One becomes used to it and forgets after each incident; that is the only way to do—to cultivate a forgetting memory. I once started to count on my fingers how many men I had been with and when I reached my last finger I cut the counting out. I was appalled at that number. I know you could never do a thing like that, that is one reason I like you—you are so strong and yet so comprehensive.

I have absolutely no reciprocation as far as passion is concerned for a man who pays me for sex. So bent is such a man for self-gratification that he seldom bothers to find out whether the woman responds or not and if he does want response he can easily be "bluffed." Nearly all men try to buy love, if they don't do it by marrying they do it otherwise, and that is why I have such a contempt for men. Love should be worship but love seems to be with most people—ejaculation. I fear I never will love any man. I've seen too much and I am no fool. . . . And it is the wild part of me that would be unabashed in showing its love for you in front of a multitude or in a crowded room. My eyes would sparkle with love—they would follow you about and love to gaze upon you always and every part of my body would be replete with satisfaction of its expression of love. God! God! God! God!

A.

Almeda referred to Emma as her "lovely bruised purple grape—you crushed pineapple, you smothered crab apple-blossom—you beautiful odor of rotten apples." Often she would cut off her letters to "save [Emma] suffering" because she feared that she herself was a "poisonous weed—fatal to myself and everyone around me."

During the early period of their relationship it is doubtful that Emma and Almeda were actually lovers. Emma's letters indicate that she returned Sperry's affection, but with less passion and desperation. Sperry assured Goldman, however, "Never mind not feeling as I do. I find restraint to be purifying. Realization is hell for it is satisfying and degenerating." Still, Almeda wrote a poem to Emma,

O, rock of indifference, I am the warm sun.
I will shrivel you with my flame. . . .
I possess you and compel you to love me, causing your
    dissolution.

In general, though, Almeda's letters reflect her confidence that Emma understood and cared for her. In March she had written Emma about how few real men she thought there were in the world. "I never *saw* a man. I have [seen] bipeds who pose as men, but never saw a *man*. No, I have never deeply loved any man. I seem to act too much. The men are lying pimps and all they are after is sex." Yet when Almeda confided in Emma that she was pregnant, she admitted that if it were "Sash Berkman's baby" she would have it. "*He* is a *man*." And, perhaps not coincidentally, Emma's man. Although she respected Sasha, Almeda's fantasy was to possess the man who had possessed Emma, if she could not have Emma directly.

Although Almeda boasted of being free of convention, she, like Emma, was subject to feelings of confusion and jealousy, while she desperately asserted her right to free love. One of Almeda's letters indicated that Emma was aware of Almeda's promiscuity, and had admonished her to curtail it before it became a serious hazard to her health. In this case, Emma's advice came primarily not from jealousy but from concern for her friend's well-being. Ultimately it was Almeda who became jealous. Emma's involvement with the anarchist cause, which was the origin of her attraction to Emma, became the wedge between them, for it occupied Emma's time and energy, leaving little for Almeda.

Almeda was also jealous of Emma's passionate abandon with Ben, a fellow member of the underworld who treated Almeda disrespectfully because she had been a prostitute. Ben, the champion of the underclass, also needed to assert his own superiority over its members. His generosity to the hobos invited to his hobo banquets stood in stark contrast to his rudeness to Almeda. Probably he was provoked by his sexual jealousy of this young woman.

When Almeda was scheduled to visit Emma in New York, Emma had to admonish Ben not to taunt her. She warned him "not to make her realize you know of her feelings for me." But animosity grew between Almeda and Ben, as is evident in a letter from Almeda to Emma:

I don't think I used any worse language to Reitman than he has used to me; he asked Hutch Hapgood to suck one of my breasts while he sucked the other so I could have two orgasms at the same time, and that was just after I had had the most divine conversations with Hutch. He also asked me how many men there are in this town that I had not fucked yet. Dearest, if you want to know just how much Reitman has hurt me from the first day I met him, just go out on the streets awhile, as I foolishly did when I was about twenty-one, and go with strange men for money. For a woman of your knowledge you are strangely innocent. I ask for no forgiveness of the language I used toward him but I do ask forgiveness for my anger. He has received from me just what he has given me—no more—no less. He tackled the wrong woman when he tackled me. I have had a deep horror of him ever since he met me at the N.Y. station. I understood him thoroughly as soon as he grabbed my arm as we walked along the street. I used the same kind of language he did. Please ask him that, for the sake of the Cause, if he ever goes to meet another sin-laden woman who is beginning to see a glimmer of light—please ask him, for humanity's sake, for his own sake, and the woman's sake—not to begin "fuck" talk. Please ask him to remember that he stands by your side as representing anarchism.

I have shown you the secret places of my soul, thinking if I did so without any reservation that it would help the cause along. I would not care if you told my story to the public or even used my name from the platform. And there are depths I have not told you for I have not had time. . . . The thing we need most in the world is tolerance, isn't it? Perhaps Ben is the way he is thru suffering—just like myself. It warps one.

In her relationship with Almeda, Emma was again relegated to the role of mother. "I wish I had a mother like you," Almeda wrote her. "You are my mother." Emma even seems to have held her at times, like a baby. But Almeda harbored doubts about why the great Emma Goldman would care for someone as insignificant and confused as she. She wrote, "Sometimes I think, Perhaps she is just studying me—all my personalities for the good of her cause—studying this peculiar product of our civilization. Her cause is first." These doubts fed what Almeda called her "cruel side" toward Emma. She continued her conversation with herself in that letter: "But if I were really assured of this fact I would carve her heart out. Mark how the blood spurts! But by carving her heart out, Almeda, you would only acknowledge your weakness and you do love to kiss her hands, Almeda, and lay your head on her wonderful bosom." Although she lamented their physical distance, she, like Emma, thrived on intense longing for a loved one. "God, how I dream of you!" she wrote. "You say that you would like to have me near you always if you were a man, or if you felt as I do. Dearest, I would not if I could. I would soon die. . . . The thought of distance adds to my terrible pain—so pleasurable. I want no *calm* friendships. The thoughts of annihilation used to appeal to me. Today they do not."

In another letter, she made allusions to a more tangible intimacy. And, although it might have been Almeda's fantasy, it seems more likely that the all-encompassing Emma did in fact consummate her attraction for Almeda. After a visit, Almeda wrote about the feelings this new stage of their relationship had provoked in her:

Dearest: It is a good thing that I came away when I did—in fact I would have had to come away anyway. If I had only had courage enuf to kill myself when you reached the climax then—then I would have known happiness, for then at that moment I had complete possession of you. Now you see the yearning I am possessed with—the yearning to possess you at all times and it is impossible. What greater suffering can there be—what greater heaven—what greater hell? And how the will to live sticks in me when I wish to live after possessing you. Satisfied? Ah God, no! At this moment I am listening to the rhythm of the pulse coming thru your throat. I am surg[ing] along with your life blood, coursing thru the secret places of your body.

I wish to escape from you but am harried from place to place in my thots. I cannot escape from the rhythmic spurt of your love juice.

I am sitting here at East Liberty waiting for my train. One minute I have a longing for you and the next minute I pray that I never see you again. I pray for death for I have had the greatest thing in the world

To yearn for a thing with great intensity is to suffer, but to kill the yearning with satisfaction is deadly. Sweet yearning! maddening yearning—revolutionary yearning.

I am in pain, dear heart, I am in pain but you have enriched me. You have enriched me—at this moment I feel you open your mouth in sweet invitation so you see, dear heart, I can now possess you at any time (how inconsistent with what I said a moment ago) and can even spill wine upon you in mad abandon and hear you moan with the shock of it and hear you moan at the cruelty of my dalliance.

At times my hatred of you is greater than my love. I hate you that your interests are myriad. I hate you for my own cowardice in not killing you—that your life is not mine to keep or mine to take.

I can give to no other person what I have given to you my dear, my dear!—my dear whose succulence is sweet and who drips with honey.

Now I am prostrate upon the ground and the rain is beating down upon me and dark clouds loom above and around me. I am desolate   I am alone

Almeda

In the end, Almeda lowered her head in shame at thoughts she felt were unworthy of her strong friend Emma, and shifted her attention back to a more elevating image of herself in love with Emma. She ended one letter to her, "Well, I'll smoke a few more cigarettes and dream of you before I turn in. I like to think of you from the first glimpse I ever had of you. Tonight I approach you with reverence."

Almeda, like Emma, recognized that women whose ideas were ahead of their times, who had no man to match their energy and intelligence, suffered an incongruous fate. And, like Emma, she identified with Mary Wollstonecraft, though more as one who was never afforded the right environment than as the great public figure battling with herself.

> I have read *Mary Wollstonecraft* twice since I have had the book. Poor soul! The human soul is like a plant; the beauty of its maturity is wholly governed by the quality of its seed and its environment while growing. . . . Poor soul. She too had a vision of the future and was strained to the uttermost by the war between her intellect and her emotions—the fate common to all genius. People like Mary need compassionate, gentle love and yet loves that are fervent. Instead, people like Mary nearly always waste themselves upon those who are not worthy of their loyalty, for few people have lived who were as loyal both to herself and her loves as Mary. Dear Mary! Dear Mary!

Emma's relationship with Almeda Sperry had enhanced her belief in free love and strengthened her convictions about freedom from restraint, although she often characterized intimacy between women as a retreat from intimacy with men. Her friendship with Almeda was one of many close associations with lesbians and bisexuals, whom she found "far above average in terms of intelligence, ability, sensitivity, and personal charm. . . . Modern woman is no longer satisfied to be the beloved of a man," she wrote, "she looks for understanding, comradeship; she wants to be treated as a human being and not simply as an object for sexual gratification. And since man in many cases cannot offer her this, she turns to her sisters."

It is thus not surprising that the correspondence with Almeda Sperry was most frequent and intense when Emma's infatuation for Ben was waning. It is not surprising that Almeda, even with her troubling moods and occasional violent animosity toward Emma, represented a radical rebellion against, and an alternative to, Emma's helpless infatuation with her "man": Almeda fueled Emma's sense of independence.

Ben was threatened by Almeda's attraction to Emma. He derived so much of his own sense of self from his success with women as "the man with the magic touch" that he described his "'Will' shrinking" at the thought of Emma's new friendship.

Ben's brief summer visit to New York, after which he returned to his mother in Chicago, had been a disappointment to Emma. The same frictions kept resurfacing; and, after six months on the road, coming back to domestic life, to borrowing money, and to the dreary grind of running a magazine did not lend itself to great romance. After Ben apparently complained that Emma had "denied his Willie," Emma merely scoffed:

> Tuesday after phoning Hobo
>
> How dare you say I denied W. Ain't you ashamed? Dearest Hobo, in all the World I love you, but I is sad and Hobo don't understand. If he would only be patient, take me in his arms and be restful for a little while, the T-B would soon respond. But Hobo is in that like in his meals, madly racing on, then not giving the T-B a chance. Almeda Sperry writes, "most men are so bent on their own desire they do not care if the woman is satisfied and are easy bluffed into thinking she is satisfied." Don't you think there is much truth in that? My trouble is, I cannot bluff, and when I am sad cannot pretend to be glad. But Hobo will forgive me and try to understand, won't he?
>
> Good-bye, darling boy, I loves you awfully much and I kiss W.
>
> Mammy

Yet in the same breath, Emma urged Ben not to channel his sexual frustrations into masturbation. "Do not torture W., he is not yours, he belongs to the T.B., see."

Emma assured Ben that her shifts in mood, which frightened him, were not the result of any new love affair with what he had referred to as a "blue-eyed boy."

You need not worry on that score. Partly my moods and depressions are due to physical reasons; I have been suffering terribly before and during menstruation of late, which is but natural considering that I always suffered and that I have come to the "dangerous age." But more so it is because I feel a great sadness in my heart. Why? You will ask. For many reasons. Because every year, after such drudgery as ours and dangers, we come back to where we started, the same misery, the same frictions, the same worry. It has never been easy for me to, but I feel it very much this time.

In this period, Emma was in Ossining to help Alexander Berkman finish his prison memoirs, and Ben had come back to New York from Chicago to work at the *Mother Earth* office. Ben wrote her:

My darling lover

I really think that if we had time, we would have a wonderful romance. You have all the qualities of a new young lover and it all seems so strangely new and beautiful. Never did I do so much work and never did I have so much energy. And don't tell anyone, but never did my soul feel so much at peace. And never did your love feel so comforting and secure. I now really feel a part of you.

I love you and want to be with you. There is so much to do and so much to tell you that I hardly know what to say first (let alone speak for Willie, he has been so quiet and secure lately that he surprises me). But I must tell the T.B. and Mountains that they are not forgotten, not even for a minute.

Interspersed with news of his progress in preparing their tour was the text of a telegram he had received from his brother, announcing his mother's imminent arrival in New York. His mother's assumption that she could visit Ben whenever she wanted was apparent, but Ben responded with good humor: "We are some direct actionists, our Family.(!) Mother said that if I stayed away long enough she would come to me. It was a complete delightful surprise."

Emma did not balk at the arrival of her "mother-in-law": she was more than ever sensitive to the issues of aging and mothering now that she had entered "the dangerous age." Ben intentionally referred to Emma early in his letter as a "young" lover, in a clumsy effort to reassure her, at a time when she was certain that she was heading into menopause. He unselfconsciously referred to his simultaneous attachment to his mother and to his Mommy, Emma.

After his mother joined him in New York, Ben worked so incessantly to please Emma that he hardly saw his own mother. He felt himself propelled to work by the power of love:

> To live and to love is the most important thing in life, and we try so hard to keep from living and loving. . . . I am using up every bit of energy that I possess in our work these days. I see very little of my Mother or anyone else's and I have completely lost track of Willie. I can only abandon myself to my work because I have the consciousness that you love me and We are in harmony. I am sure that if we had a misunderstanding I could not do this.

A few days later he and his mother were to join Emma on the farm. "Hurrah, Hobo is coming!" wrote the "famished" Emma.

The two lovers spent October and November together, preparing for their lecture tour. By December 10, however, their mood had shifted and Emma was on the train en route to give a talk without Ben at her side. Ben's summer financial and organizational efforts had not gotten *Mother Earth* out of the red, and Emma was feeling that her work had been a failure. This sense of political failure coincided with renewed tensions in their relationship. As articulated in her letters to Ben, she was suffering another of her periodic lapses of faith in the efficacy of her work for the cause, in herself, and in her love life.

To her friend Ellen Kennan, a schoolteacher in Denver, Emma wrote frankly about the cause of her easy depression:

I need not tell you how often I get terribly depressed and discouraged: not because of my lack of faith in the intrinsic value of my work, or my ideas, but because of the thousand disagreeable things that come into the life of a public woman, and from which I shrink with every fiber of my being. I often think that to be a successful public character, one must have the hide of a Roosevelt; but if your skin is thin and transparent, every little coarse event sticks like a needle into your soul. I have so much of it that I sometimes feel as if I could not go on. Fortunately, I have the tenacity of my race, and must continue in spite of myself.

Emma planned to meet up with Reitman, but in her current mood the man whose image stood before her as that of the true revolutionary was Alexander Berkman.

Sasha had just completed his *Prison Memoirs of an Anarchist*. Emma had worked ceaselessly to edit and reshape the book, and had also struggled to keep him from falling into the despair evoked by reawakening memories. One of the missions of her speaking tour was to publicize Berkman's book and thereby expose the horrors of prison life to her audiences across the country. The work with Sasha that summer had been grueling, and Emma often felt unappreciated and resentful, yet now that the book was finished, she could see only its greatness as a work of art that was also propaganda for the cause. While she was doing the editing, she had written a letter to Ben that revealed her somewhat ambiguous relationship with Berkman and her contribution to his independence after prison.

Yes, dear, it was love that made me return to N.Y. A love nourished on 16 years of sorrow and responsibility, a love that got me used to giving without ever *receiving*, that when I realized that Alex was ill again it was as self-evident that I must return as it is evident that my lungs must breathe. But the baby has learned to walk at last, so why waste my life. Someday, dear, I will be plainer, now I would rather not talk about the subject. I am very miserable, dear. Somehow, I feel that you too may not need me someday, the end then?!!! If I thought gin fizz would bring me cheer, I should drink a whole lot. But there is a sorrow in my soul that cannot be washed away with gin fizz.

The book's appearance, however, prompted impatience, not with Sasha, but with herself and with Ben. Sasha asserted that "in his innermost soul" he felt himself to be "a revolutionist first and human afterwards." For Emma the two aspects of life were intertwined, although occasionally at war. She felt the tension most acutely in her relationship with Ben, and on this trip she was determined to reinforce the part of her that was "revolutionist first," rather than her "humanness."

But the power of Sasha's *Prison Memoirs* sprang from his "humanness." In his book, he reflected on his early life, highlighting the experiences that led him to his fateful attempt on Frick's life, as he had relived them during his harrowing incarceration. And it was this human part of Sasha's story that had the greatest impact on Emma. Its psychological depth and style were reminiscent of Dostoevsky.

Even so, Sasha's friend Jack London refused to write an introduction, because he felt compelled to give a socialist critique of this anarchist document. In the end Hutch Hapgood wrote an introduction, with the enthusiasm Emma felt was appropriate for a great work.

Setting out for her 1913 lecture tour, Emma took along Sasha's book, with all its wrenching images. Emma believed that *Prison Memoirs* "represented Sasha's real resurrection from his prison nightmare, and my own release from the gnawing regret of not having shared his fate." Plunged back into the days when she and Sasha, young and impulsive, had determined to deal a death blow to the capitalist forces by killing Frick, she tasted again what it meant to take extreme risks. And although she had developed her own critique of Sasha's use of violence, the clearest message of his book—and the message with which she still identified— was that conviction in one's beliefs gives a person the power to endure almost any hardship. It was Sasha and other prisoners with an evolved political awareness and an understanding of the context for their imprisonment, who were best able to survive the brutality of prison life, to stand against unjust authority even when their opposition was met with severe punishment.

This kinship Emma felt with Sasha under political attack was in contrast to her perceptions of Ben in San Diego. His submission to the vigilantes and his subsequent depression might have been seen as normal reactions to the shock of being subjected to personal violence, but not by Emma and Sasha. They felt that their convictions made them stronger under attack, while Ben weakened, as if surprised by political repression.

Sasha had endured his fourteen years behind bars by gradually transforming himself from an outsider among "criminals" to a true friend and leader of his fellow inmates. He had learned the language of the prison, had gained the trust of his prisonmates, and had felt the extraordinary camaraderie and love that could develop among men even under the most adverse conditions. Sasha dared to write frankly about homosexuality in prison, even about his own initial "horror and disgust" at what seemed to be "excessive physical contact" among men, which he ultimately came to see as the expression of "a very beautiful emotion." Throughout his struggles in prison, Emma, whom he refers to as "the Girl," kept writing to him, kept him in touch with the outside world, and made him sorrowfully aware of the difficulty of communicating the political perspective of a prisoner to even his closest comrade on the outside. He had felt the distance grow between them, though he knew she would support him no matter how their opinions might diverge.

Emma's effort to spread Sasha's message across the country was bound to create tension with Ben. Ben had never felt fully appreciated by Sasha, and he knew that he had never earned from Emma the great respect she had for Sasha's suffering. On this lecture tour, Sasha's spirit haunted both of them.

Perhaps in part because of his competition with Sasha, Ben became obsessed with the desire to return to the scene of his humiliation. Next time in San Diego, he figured, he could stand up to the vigilantes and bring justice and free speech back to that city. Emma sympathized, but thought that his belief that the political climate had changed enough to permit their return to that city was distorted by his need to resolve his unsettling experience of less than a year ago. Against her better judgment, Emma agreed that "Ben would not be freed from the hold of that city unless he returned to the scene of the May outrage." Not wanting him to go alone, she arranged to lecture in San Diego again. But en route, Ben's optimistic enthusiasm turned to dread.

As they stepped off their train at dawn in San Diego, they were met by five men, four of whom flashed detective badges and ordered them under arrest. The fifth man who accompanied them to the local jail looked unpleasantly familiar; he was, in fact, the same man who had come to Emma's hotel room on her last visit to say that she was wanted by the authorities. Later they found out he was a leader of the vigilantes.

Filled with anxiety, the two anarchists walked into their respective jail cells. Before long, they heard the sound of vigilantes in the street shouting, "Reitman! We want Reitman!" Automobile horns honked and the riot signal sounded. A few moments later, the chief of police appeared in Emma's cell with an offer to escort Ben, Emma, and the young comrade who had arranged their speaking engagement out of town. As always, Emma objected on principle to accepting any "protection" from the police, and thus validating their power. But when she was taken to Ben's cell and saw his face, white with fear, she was forced to reconsider. At first she thought that Ben and the young comrade should leave and that she should remain in San Diego by herself. But Ben would not leave her, although it was clear he was too afraid to be of any use politically. Rather than endanger his life and the life of their friend, she reluctantly accepted the police escort out of town.

No play was ever staged with greater melodrama than our rescue from the San Diego jail and our ride to the railroad station. At the head of the procession marched a dozen policemen, carrying a shot-gun, with revolvers sticking in their belts. Then came the Chief of Police and the Chief of Detectives, heavily armed, Ben between them. I followed with two officers at each side. Behind me was our young comrade. And behind him more police.

Our appearance was greeted with savage howls. As far as the eye could reach, there was a swaying, jostling human pack. The shrill cries of women mingled with the voices of the men, drunk with the lust of blood. The more venturesome of them tried to make a rush for Ben.

"Back, back!" shouted the Chief. "The prisoners are under the protection of the law. I demand respect for the law. Get back!"

The humiliation of the police escort left Emma with the resolve that she, too, would have to return to San Diego one day to tip the balance back in the direction of free speech. But she did not make much public mention of this humiliation. She was sure that the next trip would not include Ben, who, she felt, had proved unreliable in a critical moment.

> He was impulsive, but he lacked stamina and a sense of responsibility. These traits of his character had repeatedly clouded our lives and made me tremble for our love. I grieved to realize that Ben was not of heroic stuff. He was not of the texture of Sasha, who had courage enough for a dozen men and extraordinary coolness and presence of mind in moments of danger. . . . Inwardly I strove to exonerate Ben, to find some justification for his readiness to run away. . . . Ben's face was close to mine, his voice whispering endearments, his eyes gazing pleadingly into mine. As so often before, all my doubts and all my pain dissolved in my love for my impossible boy.

San Diego, a symbol of double defeat to both of them, was a subtle turning point in their relationship. While Emma worried about what Ben's fearfulness meant for their future struggles against repression, Ben was fixated on the horror of his first experience and the realization of the boundless hate that the "right wing" felt for the anarchist and "left-wing" spokespeople a full year later. It was as if all his work before had been mere stage management, in which he had created a dramatic spectacle but remained in the wings. To be targeted by vigilantes, to be held accountable for Emma's politics, to be threatened with death, made the danger of political struggle real. Taboos against using profanity and violence against women afforded Emma some protection against physical abuse by the mob. She was so critical of Ben's "cowardice" in part because she had not had to endure what he had. Still, taking her lesson from Sasha, she refused to admit to fear; fearlessness, she believed, was the true mark of the revolutionary.

Sasha's words resounded with a special force for Emma from the pages of his *Prison Memoirs of an Anarchist:*

> Could anything be nobler than to die for a grand, sublime Cause? Why, the very life of a true revolutionist has no other purpose, no significance whatever, save to sacrifice it on the altar of the beloved People. And what could be higher in life than to be a true revolutionist? It is to be a *man,* a complete MAN. A being who has neither personal interests nor desires above the necessities of the Cause; one who has emancipated himself from being merely human, and has risen above that, even to the heights of conviction which excludes all doubt, all regret.

Thus, Ben had failed in Emma's eyes to be "a man" in Sasha's political sense, though she still felt helplessly drawn to him sexually. She knew that she might someday have to "dedicate [herself] to the Cause in some supreme deed," even risk her life for it, and that most likely Ben would never do the same.

Ben's style was to make periodic retreats to "nurse [his] soul," temporarily surrendering to the comforts of a personal life undisturbed by stressful service to Emma's ideal. Emma was overly angry and disappointed with Ben's withdrawal after the San Diego experience perhaps because she recognized a part of herself that longed to give up the struggle.

Although the two lovers did not formally part in the spring of 1913, the implications of their second San Diego experience felt ominous to both of them. "Sex" was still an "element" in Emma's "creative work," in accordance with her lecture, but even stronger was the power of her ideal. And Ben, stricken with insomnia, still needed "to feel the Mountains to rest well . . . [and] to draw [his] inspiration from [his] precious T.B." The two continued to feel dependent on each other, but the mutuality of their commitment to anarchism was fading. Ben tried to compensate by overstating his optimism and dedication to "the revolution." He had given a talk to college students in Lawrence, Kansas, that

April, asserting that all they knew was ignorance, that there was no God, and that morals were a matter of geography and station in life. "The workers," he said, "no longer believe in the sanctity of the law, private property, religion or college education. Yes, that is why the Revolution is on. Real men hate nothing but poverty and tyranny, and want only freedom and a chance to express themselves and realize their own power to make the world a better place in which to live. THE REVOLU-TION IS ON!"

Ben could not get away with such hyperbole when it came to writing for *Mother Earth* under Sasha's editorship. Following the most recent San Diego debacle, Sasha rejected an article that Ben had written for the magazine. His rejection letter stands as a scathing critique of Ben's sloppy political thinking:

April 7, 1913

Dear Ben—

I know you are sensible and hope you'll read these lines in a friendly, unprejudiced way, so as to understand and not misjudge me.

I am doing something I hate to do. And that is I can't publish your article in *Mother Earth* in its present form.

An editor does not have to agree with the views expressed by his contributors and I have published several of your articles with which I disagreed in various points.

That is not the objection . . . No. It is rather because neither the spirit nor the contents of your article fit in *Mother Earth*. . . .

Your article misrepresents the purpose and spirit of the Anar-chist movement. Of course, you do not do it willfully or consciously. You are not aware of it, I suppose. But the result is the same.

The *whole* article makes the impression that EG speaks only to the bourgeois and bourgeois places. That the *large* size of audiences is more important than the quality of it. That people who have automobiles are what we are after in the distribution of hand-bills, etc.

There is also too much hinting that you want people with money to leave us an inheritance—rich people to contribute to the movement, etc. Too much begging for money. The whole article is like a page of Mark Twain, in a certain sense. You can't put the finger on a word or sentence of Twain, and say "Here's the humor." It pervades the whole page, the whole book. And so your whole article is pervaded by a spirit of entire misconception of the purpose and significance of the Anarchist propaganda.

Sasha went on in a moralistic tone to assert that "The persecution of Anarchists by the police is a *healthy* sign of Anarchist activity. That the police open all halls to us etc. is a very bad sign," that "as a philosophy, Anarchism includes the whole of mankind," but "as a militant movement, we deal with the proletariat that will have to make the revolution," not the intellectuals. On this Sasha disagreed with Emma, who did believe that intellectuals and professionals in the United States experienced a special form of oppression and would be key participants in the coming revolution. Sasha, on the other hand, saw them only as parasites who used anarchism as "an intellectual pastime." He then added a personal admonishment to Ben that "the horrors of San Diego were the best compliment to Anarchist activity, as a force that is *feared* as dangerous to capital, patriotism, et cetera." Ben took Sasha's rejection as an indirect message from both Emma and Sasha that he really did not belong in their ranks.

Although Ben continued his work with Emma, his attitudes toward politics and even religion had begun to change. He wished that he could stand up to Emma's self-righteousness when the pressure of his subordinate position and its concomitant danger was becoming too much for him. He felt trapped, resentful; his well-intentioned work seemed to be taken for granted and even abused. His most dominant feeling, however, was fear. The San Francisco suffragist Miriam Allen de Ford wrote a telling vignette about Ben's interaction with her husband, a leader in the Socialist Party, in her book, *Up-Hill All the Way: The Life of Maynard Shipley:*

On July 13, 1913 Maynard took part in the first debate of his life and for his opponent he had one of the most formidable debaters who ever lived, the redoubtable Emma Goldman. . . . He himself had no idea how he would come out in a contest with the famous Anarchist, who was renowned for her rough tactics and merciless quickness in dealing with her opponents. . . . [A friend of his] was horrified at Maynard's audacity in taking Emma Goldman on. "She'll eat you alive!" he predicted, and he refused to go to San Francisco to listen to the slaughter.

But early in the debate Maynard realized that he had made his opponent angry, a sure sign that she could not meet his arguments on a logical basis. She descended to personalities—even to the Prince Albert coat which was then Maynard's invariable lecture costume, for the very good reason that he had no other presentable one. There was no formal decision, but the audience, made up far more of Miss Goldman's adherents than of his, showed by its applause that it considered he had more than held his own. After the debate her "companion" and manager, Dr. Ben Reitman, came to Maynard to give him the agreed fee—which went not to him, but to *The World*. "Shipley," he whispered, as he pressed the gold-pieces into Maynard's hand, "you had her on the run, and I'm Goddamned glad of it!" They were to meet again the next month in Washington. . . . His second debate with Emma Goldman . . . took place in Everett on August 17, 1913. One morning while he was awaiting final settlement of the arrangements [for the debate] he went to the party headquarters. There was a piano in the hall, and since he was alone he sat down and began to play some of the old romantic songs. Presently he heard a sniffle, then a sob. Looking around, he found stretched out on a bench and hitherto out of sight, big, pink-cheeked Ben Reitman, Miss Goldman's manager. . . .

When he saw Maynard had noticed his presence he burst into unrestrained tears. "Oh, Shipley, I'm so tired of it all!" he cried. "I want to go home—I want to go home to my mother!"

Within the month, Ben was indeed back in Chicago with his mother, away from the pressures of political activism. He wrote to

Emma, "My lover, my wife, my all . . . This morning Mother washed my head and I thought of how Mommy used to do it." Ben now longed for the sheltering care of a mother more than anything else in the world. He hoped "to God" that Emma could someday give him a sense of safety and peace of mind. Only that could cleanse the tar and sagebrush from his memory.

SONS AND MOTHERS

Emma, too, longed for a home. Weary of travel, tired of long separations from Ben and the insecurity and misunderstandings that inevitably accompanied them, she yearned to have a place with him in New York that would be a true haven from her life on the road. Yet from her earliest memories, "home and family" had meant the stifling of emotional and intellectual life. In recent years she had managed to make annual visits to Rochester, renewing her contact with her family. Emma's mother had become an outgoing organizer in the Jewish community, and although in the past she had been withdrawn and somewhat disapproving of Emma, now she was proud to show her own medals to her daughter, even to bequeath them to her. She was known to have refused to stick to a time quota when giving a speech to a Rochester Jewish women's charity organization, claiming that if the government couldn't stop her daughter from speaking, how could this group expect to stop her. Yet, in September 1913, during a visit with her family, Emma was struck by their hostile reaction when her young nephew Saxe said he wanted to move to New York City, where he could find stimulation for his active mind. Saxe Commins eventually became a well-known editor at Random House—but without his parents' blessings. Emma believed that he was caught, as she had been, in the contradictions of a Jewish family system:

> But, then, Jewish families consider it a tragedy if one of their kin has constipation. The physical is all they are interested [in]. They'd divest themselves of every penny and stifle their desire to be near a loved one so long as his physical well-being is at stake.
>
> But let that loved one suffer spiritually, let him eat his very heart out with some soul struggle, and he will receive neither understanding nor help from his people. Thus my sister Lena would do anything for her consumptive boy, but poor Saxe is nagged sick because he will not sell his soul to money-making.

It was simpler for Emma to portray herself as having escaped the narrow provincialism of her Jewish background for a life devoted to "higher" things, and to reinforce her image as a self-created individual in opposition to society, than to see her work as deriving from her familial and cultural roots. Underlying her distaste for the family as an institution was a strong feeling that she could not rely on men to make a secure home for her; her own father had been financially and emotionally unreliable. In the Orthodox Jewish tradition of the Russian shtetl, the women provided for the family and tended to daily necessities while the men studied the Talmud together. That her mother and father had attempted to depart from that tradition and still had not found happiness in their marriage left Emma without a positive image of family. When her sisters chose a conventional family life, Emma could see only the stifling aspect of the security it entailed.

She often compared the sexual repression in her family with her experience with Ben:

Rochester, June 29th [n. d.]

Hobo treasure hobo

Now that I have tasted the invigorating breeze of your primitive, untrammeled nature, I feel the narrowness of family even more. I never could stand it. Indeed, my own family made me hate such narrow enslaving and degrading confines. I feel them more today probably because I still have you near me, oh so closely, darling mine.

Emma set herself the task of creating a new type of family. To her, the isolated nuclear family represented deadening convention. By setting up a communal household, she thought that she would have the benefits of living with Ben without the pitfalls of marriage.

The proposed household would combine the best of Ben's and Emma's worlds, even including traces of the Messianic and Talmudic traditions from her roots. They would "remain separate personalities," and neither would have to give up other important relationships. The arrangement would accommodate Ben's strong sense that "My mother is my home," and would also have space for his red-headed former lover (soon to be his stenographer), M. Eleanor Fitzgerald, otherwise known as Lioness or Fitzi. At the same time, the core members of the *Mother Earth* group would live there. Thus Emma would have the privacy of her own room and constant contact with her comrades on the staff of *Mother Earth*. She could not fail to recognize that this plan was full of pitfalls. Even though she wrote of it to Ben eagerly, she also suspected that this venture might repeat her pattern of "all-or-nothing" disappointment. She hoped that they would not quarrel that winter,

. . . when we have a decent home and some comforts and Hobo will have his mother and his heart's desire, Lioness as his stenographer. Perhaps that will make you kind to Mommy and bring you close to me. And if that too fails I shall give up everything and go away alone for several years. I could no longer live the old life any more. I need love and devotion now more than ever, and if I cannot get it from you, I shall at least need distraction in travel.

In the same letter, Emma joked about the tensions in their mother-son-lover relationship: "Dearest own Hobo, I love you, though you are a bum lover. Who ever heard a good son make a good lover, never." It was clear that they would not be able to maintain the fiction that Emma was

Ben's mommy and lover combined, when his actual mother was living with them under the same roof.

Emma had experienced the tension Ben felt when she and his mother were near. In that situation she perceived Ben's attention to her as "duty calls," while his thoughts were with his mother.

> I assure you, Hobo mine, I do not begrudge your devotion to your mother. Really and truly not. I can but regret that in all the years of our union, you have never given me . . . such care, such devotion. . . .
>
> There was a time, dear, when I thought you incapable of tenderness, devotion, and attentiveness. But since I saw your obsession for your mother I have come to the conclusion that you love her and only her beyond everyone and everything in the World; therefore you can be kind and thoughtful and attentive. It is not because of what you gave your mother that [I felt] so distant to you in Chicago and now. It is because in six years I have failed to awaken such a love, which should have made you kind and tender to me. That's my sorrow and I feel it keenly. And that's also the reason why you want me only in cheer and work. Your love has not proven big enough to take me in pain and distress, and after all that is the only criterion of love.

Emma explained her willingness to put herself in such a difficult situation:

> However, we have a great work in common. No one can take that from me, and so I must be content with that. Perhaps, I could not do the work with the same zeal if I had a satisfactory love. I really don't know, I never had such love, so I must work harder and harder to forget the everlasting craving for a great love, which can give the kind of devotion, thoughtfulness, and attention *you* give when you love.

But Emma feared the future *ménage à trois,* even with the whole *Mother Earth* staff also in attendance:

194

I want you with me, I want you to be happy, I want your mother to be comfortable, but I have a fear in my heart. You see, dearie, I know the Psychology of mothers, and your mother is so very much the mother. Will she be able to fit in her new life, with her son's sweetheart ever present. That's the question before me. If she should not it would cause friction, and if there is anything I want most to avoid [it] is to stand between you and your mother in the position of a daughter-in-law. Indeed, indeed I could not endure that.

Despite her anxieties about their new living situation, Emma enjoyed making plans:

Now, as to the arrangement of the house, the office will be in the front-room basement, just like at the Ferrer [Center], it's right from the street and will keep the rest of the house clean, it is a beautiful room, much longer than our present office, but not so wide. Back of that is a large kitchen, light and leading out into a beautiful yard.

Next is what we call the parlor floor, a long parlor, almost the style of the Ferrer, only more beautiful and with a parquet floor. I will take that, and Hobo can always come to Mommy and love her, with no one back of us to disturb our great and wonderful love, as it is at times. Back of this room is a magnificent dining room; it will be a joy to eat there, a dumb waiter leading from the kitchen to send up the food.

On the first floor are two rooms and the bath, which I have rented to Stella and Saxe, for which she pays forty dollars per month, including light and laundry. The bath is on the same floor which we will all use, but there is a separate "Tante Meyre" [toilet] from the kitchen and we expect to put one in on the second floor.

The second floor has four rooms; three are not large, and the reason I have in mind the larger room for Alex is that you will want to be with your mother and there are two rooms together close by, Alex will have the front room and Smithy the one between. That will give your mother absolute privacy, yet leave the dining room and kitchen open to her always. When you come and you do not like the arrangements, we can manage differently. But if you and mother are in the house, we will have no one else, except the floor for Stella, which is quite private. . . .

Last night I wrote you it would be foolish to ship your furniture, but since I got your letter and have seen how much it means to you and mother, I decided it is best you send what you want. What difference does it make if it costs a little more, your joy and comfort and especially the feeling of your mother really mean more to me. If we have too much we will send it to the farm. . . .

Hobo mine, I do hope all will be well and harmonious in our new house. Oh, I want peace and harmony so much and I want my lover, my darling comrade co-worker, friend and sweetheart, I want you more than everything else in the World and I want our work.

On second thought, the next day, Emma decided to change the room arrangement, to have Ben closer to her and farther from his mother. She rationalized to Ben:

I have a peach of a room for Hobo on the same floor with Mommy. Does you like it, lover mine? I found that the room next to your mother's would be entirely too small for my precious, as you need the large bed, the one you had here. Or is it absolutely necessary to be on the same floor with mother?

Her room is not very large but it is cozy, has a stationary wash stand and clothes closet. With a single bed, she can have a bureau, and with a rug and curtains, it would make up a comfy place. I want her to be happy.

Only a few days later, however, Emma chided Ben for his inappropriate attachment to his mother. In correcting an article Ben had written for *Mother Earth* about their recent and difficult trip together, she mentioned his gross exaggeration of the number of meetings they had conducted, then delicately brought up his rather comical concluding sentence, announcing that he had returned to his mother after the trip:

I have left out one thing which I hope you will forgive. I meant to call your attention to that so many times, but always dreaded to do so for fear you'll be hurt. But as my Hobo is getting sensible I did it this time. It's the sentence "I remain some with my mother." Darling, it sounds awful in an anarchist magazine. It would be different if your mother were in the work or had any sympathies with it. But she is away from it, Baby Dear, it's like a nursery rhyme, out of place in the magazine.

Whether they could work effectively with Ben's mother present remained to be seen. Emma could only hope for the best and proceed with the move, from 210 East Thirteenth Street to 74 West 119th Street. Leaving 210 marked the end of a decade for her, and although her new quarters were more spacious, she still felt a sense of loss.

There were no facilities for heating at 210, except the kitchen stove, and my room was farthest from it. It faced the yard and looked right into the windows of a large printing house. The nerve-racking buzz of its linotypes and presses never let up. My room was the living-room, dining-room, and *Mother Earth* office, all in one. I slept in a little alcove behind my bookcase. There was always someone sleeping in front, someone who had stayed too late and lived too far away or who was too shaky on his feet and needing cold compresses or who had no home to go to. . . . Everyone in distress came to us in 210 as to an oasis in the desert of their lives. It was flattering, but at the same time wearying, never to have any privacy by day or at night. . . . The entire kaleidoscope of human tragedy and comedy had been reflected in colourful variegation within the walls of 210 . . . that "home of lost dogs." . . . Taking a last look at the empty rooms, I walked out with a feeling of deep loss. Ten most interesting years of my life left behind!

Emma also recorded in *Living My Life* the working arrangements in the new *Mother Earth* headquarters:

Ben and Miss Fitzgerald were in charge of the office, Rhoda [Smith, who cleaned and cooked] of the house, while Sasha and I took care of the magazine. With each one busy in his own sphere, the differences in character and attitude had more scope for expression without mutual invasiveness. We all found "Fitzi," as we called our new co-worker, a most charming woman, and Rhoda also liked her, though she often took delight in shocking our romantic friend by her peppery jokes and stories.

Predictably, Ben's mother, Ida, had the hardest time adjusting to the household. In Chicago, she "lived among her pots and kettles, untouched by the stream outside." She adored Ben, hoping that he would become a successful doctor. Instead (as Emma intuited the older woman's response), "he had dropped his practice when he had barely begun it, 'took up' with a woman nine years his senior, and got himself involved with a dangerous lot of anarchists." Although Ida was respectful to Emma, it was always clear that she disliked her. Emma continued in her autobiography:

[Ben's mother] was given the best room in the house, supplied with her own furniture, so as to make her feel more at home. Ben always took his breakfast alone with her, with no one near to disturb their idyll. At our common meals she was given the seat of honor and treated by everybody with utmost consideration. But she felt ill at ease, out of her environment. She longed for her old Chicago place and she became dissatisfied and unhappy. . . .

At this time of adjustment, Ben began to read D. H. Lawrence's new novel, *Sons and Lovers*. Emma described this "unfortunate day" in her autobiography: "From the very first page he lived in the book with his mother. He saw in it the story of himself and of her."

Sons and Lovers treats Lawrence's relationship with his mother in fictional form. Its powerful rendition of the building of sensual closeness between a mother, estranged from her coal-miner husband, and her sons touched Ben directly, especially the story of Paul Morel, the second son, who could never fully surrender himself to the love of a woman other than his mother. Paul's relationship with his mother had always been the strongest in his life, and both passion and duty tied him to her. But Paul was torn between his mother and a woman named Miriam, with whom he had a mostly spiritual relationship. Her religious vision, which enabled her to escape the ugliness of the world, reminded Ben of Emma's determination to live out her ideal in the face of harsh reality. Miriam, like Emma, glorified sacrifice. Both inspired and diminished by her grand vision, Paul agonized over his alternate attraction to and revulsion against Miriam and all that she represented. His mother, who had never had an easy time approving of any of the relationships her sons had formed with women, felt particularly threatened by this woman whom she could not dominate and who offered Paul something that she herself could not give. Paul sensed the grief that his relationship with Miriam aroused in his mother, and began to hate and resent Miriam for it. Ben identified with the jealousy of the mother and the guilt of the son expressed in the book:

> "She exults—she exults as she carries him off from me," Mrs. Morel cried in her heart when Paul had gone. "She's not like an ordinary woman, who can leave me my share in him. She wants to absorb him. She wants to draw him out and absorb him till there is nothing left of him, even for himself. He will never be a man on his own feet—she will suck him up." So the mother sat, and battled and brooded bitterly.
>
> And he coming home from his walks with Miriam, was wild with torture. . . . It was all weird and dreadful. Why was he torn so, almost bewildered, and unable to move? Why did his mother sit home and suffer? . . . And why did he hate Miriam, and feel so cruel towards her, at the thought of his mother. If Miriam caused his mother suffering, then he hated her—and he easily hated her. Why did she make him feel as if he were uncertain of himself, insecure, an indefinite thing, as if he had not sufficient sheathing to prevent the night and the space breaking into him? How he hated her! And then, what a rush of tenderness and humility!

Suddenly he plunged on again, running home. . . .

"Why don't you like her, mother?" he cried in despair. "I don't know, my boy," she replied piteously. "I'm sure I've tried to like her. I've tried and tried, but I can't—I can't!"

And he felt dreary and hopeless between the two.

Another character, Clara, became a sexual obsession for Paul, though she did not possess his soul in the way that Miriam had; she, as well as the other characters and situations in the book, stood, for Ben, as a composite of his experiences. As long as his mother lived far from the *Mother Earth* office, where his political and sexual life was centered, he could avoid facing these conflicts. But Ida was now in New York, and he was living under the same roof with her and his powerful lover. He was overwhelmed by the situation, and by the book's congruence.

In *Sons and Lovers,* Paul Morel resolved the rivalry by devoting himself to his mother when she became ill, because he understood that while she was alive he was incapable of loving another woman or living fully. Morel perceived her on her deathbed as a love-stricken adolescent. When he was beside her then, he felt his passion for her as the girl and the mother he had loved so deeply, and he jealously protected her from being seen in her weakened state. Although many readers have been struck by the pathos of the complexities of this mother-son relationship, Ben found the novel elevating, its message simple—and directed at him. As Emma recounted it, "The office, our work, and our life were blotted out. He could think of nothing but the story and his mother, and he began to imagine that I—and everyone else—was treating her badly. He would have to take her away, he decided; he must give up everything and live only for his mother."

Ben recognized that he had disengaged from the work, and decided to "free himself from the office." No one knew that he had also been stricken by another obsession, Anna Martindale, a tall blond woman who had stopped by the office one day to pick up anarchist literature. Emma's ire grew as she completed the publication of a revision of her lecture on "Free Love" around this time. She finally lashed out at Ben in a twenty-one-page attack:

My dearest Hobo,

I have had no drink so you need not think that what I am going to say is the result of drink.

I write only because it is difficult for me to talk to you, you are so violent, so impatient, so hard, you take what I say in the wrong light, and out of despair and hopelessness I too lose my temper and grow impatient. That's why I prefer to write.

Your announcement [to] free yourself from [the] office has not come [as a] surprise, I have expected it for several weeks, not because of the reason you have given this morning, that you are no longer satisfied in the office.

But for another reason.

You said the other day, "How strange it is that people can grow away from each other." It may have been an unguarded expression, but was the truth. You have grown away from me. *Yes, Hobo dearest, you have grown away from me. . . .*

Now, please don't think I complain, or what you deemed to say the other day, I "whine," indeed not, my Hobo. I know that love cannot be forced nor that anyone can be held responsible if he grows away from love, or love from him.

But being a thinking human I have tried to find a reason for your change and I came to the conclusion it is your growing devotion to your mother which is eliminating your love for me.

Please, please, Hobo darling, don't be superficial and say it's jealousy on my part. . . .

It is the surprise of everybody because it is indeed an abnormal devotion, which excludes everything and even blurs your judgment of everything concerning your mother.

However, I know that back of your obsession for your mother is a subtler reason . . . that . . . is responsible for your attitude toward drink and smoking.

It is the decline of sex, of your physical passion, Hobo dear. In proportion as you have declined in that the child in you has awakened, and it is the child in you which is centered around your mother. . . . No, it is not the love you had for your mother when sex craved expression, and the man in you sought the love & companionship of the woman. It is not even your mother's illness, because she has been ill before.

It is just the child which craves the utter abandon, the care and presence of the other. . . .

No other mother of the old type could give more than your mother. You are her World, her religion, her all, she is so thoroughly of the old type that could not even absorb herself in the simplest social interests, and since the World of letters is closed to her, you are all in all to her. Now, if I could have given you that, you never would have grown away from me, but even if I could have done so, I should not want it, because the old-time motherhood to me is the most terrible thing imposed upon woman, it has made her so unspeakably helpless and dependent, so self-centered and unsocial as to fill me with absolute horror. . . .

Do you call that having a home with me when you brought the old home into it? . . .

The only time we have lived together was on the road and that has not been a failure. True, we have our disagreements and [stilted moments], which is natural among two humans who cannot become submerged in each other. But we have our work, we have our joys. If this month has been a failure it is due to the fact that certain elements do not mix, which you overlooked because you wanted both elements. . . .

It is true that I am utterly unfitted to minister to the child in you, though heaven knows I have done as much as your mother. Yes, I believe I have done more. I have alienated my friends, have defied my comrades and have fought the whole World for the love [of] you. . . .

I have been able to do what she has not, imbue you with an ideal, with a desire to do big things. And if I have been critical at times it was because I did not want you to waste yourself on sensations. . . . Because I wanted you to do deep and thorough work.

I have succeeded in that so I need not complain.

Dear Hobo, whatever you will do or whether you will go, my

devotion, my interest, my passionate love will follow you. I wanted you to know this, my Hobo.

Deeply and intensely,
your Mommy

By the time Emma wrote this letter, all the underlying tensions of the household had erupted. Emma was right in saying that Sasha had never approved of them all living with Ben and his mother. Ben knew Sasha had little regard for his grasp of anarchism, and perhaps felt his mother was an ally against what seemed to be a self-righteous inner core of anarchists. The clashes of the key personalities at work on *Mother Earth* became more violent and frequent, until at last Emma felt that she and everyone else had had enough.

The break came. Ben had started again the old plaint about his mother. I listened in silence for a while, and then something snapped in me. The desire seized me to make an end of Ben as far as I was concerned, to do something that would shut out for ever every thought and every memory of this creature who had possessed me all these years. In blind fury I picked up a chair and hurled it at him. It whirled through space and came crashing down at his feet.

He made a step towards me, then stopped and stared at me in wonder and fright.

"Enough!" I cried, beside myself with pain and anger. "I've had enough of you and your mother. Go, take her away—today, this very hour!"

He walked out without a word.

ABOVE: Goldman family portrait, probably taken in St. Petersburg in 1882. *Left to right:* Emma, standing; Helena, sitting with Morris in her lap; Taube; Herman; and Abraham Goldman. Emma's sister Lena had presumably already settled in Rochester, New York. (*New York Public Library*) LEFT: Emma upon her arrival in Rochester, 1886, at the age of seventeen. (*Living My Life* and International Institute of Social History)

LEFT: Johann Most, Emma's first political mentor, photographed in New York City in the 1890s. (*Living My Life* and International Institute of Social History) BOTTOM LEFT: Alexander "Sasha" Berkman, Emma's "chum of a lifetime," photographed in New York City, 1892, at the age of twenty-one. (*Living My Life* and International Institute of Social History) BOTTOM RIGHT: Edward Brady, Emma's "erudite Austrian" lover, photographed in New York City in the 1890s. (*Living My Life*)

UPPER LEFT: Hippolyte Havel, the Czech anarchist whom Emma met in London in 1899, where they became lovers. They remained friends and co-workers on *Mother Earth* until Emma's deportation in 1919. (International Institute of Social History) UPPER RIGHT: Ben L. Reitman, photographed c. 1912, Emma's lover and manager from 1908 to 1918. (Ben Lewis Reitman Papers, University of Illinois at Chicago, The Library, Manuscript Collection) LOWER LEFT: "Fedya" (Modest Stein) with his cousin, Sasha, 1928. Fedya was an artist and supporter of the anarchist cause. Between 1890 and 1891 he was a member of a ménage à trois with Emma and Sasha. (International Institute of Social History)

Emma as a young activist in New York City in the 1900s.
(International Institute of Social History)

A typical lecture schedule handbill. (Holzworth Collection, University of California, Santa Barbara, Manuscript Library)

War Department photograph of Emma captioned "anarchist disturber, lecturer and leader of radical expression of distrust of the American government and its part in the war." (National Archives Record Group 165, Records of the War Department General and Special Staffs, 165-WW-164B-5)

LEFT: Ben Reitman typically garbed, with hat and cane, in Chicago, c. 1918. (University of Illinois at Chicago, The Library, Manuscript Collection) BELOW: Ben holding a placard for Emma's early birth control lecture in Butte, Montana, June 24, 1912, with two local assistants. (University of Illinois Library, Chicago Circle Campus) BOTTOM: A young Ben Reitman giving a toast at a hobo banquet in Chicago, May 20, 1907. (University of Illinois at Chicago, The Library, Manuscript Collection)

LEFT: Ben with his son, Brutus, in 1918. (MM-B) BELOW: Berkman, pictured with crutches, was recuperating from a fall. On crutches and in pain, he spoke at the Harlem River Casino anti-conscription meeting, and for that he was arrested and eventually deported. Photograph taken in New York, 1917. (National Archives Record Group 165, Records of the War Department General and Special Staffs, 165-WW-164B-6)

ABOVE: Emma addressing a crowd in Union Square, New York City, 1917. (UPI, photo archives) LEFT: Almeda Sperry, the Pennsylvania activist and sometime prostitute, who admired Emma and fell in love with her in 1912. (Boston University, Special Collections, University Library)

8

DENYING FINALITIES

Emma needed a celebration to help her "kick out the Old with its trouble and pain and gaily meet the New no matter what it might bring." She decided to counteract her usual longing to be with Ben, on his New Year's Day birthday, by making New Year's Eve 1913–14 the occasion for her long-overdue "housewarming" party, to bring life into the home that now seemed so empty. But all her friends, though they brought with them the enthusiasm of their varied work as "poets, writers, rebels and Bohemians of various attitude," arguing about "philosophy, social theories, art and sex" as they ate and drank on this festive occasion, could not fill the void that Ben's departure had left in Emma's life. Throughout the party, the forty-four-year-old Emma "felt lonely and unutterably sad."

It had been several months since Emma had thrown Ben and his mother out of her house. At first, he and his mother had moved to a small apartment in New York, so that he could continue his work with Emma. But before long their working relationship, too, had become unbearably strained, to the point where Ben had decided to return to Chicago and resume his medical practice. Emma and Ben still pined for each other, but Ben was full of grievances against her and the whole

Mother Earth crowd, just as vehement as those she had voiced concerning him and his relationship with his mother.

According to Ben, the comrades of the *Mother Earth* office had always been suspicious and disapproving of his manner. Although he was a doctor, and in one sense the most professionally respectable of the crowd, his lack of general education and sophistication grated on the nerves of this reserved and exclusive group of anarchist intellectuals. The social and cultural milieu of the leftist bohemians was predominantly European, hence difficult for a man with "an American swagger" to penetrate. Its members generally had "the illusion of self-importance, congenial associations, freedom as to time," yet "radiate gloom constantly" and "accuse me of superficiality because I can grin at myself and the world."

Ben often helped to foster their rejection by purposely blaspheming the cause, or exhibiting what they considered to be "vulgar" behavior. He took advantage of his position as Emma's lover to get away with pranks and unconsciously conspired in minimizing his crucial role as manager and publicist. Many of the anarchists could not get past Ben's exterior, and made him feel like an outsider even when he worked as hard and as effectively as anyone else. And he provided an easy scapegoat for the displaced jealousy the others felt at his highly coveted access to, and attention from, Emma.

Ben used his thirty-fifth birthday as an occasion to reassess his life. By mid-February before taking his leave of Emma and of New York, he wrote a letter that expressed his increasingly diminished sense of self-worth and his anger.

146 Lenox Avenue

Mommy

You always write me long letters—and I answer "What do you want me to say?"— Now I have something to say. First, I have decided to leave New York—*absolutely and for good*. Mother will go to Chicago Thursday and I will ship the furniture to *Chicago*. . . .

Today I wrote my brother that he must relieve me of taking care of mother for a while.

I am determined not to have the care of mother or anyone else for a while. Not even if Mother has to go to the Poor House.

I am going to leave N.Y. Thursday. I may go to Michigan and try and find [help] in the Woods. I want to get a rest away from the world.

I have no plans, no hope, no ambition, no sweetheart calling or needing *me*.

I want to get away from mother and work and everything. If I can't stand it I'll crawl back and *ask* to be forgiven. I may tramp again, I don't know and I don't care. I feel that if once I get rid of all burdens and responsibilities I shall be free.

I am 35 years old and I haven't anything, and I am only the janitor or clown. I don't amount to a damn in the movement, and I know of no one [who] takes me serious. The kindest thing they can say about me is that I can sell literature. You are a power, Berkman is a force and Reitman is a *joke*.

I will be forgotten in 3 months or *less*. There is nothing to me. So I had to act and serve, and I did serve you and the movement as well as I knew how. Every activity of my brains, every thought I had during the last 6 years was yours. It was a voluntary service and it came naturally and I have *no regrets*.

But now it is *over*. You poor woman made a silly crack diagnosis, thinking the trouble was due to mother. No—no— You will have to guess again. I haven't any pride for I know myself. I am ignorant and superficial. I don't think in my heart. I am a coward or afraid of death or jail, maybe I am. But you must let me express my *opinion*.

You called me a *coward* again and again when I was thinking of your safety and your meetings. You stabbed me with the taunt that I spoiled Philadelphia and San Diego when I thought I was putting one over on the *police*. You robbed [me] of my joy in getting the *best of the police*. On that trip back from Paterson [New Jersey silk workers' strike] when I needed a kind word, you and Berkman made me feel like a whipped cur and you discussed my recurring *cowardice*.

On Jan. 1 [Ben's last birthday], during the few moments I slept, when I woke up irritable, something happened, a big abscess was forming in my intestines. Later it broke. When I refer to how my Intestine or Stomach or Cigarettes affected me, you scoff [at] me and are not helpful and called me brutal and a coward.

You keep reminding me how much you give up for me and how I draw your very heart's blood out . . . and so forth and so on———— It had to come to an end some time. And now is as good as any.

I feel sure that your meeting[s] will be successful and little effort will be needed to keep them up. Lioness can take care of all my work (if not, what difference), the little literature I sell is not worth half the bother.

It doesn't matter what happens. I am going away. If I don't have money to send mother away she will shift for her self.

There is little else to say. I don't understand & you don't understand, what difference does it make.

If I can't live my life without you I['ll] beg you to take me back. Well, let the future *take care of that*.

It isn't necessary to write me—I know you are always right— At least I have never heard you admit you were wrong or unjust or unkind since I have been with you

Hobo

Emma's grief upon receiving Ben's letter did not prevent her from responding quickly:

This much I want [you] to take away with you, that our life leaves me but one terrible regret, namely that my love for you failed so utterly and completely. Perhaps it is not given to me to awaken unity, harmony and oneness. Perhaps I am only good to stir up strife in other people's lives and my own. I don't know what it is. I only know I have failed in my love for you. Because if I had not you would have understood, you would have known, and no force on Earth could have separated us. I am sorry, as I said before. I hope you are saving enough of our love to think of it in kindness, not in cruel bitterness.

E

Emma's next letter to Ben was full of regret. She suggested that the San Diego incident had set off a fear in Ben that could only be quelled by a more conventional life, away from the uncertain and often dangerous path of an anarchist leader. There is an air of superiority in her attempt at "objectivity":

I fear, dearest heart, that you too are still so much in the thralls of the old, therefore you are easily overcome by the struggle of the new. The old is of course much pleasanter, warmer, more comfortable, it requires less effort and causes less pain. I do not blame anyone who prefers that to the thorny road of the new. Only that I would rather die in the new than live in the old. It's behind me long ago and there is no return for me. . . .

I love you, dearest Hobo, but you need something new in your life. I wish I were the one to give it to you. But I know I am not.

Devotedly,
Your Mommy

Ben heard only the remorse and love in Emma's tone, for life had not gone well for him since their separation. Practicing medicine did not hold his interest, and he could not bring himself to work as hard at it as he had on *Mother Earth*. Soon he began to hope that "Mommy" would take him back:

Your dear letter this morning was the first warm breeze I have had since I left N.Y. long long ago. . . . I seem to detect the faintest sort of a suggestion that maybe Hobo won't have to live his life in loneliness and despair. Your mind has been crowded. I have been quite at leisure—lots of time to think about the things that was and is, and, God, how I have missed you. Just how much you were a part of my life and just how much *Mother Earth* was in my blood . . . you can never know— Every moment you have filled my brain cells—every thought has been of you and for you. . . .

—my previous training and work was just a preparation for you and the work.

I cannot see, I cannot think of a work and a life without you. Oh, my firstborn. I never fully realized how absolutely dependent I am upon you.

The repentant Reitman came the closest to proposing marriage than he ever had ("I shall always remain wedded to you"). He begged Emma to take him back, and once again made himself completely vulnerable:

Ten days in Chicago effected the *cure*. I want to come back to Mommy and to *my* work on *Mother Earth*. . . . Oh, six wonderful years with you have made me unfit for the conservative world. Mommy's love and work shall hold me and the rest can go to hell. I have thought it all out and now I am *convinced* that life and work without you is *impossible*.

What the hell do I care about success and business. . . . What do I [need] money for—for my mother, nothing doing, that I should sell my soul for her. . . .

No, Baby, I want to come back. I hate business and can't stand the practice of *medicine*. . . . Outside of a religious streak, I am far removed from the *conservative world* and can never *get back*. No, never, and you know that, I am sure it would be easier for Berkman . . . to live among conservatives or business people than I. . . .

I do know that I am wedded to you and *Mother Earth* for life. . . .

Baby, does you love me? . . . I want to live and work and die with *you*.

You are my religion. You *are all I have*. Since I met you there has been no sex or excitement outside of you. What about our tour, I want to begin to plan it. . . .

In spite of all the varietism talk, I am sure that there is but one woman in all the world. . . . Oh, baby dear, want me, love me

Hobo

Ben's change of heart and offer to come to her immediately took Emma by surprise. But she found that she, too, had fallen into "a dead inertia. . . . I love you, dearest heart, but that does not seem enough."

Still, their trust was renewed enough to allow them to discuss what had gone wrong. Emma had written Ben a letter that he characterized as loving but strange, in which she both declared her undying love and charged that Ben's attitude toward their work had changed in the months before he left. She had attributed his restlessness to his waning faith in the cause. Ben responded with a critique of the "gloominess of the Anarchist politicos" and a defense of himself:

I have no explanation to offer. Only this, that the new house did not bring cheer to me—Mother was a constant source of discomfort and *unhappiness*. I did not seem to have a secure hold upon affairs, and, dear heart, you will not admit it. You did not pay a great deal of attention to me, or shall I say, my need. But what difference does it make? Your work is my work, and *Mother Earth*'s struggle and debts have been mine. You are the big force in my life and the only love. And I am sure, more than that, I want to go with you—if you want me. Sasha bothered me not a little—but what difference does it make. I have said to others, if I have not to you, I don't feel that I have had an opportunity to expand as I could at 74 [West 119th Street]. . . . Seems to me that a good deal of gloom and irritation radiate from the home—I can't tell you what pain, what sorrow, it has been to do some things. . . . You and Sasha do not realize, and I am afraid you never will, how much you prevent 74 from being a household of *cheer*.

You say you are not sure you want to tour with me unless [you] think [I] am different. What can I say, lover, I want to tour with you, I cannot imagine any more desirable work or greater *happiness*.

The *office* I love—OH, darling, I have not grown tired of it. To work, to plan, to scheme for it, has been my great hope. To have Sasha and you scowl at my plans, and check them, has been my greatest sorrow.

But what difference does it make, *lover*. I love you more than life, more than all else, and I want to be with you.

I shall not settle down in Chicago, no matter what you decide to do. . . . You are so wonderful a creature and too powerful a force in my life [for me] to let you go out without a *struggle*—now, as often I think, maybe you will be better off without me, and you will go on to a larger life. Who can say, who knows.

Tonight I go to hear Thurston Brown lecture on the "Art of *Love*." May [be] I will learn something that will make me a more desirable love. I fully realize I have not been a satisfactory lover to *you*.

Baby blue eyes, I love you, I want to climb way up in the mountains and feel secure. I want to find sweet abandon in the life-giving treasure box. . . . I am waiting to come to you. I am not fixed to anything but you. With all my love

Hobo

Emma was glad that Ben wished to return to her, but she was too preoccupied with the completion of her book on *The Social Significance of the Modern Drama* to respond attentively. However resentful she might be at his leaving her to write the book alone, she acknowledged that it was he who, in his capacity as her manager, had secured a publisher for the book. Nearing its completion, she wrote to him:

Today I put the finishing touches to the first part of the book. If writing with blood makes good literature mine ought to be. Oh, god, the pain I have endured, the doubts, the wretched conflict. If only it were all over, but I still have three terrible weeks of it. Perhaps it will be easier now, with the load of publications off my back. Anyhow, I thank you, dear. . . . Hobo, six years in blood and spirit with you have impaired my independence. . . . Hobo, my hobo, give me back my faith. I cannot live or work without it. Six years, strangely terrible and fascinating years. Hobo! Hobo!

Mommy

Emma's longing for Ben was mingled with her economic need for his services. She was tired of financial struggle, and it was clear that she had become dependent on Ben's skills at drawing large audiences, selling literature, and expanding the circulation of *Mother Earth*: "Work, work, and no end. Hobo, oh, Hobo why did you go away and leave me with all the work, no one in all the World can do it as you. Hobo is cruel but I love him just the same and the m—— and t-b love him even more."

Although Emma was not ready to take him back, Ben vowed to remain ready for her. At first he was horrified at her lack of enthusiasm for his return:

My great lover:
    Seems strange that I should be pleading "Mommy, take me back" and you should explain what is best for me—not to come——
    The special letter you wrote Friday night nearly killed me. Freud calls it "Psychic Trauma." That letter lies on my bookcase like a corpse. It gives me the shivers. All men kill the things they love. . . . I feel alone and lonely. Really, I have not one friend here. . . . I am removed from the World and from activities. And I sit and think about the things that was.
    Well, no one can rob me of the last 6 years, no one will ever take the sweetness of the mountains and the fragrance of the Treasure Box from me. You will always be my Mommy and my lover.
    I am convinced that if you ever want me, you will ask me to come. And that, I trust, will only be when all that is in you cries out for me. I shall work on quietly here and will be ready when you call, if it is in one week, or one year. . . .

As they approached the sixth anniversary of their meeting, the two lovers planned a rendezvous in Chicago. The knowledge that they would soon meet prompted a series of impassioned letters. However, politics intervened, forcing a posponement of their meeting.

The young, unassuming Frank Tannenbaum, who frequently volunteered his help at the *Mother Earth* office, spontaneously led the unemployed in several marches to individual churches in Manhattan demanding shelter and food. Emma rejoiced in his victories. But on March 4, 1914, the priest of The Church of St. Alphonsus refused the marchers refuge and called the police. Tannenbaum and almost two hundred others, including Sasha, were arrested. Emma took this affront quite personally. When a photographer's flashbulb popped so loudly that both the marchers and the police thought a bomb had exploded, a small riot ensued. Although Sasha and most of the others were released, she agonized over Tannenbaum's one-year prison sentence and five-hundred-dollar fine. Emma was furious with the IWW and socialist left for their lack of support for Tannenbaum's "direct-action" tactics, and worried about what violent repercussions would follow at the forthcoming demonstrations and mass meeting, the Conference of the Unemployed. In this context, her relationship with Ben, with all its turbulence, seemed like an oasis of intimacy in a hostile world, and she clung to him.

> It's the realization of how utterly alone we anarchists are that makes me so uneasy about next Saturday's meeting on Union Square. The meeting itself may not be interfered with but any attempt at a demonstration up 5th Avenue will be choked in blood, I am sure of that. And the only one who will pay for it will be Alex. . . . If only I did not have the anxiety about next Saturday's outcome, I should be most happy to leave. I am coming to you with a deep love in my heart for you, my darling, and a great soul hunger for your love and devotion. I am looking forward to our meeting as to a new life. My dearest one in all the World. I love you deeply. . . . We will have to hustle more than ever, such is our life. Yet with it all we are bitterly attacked by our own people. . . . Elizabeth Gurley [Flynn] has been very ill, she is in danger of losing her voice, she needs a rest and warm climate, I have collected some money to send her away. I am going to see her now.
>
> When I think of how cruelly indifferent the radicals are to those who drudge in the work I lose faith.

Emma proceeded to tell Ben that when the IWW turned against Flynn in the Paterson strike, Flynn had remarked to her that she could only work without their backing if she had "someone like Ben." The desolate state of the movement, the ominous war preparations in Europe accentuated Emma's feeling of isolation and made her long once again for a secure relationship with Ben. But she could not forget the anger and pain of their past:

Hobo, my hobo, I love you. I never stopped loving you for a moment but your leaving me has been an awful blow. It has stabbed [me] to the quick. Perhaps if I had not suffered so much since your return to N.Y. last Fall, I should have been better prepared for the pain your going has caused me. But I have endured too much, dear, more than you will ever guess. . . .

I am sure, dearest, you could not have stood so much had you been in my place. . . . And when on top of it all you went away and left me with all the pain and burdens, everything in me cried out against you, against the fact that you fail me when I need you most. And that is why I did not wish to see you or work with you again. That is why I would not call you back, if only I had the strength, dear, if only I did not love you so.

But I do, hobo, I love you with an intensity, with a devotion which knows no bounds, and which must die if [I am] away from you, die of lack of light, lack of warmth, lack of the dew of life.

You are gone 3 weeks but to me they have been months, terrible months. Especially the nights, sleepless, restless, maddening, I cannot begin to tell you how terrible they have been.

I have thought much and deeply, dearest, and whether I am like the drowning man grabbing at a straw or whether our love really has vitality, I want to give it one more chance, one more opportunity. I know of course that you and I have never had a chance in N.Y. (though we had any amount of it on the road and we had friction). I want to arrange it so that if you come to me again, I shall be alone, with no one to break the harmony.

I will have a little flat of my own, as I am no longer able to stand the clash of temperaments. Perhaps then you will be able to be yourself with me.

Until then, I want you with me on tour, after all, the little happiness you and I have ever had was on the road. . . . If you really love me and want to work with me again, you can go ahead with the arrangements of the Chicago meetings for the date stated last night, Tuesday, April 7th. . . . Hobo, my own, I love you, I want you. I am coming to you. Oh, my hobo, if only you would be kind, if only you would understand Mommy's great longing. . . .

And so Emma plodded through a cold March, demoralized by the poorly attended meetings, which were proof of her dependence on Ben's contribution. She hated to speak to only a few people in a large hall, dreading most the late-night return to "74, chilled to the bones and hungry, everybody . . . asleep [while she] sat alone at the kitchen table eating."

In the next weeks, Ben anxiously prepared for their tour together—including another try at speaking in San Diego—while Emma and Sasha finished up the editing and proofreading of the manuscript of her book on the drama. Only a year before, Emma had edited Sasha's book. She was exasperated by his efforts in the role. "Alex is so slow and so pedantic, he will argue over every sentence until I feel as if I'd like to throw the damned thing in the fire." She welcomed the opportunity to get away.

The only thing that Emma thought might hinder their plans would be an arrest at the demonstration for the unemployed that was planned for the Saturday before she was to leave. "I want nothing to interfere in our love and work," she wrote Ben, "but Mommy is a fighter and when she hears the bugle she has got to go." Ben, bent on being supportive, unsure of whether he was "a coward or a dreamer" to be so determined "to have a peaceful happy trip," was also certain that he "never wanted to be a conservative force in [Emma's] life." He knew that if Sasha, one of the key organizers, were arrested or in serious trouble, they would have an unhappy tour. "I want you always to be big and brave and free. I love you and am anxious that you will always follow your natural impulses."

Such statements eased Emma's doubts about Ben's anarchist commitment, and she waited eagerly to hold him in her arms "in wild and passionate abandon."

Is it really true that I will be with Hobo in love and joy? Sometimes, I am afraid to hope for it. What if it will not come to pass, what if Hobo & Me will not be happy! Oh, dearest own boy, we *must*, we must find happiness, it would be too terrible if we failed. Please not, darling mine. . . . Hobo my precious, good morning, the TB was so terribly unruly & Mommy did something, but it was not nice, only Hobo can give joy, six more days! . . .

Soon I will see the beautiful face of my love, the big hat and stick, just as I saw him 6 years ago. Soon he will strike fire in my soul as he did six years ago, soon he will say, "Do I hurt you?" Oh, Hobo, you have become part of me so much, I cannot even think in terms other than "Hobo will do this and Ben will do that and Hobo will look after everything." You don't know what a relief it is to be able to [look] forward to your cooperation.

Years later, in her autobiography, Emma characterized her decision to rejoin Reitman with the Russian expression: "If you drink, you'll die, and if you don't drink, you'll die. Better to drink and die." "To be away from Ben meant sleepless nights, restless days, sickening yearning. To be near him involved conflict and strife, daily denial of my pride. But it also meant ecstasy and renewed vigour for my work. I would have Ben and go with him on tour again, I decided. If the price was high, I would pay it; but I would drink, I would drink! . . ."

Ironically, although Emma's reunion with Ben matched her expectations, the highlight of her trip to Chicago was meeting Margaret Anderson and Harriet Dean, editors of *The Little Review*, a magazine "alive to new art forms and . . . free of mawkish sentimentality [with a] fearless critique of conventional standards." Emma had contacted Margaret Anderson after reading her article on anarchism in the *Little Review*; she asked if she could visit the staff when she was in Chicago. Margaret Anderson recounted their meeting in her autobiography, *My Thirty Years' War*:

She answered, thanking me graciously, but explaining that she never visited families, that she couldn't adapt herself to bourgeois life even for a few days. I replied that we weren't exactly bourgeois perhaps—that we ought to be very congenial to her, being without furniture. But she didn't believe it, I think. She wanted to see. . . .

Emma Goldman surprised me by being more human than she had seemed on the platform. When she lectured she was as serious as the deep Russian soul itself. In private she was gay, communicative, tender. Her English was the peculiar personal idiom favored by Russian Jews and she spoke only in platitudes—which I found fascinating. Her eyes were a clear, strong blue which deepened as she talked.

The two women persuaded Emma to leave her hotel room and stay with them in their large and restful apartment overlooking Lake Michigan.

I went to the Lexington [Hotel] to fetch her and her bag (it deserves mention, being so big), and as we stood at the door of the hotel waiting for a trolley car, a proletarian chose that moment to fall off a truck he was driving. He slid down from his high seat and floundered among the horses' feet with horrible noises. E.G.'s coordination was something to remark—her cry and act were simultaneous. She pulled the man from under the horses before anyone else on the street could move and administered first aid with such a grim face that I felt she might be planning to hit him on the jaw as soon as she had revived him. But I learned later that she was always grim when distressed. I have seen beggars in the street ask for money and my instinct was always to conceal myself under the sidewalk until the bout was over—she looked as if she would knock out the universe. . . .

[Later at the apartment] we dined lightly (on superlative coffee made by E.G.) and then walked on the beach as the night came down. No one else was there. E.G. sang Russian folk songs in a low and husky voice. We were intensely moved.

And then the great anarchist could control her enthusiasm no longer. She telephoned to Reitman and a few "comrades" to come out.

It's divine here, she cried. They came and found it divine.

You look rejuvenated, Emma, they exclaimed, rushing through the apartment with violence. I was glad there was no furniture. . . .

Emma was impressed by their ability to break "the shackles of their middle-class homes to find release from family bondage and bourgeois tradition" in their lesbian relationship. She felt at home in this avant-garde women's environment, though perhaps she was also asserting her independence from Ben. In any case, Ben found himself threatened by this group of "half-assed poets" who seemed to him to have no connection to the poverty and suffering of the people in his world.

This review of Emma's Chicago lectures, both glowing and shrewd, came from Margaret Anderson: "The exasperating thing about Emma Goldman is that she makes herself so indispensable to her audiences that it is always tragic when she leaves; the amazing thing about her is that her inspiration seems never to falter. Life takes on an intenser quality when she is present. . . . She is always a giant—for some reason that no one has yet expressed very well. Perhaps because, like science, she denies finalities."

9

BIRTH CONTROL AND "BLOOD AND IRON MILITARISM"

On the road again in 1914, Ben put all his skills into organizing and publicizing Emma's meetings. As they traveled from Chicago to Madison, Minneapolis, Denver, Salt Lake City, and then the West Coast, most of Emma's lectures were based on her recently published book on modern drama. But she did not hesitate to speak out against the growing mood of militarism, with Europe standing on the brink of war; nor did she ignore the killing of striking miners in Ludlow, Colorado (although the miners' organization did not want to be associated with her or anarchism). One thread that ran through all her lectures was her call to love and freedom, her insistence that the fulfillment of each person's inner needs was as vital to the general good as the most salutary political events. Because she did not wish to risk imprisonment for openly disseminating birth-control information at a time when she felt she could be more useful speaking out on other critical issues, Emma used the themes of current plays as a way of asserting the principles of birth control and free love. From Nora's decision to slam the door of *A Doll's House*, Emma extracted the lesson "that only perfect freedom and communion make a true bond between man and woman, meeting in the open, without lies, without shame, free from the bondage of duty." She moved from a discussion of Nora to Brieux's play *Maternity*, about children born in poverty, in support of "the demand that woman must be given means to prevent conception of undesired and unloved children; that she must become free and strong to choose the father of her child and to decide the number of children she is to bring into the world and under what conditions. That is the only kind of motherhood which can endure."

The new fervor of Emma's work for birth control came partly from her ties with Margaret Sanger, whose magazine, *The Woman Rebel*, had been banned from the U.S. mails: the dissemination of birth-control information in its pages was judged to be "obscene" by the Post Office. Emma wrote to Margaret that she would publicize the magazine all she could, and this she did, not only selling copies in every city of her tour, but also arranging for distribution agents to circulate it in defiance of restrictions. In one letter to Margaret from Los Angeles, on May 26, 1914, Emma wrote: "Not one of my lectures brings out such crowds as the one on the birth strike and it is the same with Woman Rebel. It sells better than anything else we have."

Yet even though millions of women and men across the country were eager to have clear information about birth control, not only in the name of free love but also in the search for economic survival, others joined with the government to oppose the birth-control movement. In fact, as Emma noted:

> I know you will be amused to learn that most of the women are up in arms against your paper; mostly women, of course, whose emancipation has been on paper and not in reality. I am kept busy answering questions as to your "brazen" method. They would not believe me when I told them that you were a little, delicate woman, refined and shrinking, but that you did believe in the daring and courage of woman in her struggle for freedom.

The two women shared their hopes as well as their disappointments. Emma had been barred from the Rockefeller-run mining town of Ludlow, Colorado, where twenty-two people had been killed in the course of a vicious anti-union attack. She wrote to Margaret from Denver:

> We are certainly living in wonderful times. The resistance offered by the striking miners of Ludlow and the solidarity extended them by even conservative unions is the most wonderful thing that has happened in this country. Of course the workers have again been misled. They allowed the troops to come in and that will kill the strike; still, the beginning was made, and the fact demonstrated that the only way the workers can command respect is when they are ready to fight. As to sabotage, it would do your heart good to know the amount of property that has been destroyed. Yes, we are living in great times.

By the next month, however, Emma wrote that she hadn't been able to answer Margaret's telegram because it had reached her when she was "in a depressed state of mind." She continued her letter to Margaret from San Francisco:

> About myself, there isn't much to say. Our meetings have been most discouraging all along, although the last few we have had in this city have improved somewhat. I am to continue here for the next three weeks in the course of Drama lectures, and as we have succeeded in securing a centrally located hall, we are more hopeful of results. Certain it is that the country is stricken by the results of the unemployment of last winter and the radical movement by a sort of mental apathy. That applies to every shade of opinion. Most of the IWW and others, including the Anarchists, haven't enough spirit to kill a fly, let alone to offer resistance to the increased reactionary tendencies infesting the country. Perhaps it is the quiet before the storm. I hope so anyway; but it is hell to be

confronted with such a state of affairs. However, we must go on to the very end.

> With much love,
> Emma

Emma was determined to "go on to the very end" in the face of all obstacles. Although the two women did not have a personal affinity, their common work for "free motherhood" (birth control) forged a strong link between them. Emma's experience, her ability to reach and move large audiences, and her motherly concern for the frail Margaret gave the early part of Sanger's birth-control struggle the support it needed.

Inwardly, Emma, the relentless believer, hoped that the issues raised in her birth-control work with Ben might finally fuse their personal and political beliefs and that perhaps at last she and Ben could truly live out her vision of love and freedom. Ben listened carefully to her lectures, and to the opposition's arguments on the blessings of a child to even the poorest family and began to realize the issue had personal implications: he approached Emma with a newly awakened longing for a home and children. If in fact Emma had been so bitterly disappointed by her earlier, false pregnancy, then Ben's reawakened urge for fatherhood was particularly insensitive, even hostile—albeit genuine. The forty-five-year-old Emma brusquely asserted that a child could only handicap her work in the movement. And anyway, she protested, Ben already had a child, whom he had abandoned years before when he divorced his wife. Given Emma's convictions about the incompatibility of love and marriage and about woman's need not to be shackled by her reproductive capacities, the childless life she led with Ben was both consistent and gratifying. But Ben was beginning to feel uneasy with this aspect of their lives, and he had no intention of going back to his ex-wife or to the child he had abandoned and barely knew. By the time their tour was over, Emma returning to New York and Ben to his mother in Chicago, he had made clear his desire for domestic security:

> . . . if I can't have a home with you, I want a home alone with my
> Mother. . . . I have lived alone with my mother all my life and I have

no desire to make a change. . . . I want to do that best with you, and next alone with my mother. . . .

I am sorry that I can give you so little, when I think about having a home it makes my heart bleed when I realize that you would not have a real home with me. What you always had, and what you will always need, is a home of your own. You will not entirely agree with me, but it is true. I feel full of life but I am insecure about you. Oh, God, my lover, I know you much better than you think I do, and often I think that you are either not honest with me, or with yourself.

Ben was also, finally, facing the obstacles to his personal well-being imposed by the triangles in his life—among himself, Emma, and his mother, and among himself, Emma, and Sasha. The fact that Ben and Sasha were not getting along made for more conflict between Ben and Emma. Still, the Ben-Emma-Sasha constellation until then had served Emma well. Eager to avoid breaking up their work team, she wrote Ben that the struggle between Ben and Sasha was

driving [her] to distraction. . . . It is impossible for me to cast out Alex, as it would be for you to cast out your mother.

He has been in my life for 24 years in every pain and sorrow and through very Hell itself. That I should now be constantly called upon to decide between you two is agony, which you evidently never realized anymore than Alex does. . . . Please, dear heart, do not misunderstand, I do not defend B as against you. I know that your prejudice against him has been roused through his prejudice against you. I know that Alex is unreasonable and that he makes blunders. But when you say that if you had the right you'd bounce Alex from *Mother Earth*, it shows that you are utterly blind to the fact that of all the people we know, no one is more fitted for the position, nor has anyone been in my life through so many common ties. . . .

Hobo, my Hobo, I wish I could tell you how I feel about the whole matter, especially my failure to bring you and Alex close to each other. But such is fate. Our tastes as regard friends and relatives differ, don't they?

But the issue went deeper than their disparate tastes in friends and relatives. Sasha would not publish Reitman's statements in *Mother Earth*, and told him again and again that he did not belong in or understand the anarchist movement. Ben refused to work under the same roof as Sasha, whom he considered too narrowly moralistic and intellectual to understand Ben's talent for publicity and financial management. When it seemed that *Mother Earth* might fall apart as a result of this conflict, Emma began to pay closer attention to both sides, looking for a compromise.

Ben finally suggested that Sasha take charge of the magazine, while he and Emma toured. He scolded Emma for being a "temperamental creature" who worried constantly about everything, and encouraged her to "rest, go to the farm soon." But Emma was tormented by the emotional chaos and unpredictability connected to her work at the office. She was furious with Sasha for neglecting the financial obligations of the magazine during the five months that she was away working on the Anti-Militarist League and his own political organizing. She acknowledged the importance of creating an organization that would focus on the growing militarism as the United States joined World War I, but the work of the magazine was too important to Emma to be thrust aside. Emma wanted Ben and Sasha to care for "her baby" with the dedication of parents, but she faced Ben's possible abandonment of her and her journal. Again she compared her commitment to *Mother Earth* with Ben's bond with his mother:

And so Hobo wants me to give up *Mother Earth* and N.Y. I am afraid, lover, I cannot comply with your requests, anymore than you could if I asked you to give up your mother.

I have suffered too much in this City, have spent nearly a quarter of a Century here, and I could not go back on it if I tried. As to the magazine, how is it you advise giving it up? Have you gone back on your love for it? Strange Hobo you are.

As to Alex, the less said the better, but you are mistaken in one thing, namely this, if ever he felt as you do about *Mother Earth*, it being mine, he certainly did not do so during the last 5½ months, for he ran it in his own way. Indeed he did as he damned please about it, as if it were his own.

Dear heart, I don't believe in ownership, Heaven knows I don't, but I have given birth to *Mother Earth* and have [nurtured] it with my blood ever since.

Don't you see, Hobo, a man might not be sure of his fatherhood but a woman always is. That is her recompense for the many limitations nature has imposed upon her.

Emma's message to Ben was clear. Her chosen family centered on her work, and her chosen child was *Mother Earth* magazine. She was willing to be a single mother if she had to be. Certainly this was no time for her to consider having a flesh-and-blood infant with Ben.

Not wanting to travel all the time or give up *Mother Earth* just because Ben did not get along with Sasha, Emma reconsidered her previous idea of taking an apartment in New York alone so that she and Ben could live and work together. Since their break-up, Emma had lost her zest for collective living. At first Ben suggested they take a separate apartment, but only a few days later he changed his mind:

My suggestion is to put the questions of moving out of your head. . . . What are you going to do with your family. Sasha, Becky, Lioness & (etc.) How are they going to get on? What will you do for an Anarchist headquarters? One is absolutely needed, and a consultant like Sasha is needed. He is valuable in that way. . . . What are you going to do with yourself? You are a social animal, you need a large home and a place to entertain and take care of your friends.

What will you do with me. (I admit I do not look forward to N.Y. with much pleasure.) . . . You are really the boss in this case, everyone is dependent upon you, and you must decide.

I shall love you and work with you, what ever you do. You know how I feel about Sasha & *Mother Earth*—I don't think we ought ever to be asked to work together.

But I am not going to worry and I hope you won't. Just work things out the best you can and let it go at that.

But Emma's mind was made up:

Sept. 14 [1914]

Dearest. To ask questions is much easier than to answer them. What do you want me to do between now and Oct. 20 [when Ben was scheduled to come to New York]? I must prepare lectures. I must attend to a lot of things, how can I also make a radical change in my "family" as you call it?

By the way, dear, Lioness is really your family, you brought her into my life, so is your mother for all that, and such members are not easily gotten rid of, as you well know.

I must do the next-best thing, get rid of the house, which is a white elephant and has brought me nothing but sorrow. That's what I am going to do; as to the anarchist headquarters, etc., I can not revolutionize the whole World, dearie.

You ask me what I will do with you. Love you, of course. As to traveling all my life because you do not like to work with Sasha, or to give up *Mother Earth* on account of it, that is expecting a little too much, Hobo.

But as you say "I should worry," don't do it, darling, it will make you thin. Besides, I have large shoulders, I will do it for both. . . .

With lots of love
Mommy

Emma had resolved to give up her communal house, at any cost: "I am tired of feeding leeches and I am tired of living with people. I know you will smile and say I am a social animal, etc., etc. But just now I feel an urgent need of having a nook for myself."

It became apparent that the dissolution of their commune would in the long run work better for Sasha and Fitzi, too. Fitzi, who had been Ben's lover before coming to the *Mother Earth* office, was by this time an indispensable part of the *Mother Earth* group. She and Sasha had been lovers briefly; she, like Ben, played a supporting role to the great actors of the anarchist movement, although she was much more modest and self-deprecating than Ben. She did what needed to be done—the mailings, the publicity work, the smoothing over of dissension within the ranks—and was often referred to as "Emma's wife," although there seems to have been an element of sexual jealousy as well as attraction between the two women. But she, too, was tired of the tensions in the large household and had decided to move out with Sasha and Becky, Sasha's long-term lover.

Emma, recognizing that she had been overprotective of Sasha and that he had come to resent her dominance and her jealousies within their household, was now ready to allow him more freedom—and he was ready to take it. Sasha and Fitzi began to plan to tour out west with their own lectures, on Ludlow and the Anti-Militarist League.

Max Baginsky and Emma's nephew, Saxe Commins, took over the editing of *Mother Earth*, and within a few months Ben would join Emma and they would be on the road again.

Once they had settled on a temporary solution to the *Mother Earth* problem, Emma and Ben's correspondence took on a more political cast. Since Ben had begun to re-evaluate his support of political violence, he wondered how Emma now stood on that issue, what with talk of war in Europe in the air and radical groups springing up all over the country. During this period, there was an upsurge of random sabotage and bombings. While they were on the West Coast, a bomb exploded in the Lexington Avenue apartment of four anarchist comrades rumored to have been preparing to bomb the Rockefeller estate in Tarrytown, New York, to protest the Ludlow massacre. Although most people in the IWW disassociated themselves from the slain anarchists, Emma and Ben sent a telegram to the funeral procession, led from the *Mother Earth* office to Union Square by Sasha and Becky, hailing them as "victims of the capitalist system" and "martyrs of labor." Emma, critical of Ben's constant shifts, was reticent even to discuss the issue with him before he had taken a strong position.

About myself, I hold this position, violence is inevitable, never mind what Jesus said. But it is not so because it is part of anarchism but because it is thrust upon the individual and the masses by conditions. Now, whether I would or would not use violence, I never have or would condemn the individual in his struggle with society if he uses violence. My place is on the side of the social outcast, . . . at the present, I believe in the right of the workers to resist, whether in Colorado, Butte or elsewhere. That has nothing to do with the Marxian influence, my lover, that has to do (1) with my revolutionary temperament, (2) with my firm conviction that what liberty man has not the courage to take, he will never get.

Emma went on to cite the acts of random violence that she did not approve of "because it is impardonable to endanger the lives of innocent people." She also acknowledged that many of the editorials and articles on the subject of violence that appeared in *Mother Earth* were "bombast" and "stupid," although as editor of the magazine she had chosen not to act as a "boss or a dictator" with regard to the decision to include or exclude these opinions.

Ben found her response to his new formulations insulting:

In re Violence. You wasted 4 pages in saying things I heard you say 100 times. Do you think I am trying to change you? Do you believe that I want to condemn anyone? No—if our boys destroyed 100 women and children—like you—I would be a "social student," never would I condemn. To cut a long story short—I am arriving at a Tolstoy-Ferrer attitude on Violence. Am I less of an anarchist for it?

Yes, sure, I may change 40 times, does that prove anything? I don't want to be a part of any group that shows the Master class what bombs can do. To me these guys are terrorists, and I don't want to frighten anyone into leaving me alone—I want a chance to prove that our ideas are correct and will help the world.

Violence never proved any truth—as far as I can see. . . . If I am opposed to Violence on top, can I condone Violence at the bottom? . . . Now I love you, all of my brains & heart is wrapped around your activities. I want to work with you. But I want to be honest. I don't want to have to stand for things I don't believe in. . . . [Perhaps] I came into the anarchist movement too late.

Perhaps as an attack on Emma, and as a way of separating himself from her, an undercurrent of anti-Semitism appeared in Ben's letters, along with frequent allusions to the teachings of Jesus. Ben complained that the Jewish audience was interested only in bettering the condition of Jews,

> and the Rest could go to hell. Also the Jews bring their Religion, their customs, into everything. Socialist, IWW, Anarchist, Jewish—they won't combine with the American and Irish. Also labor, Hebrew trade unions. I am convinced that we have to do anti-Jewish propaganda and do something [to] break down the Racial feeling. It would make a wonderful lecture, especially for the Jews.

Emma replied:

> Hobo, you are quite an anti-Semite, aren't you? I am afraid I cannot take your point of view regarding the Jews. You see, dear, you know nothing about them, since you said yourself that you never came in touch with them until you met me. You are really not in a position to judge them one way or another. But if what you say were really true I should not condemn them, because they are a persecuted people and owe their survival only to the capacity of sticking together.

Emma felt that her loyalty to her people gave her leeway to criticize them at times. She often held meetings expressly on the most solemn of all Jewish holidays, Yom Kippur, and she took a strong position against the formation of a Jewish state. She believed that the Jews had a special character because they were bound by an idea, not because they were a nation. "Owing to a lack of a country of their own, they developed, crystallized and idealized their cosmopolitan reasoning faculty . . . working for the great moment when the earth will become the home for all, without distinction of ancestry or race."

Although Ben had rejected his own birthright as a Jew, most likely part of his attraction for Emma were his Jewish physical and emotional traits—his dark hair and eyes, and what she called his intense emotionalism. Emma continued to plan her tour, including among her lectures "The Tzar and 'My' Jews" (a strong statement against Jewish nationalism or any expectation of privilege or protection within a state structure), without censoring her ideas because of Ben's prejudices. And Ben continued to work with Emma, feeling "wedded to [her] and to *Mother Earth*." Yet underlying his devotion was his need "to nurse his soul" away from Emma, to distance himself from this woman who was his lover, his boss, his "religion." They were growing apart once again, and Emma began to feel depressed and abandoned, as she had felt many times before in their relationship.

Emma had found herself a small apartment, but at first she was set off balance by the move:

My Ben, my Ben, there are days when I feel terribly bitter against you because always in the most trying periods of my life you are far away from me. Fate is kind to save you the struggle and annoyance always.

Then again, my love breaks forth like brilliant sunlight after a storm and envelops you in warmth and devotion. Then I am glad that you at least are saved the sordidness, the paralyzing daily routine, the pots and kettles, books and boxes, until it seems as if I'd choke to death. I know then that no matter how hard and indifferent and selfish you are, I love you profoundly, devotedly, passionately.

Perhaps it will only be one more disappointment in my life, but somehow I feel that in giving up the house and old galling arrangement I have made a move toward peace, gradually other matters will be adjusted. Perhaps some day soon I can rest for a year and devote myself to *Mother Earth*. I am so tired of lectures, meetings, and the mad chase, I want rest, I want time to read and think and love. Meanwhile we have a beautiful large airy office, the very best we have had. And I shall have a beautiful sunny room with a darling kitchenette. If only I had a bath my dream would be complete. But one cannot have everything. . . . Baby mine, tonight is my last night in the house which was cursed from the very beginning. I don't remember any place where so much friction and sorrow were cramped in one year. I shall be glad to get out of it and look forward to cheer and peace in my new home. Perhaps then I shall be kind and Hobo will know—I love him.

In another letter, Emma continued in the same vein:

Life is an eternal merry-go-around only it is rarely merry. Years ago, when I came to N.Y., I lived in a furnished room. Today I have gotten back to that starting point. . . . Hobo, my Hobo, I love you but I am weary with the World, with people, with myself. I shall be cheerful soon—have patience, dear. . . .

Having made it through the upheaval of the summer, the disarray of the *Mother Earth* office, she was ready to start over.

At the end of their period of temporary estrangement, the two lovers were anxious to see each other again. They had been apart for the months of September and October, during which time both Emma and Ben claimed to have been sexually and emotionally loyal to each other. But with no competition from other men for Emma, Ben jealously worried that Emma was now drawn to other women. Almeda Sperry had visited her in September, and Ben wrote to Emma, "Baby, I love you and I am completely yours. I hope you enjoy your visit with Sperry and I trust you will not develop any TECHNIQUE whereby you can displace me."

And when Margaret Anderson, of *The Little Review*, came to visit her, Emma felt she had to assure Ben that she was still heterosexual, although there was an edge to her assurances:

Yes, Margaret is coming and I am glad of that. But I do not incline that way. I love your damned sex. Most of the men I'd love to exchange for you are too madly absorbed in their own women—Roe, Middleton, etc., etc. So I have to stick to you, out of necessity, you know. . . . I don't know why I love you, but I know how I love you, Hobo, lover, my all.

Mommy

Given the continuing complexity of their relationship, it was no wonder that Emma included among her new lectures "Misconceptions of

Free Love," a response partly to her own experience with Ben, and partly to the socialists who denounced Emma and free love. In it, Emma distinguished between open, honest sexual relations outside of the confines of monogamy and marriage, and hidden, illicit, and indiscriminate promiscuity—between good and bad forms of nonmonogamous relationships. The good involved a spiritual union between two people, the bad only a physical union. In part Emma's talk was an effort to dispel the view that she was a dangerous advocate of free love with no sense of morality, out to destroy the social fabric. According to Emma, personal stability could never come from the dictates of social norms and the law, but would have to come from true commitment and love among people.

Emma met Ben in Chicago for three weeks of lectures on war—its psychology, effect on women, and link to religion—and on modern drama. Then she traveled to Grand Rapids, Detroit, Ann Arbor, Peoria, and St. Louis; in print, she attributed the success of her tour to the "invaluable organizing and managing force behind my co-worker, Ben Reitman."

After her tour, Emma returned to New York, without Ben, to continue her anti-militarist and free-love talks while planning her next series of lectures. She was eager to put together public talks that would both address the war and embrace the birth-control issue, to help produce a new unity of vision for a radical movement experiencing the effects of growing repression as the United States anticipated going to war. It was no coincidence that governmental repression coincided with the outbreak of war in Europe: a country at war needs to maintain tight control over its people, to assure the subordination of individual needs to the needs of the state. Socialists' and anarchists' opposition to the impending conflict isolated them from the mainstream, which heretofore had been more tolerant of them. Emma was determined that her work should serve as an inspiration, "because there is such despair in the radical ranks." But even she could not revitalize a movement single-handedly.

Emma was glad to come home to her own apartment, quiet enough to allow her to collect her thoughts for writing. After years of being the hostess for all holiday meals, she even had Christmas dinner away, at her niece Stella's, after having danced until 4:00 A.M. the night before at the

Futurist Masses Ball. She wrote to Ben: "I can't say I minded, because the care and burden of a large family which I have carried so many years have made domesticity very hateful to me. I really enjoy my bachelor quarters and the quiet and peace it contains. . . . No one disagreeable to me is in the house to tear my nerves and sap my energies. It's a wonderful sensation."

The comfort of her new living arrangements was, however, offset by loneliness and a longing for Ben. Though she claimed she did not want him if he felt coerced, thus paying homage to the principle of free choice, she went on to use her powers of persuasion to encourage him to join her:

Indeed, dearest, I will not say "If you love me you will come to N.Y."

But I will say, whatever is the most dominant urge in your being will lure you. If your love for me and your interest in the work are that dominant urge, why, of course, you'll come to N.Y. As a good follower of Jesus you ought to know this idea that man is known by his deeds. . . . I have already written you that if my very life depended on your coming and I knew you'd rather not come, I certainly would prefer to be without you than play upon your love, your sex, your devotion I simply cannot do that, baby mine. You must act as the spirit moves you, else there is no joy with you.

Ben was leaning toward joining Emma, but as his thirty-sixth birthday approached he was assailed again, as he had been the year before, with the feeling that he was growing old. He doubted that he had chosen the right path as Emma's road manager. Emma, at forty-five, tried to comfort him.

You speak of being old, you are funny—36 years of age. Why, it's the greatest time in a man's life, and especially such a life as we have lived. Hobo, Hobo, there is not another man in America who has crowded so much in 36 years as you, but you are a puritan, dear. . . . Happy New Year to you, my darling. May you find joy and peace and purpose. May you regain your reckless youth, your savage fancy, may you fall in love with Mommy.

Ben spent his birthday with his mother, who, as Emma pointed out, "replaced wife, kiddies and home" to him. But Ben had decided that what he wanted now was a real wife and family. Since he and Emma could not see their way clear to such a stable future, he arrived in New York with a somewhat cold-blooded resolve to search for a woman with whom he could settle down.

Thus he leaped at the opportunity to renew his acquaintance with the tall blond Englishwoman who had attracted his attention in the *Mother Earth* office the previous winter, when he and Emma were splitting up. After seeing her again at Emma's meetings, Ben sought her out. He recounted the early stages of this romance in his unpublished autobiography, "Following the Monkey":

> After the meetings I would ride home with her occasionally on the top of the bus and once in a while we walked through Central Park. I became infatuated with Miss Martindale and for the first time in my life I wanted to marry a woman, and have a home and children. We had a sort of strange romance. All this time I was living and working with Emma Goldman. The call of honor became stronger and more powerful. I became irritable with Emma and the rest of the Anarchists. I was constantly finding fault with the propaganda and criticizing the individuals.

Ben kept up the charade of his loyal intimacy with Emma while he spent his romantic energy on Anna Martindale, a labor activist who respected Ben's work with Emma. He organized and presided over Emma's meetings, from Albany to Boston and later on the West Coast. Emma's lectures continued to reflect her insistence on connecting personal and political life, ranging from "Anarchism and Literature" and "Nietszche: The Intellectual Storm Center of the Great War," to "Feminism: A Criticism of Women's Struggle for the Vote and 'Freedom,'" to "The Limitation of Offspring," "The Intermediate Sex: A Discussion of Homosexuality," and "Man: Monogamist or Varietist."

As their trip progressed, she even gave a talk on "Jealousy: Its Possible Causes and Cures." Still unaware of the significance of Ben's affair with Anna, she recognized the symptoms, and she tried to root out her own jealousy in the name of free love. The effort to universalize her own inner struggle provided the force behind her speeches.

The direction of her public positions shifted in response to significant historical events. In January 1915, just before Ben and Emma were to begin planning their next trip across the country, Margaret Sanger's husband, William, was arrested for giving a visitor in his home a copy of his wife's pamphlet *Family Limitation*. As *Mother Earth* pointed out, such legal censorship was now almost unheard of.

Ten years after the founding of *Mother Earth*, Emma was determined to take on the birth-control issue through the magazine. Although the staff, to avoid arrest, did not distribute Margaret Sanger's technical manual on the *Limitation of Offspring*, they did send Sanger's pamphlets *What Every Mother Should Know* and *What Every Girl Should Know* through the mail to those who deluged the *Mother Earth* office with requests for birth-control literature. Nevertheless, Margaret Sanger felt that she had been neglected by the *Mother Earth* staff, that they had not given her sufficient support. She sent an angry letter to the editors, which was published in April 1915:

> I will frankly say that I was keenly disappointed at the silence of *Mother Earth* in regard to this outrageous tyrannical attitude of the Post Office authorities toward the *Woman Rebel*. I expect very little publicity on this "delicate subject" from the capitalist press, but naturally I look for an attitude of solidarity and comradeship from the radical press.
>
> But as the indictments were returned in August and there were 3 suppressions since March—and not a word in any paper until November, it makes one feel quite alone in a fight that so concerns the workers and all of us.

Emma, never one to accept criticism with grace, was in this case justifiably offended by Sanger's abrupt assumption that she was "alone" in the birth-control fight—in which Emma had dared to speak out long before Sanger.

> During all of that time [while Sanger felt she was alone in furthering the cause] we pushed *The Woman Rebel* and discussed its editor's case before thousands of people throughout the country. Under the circumstances it seems very unfair on the part of our comrade to accuse *Mother Earth* of indifference. But then it is human to feel neglected when one faces one's first great battle with the powers that be, in behalf of an unpopular cause.
>
> We understand our comrade and assure her that *Mother Earth* and those connected with her never have and never will hesitate to stand by our brave friend, Margaret H. Sanger.

The exchange of letters reflected a growing tension within the ranks of the free-motherhood movement. Gradually Margaret Sanger was severing her links with her initial, left-wing supporters, taking the issue of birth control to more moderate forums in an effort to gain wider support and respectability for the issue. Although her strategy seemed to work, and was adaptive to the repression that plagued the labor movement, she herself gradually altered her basic informational pamphlet to eliminate the focus on working people, socialists, and anarchists, who linked the issue of birth control to economic and social conditions.

Sanger, a woman with a single purpose, was pragmatic in her approach to the birth-control issue. She was willing to compromise to reach her desired end. Emma, who hoped to improve the fundamental fabric of human relationships, saw birth control as only one facet of the larger issue of freedom and love. She would not consciously compromise on anything, wanting all or nothing. The relationship between the two women was typical of others in Emma's life. At first she was a mentor and support to Sanger, but when Sanger developed a substantial movement stamped with her own political approach, a competitive animosity developed. Emma would give her all for others, but she expected gratitude—in this case, public acknowledgment of her role in the beginnings of the birth-control movement.

Still, she continued to raise the issue in her own way. She lectured on the "Limitation of Offspring." She reviewed a new book by Dr. William Robinson as a way of bringing attention to the history of the birth-control movement and exposing the idiocy of the postal laws, which prompted the author to leave blank pages where he wanted to describe birth-control "remedies." Ben and Emma, possibly with the help of Dr. Robinson, distributed a four-page pamphlet, *Why and How the Poor Should Not Have Many Children*. It gave explicit instructions for various contraceptives and included a brief political argument: "although normal people love and want children, society today is a wretched place for poor children, who are not only a burden to their mothers and families, but also glut the labor market, tend to lower wages, and are a menace to the welfare of the working class. . . . If you think that the teaching of the prevention of conception will help working men and women, spread the glad tidings."

Emma Goldman and Ben Reitman were among the first radicals in the United States to take risks in the name of the birth-control movement. They fought not only against right-wing conservative forces, but also, in one instance, against the Catholic socialists. Ben organized, with special gusto, meetings in Paterson, New Jersey, against the evangelical Billy Sunday's morality; he even wrote a poem to God about it. Anna Martindale worked on the Paterson meeting, and a similar event in Philadelphia. Emma and Ben enjoyed the fight, for it enabled them to raise critical issues in a charged political setting, and no doubt the presence of the attractive Anna enhanced his pleasure. Ben summed up the 1915 tour as the most satisfactory of his nine trips across the country:

Four wonderful months in New York, crowded meetings almost every night; six glorious weeks in Chicago; a delightful month in Los Angeles; a perfect month in San Francisco, and most interesting weeks in Minneapolis, Cleveland, Pittsburgh, Denver, Portland, and Seattle. . . . O Brave Margaret Sanger! You can be glad even if they hang you or send you to penitentiary for life, your pamphlet has found its way into nearly every hamlet or village in America, and dozens of other men or women have republished your pamphlet or similar one, and scattered them broadcast throughout the land and Anthony Comstock [who had been responsible for framing William Sanger], though aided by all the powers of government or hell, cannot stop this stupendous movement. . . . Now the tour is over. I am going back to Chicago to write a book on "Safety First in Sex."

In his enthusiasm, Ben even seemed undefensive about Emma's returning to San Diego without him. He toured the city with his mother anonymously shortly after Sasha, Fitzi, their old anarchist comrade Ben Capes, and an Albany anarchist named Leon Malmed cautiously arranged Emma's San Diego talks. Emma scored a victory for free speech, and Ben's mother said that she had had the best time in her life since her childhood. Although Ben reported that "the free speech fight . . . was won in San Diego without my aid and abetment," Emma was glad that Ben had returned to the city, "thereby breaking the nervous tension that was his for three years." Emma felt that her "triumph was due mostly to the comrades martyred for free speech three years previously—to Joseph Mikolasek, who had been murdered in the fight, and the hundreds of IWW's and other victims, including Ben, who had been beaten, thrown into prison and driven out of town." The sense of victory, as well as the focus on issues that were central to her life, both politically and personally, gave Emma's trip its vitality. And her visionary talks on birth control, free love, homosexuality—essentially women's right to the control and appreciation of their own bodies—were reinforced by her enjoyable sexual experiences with Ben.

Such pleasure did not preclude erratic behavior, this time on Emma's part. On her ritual September break, she and Ben entered into yet another battle over the issue of "variety" as it affected their own lives, after she had an active flirtation with Leon Malmed. Her honesty on the subject with Ben provoked his jealousy and resentment of her vast circle of friends and admirers, particularly because he had not been feeling well physically, and feared being replaced in Emma's life.

My dear Hobo

If you really have even one hundred part of your love for me, please, please stop torturing me with my "variety" with the many friends I need and have. I really can't stand it anymore. I do not want to quarrel, dear heart, but you are really wearing me out, as indeed you have all these 7 years every time I showed the least interest in man, woman or child.

Of all men you are the last to do it, Hobo mine. . . . Even if I really had all the lovers you have imagined, you should grant me the right. I have granted you. Don't you think so, dear? . . .

If only you would once in your life practice what you preach, perhaps you'd understand. But to use your term, You are as you are. . . .

But, Hobo mine, all the reason in the World has not helped to explain emotions. Greater men and Women than you and I have attempted the task and have failed. What hope have we?

If needing companionship, community of taste, if the creative things of life, if friendship & kindness originate from sex, I am indeed the greatest varietest who ever lived, for I need all that and more. But if love, a deep, large, all-understanding, all-forgiving, passionate love be the ultimate exaltant expression of sex then I have been the most rigid monogamist since March 1908. Nor was it the strong factor of our work which has held me bound to you, my Hobo. It is my love, my wild primitive passion, my deep devotion to you and for you alone and nothing else. . . .

You must have faith in me, Hobo, because love needs faith and trust and confidence just as the rose needs sunshine and dew. Please don't keep on tearing and pulling at its petals. Do you think because we do not see the twitchings of the plant it has no nerves? Now, you wouldn't attempt to cut my flesh to see my blood flow, would you, Darling? Why then do you pierce my soul? I love you, that's all I know. . . .

Hobo, my Dearest, my Lover. I am tired to death of arguments, please let me love in my own way, since that's the only way I can love, the only way you love. Do you think I am satisfied with your way? But I know you cannot love otherwise and I take you as you are without everlasting dissection. Let's leave the operating and dissecting room; let's rise to the Glory & Warmth of our love.

The two lovers were on the road again within the month, resolving simply "to not discuss last month."

While Emma was touring, Margaret Sanger's daughter Peggy died. Sanger was extremely depressed, full of self-blame for having been away from home so much. Emma wrote from her tour, somewhat callously: "I feel deeply with your loss, but I also feel that you owe it to yourself and the work you have before you to collect your strength. After all, dear, it is a thing which has passed and cannot be redeemed, whereas you need your vitality and unless you will take hold of yourself you will lose whatever little you have, and yet not change the inexorable."

At the same time, Margaret Sanger's trial was approaching. Emma had heard that many of Margaret's liberal friends in the birth-control movement (in particular, Theodore Schroeder, her lawyer) were urging her to plead guilty to try to shorten her jail sentence. In her unhappy state of mind, Margaret felt pressured, concerned about the effect on her other children. Emma, who always believed in asserting principle over expediency, urged Margaret not to give way on her position that referring to birth control did *not* constitute obscenity. Emma wrote to her from St. Louis: "That would be too awful. Just kill the movement you have helped to advance in 50 years. I hope you will do no such a thing, that you will be as brave as you have so far. . . . You have friends all over the country, you can have whatever means will be needed to fight. You have aroused the interest as no one ever has. Think of losing it all by declaring yourself guilty. Don't do it."

Emma urged Margaret not to make a decision until she returned from her trip at the end of the month, and to give herself time to rest and talk with Emma at a resort in Lakewood, New Jersey. "We'd both gain much and I would help you find yourself."

From Columbus, Ohio, Emma wrote Margaret that her meetings in Indianapolis had been sparsely attended, but the interest in birth control was tremendous. Emma sent Margaret the money she had collected for her trial and some subscriptions to *The Woman Rebel*. "How I wish I were rich enough to take you and the children with me to Lakewood. Will you at least come with them to my Christmas Dinner I intend to have at my place. . . ."

Sanger's trial was postponed until January 4; since Emma was sure to see her before then, the urgency of her letters to persuade Margaret to stand firm abated. Emma held true to her promise to use all her lectures on birth control as a means of collecting money for Margaret Sanger. She had written, "I know that it is not enough to express my affection for you and my devotion to the thing we both love so much, but in our materialistic age, the money question is very pressing indeed."

Ultimately, Sanger decided "to enter a plea of not guilty in order to separate the idea of prevention of conception and birth control from the sphere of pornography, from the gutter of slime and filth where the lily-livered legislators have placed it, under the direction of the late unlamented Anthony Comstock, and in which the forces of reaction are still attempting to hold it." Emma, pleased with Margaret's decision, entered a generous postscript in *Mother Earth*: ". . . what our readers do not know is that Margaret Sanger has gone through untold hardships the last year. . . . To face trial under such conditions requires more than ordinary strength. . . . To sustain her in this crucial moment [she needs] the moral and material support of all rebels."

Emma continued to speak forcefully on the birth-control issue and to raise money for the Sanger case. *The New York Times* of January 17, 1916, reporting on a talk she gave, headlined the article: TEDDY ROOSEVELT WRONG, SAYS ANARCHIST—EMMA GOLDMAN ASSERTS CHILD HAS A RIGHT NOT TO BE BORN. The reporter quoted her as saying, "If everyone followed the injunction of the Bible and Teddy Roosevelt to be fruitful and multiply, every tenement house would be turned into a lunatic asylum by the excessive number of children."

After she had taken her birth-control lecture coast to coast, and had delivered it eight times in New York City alone, Emma was suddenly arrested there on February 11, 1916. *The New York Times* took time out from stories on preparedness and the European war to cover Emma's arrest, an event symptomatic of the growing mood of repression in the country:

EMMA GOLDMAN ARRESTED

. . . charged with having lectured on a medical question in defiance of Section 1142 of the Penal Code. . . .

Dr. B. Reitman . . . said that though Miss Goldman could have been arrested at her home, the police waited until nearly a thousand persons were about the door of the hall. When she appeared they refused to allow her to enter the hall for a moment. Some 500 followed, cheered Miss Goldman, and scoffed at the police.

Her arrest, which she described in *Mother Earth*, was accompanied by a search done "in the most vulgar manner by a coarse looking matron in the presence of two detectives, a thing which would outrage the most hardened criminal." Ironically, she was arrested while on her way to deliver a lecture on atheism, not birth control. At her preliminary hearing on February 28, she chose to have no legal counsel and insisted on cross-examining witnesses herself; she moved for a dismissal of her case, but her request was denied. Determined to use the occasion of her impending jail sentence to launch a nationwide publicity campaign for birth control, Emma reiterated that although she would fight to the end "for the right of the masses, and especially women, to decide whether or not they shall bring forth life in a system which rests on the degradation and humiliation as well as the destruction of life," she believed "more than ever that [her] fight is in behalf of freedom of speech and press on the great social problems of our time."

At the same time that Emma's case was growing more serious, Margaret Sanger's was dismissed by the courts. Sanger defended herself in the pages of *Mother Earth* against left-wing criticism by asserting that there was no guarantee that going to jail would ultimately change any law. Her husband had gone to jail for giving the pamphlet *Family Limitation* to a detective, and the law remained the same. Margaret Sanger claimed that perhaps dismissal of her case by the government was of far greater value as a precedent than an acquittal by a jury. She urged the people who had begun to factionalize the birth-control movement to continue their common work "without quibbling."

Despite this noble sentiment, Emma's arrest and the attention it brought to her spurred a rivalry between the two women. Emma still resented Margaret's assumption that it was only Sanger's issue, and wrote to her friend Ellen Kennan that she had "started out on birth control agitation long before the Sangers thought of it and gave the information from the pamphlet before Mrs. Sanger sent out her pamphlet." William Sanger himself wrote Emma an irate letter about the rift that had developed between his wife and Emma on their respective prominence in the birth-control movement: "But getting back to the original proposition, Margaret's work stands out clear cut and revolutionary. . . . She was the first one, to my mind, to attack the statutes *involving long terms of imprisonment*. Your arrests have been based on only misdemeanors and disorderly conduct."

Emma neither replied nor deferred to the Sangers. Instead, she continued to wage the battle for birth control in her own way, assuring readers of *Mother Earth*: "I may be arrested, I may be tried and thrown into jail, but I never will be silent; I never will acquiesce or submit to authority, nor will I make peace with a system which degrades woman to a mere incubator and which fattens on her innocent victims [children who become exploited workers]. I now and here declare war upon this system and shall not rest until the path has been cleared for a free motherhood and a healthy, joyous and happy childhood."

Given the choice between a fine of $100 or fifteen days in the Queens County jail, Emma opted for "the Workhouse." For advocating that "women need not always keep their mouths shut, and their wombs open," she went to prison. She always preferred the symbolic act of defiance, and besides, as she wrote to a woman friend, her jail term gave her a convenient opportunity to diet.

Emma's only lament was that the prison didn't have Swedish exercises. True to form, Ben noted in a *Mother Earth* article that "her blue prison uniform is not at all unbecoming." Worried about what Emma would get to eat in prison, Ben wrote to her friend Ellen Kennan: "I took your loving contribution and bought some eggs and some fish and some matzos and tried to bring them to Emma, but they wouldn't let me get to her. Just think of it, our Emma not allowed to have a little food that she likes but compelled to eat the most miserable kind of food which absolutely disagrees with her."

Emma described to Margaret Anderson how she felt about her conviction, in a letter from prison: "Oh, I am not sorry I was sentenced. In fact I am glad. I needed to get to these pariahs who are the butt of all the horrors. It would be well if every rebel were sent to prison for a time; it would fan his smouldering flame of hate of the things that make prisons possible. I am really glad."

Ben continued to take on "the anxiety and the worry" of arranging future meetings. He had his own apartment now, apart from the *Mother Earth* office, but worked faithfully. While Emma was in jail, he organized a meeting at the Harlem Masonic Temple to protest her conviction. Ben announced at the meeting that he was going to distribute a pamphlet containing information on all methods of birth control, and called for volunteers to help. Within a few days he was served with a warrant for his arrest at the *Mother Earth* office, then released on $500 bail and scheduled to appear in court on May 8, 1916. Proud of his arrest, he wrote an article in *Mother Earth* entitled "Pinched": "If the authorities think that we are going like lambs to the slaughter they are mistaken. We believe in Birth Control—yes, believe in it enough to go to jail, to the gallows, if necessary." In this spirit Ben accepted his sentence of imprisonment in the workhouse for sixty days.

Shortly before his arrest, Ben had organized a meeting at Carnegie Hall to celebrate Emma's release from prison. Replete with public figures who favored the distribution and accessibility of birth-control information, that meeting, coupled with news of Emma and Ben's arrests, spurred renewed interest in birth control throughout the country, including a declaration signed by forty prominent San Francisco women pledging their willingness to distribute pamphlets and go to prison in solidarity with Emma and Ben. But Max Eastman, editor of *The Masses* (the socialist equivalent of *Mother Earth*), refused to preside over the meeting if Ben was allowed to speak. A respected writer and editor in socialist circles, Eastman was one of many who could not overcome a personal dislike for Ben. He described Ben as a "white fleshed, waxy-looking doctor, who thought it was radical to shock people with crude allusion to their sexual physiology." The incident left Ben, during his sixty days in jail, with a sense of isolation from a movement that he felt he had served with all his heart. For Emma, it was just another sign of what she took to be socialist pettiness. She continued to support Ben and even arranged a large meeting at Union Square to protest his arrest. The meeting was well attended, confirming Ben's description of himself to the jury not as Emma Goldman's advertising man (as the prosecutor had referred to him) but as a "sort of advance agent for social revolution."

In prison, Ben, like Emma, was brought back in direct touch with society's victims. At first he enjoyed the shock he could provoke by identifying himself as "a physician and a poet" and then proceeding to shovel coal faster than the other men, who prided themselves on strength gained through lifelong manual labor. Ben didn't think prisoners were made to do such terrible things, as Emma did: he relished a chance to get back to working hard in the open air. He was so enthusiastic that, according to Ben's autobiography, when a well-known society woman came to visit him one day and offered to have him pardoned, Ben refused. "No, don't bother about getting me a pardon—I'm very happy here—I'm getting a good rest and I needed it so. I am doing some physical labor and I needed that more than you think. Also, I've got plenty of time to read and plenty of books. I average reading two books a day while I am here. I don't want to get out," he replied. When asked if there was anything he *would* like, he answered, "Yes, get a couple of indoor balls and some bats for the boys and send me in a nice big apple pie, that's all I need in the world." When the pie came, and Ben was told that he couldn't eat it because the other prisoners would take it as an unfair privilege, instead he asked whether he could kiss the pie. The warden said he could do it if he promised not to stick his tongue into it, so, "I gave the pie a very chaste kiss."

Although Ben complained about the food in prison, Emma expected he would leave in better shape and even more handsome than before. His main complaint was that some of the prisoners cadged the names and addresses of his female correspondents, took the liberty of writing them letters, and then punched him for getting angry. Eventually they apologized. Ben shared his books with them; Berkman's *Prison Memoirs of an Anarchist* was popular. But when it rained and Ben could not go outside, he knew the horrors of confinement, the constant surveillance, the isolation, the longing for women and affection. His suffering in prison stimulated Ben's identification with the story of Christ, and spurred him on to serve the revolution despite the temptations to surrender himself to the conflicting forces of promiscuity, politics, and family. In a poem he wrote entitled "Vengeance," which appeared in the July 1916 issue of *Mother Earth*, he spelled out his desire for martyrdom:

Let not my love for love or desire for life or
duty toward Mother hold me.
Let me be thine avenging sword, Oh God of
Liberty!

Emma worried about Ben in jail, but felt that his letters had a
serenity she had never seen in him before. Since she was scheduled to
begin her tour to the West Coast, she reluctantly went without him,
anticipating a glorious reunion in California. It would be the first time in
eight years that she would tour without Ben. She wondered how it
would be "without his elemental activity," which had helped so much to
make her meetings a success. She wondered, too, whether she could bear
the strain of the struggle without Ben's affection and the comfort of his
presence.

Emma had originally encouraged Ben to appeal his case in order to
gain time and to have him with her on tour. From an ideological
viewpoint she was glad that he had turned down the appeal, but she was
personally apprehensive. And once on the road, she missed him so much
that she had some regrets about not having waited for him. Still, Emma
managed without "her manager." She wrote to him from Denver: "Hobo
mine. What do you think of Mommy getting up at seven all by myself?
And I went to bed at one, too, ain't I smart? And what do you think is
the morning prayer? Hobo, I love you and I am glad I will see you soon."
Though she tried to handle her own ads and publicity without Ben, she
felt inadequate:

One thing is certain, Hobo, if my public work would depend on
going after the newspapers, I would give up the job. I loathe it and
feel as if I were prostituting myself, in fact I have never all these
years given them the satisfaction and I never will again. Hobo is
born for it just as he is born to be a manager; he is born to love
Mommy, that's why he does it so badly, almost as badly as I do
when I have to ask the papers for favors.

In California, Emma had to devote all her attention to the immediate political situation. She had come to Los Angeles to speak on

"preparedness" on the day of the Preparedness Day Parade, and the entire city was like a military encampment. Emma worked closely with Sasha and Fitzi, who were now living in San Francisco, the base for their new labor magazine, *The Blast*. The next meeting, which was scheduled for San Francisco, conflicted with an anti-preparedness mass meeting, so she postponed it until the evening of July 22. On that afternoon, a bomb exploded at the Preparedness Day Parade in San Francisco. Everyone connected with the local anti-preparedness campaign came under suspicion. The fact that Emma had postponed her meeting meant that the people associated directly with her were not immediately suspect. It was a narrow escape for her, but the five leaders of the most prominent local labor unions were not so fortunate. Tom Mooney and his wife, Rena, Warren Billings, Edward Nolan, and Israel Weinberg were arrested, in a deliberate blow to the labor movement. Any claims of a frame-up as a defense were precluded by the active role the labor movement had assumed a few years before in fighting for the acquittal of the McNamara brothers on the charge of bombing the *Los Angeles Times* building—before they confessed to the act. Emma's July 22 lecture attracted only fifty paying customers, most of them detectives. She recollected this evening in her autobiography: "The atmosphere was very tense, everybody fidgeting about, apparently in terror of another bomb." Emma's lecture dealt "with the tragedy of the afternoon as proving more convincingly than theoretic dissertations that violence begets violence." She accurately predicted that the events that followed the bombing could turn into "an official reign of terror." The government was concerned, above all, with readiness for war; they would come down hard on all forms of dissent.

It was in this atmosphere that Ben joined Emma in San Francisco. People were afraid to attend her lectures, and Ben could not stand seeing a hall that was meant to hold a thousand people with only a handful in the audience. He urged Emma to cancel her tour and go home, but she felt committed to completing her schedule. Sasha and Fitzi's magazine continued to give unconditional support to those who had been arrested; as Emma and Ben left for Portland to complete their tour, the police ransacked the office of *The Blast* and threatened to arrest Sasha and Fitzi.

In the midst of the growing repression, Ben had an urge to escape home, "to tabulate his ideas, and get acquainted with himself." He was not driven so much by a wish to bow out of the struggle, although it was becoming more terrifying with each day, as he was by his desire to be with his "other sweethearts"—in particular, Anna Martindale. Under renewed political pressure, he longed for the calm of his new-found love.

At first Ben said he wanted to go away to have a chance to write, that he was tired of being "a mere office boy," carrying bundles and selling literature. Ben claimed that Emma had always been truer and more respectful to Sasha than she had been to him, and that he had never been permitted to do anything he really wanted to do with her, not even to have a child. Emma's categorical rejection of that notion had, Ben claimed, thrown him into a deep depression, which he escaped through his fantasies of having a home and family with Anna Martindale. He had been afraid to tell Emma that while he and Emma were working together and still lovers, he had often spent a good deal of time with Anna Martindale in her New York apartment. This explained the new serenity that Emma thought he had acquired in the last year.

In his autobiography, Ben ascribed his change of heart toward Emma to his desire to have a child with Anna:

> At the time I developed a psychology that made it impossible for me to continue my work in the Anarchist movement, a number of forces were at work.
>
> When does love die? When does a person begin to be indifferent about his work or his religion? . . .
>
> During the birth control trial in New York, Anna stood by me, and in the sixty days that I lived in the New York jail her letters and love helped sustain me. When I was released from the Long Island Prison in July, 1916, Anna Martindale and I decided to be united as soon as possible. I was to leave the propaganda, go to Chicago and resume the practice of medicine, and we would have a home and a life of our own.

Ben claimed it was his feelings of inferiority that had contributed to his gradual disenchantment with Emma Goldman and her circle of unac-cepting comrades.

I think another tremendous factor that was responsible for my alienation from the Anarchist movement was some sort of an inferiority complex. I had not been in the Anarchist movement long before I began to realize that the other men, Berkman, Havel, Baginsky, [writer Leonard] Abbott, and many others were decidedly my intellectual superiors. In the beginning that was all right. At first they looked upon me as a novelty, a boy, a janitor, a clown, and a necessary evil. But as I began to develop a soul of my own and showed a faint spark of intelligence and was beginning to be a power, and an influence, I felt a real or imaginary increase in opposition on the part of some of the comrades.

I developed a decided antagonism to Berkman. As I saw Emma leaning more and more on him, as the propaganda grew more exciting and the labor, free-speech, birth control and especially the anti-militarist propaganda grew more intense, I perhaps became jealous of him. It was evident to Emma Goldman and Berkman that tragedy was in the air and that they were going to be killed, or at least to be sent to jail. There was no question but the impending danger which we all sensed threw Berkman and Miss Goldman closer together and she leaned less on me.

Indeed, Emma did lean more on Sasha, particularly when she felt completely abandoned by Ben in a moment of need. Although she had long known of Ben's duplicity in matters of love and sex, she was now taken by surprise. His confession of multiple affairs during the first year of their love had set the tone of doubt that had characterized their relationship ever since, but there were times when she wished she could close her eyes and relax into the comforts of the relationship. This time, though, it was not just her wayward boy's brief desire for a moment of passion away from Mommy. The deep urge to have a family was a clear rejection of Emma's application of anarchist principles to her life—and of the forty-seven-year-old Emma herself.

Ben's betrayal and dishonesty, and the irony of her outpourings of concern for him in jail while he was so involved with another woman, numbed Emma. She remembered this episode in her autobiography as "absurd and grotesque" and wrote: "I felt unutterably weary and possessed only of a desire to get away somewhere and forget the failure of my personal life, to forget even the cruel urge to struggle for an ideal."

Just as the fight for birth control had brought her closer to Ben than any other political issue, now she felt further from him than ever, because of his resolve to have a child of his own. She did not question that he would continue his work with her on tour, but she was crushed by the prospect of their waning relationship.

In the summer, Emma tried to find a month's respite from public life in Provincetown, taking solace in family and friends. She enjoyed the company of her niece, Stella. Yet there, too, the subject of children was very much present: on February 15, 1916, Stella gave birth to a boy, Ian, who was said to resemble Emma's brother who had died as a young child. Emma was reminded of the joys of new life and also of the constant demands a baby placed on a woman. Although she deeply loved her niece, she had often distanced herself through letters expressing her judgments on the mental and physical stagnation that a preoccupation with children breeds, and her strong belief that "the family, the home, even at best they crush the individual, the man, the woman and above all, the child." She contended that "The hardest and most trying life in a large sphere is better than the most sheltered existence in a little bit of a provincial town." Still, Emma felt her spirit replenished and hoped that her month would make her strong enough to counter the blow from Ben.

Emma turned to her old lover Max Baginsky for affirmation of her desirability, and to the Provincetown community of theater people and intellectuals, writers, and political activists for validation of her importance. All the while, Sasha was bombarding her with letters and telegrams asking her to end her vacation and go to work for the people accused of the Preparedness Day bombing. They needed money for lawyers, and people to help dispel the prejudice against them—how could Emma continue to relax when their lives were in danger? Sasha played on Emma's susceptibility to guilt as well as her sense of duty to the cause. Undecided, and resenting the intrusion on her hard-earned rest, Emma had made up her mind to stay when word reached her that one of the defendants had been convicted and sentenced to prison for life. She immediately cut her vacation short, set aside her disappointment with Ben, and joined the struggle against war fever by organizing a new tour with Ben.

Emma planned to travel between New York and Chicago for the next three months, lecturing on war preparedness and birth control. Although Emma considered birth control nowhere near as hot an issue as the madness of war, the authorities did not agree. Because she and Ben were anarchists, and because they dealt directly with issues of sexual oppression, they were vulnerable to the new wave of opposition facing birth-control supporters.

In Cleveland, Emma had long benefited from the influence of the liberal mayor, Tom Johnson. She was shocked, therefore, to see that when Ben (who was trying to show extra gusto for the work, to prove to Emma that his new affair did not imply that he had left the ranks) asked for volunteers to distribute birth-control pamphlets and several people from the audience responded, only Ben was arrested and held for trial. One hundred people followed him to jail, which encouraged a united effort by a local birth-control organization and the Free Speech League to fight Ben's case. Ben was released on $1,000 bail and his court date set for the following month.

In Rochester, Ben was arrested for selling a copy of Dr. William Robinson's *Family Limitation* and Margaret Sanger's *What Every Woman Should Know* at one of Emma's meetings—pamphlets that were already available in New York bookstores and through the mails. Then he was confronted at the police station with a trumped-up charge that he had placed inside Dr. Robinson's book a pamphlet containing explicit information on contraceptives. Ben was outraged, insisting that such deviousness would violate the principles of an anarchist propagandist.

Emma worked hard to show that Ben would not have stooped to such a ruse. But both Emma and Ben were weary, and feeling the strain of their changed relationship. They no longer were invincible warriors inspired by love.

Emma had been arrested again in October in New York for lecturing on birth control, along with other notables of the birth-control movement, and then released on $1,000 bail. Margaret Sanger was also arrested in the same month, for giving birth-control information at the Sanger Clinic to a detective posing as a poor woman with four children.

The rift grew between the Reitman-and-Goldman-led forces of the birth-control movement and the Sanger-led group. Although in the broadest sense they still cooperated, each side conspicuously left the other out of major articles and speeches. Emma was clearly hurt by what she claimed was Sanger's shortsightedness:

> It is tragic but yet true that she is not big enough to give credit to those who have paved the way for her. Then, too, she is evidently trying to interest people of means, so of course it will not do to mention the name of Emma Goldman. It is pitiful to be so small, but who cares? Each one of us must stand on his own merits, after all, only she is really hurting herself much more than she can possibly injure us.

When Margaret Sanger officially split with the more traditional working-class and socialist left, *The Masses* published a tribute to Emma Goldman as the woman who had done the most in the country to champion the cause of birth control.

Ben was in New York, testifying for Emma at her birth-control trial, when his own trial date came up in Cleveland, although he had thought that he had adequately arranged a postponement. Within a few days he was notified that he was in contempt of court and his bond had been forfeited, charges that it took several days to have dropped. When Ben came before a jury, the prosecutor denounced him as "an Anarchist, who comes to our fair city to defy our laws. . . . If you will let him break the law on birth control, our property and our wives and daughters will not be safe . . . [from the] dirty, filthy, stinking birth control literature." Ben was never given a chance to explain either the meaning of his birth-control literature, or his views on anarchism. The jury deliberated from 11:00 A.M. to midnight. Ben hoped that they were busy copying down the information in his birth-control pamphlet, but the verdict they entered was "guilty." Ben told the judge that "no matter what he or any jury should say, the birth control propaganda would go on, and that as long as there are laws which interfere with people acquiring knowledge or living a free harmonious life, I and others would defy such laws and take the consequences." He was "given the limit of the law, six months workhouse, $1,000 fines and costs. This would mean over 5 years imprisonment, as Cleveland allows only 60 cts. a day working out a fine. Several hours later some Italian comrades went my bail."

Ben was released on $2,500 bail pending an appeal. The Cleveland trial ended just in time for Ben to go to Rochester to face that trial.

In Rochester, Ben received a more humane response to his work. In fact, the judge saw the absurdity of his arrest for the distribution of literature that was readily available in bookstores and through the mails. Admitting that he had given out birth-control pamphlets in the past, Ben argued that a law forbidding the distribution of such information was unjust, and again promised to break it whenever he could. However, he testified that he had not known of the birth-control pamphlet planted in Dr. Robinson's book. "The jury was out long enough to smoke a cigarette and returned a verdict of not guilty which was received with wild cheering from the court room," Ben later wrote in his memoirs.

According to Emma, Ben came back from his case "a little paler than he left, but the same old gay and optimistic Ben," although he dreaded the possibility of a long prison sentence. He and Emma continued to work furiously to raise legal funds for their trials, and popular opposition to their impending jail sentences, as the new year began.

By the spring of 1917, Emma had a new mass struggle on which to focus: this time, against conscription. She was already contemplating a tour, despite the "blood and iron militarism" that had swept the country; it was no coincidence that Ben was busy trying to have a child with Anna.

10

"1917—
EXCRUCIATING EVEN
NOW TO WRITE
ABOUT IT"

Nineteen-seventeen was the most important year of Emma's American life—"excruciating even now to write about it," she described it in 1930, when she was at work on her autobiography. It was a year in which "everything [was] so uncertain." Besides shifting her focus from birth control to opposing conscription, Emma was torn between her desire to join the Russian revolutionaries and rebuild her mother country, and her commitment to stay in America and fight the mounting repression and intolerance of any deviation from the norm in all areas of life that accompanied America's entry into World War I. That she even considered leaving the country, given the risk of being denied re-entry, was perhaps a sign that she felt her work with Ben in America had little future.

Emma decided to stay and fight, partly because she perceived an urgent need to oppose war fever in the United States, and partly because many of the people who attempted to return to Russia were being detained in England anyway: the allies, including Russia, did not want revolutionists opposed to war to enter Russia. And, too, Emma felt some duty to support Ben, who was facing yet another trial in May. She vowed that if Ben was to be jailed for his Cleveland birth-control conviction, she would not tour.

Ben himself was still committed to the principles to which he had devoted all those years of his life with Emma. An article he wrote for *Mother Earth*, "Why You Shouldn't Go to War—Refuse to Kill or Be Killed," opposed the war so explicitly and dramatically that many people thought Emma had written it, though Emma herself thought it lacked tact and literary polish.

Yet when Ben's case was postponed until October, he decided he needed peace of mind. Rather than continuing his work with Emma at the *Mother Earth* office, or even supporting her long enough to make another tour, he planned to leave New York, perhaps even to take his mother to California.

Without Ben, Emma could not bear to make another tour. In June she threw herself into organizing a No-Conscription League in New York, so successfully that only two weeks after the No-Conscription League was started, eight thousand people pledged their determination not to register. Emma, inspired by a degree of receptiveness she had not encountered in years, spoke to the crowds "as if possessed by divine fire."

Excited to be part of a mass movement once again, Emma was also pleased that for the first time in years she and Berkman were working together in the same city. Sasha's work in organizing an Anti-Militarist League in San Francisco had made him an easy target for the government, which looked for any excuse to implicate as many anarchists as possible along with him in the San Francisco bombing. When *The Blast*'s office was raided, Sasha and Fitzi felt they had to come back to New York to continue their work.

Ben was to join Emma for the early anti-conscription meetings, but, as described in his autobiography:

In 1916 and '17, it was an extremely dangerous thing for a man to be an Anarchist and anti-militarist, an active I.W.W., or to be associated with the Anarchist group. I have stated before, and I want to emphasize, that it was evident to all of us of the *Mother Earth* group that the jail and maybe the gallows were before us. Many of the Anarchists and Radicals took to cover. Some found safety in joining the Army, others in getting married, others in going to Mexico, and still others by changing their names and their nationalities. Not so with Emma and Berkman. They became more revolutionary, more violent, and less compromising.

Ben was sure that if he had felt as certain about the war as he had about birth control and free speech, he would have faced all the consequences that Sasha and Emma faced. But, although he had been active in the early anti-conscription campaign, by the end of the war he had changed his mind: "if my brother, my fellow citizen, was willing to fight and die for [his] country, whether wars be right or whether wars be wrong, whether it does good or does harm to be a soldier, my place is with my fellow man." Ben even tried to enlist in the medical corps, but was refused because of his anarchist past. He believed that his temperament needed more excitement than constant propaganda work could provide:

The Anarchist movement had become monotonous to me. For ten years I had been in on the big parade. When the scenes were shifting in the early part of my Anarchist experience I was always in action. As time went on I gradually worked my way into the grind of propaganda, which was deadening for such a temperament as mine. . . . While I had worked hard with excitement for breakfast, police for dinner and riot for supper, I was taking part in a different way. I was becoming a drudge in the battle. . . .

I began to dream of a home with my mother, my wife and baby and a steady practice. I had visions of myself teaching in a medical college, of being a reformer to the outcasts and an active worker in the church. All this added to my growing unhappiness with the Anarchist movement in 1916 and 1917.

While Emma's work was becoming more intense, involving greater risks, Ben was heading toward a safer and more predictable life. The distance between them was increased by the growing national emphasis on the danger of "foreign infiltration," which made Emma more, and Ben less, vulnerable.

By the time June 5, 1917, registration day for the army, arrived, thousands of resisters throughout the country were organized against the draft. Headlines—SHOTS FIRED IN BUTTE, ANTIWAR DEMONSTRATIONS BROKEN UP BY TROOPS, TROOPS CALLED OUT TO HANDLE DRAFT RIOT-ERS—ran above stories from Springfield, Massachusetts, to Centerville, Iowa, to Red Lodge, Montana, on June 6 and 7, 1917. The U.S. Post Office hoped to suppress *Mother Earth*'s special June 5 issue "In Memoriam: American Democracy" for its inflammatory statements against the induction of youth into the army, but twenty thousand copies were distributed anyway. Some newspapers even published Emma's no-conscription manifesto, which began, "On June 5th the Moloch militarism will sit in pompous state awaiting its victims who are to be dedicated to its gluttonous appetite."

For the previous month Emma had been speaking openly against what she called "the political clap-trap" and urged workers to follow the leadership of the victorious Russian revolutionaries who had overthrown the Czar in February 1917. Emma estimated that at her most recent meeting there had been five thousand people inside and thirty thousand outside on the street. Yet even the newspaper headlines noted that there were no arrests; the police were just taking notes. As the newspaper reports indicate, Emma was careful to avoid arrest:

> "Are you advising men of the ages affected by the draft act not to register" she was asked. "No, we are not doing that. What we are doing is to make the issue plain to them and then leave it to them to act on their own initiative. But we will stand behind all who refuse to register and will see to it that they get all legal protection and that their rights in this matter are maintained."

An article describing a mass meeting on registration day, packed with government stenographers and a hundred policemen, pointed out that all the major speakers avoided any references to registration: "Then came Emma Goldman. Even the Government officials present had an idea she would say something about conscription. Instead she told of her girlhood in Russia and how she has hated militarism ever since she was 9 years old. . . . She ended as did others by denouncing militarism."

But the government was set on arresting Emma, and at a draft protest meeting organized under the auspices of the Collegiate League for Peace and Harmony by a Columbia University student, thirty young men were arrested for not having their registration cards. Emma commented that this was like old Russia. Marshall said in a fury, "I will arrest this Goldman woman, if she organizes more such meetings." Emma had been in her glory at that meeting: "Her face looked like a prize red poppy at a flower show. She denounced everything in sight. . . . The state is taking a census, she added, to draft men into the militia to shoot down labouring men."

Emma was experiencing the consequences of the transition away from a relatively liberal social and political atmosphere as the United States prepared to enter World War I. Government repression grew and most of the available surveillance methods were tried first on the anarchists and labor organizers. The birth-control arrests were merely a preview of what was to come. Detectives from intelligence units of the Military and the Justice departments came with a group of stenographers to document Emma's talks, collecting material that might be used against her at the appropriate moment.

On the day of an anti-conscription meeting planned for Forwarts Hall in Manhattan, Emma received a call warning of a plot to kill her. Although she joked about living to "a disgusting old age," she made out a will before going to the meeting. When she arrived at the street where the meeting was to be held, hordes of people were being kept back by what seemed to be the entire New York Police Department. Inside, the hall was mobbed, and the level of surveillance made it seem like a prison. Although the meeting was a success in terms of attendance, the arrests of hundreds of draft resisters afterward convinced Emma that in the future she must rely on the printed word. She would not allow her meetings to serve as the occasion for the entrapment and arrest of prospective war resisters.

Late the next afternoon, June 15, 1917, as Emma was preparing circulars in the *Mother Earth* office and Fitzi and Sasha were upstairs working in the relocated office of *The Blast*, U.S. Marshal Thomas McCarthy himself came up the stairs, accompanied by twelve other officers to fend off any protest, and announced that both Goldman and Berkman were under arrest. What he held, instead of an official warrant, was a copy of the June issue of *Mother Earth*, which he claimed had enough treasonable matter in it to land Emma and Sasha in jail for years. Before leaving, Emma quickly changed into a "royal purple dress" and grabbed a small toilet case and a copy of James Joyce's *Portrait of the Artist as a Young Man*. Harry Weinberger, Emma and Sasha's lawyer, asked for an immediate arraignment and release on bail, but the arrest, it turned out, had been made in the afternoon to assure that they would have to spend the night in prison.

The next day formal charges were made—"conspiracy against the draft"—and bail was set at $25,000 each. While they were incommunicado in jail for several days, the New York branch of the Justice Department and the police ransacked the *Mother Earth* office, seizing letters, mailing lists, checkbooks, and manuscripts; this was part of a program of raids being conducted on radical offices throughout the country at that time. Still, Emma retained her optimism. From prison, she wrote to Agnes Inglis, a friend from Ann Arbor who had offered to mortgage her house for Emma:

> You see, dear, the upholders of law have never learned that our Ideal can never be suppressed nor can truth ever be silenced. Thus our voices from prison will call louder than those on the outside. . . . About B . . . It was a terrible wrench to me. But I have always held that each must be free to go his way no matter how painful to the other. Only there is no justification in his going when he was needed.

The "terrible wrench" was that Ben had returned to Chicago to be with the now pregnant Anna. Though she remained strong in her public stance, Emma felt aggrieved and humiliated because he had not rushed to her side in her moment of need. With the hostility of the U.S.

government directed against her, Ben's absence was devastating—she felt as profoundly abandoned as she had ever felt in her life. The child Ben and Anna were expecting made the separation even more final.

Emma and Sasha decided to stand trial without an attorney, as a symbol of their defiance of the law and its machinery. At first, they thought that they would be most effective by refusing to speak at the trial at all. Then, with the advice of friends and comrades (including John Reed, Frank Harris, Max Eastman, and Gilbert Roe), they decided that speaking out against conscription would be more dramatic and less likely to be misinterpreted.

On Emma's forty-eighth birthday, she was greeted in court with flowers and gifts. Her lawyer, Harry Weinberger, requested a postponement, which was immediately denied. The next three days were devoted to jury selection. She and Sasha began by quizzing the prospective jurors—but none met their standards of openness on social, political, or religious matters.

The prosecution opened the trial on July 2 by supporting the charge that Emma and Sasha had conspired to obstruct the draft by claiming that Emma advocated violence at the anti-conscription meeting at the Harlem River Casino on May 18. The prosecution also asserted that Alexander Berkman had advised people not to register for the draft; and it insinuated that Emma and Sasha were agents of the German government.

Later, when Emma took the stand, she described their arrest and was quick to note that it was improbable that the police would enter the office of a Morgan or a Rockefeller without a search warrant, as they had done with the offices of *Mother Earth*, *The Blast*, and the No-Conscription League. Emma identified herself as a social student, whose business in life was to diagnose social wrongs. She and Sasha disproved the prosecutor's claim that they had directly advised people not to register for the draft and that the large sum of money in their bank account had come from Germany. (It was a donation to their work from James Hallbeck, an aging Swedish grape grower in California.) Most important, Emma insisted that the government stenographer had not done his job very well; she had never said, "We believe in Violence, we will use Violence," although those words had once appeared in the pages of *Mother Earth*. Instead, she defended the path of the conscientious objectors, reminding the jurors of the historical roots of their civil liberties: "Whatever liberties you have, those who established the constitutional right of free speech . . . were not within the law . . . they were the Anarchists of their time."

Testimony was heard from their influential associates (among whom were John Reed and Lincoln Steffens), who asserted that neither Emma nor Sasha were violent anarchists. Emma and Sasha took the stand to speak for over an hour each on true Americanism and how conscription violated the best of its principles. Emma even read from the Declaration of Independence, although the two anarchists had remained seated during the Star-Spangled Banner. Sasha was less composed than Emma, often yelling at the judge for interrupting him. During recesses from the trial, Emma and Sasha lunched with Margaret Anderson and Harriet Dean and jabbered optimistically about their ability to persuade the jury of the value of their work.

The prosecutor claimed that the well-bred lady the jury saw in the courtroom was not the real Emma Goldman. "The real Emma Goldman can be seen only on the platform. There she is in her true element, sweeping all caution to the winds! There she inflames the young and drives them to violent deeds. If you could see Emma Goldman at her meetings, you would realize that she is a menace to our well-ordered institutions."

The judge, after lamenting that they did not use their powers of persuasion in behalf of the government instead of against it, admonished the jury that "whether you think these people are wrong or right has nothing to do with the verdict." On July 9, 1917, the verdict of guilty was announced, after only thirty-nine minutes of deliberation. The judge denied the defendants' request for a two-day stay before they had to begin serving their time in jail. Declaring that Emma Goldman was probably "the greatest woman of her time," he proceeded to impose the maximum penalty for conspiracy against the draft—two years' imprisonment and a $10,000 fine. Emma and Sasha, however, would not go down without an eloquent fight. They stood up in anger to condemn the judge for his harsh decision, for treating them as if they were the most "heinous of criminals."

That night, Emma was forced to sleep in the same room as the male deputy. The next day, she was sent to Jefferson City's Missouri State Prison, while Sasha was sent to Atlanta. Once in prison, Emma pitied Fitzi and Ben, who were outside but isolated. She and Sasha could be comfortable in the "exalted sense of having been absolutely true to [their] Ideal. . . . All else is immaterial."

Ironically, Emma's job in prison was once again needlework:

> Friedrich Nietzsche was right when he spoke of life as the eternal recurrence. Life indeed is nothing else. Thirty-two years ago, when I came to America with exultation in my heart about liberty and opportunity, I was given a taste of both in a large clothing factory, making coats ten hours a day at $2.50 per week. In Jefferson Prison, the very morning after a suffocating journey, I tasted the blessings of democracy making coats, with this difference: my lucrative wage of thirty-two years ago was reduced to three meals a day and a cell. Progress moves imperceptibly indeed.

Fitzi worked with a much-reduced staff to produce the July issue of *Mother Earth*, which included transcripts and analyses of Emma's and Sasha's speeches and trial proceedings, as well as an article entitled "How One Young Man Met the Challenge of Conscription." But when they mailed it, the *Mother Earth* staff received a card advising them that the issue was being held up by the Post Office pending a decision from Washington. The August 1917 issue of the socialist periodical, *The Masses*, which contained "A Tribute" to Emma and Sasha for "working on our destinies . . . forging the love of nations," was considered so objectionable that it was barred from the mails as well. Ben visited Emma in July; immediately afterward, he wrote a polite but angry letter to the Postmaster in behalf of *Mother Earth*.

A steady erosion of normal civil liberties accompanied the United States' entry into the world war. Prewar progressivism and liberalism collapsed into uncritical support of the war effort. Many people in the Wilson administration, even liberals, were willing to live with the new suspension of constitutional rights on the grounds of national emergency. Emma's mail from prison was transcribed and put on file by the War Department. Even the communications with her lawyer, which should have been protected and confidential, were intercepted and recorded. Harry Weinberger worked day and night within this charged atmosphere to find a Justice of the U.S. Supreme Court who would agree that the convictions should be reviewed.

On July 20, Justice Louis D. Brandeis signed an order directing the release of Berkman and Goldman on bail of $25,000 each, pending decision of their appeal. Two weeks after they had been imprisoned, Emma and Sasha were on their way back to the New York "Tombs," from which they would be released. Bail was raised quickly for Emma, but an unexpected barrier blocked the road to freedom for Sasha. In late July, when Emma was met on her arrival and release in New York by Weinberger, Fitzi, and Stella, she learned that Sasha had been charged with murder by the San Francisco district attorney in connection with the 1916 Preparedness Day bombing.

Rather than raising bail money for Sasha's release, the comrades decided that Sasha was actually safer in the Tombs than on the streets of New York. It was not unusual for a representative of a state seeking to prosecute a person living in another state outside its jurisdiction to kidnap that person and bring him to trial. With the memory of the kidnapping of the McNamara brothers from Indiana to California in 1910, and Haywood, Moyer, and Pettibone's abduction from Colorado to Utah, Weinberger decided to take no legal action to compel Sasha's release as yet. They stalled until September 10 to admit Sasha to bail.

Immediately after he was released on bail by the federal authorities, the New York City police arrested Sasha on the murder charge at the request of the San Francisco district attorney. The state of California requested Sasha's extradition to California to stand trial. New York authorities could hold him without bail no more than thirty days while the San Francisco district attorney pursued the extradition effort. Soon the federal authorities became involved in this transaction because they had their own strong interests in Berkman's legal fate. Among other things, they were concerned that the Supreme Court might reverse the anti-conscription conspiracy convictions and order a retrial. They believed that the extradition could cause problems, whether the Supreme Court eventually affirmed or reversed Berkman's conviction. In the event the conviction was affirmed, the extradition would reduce the effectiveness of his bail to compel him to surrender himself. A reversal would pose a different problem, as U.S. Attorney Caffey explained to San Francisco District Attorney Fickert:

> Another situation might arise which would add to the difficulty if Berkman were removed to California. In the event that the United States Supreme Court should reverse the judgment of conviction and order a retrial, it would probably be the desire of the Federal Government to retry both Berkman and Emma Goldman immediately. The evidence in the federal case is of such a nature that it would be exceedingly embarrassing to be forced to try one defendant on a conspiracy charge without the other defendant being present in court and on trial at the same time.

While vigorously asserting these concerns, Caffey also acknowledged that the federal government did not actually have the authority to resist the extradition. This was conveyed in a coded telegram from U.S. Attorney Caffey to U.S. Attorney General Gregory assigning the humorous aliases "Indistinguishable of Dreamer" to the Governor of California and "Indistinguishable of Overdoer" to the Governor of New York.

No doubt the national uproar protesting Sasha's extradition played some role in the federal government's willingness to exert pressure against the extradition. One hundred labor leaders, representing one million workers, marched into New York Governor Whitman's office to assert that Sasha was not alone. President Wilson, advised of this show of strength, appointed a commission to counsel him on the rights of the federal government to intervene in Sasha's extradition.

As soon as Emma was released, she seized her brief period of freedom to speak out against conscription and to muster opposition to the new charges against Sasha, not yet knowing that the federal government had its own reasons to prevent Sasha's extradition. U.S. Marshal McCarthy was so angry at Emma, and at the fact that she was again giving speeches, that he personally tried to stop each of her speeches in New York. In one instance, Emma appeared on stage with a symbolic gag over her mouth; the audience rolled with laughter. Yet while McCarthy was supervising Emma's visit to Sasha in jail, he claimed that although he was sure Emma hated him, someday she and Sasha would thank him for arresting them before the espionage bill was passed. He said to her, "Now you get only two years, but later you would get twenty. Own up, wasn't I your friend?"

Harry Weinberger had instituted extensive correspondence with Washington's Committee on Public Information, complaining about U.S. Marshal McCarthy's threats and interference with Emma's legal rights to hold meetings on drama and literature and to raise support funds for Sasha and the Mooney case. Weinberger's complaints prompted a confidential warning letter to McCarthy from the U.S. Attorney General. Asked to defend his actions to McCarthy, he admitted that he could not imagine that Emma Goldman could give voice to anything but "seditious utterances," and therefore felt justified in preventing her from speaking. He acknowledged an extraordinary zeal; had the Attorney General's staff not ordered him to wait, he would have arrested Emma and Sasha the day before they were actually arrested. If he erred, he wrote, it was because he believed that a crime had been committed in the seditious utterances given at their meetings. The Attorney General found it necessary to admonish McCarthy against further violations of Emma Goldman's right to free speech: "I now instruct you in writing to refrain from telling speakers at public meetings that they cannot address the crowd, or from saying to the chairmen of such meetings that they must make certain announcements at your dictation, or the meeting will not be allowed to proceed."

There was dissension within the government about both the legality and the advisability, given public opinion, of silencing Emma, and also about Sasha's extradition.

Even Ben was hounded again, this time not for his current activity (he was doing some *Mother Earth* work in hiding in New York, even though he had already launched his new life in Chicago) but for his past connections. The government was trying to locate a man named Jean Crones accused of poisoning the soup at a Chicago banquet given in honor of Archbishop Mundelein, as a protest against religion. They turned to Reitman as a potential informer. Ben had an unusually trusting relationship with his old friend Chicago Police Chief Herman Schuettler, which Captain Evans of the War Department tried to exploit.

Evans pressured Schuettler to arrange a secret meeting with Ben in New York, in order to get him to reveal the whereabouts of Jean Crones. Although Ben claims, in his autobiography, to have turned down Schuettler immediately, feigning ignorance on the matter and asserting that he wanted "to be able to have the respect of Emma Goldman and the comrades [whom he had] worked with for ten years," and that he would "rather go to jail or die than to be a traitor," Schuettler's report indicates Ben partly cooperated with the police. Schuettler claimed that Ben offered to put a personal ad in the IWW paper *Solidarity* to which he thought Crones might respond. After that Captain Evans insisted on meeting with Schuettler and Reitman, this time pushing Ben to go further than he was willing to go—to be a general informant. Ben affirmed his own ideals in a letter to the chief, even declining his and Evans's offer to arrange for the dismissal of his birth-control charges. He was stricken with "deep gloom" at the thought of betraying the people and the cause to which he had given "the ten best years" of his life. He wanted to go back to practicing medicine "with clean hands and a pure heart." Ben believed that his work for birth control was not a crime, but wrote, "If Ohio wants to lock me up, I am ready." He thanked Schuettler for the kindness and humanity he had always shown in his dealings with Ben, and ended his letter with the salutation, "I remain yours for a better World."

In this atmosphere of repression, Ben continued to work with Emma, though with half a heart. She was trying to do as much political work as possible, in anticipation of a two-year jail sentence. Even her letters could not be sent directly to her friends and comrades because of the heavy postal surveillance. Instead she arranged for "mail drops" —other people would receive and transfer letters to the proper correspondents.

With Ben's help on occasion, Emma worked to build support against Sasha's threatened extradition, which by that time was a popular cause on the left—even in Russia there was a Berkman solidarity demonstration. In fact, the sailors of Kronstadt called for the arrest of David Rowland Francis, the U.S. Ambassador in Russia, who was to be held as hostage until the San Francisco defendants and Sasha were freed. By November, unrest was sufficient throughout the country to pressure San Francisco District Attorney Charles Fickert to withdraw his extradition demand. Sasha was released by a writ of habeas corpus on November 14, 1917. He and Emma redoubled their efforts with a new sense of urgency; the Espionage Act had just passed, and speaking out against the war and conscription became still more dangerous.

In December 1917, even the underground *Mother Earth Bulletin*—which Fitzi, Ben, and Stella had initiated when most of the staff were scattered or in prison; all its funds had been funneled into legal fees—and *Mother Earth* itself, officially defunct, were suppressed under the Espionage Act, along with a long list of other periodicals, including Margaret Anderson's *Little Review*. "This circular letter of ill-smelling Mother Earth people should not be given freedom of the mails," was the Post Office communiqué to the Superintendent of Second Class Matter.

The December 1917 *Mother Earth Bulletin* was barred from the mails because of its report on the mysterious hanging of thirteen "Negro soldiers" on an army base in Texas. The article deplored the public silence about the case: "Not a word has been said about the trial, the evidence—not a line, until 13 bodies were stiff in death and dangling at the end of a rope, 41 others—in prison for life. . . . First time since the Mexican War of 1848 that such a thing has been possible under the cover of journalistic silence. Not even the terrible Civil War produced such horror. . . ."

Military Intelligence was naturally sensitive to such bad press and accusations of racism. It was widely thought by the military intelligence division of the War Department that any opposition within the military was the result of the subversive efforts of radicals intent on disrupting the army from the inside. There was even supposed to have been a quiet campaign among the IWW "to destroy everything that was to be shipped to foreign countries to carry on this war." Military intelligence claimed that Emma herself was "secretly sending in three or four wrappers [of] seditious newspapers to military camps and garrisons for the purpose of arousing the soldiers against the Government." And according to an agent who infiltrated Emma's group, Emma said that Roger Baldwin had "the best known system of anti-draft organization . . . quietly and safely [enrolling] 10,000 young men throughout the country who are being educated by his agents."

It was also thought that there was a sympathetic leak in the government ranks letting Emma know of raids before they happened, so that she could safeguard her papers and lists of contacts. But by far the most dramatic and wildly improbable aspect of the intelligence reports on Emma's activity during this period was the claim that she was complicitous in organizing "a committee of five, in all important cities, to act at a given hour by killing the President, District Attorneys and prominent State Officials. . . . This organization is called the Guillotine." Although the highest level of army intelligence doubted whether any acts of violence would be attempted, at least not until the end of the trial of the IWW in Chicago at the end of August 1918, such rumors exemplified the government's growing fear of Emma, and its desperate efforts to prove that she must be taken out of circulation in the interest of national security. Given the information gathered by Military Intelligence, the recommendation to arrest and confine Emma for the duration of the war went directly to the chief of staff.

The extraordinary levels of surveillance used against her are illustrated by one agent's report on his attendance at a dance performance by Isadora Duncan, who he said was reputed to be a close friend of Emma Goldman. He described Duncan dancing to the "Marseillaise" in a red costume. By this time almost every known friend of Emma and Ben's had a file and was under suspicion. Officials within the government were not above suspicion as the Military Intelligence staff of the War Department looked for ties between the anarchists and those high in government, who might have influenced President Wilson to ask New York's Governor Whitman to postpone Berkman's extradition.

Intelligence reports on Ben had taken quite a different turn. An agent had infiltrated an "anarchist intellectual organization of radical elements" called the Dill Pickle Club in Chicago. It was an extraordinary organization that invited everyone from hobo poets to bohemian intellectuals to speak, with an open forum that was progressive and avant-garde. On its Tooker Alley door read the motto: "Step high, stoop low, leave your dignity behind." The agent reported:

Ben Reitman now acts as chairman of our meetings. Ben is very mild these days. He is now living at 25 East Walton Place with [Anna] Martindale. I am not sure whether they are legally married or not. I had tea with them Sunday night and was splendidly treated. Reitman has opened an office in the Bush Temple for the practice of medicine, his profession. He evidently intends to settle down and be a good citizen.

Among other conservative influences in Ben's life were the effects of a letter Sasha had sent to him calling him "an ostrich" and declining both his offer to help with the San Francisco case and even his sympathy for Sasha's situation. Sasha wrote to Ben, "there is something in your view of things that I strongly resent." Sasha had "no use for any sickly sentimentality," nor did he wish to be taken as "a fool." Ben thought he was comforting Sasha with the assurance that everything would work out, that Mooney would not be hanged, but Sasha distinguished between an optimist, who could "face facts" and "keep up his courage, in spite of the blackest truth," and an ostrich, who "fools himself by hiding his head in the bushes, and pretending not to see things." He predicted that Mooney would be hanged, that he himself would be sentenced to death, and that Billings and Weinberg would get life sentences, as tactics to "terrorize the unions and paralyze their power" in the strong union city of San Francisco. A real revolutionist, he claimed, expects such things and has no reason "for tears or whining." "Anyone who is not willing to take the consequences of being a revolutionist should get out of the danger zone—the movement." "In fighting every inch," even if some "have to pay with their lives," is "the hope of enlightening the people."

Ben smarted at being treated as a political fool. When *Mother Earth* was suppressed, he was among supporters of the *Mother Earth Bulletin*, but warned that "it was reckless to defy the war sentiment of the country." He felt they should not include material on the war because "they could not afford to get in trouble."

Although Ben's initial enthusiasm for the *Bulletin* was what gave it life, he and Emma had drifted too far apart, politically and personally. In her autobiography, Emma wrote: "Our strained relations could not last. One day the storm burst, and Ben left. For good. Listless and dry-eyed, I sank into a chair. Fitzi was near me, soothingly stroking my head."

Emma sadly continued her work without Ben, and, uncharacteristically, scarcely wrote a letter to anyone. She and Ben had been intermittent lovers up until the end, but his attention had ceased to be focused on her. Under the circumstances, it was easier in some ways to be apart.

Just before Emma's appeal was heard by the Supreme Court, she made a whirlwind tour, taking up the issue of the Russian Revolution with the mission of developing public sympathy for the Bolsheviks, who took power in October 1917. Thus Emma again latched on to something distant, which partook of a grander vision, to save her (and not incidentally humankind) from the bleakness of the reality in which she found herself.

Defying the sentence that awaited them, she and Sasha staged a family New Year's party for forty or fifty people, which Emma called the "big blow out of the year. . . . Life was alluring and every hour of freedom precious. Atlanta and Jefferson [prisons] were far away." Emma sent out New Year's cards that expressed her sense of the links between personal and political life in frightening times: "Wishes for any personal joy in the world's madness seem [so] commonplace that I can't gather up the courage to wish such things for the New Year, except that the world may come to its senses. I know that will bring us all joy."

11

THE LAST PAGE OF A STORMY CHAPTER— 1918–1919

Only a few days into the new year, while Emma was on tour in the Midwest hailing the accomplishments of her most recent inspiration, the Bolsheviks, the Supreme Court rejected the Berkman-Goldman appeal. Sasha and Emma had appealed the conspiracy convictions for their anti-conscription work with a challenge to the constitutionality of the Draft Law. When the Draft Law was upheld as constitutional, their appeal failed. Facing incarceration on February 5, Emma spent her last month of freedom with friends and in the organization of the Political Prisoners' Amnesty League. Before returning to jail, she was able to put the finishing touches on a pamphlet she had been writing called *The Truth About the Bolsheviki*, her way of affirming that even though the political situation in the United States was so dismal, there was still hope in Russia. She asked that her friends "take care of my love child, the *Mother Earth Bulletin*. . . . I know that you will look after her tenderly, so that I may find her bigger, stronger and more worth while when I return from

Jefferson." Then Emma and Sasha surrendered themselves to begin serving their two-year sentences. They were taken under maximum security back to Jefferson City and Atlanta. Even as Emma felt the prison doors closing on an epoch of relative political freedom, she consoled herself with the thought that perhaps the solid barriers of a jail cell could protect her from any lingering yearnings for Ben.

Ben had joined Emma briefly in New York and witnessed her final sentencing; on his trip home, he felt especially solemn.

Joy and sorrow mingled as I reflected [on] the past and contemplated the future.

Emma Goldman was in jail in Jefferson City. Lioness was in New York trying to hold together the tattered and scattered ends of the Anarchist, Anti-Militarist and Birth Control propaganda. America was in the throes of a terrible war. . . .

Mother, a loving wife, a devoted brother, and a big automobile met me and drove us to my first real home in Chicago.

So absorbed was Ben in setting up his medical practice in Chicago and establishing a home before the birth of his child that he did not take the time to visit Emma in prison soon enough to please her. Yet, despite his new life, he could not let go of his old stance in his letters as her lover-manager. For Emma, the weeks away from Ben seemed like months. Her loyal old friend Benny Capes, the St. Louis anarchist, affectionately called "Little Ben," visited her religiously. But as she wrote later in her autobiography, his visits served only to increase her disappointment with "Big Ben."

The grief he had caused me, especially in the course of the last two years of our life, undermined my faith in him and filled my cup with bitterness. I had determined after his last departure from New York to break the bond that had chained me so long. Two years in prison would, I hoped, help me do it. But Ben kept on writing as if nothing had happened. His letters, breathing the old assurance of his love, were like coals of fire. I could not believe him any more, yet I wanted to believe. I refused his plea to permit him to visit me. I even intended to ask him to stop writing, but he himself was facing a prison sentence, incurred during the period of our association, and that still linked him to me. His approaching fatherhood added fuel to my emotional stress. His minute description of the feelings engendered in him, and his delight in the little garments prepared for the expected child, afforded me a glimpse into an unsuspected aspect of Ben's character. Whether it was the defeat of my own motherhood or the pain that another should have given Ben what I would not, his rhapsodies increased my resentment against him and everyone connected with him.

Finally, after a few weeks, Ben made a solemn visit to see Emma:

It was strange to see my little blue-eyed "Mommy" in prison garb, with the pain of compulsory confinement and forced labor written upon her face. We could not say the things we felt; hostile eyes were upon us. Emma and I were conscious of my "desertion of her and the cause." It was a painful visit. I had a cheap way of comforting myself. I was able to buy her a few dollars' worth of food.

There was no message that I could give her and none that I could take. I stood like a traitor before his confessor but could not confess. As I looked into her face I saw none of the reproach I felt for myself. As they led her back to her toil I was heartbroken. I felt that if I had done my duty I should have been in jail with her. But I turned in to another path. I had been seduced by the ordinary man's desire for a home, a wife and a child.

When Ben's child was born, he named him Brutus. As Brutus had betrayed Caesar, Ben felt that he had betrayed Emma by choosing marriage and family over the cause. From an anarchist point of view, the historical Brutus represented a man who was not in thrall to a world ruled exclusively by considerations of state power. News of Brutus's birth coincided with the Ohio Appellate Court's decision to affirm Ben's conviction. Within the month, he was forced to leave his child, close his medical practice, and return to prison, to serve six months in the workhouse.

Ben wrote to his newborn son from prison. Wanting his son to know he was welcome even though his father firmly believed in birth control, Ben wrote in elegiac tones, as if from beyond the grave:

> My boy, I am glad you are on earth. I wanted you, your Mother and I hoped and planned for you—you are *welcome*. . . . Your Father loved life and lived life. I hope you will see and enjoy as much of the world as I did. I hope you will love men and women and have as much joy from loving as I did, and even more. . . . Your Father loved people and wanted them to be happy, well and free, and he did his best with the light he had to build a world where you and all children would not have to see misery, poverty, tyranny, wars and ignorance. . . .
>
> Little Ben, . . . I hope you will . . . especially love poor people, the tramps, the criminals and the outcasts—men whom your Father devoted most of his life to.
>
> Oh, my boy, I am glad I have you. May you comfort your Mother as you do me, and may you serve humanity and live a big, rich free unselfish life is your Father's prayer.
>
> Lovingly your Father,
Ben L. Reitman

In jail, the new father felt forsaken by his anarchist friends. Why had they failed to raise enough money to free him, as he had done for so many others? When Emma heard of Ben's situation, she once again reached out to him in sympathy, inquiring after him in a letter to Agnes Inglis: "How about Ben. I am very anxious to make sure what his status is. . . . Please tell him he need never fear I will forsake him. Please see him, you will relieve my mind very much."

Emma wrote to her niece, Stella, asking her, too, to look after Ben and to visit him, Anna, and the baby. Emma wrote frankly to Stella about her feelings for Ben, without the somewhat exaggerated neediness in her letters to Agnes Inglis, which generally had the dual purpose of affirming their continued friendship and requesting monetary support for her work.

> I suppose you think I am sentimental about Ben's fine. Darling, it is not that at all. It is merely wanting to get through with the last of a stormy chapter. Ben's in prison in connection with my work, hence the responsibility is mine. Once he is free and in the folds of his family, the page of reading will be done. . . . I guess you and most of my dear ones think that I was blind to the real BR. I wish I had been; that would have saved me much pain. But *I saw*, dear, and yet the pain was not because of what I saw. . . . No one can hurt you quite so much as you can hurt yourself. But, then, who would avoid hurting oneself through a rich and intense experience?

Stella complied with Emma's request and visited Ben, then wrote to Sasha, with some disgust, "All his interest centered around himself and his mother—hardly a word of inquiry about our dear girl, except the most perfunctory." The unknowing Emma meanwhile decided that upon her release from prison, she would visit Ben and his new family. Even if the visit would be painful, she needed to see him in his new life:

> . . . why fear pain? Are we not made or unmade by our capacity for pain? We come from a race that has known nothing but pain, yet it has survived. So I too will survive. I hope I shall come out with a deeper understanding and greater sympathy for B. I certainly never want to feel bitter or indifferent. After all, ten years of a common struggle are not to be thrust out of one's life. My desire to stop off in Chicago, if I do at all, is mainly due to the uncertainty of my life after I come out. Should the inevitable [deportation] happen, I would feel most miserable to go away without seeing B. once more.

Letters full of reflections about Ben indicated how much of Emma's time in prison was spent mulling over the past. Her discomfort, however, was not exclusively emotional. The long hours of garment work had given her a chronic neck pain, exacerbated by prison conditions: "Nothing new about myself. Some days, I feel comparatively free from pain, other days it is excruciating. But one must meet every emergency. Fortunately there is the Eve[ning] and Saturday and Sunday, when I forget the shop and live in my books, in the memories of the past, and the hope for the future."

Emma's release from prison, however, was not imminent. She could not go on living in the past, yet she was unable to resign herself to the starkness of prison, with its total absence of sensuous comforts. Eugene O'Neill sent her a volume of his plays. Emma asked her friends for food and for stockings and nightgowns, requests they evidently found amusing. "I can see you smile at my request for so many feminine things," Emma responded. "But, then, I always was more feminine than is good for a dyed-in-the-blood revolutionist."

In prison, because the issue of birth control for which he had fought was less controversial than the national issue of conscription, which Emma had taken on, Ben was treated less harshly than Emma. A Chicago alderman and some newspaperman investigating penal institutions in America visited the Warrensville House of Correction and requested that Ben be treated well. He was even allowed to have dinner with Anna and Brutus in the prison garden. As a doctor, he was permitted to make medical visits to the city tuberculosis hospital near City Hall to practice his medical specialty—the treatment of syphilis.

Some of the guards and a Catholic priest objected to Ben's privileges and led a successful campaign to rescind them, but Ben did not go back to the life of an ordinary prisoner. He was, in his own words, put in charge of helping "dope fiends" in the prison "kick the habit." Ben not only treated them, but also helped break the drug rings that had developed within the jail.

Although Ben was glad to do useful work during his time in prison, and considered that he had to some extent proved himself to Emma while she also was behind bars, this did not stop him from asking her for money to pay his fine, so that he would not have to stay in jail longer than six months. When the money was partially raised, a judge lowered Ben's fine by half because of Ben's good behavior and mounting public pressure for his release. Emma continued her work without realizing that it was now unnecessary, since Ben never told her; instead he wrote her a long letter about his son, his mother, and his wife. When she found out, Emma was furious. Ben wanted her to come see him eventually, after her own release, but she had a hard time even bringing herself to write to him once he was out of jail: on top of his dishonest omission of information about his reduced fine, he had committed the fatal error of withholding his gratitude. Her chronic disappointment in him dragged her back into what she called her "emotional bondage to Ben" at a time when she had hoped her work would free her from him.

After Ben left prison, he re-established his medical practice and settled into family life. In his letters he boasted to Emma about his new accomplishments—working for the Health Department, in a clinic, and for the Hobo College—and urged her to let him visit her in prison. But it took some complaints on his part about newly developed stomach trouble to arouse Emma's sympathies enough for her to answer his letter, and in that reply Emma distanced herself further from Ben by asserting that he had never been a revolutionary, but merely a reformer: "You are by nature a reformer, Ben dear. Your revolutionary period was like a fever, it lasted for ten years, and, like some fevers, it seems to have left a void. So I am not surprised that you went back to where you left off ten years ago—reform. But for goodness' sakes—don't do it with such a force as a moral squad, it would be really ridiculous." She went on to say that his visit could do nothing to help her in prison. She had to get her "sustenance from the Outside World, the heroic struggle of the Bolsheviki against organized stupidity and brutality." Besides, Ben's praise for his wife and motherhood in general struck Emma as being overblown. Anna was merely a mother who loved her son. "So what?" wrote Emma.

Emma's disappointment was not only with Ben: already there were strong indications that her idealized Bolsheviks had not lived up to their promise, either. Catherine Breshkovskaya, known as the grandmother of the Russian Revolution, whose "fifty years of anarchist revolutionary work had paved the way for the October upheaval," had taken a bitter stand against Emma's new great hope—the Bolshevik Revolution. Because it seemed to Emma that Breshkovskaya's criticism played into the hands of both the United States government and White Russia, she smuggled letters out of prison through Stella, pleading with "Babushka" to rethink her position and the effect it would have on a country already hostile to the Russian dream.

In the meantime, Emma shifted her attention to younger rebels in the United States, like Mollie Steimer, the young, uncompromising anarchist companion of the photographer Senya Fleshine, who had done layouts for *Mother Earth*. Mollie had been arrested for distributing leaflets protesting U.S. intervention in Russia.

Repression in the United States had taken on unprecedented dimensions. The invocation of the recent Espionage Act, which broadly defined seditious utterances that might weaken the war effort, led to thousands of arrests, particularly of alien anti-militarists and radicals of any kind. Among those given the longest sentences were Bill Haywood of the IWW; Eugene Debs, the leader of the Socialist Party; and Kate Richards O'Hare, the prominent Socialist Party activist and reformer. Mail censorship had tightened. Anarchist theoretician Peter Kropotkin's pamphlet *Anarchist Morality* was banned from the mails, because the Postmaster believed that "dwelling in such utopias" might "interfere with the waging of the war." Among the leaflets considered to be most dangerous was the Wobbly appeal for *Justice for the Negro*, a publication that pointed out, among other things, that "while colored soldiers were being obligated to 'fight for democracy' abroad, ninety-one of their race were lynched at home." The suppression of this leaflet, like the article in *Mother Earth* that had called attention to the lynching of black soldiers in the army, indicated that the government would try to stamp out any possible alliance between anarchist forces and black minority forces. Accordingly, all eight thousand remaining subscribers to *Mother Earth* were considered suspect and had files in Military Intelligence. Voltairine de Cleyre's posthumously published book of essays, including a piece on Emma Goldman and one on sexual slavery, was banned as well. In particular, her linking of sexual freedom and anti-military senti-ment elicited an almost hysterical condemnation from the Postmaster: "To her Emma Goldman was a prophetess of light—one of the elect of the ages—God, it may be said parenthetically, not being in good repute with this misguided creature. The book is harmful, not without the germ of a basic truth, but utterly perverted and to be reprehended, but there are other and more vital things for the world to think about today."

Not only were publications that extolled Emma's contribution to society banned from the mails, but all of her friends and family were watched, as were comrades around the country who had housed her or helped organize her tours.

Ironically, Fitzi, one of Emma's closest associates and an untiring worker for the *Mother Earth* organization, was relatively untouched by the federal authorities. Although she had been harassed and arrested in connection with *The Blast* and Alexander Berkman's alleged connection to the San Francisco bombing, now she was free to function as efficiently as she could with the few comrades who were left. Fitzi did so much of the background work of the organization that she had contacts with anarchists everywhere. For this reason, Military Intelligence figured that she was more valuable to them on the loose, as long as they could keep track of her comings and goings and the people with whom she talked and worked, than she would be in jail. They decided "to use her as bait with which to catch the other leaders." And Fitzi, in her quiet way, did in fact occupy a critical place in the work of the *Mother Earth* group. Emma continued to count on her from prison.

Government eyes were everywhere. Emma's and Sasha's letters were intercepted and read, even confiscated from the various secret "name-drops" that she used. But the organizations supporting them and the other victims of the new repression grew nevertheless. The Political Prisoners' Amnesty League, which Emma had worked to establish before returning to prison, had active branches in Rochester, Detroit, Chicago, Cleveland, Ann Arbor, San Francisco, St. Louis, Los Angeles, and New York, and they hoped for international support.

Among the means of communication with those in sympathy with Emma and Sasha was a multigraphed newsletter that Stella sent out. With both *Mother Earth* and the *Mother Earth Bulletin* barred from the mails, Stella entitled her new bulletin *Instead of a Magazine*. Military intelligence authorities may have been proud of "killing" most of the anarchist publications, but while they were suppressing each one, the anarchists had some lag time to work up another.

Instead of a Magazine informed its readers which of the former issues and publications of the *Mother Earth* office had been labeled "unmailable" by the Post Office. In the June 29, 1918, issue, Stella wrote an account of her six visits to Emma in jail:

A trustee brought her in through an iron gate, and we sat on a couch in the matron's office—two days the matron sat near us and the last day, Sunday, a guard watched us. At first I could hardly speak. Our Dear Emma looked as usual, her eyes bright, her lovely complexion rosy, I still felt as if I were dreaming in a topsy turvy world, and that presently I would wake up.

We talked of many things, mostly of her beloved comrades and friends on the outside, the world situation and her future plans. She was loath to talk of the disabilities of her prison life. She spoke of the few privileges she enjoyed, such as being permitted to get her food from the outside, to have all the books and papers sent to her, that she is given all letters written her. . . . One must no longer address her as "political prisoner," because they are not recognized in this country.

I asked her to take off her glasses so that I might see her eyes. There are many new "crowsfeet" about them, and they look so sad and tired. . . . There seems to be no relief from the tailor shop as sewing is the only work given the women prisoners. . . .

She told me . . . when the lights are turned out she forgets she is in prison. She turns to her books, reads her papers, and communes with the outside world.

She sends every one of you her greetings and looks forward to the day of her release when she may again walk among you bearing witness to truth. In the meantime, each one of us can hold out his hand to her in the dark to show we are still here.

Emma's lawyer, Harry Weinberger, made several formal pleas to have Emma's prison work changed to waitressing or nursing, which might be less stressful, "on account of a change of period in her life, she being just fifty years of age, and because her eyesight is so bad that she has to work with a curved back, while working on jackets."

Stella's reports on Berkman were even grimmer. He was not permitted any food from outside, or any radical papers or books. "The prison authorities show the parcel to him and then take them away, which is more tantalizing." Never mind that his old stomach problem had returned; Sasha assured his comrades that he could serve his time easily, because he lived "above the stomach."

Even in prison, Emma and Sasha were not immune from the new paranoia about "outside agitators" from foreign countries, who might be allied with enemies of the United States in battle. The world war had fostered anti-German sentiment in the United States to the point where anyone with ties to Germany was suspect. Russian immigrants, sympathetic to the Bolsheviks, were equally suspect. The Justice Department tried to link Emma to a German spy ring. On January 18, 1919, her former husband, Joseph Kershner, died. The government proceeded after his death to implement a plan they had devised back in 1907 to deport Emma now that her marital status could no longer support her claim to legal citizenship. A quiet, methodical search for a way to deport "Red Emma" had begun, although she herself did not learn of it till the end of the year. Attorney General A. Mitchell Palmer was busy preparing the evidence to invoke the Alien Immigration Act of February 5, 1917, which gave the government the jurisdiction to deport or exclude aliens who were anarchists or any sort of disbelievers in organized government.

Emma's letters from prison were all systematically monitored, transcribed, and forwarded to the Attorney General by the president of the Missouri State Prison Board. Her active involvement in political work on the outside was highly disturbing to the officials, and they suggested that "something should be done and done quick." Her written expressions of grief when her nephew David Hochstein (Helena's son)— whom she had loved and encouraged as a great violinist before he shocked her with his enlistment—died in the war was transcribed by the prison officials as carefully as her elation at the amnesty of 113 conscientious objectors. Sasha's most intimate love letters, including daily letters from Fitzi, and other letters from an array of women admirers were transcribed, as well.

And so the two prisoners served out their sentences. Berkman was put into solitary confinement for protesting the death of a black convict who was shot in the back by a guard. He could not receive his mail, and, cruelest of all his punishments, he could talk with no one.

Unlike Sasha, Emma had companionship in prison, especially in the person of Kate Richards O'Hare, the well-known socialist leader, who had been jailed for her anti-war activities under the Espionage Act. Emma wrote to her friends that the differences between anarchism and socialism faded in jail: "Don't think we compete in 'isms.' We compete in feeding hungry sparrows." O'Hare and Goldman's friendship made the harshness of prison life endurable, and Kate's steadier personality balanced Emma's periodic depressions. Emma wrote that Kate worked well with the other women because she "doesn't have a Jewish soul, which resists submission. . . . O'Hare is optimistic, which EG and her Jewish compound cannot have." Both women were later to write with affection and appreciation about the time they spent together in prison. Kate referred to Emma as her "loyal comrade and cosmic mother," with "a passionate maternal spirit" that appealed to the inmates, "not her anarchist philosophy." Kate noted that after Emma was released, she herself "could not fill Emma's place in their hearts."

Still, prison camaraderie could not alleviate the pain of being cut off from friends and meaningful activity. She thought of her friend, W. S. Van Valkenburgh, the journalist, who was happiest in a small upstate New York town living a quiet life. Emma likened herself to a wildflower that could never grow in a hothouse. She was "a child of the open, of an intense wild stormy life," she wrote to her friend Van: "I can truthfully say I am here only in the physical sense. But I live and dream in the world at large—in the events of Russia—of Germania—of Hungary." Emma managed to read the radical press even behind bars, and claimed that she "live[d] the events now changing in the world at large with greater passion than I would were I on the outside."

It was in the Missouri State Penitentiary that Emma celebrated her fiftieth birthday. Flowers and telegrams streamed in, including a cable from Ben and his friends: "ON THIS YOUR BIRTHDAY IN THE CITY WHERE YOU WORKED AND STRUGGLED AND HAVE MOST FRIENDS, WE SEND YOU LOVE AND ASSURANCE AND DEVOTION. HOPE THAT THE NEXT HALF CENTURY WILL HAVE GREATER POSSIBILITIES FOR SERVICE AND SELF-ASSERTION. TRUST THE COMING YEAR WILL SET YOU FREE."

For a solid month Ben had been trying to persuade Emma to allow him to visit her, but Emma refused: she felt that he had dealt her an unforgivable blow by abandoning her and the cause when she was imprisoned and needed the most support. And his retraction of his anti-military and anti-war positions "have all but killed me. . . . It took the bottom out from under me." She hoped to emerge from prison healed, whereas seeing Ben would only reopen the wound. She begged him to stop insisting on seeing her—"it only hurts."

Meanwhile, Emma became completely absorbed in her new political hope for the Russian Revolution. She wrote to her friend Ellen Kennan, "I have set my face toward the red glow on the social horizon: after all that is the only real and worthwhile love." She even rejected professions of love sent her by an old comrade, Leon Malmed, who had accompanied her to San Diego on her 1915 West Coast *Mother Earth* tour and was now both a friend and a supplier of exotic foods from his Albany delicatessen. "Dearest boy," she wrote to him, "what greater love is there than one which binds two people in a great ideal? And ours is that, is it not?" She had sworn off "personal love" and was determined to simplify and purify her commitment to the cause during this trying period of her life:

> . . . it has brought me much pain and little joy. More and more I came to the conclusion that a personal love is not for one who dedicates himself to an ideal. Somehow it is like serving two Gods. Of course one longs for a personal love, for a real home and the comforts that come from deep personal affections and devotion such as yours, for instance. But no man could be satisfied to give all of himself and to receive in return only a small part of the woman he loves, and how is she to give all when every nerve of her pulls towards the impersonal, the universal love? She need not expect to have both, the man and the universe. And so she must forswear the one for the other. When one is young, one is easily content to go without a personal love. But when the years begin to pile up, one finds it rather cold and lonely in the universe. No, there can be no personal life for me.

Her disillusionment with Ben also led her to dwell on the unhappiness of her past. As Emma's attachment to Ben faded, her evaluation of his integrity declined. She reminded herself of her earlier suspicions of his spying and cooperation with the police—and even wrote that she felt sorry his son should have such an unstable father.

It was a challenge to Emma's great idealism that she could maintain her vision of the future when almost everything in the present seemed so hopeless. Sasha, too, mustered the courage to survive his prison term with his ideals intact. He wrote to Fitzi, "The ultimate goal is 6 feet of clay, but I'd rather die the victim of my faith than live the dupe of vain self-aggrandizement in ambition. It's all in the point of view. I do not think we 'get it in the neck,' except on the practical plane."

On the practical plane, Berkman and Goldman were not even assured of freedom once their prison sentences ended. In the fall of 1919, while Emma was serving her last month, U.S. Attorney General Palmer personally issued a warrant for her arrest as part of the round-up under the Alien Immigration Act of February 5, 1917, and the Anti-Anarchist Act of October 16, 1918, which authorized the deportation of all alien anarchists.

Emma and Sasha had been arrested during the early wave of cultural-political chauvinism just before the United States entered World War I. Then came the Bolshevik Revolution, which effectively took Russia out of the war; general anti-radicalism was joined with anti-foreign sentiment, and arrests became more arbitrary. By the time Emma and Sasha were threatened with deportation in 1919, the country's postwar hysteria had led to the Palmer raids—a systematic crackdown on offices and organizations linked to foreign, anti-war, and radical activity. Although Emma and Sasha were not direct victims of Palmer's raids, the violently repressive mood of the country and the general fear of the Russian Revolution were bound to affect the outcome of the hearings about their deportation.

Both Emma and Sasha were scheduled for deportation proceedings upon their release. Berkman was questioned while still in prison. He asserted that since any court set up to determine a person's "attitude of mind" was an invasion of his conscience, he would not participate in its proceedings. Each refused to "swear" to tell the truth and made a point of "affirming" it instead. Using the Immigration Act and the Anti-Anarchist Act, the federal government laid the foundation for Emma's and Sasha's deportations. At the immigration proceedings, Emma, too, objected to the barrage of questions about her past, her beliefs, and her political activities. She refused to answer on the grounds that thoughts should be free. She insisted that such despotic star-chamber treatment was reminiscent of the "Spanish Inquisition or the more recently defunct Third Degree system of Czarist Russia." She called attention to the attack against personal freedom that these deportation proceedings symbolized. "Today, so-called aliens are deported; tomorrow native Americans will be banished." Such severe repression was "the spirit of an irresponsible hysteria, the result of the terrible war, and of the evil tendencies of bigotry and persecution and violence which are the epilogue of five years of bloodshed."

Pending a decision on their deportation, both Emma and Sasha were released on bail; Harry Weinberger secured the necessary $15,000 from individuals who protested her arrest by cashing in their Liberty Bonds. Barely taking time to catch their breath after a year and a half in prison, they went right out speaking and touring again. Sasha even published a scathing article in the Atlanta Constitution to expose the cruelty of the warden and deputy warden in the federal penitentiary there. The state intelligence bureau managed to have Emma and Sasha's activities under surveillance by hiring a young woman, Marion Barling, using the alias Margaret M. Scully, to infiltrate their ranks as Emma's secretary. She wined and dined with the anarchist men in Emma's circle, then reported on the subversive work of "those damned kikes."

What time Emma did take away from politics to recuperate was spent in Bearsville, New York, with Stella and her husband, the actor Teddy Ballantine, and their son, Ian, who by now was three years old. Emma took care of her great-nephew while her niece worked. Ben came to visit her at Stella's, but was restless, as usual, and could not stay long enough to establish the rapport that might have eased their long separation. Emma wrote to Agnes Inglis:

> The tragic part is Ben does not realize that so long as we take ourselves along wherever we go, nothing can be changed. No, it is not the particular City which gives us comparative peace, it is what we give to the City, or the work we do. Ben has never learned that, he goes back and forth, finds peace nowhere, nor does anyone else.

It has been a bitter time, but it is over now.... The only way to endure the blackness of life is to absorb oneself in the work.

Emma did indeed absorb herself in the work of speaking out against prison conditions, the rash of deportations, and the blatant assaults on the principles of free speech. She and Sasha planned a Thanksgiving speaking tour that would take them as far as Detroit and Chicago. Everywhere banquets were given in their honor, to celebrate the release of the two prison-weary anarchists. Yet, with the deportation fever taking hold of the government, there was also a sense of impending doom mingled with these festivities. The fact that Mollie Steimer was on a hunger strike on Ellis Island gave a somber tone to their elaborate meal. And since no one knew how long Emma and Sasha would be allowed to remain in the United States, the speeches accordingly became tributes to their life and times. The banquets were surprisingly expensive, and the menus elaborate—Hors d'Oeuvres Assortis, Huîtres Blue Points, Potage Ledoyen, Filet de Bass Vert-Pré, Pommes au Beurre, Poulet Grillé Maître-d'Hôtel, Haricots Verts Sautés, Salade Mélangé, Mousse à la Vanille, Petit Fours, Café—with no extravagance spared for the "Anarchist Queen." One hundred and eighty people crowded into the Hotel Brevoort in New York City. One man commented to Emma's lawyer, "with prohibition coming in and Emma Goldman going out, 'twill be a dull country."

On November 29, 1919, while Emma and Sasha were touring the Midwest, they received word that the order for their deportation had been signed. Harry Weinberger appealed the decision on Emma's case on the grounds that she was not an alien, and therefore not subject to deportation under the Anti-Anarchist Act. He asserted that Emma had obtained her citizenship long ago through her husband, Jacob Kershner. Her case would rely on proving that Kershner was either dead before his citizenship was revoked in 1909 or that he was still alive to prove that his citizenship had been taken away illegally. The young J. Edgar Hoover of the General Intelligence Division of the Department of Justice, as Attorney General Palmer's special assistant, took an interest in the swift expulsion of Emma and Sasha. Every detail of Emma's past would now be subject to scrutiny and used against her. Hoover wrote a memo stating,

"Emma Goldman and Alexander Berkman are, beyond doubt, two of the most dangerous anarchists in this country and if permitted to return to the community will result in undue harm." The government tracked down Kershner, who had lived in Chicago under the alias of Jake Lewis, and discovered that he had died in January 1919. The government had revoked the now dead Kershner's citizenship ten years before on the grounds that he had been granted it illegally, before he was twenty-one years old. They further discredited Kershner by uncovering a grand larceny charge against him after Emma had left him, in June of 1894. He had pleaded guilty to having embezzled $680 from the Lodge of Oddfellows, of which he was a member. He had served a term in prison until September 1895. There is no indication that Emma had known about Kershner's disreputable life after they had separated. To make a foolproof case, the government was also prepared to argue that Emma's marriage to Kershner had not been performed by an ordained rabbi, but instead by a "shokhet," a learned man who mainly performs the ritual slaughtering of animals and, on occasion, presides over marriages in the Jewish community. The government tried to make this the technical basis for invalidating Emma's marriage. The court hearing on Emma's appeal was scheduled for December 8, 1919.

At this critical juncture in Emma's life, Ben stood up at a farewell banquet in Chicago and announced that, despite ten wonderful years as Emma's co-worker, he was now through with anarchism: "Emma came into my life years ago and seduced me from the old world. I dropped my old ideas. I dropped Jesus Christ. But today I'm thanking God I've learned the right road—and I learned it when I came back to Jesus."

Ben's proclamation infuriated Emma, but it helped strengthen her inner resolve that there was nothing to return to with Ben. In contrast, she could not allow the government to sever her relationship with Sasha, with its basis of loyalty and love. The legal efforts to prove that Emma could not be denied the citizenship that was her right through her late husband had some chance of success, but there was no such chance for Sasha, who had never been a citizen.

At the December hearing, the government defeated her appeal. At first Emma had her lawyer file another appeal with the Supreme Court on the issue of her citizenship. Then she abandoned her appeal. She decided to leave the country with her staunchest comrade, hoping to find more fertile ground for their ideals in their mother country. Although there was no guarantee that the government would send them where they wanted to go, she wanted, together with Sasha, to be part of the great revolutionary events in Russia, and the thought of fighting her battle in America without him was too dismal. She did not even allow herself to imagine that she might face a disappointment in Russia as well, nor did she admit how deep was her love of America. Her judgment clouded by the pain of losing Ben, she made this decision to enforce a physical break with Ben and thus give that relationship the dramatic finality she so desperately needed. When she waved good-bye to Ben at Chicago's LaSalle Street station, she felt that perhaps she would never see him again.

Condemned to Ellis Island, the departure point for deportees, Emma wrote Ben a sentimental farewell. In it she told him that she had decided to accept deportation rather than endure the antagonism of the government by appealing the flimsy charges on which her citizenship had been revoked.

One does not live in a country 34 years, live as I have lived, and find it easy to go. I found my spiritual birth here. All I know, I gained here. All the turmoil of body and soul, all the love and all the hate that come to an intense human being in a lifetime, have come to me in this Country. All my dreams, hopes, aspirations, all the woe and pain, all the joy and ecstasy, I have found them here. Yes, it is bitter hard to go. But I am proud. . . . The mad rush in getting us out of the Country is the greatest proof to me that I have served the cause of humanity, that I have never waivered or compromised. I really feel proud of my achievement. Then, too, I feel that no matter where I am my work for the American Revolution can go on. I feel very deeply about the future of this Country. I have helped to sow the seeds. I hope to see their growth and their fruition even if I will be too far away to participate in the harvest. . . .

I was glad to have been in Chicago and to see you again, dearest hobo. I never realized quite so well how far apart we have travelled.

But it is all right, nothing you have done since you left me, or will yet do, can take away the 10 wonderful years with you. If it is true that the power of endurance is the greatest test of love, Hobo mine, I have loved you much. But I have been rewarded not only in pain but in real joy—in ecstasy—in all that makes life full & rich & sparkling. I really owe much to you. During our years together, I have done my best and most valuable work. My two books, the continuance of *Mother Earth* during all the years—I owe them to you. Your devotion, your untiring work, your tremendous energy. If I owe also much heartache, much soul-tearing misery to you, what of it? Nothing in life can be achieved without pain. I am glad to have paid the price. I only hope I too have given you something worth whatever price you have paid for your love. I shall feel proud and glad.

Emma even seemed to have made her peace with Ben's new family:

I know you are not happy now, you are too restless to be that, or to be contented. You will yet have many changes. I hope, though, that dear sweet little Brutus will bring much in your life. That he will grow up as fascinating as his father but with deeper social con-secration for a great ideal. I love Brutus as if he were my own. Tell him so when he grows a little older to understand. Tell Anna, I regret we were not thrown together more, to know her better. She seemed to have warmed up a little more during my stay this time. Perhaps some day in the not too distant future, we will meet again in free Russia—or some other place where human beings have stopped hating and have begun loving. Anyway, you, dearest Hobo, are going to be in my life for ever and ever.

Irrepressible when it came to furthering the anarchist cause, Emma also included a last request that Ben continue the promotional work he had done for her: "Dear, you will push my Essays & prison pamphlets. We are now working on one dealing with deportation which will also be pub-lished soon. I want you . . . to push things—to keep my memory alive."

All the letters written to friends during her last days on Ellis

Island—"the worst dump I have ever stayed in"—had the same message: a sadness about saying good-bye, an appreciation for all the support that she had received from friends and comrades, and a statement about her hopes for Russia and the second revolution that was still evolving in America. In extreme and unambiguous situations that required courage, that brought her to public attention, and that provided her with the love and support of her comrades, Emma was at her best. To W. S. Van Valkenburgh she wrote: "I never felt more peaceful in all my life. I think it is because my faith in the future of America is deeper now than ever in my 30 years of struggle. Then, too, I feel that I shall yet play a part in the American revolution. Oh, I know you will think me naive. That is all right. But remember, so were the Russian pioneers and rebels once called naive. Yet now they are the fiery symbol for the whole world." She said her good-byes with a transcendent sense of herself as a heroine.

Emma's letters to Fitzi from Ellis Island conveyed more of a feeling of regret. Fitzi was in a panic at the thought of losing Emma and Sasha; she even—according to J. Edgar Hoover—"made every effort to get deported with them." The two women, who had worked together over the last ten years, had never felt as close as they did now. A staunch worker and a great proponent of sexual freedom, thought by some to be bisexual, Fitzi had found her identity and her surrogate parents in Emma and Sasha's anarchist movement. There is little doubt that Emma felt some jealousy of this red-headed Lioness, almost six feet tall, who had been a lover and confidante of both Ben and Sasha. The fact that Fitzi rarely mentioned Emma in her daily letters to Sasha in prison must have indicated that the distance between the two women was mutual. In her letter, Emma reflected on what she consciously perceived as having stood between them:

My dearest Fitzi,

I too feel the pain and the tragedy that you and I united by a thousand ties should yet be so far apart. Sometimes it makes me feel as if some cruel force were bent on separating us. Think of it. Ever since you came to us, we were prevented from close communion. At first it was the terrible bitter and cruel struggle I went through with Ben and his impossible mother. . . . Sasha too was terribly trying, with his obsession for B[ecky] E[delson]. And there were a hundred matters all sapping my strength and tearing my body and soul.

When I met you again in San Francisco the first week of that memorable month in 1916, I wanted so very, very much to get close to you. But you seemed very aloof—wrapped up . . . for which I was very glad, in *The Blast*, in your home and your friends. I felt a [barrier] between us, even between B and myself. I was terribly unhappy and lonely. Then the Catastrophe of July 1916 [the San Francisco bombing] broke over us and all personal interests swept aside. And since then our life has been so tense—so nerve-destroying, so chaotic. How was one to seek and find a kindred soul?

It seems to me that only since our return from prison and the fact that you too were terribly distraught and unhappy have you really come very close to me. Sorrow often brings people together more than joy. Day after day I planned to take you away from the tear and wear with Sasha, your fatigued condition and the numerous things you were engaged in. I wanted to take you away, all to myself, so you and I could really learn to know one another. . . . Good night, dearest Fitz. I love you very much. I hope some day to be called upon to prove my love. Meanwhile, I want you to believe in it. I know you love me a little anyway. I hope some day we two can be close enough to each other and under less stress and strain, so you can love me more. I want your friendship and your love very much.

I embrace you and kiss you tenderly.

Your EG

. . . I ought to be used to [loneliness] by this time. I have been very very lonely since foolish Ben killed the thing he loved. Life is strange, yet very fascinating.

Good night, dearest
EG

Louis Post, Assistant Secretary of Labor, was largely responsible for any leniency the government showed toward Emma. He had turned down the initial requests for her deportation, though J. Edgar Hoover made an additional investigation to circumvent his more sympathetic reading of the situation. Post gradually grew to appreciate Emma for her integrity, and he took it upon himself to make sure of her safety, secretly ensuring that she and Sasha would not be sent to a prison camp in the Philippines or delivered into the hands of White Russians; he did not have the authority, however, to grant Sasha's request to pay his own fare to France, Mexico, or Hamburg, Germany. Ashamed of the mass deportations, Post revealed in his memoirs the guilt he felt for being an integral part of the government repressions, even as he rationalized the aspect of his personality that enabled him to go on working with the government. It was Post who arranged for Emma and Sasha to be sent to their mother country, Red Russia. But they were not officially notified of their destination until they were at sea, although a newspaper reported that Ludwig C. A. K. Martens, "Bolshevik Ambassador to the U.S.," said that Emma Goldman was welcome to the "Workers' Republic of Russia." The relative confidence they had in their future enabled Emma and Sasha to speak for the thousands of people being held on Ellis Island. They wrote a pamphlet from confinement, *Deportation: Its Meaning and Menace*, which listed all the "great American" and foreign authors who might have found themselves silenced under the Criminal Anarchy Law and Espionage Act if they had lived in 1919—Thomas Paine, Henry George, Henry David Thoreau, Ralph Waldo Emerson, Edmund Burke, John Stuart Mill, Herbert Spencer, Leo Tolstoy. And they reminded their readers of Lincoln's edict: "The Cause of Civil Liberty must not be surrendered at the end of one or even one hundred defeats."

Emma and Sasha wrote a general letter to their friends:

We have been told this afternoon that we must get ready as we may be shipped any moment. This, then, is our last chance to speak to you once more while still on American soil. . . . To you, dear, faithful friends, we want to send a parting word.

Do not be sad about our forced departure. Rather, rejoice with us that our common enemies, prompted by fear and stupidity, have resorted to this mad act of driving political refugees out of the land. This act must ultimately lead to the undoing of the madmen themselves. For now the American people will see more clearly than our ardent work of thirty years could prove to them, that liberty in America has been sold into bondage, that justice has been outraged, and life made cheap and ugly. . . .

We go strengthened by our conviction that America will free herself not merely from the sham of paper guarantees, but in a fundamental sense, in her economic, social and spiritual life.

Dear friends, it is an old truism which most of you have surely experienced: He who ascends to the greatest heights of faith is often hurled into the depths of doubt. We have known the ecstasy of the one and the torture of the other. If we have not despaired utterly, it is because of the boundless love and devotion of our friends. That has been our sustaining power. Few fighters in the struggle for human freedom have known such beautiful comradeship. If we have been among the most hated, reviled, and persecuted, we have also been the most beloved. What greater tribute to one's integrity can one wish? . . .

We can only say that our physical separation can have no effect on our appreciation of your loyalty—it can only enhance it. . . . These are trying but wonderful times. Clear heads and brave hearts were never more needed. There is great work to do. May each one of you give the best that is in him to the great struggle, the last struggle between liberty and bondage, between well-being and poverty, between beauty and ugliness.

In the small hours of the morning of December 21, 1919, one of the coldest days of the year, Emma and Sasha and the other 247 exiles were shunted into a dilapidated military ship, the *Buford*, and cast off from American soil. Two hundred fifty soldiers each armed with a rifle and two pistols guarded them. The secret departure time prevented friends from coming to say their last farewells or bringing extra overcoats and food. Sasha dressed like a Cossack soldier, with a flowing cravat and gray breeches in a military cut. Emma carried her typewriter and sat with her friends Ethel Bernstein and Dora Lipkin. Zealous government officials, among them the twenty-five-year-old J. Edgar Hoover, came to see the result of their long effort to dispatch this "Red Ark." Hoover even began collecting a personal scrapbook of newspaper clippings relating to the deportation. When Hoover asked Emma if she agreed that he had given her a square deal, she said that she supposed that he had done what he could—"We shouldn't expect from any person something beyond his capacity." Emma is said to have thumbed her nose at Hoover as her last act of defiance as she sailed away.

Emma wrote a sad letter to Stella Ballantine from the *Buford*. She had always dreamed of a sea voyage as an escape, she said, but a ship was now her prison. The year 1919 ended at sea for Emma; she did indeed assume that this voyage was "the last page of a stormy chapter."

12

MOTHER RUSSIA

For twenty-eight days, the 249 prisoners of the *Buford* withstood the hardships of their voyage at sea by focusing not on the lack of food, sunshine, and freedom but on a vision of the newly free Russia ahead of them. Emma longed for reassurance and renewed faith as she withdrew emotionally from her shattered relationships with Ben and with America. She believed that working to realize the Bolshevik Revolution offered the possibility of a pure, all-encompassing love, which—unlike sexual love—would not fail her.

The *Buford* docked in Hangö, a Finnish port, where the deportees were transferred to a train that took them to Terjoki, on the Finnish-Russian border. Once across the border, the exiles were greeted like long-lost brothers and sisters by a Soviet committee and then transported to several Russian villages where they also got an enthusiastic reception. Emma was moved by the warmth, so different from the officialness and hatred that had marked her departure from the United States. As if in a dream, Emma suddenly found herself on a platform. "I could only blurt out that like my comrades I had not come to Russia to teach: I had come to learn, to draw sustenance and hope from her, to lay down my life on the altar of the Revolution."

In Petrograd, she and Sasha were housed in an apartment hotel for deportees that turned out to be quite a bit more comfortable than those to which their shipmates were assigned. It felt odd for Emma to return to the St. Petersburg of her youth, now so changed and full of promise. The two travel-weary deportees basked in the spirit of the revolution, as yet unaware that darker forces were at work around them. They cabled their friends in the United States to convey their relief and even elation at being in the presence of a world-historical revolution. But their cable was intercepted by the Department of State; and perhaps it was never received by their friends at home:

PREMET [MET IN ADVANCE] AT SOVIET BORDER AND PETROGRAD WITH TREMENDOUS ENTHUSIASM RECEPTION WEEPING. ENJOYING HOSPITALITY PETROGRAD. DEPORTEES WILL BE SENT TO WORK WHEREVER THEY DESIRE. PEOPLE COLD AND HUNGRY BUT SPIRIT AND DEVOTION MARVELOUS. AFTER WEEKS WILL GO TO MOSCOW CABLED WORLD FINLAND.

EMMA GOLDMAN

ALEXANDER BERKMAN

Emma, who felt she was free of U.S. surveillance and in the land of her dreams, could hardly contain her joy. And short of sharing her happiness directly with the loved ones she had left behind, the next-best pleasure was seeing the comrades who had left America before her to aid the revolution—in particular, her old friend Bill Shatoff. He had come to the United States from Russia in 1907, had a colorful and varied career as a proletarian worker and organizer, but decided to return to Russia in 1917 and work for the revolution.

Emma was glad to see Shatoff, who had last communicated with her through the flowers he had arranged to have sent to her—from Russia—while she was in the Missouri State Prison, but she sensed a change in him. Now the military commissar of Petrograd, he said very little, seeming to be determined to let Emma form her own opinion of this war-torn country that was struggling for its survival. But Emma, whom he called "the same old persistent pest," pushed him far enough to discover how hampered he felt by the restrictions of the communist state, particularly those on his freedom to move around without permission, since he had fallen into disfavor. He was sure that Emma, too, would eventually share his uneasiness over the Russia of their dreams.

But Emma, like Bill, was determined to give Russia her best effort, to work to make it the beacon of worldwide revolution. Perhaps there were problems; Emma had never said that massive revolutionary change would immediately result in perfection. She was aware that, so soon after fighting the revolution at home, Russia was plagued with a war on her Polish border, and that the White Russians were still hoping to defeat the revolution. The poverty, the scarcity of resources, the massive challenge of clothing, feeding, and educating the people were all evident. Emma felt aligned with the anarchists who had helped to win the revolution, and now she was determined to carry out the principles of their struggle. She had pledged herself to the Bolsheviks; she was an anarchist, and usually did not believe in the centralization of state power, but she had to admit that the Bolshevik leadership seemed to embody anarchist tactics and principles.

Emma went out daily to acclimatize herself to her new home and to talk to the people who had been the source of her inspiration. Everywhere she found suffering and discontent. At first, she could not hear the volume of dissent around her, for she tempered it with her own sense of revolutionary timing and necessary patience.

Emma's knowledge of the Russian language, her extensive contacts among radicals who had made the pilgrimage to Russia from other parts of the world to help build the country, and her stature as a leader and propagandist in the United States gave her special access to the people and the life around her. She was not limited to seeing only model schools and hospitals or restricted to having conversations with only the most avid devotees of the Bolshevik regime. The contradictions loomed over her, and began to occupy her every thought. The leaders, including Zorin, Zinoviev, and even her old American comrade John Reed, viewed the misery around them as a temporary stage in the great struggle forward. She met with Alexandra Kollontai, the great communist theoretician who, like Emma, had written openly about sexual freedom, but found no resonance in their perspectives on the misery of the Russian masses; Kollontai belittled Emma's observations as "a few dull grey spots." Emma began to see that some of the leaders of the anarchist movement who had played a crucial role in the victory of the Russian Revolution were now being discriminated against, assigned poor housing, given short rations, sent to work in remote, cold regions of the country, and even imprisoned. In particular, the sorry treatment of Angelica Balabanoff, the compassionate theorist of the revolution, convinced Emma that she needed to go directly to Lenin to challenge him with this information of which she hoped he was unaware.

Emma worked out a memorandum containing what she called "the most salient contradictions in Soviet life" to present to Lenin. Although Sasha shared many of Emma's doubts, at this point he felt more hesitant about asserting them; yet, as usual, when in doubt, he supported Emma. Together they were driven to the Kremlin, where they addressed Lenin in his meticulously neat office. Lenin was more curious at first to hear from them about conditions in the United States, about the labor movement, the IWW, and their own trials. He expressed regret that the two anarchist leaders had not been able to stay behind in the United States, where they could have done so much to promote revolution. At one point, Sasha began to talk in English; Lenin interrupted him instantly, since he did not know the language. In Russian, therefore, Sasha asked why there were anarchists in Soviet prisons. Lenin asserted that only bandits were in prison and that none of them were anarchists, who were truly "with" Soviet Russia. When Emma argued that these people were being denied their freedom of speech, she was immediately quelled by Lenin's equally adamant assertion that placing high value on freedom of speech is a bourgeois prejudice, for it is not so critical as economic well-being. Sasha handed Lenin the resolutions of a recent anarchist conference, emphasizing his belief that the anarchists behind bars were not bandits. Although Lenin took the resolutions with the aloof promise that he would consider them carefully and come to a decision, he then proceeded, in a condescending tone, to encourage the two of them to find meaningful work in building the revolution, in order "to regain their revolutionary balance." Actually, Emma thought Lenin might be right and suggested that they form a society of Russian Friends of American Freedom to support the revolutionary political movements in the United States, as the American Friends of Russian Freedom had done in aid of the Russian people against the czarist regime. When Lenin approved the idea and encouraged them to write up a proposal to be approved by the Third International, Emma balked: any affiliation with Bolshevik organizations might make it difficult to organize the American people. But before they realized it, they were shaking hands good-bye and being shunted out of Lenin's office.

Confused, Emma and Sasha made a pilgrimage to visit Peter Kropotkin in Dmitrov outside of Petrograd, to clarify their experience with Lenin. Kropotkin was in poor health, but lived in voluntary poverty because, on principle, he had decided to refuse any money or privilege from the Bolsheviks; he believed they had betrayed the anarchists who had fought to put them in power. Kropotkin discouraged Emma and Sasha from creating an organization that would tie them to the apron strings of the party, suggesting that instead they find work that would be directly useful to the people.

When they returned to Petrograd, Emma and Sasha managed to find work arranging a welcoming party for the next arrival of American deportees. But their efforts were all for naught: without any explanation, no other American deportees ever arrived. At Emma's suggestion, a project was undertaken to renovate the building that had been prepared for the deportees into a rest home for workers. But the work slowed nearly to a halt as the morale among the assigned workers plummeted: it had become obvious that they had been divided into first- and second-class groupings, receiving very different treatment with respect to breaks, food, and shelter. When the rest homes were finally inaugurated, Emma predicted sadly that no workers except those well established in the party would ever find themselves within its walls.

Sasha next tried to organize the dismal local soup kitchens into efficient cafeterias that could be spread throughout the city. But despite his great plans and the obvious need that his project would fill, the work was squelched by the slow-moving Soviet bureaucracy. At the same time, Emma decided to use her nursing skills and volunteered to work in a Soviet hospital, or even on the front lines, where the fighting against White Russians was still going on. Although her offer was initially met with enthusiasm, when it came to her actually going to the hospital, her sponsoring doctor mysteriously never showed up to take her there. In utter frustration, she and Sasha followed the suggestion of a friend to help the Museum of the Revolution by initiating an expedition to the various regions of the Russian countryside to collect and document the stories of heroism and suffering involved in making the revolution. Here, at last, they were given the freedom to follow their own initiative, and they could go out among the people to find out first-hand what had happened to them since the revolution.

On June 30, 1920, only seven months after they had arrived in Soviet Russia, Emma and Sasha set out in a renovated train car with a small staff to begin their search. They hoped that their work would keep the heroism of the revolution alive.

But everywhere they went, they were met initially with hostility. They managed to break through the general suspicion of Bolshevik representatives by assuring them that they were Americans who had come to find out about the great heroism that had made the revolution possible, and that the Museum of the Revolution would be an inspiration to the world. Gradually, people became less defensive; along with the stories of the old, high-principled times came those of newer disillusionment, of poverty, and the feeling of powerlessness against the Communist Party and its police arm, the Cheka. It was in this context that Emma and Sasha learned of the terrible conditions inside prisons, the discrimination against intellectuals and professors, the anti-Semitism, which was rampant, and the hunger of the children of the revolution. In their nightmarish trip through the purgatory of postrevolutionary Russia, they were able to unearth early pamphlets, personal notes and diaries, and other artifacts bespeaking the hopes of the people. They were inspired with a mission as they made their way from town to town.

The popular leader of a guerrilla army in the Ukraine, who had fought against the White Russians and was dedicated to resisting domination of any kind, managed to contact Emma. Nestor Makhno, the anarchist hero of the Russian Revolution, had turned against the Soviets, set up independent zones, and was now being hunted by the Bolsheviks for what they considered his treasonous activities. He surreptitiously sent his wife, Galina, to ask Emma and Sasha to approve a coup he was planning, even to allow themselves to be imprisoned by Makhno's men in a charade to clear her of blame. But Emma was not ready to be so directly involved in a plan to defeat the Bolsheviks. Although she was increasingly distancing herself intellectually from the regime, she could not break her emotional tie to the Bolshevik dream, and to the people behind it, whom she was still struggling to understand.

When their first tour had ended, Emma and Sasha spent a little time at the Hotel International in Petrograd, meant to lodge foreign visitors and the noncommunist population. They had scarcely begun to enjoy the relative comfort and free time to rethink their four months on the road when they were sent to Archangel, at the mouth of the Northern Dvina, and arrived on a day when the temperature was fifty degrees below zero. But the cold air was balanced by the warm camaraderie and the relative optimism of these former members of the bourgeoisie—ex-nuns, monks, and White officers. These people, unlike the active anarchists, felt that they had not been discriminated against because of their past, and that the Soviets were sincere in their efforts to reclaim the country. All too soon, Emma and Sasha had to leave this oasis of contentment to continue their work for the museum. Held up by snowstorms, they spent a miserable Christmas on the road, fifty miles from Petrograd.

When they got back to the city, they found that their plans to continue working for the Museum of the Revolution had been pre-empted by a newly formed commission, "Ispart," created for the purpose of collecting data on the history of the Communist Party. The new organization's leadership had decided that Emma and Sasha's work was no longer necessary. Such arbitrariness incensed all those who had partici-pated in the Museum of the Revolution. Zinoviev himself wrote a letter of protest over the new arrangements, which he sent Emma and Sasha to Moscow to deliver. But their efforts had no effect.

They received word that Kropotkin was dying and tried to change their plans so they could visit him one last time, but the family asked that they wait. Sasha was called back to Petrograd to deliver a report on the state of their work for the museum. Emma stayed in Moscow, hoping to get word of Kropotkin's health. She took no news to be good news and proceeded on to Petrograd. But within an hour of her arrival, the Kropotkin family called her to his deathbed. Delayed by work obliga-tions, bad weather, broken telephone lines, and irregular train schedules, by the time she arrived, early in the morning of February 8, it was too late; the grandfather of the anarchist movement had died just an hour before. Emma stayed to help prepare for the transfer of Kropotkin's body to Moscow and to mourn with his closest family and friends. Sasha came with some comrades to assist in moving the body. Just before, in Moscow, he had organized the Kropotkin Funeral Commission and initiated a formal request to Lenin to release the anarchists imprisoned in Moscow just long enough to attend the funeral. To bypass the official line that there were no anarchists in Soviet prisons, Sasha threatened that the wreaths donated by the communist organizations and soviets would be removed from Kropotkin's coffin in protest unless the prisoners were released.

In the end, only seven prisoners were released, to lead the funeral procession as pallbearers. A massive outpouring of mourners from every walk of life, bearing armbands in red and black, showed up to honor their beloved Kropotkin. Speeches erupted spontaneously, and even Emma found herself on the platform once again. This obvious show of support for Kropotkin inspired Emma and Sasha to stop fighting for their positions at the Museum of the Revolution so they could begin laying the groundwork for a Kropotkin museum.

But when they returned to Petrograd in late February, they found the city paralyzed by a massive strike. Workers who could no longer bear the grinding poverty and the lack of fuel to temper the cold of the long winter had rebelled, convinced that resources and money were being hoarded by the more privileged classes that still existed within the Soviet Union. The Bolshevik leadership, plagued by war and blockades of food and supplies, viewed the strike as a complete abandonment of the principles of the revolution. They declared martial law and ordered the workers back to their factories. But the workers did not acquiesce; instead, the strike spread and the jails filled. Then, just when it seemed that the workers might be starved into submission, the sailors of Kronstadt decided to join the protest, expanding the demands of the strike to include the democratization of the Bolshevik state. They demanded free elections by secret ballot, freedom of the press and assembly for labor unions and peasant organizations, individually run, small-scale production, the abolition of all political bureaus that repre-

sented undue privilege and power, and the disbanding of armed Bolshevik units. The general strike had now taken on a more democratic cast.

Lenin and Trotsky panicked and signed an order proclaiming that
the Kronstadt sailors had mutinied against the Soviet government, and
that the sailors were "tools of former tsarist generals who together with
Socialist-Revolutionist traitors staged a counter-revolutionary conspiracy
against the proletarian Republic." The situation escalated, and threats of
violence emanated from the Kremlin. By this time Sasha and Emma were
both convinced that they could no longer remain silent. On March 5
they wrote to Chairman Zinoviev of the Petrograd Soviet of Labor and
Defense:

> To remain silent now is impossible, even criminal. Recent events
> impel us Anarchists to speak out and to declare our attitude on the
> present situation. The spirit of ferment and dissatisfaction manifest
> among the workers and sailors is the result of causes that demand
> our serious attention. Cold and hunger have produced dissatisfac-
> tion, and the absence of any opportunity for discussion and criti-
> cism is forcing the workers and sailors to air their grievances in the
> open.
>
> More important still, the use of force by the Workers' and
> Peasants' Government against workers and sailors will have a
> reactionary effect upon the international revolutionary movement
> and will everywhere result in incalculable harm to the Social
> Revolution.
>
> Comrades Bolsheviki, bethink yourselves before it is too late. Do
> not play with fire: you are about to make a most serious and
> decisive step. We hereby submit to you the following proposition:
> let a Commission be selected to consist of five persons, inclusive of
> two Anarchists, the Commission ... to settle the dispute by
> peaceful means. In the given situation this is the most radical
> method. It will be of international revolutionary significance.
>
> EG. AB. Perkus, Petrovsky.

Their plea went unanswered, although the next day, March 6, the
Petrograd Soviet telegraphed the Revolutionary Committee, asking if a

delegation of both party and nonparty members of the Soviet might visit Kronstadt. So much mistrust had developed by this time that the beleaguered sailors rejected the Soviet conciliatory gesture. Time had run out. The Cheka and the army were ordered to attack. From March 7 through March 17, 1921, the days and nights were filled with gunfire, and tens of thousands of sailors and soldiers were slain.

Lenin explained the Kronstadt rebellion in his discussion of the New Economic Policy:

In the spring of 1921, mainly as a result of the failure of the harvest and the dying of cattle, the condition of the peasantry, which was extremely bad already as a consequence of the war and blockade, became very much worse. This resulted in political vacillation which, generally speaking, expresses the very "nature" of the small producer. The most striking expression of this vacillation was the Kronstadt mutiny.

The most characteristic feature of the Kronstadt events was precisely the vacillation of the petty-bourgeois element. There was very little of anything that was fully formed, clear and definite. We heard nebulous slogans about "liberty," "free trade," "emancipation from serfdom," "Soviets without the Bolsheviks," or new elections to the Soviets, or relief from "Party dictatorship," and so on and so forth. Both the Mensheviks and the Socialist-Revolutionaries declared the Kronstadt movement to be "their own." . . . The big banks, all the forces of finance capital, are collecting funds to assist the Kronstadt. . . .

The events of the spring of 1921 once again revealed the role of the Socialist-Revolutionaries and Mensheviks: they are helping the vacillating petty-bourgeois element to recoil from the Bolsheviks, to cause a "shifting of power" for the benefit of the capitalists and landlords. . . .

We are surrounded by the world bourgeoisie, who are watching every moment of vacillation in order to bring back "their own fold," to restore the landlords and the bourgeoisie. We will keep the Mensheviks and Socialist-Revolutionaries, whether open or disguised as "non-party," in prison . . . or packed off to Berlin . . . so they may freely enjoy all the charms of pure democracy.

When it was over, Emma was haunted by the stillness that had fallen on this "city drenched in blood." For the first time, she entertained the idea of fleeing Soviet Russia, to tell the world of the atrocities she had witnessed in her motherland. The death of the Kronstadt sailors had given Emma a new mission; perhaps international outrage would change the course of postrevolutionary Russia.

Sasha was also convinced that they had to leave. He could not tolerate the New Economic Plan adopted by the Bolsheviks following Kronstadt. He was angered by Lenin's economic flexibility and political rigidity. The plan seemed to offer too many concessions to Russia's lingering capitalist constituency. While he was planning a secret escape, they got word of an anarchist congress to take place in Berlin in December. They seized the opportunity, applied for official permission to attend, and made arrangements to leave.

In the meantime, while Emma and Sasha waited to be "packed off to Berlin," they clashed with some of the more zealous pilgrims from the United States. Bill Haywood, in particular, saw Emma's critique as playing into the hands of the right wing in the United States, and even went so far as to imply that perhaps her vocal opposition to the Soviet regime was a way of winning favor for herself in the eyes of the government in the United States. His reaction offered a small taste of the new anger Emma's views were to incur in radical circles. Well accustomed to championing unpopular causes, she handled such criticisms without flinching in her beliefs.

She remembered that even John Reed, the American communist whose early enthusiasm was expressed in his book *Ten Days That Shook the World,* had died in Soviet Russia in a typhus delirium shouting about being caught in a trap. Memories of the anarchists in Russia who had suffered, been killed, or been forced to die a slow death by starvation haunted her. Emma's desire to reveal the offenses of postrevolutionary Russia, its extreme forms of repression, and the betrayal and suppression of the anarchists was fueled by her loyalty to the anarchists and her terrible fear that their voices would never be heard, that justice would never triumph.

I would return to the National [hotel] bruised and battered, my illusions gradually shattered, my foundations crumbling. But I would not let go. After all, I thought, the common people could not understand the tremendous difficulties confronting the Soviet Government: the imperialist forces arraigned against Russia, the many attacks which drained her of her men who otherwise would be employed in productive labor, the blockade which was relentlessly slaying Russia's young and weak. Of course, the people could not understand these things, and I must not be misled by their bitterness born of suffering. I must be patient. I must get to the source of the evils confronting me. . . . Was this the Revolution I had believed in all my life, yearned for and strove to interest others in, or was it a caricature—a hideous monster which had come to jeer and mock me? . . .

I was no longer deceived by their mask, but my real problem lay much deeper. It was the Revolution itself. Its manifestations were so completely at variance with what I had conceived and propagated as revolution that I did not know any more which was right. My old values had been shipwrecked and I myself thrown overboard to sink or swim. All I could do was to try to keep my head above water and trust to time to bring me to safe shores.

Emma began to write to her friends about her disillusioning experiences in Soviet Russia, in part to share and spread the word, and in part to think out her position on paper. She described herself in Russia as a rabbit in a trap: the issues were complex, and her loyalties divided. She also ached to escape the isolation and confusion she felt, and to recapture a measure of her former sense of identity, which had grown dim in the last two years. Seemingly out of nowhere, a man had approached her in Kiev with a bundle of *Mother Earth* magazines. Instead of surprise and pride, Emma had felt a sense of hopeless longing for the past. "In the Russian cataclysm, my former life in America had receded into pale memory, becoming a dream bereft of living fibre and I myself a mere shadow without firm hold, all my values turned to vapor. The sudden appearance of *Mother Earth* copies revived the poignancy of my aimless and useless existence. Yearning, sickening yearning, possessed me, chilling the very marrow of my being."

Emma wrote to the *New York World,* "I wish I had a tongue of fire; I would burn it into the hearts of the American people what a crime is being committed against this great country."

To her lawyer and friend Harry Weinberger, who had worked so untiringly to keep her in America, she wrote:

The only difference between Russia and other countries is that in Russia the very elements who have helped unfurl the revolution have also helped to carry the revolution to her grave—and that pain eats more into one's vitals than the existence of reaction in other lands.

She summed up her feelings to Stella:

It was excruciating to go through the last two years. But you need not think it will be easy to go away. All my life I fed on the wonderful spirit of Russia, all my life I longed to see it free. Then to have found it prostrate, kicked into the gutter, attacked on all sides, enduring tortures Dante's Inferno did not contain. Above all stabbed to the heart by its own friends. And then not to be able to help even a little bit. Yes, that was the hardest to bear, for never in all my life did I [so much] long to help, to be of service, to give out of my overflowing heart to the people of Russia. But it was impossible. So if we go, we will have given nothing and no one will know the yearning that was ours since we set foot on Russian soil. Will I be able to give anything in other lands? I am not deceived. I know only too well how rooted I have become. I know how little I could do now in America, which seems to have gone mad with reaction. Yet I feel I belong there and nowhere else. However, I must try other shores, get away from the nightmare, look at the tremendous panorama of Russia at a distance. That is necessary if one is not to judge too [sub]jectively.

And Emma confided in her niece Stella that even Sasha was getting on her nerves, with his ability to take and take as "a matter of fact." Still, "often when I feel I can stand it no longer, the Western Penitentiary looms up as black as night and all else is forgotten."

Emma wrote to Agnes Inglis likening her shattered Russian dream to her struggle to stay in love with Ben once she knew the true nature of their relationship:

Ah, dearest girl. How we used to dream of the wonderful thing come true in Russia. But like all dreams there is an awakening which is hard to bear even for the strongest of us. One could not bear it if one did not know that other dreams will come and that the ideal must always remain real. Do I speak riddles? . . .

You remember my saying that the love which sees is a tragic love. But it is the only love worth while. So if we will love Russia, we must cease to be blind among the blind. . . . Out of the ruins, out of all that is crushed and shattered, must come new life. . . .

Do you ever hear from Ben R? If you write him send him my greetings. I wonder how he is.

In fact, Emma had thought of Ben quite often. She first wrote to him in March of 1920, three months after she had waved good-bye to him at the LaSalle Street Station. In those three months what she had experienced made her "absence seem like many years." She had written to him and many other friends from her "floating prison," but so far not a word had reached her from anyone in the United States. "You can imagine how I feel about it. It is very difficult for one at my age to acclimatize himself in a new country, even under the best conditions, in normal times. But Russia, bled white by over four years of war and starved by the inhuman blockade, is not a place where one may hope to take root easily. However, if I could at least hear from those dear to me I left behind, life would not be so difficult."

What she did not know—but might have expected—was that her mail and her activities were being watched by agents of the United States government, who perceived her as a threat to national security even from her exile in Soviet Russia.

Her letter to Ben was transcribed and sent to the Director of Military Intelligence as part of the "Weekly Situation Survey." Emma's earliest accounts of her enthusiasm for the arts in the Soviet Union was considered of enough interest to national security to be included in the surveillance materials: "The one great delight we have had so far has been the Art Theatre and the Studio of Stanislavsky, of whose work, as you will remember, I have often spoken in my lectures. The acting is superb, the scenery and setting most wonderful in their simplicity. Besides that, we have seen some wonderful art galleries, in which Moscow in particular seems to be very rich."

Ben unknowingly leaked information to an agent that this was the first communiqué he had received from Emma since her deportation and that all mail went through Stella.

Without ever receiving an answer, Emma wrote to Ben again from Petrograd on May Day. "I think of you often and of the things that were. You used to say 'life is strange.' I am only now realizing how very strange it really is. One longs and dreams for what often seems the unattainable. Yet when one realizes one's dreams, one finds reality so very different from one's dreams. After all to be ever alluring and ever receding."

For her birthday Ben wrote her a rambling, nostalgic letter on the ironies of life.

> Dear little Mommy:
> It's June 27th again.
> Your birthday.
> My heart turns to you.
> Brain is flooded with memories.
> Of our happy years together.
> Especially of your Birthdays.
> Do you remember the first one?
> We spent together in Sunny Calif.
> Remember the corals and the flowers.
> Was it on your birthday.
> When we were in the Bellingham jail.

Jail that makes me think.
It was or is 5 years since.
We spent your birthday together.
Four years ago I in Queens County.
Three years ago in Calif.
(And you on trial) in New York.
Two years I in Warrensville.
And you in Jefferson City.

Yes life is strange.
And when I thinks about the things
That was and is, I am glad:
Grateful for those glorious years.
That we worked, played and loved.
We did things, you carved.
Your name in history (I helped a little)
And made thousands love and revere you.

It was here (Chicago, March 1908.)
Now you are in far off Russia.
Exiled, but not isolated.
Deported but not Cast out.
You will come back.
America is big, beautiful.
And when she awakens to your usefulness
She will welcome you back.

He continued his letter with news of his own new life.

A successful Dr. business is very good.
A well liked prison physician.
As popular with prisoners as I was with outcasts.
A sort of a 3rd class politician. . . .
Still talking much in Hall and Street.
Talked at Theological seminary and to Bartenders Union.

Was arrested at Press Club banquet at Sherman Hotel.
For carrying a half pint on hip.
Being "respectable," case dismissed without a trial. . . .

Many of our old friends have stayed at our home. . . .
All comrades not in jail seem prosperous.
Home life apparently successful.
Brutus big, happy and a joygiver.
Anna well, lovely and devoted.
Mother, ill, cheerless wants Calif.
Hobo "he will get by somehow."
Willie not all together idle.
But he always hankers for Miss T. B. . . .
Are the Bolsheviks good lovers? . . .
Someday we will meet.

Within the year, Ben attempted to obtain a visa to visit Emma in
Russia, his trip to follow a visit to his wife's relatives in London. The
United States Embassy in London investigated Reitman after his request,
which was denied when they learned from the Department of Justice
that he "was formerly a close associate of Emma Goldman." The denial
was signed by J. Edgar Hoover, who had a political vendetta that
bordered on the personal against Emma and all her associates.

Although Ben had chosen domesticity and religion over politics, he
still sympathized with Emma and the anarchist cause. In fact, he tried to
arrange, through the Dill Pickle Club in Chicago, a relief fund for
anarchists imprisoned by the Russian Bolshevik government.

Emma reminded herself, on the point of leaving Russia, that she
had also been able to pry herself away from Ben, from his abuses and
ultimate rejection of her. She still loved him, as she loved America,
feeling her departure as "a tragic end of a great love to which one clings
long after it is no more." Now, when her train pulled away from Moscow
on December 1, 1921, she felt that her "radiant dream," her "burning
faith," was crushed. She could hardly suppress her sobs.

But she had not lost faith in her great ideal, anarchism. In her later

315

writing, she attributed any last vestige of civil rights in the Soviet Union to the prior existence of an independent anarchist movement there. Emma believed that a revolution would ultimately fail unless the means and the ends were identical in spirit.

> [Revolution] is the herald of NEW VALUES, ushering in a transformation of the basic relations of man to man, and of man to society. It is not a mere reformer, pitching up some social evils; not a mere changer of forms and institutions; not only a re-distributor of social well-being. It is all that, yet more, much more. It is, first and foremost, the TRANSVALUATOR, the bearer of "new" values. It is the great TEACHER of the NEW ETHICS, inspiring man with a new concept of life and its manifestations in social relationships. . . . It is the mental and spiritual regenerator. . . .
>
> Revolution . . . signifies not mere "external" change, but "internal," basic fundamental change. . . .
>
> Revolution is the mirror of the coming day; it is the child that is to be the Man of To-morrow.

News of Emma's departure threw Hoover and the intelligence agencies of the United States military, the Department of Justice, and the Immigration and Naturalization Service into a frenzy. Photographs of her were sent to immigration officers throughout the country, in case she married and tried to re-enter. A U.S. Secret Service agent posing as an Associated Press reporter had interviewed someone who knew Emma in Moscow, and reported that Trotsky and Lenin were afraid of Emma "for the reason that she may be too smart for them, and through her influence overthrow their present form of government. Emma Goldman is closely watched, and if she were to do anything out of the way against the government she would no doubt pass out of existence." Such reports led to increased U.S. surveillance of Emma, because it was feared that, once she was out of Russia, her access to the Western press would bring her back forcefully into American public life. The Secret Service Commission filed a report with the Secretary of State, concerning the departure of Berkman, Goldman, and their friend Alexander Shapiro from Soviet Russia:

The parties mentioned arrived in Riga from Moscow Dec. 5th and proceeded directly to the residence occupied by the Bolshevik Consulate, where they remained during practically all of their stay in Riga.

On Dec. 22, they departed by the afternoon train for Reval only to be taken off the train a few stations down the line by agents of the Latvian secret service and brought back to Riga, where they remained in jail until yesterday [Dec. 30], when they were released from confinement. They, of course, are being carefully watched, and I anticipate no difficulty in keeping myself informed regarding their movements.

The object of the action of the Latvian secret service in removing them from the train was to afford their agents an opportunity to search the baggage, personal effects, etc., and to examine all of their papers and documents, which of course could not be done while they were housed in the Bolshevik Consulate.

All of the papers and documents found in the possession of these three parties came into my hands for a few hours. Every effort was made during this brief period of time to make copies of those which it was thought would be of interest to the Department. These papers and documents clearly establish the fact that Goldman, Berkman, and Shapiro were proceeding to Berlin to attend an international congress of anarchists which was to convene at Berlin on Dec. 25.

Emma and Sasha had spent Christmas in prison again—this time in Latvia. Finally Sweden agreed to allow them a month's asylum, while the Germans deliberated over their request to enter the country. All of the letters Emma sent from Riga were intercepted, excerpted, and dispatched to the U.S. Secretary of State, including her instructions on how to send letters and to whom. In Berkman's diary notes, which were confiscated, he had chronicled the progression of his inner feelings through this ordeal:

Dec. 21st . . . This is just the day two years ago that we were taken aboard the *Buford*. It was midnight, Dec. 20-21, 1919, when we were called out, going aboard about 7:05 A.M. December 21st. Just two years! What joy and woe crowded those last two years, but mostly grief, disappointment and disillusion. Really terrible when I stop to think of it. The enthusiasm of those days at the thought of nearing the promised land! Where has it all gone? . . . Where shall we be this Christmas? and New Year's? It seems to me we are just drifting, going where we could not stay.

13

BLOWN TO THE WINDS

On January 2, 1922, Emma and Sasha boarded a steamer from the port of Reval in Estonia for Stockholm. The United States consulates in all the countries of Europe were sent notices about the two aliens, who were suspected of intending to return to the United States. Officials at every border and port of entry in Europe and the United States were sent photographs and warnings about Emma and Sasha. The United States also tried to encourage its allies to lock out or harass the two exiles wherever else they might go. They no longer had any hope of attending the conference, but at this point the two were relieved just to be out of the Soviet Union. They were also anxious to publish articles about their Russian experience as soon as possible. Sweden, with its generally tolerant attitudes, was a good place to begin.

Their arrival was heralded by a low-key reception from syndicalist friends, who provided housing, food, camaraderie, and some protection from the curious reporters who, Emma feared, wanted only to seize and distort her first words about the Soviet Union and make them international news.

It was not long before Emma and Sasha had written several articles of their own, and agreed to be interviewed in the friendly local press. During this time, Emma reluctantly accepted an offer to write a series of articles for the *New York World* on her Russian experience, for she wanted her views known in the United States above all. But the labor papers there had already turned down her articles, and she was running out of money. Sasha felt that writing against the Bolsheviks in a capitalist newspaper was a mistake, and he made his disapproval plain. Predictably, Emma's new cause was not well received by her old comrades. Bill Haywood called the articles

> false, malicious, but well suited for the purpose intended. It is Emma's desire to return to the United States where she was formerly able to obtain the good will of illiterate audiences. The people of Soviet Russia stand far above the most radical ideal Miss Goldman has ever had. . . .
>
> The articles must be viewed from the point of view of their mission; a polite knocking at the doors of the United States, these doors which she states with a sigh are closed and sealed. She shows no ill feeling towards the United States though she stated that this country has robbed her of home and heart but she is furious at Soviet Russia which offered her work, a home and a living. Is not her attitude towards the Soviet Government more than pure ingratitude?

He went so far as to attribute some of her misguided zeal to the fact that she was a woman:

> . . . when a woman falls, there are no limits to which she cannot go. No doubt similar articles will be flowing from her pen, that instrument [with] which she tries to open the locks of the doors closed to her, though every work she writes will condemn her in the opinion of former friends as they know she was made welcome when she came to Russia and given an influential post by the Soviet Government. . . . It is not her friends who have made her impossible. She has sealed her own doom.

Emma found herself suffering the practical consequences of voicing her passionate beliefs. Exiled from her beloved Russia, she was forced to search for a place to live while all the world seemed to be closing its doors to her. She had lost the only home she had ever had, in America, and her hope for the revolution in Russia as well.

But Emma had a new source of emotional sustenance. Rebounding quickly from her disappointment, she met a man who was more than twenty years her junior. Emma called him her "sunbeam," and, as photographs of Emma taken at the time show, a softness, nearly vanished during the two years in prison and her subsequent two years in Russia, resurfaced in her face.

Emma had met Arthur Swenson in Swedish anarchist circles, the "one comforting association of [her] dismal sojourn in Stockholm." With her visa running out, she was desperately seeking another place to live. She and Swenson even tried to stow away together on a boat to Denmark. A policeman who found them entangled under a blanket accepted Emma's story that they were destitute lovers and agreed not to arrest them if they left the boat. Still without anywhere to go, thanks to the efforts of the U.S. State Department and the Russian Cheka, Emma and Arthur returned to Stockholm. When a visa from Germany finally came through, Emma hoped to start a new life in Berlin, where she would wait for Swenson.

In Berlin, Emma had good friends from her 1907 trip, the German anarchists Millie and Rudolf Rocker, and the advantage of speaking fluent German. There she would write a book about her experiences in Russia and bask in the glow of her "sunbeam."

Arthur wrote to her from Copenhagen that he not only wanted to be *near* her, he wanted to be *like* her, which he considered synonymous with "good":

I want to work, to work for your great ideals because they are mine. Oh, I want to devote my life for the good of all mankind. Before I met you I did not live; I doubted everybody and condemned almost everything. Now the sun shines with a radiant glow and I know that all mankind is of good and not of evil. Oh, Emma, make me good, I want to be good in every way! Oh,

I love you so much, there is no limit to my love to you, my darling
Emma!

Despite his effusiveness, Emma could not quite believe that her
"infant," as she called him, could stay erotically interested in someone
her age. She knew she had his admiration, but what she wanted most was
reassurance of his physical attraction. So, while their separation enhanced the fantasy of romantic passion, it also increased Emma's insecurity. She wondered whether he wouldn't be more attracted to the young
women of Berlin than to her. Swenson acknowledged that many women
were attracted to him, even in Sweden, but his heart belonged to Emma:
"You tell me of all the young attractive girls in Berlin. Ah, there are lots
of them here too, but my love belongs to you and only you. . . . My Emma
is the youngest and most attractive of them all. And by God, I love her!"

Swenson obtained a travel visa on his own, but did not hesitate to
ask Emma for money to finance his trip. In fact, her "infant" seemed
repeatedly to squander the precious money Emma scraped together from
her *New York World* articles to send him. Yet, despite his growing financial
dependence on Emma, when she offered to formalize her support for
him, he felt threatened. More than anything else, he wanted Emma to
help him find his life's work; he rejected "the idea of being kept and fed
like a baby, altogether without possibilities to do a damned thing myself.
Anybody else is quite different. They can still do something but I don't
know of a goddamned valuable thing I could do."

"All that is high and noble and beautiful within me belongs to you,
my dearest beloved Emma," he wrote her. "I love you as much as a man is
capable of loving a woman. And I love the greatest woman on earth." But
by the time he arrived in Berlin, after a separation of just four weeks, it
was obvious to Emma that his passion had cooled. They clung to each
other nevertheless—Emma hoping that close contact would rekindle
passion and Arthur lacking either another place to go or the courage to
reject his idol. Emma later wrote about living with Swenson as "eight
months of purgatory."

Loneliness, the yearning to be cared for in an intimate sense, made
me cling to the boy. He admired me as a rebel and as a fighter; as a

friend and companion I had awakened his spirit and had opened to him a new world of ideas, books, music, art. He did not want to live away from me and he needed the fellowship and understanding that he found in our relationship, he said. But the difference, the ever present difference of twenty-four years, he could not forget.

In constant turmoil, Emma could neither write nor even think of anything else. She engaged in endless correspondence to escape her lethargy. She went so far as to write to men, such as Leon Malmed, who had expressed sexual interest in her, to counteract her current feelings of rejection. Everything was uncertain: forced to live from month to month, awaiting visa extensions, she also had to endure Sasha's intolerance of her obsession, and that of her devoted niece, Stella, who had come to visit. Stella had always kept her on a pedestal, and "could not bear to see [Emma's] feet of clay."

Emma made a breakthrough in her work only when Arthur went to the seashore, ostensibly to leave her alone with her niece and her grandnephew, Ian. Once again, complete immersion in work was her way of avoiding despair. It was the spring of 1922 when she finally began her book on Russia, temporarily removing her attention from her obsessive and unhappy love.

Almost as soon as Swenson returned, however, he fell in love with the young secretary who was helping Emma type the manuscript of her book. Naïvely, the two young lovers thought that they could hide their attraction for each other by arguing incessantly in Emma's presence. When the secretary moved into the apartment with Emma and Arthur, the humiliating situation grew worse. Emma wrote:

The two young people had fallen in love with each other and were fighting to distract my attention from their real feelings. They were too unsophisticated to be guilty of deliberate deception. They simply lacked the courage to speak and were perhaps afraid to hurt me. As if their frankness could have been more lacerating than my realization that their show of indifference was only a shield: at heart I had not ceased to believe that my love would rekindle his affection, so rich and abundant during our months in Stockholm.

Emma demanded that they find other living quarters, although she tried to retain separate friendships with both of them. But it did not take her long to realize that she could not handle a platonic relationship with Arthur.

Dear, dear Arthur

When one's life depends upon a surgical operation it is folly to postpone the painful process. One's condition only grows worse and brings one near to death.

For months I have seen with absolute clarity that my peace of mind and soul and my very life depend upon our *separation*. But I have gone on postponing the painful operation until I can bear it no longer.

I am not sure that you have understood the conflict that has lacerated my being and has been daily torture to me since your arrival in Berlin. . . . During all these painful months, in fact the first few days of your arrival, I saw with certainty that one month's separation had killed your love for me. I am often beset by doubts whether you ever really loved me, whether it was not self-deception on your part. Still I clung to the idea that nothing so cruel could happen. . . .

Then, after the first dreadful months in this apartment, and all through Stella's visit—your cruel disappearance until now—you have made me realize that it is futile to hope for the impossible. Still I kept on clinging, I thought the boy cannot help the death of his love, at least his friendship will assert itself somehow, it will help me with tenderness and understanding to overcome the storm within me. But even that was not to be, the elemental force which makes for love and which has died in you has also affected your entire attitude towards me. Your friendship and comradeship became of an indifferent sort, detached, cold and often even brutal. You continued near me all these months an entire stranger, you said repeatedly "I am a coward"! . . . You meant that you would have gone away long ago if you had the strength. . . . You have gotten yourself to be hard as nails, cruelly indifferent to me.

Don't for one minute think I am blaming you, my Arthur. My

brain sees, even if my heart refuses to submit to the verdict of my mind. You are thirty and I am fifty-two. From the ordinary point of view it is natural that your love for me should have died. It is a wonder it should ever have been born. How, then, can it be your fault? Traditions of centuries have created the cruel injustice which grants the man the right to ask and receive love from one much younger than himself and does not grant the same right to the woman. Every day one sees decrepit men of more than 52 with girls of twenty, nor is it true that these girls are with such men only for money. I have known several cases where girls of twenty were passionately devoted to men of sixty. No one saw anything unusual in that. Yet even the most advanced people cannot reconcile themselves to the love of a man of thirty for one much older than he. You certainly could not. . . .

I have stood the strain first because I could not get myself to accept the inevitable. I then stood it because I thought, I am helping you to grow finer, kinder, freer and more understanding. Above all because I thought I might help you to a purpose in life, to some strong glowing ideal. . . . What, then, should be the purpose of all my struggle, why spend sleepless nights and agonized days? Why see my love mortally wounded by an unkind look or wound in my flesh every hour of the day? *I must therefore ask you to go away.* . . .

Because if I wait much longer, you will grow still harder and my poor love will be crushed. I won't have that. I want to retain the memory of three glorious months, so full of beauty and warmth—

I am your friend whom you can always call upon, I will never fail you.

Always devotedly,
Emma

Emma put this letter in her drawer, unable to mail it, unable to expose herself. Finally, weeks later, she sent it, after spending an evening with Arthur at a Beethoven concert that, contrary to her expectations, had failed to bring them closer. Once her passion for Swenson had faded and she was back at the difficult task of writing about

Russia, her comrade Sasha re-entered her life to see her through the editing of the book. In sharing his notes with Emma, Sasha felt that in some ways he had provided her with the "meat" of his own book on Russia, out of deference and to overcome some awkwardness in their friendship.

Stella, who had been staying with Emma for three months, suddenly developed a serious ailment that threatened to blind her. Having finished most of the book, Emma welcomed the opportunity to devote herself to her niece. With the remainder of the book's advance money in hand, they went to Liebenstein in Germany, for Stella's treatments. During this time, Emma took the opportunity to visit with many old friends from Europe and America: Fitzi and a woman named Paula, who had also worked on *Mother Earth*; Ellen Kennan from Denver; Henry Alsberg, an American journalist with whom Emma had become friends in the Soviet Union; Rudolf and Millie Rocker, the German anarchists; Agnes Smedley, an American writer, and her lover from India, Chatto (Virendranath Chattopadhyaya, the Indian revolutionary then living in Berlin); and some comrades from England all convened at "Queen Emma's court." As Stella's health improved, Emma's spirits revived.

If Emma had retained her popularity among old friends and had made some new ones in Europe, she also encountered a wave of angry criticism from the left.

Support for the Soviet Union had grown among radical groups, and when her articles and book about Russia were published, she was fiercely attacked. That her literary agent at first suggested, however unsuccessfully, that Hoover write the introduction, and that her publisher had renamed her book *My Disillusionment in Russia* (1923)—and then claimed never to have received her second part and had omitted the last twelve chapters, which articulated what she thought a true revolution could mean—did not serve Emma well. When her publisher finally agreed to issue her afterword in a separate volume, it was titled *My Further Disillusionment with Russia* (1924), which once again belied her sympathy and understanding with the causes and original goals of the Russian Revolution. William Z. Foster, a leading American communist, went so far as to say that "everybody in Moscow was aware that Emma Goldman was receiving support from the American Secret Service

Department." And, in fact, the United States Ambassador in London wrote to the State Department and the FBI expressing how delighted they would be to receive a copy of Emma's book. Big Bill Haywood, nurturing his vendetta, wrote, "Emma Goldman did not get the soft jobs she was looking for; that was why she wrote against the Dictatorship of the Proletariat." And the labor leader Rose Pastor Stokes, who was once a friend of Emma's, suggested that she be burned in effigy.

In the face of all the indignities and personal insults, Emma continued to lecture, to write, and to try to persuade others that they, too, must speak out against the shocking brutality of the new regime in Russia. Many of her comrades, however, believing that she was too quick to condemn this world-historical experiment, urged her to be patient. Emma fought their "complacency" and "blindness." She felt that the Russian situation was steadily worsening, atrocities mounting. Even her staunch comrades Mollie Steimer and Senya Fleshine, who had been arrested years before in the United States for their work against U.S. intervention in Russia, were deported from the United States to Russia, then persecuted and jailed by the Soviets for their attempt to raise funds for food for the anarchist prisoners, and finally cast out, destitute and in bad health, onto Emma's doorstep in Berlin.

Emma's view of the Soviet Union made her position as an exile even more untenable, for many of those in the radical communities of Europe and the United States were antagonistic to her. In one letter that was intercepted by the Department of State, Emma wrote about the added despair of being an exile: "I have come to realize that there is no greater punishment for an active spirit than to be torn out of one's sphere." Eventually, she was forced to leave Germany. She wrote to her old friend Max Nettlau about her fears for herself and many old comrades: "Often I think that we revolutionists are like the capitalist system, we drain men and women of the best that is in them and then stand quietly by to see them end their days in destitution and loneliness. . . . Anarchism must be lived now in our relations to each other, not in the future."

Emma decided to move to England. In order to be granted a visa, she had only to prove that she knew people there who could support her financially. With the help of friends, and friends of friends, she put together a list of sponsors, then, in the summer of 1924, traveled to London via Holland and France.

She described her stay in Paris in a letter to Max Nettlau: "I myself have for 30 years built for the future and have hardly ever permitted myself to enjoy the moment. Then all was wiped out, root and all. Tossed about by the terrific tide, I now find it impossible to make plans, or work out a line of action. Perhaps that explains why I feel Paris so keenly, much more than 17 years ago, when I myself was much younger."

Emma wrote to Roger Baldwin that her seven weeks in Paris were the first time in seven years that she had felt free to breathe and move about. She even wrote a postcard to Ben, promising to write more "when I get settled somewhere between heaven and hell." To her old friend Agnes Inglis she wrote that she felt fifteen years younger. Yet she knew that the world had begun to see her as an aging woman. As her fifty-sixth birthday approached, she wrote to Minna Lowensohn, a friend in New York: "To be sure I am young in heart, but that is most unfortunate in the case of a woman. Such a luxury is permissible only to men. The lucky dogs, everything is permissible to them, no wonder they think themselves the superior sex. And what is more they are, in their achievements and their rights to drain life to the last drop. But enough of 'mere males.'"

To Van Valkenburgh Emma wrote: "My trouble is not that I am poor myself, nor that I am getting on in years, but that I cannot tone my spirit down to suit my years. Nothing more terrible for a woman, especially to have many years on her shoulders and yet retain a young spirit. That is nothing short of a crime in this world of ours."

Emma hoped to use the British Museum to finish her preliminary articles for a book on "Women and their Creativity." Despite her reputation as "a man's woman by feminists," Emma was acutely aware of the barriers to women's creativity, and of how undervalued many of their accomplishments were:

> . . . the opponents of woman as a creative factor do not deny that she has at all times inspired the "creators." [No] more do they gainsay her courage and heroism. They do deny, however, that woman can do original work of lasting quality. The usual argument

is there is no female Newton, Shakespeare, Goethe, Beethoven, etc. And there is not. But, then, the Newtons and the others mentioned are no indication for man's superior creative quality. They are very rare spirits, very solitary even among men.

What I want to prove is that in the average, there are creative women whose quality of work is on par with the men of their time. I agree with you that cooking and housekeeping are as much an art as painting. I must therefore find whether women have added to the comforts of home by simplifying the means of housekeeping, have they invented such things [as] have reduced the drudgery of housekeeping and have raised it to an art. Are women on par in the art of cooking with the great chefs who have developed it to an art. Anyhow, I mean to take up every phase of woman's creative efforts.

She had come to see that as a woman who had challenged laws and convention, she had something special to contribute to, and something to learn from, other women who had dared to assert themselves. She looked to American women as the beacon of the future:

Already the new American youth is making history in the social struggle, in woman's emancipation, in the new approach to the child and education. Above all, the creative forces now at play in America are most encouraging. Thus, America's thinking woman. What virile, alert and significant type there is being developed. Their freedom from care and hypocrisy, their love of life and beauty, their intense interest in the social struggle—far more than political suffrage—make of the American women an outstanding figure in the new conception of womanhood.

It soon became clear that no publisher was interested enough in her historical research at the British Museum to advance her money. Emma tried with limited success to sell her articles. Only interviews with contemporary women in the creative arts elicited any interest from publishers, and even that was no solid assurance.

The need to find a way to support herself was urgent. One friend suggested that she use the potential income from her book on Russia to start a magazine, but her recollections of the travails of sustaining a periodical were so vivid that she ruled out that possibility.

During this time of economic uncertainty, she tried to make sense of her own life experiences through her work. An essay she had written in 1924, "America by Comparison," hinted that she had been profoundly changed by "the curse" that had touched her life since 1917.

> In my childhood I was taught that people are imbued with conflicting impulses: the one which makes for good, the other for evil: and he who is strong enough to overcome "evil" is good. In that conception the saints and holy men were good, for which they were to be rewarded—if not on earth, surely in heaven. The others were bad and would suffer dire punishment.
>
> In later years I realized that the impulses which move the individual as well as the masses are not quite so simple and easily defined as I was led to believe by my well-intentioned parents and teachers. I have found that there is no straight and clearly marked line between good and evil. Both are interwoven, they overlap each other, cross and recross, and can frequently not be distinguished one from the other. Surely neither good nor evil can be chosen by one's mere "free will." I have found that good and evil are terms for human actions conditioned by various forces outside of man. Their meaning and content are subject to modifications and development in accordance with the changes constantly going on in the social and ethical values at various periods of human life.
>
> The most important lesson, however, which life has taught me is the relativity of things. Every institution, be it ever so evil, may yet become worse. On the other hand, the best in man and society can become better. That is the law of evolution and growth without which life would decay, and society become extinct.

Her research at the British Museum turned to the Russian dramatists, but even though digging into old archives and reconstructing the life and spirit of these writers excited Emma, it did not pay the rent. At one point she even toyed with the idea of opening a shampoo, facial, and scalp-massage parlor, as she had once done in New York.

Emma tried to sell articles about women and feminism, about Russia, the drama, even about the pros and cons of America, and about herself as the striking example of the disenchanted radical. In an essay "On the Equality of the Sexes," Emma affirmed "the function of the strong intelligent old maid . . . in the making of the New Woman." The unmarried woman had "the time and energy to examine closely the puzzle in which women were involved. . . . Also, as time went on, these childless women were free to demonstrate in their own persons that women have abilities and aspirations other than those represented by reproduction and manual work." She expanded her writing on women to include a defense of homosexuality, with an attack on the charge that Louise Michel, the great French revolutionary, had been a lesbian. Michel, she claimed, was "one of the truly great saints, utterly oblivious to personal feelings and desires."

Emma, unlike Louise Michel, could never be oblivious to personal feelings and desires. She confided to Sasha her desperate need for love, particularly as she felt herself aging:

We all need love and affection and understanding, and woman needs a damn sight more of it when she grows older. I am sure that is the main cause of my misery since I left A[merica]. For since then I have had no one, or met anyone who gave a fig for what I do and what becomes of me. Of course, you, dear, I am not speaking of our friendship, that is a thing apart. But I mean exactly what you mean, someone intimate, someone personal who would take some interest, show affection and really care. I think in the case of one who gave out so much in her life, it is doubly tragic not to have anyone, to really be quite alone. Oh, I know, I have the kids at home and a few dear comrades in A. But it is not that. I am consumed by longing for love and affection for some human being of my own. I know the agony of loneliness and yearning. I therefore agree fully with you that both men and women need some person who really cares. The woman needs it more and finds it impossible to meet anyone when she has reached a certain age. That is her tragedy.

When Ellen Kennan wrote to Emma how lovingly Ben Reitman had spoken of her in the United States, Emma replied:

> I only wish he would have demonstrated his feelings in my most crucial moment, it would have been so much easier to bear the two years in the Missouri Penitentiary. Even ghastly disappointment in Russia would have been easier to bear. For I would have been one faith richer, that Ben was dependable and really cared. . . . Ben was my Grande Passion. But my life would not be quite so desolate as it is if Ben too had not broken faith. . . . The ten years of our work and travel will always stand out as the most worthwhile and attractive in my life.

No one had ever replaced Ben, and Emma increasingly felt the weight of her life of successive disappointments. She tried to concentrate on the mundane tasks of surviving as an exile, and on reminiscence. In a letter to Frank Harris, she recalled her early dispute with Kropotkin, when he had criticized the stress placed by a San Francisco anarchist paper on the sexual emancipation of women:

> Peter Kropotkin was very much opposed to that. . . . He insisted that if Woman will be educated and advanced politically, she will be able to arrange her own sexual life. I, on the other hand, hotly defended the need of sex propaganda and enlightenment along with the education along other lines. Peter became terribly excited during the argument and denounced us as "heretics" in no [uncertain terms]. I was then 24 years younger, you see, and Kropotkin was about 58. I said, "Dear Peter, when I will be your age the sex question may be settled for me; just now, it is a very dominant factor. I demand freedom for expression in the love relation as I do in any other phase of life." Peter stopped short, looked at me for a moment, and then began to roar. With a most gracious smile on his face, he said: "What a fool I am. I forgot that Youth cannot consider what is most practical or impractical for propaganda."

Now she was almost the age Kropotkin had been when they had that meeting, and Emma's face was etched with lines of disappointment and bitterness. She wrote to her old friend and cellmate, Kate Richards O'Hare:

I wish I could say that I look as youthful as you seem to be: at least I can say I feel youthful. Sometimes a youthful spirit in an old body is a very unfortunate thing. Especially in the case of woman. The world, whether Conservative or Radical, will go on judging woman by her looks and not by her spirit; that is where man has so much advantage over her. . . .

The only thing to survive this cruel inequality is to devote one's life to a great cause: to something worthwhile living for.

Emma had always been concerned about her appearance. Although she wasn't conventionally beautiful, she had an attractiveness rooted in her best qualities, especially in her dynamism. When she couldn't express herself through her politics or a love relationship, Emma knew that the frustration and disappointment affected her looks, and that made her feel even worse.

In 1925, Emma was stunned at receiving a letter from Ben. She daydreamed about her former life with Ben and toyed with writing her memoirs, to re-create the feelings they had shared in 1908. Living in exile in itself forced her constantly to reassess her life: her sense of not living fully in the present and yet never being able to recapture her past made Emma feel "nowhere at home." It was no surprise, then, that she took four months to respond to Ben, who had received two and three letters a day when their love affair was most intense. She explained to her "Dear old Ben" that the late reply did not mean she had forgotten him:

It is because it is extremely hard for me to pick up torn threads and piece them together. There is so much that has passed in the last eight years which has thrown us upon such opposite shores, and has created such a wide gulf I do not know how to go about to reach you. That does not mean that there is bitterness in my soul, or anything of that sort to prevent my writing you as I would like.

It is only that I fear you might misunderstand anything I would say, as hurt, or a desire to make you unhappy. I certainly do not want you to feel that way. So how am I to begin the old long ago?

Emma began by reasserting that she was glad Ben had found happiness in his family and work. Although she would never dare accuse him of being "respectable" after the life they had led together, she did say:

You are of the Jewish race no matter how much you are absorbed in Jesus, and I have never known Jews who are settled down, though many of them do become disagreeably respectable.

But whatever you have become, I shall never think of you in any other way except as you appeared to me 17 years ago last March, vivid, intense, irresponsible, fascinating and irritating at the same time.

She went on to sketch their differences, particularly given her experiences over the last several years. Ben had recently been given the management of the Grandville Hotel of Chicago, by vice-syndicate leaders, "for one month as a haven for hoboes." And he was staff physician to a Mafia-run house of prostitution.

As I have often told you, you are of a different world than mine, now perhaps more than when we first met. The events of the last eight years have crowded in so many heartbreaking experiences in my life and my world that yours seems even more removed than in 1908. But I have come to realize that there may be much of value in the worlds of others though they are not like mine. And that my world may have many aspects not so very much worthwhile as I had imagined. But of whatever natures our worlds are, we cannot get away from them, each remains in his separate hell, or heaven—just as one chooses to look upon. You are more inclined to see your world as heaven. I have remained irreconcilable and discontented and see the world as anything but "divine." Never mind, old Ben, we remain as always tied to the inmost depths of our beings. [There] is no reason why people who are so very different as we

two have ever been should not be friends, and remember each
other in affection. I certainly remember you in that sense. And I am
grateful to whatever queer forces there may be in life for having
brought you to me. Not for Morgan's fortunes would I have missed
knowing and having you in my life.

Emma wrote that she would have an easier time expressing her
thoughts to Ben in person, and encouraged him to visit her in London.
"Forgive me if I seem aloof and cold, I do not want to be either. But I
really find it impossible to put down what is in my mind and if I wait
much longer I shall probably not be able to write at all, and expose
myself to your wrong interpretation as if I did not care to hear from you."

Remembering the excitement of her association with Ben, she
lamented the slow pace of her life now, in which

> there is no Calif., where one can go on a tour, and no Hobo to
> organize meetings. . . . One in my position can make no plans, I am
> just drifting, living from day to day. Interesting in a way, but not
> very secure for an old lady like myself.
>
> Yes, many people speak kindly of me as they do of the dead. The
> dead can live on praise, not so the living. And that I am very much
> alive I hardly need to tell you, hence the "kind" things my erstwhile
> or present friends say about me may be nice, but . . . you see I am still
> the old skeptic. I still do not believe in friendships which [are] ex-
> pressed in words merely. But it is all right, I do not mind, I am rather
> amused with the stuff that appears in the [American] papers. The
> praise is no more to be taken seriously than the condemnation used
> to be. One must learn to go one's way and remain true to oneself.
>
> You are as extravagant in your praise, Ben dear, as you used to be. I
> am not at all great. If I were that, I would have made the world see the
> things which to me are still the most and only worthwhile living and
> struggling for. I know too much of myself to [think] that I have
> succeeded, hence am not great. I do not mean success in the ordi-
> nary term of the word, you understand that, do you not, dear Ben? . . .
>
> Affectionately
>
> EG

Ben seemed to leap at the opportunity to see Emma again, and arranged to come to England. But as their rendezvous approached, his letters reflected some of his old feelings that he was undermined in his own struggles by Emma and Sasha, who were too caught up in their own pain "to see or to feel what was happening to *me.*"

As the date of Ben's arrival approached, Emma could hardly wait to see him. She chided him for not remembering her birthday in his June 27 letter to her, but then wrote nostalgically, "It will be almost six years since I saw you last. . . . Well, I will be very glad to see you, dear, old Ben."

Emma hoped that this opportunity to re-establish contact with her past would revive her spirits. Since she needed them as a resource for her projected autobiography, she asked Ben to bring her the five hundred letters she had written him. Ben felt complimented, and hoped that he would have a place in history next to hers. He, too, wanted to write an autobiography. Yet their nostalgia was necessarily accompanied by a residue of resentment. Before leaving for England, Ben expressed his conflicting feelings, warning her not to "always [be] knocking, kicking, criticizing, seeing the worst side of everything, whining," in her autobiography as she had been in her book about Russia:

It is good, it is wonderful to have you pay so much attention to me again.

Many many things crowd my mind. I have so much to say to you. What I am interested most in is, of course, your autobiography, and in mine. All your Letters, I have about 500 of them, and clippings and everything else is at your disposal. I am hoping to be able to talk to you soon. You have enough material for not only two volumes but for ten volumes. . . . Your first book on Russia left me sympathetic to Russia. I felt that Russia gave you every chance in the world, that they put themselves out to . . . you and Sasha. . . . YOU WERE AS YOU ALWAYS WERE HARD*CRITICAL* BITTER*SELF-DETERMINED*UNWILLING TO FALL IN WITH NEEDS OF THE COMMUNITY* (Now, don't label this refusal to compromise.) What I am trying to say [is] that you and Sasha wanted your way (and that is characteristic of the ANTI-MIND) and refused to work for God, for Society or Humanity, or whatever you may call it—unless it was your way.

There is no question that your way may have been best. . . .

Little blue-eyed Mommy, I want you to write a GREAT HAPPY HONEST WONDERFUL Autobiography—write as a mature philosopher, write as a student of life and social movements—Joy and many good things have passed your way, the Gods have been good to you. DON'T LEAVE THE WORLD WITH ONLY A HARSH CRITIC and an AGITATOR RECORD BEHIND YOU. Mommy dear, you have no idea of your whinefulness and bitterness and unjust critical attitude. Wake up and be happy.

Please don't tell me about the Poverty, misery, disease, tyranny and stupidity in the world. Sure there is—BUT THERE IS LESS OF IT IN THE WORLD THAN THERE WAS BEFORE YOU STARTED YOUR WORK. You see, Mommy, you have to be honest and just, even though the other fellow is not. . . . But when I understood that the Bolsheviks had to deal with minds like yours I was not surprised at the Kronstadt bombardment and Prisons and all the terrible things they did to the ANTI-MINDS—yes, you are a typical anti-mind, you always oppose the thing that is. Can't you be a philosopher and a thinker and not justify the right to live and thrive—the right to be—How in the hell could the bolshevists live and thrive if they allowed you and minds like you to have power? I am not saying that they knew what was best for the human race and I am less sure that the Anarchistic type of mind knows what is best. . . .

Be that as it may, I am glad you are to write the Story of EG, I am sure it will go over big. For there is no other woman that ever lived that had as many and as varied contacts with pulsating thrilling life as you have had, you can tell a wonderful story and I can see how you can make a most valuable contribution.

Unfortunately, Ben was forced to postpone his trip. His wife, Anna, was not well, nor was his brother, Lew. The British Consulate in Chicago, suspecting Ben's violent tendencies and strongly warned about him by the U.S. State Department, refused to grant him a passport and referred the matter to London, where it could take a month to produce an answer. Ben himself had recently finished writing a book on pimps and prostitutes, *The Second Oldest Profession,* which was with a publisher, awaiting a decision on publication. Besides, Ben realized that he needed to voice his long-accumulated anger with Emma to clear the air before their reunion. The two old lovers had their own separate interpretations of the past. Ben had to justify the changes in his life eventually to write his autobiography, and Emma had to unearth her old feelings for Ben to make her forthcoming book ring true.

When Emma answered Ben's letter, she matched his warning against bitterness by admonishing him to beware of sensationalistic tendencies in his own writing, then allowed herself some sarcasm: "So you are trying to write a better book than Sasha and I wrote. I certainly hope you will succeed. The world would then be enriched by a great work. So fire ahead, old Ben. I wish you all the success in the world."

She was infuriated by Ben's references to her ANTI-MIND, but, struggling to keep some perspective, she managed to find some of his accusations funny. Still, she could not resist another argument:

> You must have thought that you are preparing a sermon for your congregation, a regular Billy Sunday sermon, fire and brimstone upon the heads of us poor sinners. . . . You upbraid me for my "anti" mind, as you call it, by the way, where did you get this term? I am sure it is not yours. . . . Why, then, keep up such petty accusations? . . . Do you think Berkman and I were jealous of your literary output of that time? Really, Ben, it would be funny if it were not so sad that you should not rise above petty grievances.
>
> Imagine if I should indulge in such recriminations, I might throw it into your face that though we were together ten years and shared everything, the good as well as the bad, you have not been sufficiently interested since I left America to find out whether I am hungry or fed, warm or famished, distressed or at ease. . . . Would you like me to repeat my plaints about your neglect in every letter? Of course not. I would never have breathed a word, nor do I do so now in the sense of complaint. I merely mention it because you keep your complaints up in every letter. . . .

I have so many beautiful things in our common life to remember, there is no time left for the bitter things. Now won't you do the same, or have you nothing beautiful to remember?

If you are going to say the same things about me in your book as you have in your last letter, your book will be a great seller, the Communists will buy up the entire edition. . . .

Dear, dear Ben, please don't think I am hurt, or angry, really, really not. I don't mind your criticism in the least. I am certain you mean for my best, everybody knows what is best for the other fellow. I too used to know. I am not so sure now. You seem to be more sure than ever. I am glad for your sake. . . . Funny Ben. . . .

Goodbye, old scold.

Affectionately,
EG

Ben's answer to this: "Baby dear, I have seen you argue and debate with 1,000 different people and know that no one ever got the best of you. I have no desire to do so."

When Ben finally did see Emma in England the next year, their visit was a disaster. Too much time had passed, each had too much distaste for the other's changed world, and Emma's expectations of a reconciliation were too high. She experienced an added disappointment when he did not bring the old love letters he promised to lend her. After Ben returned to Chicago, she wrote: "Now that the old Mommy is dead, you ought to be able to be more frank than in the past. . . . No, our visit was not satisfactory, largely because you came to do enough work [on your book] for three months in two weeks. The gulf created in 8 years could not be bridged in two weeks. Well, it cannot be helped. Perhaps you will come back to Europe some day before I am too decrepit, then we might come nearer again."

Ben's visit heightened the pain of Emma's isolation and rekindled her anger at what she perceived as his insensitivity to her situation. Strong feelings of both attraction and repulsion overwhelmed her—but her dominant feeling toward Ben was, as always, deep disappointment. She knew that if she ever returned to the United States or Canada, she would have to limit her contact with him.

Emma's estrangement from men yielded a more adamantly feminist theme in her correspondence than at any other phase of her life. She saw in her close women friends the plight of the modern woman, who was paying dearly for her freedom. When Fitzi came to visit, Emma's intense identification with her was reflected in a letter to Sasha:

Of course the price we modern women and men too pay for our own development and growth is very great and painful, but one must go ahead or remain in the dull state of the cow. For it is not only the modern woman, but all civilized people who pay a certain price for their awakening. Another thing is that even the ordinary woman is not secure that she will have her children, her man, her home in her old age.

Nothing is certain in our time, or perhaps never was at any time for those who must struggle for their existence. In what way, then, is the ordinary woman better off than we are? I rather think she is worse off. For while the modern woman is more exacting and has greater and deeper needs, so too she has considerable richness out of her finer sensibilities and deeper understanding. There is nothing without a price and we must be ready to pay it. Fact is, we have no choice. There is the terrific urge towards freedom, towards the struggle for higher ideals, which no one can resist. What, then, is to be done? . . .

The one intrinsic cause is the tragedy of all of us women, Agnes Smedley, Ellen Kennan, Fitzi, Kitty Beck [who committed suicide], and nearly everyone I have known: it is the tragedy of getting on in age without anything worthwhile to make life warm and beautiful, without a purpose. I did not feel this so much as long as I was in America, had my work, and still believed in it. But since the Russian experience I have lost my faith and having nothing else in life, man, child, home, or even some profession to support me, I feel the utter void of life so much more. And for this very reason, I can understand Fitzi's void. . . .

Fitzi's main tragedy, which is pulling at her heart, is really the tragedy of all of us modern women. It is a fact that we are removed only by a very short period from our traditions, the traditions of being loved, cared for, protected, secured, and above all, the time when women could look forward to an old age of children, a home and someone to brighten their lives. Being away from all that by a mere fraction of time, most modern women, especially when they see age growing upon them, and if they have given out of themselves so abundantly, begin to feel the utter emptiness of their existence, the lack of *the man*, whom they love and who loves them, the comradeship and companionship that grows out of such a relation, the home, a child. And above all the economic security either through the man or their own definite independent efforts. Nearly every modern woman I have known and have read about has come to the condition of Fitzi. All have felt and feel that their lives are empty and that they have nothing to look forward to. . . .

The modern woman cannot be the wife and mother in the old sense, and the new medium has not yet been devised, I mean the way of being wife, mother, friend and yet retain one's complete freedom. Will it ever? . . .

In the meantime, the women had each other. Emma denied any sexual attraction to women, but found that many of her staunch supporters and most stimulating friends were lesbians. She wrote to Sasha about one friend who reminded her of Almeda Sperry (whose name she could not remember):

The only interesting person I have met in this city is Marjorie Peacock, an anarchist of a rather hazy kind. I believe she is a Homo, something like that woman who once corresponded with me and who came to Ossining, you remember. I wish I had her letters. Funny, I have even forgotten her name. I should like to write about her if ever I write my biography. Marjorie Peacock is terribly reserved, still I suspect she is a lady bug. She is as crude and primitive as anyone I have met . . . [and] as refreshing as an autumn day in New York. You'd like her, she is a little thing, very quaint and dark. I really enjoy being with her. No suspicion, please, it's all very platonic. But she helped me to throw off the gloom that was upon me Saturday evening and yesterday.

Although Emma could speak to London audiences in English, and had many devoted friends in the city, among them Ethel Mannin and Paul and Eslanda Robeson, she could not shake her depression there. She blamed it on the cold climate, and on the formality and lack of overt warmth which were part of the British culture. Emma wrote to Frank Harris from London complaining that she was "unable to earn something by my pen and finding it impossible to realize anything by means of lectures—at a loss for what to do—pushed by the eternal urge of life and the necessity of finding an outlet for my unquenchable thirst for new efforts and experiences."

To her surprise, Emma found that she was happier doing research and writing at the British Museum than she was speaking on the public platform. The strong communist movement in England was a critical factor here. Bertrand Russell recollected, in his autobiography, a dinner in London given in Emma's honor: "When she rose to speak, she was welcomed enthusiastically; but when she sat down, there was dead silence. This was because almost the whole speech was against the Bolsheviks."

With nowhere else to go, Emma was receptive to her friends' suggestion that she might legalize her stay in England through marriage. Her friend Harry Kelly, the Missouri-born union printer who had admired Emma ever since he launched the magazine *The Rebel* in 1895, and later worked with her editing a monthly bulletin for the Ferrer Center, in 1909, had offered to marry her in the past, to keep her from deportation, but Emma had refused on principle, being opposed to the institution of marriage. However, as she recalled in her autobiography, "the glowing dream [of Russia] was dead now, together with the notion that one could remain on earth without making compromises."

A sixty-five-year-old Welsh coal miner named James Colton, who had been her long-time supporter and friend, gave her his hand in marriage, although they were neither lovers nor even very close friends and certainly did not intend to live together. The press, confirming her fears, chose to see her act as a sign that she had betrayed her principles.

But, with British citizenship, Emma was now free. She could even escape the winter. When she suffered from fever and chills, she could accept an invitation from Frank and Nellie Harris to visit them in the south of France.

Emma began to see herself and her work in a new perspective. She was not happy trying to make a living lecturing and writing on subjects unconnected to the immediate economic and political situation of the country in which she lived. Asking for money from underpaid coal miners and cotton-mill workers was agony for her. And the lectures that she prepared with more research and care than she had ever had time for in the United States were too sparsely attended to satisfy her. What she needed was the immediate response of large audiences, and her words in print.

She wrote in her autobiography: "I did not have many more years to throw about. Meanwhile I was faced with the problem of making ends meet. Not till my deportation had I ever given a thought to this question; I had felt that as long as I could use my voice and pen, I could easily earn my living. Since then I had been haunted by the spectre of dependence."

Encouragement from a publisher to transcribe her lectures into a book, "The Origin and Development of the Russian Drama," eventually retitled in 1926, *Foremost Russian Dramatists,* and an invitation for a paid tour to Canada offered at least a temporary solution. For four months she lived and wrote in a beautiful little cottage called "Bon Esprit," found by Nellie and Frank Harris and ultimately purchased for Emma with the help of Peggy Guggenheim, in St.-Tropez, then just a fishing village. Neither of her prospects materialized, however. A general strike in England delayed the publication of her book indefinitely, and the lack of funds and fear of outright physical hostility by communists in Canada made the tour unlikely as well. But something of Emma's old spirit was renewed in her country house. For the first time since her exile, she could dig in the soil as she had done in Ossining, and surround herself with flowers, her lifelong passion. Gardening gave her the peace that she needed, and she wrote and visited with the many old friends from America and other parts of the world who lived nearby. Margaret Anderson, Peggy Guggenheim and her husband Lawrence Vail, Kathleen

Millay (the sister of Edna St. Vincent Millay) all made their way to her cottage. Some of them came every day for the stimulating conversation over coffee and pastries.

These friends encouraged Emma to write her autobiography. Once inspired, she was driven to find financial backing. Life as an exile had convinced her that she had made her greatest contribution in the past; she yearned to retell her story for posterity and for herself. As early as 1924, she had mentioned the idea to Agnes Inglis, but lamented the lack of money to support herself for the two years the work would take, collecting her letters and papers from friends all over the world as well as actually writing.

Emma's plan was to start writing while others raised money for her book. She insisted that she would not accept money with any strings—that without freedom, intellectual work was drudgery. She had made a point of seeing every statement, every fund-raising letter that went out of the New York-based Emma Goldman Memoirs Fund office, headed by her old friend W. S. Van Valkenburgh, her friend and benefactor Peggy Guggenheim, and the writer Howard Young, to make sure that they truly reflected her own wishes. People who had worked with her began to resent her possessiveness about raising money for her "magnum opus." Kathleen Millay, who worked on the fund-raising committee, complained to their mutual friend Van Valkenburgh about Emma: "I don't want to have started something and then lay down on the job; but I told Howard [Young] after he talked to Emma in Europe that she would be difficult and that she was demanding a lot without realizing she was demanding it. She is spoiled in her way, even if she has had such a hard life. And I have wasted too much time already on 'spoiled' people."

Indeed, Emma was not conscious of the ways she exploited people's generosity, particularly that of other women. The women who put Emma up in their homes would later complain that she had no regard for their needs, or the extent to which her busy schedule completely dominated their households. Emma acted as though it were her right to demand so much, because she gave so much to the cause. Many married women felt Emma to be a sexual threat, for although she did not always act on her impulses (as did Reitman), she did not hide them. Other women found

Emma abrasive: the softness that was part of her self-image was rarely apparent when she felt threatened or needy.

Among the autobiographies Emma read before embarking on her own was that of Isadora Duncan. Emma had always been critical of Isadora because of what she perceived to be her lack of sympathy for other women. Only Isadora's tragic death could elicit Emma's forgiveness for her offenses:

> Isadora Duncan's life . . . is a beautiful piece of work, and it is one of the simplest and frankest records of a human life. Her description of the death of her children really broke my heart. It is so vivid and so tremendously gripping. In fact her whole life seems to me to have been fated, one fierce disillusionment after another, but, then, there can be no greatness without the dreadful price it is called upon to pay, so if Isadora had many clouds in her life, so too did she have many brilliant days. I am sorry in a way that I permitted her antagonism to our sex to stand in the way of knowing her better. I confess I was repelled by the rather superior way Isadora displayed in her attitude towards women, not towards me personally, but towards other women. I never could stand that, but one should be big enough to overlook such frailties.

Emma made plans once again to go to Canada to speak and to raise money for her projected autobiography. The trip held out the prospect of financial security, rewarding work, and a reason to get back in touch with friends and lovers. The threat of communist harassment could not stop her this time.

So determined was Emma to go to Canada that when other financial arrangements fell through, she borrowed the money from her old admirer Leon Malmed and set sail in the fall of 1926. Emma wrote him a suggestive letter from St.-Tropez before she left: "I just got your letter and the check enclosed. . . . When we meet, as I now feel we might, I will be able to express better than in a letter how much your coming to the rescue means to me. I cannot do it in a letter. But you must believe me when I say you are helping to save me from utter despair."

As the boat left England, she felt herself moving closer to her youth.

14

BORDER CROSSINGS

Emma's anticipation mounted as she neared America. Although she would be confined to Canada, she hoped to recapture her past sense of self and to continue her political work. She especially hoped that friends and comrades would visit her to lend support and to confirm her belief that her years in the United States were her period of greatest effectiveness. More recent events had accentuated her early fear of being invisible, her recurring sense that she did not exist unless someone else validated her.

Emma needed public attention almost to prove to herself that she was alive. Even the body of correspondence that she had built up over the years had become a way of guaranteeing that her intense emotions and thoughts would have a tangible form. Writing letters enabled her to speak to herself as well as to others.

And Emma wondered whether Leon Malmed's offer of money to finance her trip carried the promise of something more. His support had clinched her decision to come to Canada, and she had telegraphed him announcing her arrival in October, adding, "HOPE YOU CAN COME SOON." After Emma had settled with some friends in Montreal and weathered a chilly and sparsely attended political welcome, Malmed did indeed come to see her. It was no surprise that the two old comrades, whose relationship had been enhanced by the fantasies that distance often imparts, were tempted to cross the border between friendship and desire:

> . . . how cold it feels in this city since I waved you goodby. I too would have given anything if only you could have stayed and I would have had a place of my own. How I would have loved to show you what beauty and love and an inflamed spirit can do. But it was not to be for the present. I am hoping that it may yet be within the near future. I am famished for love and devotion, terribly starved for both. . . . If all my meetings fail I shall yet rejoice in having come to Canada, for I found a new Leon here and new hope for life and beauty. . . . I stretch out my arms to clasp you to my throbbing heart, my own newfound, old, young boy.
>
> Devotedly,
> E

Emma, who years before had written to Ben that she "missed [him] more than food," was falling in love with a delicatessen owner. Leon Malmed had provided her with his finest culinary delights while she was imprisoned in Jefferson City, before her deportation. A comrade from Albany, Malmed had been intermittently involved with Emma's work. He had arranged her meetings in upstate New York, and in 1915 had even gone on a West Coast tour with her. One State Department agent's surveillance report noted that Emma had used his store as her headquarters whenever she lectured in Albany, though the agent concluded that Malmed's current prosperity had cooled his ardor for radicalism. They had kept the flirtation between them within bounds, to allow Emma's relationship with Ben and Malmed's with his wife to take precedence. Not that Emma had not teased Ben with the mystery of whether or not she had exercised her prerogative of free love in 1915; and when she admitted that she was attracted to Malmed it had been enough to challenge Ben's assumptions about the practice—one-sided, he had thought—of sexual variety. But many constraints had always prevented Emma and Leon from acting on their sexual feelings. Over the years, however, Emma's loneliness had built to desperation and Malmed's boredom with his business, his small-town life, and his marriage had made them draw closer together through letters.

With Ben, the fear of the police and the proprieties of the lecture circuit had kept Emma's passion ignited. This time, the barrier was the hostile force of convention—Malmed's wife and family. But Emma's desperation was too great for her to consider Malmed's personal life, his wife's feelings, or his business affairs—she encouraged him to "be reckless and live dangerously for once in [his] life."

It wasn't long before Emma felt completely dependent upon Malmed's love, waiting daily for his letters and telephone calls. As in the past, having a man in her life made Emma feel content and arrested her gnawing feeling of incompleteness.

Emma decided to look for a small apartment in Montreal, so that she could have a hideaway to which she could lure Malmed, to share in what she called her "sublime festival of love." Their relationship made her forget that she was "a stranger among strangers" and consumed her with "a mad longing for all that was denied [her] for so many years." She described to Leon the elation that was prompted by a surprise call from him:

> I got so worked up, I am shaking from head to my feet, hearing your voice so unexpectedly aroused me to a wild pitch and lifted the depression like a thunderstorm. I am myself amazed at this new terrific force that you helped to unloose in my soul. All these many years I had the deepest affection for you as a devoted friend and comrade. But it is only since I saw you last that all the suppressed elemental forces have broken loose in me. . . . I hold you pressed to my throbbing heart.
>
> E

Nevertheless, when Leon visited her in Canada, she chose to have him come directly to her apartment so as not to display her affection in public: with Malmed as with Ben, she wanted to avoid any scandal that might detract from her political effectiveness. Rumor had it that Emma was having an affair with a young sailor.

At a time when Emma despaired over her inability to realize her ideals—her lectures were poorly attended and she was falling deeper in debt with every passing day—Malmed was "the one star on the dark horizon." She wrote of her new love:

> ... if that too should fail me, life would be utterly impossible, too hideous to go on. Oh, Leon, Leon darling, do not fail me, let me see that you can respond to a great, a wonderful, a mysterious power that has come into our lives. Let us live that power, for life is fleeting as the years go by. Let us abandon ourselves to the moment so rare, so precious, so wondrously beautiful. Let us shut out the world, and worry and doubts. Let us drink the goblet to the last drop. Oh, Leon mine.

No extravagance had been spared for the consummation of their love affair. Her last two weeks in Montreal, Emma had paid $65 for a small apartment, just to ensure some privacy with Malmed. She justified the expense by asserting to Leon that "only extravagant and crazy people know the meaning and mystery of life. . . . The greatest beauty springs from aristocracy of the spirit." To Emma extravagance had always meant abundance and freedom from want. She and Leon even planned a November rendezvous in the expensive resort town of Napierville.

In her letters, Emma referred to herself as Leon's "maidale," his little girl. Yet she signed herself, "Your maidale, who is your mother— sweetheart, chum and lover all in one." If she was his "maidale," he was also her "child," her "boy," as well as her "best beloved," for her love for Leon was no less permeated with Oedipal tension than her relationships with Ben and Swenson had been. She and Malmed were closer in age and family background, however, which gave her the illusion that this time her love could be a "work of art" created by equals. She wrote to Malmed of her love:

> My darling boy, how wonderful it is to have something fresh and new come into your life after you have given up all hopes. In me it is the awakening of spring, only more wonderful than that because of the maturity, the experience and the art life has taught me. Yes, I want our love to be a true work of art, something so fascinating

and stirring that nothing else will matter. After all, love in all its beauty and splendor is the most abiding and the most inspiring of events. In my case, it will help me over all the rocks and difficulties of the future. For now, I have someone in my life, in my heart and mind, who really cares, whose love has been tested by the fire of time and space and yet has emerged stronger and more beautiful than in the beginning. That is the wonder, the marvelous miracle that has come to me. May the stars, or fate, or whatever it is that has brought me to you be blessed.

My Leon, I hold you close to my throbbing heart and cover you with the whole intensity of my being.

Your Maidale
E

Emma did in fact nearly smother Leon. When he did not respond to her letters quickly enough, she expressed the full weight of her disappointment; thus Malmed gradually was made to feel responsible for her acute shifts in mood. She could not bear a day without contact with him. She even claimed that she wanted to drop the intrigue and that she did not "give a damn who knows about it."

Meanwhile, now that she was so near, Ben wanted to see her—but Emma refused. The aging former King of the Hobos knew what Emma needed for the success of her public-speaking tours and fantasized that he could still provide it; as her manager, he could spread the word that the great Emma Goldman had something important to say. Although she felt nostalgia for the work they had done together in the past, the anger and disappointment of their last meeting, and Emma's resolve not to leave herself vulnerable to Ben, gave her the strength to refuse all his offers. Because no other relationship with a man had ever affected Emma so deeply, she had to guard herself against opening herself again, emotionally or physically, to Ben.

I am afraid I cannot ask you to come to see me; our meeting again in London has left me too disturbed to repeat the experience. Besides, what is there we can talk about? Our worlds are more than ever apart. Really, Ben, let's not be sentimental; let's bury the dead.

I say this in the kindliest of spirits, because I know that you too got nothing out of our meeting. Why tear open the old scars?

Yes, indeed, I remember our work in Canada. I always remember with appreciation your splendid work while you were with me. But then you believed in what you were doing and you believed in me. All that is no more, so I would rather not see you again in C. than have what is very vivid in my mind of the past blurred by the present.

If the miracle should happen and I should get to the States I will see you, of course, but we need not bank on that. Thanks for offering to do something that "will make me happy." I don't know what that can be; certainly not money.

Goodby, old man, let's cherish the past and not spoil the present.

Affectionately,

E

But when Ben persisted, trying to find some way to help her re-enter the United States, Emma softened, realizing that he genuinely wanted to be involved in her life again. "Thanks, dear, for wanting to do something for me, I am 'Beyond help.' I really need nothing that money could buy anyway. And unpurchasable things do not come often in one's life. They did come with a gush when we first met. But that is long ago, buried, but not forgotten." Emma concluded this letter by saying that one thing that Ben could do for her was to return the letters she had written to him, so that she might be better able to write her autobiography. She would arrange a meeting in order to borrow the letters from him.

What I really want the letters for is to refresh my mind of the events that took place in the years of our common efforts. That those years will have a very important place in my autobiography I do not have to tell you. They were among the most significant years in my life—bright lights and dark together. Tell me, Ben, if I may have the material. . . .

I have a phone in my apartment. I understand that the rates are

very cheap after midnight. . . . I am sure to be in until noon and
after midnight.

> Goodby dear Ben,
> Always affectionately,
> EG

Emma used her telephone sparingly—it was costly, and she knew
that it was being tapped. But because she had now begun to rely on it
where in the past she would have written, there is no record of some of
her interchanges from Canada with friends and comrades in the United
States. On the phone, she and Ben reverted to their old pattern of fights
and misunderstandings. One night Ben woke Emma with a call in the
small hours of the morning. She was furious, bent on thinking that
he had been drinking and therefore was not seriously prepared to talk
with her.

It was clear that Ben was no truer to Anna than he had been to
Emma. He wrote to clarify his intentions and to wax nostalgic:

Dearest Mommy,
Where did we used to be at this time of the year.
New York or on the road
How often the old days come back to me.
Yes they were great old days.
And the memory of them shall always be sacred.
You misunderstood me over the phone.
I was not out celebrating.
I haven't been out or had a drink. . . .
It is the simple life of the hard worker
That I live.

There is nothing to explain. . . .

The "things I cannot say"
Is what bothers me.
My inability to cheer you.
Or do things for you.

Is what makes me unhappy. . . .
Tell me what you want me to bring.
I have much of your personal letters.
About 500 I think.
And some other things.
I will bring them all.
I want you to write the biography of the
Century. . . .
I do want to wipe out the London experience.
Oh it was so terrible
And Paris with Sasha was awful. . . .
Business is good.
Seeing 40 people a day.
Mostly prostitutes and crooks.
Trying to be kind and helpful.
The little family well.
And kind to me.

No speeches.
No Hobo College.
No publicity.
Good
by
Mommy.

                                        Hobo.

Emma tried to write to Ben with affection, but the old bitterness remained, and she turned down his request to spend New Year's with her.

Dear Ben.
    I shall not need the letters until I sail back to Europe. . . . Funny you should want to come at that time [New Year's]. In all the years we were together you used to dash back home and [see] mother. We were together only one New Year, when I arranged a birthday party for you, you see I have not forgotten that you were born Jan.

first. And about two Christmastimes. All others there was no
holding you. Strange indeed that you should want to come this
year. I am sorry, old man, but this time I cannot have you, unless
you come after the holidays.

In a letter to Leon, Emma elaborated on her feelings.

Just like Ben not to consider the other fellow in his own momen-
tary mood. . . . I don't object to seeing Ben; I am the last to harbor
a harsh feeling against anyone who has been in my life, least of all
Ben, who has certainly given everything he could to my work, but I
do not wish to start the New Year with old ghastly memories. I
want it to begin with new hope, new faith, new vigour. . . . Oh,
Leon mine . . . my dearest, my child, my comrade, my lover

Your Maidale
E

Ben felt that Emma was avoiding him. She protested that it was just
that she was preoccupied with preparing for her lectures and, as always,
needed to be completely alone the whole day before a talk or she would
be "no good" on the platform. In thanking him for his persistence, she
got in yet another sharp reminder of their last visit: "But it is good to
know that I am again wanted and appreciated. One may have to be
strong and stand alone—but it is deucedly lonely and chilly to stand
alone. You did not make allowance for that when you were in London.
How would you, never having known the pain and isolation of being an
alien in a strange land?" By the end of January 1927, Emma felt fortified
enough by the support of other comrades to write to Ben in a conciliatory tone: "love of my comrades has acted upon my famished spirit like
Sun on Ice; it has melted away much of the misery that was mine for so
many years." She would see him in the spring.

Whatever other work Emma was engaged in in Canada—lectures,
social engagements, writing—her emotional center was now firmly
established in her relationship with Malmed. When apart from him, she
fantasized his presence: "If only you were here tonight, I would talk with
a tongue of fire and I would sing the most marvelous song to you of love,

of passion, of complete abandon. . . . My darling is far away but so near, I can embrace you almost and can feel you penetrate my whole being. . . . Good night, my lover."

She tried desperately to convince Leon that the institution of the family, a small town, and a small business would destroy his soul, that he must leave them and come to live with her. She wrote to him about their mutual friend Ben Capes, who "is one of the few truly big souls in our movement and one of the still fewer friends I have; his devotion is wonderful. Ben could have made much of himself if he had not been saddled by a family. It is terrible what the family does to its members, just saps them dry. How my lover managed to escape the monster's influence I do not know."

Emma decided to stay in Canada at least until May, to be near Leon. There was nothing so compelling waiting for her in Europe, and the reception for her in Toronto was more enthusiastic than it had been in Montreal. As far as Emma was concerned, "the platform" was Leon's only "rival."

Although the anarchist comrades in Montreal had not given her the extravagant welcome that she had wished, and warnings about the hostility of Canadian communists to any criticism of the Soviet Union proved true, after several months Emma began to feel settled in Canada; in Toronto the hospitality and the generally enthusiastic reception were gratifying. She lectured and gave interviews to the Toronto press. Once again the papers were filled with Emma, from reminiscences—"Once I had to choose between buying food and buying flowers and I chose the flowers"—to her comments on modern-day education—"Present day schools turn out automatons"—and on anarchism as "the spirit of youth against outworn traditions." From France, Sasha wrote that the enthusiasm in Emma's letters during this period showed that she had found what she needed. He confided to a mutual friend that Emma's trip to Canada had been psychologically necessary for her, to pull her out of the acute depression she had suffered before she went.

Emma missed Sasha; she would need his critical advice more than anyone else's in writing her autobiography. Resourcefully, she concocted the idea of having him come to Canada, or perhaps Mexico, to start a new magazine. But Sasha wanted more time to think about it before uprooting himself and his companion, Emmy Eckstein.

Sasha had fallen in love with the very young and attractive Emmy in Berlin, and they had moved to St.-Cloud, outside of Paris, and then to Nice, which was within a few hours of St.-Tropez. He wondered why Emma had suddenly decided to stay in Canada instead of following her original plan of returning to Bon Esprit to write her autobiography. Neither Sasha nor Ben knew that Emma had recently fallen in love.

In November 1926, Emma and Leon had dared to meet in the resort town of Napierville. There she and Leon indulged in complete sexual abandonment. "Naperville," as they referred to their secret retreat, became the symbol of the passionate turning point in their relationship. Once again sexual passion felt like a force outside of herself; she even experienced her genitals as a separate being and called physical love her "child" in her letters to Leon. The fact that her relationship with Leon was illicit only fed her general tendency to experience love as something removed from daily life. Societal pressures, her deeper longing for a child, and her striving for a feeling of completion all added resonance to this metaphor of giving birth to a child. Although, in the abstract, Emma wanted Leon to leave his wife, she had never thought through what he would do, or what they would do together, if he did. Perhaps she believed that it would be enough for Leon to act as a benevolent father to his "Maidale" and somehow protect her from her isolation. To try to pry him away from his family, she wrote in appreciation of a gift and of their love experiences in Napierville:

In fact my longing for you and my need of you are so great that I dreamed last night that you came into my room laden with packages and this was what you said, "Maidale, I have come to you for good. I will not go back to Albany." I screamed with delight. . . . I am sick with longing for my child that was born to me in such a miraculous way at Napierville. . . . Leon, Leon, the years go past and you have not yet lived. There is much in joy and beauty awaiting—in undreamed ecstasies. Do not wait too long, do not delay too much—live recklessly—live dangerously. It is the only way worth living—I am waiting.

Emma sometimes fantasized that Leon was her wealthy suitor. She knew he was in debt, but he had chipped in with some other comrades to give her a gold watch, and he had given her dozens of red roses, had driven her about in his green Packard, and always sent her food from his delicatessen. She chose not to notice that Malmed had sacrificed all luxuries for his family to support his reckless affair with her. With complete disregard for anything or anyone else in his life, she encouraged Leon to give up his stores and get out of debt by claiming bankruptcy, and to give up his family and move beyond his guilt. He gave to Emma, and he gave generously, but he would not give her all that she asked: he would not leave his life in Albany, his wife, and his child.

The lovers continued to meet in large hotels where they would not be recognized, in towns not inhibited by "the pest of prohibition," so that they could drink and enhance the intoxicating effect of "the dew of her rosedrops." Emma sustained the relationship with her capacity to live in a vision of reality that she constructed: "My darling, how marvelous life would be if you could come away with me, far away from all your worries, from all the terrible vulgarity that pierces your sensitive spirit. I would weave a new world for you of such marvelous color, such deep sounds, such glowing sunrise, I would give you such delights in love and passion and such tender comradeship, your famished soul would break forth like the gladiolas."

She now recognized that as early as 1915 there had been an element of romance in their relationship, but the time had not been right:

In 1915 the gap between Ben and myself had already begun, growing wider and wider every day. I was deeply unhappy and in great need of an understanding soul. You were near—you had your arms open. But I saw nothing, rather, did not wish to see. For I knew long before that how much you cared for me. How strange is life—how mysterious are the ways of love. . . . Eleven years had to pass until the magic hand of love touched my soul and awakened it to a love more wonderful than I have known before—a love matured by experience, made rich by sorrow, imbued by the fires of reborn youth. . . . It is no use to fathom its ways. One can only give oneself over completely to its charm, its beauty, its miracle—

When Emma had planned her trip to Canada, although Leon had financed it, she had anticipated only a renewed political life, but the force of Leon's unexpected love had become her "one hope":

Everything was empty in me when I came to Canada. I had no hope of a private, personal character, and I expected nothing much from my lectures. But you came into my life; or, rather, you awakened everything to life like the spring sun kissing the earth into bloom, and now I can think of nothing except our love and our future. Our future, remember that, Leon. We must have it, we simply must, no matter what happens. . . . We will have something to work and live for then, my precious Leon, my great miracle, my savage-tender lover.

She teased him with the promise of even more subtle and inspiring lovemaking:

You do not know the depths of my love for you, the thousand hidden subtleties, the fires that would scourge you and raise you to a mad delight. You will never know them unless we can be away from everybody and everything, unless we have beauty and freedom and no grinding material worries. Only then will you know the charm of a great and marvelous love—only then. . . . I press you in my arms, your head to the rosebuds—my lips to the fountain of life. I drink to our future, our golden future.

Your Maidale

Emma was in love with love, and with being loved. Everyone remarked on how energetic she was, and how much younger she seemed:

Oh, my darling, how wonderful it is to be loved and to love. Life seems so full of meaning, of great possibilities. No wonder the comrades at the station, they were all present, bless them, said what an amount of pep E has. Do they know what has put the pep into me? Can they know that the elixir of life has penetrated my blood, has lifted the weight from my heart and has made me young again? No, they cannot know, no one can except my treasure, my Leon. He alone knows the miracle that has come to both of us—our rebirth, our new marvelous spring.

Yet she wondered if Leon would have loved her as much if they were living together:

Or has my Leon loved me 25 years only because I seemed unattainable? Such things sometimes happen. But I am not afraid. I would surround my boy with so much love, with so much beauty, I would pour such burning lava in his blood, I would wind my heart around his so strongly, he would have to love me more and more all the time. . . .

You see, my Leon, I can never, and never could, give myself in snatches. It was and is always *all or nothing.* It takes me days and often weeks to grow into the one I love, to break through the barriers which life and necessity have placed upon me. For how else could I have endured all the terrible things in my life? . . . But when you will be with me, *really* with me, with everything left behind you, in freedom and in the open, you will see the real EG as only very few have seen her, perhaps as no one has seen her.

Although Emma did not think of herself as "the type of woman who wants to monopolize the man" she loved or who made demands on him, she could not stand their short visits, always clouded by mundane worries. She escalated her criticism of Malmed's "worry about a home which never was a home. . . . We must come to it free from everything and everybody, we must give ourselves to it as the birds and flowers do, in utter beauty and abandon. Do you know, my Leon, I am strong enough not to see you for months rather than to see you under the conditions of your last visit."

Emma was desperate to find a sanctuary for her affair. Yet when

Leon suggested that she might live in a little house by a lake, closer to his home, so that he could visit her for two or three days or even a week at a time, Emma could not stand the idea of being a "kept" woman.

But to sit around to wait for snatches of your love for 2 or 3 days each time or even a week, only to know you are going back to your worries and anxieties while I remain doing nothing, just waiting for your return, I could not do that. It would make me feel like the majority of wives and mistresses, who lazy around at summer resorts while their men sweat to raise the money for them to squander. I cannot imagine anything more humiliating and insulting. I just could not do it.

Emma was beginning to think that her only hope of keeping Leon was to frighten him with her inaccessibility, by planning her return to St.-Tropez. Living in Canada and being so preoccupied with Leon was not conducive to writing her autobiography. When she booked passage to Europe, she attempted to induce him to return with her, but the pressure seems to have made Leon withdraw from Emma. As a fallback position, she begged for just one full week together before her ship set sail. She dared him into being with her, and defensively hurled insults at him, indulging in self-pity: "there is no use hiding our heads in the sand, my darling. You are bound and fettered, rooted, and I am without roots, doomed to just drift."

Leon had hoped that her public life would give her the completeness that he could not, but her meetings in Winnipeg had been a failure: "Leon mine, you seem to think that meetings can fill the yearning heart. Do you know what it is to face empty halls night after night. What it means to feel the air surcharged with antagonism, as I did last Sunday? . . ."

You see, lover mine, the abyss between my life and work in New York and my present desperate struggle is so deep, it makes me feel every failure and mishap more poignantly. I am just crying my heart out over the collapse of all that was once so dear to me. I go frantic when I see how little our own comrades know about me or my work, and how little they care. Since I am here I have wept myself into a stupor over the irony that I have to drag myself, with a heavy cold, to meetings to speak before fifty Jews all of whom are secure and comfortable while I am more than ever the outcast.

Emma began to liken the hold that Leon's wife had on him to the hold that she had always had on Ben.

But you must not think I was so naïve that I did not know what was going on behind my back. No wonder Ben used to call me Sherlock Holmes. I was sorry for the women because I know that even if they lure Ben away, they will have a rude awakening. To this day, I would but have to stretch out my hand to have Ben back at my side. I have actually had to fight against this since I reached Canada, so of what good was it to lure Ben away, and I know it would be the same if you could be lured away, which I know is not possible.

She did not give up trying, or stop complaining that their two days each month felt like prison visits, but she decided against trying to sneak into the United States to see him, an idea she and Leon had concocted for the shock value of having America deport her twice. It would be preferable for him to come to Europe to join her. "There are only the chains which you yourself have forged. A home, which is no home . . . a relationship which according to your own statement gives you nothing, and finally business considerations, material things which chain you. Why, if your love is so great, should you not try to break loose? Why? You see, my boy, one cannot always do as one would like, so there is no answer to the why."

On a tour of Canada in March, Emma was reinvigorated by her reception in Edmonton. Everyone wanted her to speak, from the Kiwanis Club, to Hadassah, to the Arbeiter Ring. "One would think Queen Mary arrived to see the excitement, every society imaginable asked me to speak," Emma wrote to Leon. Finally feeling properly received, she worked harder than she had for months. The combination of her newly successful work and her inability to let go of Leon convinced her to postpone her departure at least until fall, in case Leon were to change his mind. Various groups had finally rallied to Emma's support, giving her a platform to speak on modern drama, on the Soviet Union, on women, sexuality, and, indirectly, on America. Young people gathered around her, as Emma delegated tasks down to darning her socks, which she had no time for. "I am leading such a crazy hectic life. I really haven't an hour to myself. Ever since I landed here, it has been a mad rush from one thing to another. In fact I can say that never in my career was there such a demand for your poor Maidale. . . . If all this would pay, I'd go away rich. . . . My precious Leon, if I had not been so busy, our long separation would drive me frantic."

Following her enthusiastic treatment in Edmonton, Emma asked influential friends in America to try to get Washington to reopen her case and allow her back into the country. But the campaign failed, leaving Emma especially vulnerable when the next blow landed. Leon's wife discovered the letters Emma had sent to him at his store, which he had "carelessly" left in a desk at home. Emma was unsympathetic either to Malmed, who now felt shamefully exposed, or to his wife, who felt cruelly betrayed. Malmed's wife knew Emma, had opened her home to her in the early days, before her deportation, and had once even given her her bed to sleep in. Outraged and indignant over the sham of her marriage and of what felt like the private ruthlessness underlying Emma's public generosity, she nevertheless would not leave her husband.

Fearful for her reputation—she could not risk embarrassment, particularly at a time when she still hoped to return to America—Emma wrote Malmed a scathing letter, which she vowed would be her last.

That you could consider [the letters] of so little value as to expose them to the possibility of getting into the hands of your wife, shows such utter carelessness on your part and such lack of concern for my position that I am shocked beyond words. . . .

Now, if only a small part of your regard for me is true, I must insist that you return my letters. I have repeatedly asked you for the letters of the past, which you knew I needed for an important purpose. You have evaded my request until now. Your sense of possession seems to have turned into a disease with you. All right, if you must, cling to these letters. But I must insist seriously that you return my letters of recent months. . . . I have never in my life been mixed up in a sordid matrimonial affair. I don't propose to be mixed up in yours. And I know that is likely to happen any moment now that Mrs. M. has a key to your desk. . . . You do not seem to realize that you are but human, that something might happen to you. And that Mrs. M. would then drag me through the mire. I don't think I have deserved that of you, Leon. Really, your callousness shows precious little regard or concern for what is likely to happen to me or my name.

The tirade continued in another letter a few days later:

If you think I enjoy being harsh with you, you are mistaken . . . but your childish way of assuming that no one knows what you are doing, or whom you are corresponding with, and your utter lack of consideration for the fact that while you are a "private man" I am in public life, have simply frozen my blood. . . . You are great in words, Leon, but you have never made a step to do anything that would in the least inconvenience you, or bring you the least unpleasantness. I do not understand love in that way, nor am I satisfied with the kind of affection which talks but does not act. . . . You say the letters are all you have in this "miserable" life. But how do you value them, Leon, if you could keep them in the house. . . . It is not the scandal I object to so much, though it would make me sick to my stomach to be involved in a wretched family squabble, but it is that you should have kept the letters in the house, exposed to what exactly happened. . . . You are naïve, and you are too busy with your transactions to realize what is going on. . . . Oh, Leon, is there nothing great and strong enough to make you give up the idle chase for wealth, and really begin living and enjoying what you claim means all to you? It is all so sad for one who once had an ideal, still proclaims to have it. . . . We are not children anymore, Leon, we must face facts. And the facts are that you are chained for life to a situation which I cannot share. And that I cannot have every Tom, Dick and Harry tear the innermost secrets of my soul into the gutter. Really, if I tried I could not write you anymore as I feel. I could not write you at the store, not so long as I know that you go on having my letters in your house. . . . Remember, what my letters contain represents the deepest and most radiant emotions I was capable of giving, it was all meant for you, for no one else.

Emma's desire to have her letters back became an obsession. Others had cooperated; why did Leon keep her letters, relishing his power over her in this instance? Even their mutual friend Van Valkenburgh, who lived close to Albany, pleaded Emma's case to Leon. "The very reasons why you don't want the world to know the sentimental side of EG are the very best reasons why they should be carved in printer's ink for time eternal."

Although it seems that Malmed never delivered the letters to Emma, some reconciliation took place, for letters between them continued. But now Emma ended them with salutations of "affection," not "passion." By the time Malmed was to have secured a post-office box, the spell was broken. Emma shifted her attention to other friendships. When her faithful friend Benny Capes came to see her, he seemed to her a ray of sunshine from a dark sky. Even her contentious correspondence with Ben was revived:

Whatever makes you think that I will ever be your guest in America? I suppose it is your Christian optimism? Isn't it? Well, I am quite certain that unless there is some very great radical change in the political character of the States, you will never see me there. . . . You will have to come to me, dear, old Ben, for I will certainly never come to you. . . . You write me of your home, your religion, your work, your God, your wife, your love and duty so often that I sometimes feel perhaps it is not all so very smooth in your life. But, then, I still believe that smooth and contented lives are usually very empty and commonplace. I hope yours is not that. . . .

Ben once again planned to pay Emma a visit. Swayed by his ill health (a mild case of hepatitis) and his offer to bring her all his letters, besides the gradual dissolution of her affair with Leon, she decided to allow him back into her life. She wrote to Malmed:

> It is awful to think that so strong a man as Ben, a giant that he was, should be stricken. Of course I let him come. . . .
>
> Ben R has been with me since Friday, he leaves tonight. You would not recognize him, he is completely broken in health and spirit—a very sick man. His main trouble is his lack of hope that he will get well. To see the wild, spirited Ben so listless and inert is quite awful. . . . Ben brought me all my letters and a complete set of *ME,* also clippings.

When Leon came to see Emma again, she was still angry, and refused to make love with him as long as he withheld his letters from her. The wedge between them was growing: Emma felt Malmed's preoccupation with his life in Albany as a barrier between them. He had opened a new store and had even less attention to spare for Emma, who undoubtedly was increasingly difficult to be with. She wrote to him about her disappointment during his visits:

> No girl of eighteen waits for the arrival of her lover as I wait for yours. My imagination is aflame with a thousand wild fancies. But the moment you are before me I see what you have left behind, like a shadow, follow you.
>
> I hear you talk of nothing else but Albany and all my visions are wiped out, my heart contracts and I have a feeling as if someone would hold me by the throat. I am telling you this so you may understand why I am unable to respond to what my soul craves so violently. My Leon, will it always be thus? I shudder to think that I might continue to be so near you and yet never know complete abandon, then return to Europe starved for the fulfillment of the miracle that was born in Napierville.

Emma even blamed the failure of her fifty-eighth birthday party on Leon's not calling her as promised. He could do nothing to please her anymore. When he accused her of killing their love, she responded:

"How can you say to *me* 'don't kill my love.' If there were any charge like that it is I who would be justified in making it. But it is ridiculous for either of us to say such things. So let's not do it."

As their relationship faded, the number of letters between them diminished. Emma wrote: "It is something you are unwilling to face— your change towards Napierville. Since your last visit the change has come. It cannot be helped, I understand. Gone is the intensity, the flowers, the daily telephone calls, the daily outpourings. Why not face it, Leon, and be honest with yourself and with me?"

She tried to salvage the friendship they had established: "I am not able to be content with mere assurances of affection. But what does it matter, dear Leon, our friendship is so old and so strong it is not going to die no matter what happens. For the rest, I have had so many disappointments in my life, the disappointment over the Napierville experience will also have to be endured. It was certainly beautiful while it lasted."

Indeed, the pattern was so familiar that Emma, who conspired in her own disappointment, could absorb this new blow: she had become infatuated with Leon, then obsessed by his inaccessibility, and ultimately disappointed in his inability to give her what she needed. Her disappointment masked her anger at not being able to control the course of her love relationship, and allowed her to see herself as the victim of someone else's inadequacy rather than her own.

At the same time, Emma was feeling her ineffectiveness on another level, in the larger world. On August 23, 1927, Sacco and Vanzetti were executed, after seven years' imprisonment, during which time their guilt or innocence of killing two men on a payroll robbery was debated in the United States, Europe, and Canada. Emma felt that her status as an alien had hampered her ability to affect the course of their trial. Emma had organized a protest meeting in Toronto where she raised money for the Sacco and Vanzetti Defense Committee. She had written letters to everyone she could think of who might be able to exert public pressure in their behalf. After the executions, she even imagined adopting Sacco's child, Dante, if only she had "a small income and the boy were willing."

Emma believed that both she and Malmed, each for his or her own reasons, were blocked from meaningful political action. She herself felt helpless in a strange country, cut off from her past activities; Leon was "caught in the chariot wheel of commercialism without the time or energy left for [her] or anyone else." This, too, was a source of depression: "Oh, dear Leon, both our lives though for different reasons have become useless. We might as well be honest enough to admit it. As to my work here, it never seemed more futile, inadequate and stupid. Drama, Sex, other idiotic things, when even the savage murder of two innocent men fails to move the masses to real reaction. . . ."

Emma was more determined than ever to write her autobiography, to use it as an opportunity to remember when she had had an impact on the world, and perhaps, in doing so, to have such an impact again. In the fall of 1927, she began to make plans to go back to Europe. "I am absolutely determined to sail when I have finished my lectures," she wrote Malmed. "My great hopes in coming here, my plans to establish myself in Canada, all went up in smoke. I am now counting the days [till] I can sail back and bury myself somewhere."

She had stayed through the summer, waiting without success for Leon's change of heart. Now that she realized she was alone once more, Emma resented that Leon had not given her more financial help: she would not have had to continue her lecture tour at a grueling pace until she left.

In the meantime, Emma thought that Ben was trying to sneak back into her life. He had managed to pass on some information leaked to him from the Anarchist Squad of the Chicago Police Department that there was a serious attempt under way to frame Berkman for the dynamiting of an American Legion train in France. Far from appreciating Ben's efforts, Emma looked askance at what seemed to her his all-too-intimate relationship with the Chicago police. Defensively, Ben asserted that the chief of police was a better friend than Sasha had ever been. On the margin of his letter next to this comment Emma wrote "STUPID!"

She was not ready for a visit from Ben; she had to be sure that they understood each other—in particular, that he understood that their love affair was over. Ben assured her that he would come to visit, "not as a publicity hound of the last year in London, nor the whining and pining hobo of last May, but now brilliant in mind—strong in body—secure of soul, humorous, tolerant and loving."

Emma softened, realizing that Ben wanted her to see him virile and loving once again, but made a point of rejecting any renewal of their sexual relationship, even misquoting him in her reply:

What happened, did you have a monkey gland transferred to you? Funny, funny Ben. . . . I am not sure I can present you to your old-time blue-eyed Mommy. In fact I know I can't. The past is gone. . . .

But I certainly want to be a loving friend, "tolerant and under-standing." I want always to be that to you, dear Ben. *I want nothing more.* Nor do I want you to come to me under false hopes. Let us see if we cannot really establish a beautiful friendship without the things that have been in the past, the good as well as the bad. Do you think we might?

Ben courted Emma once more. Perhaps it was the influence of her letters, which he had unearthed from a trunk for her autobiography:

I am sure when you read over some of your letters to me, you will be surprised, once you loved me. . . .

Daily you are on my mind. And daily I would write you. The only thing we have left each other appears [to be] the power to hurt (not help).

Strange that it should have turned out thus. . . . I suppose you will be going to Sunny France soon. And be starting on your book. I do hope you will write a great book. . . .

Only the hurt remains.

And life can never be the same again.

Kindly
BLR

PLEASE LET ME ADD, IF YOU REALLY WANT TO SEE ME, I COULD RUN DOWN FOR A DAY MOST ANY TIME, PREFER-ABLY SUNDAYS OR HOLIDAYS.

Ben did visit her. Although Emma hoped there was a chance to salvage their friendship from the wreckage of their ill-fated love affair of ten years before, Ben, reinvigorated, wanted to make love to her once

369

again. Emma was outraged at his audacity in thinking that he could obliterate years of neglect in one embrace. And, in turn, he was furious at her lack of affection. One letter from Emma, written with the eloquence of anger, gave Ben the most succinct summation of her view of their relationship since their break-up. Emma hoped this final and dramatic rejection would make him feel the pain she had experienced at his withdrawal of love and support at a critical moment in her life, which she attributed to his "spiritual colorblindness."

For eight years, between the dreadful year of 1917 and 1925, you took yourself out of my life as if you had never been there. As far as you were concerned, I did not exist, nor any trouble, hardships or suffering that were in my life. All right, then you came to London, ostensibly to see me. I am not going to dwell on that terrible visit, since you yourself have given it the names it deserved. All right. Then I came to Canada and we began to get somewhat close to each other. Not that I ever could blot out the last ten years from my soul to begin anew the relationship which you yourself broke into bits in 1917. Still, we were on the way [toward] some kind of friendship rescued from the avalanche which killed our love. As weeks and months went on (though it never occurred to you to ask how I was getting along in a strange unyielding country) our correspondence helped to ease the pain of the past. When you wrote me of your illness my heart went out to you with all the affection and friendliness of real concern and devotion. I would have done anything in my power to get you back to health. I was glad for your visit. I was sick with pain when I saw you so ill and worn and dead. It was to me like seeing a beautiful strong tree broken and dying. But even on that visit you had to show your impatience and violence at the last minute. But that did not matter. You were ill and nothing else mattered to me. I was terribly anxious and when I finally learned that you were on the way [toward] recovery I felt exceeding glad. All right.

Then you continued writing in a tone I had almost forgotten, it was so long ago since I heard it. You announced your coming. You wrote me to let you know whether it was convenient for me to see you at that particular time. . . . I wanted you to know that while I was glad to have you come and while I hoped we could meet as real friends, two people who have had much in common, had struggled, dreamed and hoped together for so many years, two people who had lost the one precious thing in their lives—their love—but at least who were able to retain their friendship, I wrote in this spirit. But you understood nothing of it. You were colorblind to the beauty of friendship. You could not endure the idea that I should not be ready to receive you as my lover as if there had been no terrible ten years between the time when you left me to the storm which swept over me and destroyed all I had built in pain and tears for 28 years, ten of which I had shared with you. No, you could not understand, you never have understood. . . .

If I had still a vestige of hope that you could meet me in friendship, without demanding more than I can give, just meeting me in kindness and understanding, I would certainly ask you to come before I leave T. or C. altogether. But you have taken even the last ray of hope from me, so what would be the use of our meeting again?

Ben responded with anger to match Emma's "avalanche of vituperation."

I hope in your autobiography,
You will give the details of my crookedness.
As I am sure you will my extreme selfishness.
And colossal egotism.
What right have you to ask me if I want MY set
of *Mother Earth*
Returned to me.
If you don't think my ten years service to you.
Entitle me to them.
Then give them to A[lexander] B[erkman]
I will be able to live without them. . . .
Some day I want to write a real story. Of Ten
Years with EG
For that I will need my letters.

When you are thru with them, please return.
It was you who taught me Ibsen's great message.
"The futility of sacrifice"
And Lord Douglas' "The bitterness of a
disappointed Lover"
It is Xmas time.
Peace and good will to men.
    Let us see what time will do for both of us.

                        Ben

In the end, Emma was afraid that such bitterness would be used against her in her public life. Rereading her letters to Ben, she realized how critical it was to keep them private while she was alive. She recognized that they showed a side of herself that she rarely if ever revealed to her public—the weak, dependent, jealous woman, lusting for a man. She promised to return the letters to Ben after they were copied by a secretary, but she needed his assurance that he would keep them out of his book. Nor would she include them in her book: it would be painful enough just working with them. Trying to cool their argument with friendship, she wished him a happy birthday at the very beginning of 1928, assuring him that he was entitled to his volumes of *Mother Earth* and the letters she had written to him so long ago. Significantly, Emma never considered the possibility of destroying her occasionally exhibitionistic letters, wishing only that the story of her intimate life would not emerge till after her death:

> I hope, Ben, you will never use my letters in your story any more than I use them. Letters should only be published as letters, and after the death of the writer, not that I am ashamed of anything I might have written. But love letters are written to a lover, not for every Tom, Dick and Harry. I feel sure that you will comply with my request *never to use my letters in your story.* Good night, old Ben. Do not be so bitter even if you are a disappointed lover. Above all, never go down to the level of that terrible Lord Douglas. You have too many fine traits for that. . . .
>   Your friend, though you do not realize it,
>
>   E

Ben assured Emma she should "fear no evil." He would not publish any of her letters "in a way that would hurt or embarrass" her. "The worst I would do," he wrote, "would be to try and shine in a little of your reflected glory."

Emma pored over the hundreds of letters—"the living documents of my dead past sins"—that Ben had brought with him to Canada. After spending two full weeks in Toronto rereading all these letters, she decided that she could not let anyone else see them:

> I came to the conclusion that it is impossible for me to let an outsider copy any of my letters. . . . It is like tearing off my clothes to let them see the mad outpouring of my tortured spirit, the frantic struggle for my love, the all-absorbing devotion each letter breathes. I can't do it. Inasmuch as every letter sings the same wild song of love and passion there is really no need of copying them all; besides, it would be the work of months.

Although Emma could claim legal ownership of all the letters, she begged Ben for permission to take eighty-five of them with her to France—"letters which contain reference to the people we met and the most important fights we have made"—with the promise to return them when the autobiography was written.

Reading the letters had reopened some old wounds, which "no medicine could heal." She wrote, disingenuously, that Ben must not have reread the letters for quite some time; otherwise he would not have said that she had residual feelings of "sacrifice and the bitterness of a disappointed lover."

> If I would believe in such nonsense as sacrifice between two people held together by love I would be willing to let the world judge who did all the sacrificing. But it is foolish to even breathe such a term in a relationship like ours. However, if you feel that you have sacrificed it merely shows that our love and life and work of nine years gave you nothing. I am sorry for that. Indeed I am. With all the pathos over your complete indifference to my fate since 1917, I can truthfully say the nine years gave me so much that it will never

be weighed in numbers. I would not be human if I did not feel sad over our misunderstandings, over your bitterness, your unreasonable demands while the nine years lasted, and your utter lack of interest since my imprisonment. But I realize that two such extremes as we are could never avoid an ever-growing gap. . . . It seems to be the fate of all complex people to pay a heavy toll for their love. I think I have paid it. And I am glad to say I have no regrets. It is too bad that you should have any.

Emma told Ben that Fitzi had visited her in Canada, and the two women had reminisced:

It is a long time since I had such a wonderful visit with Fitz as these 8 days. We talked much of the past, of you of course, of the ecstatic and painful in our relation to you. We talked of the strangeness of life. Fitz, who came to us at your insistence and who remained one of the staunchest, most generous, most dependable of friends. You, who came to me with the sweep of a cyclone only to take yourself out with the same force.

Emma was not entirely happy about the prospect of her return to Europe, and regretted leaving the friends she had made in Toronto. But she knew that she had to get her memoirs out of her system, and that Toronto had "absolutely no intellectual inspiration" for her, whereas there was a lively intellectual community in France—and Sasha to count on when she needed help in making sense of her past.

One hundred people came to Emma's farewell dinner, but there was no word from Ben. She wrote to him that in the end, "friendship is often more enduring than love and less exacting." She had invited Leon to the farewell banquet, feeling that he would be the only kindred spirit at the dinner. "After 15 months, I feel like a desert wanderer. Nobody knows or cares about my work, or my value to the world. It chills my bones," she wrote to him. Yet when Leon came to see her, she claimed that all she got from him was his cold, "only in a worse form." Feeling abandoned, she likened Malmed to Reitman, and continued, "It is to laugh if it were not so sad, Ben Reitman and Leon Malmed remain indifferent to the appeal for the fund [for the autobiography], such is the intensity of their love."

Emma claimed that she was not angry, yet she complained about the poor workings of the gold wristwatch that Malmed and some friends had given her upon her arrival in Canada, which she now suspected was "bought for a song." In a symbolic exchange, Emma had given Leon her own gold watch. Now, she wanted it back, explaining, "Life is full of bitter disappointments. Your last visit was painfully so." She felt that Malmed's claim that they would meet again was part of his "abnormal optimism." But in February 1928, when Leon made one last romantic gesture and sent flowers to Emma on board her ship, she was disappointed because there was no accompanying message. Nothing Malmed said in subsequent letters could convince Emma that he had not forgotten her, but by the time she was back in St.-Tropez writing her memoirs, she could at least give "Napierville" a more positive meaning. "It was beautiful while it lasted," she wrote to Leon. "This is as it should be. Adventures are only wonderful when they do not drag on."

15

RELIVING HER LIFE

Emma was relieved to get back to Bon Esprit, in early 1928, after stopovers in London and Paris. The quiet of her small cottage, her garden, and the ocean breeze were a welcome respite from the turmoil of her life in Canada. Her old friends Sasha, Mollie Steimer, and Senya Fleshine were enthusiastic about her return and anxious to contribute their ideas and reminiscences to her autobiography. They had all managed to settle as exiles within a few hours of each other, forming an anarchist circle within the progressive group of literati who had made the south of France their home.

Even before she unpacked her bags, she was engaged in a heated discussion on how much of her private love life should be chronicled in her book. Emma decided easily to conceal her most recent affair, with Leon Malmed, planning to refer to him in her book as "Leon Bass." But Ben was another story. Although she had agreed not to quote from their correspondence, she felt that it was important for people to know the struggle that had taken place within her during their ten years together. But Senya and Mollie, in particular, argued that too much detail about her relationship with Ben, or about any other love relationship for that matter, would detract from the focus on the anarchist cause and Emma's role in history.

Emma felt somewhat alienated because her comrades did not seem to see the political significance of personal life as she did, but eventually was persuaded by their arguments to play down the more outrageous aspects of her relationship with Reitman in the manuscript.

Emma counted on Sasha to help her retain her precarious emotional balance, and to enable her to find the distance necessary for her task. Sasha would act as her editor and adviser, once again occupying the center of her emotional life. She thought that he could appreciate her life's struggles as no other, and only him could she trust to restrain what she knew were the excesses of her prose. Emma believed that Sasha owed her his editing skills for the next several years; it was his duty to their friendship and to history. And Sasha was willing, though not unaware of the pitfalls he faced: it would be unreasonable of Emma to expect Sasha's undivided loyalty and editorial collaboration to serve as compensation for the loss of Malmed and her rekindled frustrations with Ben, but he knew she would try.

Emmy Eckstein, however, could not be set aside. Emma would have to contend with her competitive feelings and the loneliness of returning to France after her anticlimactic departure from Canada. The Emma-Sasha-Emmy ménage was almost bound to be another deep disappointment.

The first night that Sasha and Emmy spent at Bon Esprit, Emma prepared her own bed for Emmy to sleep in, giving herself the small guest room, and made up the couch for Sasha. In the past, Sasha had had an aversion, left over from his prison experience, to sleeping in the same bed with anyone else. Now, he sheepishly admitted to Emma that he had overcome his neurosis. Emma filled the cottage with an air of gloom.

Angry that Emma was putting him "between two fires," Sasha chided her for her "squelching effect upon other women, and particularly upon younger and inexperienced women," who were part of his life. "You are too strong for them, and they feel it, consciously or unconsciously, but every one of them has always felt it, without a single exception."

Emmy, too, was jealous of Sasha's relationships with other women: even a letter to him in a woman's handwriting would make her hysterical. She was thirty years younger than Sasha, not part of the anarchist movement, given to scenes of high drama, and bourgeois enough to feel uncomfortable living with an ex-convict, although according to Hutch Hapgood, she had been "an economic prostitute" when Sasha met her. She was completely devoted to Sasha, and her seductive manner and indulgences in the purchase of tight-fitting clothing and expensive chocolates complemented Sasha's asceticism. But every visit with Emma disturbed the balance of their lives, and was followed by an argument.

They moved from St.-Cloud to Paris and eventually to Nice, all safe distances from Emma's overbearing presence, as a way of preserving their own relationship. Emmy typed manuscripts for friends as a means of support, and during her intense work spells, Sasha found it best to visit Emma alone. When Emma had Sasha to herself, there was little friction. In fact, both of them basked in a deep intellectual and political camaraderie that neither had ever found with anyone else.

Sasha's feeling "alternately despairing and bewitched" and Emma's unwillingness to admit to the jealousy beneath her criticisms of Emmy marked their letters during this time. Emma had had premonitions about what lay in store before she had left Canada, though they ostensibly concerned Emmy and Sasha's feelings, not her own.

Will not the poor girl feel lonesome and neglected? Besides, Sasha dear, you are evidently not aware of the fact of how irritated and impatient you become when you are between two forces. I have never yet known a time when you were yourself between two women, even if only one of them was your sweetheart. You develop a sort of guilty conscience against the one or the other, the result has always been misery for all concerned. Of course it may be different now that you have your own home and your own life. I hope so with all my heart, for I certainly have no desire to be the bone of contention, to feel that I am the fifth wheel to the wagon, or that I am the innocent cause of the least suffering to E or you.

In Emma's view, Emmy was a childish, apolitical hypochondriac, who could not possibly touch Sasha's soul. But others who knew the young woman admired her devotion to Sasha and thought that she had a calming influence on him, which helped him banish some of the haunting memories of prison life. But Emma could not be objective about Sasha's love life, as this letter written from Canada indicates, with bitterness shadowing her stab at humor:

> Darling, you are a funny member of your sex. Usually you have no faith whatever in women, but the moment your emotions are aroused, you lose all sense of proportion. Thank the Lord you never were sufficiently aroused [by] me: that's why you have always been so critical of me, it hurt like hell at times, but it has been helpful just the same. But joking aside, you do get blind, deaf and dumb when you get interested in a woman.

Emma's present loneliness, coupled with her premonition of an empty future, made writing about her past an ordeal. Yet she needed to tell her story in order to make her life real to herself; and some of her experiences probably became more vivid and intelligible in the writing of the book than they had been when she lived them.

To write about her lifelong attempts to realize her higher values and to live a personal life completely attuned to her public, political life, she would be truthful—within the limits of her sense of propriety. Emma wrote to Sasha: "I want passionately to write as I talk, simple, unaffected and direct. . . . Of course it will have to be a combination of personal experiences and events. I can truthfully say that from the time I entered our movement I had no personal life which did not also reflect the movement, or my activities in it. . . . As to 'not having anything to hide,' how do you know, old chap? We all have something 'to hide.'"

Emma had had a lively exchange a few years earlier with Frank Harris, who at the time had just published a sexually explicit auto-biographical book, *Contemporary Portraits*. Believing that women's sexuality was very different from men's, Emma wondered whether she could frankly express for women what Harris had expressed so daringly for men:

Well, Frank dear, when I read your first volume, I realized, at once, how utterly impossible it is to be perfectly frank about sex experiences and to do so in an artistic and convincing manner. Believe me, it is not because I have any puritanic feeling or that I care in the least for the condemnation of people. My reasons for the impression regarding the facts of sex are that I do not consider the mere physical fact sufficient to convey the tremendous effect it has upon human emotions and sensations. Perhaps it is because to woman, sex has a far greater effect than to man. It creates a greater storm in her being and lingers on when the man is satisfied and at ease. At any rate, I feel that the effect of sexual relations is psychological and cannot be described in mere physical terms. I mean, of course, sex between two harmonious people, both equally intense. . . . For me, at any rate, it will be utterly impossible to describe the physical side, which is, after all, very limited, while the psychological is rich and varied.

Emma thought that if the public was shocked by Harris's exposé of male sexuality, complete honesty about female sexuality would cause a far worse scandal. She would be honest, within the bounds of her goal of gaining the benevolent attention of the American public. She would write *with* passion, if not about it.

The prelude to the actual writing nearly paralyzed her, given the mounting expectations from others as well as herself about the great work encompassing a great life. Before she could begin to write, Emma spent months during 1927 and 1928, in Canada and then in St.-Tropez, poring over old letters and talking with and writing to old friends about the past.

In a letter to her friend Evelyn Scott, the Tennessee-born novelist, Emma complained about how difficult it was for her to start: "To me one of the great delusions is the notion that writing is a joy. . . . In fact, some of the greatest writers have suffered agony of spirit during the process. I may not have greatness in common with them, but by Jesus, I've got the agony."

When she finally set to work, in July of 1928, her anxiety lifted. The book was at first an inspiration to her, as her speeches and lectures had always been. Ben wrote that her July letter to him "was the most cheerful in years," and Sasha lamented, in a letter of the same period, that he had missed a party in which Emma "danced the kazatzka."

Emma lived in Bon Esprit with "a mad American girl called Emily Coleman," a young, boyish-looking writer who helped her "knock her manuscript into shape" and provided Emma with the companionship, including personal conflict, she needed to function. Often such visitors as Peggy Guggenheim, who had given Emma her little house, and her husband would come to enjoy a meal with Emma. They affectionately called her the Jewish cordon bleu, with gefilte fish as her *pièce de résistance*. Lawrence remarked that Emma should have written a cookbook instead of her memoirs.

By the fall, however, she was again plunged into despair, unable to live either in the present or in the past. This restlessness and discomfort were to plague her until she finished the book, early in 1931. At first she hoped that she would complete the book in 1929, for her sixtieth birthday. But every step took longer than she expected. The writing itself was not so hard as living with the memories and the regrets in which she was immersed. "It is agony to resurrect the dead. Christ is supposed to have done it only once. I do it every day. Have done it for nearly a year."

In recalling her past, Emma had little insight into her motivations, simply recording her actions and beliefs. Never in her life had Emma allowed herself to feel pain and anger fully without transforming them into disappointment in the failure of her grand vision; she could experience pure and simple pain indirectly, only in behalf of someone else. Accordingly, in describing the break-up of her marriage, instead of re-experiencing her sadness, anger, and loneliness, she immediately shifted to a discussion of free love and the young revolutionaries of Russia, and wrote about her "disappointment" in the failure of this ideal.

It was the Haymarket martyrs' inspired final statements, she believed, that had given her the courage to leave her husband and move to New York. She even began her book with the Haymarket martyrs, because she felt that their deaths had prompted her own spiritual birth.

Emma's personal identification with the men who were hanged for their beliefs enabled her to touch others with their story as few political orators could. Yet she had been so sensitive to their tragedy because she was at that time denying her own pain at the break-up of her marriage. Ultimately, her need to deny aspects of her emotions affected her political views in turn. How much easier it was for Emma to encourage people to reach for a glowing vision than to work for small changes in their daily lives.

In writing her autobiography, she had to deal with each experience as it had occurred and stay with her feelings long enough to write about them. In some cases, perhaps in part because distance lent some protection, she found herself facing her feelings more directly than she had been able to at the time. Thus, *Living My Life* was titled more aptly than she may have imagined.

In February 1929, Emma wrote to Sasha that she was now in need of his services as a sympathetic, informed listener. Again, she chided him for refusing to be separated from Emmy long enough to help her with the book, assuring him that she would drop everything for him if the situation were reversed, even "if the separation would mean for the rest of my life." Sometimes her eyes gave out, and she would feel dizzy after writing or reading. She needed encouragement, though she fended off editorial criticisms from her visiting nephew Saxe. In fact, she forbade Sasha to do any editing until she was finished. She told Ben:

> So far Sasha has had absolutely nothing to do with my autobiography. I have even not let him read much of the Mss. The reasons are many—the main being that my present work is so absolutely part of myself I can grant no one the right to what you call "whip it into form." It is different with a work on theories or dramatic subjects than it is with a story of one's life. The latter is too deeply and painfully personal to allow anyone and especially any man in my life to "whip it into form." The form must spring from the life and both must be created by the one who has lived it, or not at all. At least that is my feeling about the quality and style of a story of one's life.

Writing her book seemed to Emma the most difficult task of her life, as she told Sasha:

> Not even when I thought I would have to go the way of Czolgosz did I feel such agony as I have since last June. It is not only the writing, it is living through what now lies in ashes and being made aware that I have nothing left in the way of personal relations from all who have been in my life and have torn my heart. You have failed to realize the deeper current of my misery since I started, and there is another year to go through with it. How, then, can anyone expect me to let others revise this child of sorrow?

She also let Sasha know about her struggle with self-doubt:

> To do our work lightly, or to be haunted by the thought that it does not matter because life itself does not matter, would mean that we could do no work at all, writing or otherwise. And without the work we care about, life itself would be impossible. It certainly would be to me, and I am inclined [to think] it would be the same with you.

In 1929, Emma reached the events of 1908 in her autobiography, including her affair with Ben. Swept back into Ben's life by their letters, she needed to ask him questions to clarify her memory of those days; in doing so, she met with the same frustrations that she had felt with him so many years earlier.

Emma tried to maintain a friendship with Ben in the present while corresponding with him about the past. Ben, for his part, was still trying to give her the support of a manager and fan:

> Lover, and friend and teacher,
> With all my heart, I wish you well.
> I want you to write a great book. I feel that in spite of all my neglect and weaknesses and brutality, your love of justice, your sense of honesty, your willingness to give the other fellow fair play, will entitle me [to] a page in your book.... If ever I amount to a

damn, if ever I give anything worthwhile to society, it will be because you loved me and worked with me. Someday we may sit on the sand and sing "until it seems no one is left alive but you and me."

At one point, Ben asked Emma to take a trip with him to North Africa. Emma eventually declined—because of the expense, and because she could not take the time now that she had a firm commitment from Knopf for her book—but not until they had both enjoyed the fantasy of an exotic reunion. Emma also wrote to ask Ben about his childhood and his medical schooling—but not about his other affairs. She had decided, after an interchange with Sasha on the subject, not to write about his or her casual affairs, to include only "such cases, whether of love or other events, that really went deep, or were of wide scope." She then wrote to Ben:

I am not asking you [for] data on your obsessions. I know all about them. Besides, in my story they are only of importance as far as they affected our life. I'd have to write another two volumes were I to mention all your ladies. I dare say you do not even remember them anymore. . . . Please, old scout, let me have the material soon. You have played a very great part in my life, I want to be able to let you stand out accordingly.

While Emma was writing about the great sexual power of her relationship with Ben, Ben became ill, and wrote to her that he was depressed because his illness had made him impotent. Sympathetic as always when he was ill, Emma provided him with some good-humored assurances that he could never lose his sexual attractiveness and that, besides, he had much more than that to recommend him. In time, Ben recovered.

Emma still thought that Ben was not only a critical figure in her own life, but that he had made a significant contribution to the anarchist movement. She debated the question with Sasha while she was writing about Ben in her autobiography, Sasha claiming that his major objection to Ben was his MANNER of activity in the movement and his uncomradely treatment of comrades, his sensationalism, etc. But all that referred ONLY to the movement. I held that he never belonged to the movement, and I am still of that opinion, and I think events proved it. His psychology did not belong there, even if he did some useful work. Were he with you and INactive in the movement, then I should have felt differently altogether.

Emma protested that Sasha had never appreciated Ben's strengths:

Ben during ten years dedicated [himself] to me and my work as no other man ever had, making it possible for me to do the best and most extensive work I had done up to my meeting him. . . . Let us be fair, dear Sash, it was Ben who helped me raise thousands of dollars which kept up a houseful of people and enabled me as well as yourself to do what we have done between 1908 and 1917. . . .

I knew Ben inside and out two weeks after we went on tour; I not only knew but loathed his sensational ways, his bombast, his braggadocio, and his promiscuity, which lacked the least sense of selection. But over and above that there was something large, primitive, unpremeditated, and simple about Ben which had terrific charm. Had you and the other friends concerned in my salvation recognized this, had you shown Ben some faith, instead of writing to the university to find out about his medical degree (which the boy never could forget), in short had you shown as much understanding for his exotic being as you did so often when you saw such types as Ben in books, Ben would not have become a renegade. The trouble with you was, dear heart, as with all our comrades, you are a puritan at heart. You all talk about how one must help the outcast and the criminal, but when you are confronted with such a creature you turn from him in disgust, do not trust him, and deliberately drive him back to the depths he sprang from. I have been too long in the movement not to know how narrow and moral[istic] it is, how unforgiving and lacking in understanding toward everyone different from [itself]. I was disappointed when I saw the same trait in you, dear.

Remembering the unhappiness the moralism of the movement had caused her, Emma deplored the unfairness of the distinction often made between a woman intimate with a younger man, and a man intimate with a younger woman—an obvious reference to her relationship with Ben and Sasha's with Emmy:

Of course it is nonsense to say that the attitude to[ward] men and women in their love for younger people is the same in the world. It is nothing of the kind, the proof of that is in the pudding. Hundreds and hundreds of men marry women much younger than themselves; they have circles of friends, they are accepted by the world. This does not happen to women, not one in a million has a love affair for any length of time with a man younger than herself. If she has, she is the butt of her dearest friends and gradually becomes that in her own eyes. . . .

Everybody objects, resents, in fact dislikes a woman who lives with a younger man; they think her a goddamned fool; no doubt she is that, but it is not the business or concern of friends to make her look and feel like a fool.

But Sasha insisted that Ben had been out of place in the movement, that it was not just because Ben was younger than Emma that he was ostracized. "Ben was a Christian at heart all the time, and psychologically, sometimes even unconsciously, antagonistic to the very spirit of our movement."

Ben himself had become humble about his role in Emma's life and in the anarchist movement:

The most important decade in my life you are going to tell, and it is unimportant whether you mention my name or give me credit for passing handbills. Outside of having been a good janitor, card distributor and bookseller and possibly fair lover, there is little of importance that you can say about me, except that most of the time I was with you I was happy. . . .

I am looking forward to your "Baby" book with all the anticipation of an expectant father.

With love and devotion, I am

As ever, yours
Ben

Ben even acknowledged that Emma had never been the dominant woman in his life. In his most direct admission of what Emma had long ago discerned, he wrote: "Yet, my obsession for my mother has continued; although she is seventy and I am more than fifty, there is a bond between us that is more than mother and son. Make your own deductions. Every man ought to be faithful to at least one woman—I have chosen my mother."

Still, Ben was now sure that, with Emma approaching sixty, he could detect a new acceptance of him and a softening in her personality, which affirmed his sense of her as a great woman: "Yes, Emma, you are a great woman, and all the comfort and rewards that a human being needs who has served humanity shall be yours. You already are the greatest female propagandist, labor leader and educator the world has ever known, and now you are going to give the world a truly great autobiography."

Emma did not hesitate to criticize Ben for exaggerating:

My god, what a romancer you are and how much like the Playboy of the Western World!! Really, old dear, for a Jew you are too much of an Irishman. . . .

I do know, however, that I am not the "greatest" propagandist or anything else in the world. Your awakened sex technique has just run away with you. And of course you assume that I have love in my life. In a way it is true. I have the love and devotion of my friends, the old and some of the new. And now I live in love of the past. But I have not the love you have in mind. So don't imagine all sorts of things.

Ben responded with even more praise: "I loved your last letter; if you don't want to be the greatest female labor leader and orator in the world, all right. You are a great letter writer and you have an extraordinary ability to express joy and pain."

Although Emma's letters to Ben were affectionate, and her letters to Sasha full of admiration for the important work Ben had done, Emma could at the same time write Sasha that she agreed that Ben "is nothing now but a Goddamned fool. . . . But he had much in him which might have been developed had not my friends knocked him on the head from the first moment he came to us."

Emma tried as best she could to write her autobiography from the perspective of the past, not from the present. "I must write as I felt at the time," she explained to Ben. They both knew that those times had been emotionally turbulent, but Ben was hopeful that the account would, on balance, be favorable. This meant a lot to him, for, in August 1929, about to embark on his first tramping trip in twenty years, he found himself keenly aware that he was no longer the young, dashing hobo; instead he felt "old, fat and ill." The memories of his dramatic past with Emma gave him a sense of his own worth, and he looked forward to shining in the glory of her autobiography.

As Emma wrote about the years immediately before her deportation, its quick-paced horror came back into focus. So absorbed was she in the lacerations of those years that she had a difficult time keeping up her correspondence with Ben. She wrote to him that only after she finished her book would she be able once more to live in the present; regression was necessary to the recounting of her story.

It is extremely difficult for me now to write letters. Especially to you. I have been for several weeks in the throes of 1918 and am going to be in the same stress of mind until I have finished 1919. These two are my prison years, which were very ghastly in more than one respect. The most painful being the process of emancipation from my mad passion for you. Living through every phase of it now, it is impossible to write you in a detached way.

Emma had felt abandoned by Ben, and her autobiography reflected it. She showed part of what she had written to Henry Alsberg, an American journalist whom she had last seen in Germany. He was impressed that Emma was able to treat "the Ben Reitman relationship beautifully." Emma had devoted eighteen chapters, 283 pages, of her book to the period from their meeting in 1908, when her "whole being was suffused with a feeling of comfort and security," to 1919, when she was released from prison, where she had "lived away from the disturbing presence of Ben. Often my heart had called for him, but I had silenced its cry." She summed up the reasons for their parting in a typically high-minded but self-deceiving way.

> Emotionalism had guided his passion as it had his life. But, like nature unleashed, he would destroy with one hand the lavish gifts of the other. I had revelled in the beauty and strength of his giving, and I had recoiled from and struggled against the self-centered egotism which ignored and annihilated obstacles in the soul of the loved one. Erotically Ben and I were of the same earth, but in a cultural sense we were separated by centuries of time.
>
> With him social impulses, sympathy with mankind, ideas, and ideals were moods of the moment, and as fleeting. He had no means of sensing basic verities or inner need to convert them into his own.
>
> My life was linked with that of the race. Its spiritual heritage was mine, and its values were transmuted into my being. The eternal struggle of man was rooted within me. That made the abyss between us.

She could not face the part she herself had played in his decision to leave her, her demands and criticisms that made it difficult for anyone to sustain a relationship with her. Having never been able to come to a recognition of her own faults, she continued to portray herself in the best light as she wrote her autobiography.

Writing about Ben resolved the end of their relationship for Emma in a way nothing had done before. She was forced to gather their scattered experiences into the form of a story—framed by a beginning and an end. In her account of her last visit with Ben after she was released from prison, Emma wrote, "The dead had buried the dead, and I felt serene." But in fact she had come to that serenity only as she relived their love affair.

When Emma had nearly finished writing about her time with Ben, news reached her that Anna had died of unknown causes. The fact that Anna had died so suddenly and mysteriously raised questions about Ben, and at the time of the funeral his possible role in her death was being investigated by the police. Although he was exonerated, the rumor spread that Anna had died of an abortion (it was commonly known that Ben performed illegal abortions in his home and office). Emma responded with the appropriate sympathy, but her feelings were double-edged. She wrote to their mutual friend Agnes Inglis:

> I suppose you know the tragedy that has come to Ben through the death of Anna. Though we were very much apart I was much shocked to hear about it. It was so sudden. She was ill only a week. I can see from Ben's last letter that he is terribly shaken and very unhappy. It isn't surprising at all, having lived with Anna all those years. She was such a yielding creature, Ben must have had it all his way, and it is hard to do without a human being who is completely wrapped up in another. I am particularly sorry for the child, although, strange to say, the love Ben never gave to his daughter, he is certainly concentrating on the boy. That is something.

Still, Ben drew comfort from Emma's assurances of love and friendship, and believed that she, unlike some of his other friends, found no satisfaction in his suffering. His mourning for Anna was sharpened by guilt about how he had behaved toward her while she was alive. "I used to weary you telling you how wonderful Anna was," he wrote Emma. "I never made her happy or was much of a husband. But oh I loved and needed her so. Now only the memory of my denial live on, with it every increasing pain."

Although Ben and Anna never actually married, he felt he had been a husband. Ben had lost the woman whom he had loved enough to leave Emma, and Emma, sensing that for the first time in his life Ben understood deep sorrow, tried to help him through his grief.

As Ben meditated on his life, and confronted his own mortality in the wake of Anna's death, he clung to his relationship with Emma for assurance that he would always be remembered. He even fantasized about being with her again. Although she did not encourage him in this, she did not have the heart to contradict him, particularly at a time when others seemed to be behaving vindictively toward him. He wrote:

Dearest Mommy.
    Into these crowded days.
    Your presence comes often.
    I have been wondering about you and your book.
    You saw what Margaret Anderson wrote about me.
    "The fantastic Dr. Reitman (who wasn't so bad if you could hastily drop all your ideas as to how human beings should look and act)"—You know I always liked Margaret and thought she was friendly.
    It was the same way about Harry Kemp. I liked and helped him, thought he was my friend, but in his book, *Tramping on Life*, he called me "A big fat nincompoop." Wonder what you will call me.

Emma, too, was insulted by Harry Kemp, the "Hobo poet" from Mornington, Ohio, who referred to her in his book as "a thick-built woman, after the gladiatorial fashion. . . . As she moved she made me think of a battleship going into action. There was something about her face . . . a squareness of jaw, a belligerency, that reminded me of Roosevelt"; Kemp did, however, go on to acknowledge Emma as a great woman. On the other hand, Reitman, "the fat nincompoop," was described as "such a weakling as great women must necessarily, it seems, fall for," revealing the jealousy and resentment that many of Emma's friends felt about Ben. Some of her friends, instead of insulting Reitman, simply ignored him. Agnes Inglis commented on Hippolyte Havel's having excluded Ben from his biographical sketch of Emma's life in *Anarchism and Other Essays*: "Did they all hate Ben or what? Ben is a sort of unmentionable person. But a tremendous character. . . . Ben touches life way down. And while it isn't the way I want to touch it, it's the way he does and he does."

Ben was determined to finish his own book on pimps, *The Second Oldest Profession*, to make the general public acknowledge the importance of his work with the conventionally unrespectable. And, despite her protests, he would dedicate it to Emma.

I SHALL D[ED]ICATE TO YOU.

For you have been the biggest force in my life.
You did more for my intellectual development than anyone else.
You showed me the beauty and possibilities of freedom.
EMMA: [in] spite of all your limitations.
You are easily the greatest woman on earth.
I have said this in my book[,] I say it to the world.
As to my book.—Hold your shirt, read it first.
I have written the best book on Pimps and Prostitution ever
    written.
And you and Berkman will admit it.
Be as fair to me as you are to Anarchi[sts].
You always say, "learn about it first and then pass judgment."

Let me go a little farther. You are going to write a great
    autobiography.
I believe that.
But my *Second Oldest Profession*
    will have a larger circulation and make more money tha[n] your
    new book. . . .
Your immor[t]ality is assured because I [dedicated] my book to
    you.

Ben's tribute read: "I dedicate this book to Emma Goldman, the most brilliant and most useful woman I have ever met. She taught me that men and women would never be free til they learned not to exploit nor be exploited."

Working on the book helped Ben make his way through the tragedy of his wife's untimely death. By Christmas 1930, he was living with a twenty-two-year-old woman. He continued to scrape by financially as a venereal-disease specialist.

As Emma was finishing her manuscript, Ben's book on pimps and prostitutes was about to be published. He called it his "baby," perhaps echoing Emma, who always described the process as though she had given birth: "Hurrah! The baby is born at last. The labor pains were excruciating enough to give birth to a dozen puppies." In any case, Ben awaited the parental judgment of Emma and Sasha, whom he wanted to love his book and be proud of him. In a somewhat grotesque metaphorical mood, he summed up his accomplishments to Emma:

> . . . I have told the story of the people
> Who have buttered my bread with Gonorrhea.
> And sweetened my coffee with Syphilis.
> And bought gas for my car with their misery.
> . . . Tell Sasha, a fellow author salutes him.
>
> > Love
> > Hobo

Although Emma's book would not be published until the following fall, her relief at finishing was enormous. She recuperated from "fallen arches, swollen veins, general fatigue" with a brief trip to Paris, then returned to St.-Tropez to tend to her roses and enjoy the company of her niece, Stella.

When Ben's book came out that spring, it was favorably reviewed and sold well, winning him some public recognition. Yet the disparity between Ben's success and the lives of the pimps and prostitutes who were the focus of his book made him uncomfortable. He began to think that he was better at being a promoter than an author. He had not anticipated the complexity of feelings that publishing the book aroused in him, including the sense of having exposed himself and other people. To Emma he wrote:

I would just like to lay my head in your lap and weep. It is no fun
    climbing and achieving and having.
With half of your friends and comrades starving. . . .
I have had my fill of being an Author, etc.
I got much more joy when *Anarchism and Other Essays*.
And the *Modern Drama* came out.
Guess I am one of those fit to play second fiddle.
Or bask in someone else's sun.
I did best when I was your manager. . . .
Hope all is well with you, dear heart.
And some day I can sit at your feet again.

Loving you
Hobo

Ben still craved publicity: he added "Author, *Second Oldest Profession*"
to "Dr. Ben L. Reitman, M.D. and sociologist" on his stationery. Even
before seeing Emma's autobiography, he wrote to Knopf without her
knowledge to ask if they would hire him to promote the book. When
Emma found out, she was outraged that Ben had tried once more to
interfere in her life.

Ben's book had been received as a serious treatment of the exploitation of women prostitutes by their pimps. Yet he felt personally too
close to the "purely negative, pimp evil," and wanted to reassociate
himself with Emma's exalted world at this time when so much attention
was being focused on his connection with the underworld.

Emma voiced her opinions to Agnes Inglis: "I do not think any part
of Ben's book is great. The material in itself is, but not the understanding
in the treatment of the material. Ben not only lacks ability to write but
he cannot enter into his subject deeply enough to bring up what he
finds. He only sees the surface."

Still unaware of how pervasive Emma's criticism of him and his
work was, however, Ben hoped for her love and respect more than
anything in the world. After collecting and organizing his papers for a
university archive to make sure that the artifacts of their life together
would be preserved, he wrote to Emma with characteristic enthusiasm,
still waiting to see her book:

I went over old trunks, boxes, and files and found

    Dozens of your letters, hundreds of clippings and thousands of
Cards and announcements of your meetings.

    Had you the material I found about you and your meetings, I am
sure you could have used it to advantage.

    You cannot use it now.

    But the Biographers (and there will be many) of EG

    Will find my material to great advantage.

Ben generously offered Emma her choice of all the materials he had
been working on for weeks, for any last-minute additions to her book.
Perhaps acting on a premonition, however, he wrote that his admiration
for her greatness did not blind him to her capacity for cruelty:

> You are unfair to me if you say I ever changed my mind about YOU
> BEING A GREAT WOMAN. . . . YOU ARE ALWAYS GREAT.
> Even when you are CRUEL and UNFAIR. Some day I shall write
> about [you]. . . . Yes, Emma, in spite of the fact that you never
> understood me, and every time I would climb, you kick me in the
> face and Step on my fingers. . . .
>
>   Every effort I have made to find joy or a place in the Sun, you
> would crush me.
>
>   You are so constituted that ONLY THOSE who serve you body
> and soul, Can you love. YES, THAT MAKES YOU GREAT. . . .
>
>   Yes, BLUE-EYED MOMMY . . . I know my ten years as your
> servant and LOVER give me a page not only in *Living My Life* but in
> history.

Emma did give Ben more than a few pages in her life history.
When the autobiography appeared, in the fall of 1931, Ben was stricken
by her account of their relationship, and overwhelmed by what seemed
to be a devastating expression of cruelty:

> *Living My Life* will be a powerful book.
>   If it affects everyone as it did me.
>   You win. . . . You always win. . . .

I knew you would be recognized as a great woman.

Your book took all of the bombast, spirit and ego out of me. I had a half dozen lectures including the Anarchist Memorial

But I have been ashamed to show my face in any radical meeting. (Your book kept one man off the platform)

Thank you for showing me what a :::: I am.

If I hadn't read *Living My Life*, I never would have believed it. I shall be glad to have an autographed copy of your book.

Maybe if I live through it, I will write you again.

It may mean nothing to you, but please let me say again.

For many years I gave you my tenderest love, my truest loyalty, my best service, I just gave you the best that was in me

And now you have crushed me.

Ben

Emma's autobiography consisted of close to a thousand pages. She had tried to encompass the years from 1869 to 1927-28, when she had begun writing the book, and it included so many people and events of significance in her life, political as well as personal, that it gave the illusion of holding back on nothing. She wrote of her love affairs—with Ed Brady, Sasha, Fedya, and Ben. With each failure of love came a variation on the same theme:

> There were other forces at work to deny me permanency in love. Were they part of some passionate yearning in me that no man could completely fulfill or were they inherent in those who forever reach out for the heights, for some ideal or exalted aim that excludes aught else? . . . If one soared high, could he hope to dwell for long in the absorbing depths of passion and love? Like all who paid for their faith, I too would have to face the inevitable. Occasional snatches of love; nothing permanent in my life except my ideal.

Emma's account of her relationship with Ben revealed her infatuation with him as "an exotic picturesque figure with a large black cowboy hat, flowing silk tie, and huge cane." She chronicled their tours together, their great successes, but also built a case against him for his infidelity, dishonesty, vulgarity, and disaffection from the anarchist movement. She did not hide her own ambivalence toward Ben—how she would run back to him even after feeling wronged by him—yet she did not show how much despair she experienced, how much her relationship with Ben made her doubt herself and the contradictions inherent in her role in the anarchist movement. With Ben more than in any other relationship, Emma confronted the disparity between her public vision and her private life. Rather than looking within herself for causes, she pointed the finger of blame at him.

Ben felt most exposed by Emma's account of his early lies to her about other affairs, her portrayal of his symbiotic relationship with his mother, including his willingness to expropriate money from anarchist funds for her, and his desertion of Emma at the end, before her deportation.

When *Living My Life* was published, Ben was ill with diabetes and nephritis—what he had described earlier as "weakness of the body, an inferiority complex, unmanageable balls." His young girl friend, Retta Toble, had gotten word of a crisis in her family and had to go back to North Dakota; to the list of ills he sent Emma, he had added the complaint that he had "no Mommy, no Anna, no Retta to ease the turmoil in my soul, and pains of my body and the longings of my heart." Ben had worshipped Emma. Now, after reading her account of him, he felt forsaken.

Emma's reply was tinged with the arrogant aloofness of someone who had won a battle:

> In the Postscript George Bernard Shaw wrote to Frank Harris' Life of him, there is one passage I wish you could take to heart. Here it is.
>
> ". . . No man is a good judge of his own portrait; and if it be well painted he has no right to prevent the artist exhibiting it, or even, when the artist is a deceased friend, to refuse to varnish it before the show is open. . . ."
>
> If you were able to realize this you would not feel as you do about your portrait in *Living My Life*. True, I am not yet deceased and you

had not been called upon to "varnish it." You probably will one day put on the varnish heavy and thick. I don't think I shall mind. For I have learned ages ago that one cannot see oneself through the eyes of another, not even our closest and dearest friends.

Emma even boasted to Agnes Inglis: "he tells me I have taken all the bombast and egoism out of him. I wish it were true, then I should consider it a great accomplishment, but I am afraid Ben will die as he lived, believing himself abused by those who cared for him the most. It can't be helped. Perhaps none of us gets out of our skin." Hutch Hapgood thought her portrayal of Ben was a striking illustration of her spontaneous sympathy with the underdog.

Although Ben was personally hurt by Emma's treatment of him, he was also concerned about his role in history, and he could not ignore the damage he felt had been done to his public image. While she had gained distance from him in the writing of her book, he had considered himself growing closer to her: he had supported her writing efforts, helped her whenever he could, and offered her love and encouragement. After publication, he was ready to start a campaign against what he perceived as her betrayal of all they had built together. But he backed down and, characteristically, remained loyal to Emma. In December 1931, he wrote to her with some humor about his new stance:

My Dear Mommy.
> For a month I have been ill.
> And in the depth of despair.
> As you so often put it.
> "You were sitting on my chest choking me."
> Never in my whole life was I outraged, humiliated, bitter, disappointed and crushed,
> And never was I so near coming back at you.
> In a way that I should have regretted all my life.
> You wrote your book, it is finished, you "were honest"
> And "true to your self," so that is all that is needed.
> I am doing a good many talks on your book and I shall review it soon.

> And you will see that I HAVE BEEN LOYAL AND FAITHFUL
> TO YOU. . . .
> Someday when I am stronger and less hurt I will
> Write Berkman a letter about *Living My Life*. . . .
> *Living My Life* cost me 20 pounds, I lost my big belly, Thanks.

Ben proved his new commitment by writing to reviewers about Emma's book, emphasizing, "She was not only America's greatest female orator, but was powerful beyond any man." And:

> . . . she interested the multitudes in Good literature, the Drama, Music, Arts . . . to people who had never come in contact with good literature before. . . . The outstanding figure in *Living My Life* is Alexander Berkman, he is a colossal figure. And if anything is underrated in her book, her tender devotion and comradely loyalty to him makes one of the most beautiful love stories in history. All that Emma Goldman said about me is true.

Although some people who read the autobiography remarked to Ben that "Emma certainly had it in for you," he tried to maintain a positive stance in public. But in private, his reactions ranged from getting angry with Emma, to deprecating himself, to glorifying her, and finally to taking credit for all the public attention that Emma had ever gained. By August 1932, he wrote to her, "Your page in history depends on Ben Reitman."

With the publication of the autobiography, Emma felt relieved of the weight of her past, and her focus had shifted away from Ben's reaction as she prepared herself to face the general reviews of her magnum opus. Naturally, she was apprehensive. Her life story covered almost sixty years of people and events, and Emma knew that she could be challenged at every turn.

She had decided not to end with her Russian experiences, not because she feared criticism, but because she wanted to avoid making the book too depressing. Privately, however, she was quite pessimistic about the state of the world. She had written to Millie Rocker, "the whole world is a prison and most people have turned into jailers. It's awful."

And to Max Nettlau, after finishing the autobiography, she wrote: "The events since 1914, perhaps I should say more specifically since 1917, have cured me from ever holding out much hope for a glowing future. Please do not think I have stopped believing in the beauty and justice of our ideal. I have not." Despite her ambivalence, she had given the world an inspiring account of her life. She hoped to represent an ideal that might seem distant to her contemporary readers but that time would show to be "the most real thing in any sane society."

Her new political attitude was translated into her personal life. Emma may have complained that she had become "a grouchy old thing," but she had become more accepting of her real situation than previously. Life as an exile, with its constant struggles to stay afloat financially and emotionally, had wearied her. She wrote to Agnes Inglis, "It seems to have been sung at our cradle that there shall be storm and strife in our life until the end. I am beginning to think that one cannot escape his fate. One must learn to meet it."

Although most reviews of the book were favorable, some even calling it a classic, others were critical. The staunchly pro-Soviet playwright Laurence Stallings reviewed her book for the *New York Sun*, redubbing it, "The Unmarried Life of Emma and Co[mpany] or Goldman, Goldman über Alles." Freda Kirchwey of *The Nation* praised *Living My Life* and the intense emotions from which it was written, but added: "Herein lies her undeniable power. Her emotion is both intense and universal, her expression of it—in words and actions—unrestrained, her courage completely instinctive. She is contemptuous of any intellectualizing that stands in the way of faith and action. Always she feels first and thinks later—and less."

At first Emma did not take Kirchwey's judgment to be in any way admiring, but eventually she could see that the criticism contained a backhanded compliment. This was a common criticism of her book; she answered it in a letter to John Haynes Holmes, a minister who had also commented on her "intense emotionalism" in reviewing the book:

I feel that you are wrong in emphasizing that I have "often run away with intense emotionalism, bordering on hysteria," or that parts of my book are "screaming with feeling, sobbing uncontrolled temperament, explosives, eruptions, like from a volcano." No one who knows me intimately has ever credited me with all these attributes. True, I am not very patient in private life. I often lose my temper over seemingly insignificant things, but, then, there is more truth than fiction in the saying that pinpricks have more disastrous effect on the nervous system than powerful thrusts. The fact is that in important matters I have remained cool and unperturbed. Strange as it may seem to you, I never felt greater peace in my soul than when I faced trial, or was locked in my cell. But, then, I know how kindly you have approached my work, and the sincerity of your splendid tribute. I do not in the least find anything you say contrary to my real being.

Emma handled the response to her autobiography more confidently than she had the critical uproar that had followed her book on Russia. She responded well to the criticisms of her personal life, her loves, and her inner life, perhaps because so many reviewers treated her book as a masterpiece. Friends and acquaintances wrote glowing letters of praise, comparing her book to Rousseau's *Confessions*.

The autobiography mirrored the high drama that had marked Emma's life. It was gripping, and more open about intimate issues than most publications during that period. Emma succeeded in connecting her personal life with the great events of the time, and in illuminating her belief "that no life is worth anything which does not contain a great ideal, and which does not bring forth determination to serve it to the uttermost." And yet she could not be completely honest with her readers or herself; she could not overcome her pattern of denial. She could not acknowledge how deeply conflicted she felt about many of her most adamant public stands, especially on marriage, marital stability, and love, or about the manifestations of this ambivalence in her private and public life. She portrayed her life as a kind of morality play—with good always pitted against evil. Although Emma was frank, even courageous, about exposing the connection between her private and public lives, she was rarely self-critical. She blamed outside forces for tarnishing her loosely defined "beautiful vision" and her unshakable commitment to freedom. She was the heroine of her own story, in love with and devoted to her ideal.

Finished with "the great obsession" of writing and publishing her autobiography, Emma was restless. Now that the project was completed and well received, she felt too empty to draw pleasure from it. While Emma had been at work on her autobiography, she had been content to live in the past. Without this excuse, she felt she had to resume her political activity, yet she found herself unmotivated.

Speaking tours and lectures on her autobiography were sure to follow, but she did not know when they would take place. Meanwhile, her friend Henry Alsberg had aptly suggested that she add to her autobiography a postscript in the form of a want ad: "Young active person (female) looking for more and better adventures. Excellent at handling police; unruly mobs a specialty."

ABOVE: Elizabeth Gurley Flynn, pictured here with organizers from the I.W.W. silkworkers' strike at Paterson, New Jersey, in 1913. Following the strike, Flynn, politically and emotionally exhausted, took refuge in Emma's care. *Left to right:* Pat Quinlan, Carlo Tresca, Elizabeth Gurley Flynn, Adolph Lessing, and William D. Haywood. (Archives of Labor and Urban Affairs, Wayne State University) RIGHT: Margaret Sanger, who was encouraged in her early work in the birth control movement by Emma Goldman. (The Sophia Smith Collection, Women's History Archive, Smith College)

UPPER LEFT: Kate Richards O'Hare, socialist prison reformer who became Emma's close friend during their prison stay in 1918. (New York University, Tamiment Library) UPPER RIGHT: Voltairine de Cleyre, anarchist contemporary of Emma's. (International Institute of Social History) LOWER LEFT: Peter Kropotkin, anarchist theorist, who inspired Emma. (International Institute of Social History)

ABOVE: Alexander Berkman at Kropotkin Funeral Committee meeting in Russia, 1921. (International Institute of Social History) RIGHT: Arthur Swenson, Emma's "Swedish sunbeam," 1922. (National Archives Record Group 59, DoS, Records of the Office of the Counselor, file #800. 11-433)

ABOVE LEFT AND RIGHT: Rudolf Rocker and Millie, Emma's personal and political friends. Many of Emma's most heartfelt letters were written to Millie. (Johanna Boetz) LEFT: Leon Malmed, Emma's friend and lover, 1915. (Courtesy of Malmed family)

RIGHT: Photograph of Ben Reitman, titled "De Profundus," about which he bragged to Emma on the occasion of its exhibition in Paris in 1931. (Max Thorak, M.D., University of Illinois at Chicago, The Library, Manuscript Collection)

LEFT: The aging Ben Reitman in Chicago, c. 1939. (University of Illinois at Chicago, The Library, Manuscript Collection)

ABOVE RIGHT: Mortally ill, Sasha is visited by friends in St. Tropez, before his suicide on June 27, 1936. (Left to right: Sasha, Mollie Steimer, an unknown friend, and Fedya.) (International Institute of Social History)
BELOW LEFT: A saddened Emma Goldman, photographed by Senya Fleshine. (SEMO, from Mollie Steimer's personal collection, courtesy Pacific Street Film Collection, New York)

ABOVE: Emma, after Sasha's death, once again heroic, with her CNT-FAI comrades in Spain in 1938. (Senya Fleshine) RIGHT: Stella Ballantine, Emma's niece, who was devoted to Emma and her work throughout Emma's life, and who was with Emma at her death. (Senya Fleshine)

16

BLIND FAITH

At the end of 1931, Emma wrote that she had "never felt so beaten." The fall from her expectations about what would follow the completion of her autobiography was very steep. Returning from the past, she faced her life in exile—a life without a home or a base for political activity. She wrote to a friend, "I feel completely torn out from my moorings." Lectures on her book in England, Amsterdam, Denmark, and Germany were often broken up by communists who focused only on Emma's account of her experiences in the Soviet Union, deeming it a vicious attack on a revolution struggling to survive. She was thrown out of Holland for making a speech against the imminent rise of Nazism, which the government thought too threatening to their fragile diplomatic ties with Germany. In Germany itself, the police threatened that she might end up getting shot, as was her European socialist counterpart, Rosa Luxemburg.

That her attackers came from both left and right underscored Emma's position as an outcast. The rise of fascism and the danger of war seemed to Emma to parallel the disregard for the individual that she had seen emerge in Lenin's Soviet Union. Such a viewpoint distanced her from much of the European left. A pervasive feeling of depression, of helplessness, of lovelessness and loneliness, marked this period of her life.

Emma's candid letters to Sasha dwelled on her feeling of being out of place and unfulfilled:

> . . . as regards myself, I seem to fit in nowhere, between you, me and the lamp post, not even in our own ranks. Certainly not in any other. That would perhaps not be such a tragedy if I were not still consumed with the need for activity. I am in the worst state of turmoil I have been in years. I wrote you that line some time ago. In addition to being neither able nor willing to be caught in the muddy mob stream, I also feel an alien everywhere.

She could still rise to the occasion, organizing support for Sasha when he was struggling to avoid deportation from France. Periodically she had to write to her influential European friends to ask that they use their influence with the French officials on Sasha's behalf, while Sasha rode the railroad back and forth to avoid arrest. He often complained that "the only place where he could go freely was up or down." Emma could battle for him, even encourage him to keep his spirits up, but for the most part she retreated into her garden and kitchen, where she sought to create beauty and sensuous pleasure in a life that seemed to have come to a premature halt.

Stuck in her small house in St.-Tropez, Emma, too, hung on the hope that her friends would exert enough pressure on the United States government for her to obtain a travel visa to make a lecture tour. Emma still believed that only in America would she find her true audience, and revive her own optimism and sense of purpose.

Her banishment from the United States amounted to political assassination. It had become difficult to function in Europe, given the precarious nature of her political asylum and the fact that the U.S. government campaign against her had spread there: all customs agencies had photographs of Emma labeling her as a possible security danger. Even in England, where she enjoyed citizenship and the friendship of various people in the arts and politics, she had run up against a wall of anti-Semitism. The clash between her effusive Jewish style and the reserve of the English made life there intolerable for Emma. In the south of France, she lived among a small exile community that provided a social outlet, but she had no part in the political life of the country. For better or worse, she felt herself to be American, and now, more than ever, she wished to return. She saw her opportunity in the favorable reception of her autobiography.

Her old friends tended to react personally. Former lovers felt closer to her again, and more concerned about their treatment in her book than about how she was currently managing her life. When Leon, for instance, complained that she hadn't given their relationship the space it deserved in her book, she explained "why I did not mention our episode which began at Napierville":

> Well, to a large extent because it ended so disastrously. I can now understand that it was largely due to your business and schemes obsession, which had so jarred on my nerves. Perhaps also because I felt it should never have happened. Our old friendship should have remained free from anything erotic. The main reason, however, was I did not wish to add to the conflict in your home. It was hardly worthwhile to make the affair known. However, it is not necessary for me to tell you that if I failed to write about it it was not because I did not feel most deeply at the time all I told you and gave you, or that the end had in any way affected our old sweet friendship and camaraderie. You have been and will remain always my dear old romantic knight, capable of beautiful emotions and fine actions along with your other traits with which I never could reconcile myself. Your marital life and your pursuit of wealth. But these were after all your affairs. What you gave me was always beautiful and always will stand out as something very precious.

Perhaps not coincidentally, Ben began work on a book about "outcasts" at this time, which included another tribute to Emma—though this hardly cheered her spirits—and he had begun to write his own memoirs. Ben had gone from bad to worse in Emma's eyes, having shifted his loyalties once again, from religion to communism.

He was "flirting with Communism," Ben wrote Emma, though, as he added with some irony, "fortunately the communists dislike me." Emma did not find his latest enthusiasm amusing and asked him not to write to her anymore, but Ben felt he had a new perspective from which to criticize her: "You didn't want capitalism destroyed. You wanted some sort of a visionary scheme in your mind to come to pass, and anything that wasn't EG and AB you wouldn't have, no matter how many people were rescued from ignorance and starvation. A few of your comrades suffering in jail meant more to you than a hundred million peasants living in freedom and in beauty."

This attack on Emma's integrity prompted a sharp response:

I have never considered you particularly profound in your judge-ment of the forces that move human actions. Still, I had thought that ten years with me had given you enough of my being to prevent you ever from charging me with lust for power, or glory. But I see you know no more of my real being than my other detractors, who had never met me. Else how could you think for a moment that I am led by personal chagrin and peevishness in my stand against the colossal fake that passes as revolution in Russia. Surely, you would have known that I must have gone through a bitter struggle before I decided on my stand. Of course, you and your Communist friends have the right to question the accuracy of my reasoning. But what have ten years with me given you that you dare to impugn my integrity and sincerity? Nothing, it seems. That, however, is your loss, not mine, old man.

Ben's belief that Emma had been unfair to the communists was reinforced by his observation that the communist movement was spread-ing quickly in the United States. Communists were multiplying, he asserted, like "Kansas grasshoppers in August." His fervor recalled his infatuation with anarchism.

You see them everywhere in every forum. They have locals in schools and jails and poorhouses, and I wouldn't be surprised if the whores and the pimps develop a local. Oh, dear Emma, don't be petty or jealous. Accept the inevitable. The Communists are going to win in America. Of course it will be very much unlike that which we have in Russia. . . . I wish you could see what

Communism has brought to the American negro. . . . And I think you are mistaken if you assume that the American negro cannot lead the white workers on to a successful social revolution. They have such a fine rebellious spirit. . . . And the new day, the new society is not that far off. As I said before, in spite of all the unemployment, stock depression, bank failures and everything else, the people of America are eating and smoking and thinking and are preparing to fight. There is no despair in America. There is a good deal of disgust, and people are provoked because the Radicals don't get together, but they are getting closer and closer together every day. . . .

This thinly veiled attack on Emma enabled Ben to take a more magnanimous view of her autobiography. "Although *Living My Life* paralyzed me in the original reading and each rereading brings tears, I still am trying to be loyal to you and grateful for the wonderful 10 years with you."

In another letter, he equated his relationships with Emma and Jesus:

I AM SAVED. I lost all of my Religion. . . . I no longer call myself a Christian. They have taken away my Jesus & I know not where they have laid him. . . .

And now Poor Jesus is gone. . . . But he was a wonderful lover. And I am grateful for having been permitted to serve him, as I am so happy to have had ten big, fine years with you.

When he was a small boy, the story of Jesus had helped Ben to survive in dire poverty. Then he had abandoned his all-encompassing faith in religion and Jesus to embrace anarchism and Emma:

I shall feel the same towards Emma Goldman. She found me an intellectual ragamuffin and half-assed reformer, she taught me the possibilities of building a new and better society. . . . She was responsible for most of the good and beautiful things in my life and although I saw many weaknesses and limitations in her I shall always love and appreciate her. Really, Emma, you are too precious to me [for me] to quarrel with you.

After receiving what she called Ben's "sermon on the mount," Emma waited four months to answer—and then she asked him to stop badgering her with letters. Ben was in such a panic that he wrote to Berkman for help. Not knowing of this new rift between Ben and Emma, Sasha replied:

You begin, "As you know, EG asked me not to write her again." Well, I really didn't know anything about it. If she asked you not to write to her again, she must have her good reasons for it. But what I want to say is this: do not assume, as you evidently did when you wrote to me, that I know anything about your correspondence with EG. For I don't. And as you surely know by this time, EG is a woman who can keep her own counsel.

Ben still respected Sasha, as he did Emma. No matter how many times they criticized him, they remained his political parents, from whom he needed approval. Besides, Emma refused to engage in a personal battle with Ben. She was more involved in responding to criticisms of her position on the Soviet Union. Emma felt that very few people understood that she was not "disillusioned" by the Russian Revolution, as her publisher's title for her book on Russia had stated, but that she had no liking for dictators. Emma was attacked for her position on Soviet Russia from within the anarchist ranks, as well.

A 1932 critique of her autobiography used Emma's stance on Russia to launch an attack on every aspect of her personality and politics. Marcus Graham, fellow anarchist and author of the article, focused on Emma's individualism in Soviet Russia, her compulsion to be at the center of every activity, thereby assuring its failure if she, on a whim, did not choose to stay involved. Among other accusations, he implied that even Sasha was exasperated by Emma's manner of engaging in political activity in Russia; then Graham's comments dug deeper by asserting that her support came mostly from "parlor liberals." She wrote to Sasha: ". . . that rotten putrid attack. If it were on my love or private life, I wouldn't give a damn. You can't say I have ever replied to any attacks made on me. But this is on my stand on Russia, the movement, the work I had done and paid for in tears and blood. This ought not to go unchallenged. It is a rotten shame that no one in America has done it."

Emma tried to break her downward emotional spiral by taking a brief vacation in Marseilles. She even tried bicycling. But being there made her more aware of how tired she was of being alone. "A man can knock about, not a woman, not in France, even if she be the age of Methuselah. Besides, I have been alone enough, dear. It is no picnic."

Emma's isolation was not entirely a result of her exile: she had become progressively more difficult to be around. Sasha confided to their old friend Fitzi how miserable one could feel in Emma's presence:

(And, strictly between me and you, dear, I could save money by living with Emmy and Emma in St.-Tropez, but—the atmosphere EG creates is impossible. A short visit is all right, but nothing more than a short visit. . . .

It's EG's character, my dear, and it is not improving with years. I am sorry to tell you that everyone who has stayed there for a week or more had the same complaints. EG is dictatorial and interfering, and she has a way of making life miserable for you without saying anything to which you can give a rough and suitable answer. The more is the pity. And the worst of it is that EG herself has not the least idea of it. She is a great woman in some ways, no doubt of that; but living close with her is just impossible. It is too bad, but it is so. Even when I visit her alone, I can't stand it there very long. There is no one, of course, to call her attention to those things except myself. As a good friend I do it, though very rarely. And then EG just gets mad. It is useless. But all this [is] in strictest confidence, my dear. For I know you will understand. I would not dream of saying this to anyone else.)

Emma continued to travel around Europe lecturing, but with dwindling energy. Growing repression and a lack of able supporters made the outlook for anarchism gloomy. By March of 1933, Emma wrote to Sasha that she was

> so tired of chasing windmills. . . . Yes, dear, hard as it is to admit even to myself, I am beginning to think that my enthusiasm, or, rather, my expectations, which seemed so much likelier of attainment this time, look discouraging. As eight years ago, there is no lack of social engagements. I could live for months and not have to spend a penny on food. But that is as far as the interest goes. I am tired to death from all the people I have already seen who claimed interest. But I see no indication of any real support in what I have come here to do. Our own people are as everywhere ineffectual. Besides, we have no one of any ability whatever. The groups consist of living corpses. . . .
>
> You are right, dear heart, the masses are anything but hopeful. And yet we must go on in our work. We are voices in the wilderness, much more so now than forty years ago. I mean voices for liberty. No one wants it any more. Yet it seems to me that just because of the present mad clamor for dictatorship, we of all people should not give up. Someday, sometime long after we are gone, liberty may again raise its proud head. It is up to us to blaze its way—dim as our torch may seem today—it is still the one flame.

This letter was written just before Emma was to tour for the Birth Control League in Germany; when Hitler assumed power, her tour was canceled.

Emma's moods fluctuated. She felt great urgency and desire for activity, yet at the same time was increasingly pessimistic. She wrote to her friends Rudolf and Millie Rocker that her faith in the workers was beginning to diminish. "They hug their chains, the deeper it eats into their flesh, the better they admire their masters. . . ." "It is disheartening," she wrote to Millie later. "But we must face facts. We are living through an awful period. And all we can do is for the few to hold together." But Emma herself was not holding together well. Plans for a Canadian tour seemed premature, permission to enter the United States unlikely. In despair Emma wrote to Millie:

Perhaps it would be the wisest to get out of the whole mess. Without means, or any possibility of earning anything, without someone close who cares a damn about you, and with every avenue of usefulness closed, what is the sense of going on? I ask myself this question every day now. Perhaps I will find an answer soon. Then there will be no need to go begging to be allowed to do the work the comrades have not the ability to do. Or wait until one is entirely decrepit and has to depend on public collections for one's bread.

Goodby, dearest. I feel madly depressed, and so restless I could jump out of my skin.

In the same vein, Emma wrote to Sasha:

Yesterday was the sixth anniversary of Sacco and Vanzetti's death. I wonder if they had been remembered even by our own comrades. Human memory is so fleeting. The thought of them added to my depression. It made me feel how crazy I am, wanting to keep up work for our ideas, when nothing changes in the world. What is the use of it all? I wish I could at least make my peace with the world, as behooves an old lady. I get disgusted with myself for the fire that is consuming me at my age. But what will you? No one can get out of his skin.

Emma considered herself to have "vegetated the summer" of 1933, until she believed her path was clear to go to Canada. She begged Sasha to come to Canada and the United States with her, but he refused, knowing that it could happen only if strings were pulled by Mabel Crouch, an influential liberal who could put pressure on the Democrats in power in Washington. Mabel Crouch knew that Frances Perkins, the Secretary of Labor, was the U.S. official most sympathetic to Emma's case, and perhaps Sasha would have a chance to re-enter with Emma if Frances Perkins could rally enough support within the government. Sasha's situation in Nice was precarious enough, but he refused to try to get back into the United States unless a total retraction of their deportation were made. Besides, he wrote, "I hate America now and don't want ever to see it again."

Emma, however, felt that Sasha was too much the purist in criticizing her willingness to have people of influence try to secure a visa for her in the United States and Canada. And she knew that her marriage to a British subject lifted any legal grounds for a refusal of a temporary visa. It was now a question of policy. She wrote, "it is really my last resort to justify my life before myself."

Emma was enough of a celebrity to have access to people of influence and wealth, and she was willing to use her access. The work of a support committee, organized by Mabel Crouch, that included Theodore Dreiser, H. L. Mencken, Isaac Don Levine, John Dewey, Dorothy Canfield Fisher, Sherwood Anderson, Roger Baldwin, Sinclair Lewis, and many other prominent persons, made her re-entry possible. Emma was granted a ninety-day visa, to begin in January 1934.

Emma's forgiveness of the United States even extended to Ben, who was no longer either a major issue for her or an obstacle to her plans to return. Ben had apologized for the letter attacking her politics, which had added to her unhappiness over the past year. "It enabled me to get the grievance or self-pity or the delusion or whatever you choose to call it out of my soul. I have never harbored an unkind or a bitter thought towards you since I wrote the letter, and whether you believe it or not, no one has ever seen the letter but myself."

Ben had also finished outlining the tribute to Emma he planned to make in his book on outcasts and in his autobiography:

I think you'll be very happy and pleased about my treatment of EG. I hope I knew you well enough and loved you deep enough and heard you often enough to see you in all of your beauty and power. Your prejudices, your limitations are all small and unimportant. I'm going to try to portray you with all of the honesty and illumination that I am capable of. And you can depend upon me to be more than fair and just to the Anarchist movement. The Anarchists may have thought me superficial and a playboy and non-revolutionary, but I think some of them have been brilliant, all of them social-minded and most of them tremendously worthwhile men and women. . . . I shall show my appreciation and loyalty to

you, Emma Goldman, who did more for my intellectual development than any person in the world.

In fact, his description of her in his book of portraits of outcasts
not only took note of her political contribution, but also portrayed her as
beautiful:

> EG was a wonderful woman.
> She had a beautiful, strong face,
> And a blue eye that flashed power and love.
> Governments feared her;
> The interests hated her;
> But the common people loved her.

And much of his autobiography was devoted to his time with Emma,
with some serious self-criticism. ("Following the Monkey," titled for his
first childhood experience of wandering off after an organ grinder, was
rejected in 1933 and never published.)

The eagerly conciliatory tone of Ben's letters reflected his own
nostalgia and loneliness. In one letter he complained that he had been
sleeping alone for four years, except during brief affairs—"the Irish
Queen, half-mad Sarah, Lovely Countess, the Lawyer, the Doctor who
got tired of me in 3 days, but I learned about women from her, and the
Orphan Asylum Teacher." He lived with his son, Brutus, now, and still
missed Anna.

By November 1933, the tone of Ben's letters to Emma changed. He
looked forward to her coming to Canada, encouraging her not to let
anything keep her away, "even if you must swim." He wrote that he
preferred to see her as two separate people—"My Mommy who thrilled
and loved me for ten years and who permitted me to serve her could not
have said the things EG said about me in her book." And so he took the
opportunity, once again, "to discuss two things . . . One is Emma
Goldman and the other is her former lover Ben." Disturbed by her last
letter, in which Emma had asserted that "the race had deteriorated to an
alarming degree," and had expressed her general sense that there was no

place for her to work and that no one wanted her, Ben began to
sermonize to Emma:

> If all the friends you made, if all the service you rendered Society,
> and if the knowledge that millions of people heard you lecture and
> read your books and pamphlets can't sustain you and give you a
> little comfort in your old age, then I have no hesitancy in saying
> you never gave much joy or good to the world.
>
> For we have what we GAVE TO THE WORLD. If you have
> bitterness, despair and misery, then that is what you gave to the
> world and that is what you deserve. . . .
>
> What I am trying to tell you is why I am optimistic about the
> world, and to ask why you are so miserable and discouraged, and
> your pessimism and despair is so common among the old
> Comrades. . . .
>
> The world is getting better. Men and women are happier,
> cleaner, finer, more noble, better educated and enjoying life
> more. There is a much greater sentiment for liberty and jus-
> tice. More people are willing to cooperate and fight for a better
> world.
>
> It is you who have FAILED—not the PEOPLE. It was you who
> were WITHOUT A CLEAR VISION—not the MASSES. Because
> you couldn't understand the psychology of the race from which you
> sprang—the Russians—you cursed their New Leaders. Because
> you lacked sufficient illumination to comprehend fundamental
> human nature and behaviour, you were broken-hearted and disap-
> pointed at a purely natural demonstration of a social phe-
> nomenon. . . . And had you had the heart of a Tolstoy or a
> Kropotkin, and been a genuine lover of Humanity, you would have
> sunk your ego and worked with the Russians to bring peace and
> plenty to them. . . .
>
> YES, MOMMY, THE WORLD IS SAFE, and we are not going
> to Hell.
>
> I sometimes feel that you and other rebels like you do not want a
> world of joy, beauty and cooperation. YOU HAVE *YOUR* PETTY
> WORLD. You want YOUR ideas to be put in practice. . . .

Ben continued his letter in a more conservative vein, by asserting that "if people don't want [liberty, justice and brotherhood] and love Masters, Rulers, Kings and Exploiters, it is O.K. with me." Ben, himself, was happy—"I have all I need, and more than I deserve. I enjoy life daily. I live at home with Mother. At seventy-three Mother still overfeeds me. I enjoy my son Brutus.... I was right when I chose between you and Anna and a son. My son has lived to give me joy—and YOU ..."

If you have the truth, why doesn't the truth make you happy and free? Ah, I will tell you, it is because the Truth and Freedom are not enough. You have to have LOVE—the kind of Love that Jesus talked about. And you did not have it. Don't laugh. I know more about Jesus than you do. I don't know or care if he really lived or not. I only know that if you really want to help the world and if you are to get the joy of service, you have to love the world. Yes, love the world more than Emma Goldman did. I think you loved yourself and your own ideas more than you did the people.

Emma wrote back to Ben when she reached Toronto:

You certainly have not changed. Both in your violent moods and those that used to soothe my ruffled spirit, you have remained the same. No one could beat you in your capacity [for] wounding those who loved you. Or hypnotising them by your capacity to cajole, plead and abase yourself to make one set aside one's hurt. No, you have not changed. Only your appeal has lost its force. At least to me.... For a moment it seemed as if we had never been torn asunder with years of pain between us. Everything seemed wiped out. But it was a rude awakening, the awakening, the awakening to reality.... The struggle to overcome the past had taken more than half the years since you had gone the way of all flesh. It had been very bitter indeed. I could not face another dose. I feel I owed you this frank admission. So when we do meet again whether in the states or here you should not make the mistake that all is as it had been between us. Let us be friends and meet as such when the time comes. It will save us both much heartache.

In characteristic fashion, Ben's next letter was, as Emma described it, "buoyant" and "boastful as ever about your sex technique." Emma had bronchitis with a high temperature and hardly cared about Ben's assertion that "the ladies still find you so efficient, such a conqueror of their hearts and all else."

Emma had finally reached Canada in December 1933. She would wait there until the technicalities of her U.S. visa were resolved. What enticed her about entering the United States was obviously not the proximity of Reitman, but the opportunity to regain a sense of continuity with her political past. Her spirits lifted when, in February 1934, she crossed the border at Niagara Falls. The customs officer noted her physical characteristics: "age, 64; height, 5′ ½″; eyes, blue; hair, blonde-grey; face, round." A newspaper reporter described her as "a grand-motherly person with a blue twinkling eye."

The one major proviso of her entry permit was that her talks be restricted to themes relating to the drama. Eager though she was to come back, Emma refused to undertake her tour until it was clear that her entry might be used as a precedent for other deportees to modify the immigration laws, and that she could use her own definition of the drama. In a lecture at the Brooklyn Academy of Music she planned to begin by asking, "Is there a greater drama in the world than the drama of Germany and Austria today?" Still, despite her bravado, she was nervous about facing the press and publicity in the United States, and asked her old friend Roger Baldwin to be with her during her press conferences—to hold her hand and give her moral support.

She had retained her capacity for terse political comments. When asked by a film news crew about Italy she said that it was a beautiful country—minus Mussolini. What did she think of Hitler? "I don't know him, don't want to." When asked about her own precarious political future she said, "Only liberty is worth fighting for. This is the job I'll keep at until I am either hanged or fall asleep in some other way." Spain was the country Emma targeted as the most favorable to anarchism. "I am delighted to be back in the United States, my hunting ground of thirty-five years, the country where I had my innings in the social and economic struggle and where I decided to devote myself to the presentation of anarchism, a social philosophy which aims at the emancipation,

economic, social, political and spiritual of the human race." Reminiscing
about her life in the United States, she remembered her arrest in 1893 for
saying to a group of striking cloak-makers that "a hungry man has a
right to share his neighbor's bread," and her arrest in 1916 for lecturing
on birth control, which was, by 1934, a respectable subject. She recalled
that some of her best lectures were prepared in jail.

When Emma arrived at Grand Central Station in New York in
February 1934, she walked to her hotel to avoid violating the city's taxi
strike. She failed to notice, however, that hotel workers were also on
strike. Thus, practically from the moment she entered New York, the
wrath of the left was upon her. Emma had expected the communists to
be as angry with her as the government was, but her inadvertent
crossing of a picket line gave them extra ammunition.

The press surrounded Emma in her hotel room, barraging her with
questions about her past and future. At one point a camera man knocked
over a waste paper basket full of used flash bulbs. Emma jumped, fearing
it was an explosion, then quickly joked that if it had been a bomb, "I'll
certainly be blamed for it. Please don't have an explosion until I get
through with this interview. Why they used to say that all the bombings
and acts of violence for the last fifty years could be blamed on me. Please
let's not have any explosions until I leave." "Are you in favor of steriliza-
tion?" she was asked. "Oh my God, I think there are plenty of people
who should be sterilized. But, of course, the rich would get themselves
exempted, and I have always believed that there is a maximum of insanity
and idiocy in high places." Responding to whether she still considered
herself a "philosophical anarchist," she replied, "Philosophical anarchist?
I never was a philosophical anarchist: I am an anarchist, just plain
anarchist. A philosophical anarchist is like a Christian Scientist, it is
neither Christian nor scientific."

Among the tributes Emma received was a formal testimonial
dinner in her honor at New York's Town Hall, where three hundred—of
the eight hundred who had applied—fêted her.

Two thousand people came to the Community Church in Town
Hall a few days later to hear Emma's "calmly delivered eulogy on the
Russian anarchist Peter Kropotkin, whose death thirteen years ago was
commemorated at the church's service." A crowd waited outside the hall

for two hours, just to catch a glimpse of Emma as she left. *The New York Times* remarked that this "mild, gray-haired woman who had come on the platform with a red-and-gold shawl thrown over her black dress, betrayed the Emma Goldman of old as she waxed indignant over war."

Emma assured her audiences that although she may have suffered for her beliefs, she did not consider herself a martyr. In Rochester, her first home in the United States, she spoke to an audience of seven hundred who stayed until 3:00 A.M. to hear her inspirational story and ask her questions. She told them: "Please don't feel that I have made sacrifices. That I'm a martyr. I have followed my bent, lived my life as I chose and no one owes me anything. I'm no more respectable than I ever was. It's you who have become a little more liberal and it's never too late to progress. You are progressing."

Emma's unabated political intensity led some to view her as "a she Peter Pan, she has never grown up emotionally, which means she has not lost the naïve courage and consistency of childhood and adolescence. . . . Fanatics who, like Emma, have rocked the world, are people whose intellects get out in front of their emotional adjustments and stay there."

Yet a reporter in Madison, Wisconsin, saw only the ageless side of Emma's personality:

> The intelligence and vitality of Emma Goldman impressed deeply her four hundred hearers in Madison. Old, but ageless, she radiated what the charm-school ads call "personality," that rare and distinctive halo which sets apart an individual from the herd. Battered by life, life flows from her, steadily, hotly; her blood and passion are the weapons she has dedicated to her revolutionary cause. She has spent herself in the tortuous quest of freedom for others. Freedom for herself she has always had,—whether in jail or in exile her winged words hunted out her persecutors, stinging them where they wallowed in beefy complacency, and fettered to smugness which is more degrading than bars.

Still, outside of New York City and Rochester, Emma did not often find the huge audiences that marked her earlier tours. This time she found large halls with sparse attendance. The manager she had hired,

James Pond, emphasized the spectacle of her arrival and hired such expensive halls that many in her constituency could not afford to hear her lecture. A young woman named Ann Lord offered Emma her assistance, but she had already committed herself to Pond. Emma wrote to a friend, "There is nothing more excruciating than to speak into a void of empty benches." In most cases, the turnout was so poor that she had to borrow money for living expenses, telegrams, telephones, and postage. Besides Pond's poor management, the rise of the communist movement in the United States also kept Emma from receiving the hero's welcome of her dreams. She had had a premonition of the financial failure of her tour when she decided to turn down Reitman's proposition to be her manager again. As she wrote to her friend Benny Capes before she entered the United States:

> The moment Ben Reitman learned of my possible readmission to the States his imagination caught fire and he offered to organize a tour for me. Of course that is out of the question for more than one reason, the two outstanding being that I will have to appear under the backing of my New York Committee, hence avoid sensationalism of every hue (not that I ever enjoyed sensationalism).
>
> And secondly because the dead have buried the dead.
>
> I don't care for a resurrection of my past with Ben. But I dare say he would make a rousing material success of my tour. But I have learned long ago that one does not live by bread alone.

She wrote directly to Ben that she would not allow him to "manage" her ever again, and that she did not even want him to come to Canada to see her before her tour began. Ben received this rejection note at his office in Chicago, and was so distraught that he ordered everyone out. Yet he could neither curse nor weep. "And so my Mommy will have none of me, not even a visit for an hour. The memory of a half dozen happy years, of tours, of conquests. Of glorious days of work and maddening nights of passion. All failed. You said, 'there was no resurrection.' I think there is."

Although Emma had rejected Reitman as a traveling companion, she did not wish to travel with a woman, either: "A handsome young lady as a traveling companion may be all right if I were a lesbian. Not for nothing did a woman's-rights woman once charge me with being a man's woman. However, I will not wrangle about the company of a manager except that I love to keep silent when I travel. It is the only time when I can rest, invite my soul and think about my subjects."

Ben wrote to her again, in a melodramatic, self-pitying mood. Oddly, he buoyed himself with his good deeds, which included defending a rapist in court:

Dear Mommy:

I shall follow you in your triumphant journey into the States and shall be with you as you visit your beloved relations. . . .

I recall our first visit to Rochester.

And you will not see me as the crowd meets you at the Depot in New York, but I will be there and see the photographers and the movie men and the reporters. . . .

I shall weep that I cannot stand by your side but shall rejoice that love and fame and honor and prosperity have come to you.

I suppose I shall see you in Chicago. That is unimportant. What is important, and what no one can ever take away from me, was a decade spent at your side.

Perhaps some time in a crowded lecture hall, someone will ask about your old Hobo manager. I ask that you be charitable and speak kindly of the "dead." Say that today, January 31, 1934, he was in Court defending a rapist and yesterday he wrote a report on Shelter House Men that helped to get them a little better food, shelter and medical care. And after you've said that, add, "as I said in my book, Ben was a coward. He deserted us in our hour of great need when the war was on. He short-changed the book funds. He was scared to death when he went to San Diego. He was always hiding behind Jesus and under women's skirts," and when you say that, I shall weep many tearless sobs. But, whether true or not, I shall reach out my arms for you and say, as I so often did, "Where can I go or hide? What's left for me to do? Oh, God, I loved you so."

Meanwhile, the years pass on.

Hobo—Ben L. Reitman

As the time approached for Emma's scheduled trip to Chicago, Ben wrote to her that there had been inadequate publicity and preparation for her arrival. He had dreamed of her having a "triumphant tour; daily meetings with the unemployed, with students and with the masses. But the milk is spilt, and I cannot help but say 'That's just the way God wants it.' Nevertheless, I cannot help but wonder what might have been had you taken my suggestion." Ben added some naïve but nonetheless astute insights into Emma's fear of intimacy, which he believed might have been behind her discrediting him in her autobiography:

> Another thing that I have thought often about was your reluctance, or your hesitancy, or your fear, that if I saw much of you there was danger of you being raped or giving in against your wishes. Your psychology is interesting to me. Especially now, as I am about to start a book on women and I want to write considerable about you. I'm too happy now and too much blessed and too devoid of bitterness to want to say anything that might hurt you, but as an amateur psychologist and as a beginning psychiatrist, I can't help but wonder what it is that is in your soul that made you discredit me in your book and fear to have anything to do with me.

Ben was writing an outline for yet another book, this time on "wandering women," mostly about women hobos. It was to be based on his own experience, and would be honest about sexuality. In his book, he planned to experiment with the role of "social psychiatrist." He intended to have a chapter on homosexual women, "because they make up a large proportion of the hitch-hiking, intellectual women of the day." And he would have a section on radical women, including, of course, Emma: "We have no men in the Anarchist movement that were equal to Emma Goldman and Voltairine de Cleyre—at least, not since the Haymarket Riot. You would be surprised, wouldn't you, if some day you will be compared to Mary Eddy and the Anarchist movement will be known as a feminist movement. And you'd be shocked to have anyone infer that Emma Goldman was a plural-glandular type. But enough of this."

In the context of his unflagging interest in documenting "social outcasts," Ben had always been fascinated with and sympathetic to homosexuality. Emma's close friendships with Almeda Sperry, and later with Margaret Anderson and Harriet Dean, who were lovers, had led him to believe that Emma was probably attracted to lesbians. Her friendship with Almeda was openly affectionate and more intimate than most of her friendships with women, and it seems that she and Almeda had been sexually involved but lamented Emma's primarily heterosexual preferences. Ben was convinced that Emma's passions and attractions were bisexual, whether she acted on them or not, and he was determined to be the first to write about this unknown side of Emma Goldman. For her part, although Emma refused to be labeled as a lesbian, she enjoyed Ben's interest in her as a sexual creature.

The two did, in fact, see each other in Chicago, which Emma considered her most successful stop. Emma had sent Ben a copy of a scathing letter she had written to Pond, criticizing his poor management. She even asked Ben to destroy the letter, lest it be misconstrued as an accusation that Pond was a mercenary. Ben and other comrades responded, and saw to it that the cost of admission was lowered and did a good bit of promotion on their own. Consequently, thousands of people came to hear Emma's talks. Her meeting with Ben was more amicable than either expected, though Ben, who had hoped for "a passionate word" from Emma, had to console himself with the thought that "we warhorses are fit for little else but *work*."

After they met, Ben wrote to Emma every few days. Finally she wrote him a sympathetic letter explaining why they did not belong together. Ben was grateful for the tone of her rejection—"the best and most understanding letter you have written me in over 15 years"—and was glad that at least they had their own work to do and were not too dependent on each other. Something of an affectionate resolution was reached by the time Emma was scheduled to leave.

But the most gratifying thing that happened during Emma's stay in Chicago was that she fell in love again there. After one of her lectures, she had met Frank Heiner, a thirty-six-year-old former osteopath, who was blind, married, and a doctoral student in sociology at the University of Chicago. He was a tall, handsome man, with wide blue eyes, blinded by an accident when he was six months old. Frank had imagined himself in love with Emma ever since he had had *Anarchism and Other Essays* read to him ten years before. Meeting her was the fulfillment of a dream for him. Emma, after so many years without it, was open to love and, back in the country of her choosing, was perhaps more vibrant and energetic than she had been since being deported. She responded to his adulation eagerly.

Although they were an unlikely match—with their great age difference, Frank's marriage and physical handicap, and the severe governmental restriction on Emma's freedom—their brief period together in Chicago haunted Emma throughout her three-month tour. By the time she returned to Canada, she had acquired a new sense of purpose: she would set herself up in a small apartment, where the two of them could consummate their new love.

Heiner's youth made Emma feel younger. His blindness seemed to validate her belief in the primacy of an inner life and an inner vision of a more beautiful world; at the same time, it relieved her of self-consciousness about her aging body. Like her, Frank had triumphed over adversity; like her, she thought, he was committed to free love. Even his wife supported his relationship with Emma, requesting only that Emma encourage him to overcome his procrastination in writing his doctoral thesis. Emma found herself once again the passionate lover-mother.

Emma's happiness also alleviated her sense of exclusion from Sasha and Emmy's relationship. Emmy was among the first to receive Emma's confidences, but Emma's enthusiasm did not conceal her recognition that this was far from an uncomplicated love:

> My dearest, I have indeed found a loving Herz. But of what avail? The man in question has his own life, with a very beautiful wife and child. He is tragically handicapped so that even if he had means and all else were harmonious he could not join me for any length of time. And for a brief episode it would be altogether too painful to take what he so generously and beautifully offers. Besides, Dr. Heiner sees me through his inner vision and with the intensity of his poetic soul. How can I get rid of the feeling that he would not feel as he does if he could see me as I am. My darling child, I am sixty-five years of age. He is probably only forty, if that. . . . But more than anything else is the knowledge that the

miracle would only last a short period. Perhaps miracles never last long or they would not be so marvelous. One does not mind when one is young. But at my age one hates to be bruised, one cannot easily tear oneself away. And more important, one is no longer content with the mere ethereal phase of love. So you see, my dear, the situation does not look so promising. But it is a comfort to know that I am still able to awaken a beautiful love. . . . Heiner's coming into my life is indeed a wonderful event. He is like you in a way, he never cared for women younger than himself, he wrote me. His wife is older than he. And he has caught fire. His letters are symphonies of love. His spirit so pure and fine. And yet, and yet, nothing can come of the whole thing. Frankly I am afraid of it. I have suffered too much in my love life to want more such misery. Not that Heiner would cause me pain. But the conditions are not favorable. Anyway, it is very platonic so far, this new experience.

Heiner's wife is a rare and fine spirit. She knows all about his infatuation. She writes me beautiful letters. I should hate to be the conscious cause of even a moment of pain to her. Life is terribly involved, Emmicken. . . .

Well, whatever will come of the strange yet fascinating affair, I am happy to have discovered Heiner. He will become a power in our ranks. So if complete union with him should be denied me I shall still bless the moment when he came into my life and when I heard his marvelous voice sing a paean song to America.

Emma wrote to Heiner discouraging his offer to come to Toronto to consummate their affair. She reminisced about the times she had been hurt by younger men and the public humiliation she had experienced:

But I know the vulgarity and the hurt it causes when something sublimely beautiful is dragged through the mire. . . .

I am so constituted that I cannot lightly respond to love, or give it up lightly. It took me years to outgrow the terrific hold my passion for Ben Reitman had on me. And again a long excruciating process to overcome a love affair in Sweden with a man thirty years younger than myself. Though that is already 12 years, I have loved no one else. . . .

And yet, while I cannot accept your rich offer, I feel proud beyond words that you have made it. Mine has been and is a very lonely life since I have been exiled. Lonelier and an inner void much more so than my outer appearance suggests. . . .

I embrace you, my dear exuberant soul.

In another letter she described the conflicts between her inner and outer lives:

Dearest, you say you know me and that you had followed me through the years. I do not doubt that. But also I am sure you do not and cannot know the inward being and the inward life, always torn by conflict between my ideal and my own personal needs. How should you know that side of me when people close and intimate for years did not know or even suspect the ache and the hunger that longed to be stilled. No one has ever understood that, dearest mine. Yes, the test of fire in my life had never been the persecution, the hardships, the obloquy I had to face. The test that burned like red-white heat was that I had to forswear what I longed for most, for passionate response to the wild passion in my body. Love in all its ecstatic form. Ben had come near the one. But our worlds of beauty were too apart to ever meet. And the price I paid often proved too high for the few moments of exaltation Ben had offered. The Swedish experience proved altogether terrible. My own fault, of course. For how could a sane person believe that a woman of fifty-two can hold a man of 29 for any length of time? The only justification for my folly was my loneliness after Russia and what then had seemed to me the debacle of all my social and revolutionary values. I should have ended it all while in Sweden had not the boy come along. . . . You can see, my splendid Frank, my fear is not imaginary. . . . It paralyzes me. . . . A thousand times would I [rather] never taste of the rich fount of the wondrous things you are offering me than face the moment when you will and must realize that there is a gulf of years between us. . . . Better not begin the climb than to be hurled back [over] the precipice of isolation and despair. No, I could not face it.

Emma then likened her relation to Frank's wife, Mary, to her own position vis-à-vis Ben's lovers.

Mary may not ever have admitted to herself how profoundly she had been stirred by your amours for other women. I know whereof I speak. For I had been confronted by dozens of women who had been Ben's fancy during the ten years of our common life. It was not that I denied Ben his right to have his sex "obsessions" as he used to call them. I believe too passionately in the freedom of love to have denied that to anyone who loved me. Yet I would lie were I to tell you they left me indifferent. Perhaps it was due to the kind of women Ben picked up on all occasions, . . . also imposing them on me. . . . I do know that women of refinement and delicacy do not remain indifferent to the many sexual fancies of the men they love. Especially in cases of a deep bond of years with the man who is also the father of their child or children. You see I am perfectly frank with you, my dearest. I want you to know that I cannot take my joy lightly if it means trampling the feelings of another in the process.

Emma's feelings about hurting Frank's wife were complicated by the fact that it was Mary who read Emma's letters to him, so that Emma was also in effect writing to her. Frank typed his own letters, but since Mary mailed them, she couldn't help knowing whenever he wrote Emma.

The role of the "other woman" was not one that Emma would have consciously chosen, but there were advantages. Since her relationship with Ed Brady, most of her love affairs had either started or ended in a triangle, with the men being unavailable for a permanent commitment to her. As in the past, her role as the "other woman" with Frank yielded a heightened emotional charge, a certain distance, and another version of the mother-lover persona that she preferred. It also contributed to her avoidance of, and ambivalence about, commitment, while allowing her the benefits of temporary intimacy. In any event, a woman of sixty-five did not have many options, and Emma was starved for passion. Cautiously, she opened herself to Heiner. She arranged for him to visit for two weeks in August. Her letters before his visit suggest a halfhearted effort to play down the event: "Only, please, please do not come with hopes too high. Accept me as your friend, I know our comradeship is already sealed. Let us be content with that. It will be less painful in the end."

Still, they both fantasized about their meeting. As Heiner's letters became more passionate and poetic, Emma's defenses began to crumble.

Your letters are like a brook to the weary and parched desert wanderer. . . . Your coming into my life, so unexpectedly and not sought for, and your glorious love have completely swept me off my feet. I reach out hungrily for your presence and your embrace. And yet I dare not quite believe the gift your letters hold out to me. Ah, your letters. They are like nothing I had ever received. Yes, of course, I have received many love letters. Perhaps more than any dozen women. But never before had anyone expressed his love in such poetic form, such fervor, such consuming fire. My darling, I could not do without your letters. Life would lose its richness and its beauty.

And as she began to know him better through his letters, she began to find significance in their common traits—they were both people who were most alive at night, who sought the poetry of love in life. She did not know whether she was in love or just "hungry for love." Time would tell, she wrote, whether her relationship with Heiner would be "the miracle of miracles, the Grande Passion or the sundown of [her] life." In the meantime she could only write to him with a "wildly beating heart."

Frank wanted Emma to know that he would ask nothing in return for his love, and felt he didn't really have anything to offer her: "One does not offer fragrance to the rose."

At the same time, though, he began to feel jealous of Emma's past lovers, particularly of Ben. Heiner took pleasure in criticizing Ben, while seeming to acknowledge his virtues. He reported that Ben, in lecturing to his sociology class about the declining birth rate, had joked, "Not very complimentary to the men. The women take one look at us and refuse to reproduce us." Frank went on:

> He seems to me wholly emotional. . . . He covers his frustrations and wounds with an assumed aggressiveness, and people some-times unnecessarily hurt him, and he is genuinely hurt. Though he is not always sympathetic to my temperament, I sincerely like him. He has high aspirations and like most of us, sometimes loses his way. The one thing in which he is essentially consistent—and in that, how few are—is his sympathy for the most forsaken ones of society, those who have most need of sympathy and understanding.

Emma noted on this letter that Frank's perceptions were accurate about Ben. In defense of his own past, Heiner wrote an account of his previous affairs and how he felt that they were different from Ben's. Mary's only abhorrence, he believed, was of being imposed upon by inferior people. Emma identified with Mary, remembering that only a few of Ben's obsessions were really worthwhile, and only Fitzi had become Emma's friend and co-worker; "the rest were attracted to Ben more because they knew our relations and they felt tickled to capture EG's lover than for his own sake." Emma wrote directly to Mary to express deep respect for her ability to handle Frank's relationships with other women with such "understanding and grace." She doubted her own capacity to do the same in Mary's situation: "The tragic fact that Frank cannot read my writing enforces even greater responsibility on me to be more careful and considerate of you both. I hope, I have not dug in too painfully in your soul."

Emma tried to establish a relationship with Mary that would be independent of her relationship with Frank. Egotistically, she said that the last thing she wanted to do was to flaunt her "success" with Heiner in Mary's face. Mary assured Emma of her trust that Emma would "play the game fairly." Her only concern was "not to be pushed overboard after the storm subsides." Mary even began to include a note to Emma as an addendum to Frank's letters after she prepared them for mailing. She restrained herself from correcting the mistakes that Frank made, or filling in the lines that were missing when he unwittingly typed over the edge of the page.

Just before Frank was to visit Emma in Canada, Mary confided in Emma about her life with Frank over the past thirteen years. Under the guise of a confession that would deepen their bond and help Emma understand Frank, Mary exposed her husband's personal history in a perhaps unconscious attempt to define and claim boundaries in her own relationship with him. The moment that Emma came into Frank's life had particular significance.

Because of his handicap, Frank had been coddled by his family as a boy, and had never learned to perform even the simplest daily tasks for himself. Only Mary had taught him relative independence—in dressing, bathing, typing, and the like. But he was still insecure—afraid, for example, to use a cane to walk by himself. By now, Heiner preferred to walk without a cane—lightly touching shoulders with the person next to him. When they were first married, Mary was finishing work on a master's degree and seemed to have a promising career ahead of her, but their ignorance about birth control meant she kept getting pregnant; finally they decided to have a child rather than a fourth abortion. Her work and her growing responsibilities at home left Mary with little energy for a satisfying emotional life with Frank; their relationship became filled with silent anger.

Immediately before he met Emma, Frank had fallen in love with a very maternal schoolteacher who treated him as he had been treated as a child. Mary described her as "the slave mother type. She couldn't discuss a book or an idea but she gave him profusely of herself. She put him mentally and physically back into his childhood milieu by doing every physical service it is possible for one human being to do for another." He met Emma on the night of the day he had made up his mind to leave Mary to live with his new love. Mary described Emma's effect on Frank:

> Well, hearing you brought him up with a jerk, he realized what stagnation lay ahead and, to his credit, tore himself from it, difficult though it was emotionally—you know the rest. . . .
>
> You know of course you have great power with him. He is an idealist and you meet all of his dreams. It isn't that I fear you—if he

prefers life with you to life with me and you feel the same, well, that's just that—I don't believe in chains for lovers any more than I do for workers.

She ended this letter by again denying that she herself was angry or distressed, asking only that Emma continue to encourage Frank to pursue his studies, which she felt were his only real hope for economic independence. She said she hoped that her letter would not mar Emma's image of Frank, but would round out her picture of him.

The letter was characteristic of other letters that revealed Mary's seething anger masked as altruism and the generally masochistic tendencies she played out in her relationship with Frank. Perceiving herself as the one who constantly sacrificed for Frank, she thought her motives and inner feelings were above suspicion. She hid her evident fury even from herself. Emma chose to ignore the underlying message and saw only Mary's willingness to cooperate, to deny herself; she identified with Mary's attempt to live out her belief in free love, although she did not want to focus on the implications long enough to hamper her affair with Frank. Emma even convinced herself that she and Mary were acting together in Frank's best interest.

Emma ignored the double messages in Mary's letter, assuring Mary that she would not stand between her and Frank. Emma was certain that Frank loved Mary very deeply, and she was not so anxious to bear the responsibility for the handicapped Heiner as she had been for her previous lover, Malmed, who was also bound to a wife. She claimed now that the age difference was not the only difficulty: "my life is so uncertain, so fraught with struggles and dangers, [even] if Frank were not so bound to you I should not bind him to me. It would be horribly cruel to him and to you. And I am not one to gain joy from the price others must pay."

Frank finally did visit Emma in Canada, and they spent two ecstatic weeks together. She put aside her work and spent every second talking and making love with him. Their contact with the Canadian comrades was incidental, in comparison to their great love. When Frank left, he cursed the border restrictions that would keep him from "the grove, the grotto of bliss," "[his] Goddess, [his] darling," whom he had come to love "more than the world." Once again, Emma was portrayed as the mother-lover.

Oh, my mother who put water and cigarettes by my bed, who woke me with caresses and with her beautiful voice that can sound the call to arms and lavish all the depths of a mother's tenderness. How I clung to her neck and how I still cling to her. Your child in this bleak world where there is little tenderness or understanding will always need you.

Your lover will always be with you.

When you are torn by your lectures, remember that I know the time of them; as the hour approaches and the tension [gets] more painful, I at home will be concentrating on the picture of giving you kisses of encouragement to sustain you. After the lecture, I will be thinking late that night of smoothing you and relaxing you and caressing you.

Emma wrote Frank that his visit had taken her "to sublime heights. You not only filled the whole place, you filled space itself for me." Yet her old pattern of "doubt, despair and fear" immediately returned, so that by the time she received his letter in response, a week later, she was worn out from feeling thoroughly abandoned.

Emma declared to Heiner that the spell of her long relationship with Ben was broken. "My past with Ben is as wiped out as if it had never existed, it was that before you came into my life. Now that I know what your love can give, I could not bear to have B near even in the remote sense."

Frank enjoyed his new place in Emma's life as her most passionate lover, and fed her erotic fantasies: "Oh, imagine my tongue over your whole body for an eternity. You are life, you are eternity, you are all."

After the passion of their time together, Emma was driven to distraction by having to write Frank through someone else. She tried to write in code, and felt almost as she had writing her autobiography when she could only express her emotions "in a general way, but not in the deepest sense." She had written about this dilemma: "I really feel embarrassed. It is not that I care who would know what you have roused.

It is such a miracle, so marvelous, and even I feel like shouting it from the housetops. But also it is so fragrant, and so delicate an event. I can't bear to have it exposed."

Life seemed "bereft of all its meaning" for Emma, now that Frank had gone. "The more one has to lose, the deeper the pain. . . . For good or for evil you have not only taken root in my heart, you have filled every pore of me to the end of my life." The dominant urge in her life became recapturing her two weeks of bliss with Heiner.

Amid the lecturing and writing she did in Canada, Emma wrote to her family and friends about Heiner, trying to puzzle out the future of their relationship. To Stella she wrote, "did you ever dream that your old Tante will inspire a wild love in a man half her age? Truly this is a miracle. . . . Don't think me cynical when I say it is only because the dear man is blind." Emma encouraged Stella to keep this matter to herself, because she would hate to make a damned fool of herself. And to her youngest brother, Moe, she wrote, "Your shameless sister has lost her heart entirely. . . . It is like the child that came to our forebear Sarah . . . indeed a wonder." To the novelist Evelyn Scott, she wrote, "it has been a great experience to know a human being so tragically handicapped and yet so free and brave." She even wrote to Sasha during Heiner's visit, in an effort to bring the two together; the men corresponded briefly, each anxious to meet the other. To Emmy she wrote of Heiner's capacity for romance in "the midst of our hard and cruel reality":

> Can you imagine, dearest, Heiner said to me the other day, "Even if I could regain my sight I should not want it. I am afraid seeing reality would destroy all my values." I could almost scream out with the pain of it. And yet I could not help but realize that he was right. His world is so full of [the] beauty and splendor of life it would be a greater calamity than his physical handicap if he could see the ugliness and feel the meanness of our world. . . .
>
> Frank is in a way in a more fortunate state. He sees me through that roseate picture he has created of me. And while it is very flattering and pleasant to appear so marvelous, still I dread his possible awakening and I have warned him against it. But it is

434

hopeless to convince him. For he cannot see our world. And his own is something quite distinct and apart.

In their need to create an illusory world more beautiful than reality could ever be, Emma and Frank were kindred spirits. Emma even went so far as to exaggerate to her friends Rudolf and Millie Rocker that Heiner was "the first American Anarchist since Parsons and Voltairine de Cleyre . . . with the ability and personality to impress himself on the country—planning to write about American traditions in relation to anarchism."

Emma tried to convince herself that even though her two weeks with Heiner had given her more joy than she could remember, she could be satisfied with a memory, and at long last was becoming a realist in matters of the heart. Compared with Heiner, Emma was indeed the pessimist. His optimism, she thought, was his way of surviving a world of darkness. To Sasha she confided:

But I have been too battered by life, especially my love life, to hope for much more than I have already received from Frank. I suppose I will get myself in leash. But just now I feel all smashed up. I am no fool, as you well know. Not for a moment did I expect that Frank should tie his life to mine, even if he had no wife, whom he cares a great deal about. His whole life is before him; mine is on the downward road. He belongs in America, where I cannot be. And he must work on his degree to be able to establish himself in some independent position, since he is poor, has responsibilities, and I can offer him nothing except love much deeper and [more] radiant than I have felt for a long time. You see then, dush, that I have no cause to be happy, though I am grateful to the stars that helped me discover Frank and have two marvelous weeks with him. At least, if I should not see him again, I will have the satisfaction of having given him to our movement. That is something.

Against her will, as their relationship progressed—in correspondence and in fantasy—Emma began to wish for more. Feeling that all her previous relationships paled before this one, Emma wrote to Stella:

It is strange, isn't it, dearest mine, that I should wake up at sixty-five to the realization that with all the men I had known intimately my love had never been fulfilled. Sasha was torn from me before we had time to actually know the meaning of love. Nor would we have grasped it even if he had remained. We were both too obsessed by our ideas and our work to think of anything personal. . . . There was Ed [Brady], he might have fulfilled me if I had not been [immersed] in the movement to the extent of complete self-abnegation. And since Ed, who was there to touch more than the surface of my being? Elementally and primitively speaking, both Ben R. and Arthur [Swenson] pulled me along. But in Ben's case there was the separation of our worlds, ideas and tastes. And Arthur was himself too conscious of the difference in our ages and never let me forget it for a moment. After that, years of loneliness and heart hunger and final realization that nothing will come to me anymore. Fact is, I had ceased to believe that I could be awakened anymore, or would respond if love or even a casual sex experience should come my way.

Then to meet Frank, to be taken into his world of beauty, his vision of freedom and comradeship, his warm, tender presence. Oh, my darling, it is a miracle, really it is. Don't think the overwhelming bliss of the two weeks has made me less eager to continue my work, or to want for a self-satisfied contented nook. . . . It has increased my faith in humanity to find in Frank such an indomitable will to overcome all the terrible difficulties his handicap had put in his way. . . . You see, dearest, I found in Frank complete harmony in ideas, in the world we aim to build, in our need for art and beauty, and complete fulfillment of my woman soul. Is this not a great wonder, at my age? And in this cold and ugly world?

But as the dreamlike quality of her time with Heiner began to fade, Emma felt stranded, with no real outlet for her reawakened feelings. She worked furiously, but she felt a familiar emptiness.

When he learned of Emma's new love affair, Ben was provoked to try to seduce her again. Emma was delighted to be able to say no to him from the position of strength of having another lover. That this lover was literally blind to harsh realities and lived in a world of imagined beauty meant Emma could join the crowd of people who had always mocked Ben for his vulgarity. She had found sexual fulfillment with a man who lived on a more profound and poetic plane than Ben ever could.

But Ben asserted that Emma could never exorcise him from her life, that he wouldn't be surprised if history turned the tables on her feeling of superiority: "You said that my page in history depends upon you, and you may be right. But, dear blue-eyed Mommie, history plays strange tricks and maybe your page in history depends upon Ben Reitman. But, then, we'll both be dead and probably not know anything about it, so we won't quarrel about that."

Ben was now actually transforming his book about "wandering women" into a postscript to the story of Box Car Bertha's life, as she told it to him. It was published in 1937 as *Sister of the Road*, an effort that involved analyzing women hobos and called upon his lifelong fieldwork seducing women. Among the observations with which he challenged Emma was that she, like his wife, Rose, and most of the other women who had once loved him, was now willing to "crush, sink and degrade" him and "prevent [him] from ever doing anything worthwhile, when [he was] not 'faithful' to any of you." Determined to give a more accurate portrayal of Emma than she had given of him in her autobiography, Ben was trying to write a serious essay about her. In it he asserted that she was typical of other women in that her

> standard of loyalty and love, faithfulness and friendship, apprecia-
> tion in creative work all depends whether the man sexually is
> faithful to you. . . . Now, dear Mommie, . . . I'm going to paint a
> word picture of you and describe our ten glorious years together. In
> spite of anything that you may say or do or infer, I think you are
> easily the greatest woman in the world. If you are jealous or
> unreasonable, it is very unimportant. You've got a great brain and
> soul, and remarkable courage, and Jesus, what a wonderful lover
> you were. . . . Oh, Mommie, dear, don't be afraid that I'll have a
> Lord Douglas inferiority complex, or a cheap desire to get even
> with you—oh, no! All the pain and hurt you've given me in the

past or in the present are all washed away when I think of your power, your influence in the world.

Although Ben wanted to see Emma again, to refresh his memory about her powerful presence for his essay on their relationship as well as to lift his spirits, he knew they would "live through it" if they did not see each other. When Ben learned of her connection with Heiner, he told her to tell the other men who "admire and rave" about her, "I think you're worth raving over, but warn them for the love of Louise Michel [the heroine of the French Commune] not to cross you or to leave you when you need them." He ended his letter by saying that he was writing some notes on "what the world needs from the artist and I can hear you saying, 'You know nothing about art.' Right again."

Emma ignored the humor in Ben's letter. She could not see past the accusation that she, like his first wife, was eager to watch him sink, nor could she understand his renewed interest in her. "I only wonder why you should be so eager to come now. My attitude or heart has not changed as far as you are concerned, I will never forget the past. But [we] are worlds apart, perhaps more than ever. We are both too old to change, so why try?"

Emma was moving in with some friends, and had neither the room nor the time for Ben. Since she claimed no expertise about hobo women, she turned down his request to write a three-thousand-word article for his book.

Ben was living with his mother, Brutus, and a dog named Rahja. He had become a local celebrity, and the Chicago papers often ran stories on him: "His eyes, as he talks to you, often seem to be pondering on matters far removed from the trivialities of the conversation. But they seem to be wise eyes, sad and smiling—understanding eyes. . . . People go to his office, you see, not only to be treated physically but to learn, to talk and to be consoled. Everyone leaves the place richer, some in purse, all in spirit."

Still, his commitment to his son and his mother made his life seem routine, and he missed the footloose days with Emma. In November, he sent her his new poem, "Servants, Sewers and Saviours," full of his own peculiar combination of longings, both exalted and vulgar:

I need a new woman to whom I can pour out my soul;
The other women in my life seem incomplete.
They don't seem to be able to reach me or hear my cry.
That's the terror of being a "Big Man."
You are not supposed to cry, have needs, or be lonely. . . .
The ten years I was with that Giant of All Women Propagandists,
I spent serving her and thinking in terms of her needs.
She climbed high upon my shoulders. . . .

All big souls have an enormous capacity.
They need flesh, obstacle, blood, enemies, service, goals.
And that's the pathos of life—we haven't developed
A type of man and woman who can get joy out of serving and
    loving;
Women don't want anyone to stand on their shoulders; or get ahead
    of them
They all want to stand on their own feet . . . and face the sun. . . .
I am in the market for a pound of flesh. . . .
. . . What the world needs is whores who can get joy out of ser-
    vice; . . .
Would you like to be a sewer? Sewers are so much needed. . . .
To be a Savior of the world you must be a Sewer and a Servant,
And to be able to sing that great Hymn, "Just as I am,
Without one stitch of clothes, I come to thee"

                                        Ben L. Reitman

Shortly after writing this offensive poem, Ben attempted to have
some of the letters Emma had written to him published in his new book.
Emma objected—as did the publisher, who insisted on having Emma's
permission. Emma told Ben that if he was so anxious to have the world
learn what a great lover he had been, he would have to wait until she was
dead. "You are much younger, dear Ben, and you will outlive me. Is it
asking too much to wait until then? I do not want my letters to you
published, not the part dealing with the struggle of my love for you. It
was entirely too dominant, too elemental and too all-absorbing to make
it common property during my lifetime."

The fate of their love letters became an issue of pride and principle. Emma claimed that they would be misunderstood anyway, because many of the letters from Ben to which she had been responding had been confiscated by the Department of Justice in the 1917 raids. That crucial period, from 1916 to her deportation, held the key to understanding her disappointment with Ben.

Ben objected that Emma had used one of his letters to her in her autobiography. Not so, replied Emma, she had only paraphrased the letter and did not quote it. As to his accusation that she was ashamed of the letters and of their past together, she had another explanation:

I see that age and experience have not made you more sensitive than you have been all your life. You will be crude and vindictive when you are crossed in your desires. I have no hope of helping you to understand anything, at least as far as I am concerned. And I am sure you are not more understanding to anybody else. Why then go on corresponding. Frankly, I see no sense in it. In fact I would stop now except that I want to set you right on two things.

First, I did not publish your letter. . . . I wish I had everything you wrote me. I should not hesitate for a moment to let you publish mine together with yours. It would make interesting reading of a human spirit trying to tear itself free from the iron hold of mad infatuation. . . .

One thing more. Everyone who has read *LML*, I mean those at all sensitised, asked me how I could lay bare my inner being to the extent I did when I crawled back to you like a whipped dog after you poured your confession over me. You alone felt wronged and keep on with all the venom . . . about the hurt you had suffered. Not once did you see that I have bared much more of myself than I have of you. But here too it is merely wasting words and time since you never have or will understand anything outside of your own strivings for recognition and vainglory.

By December 1934, when that letter was written, Emma had had enough of Ben, and of Canada. "Canada is all right to be buried in. But not to live and work for an ideal. Someday perhaps even Canada may be awakened," she wrote to Ben. A rift was growing in her relationship with Heiner: he had never managed to visit her again, and his letters were less frequent and more inhibited. Although distressing, the realization that she was alone again did not leave her so upset as she had been when her ties with Ben or Arthur or Leon had begun to disintegrate. Leon actually made a pilgrimage to Montreal to visit Emma at this point, accompanied by his son, who acted as a chaperon, to appease his wife. Now that Frank was in her life, Emma could receive Leon with a new calm. Frank had validated the many sides of her personality, and she had such great respect for him that even as their tie weakened, she did not feel she was belittled by an inferior; rather, she felt affirmed by what they had shared. Heiner's love had changed her, restoring some of her spirit. She thought that she had acquired enough confidence to return to the hardships of her European exile.

She wanted to return to St.-Tropez to be near Sasha. His camaraderie always served to stabilize Emma's emotional swings. After Heiner, she knew that she could regain a semblance of balance near Sasha, even with Emmy in attendance. Emma's physical distance from the younger woman during her trip to the United States and Canada seemed to have healed past wounds for both of them. For better or worse, Sasha and Emmy were the closest thing to family Emma had in her exile. Sasha was the one person to whom she could always write about the details of her relationships with people and the nuances of her political thoughts, for she knew that he would understand. With him she felt most sane, most fully herself, as their bond deepened over the years.

Their letters were consistently full of affection, respect, and honesty, without embellishment or artifice. Indeed, they stand out in Emma's correspondence as an exchange between equals. Emma relied on his rational capacity to balance her emotionalism. He relied on Emma's expressiveness to give full voice to his own feelings. Although Emma had maintained more of her public stature than Sasha since their deportation in 1919, and also relative, if marginal, financial stability, Sasha had succeeded in creating a more stable social and domestic life. He was generally well liked and respected by many who had a more difficult time relating to Emma. Generations had passed since they stopped being lovers, but their connection to each other as intimate friends had strengthened.

For Emma, Sasha stood out as the only man not relegated to son-lover status, providing almost paternal guidance to her at rocky points in her emotional and political life. In return, the maternal Emma was able to use her contacts with influential people to initiate letter-writing campaigns in his behalf, to counteract some of the official harassment that plagued him throughout his exile. As an alien with only temporary visas, always subject to revocation, he could not work legally in France and no matter how sparsely he had always prided himself on being able to live—blending necessity with principle—in the past several years he and Emmy had been poor, so poor that on occasion they had to sell Emmy's jewelry, and even the furniture that friends had given them, in order to eat and pay bills. Often they lived on bread and tea. Sasha did some translating and Emmy typed, but together they did not earn enough to survive. Emma did her best to encourage old comrades in the states to send Sasha money, and she shared whatever money she had with them both. She had even promoted Sasha's book *Now and After: The ABC of Communist Anarchism* while she toured the United States. The financial failure of Emma's tour in the United States affected all of them, and there was talk of having to sell Bon Esprit just to make ends meet.

Sometimes Emma felt that in her relationship with Sasha she had to work in order to be loved, and resentfully saw herself as the older child who had been pushed out by a new sibling. And although Sasha was always loyal to her, there were times, as in all of Emma's relationships, when she wanted more from him than he could give. But in 1935, during her absence, Sasha had written to Emma in Canada to affirm their unshakable friendship:

Well, dearest girl, do come soon. It has been long, long since I saw you last. Seems an awful long time. And it will be a great joy to see you again, dear, after all that you have gone through in the last 18 months. So for the present I just embrace you, but soon I hope to take you in my arms properly, in the right way, and to press you to my heart like a long-lost soul and my newfound sailor.

So, may it be real soon.

Love, S

Such an expression of love from Sasha opened Emma's heart to Emmy as well. Before her return, Emma had admitted to complicity in some of her conflicts with Emmy, acknowledging that much of her impatience and unkindness resulted more from her loneliness than from anything Emmy had ever done or said to her.

Dear, neither S. nor you have ever guessed how unhappy and dejected I have been these years since I came back from Russia. Nor will you ever know how I have tried to adjust myself to the inevitable, to an inactive and terribly lonely life. If I have seemed impatient and unkind to you, my dear, it was only due to my own inner void, and unsatisfied longing for what I had left behind. I am sure you would hardly have recognized your old cranky friend. Not that there were not enough reasons to be depressed and worried. The financial failure of the tour that promised to be a great success was enough to try the patience of saints. But just being in America made everything else appear of no moment. No wonder every one of our old friends felt that I had never been in better mental state and had never spoken so well. Yes, my dear, surroundings mean much to such moody people as you and I are. Or do you think I am the only moody [one] in our little family.

The new honesty in Emma's relationship with Emmy was prompted by the equality she felt with her now that Emma, too, was a woman in love. In turn, Emmy felt freer to express her sympathy for Emma's situation, noting that "in spite of your wonderful success abroad, there is emptiness in your heart. Of course, I know. One needs a heart to rest, to weep, and to be cheerful with. All those people are expecting wonders and news coming from the mouth of EG. And admiration—is not love."

Emmy acknowledged in her letter, written in her almost incomprehensible Germanic English, that she had not always gotten along well with Emma. But she was ready to turn over a new leaf, particularly as Sasha's and her own health was declining. Sasha had developed prostate trouble, and Emmy suffered from painful stomach problems.

I tell you that now, because I am completely warm to you, and I will be, never mind what I thought and felt in the past. And when you come, sweet Emma, you will feel that I share completely my happiness with Sasha and you. You will not believe me that I intended it at first. But circumstances all around did not give me the opportunity.

I went also through certain struggles and they made me greater and better [able to] understand the heart of others. I love Sasha more than ever but in a much broader way, you know. Not as being all the time after him, etc.

I know that we both in this regard will be perfectly happy, Emma, since I feel that my love and feeling for Sasha corresponds enormously with yours. And if even quite different because of the very difference of our personalities, dearie, he loves us both alike, you know, only that I, as a comrade in regard to you, am very pale, you know. But I try my best.

Emma darling, Sasha is not very strong. I have the desire and deepest hope to give him and you at least now the possible happiness there is for you both. My God, life passes so quick.

Emmy compared herself favorably with Heiner's wife, who she felt did not let Emma "be free towards him. . . . The moment I feel SOME warmth coming from you to me, I am so happy. . . . I daresay that I love Sasha much deeper, happier, when we both are near to each other. You and Sasha are one for me."

May 18, the anniversary of Sasha's freedom, became Emma's target date for departure for France. She was sure that a massive war was brewing in Europe and did not want to be far from Sasha in such a crisis.

In early February 1935, Emma booked passage for a May voyage back to Europe. To her friends in France she wrote that they would find her "a much sadder Emma, but both wiser and, though outwardly I look beastly healthy and as if I owned Rockefeller's wealth, I am inwardly more torn and empty than when I left you 15 months ago. But, then, the summer in Bon Esprit with you, my own darlings, near will help to ease the wounds I sustained since I reached these shores."

Determined to leave and not hiding from her feelings of longing and loss, Emma wrote to Heiner, "it is so difficult to write. It's like attempting to sweep back the onrushing waves of the sea with a broom." She fantasized that they would meet again, in her little house in St.-Tropez, and that their love could flourish away from the pressures of his domestic responsibility. But her main desire was to harness her obsession for Frank, and regain the balance she needed, by anchoring herself in her exile community, in her writing and touring, and in her relationship with Sasha.

She recognized her long pattern of expecting the best and meeting disappointment. In May, before leaving for France, she wrote to her friend Millie Rocker, trying to downplay her hopes about what would come next, especially the hope that by leaving Canada she would force Heiner to follow: "I refuse to expect too much. I have become hardened by the numerous disappointments."

But inwardly she mused that if life had brought her the miracle of Heiner at the age of sixty-five, there was no telling what surprises the future might hold.

17

FATAL ENDINGS

For five weeks aboard ship and in transit, Emma did not hear from
Heiner. She felt she was going mad. Her relationship with him seemed
ever more bizarre to her—an obsession with someone so far away and
unreachable. The waiting, and the lack of any real basis for her feelings,
drove Emma to distraction:

> Your letters . . . are like a fresh brook to the desert wanderer. . . .
> Oh, my Frank, it was insanity to think I could enjoy life separated
> from you by thousands of miles. It was hard enough in Canada.
> Now it is altogether impossible to endure. . . . I am alone, without
> you I am alone as I never in my life have felt. . . . It was madness,
> madness to have gone away.
>
> I say madness because I feel I should never have given way to my
> longing for you. But for our two weeks in Toronto, two fascinating,
> overpowering, ecstatic weeks, I might not have missed you so
> frightfully. Since then I have tried desperately to eliminate you
> from my being. I have reasoned with myself that we could be good
> comrades, and friends, and that I should learn to content myself
> with that. But the more I reason, the more every nerve cried out

for you, your inspiring presence, your wild passion, your magic touch, your beautifully understanding mind. Why did you have to bewitch me so, take possession of all my thoughts, ... an earthquake that shattered all my reserves ... that made me forget that I need hope for nothing personal any more. Nothing I had the right to call my own.... It was the most spontaneous, most elemental, most overpowering event in my life. Just the same I should have fought against it. For well I knew it could not last, or happen again. Yes, my precious Frank, I know you love me.

My present life would be more unbearable if I doubted your love. But is it enough? I mean, can one satisfy one's hunger when one knows there is plenty of bread in the world. Of what avail is all this knowledge if the bread is not within reach of me? ... You have love outside of me, and many interests. But I have nothing now, neither activity, nor love, nor anything I crave most.... Please don't think I blame you for anything, or anybody.... I feel empty, ... I dream about you night after night ... weary with the heart hunger for your presence and your embrace.... Yet I see nothing ... before me but space and time.... Why should this have happened at this time in my life....

I suppose I will find no rest unless I am at least on the American Continent again. There I would still have hopes of seeing you. I have none now.

I hold you close to my longing and aching heart. With love, deep intense and passionate love.

Frank echoed her despair, complaining that even anarchism could not save him from the miserable fear that they might never be together again. When he heard a Russian melody on the radio that Emma used to sing to him, he was sick with longing to be beside her again: "First, before I let you go, you must let me lie with you a long time in the most complete bliss life has to offer. Then promise that you will wake me in the morning and mother me and let me cling to you and hold you again. Oh, your caresses. My goddess, my treasure, my woman beyond all compare, you cannot know how I love you."

But Emma was more tormented than soothed by his letters. She had told him once that "there [was] no greater fool than an old fool in love," but now she could not be whimsical. St.-Tropez was indeed beautiful to come home to, but she felt that the place was incomplete without Heiner, and her reunion with Sasha and Emmy was far from what she had imagined it would be. "Such are the vagaries of the human heart," she wrote to Frank on her return, "one craves what one knows to be unattainable."

In a burst of generosity, two weeks before Emma was scheduled to return to St.-Tropez, Emmy had decided to open and clean Bon Esprit. She left Sasha in Nice, and by herself dusted every cobweb, washed every surface of the house, painted each room, including the outhouse, and weeded the garden. Her efforts were particularly valiant in light of her worsening stomach problems. Sasha, too, had been in a period of physical decline, which he tried to hide from Emma. When Sasha joined Emmy, the day before Emma's return, he saw the poignancy in her energetic attempt to erase the blemishes of her past relationship with Emma with soap and paint, to root out the weeds that had kept their friendship from flowering.

Emma returned to find Bon Esprit sparkling, flowers in bloom all around, but her senses seemed numbed by the confusion and emptiness that had accompanied her long voyage away from Heiner and from her hopes for a more stable life in North America: she arrived travel-weary and lonely for Frank. Although her letters to Emmy from afar had signaled a new warmth, when she was face to face with this young woman who claimed the affection of her soulmate, she could not contain her jealousy and resentment. No matter how cheerful Emmy and Sasha tried to make Emma's return, Emma could not see beyond her own misery, feeling more acutely alone in their presence as a couple. Her only comment about Emmy's work on Bon Esprit was critical. Why, she asked, had Emmy spent so much money on paint?

Sasha wrote to Emma's niece, Stella, explaining away Emma's inconsiderate demeanor on her return.

EG arrived from Canada pretty much exhausted, more mentally perhaps than physically. . . . Indeed, I felt she was more oppressed in spirit than at any former return home. Most probably Chicago

449

[i.e., Frank Heiner] was the cause of it. At any rate, the surprise of the renovated house and the cleared garden, the most warm welcome, etc., failed to raise her spirits, unfortunately. You know our dear Emma—even Emmy's spontaneous cheerfulness and my "celebrated" jokes were powerless to lighten the atmosphere. Indeed, I believe that the cheerfulness was resented as aggravating to a serious attitude toward life. It's too bad, of course, but there is no cure for it. Things must take their course, in their own natural manner, so to speak.

Emma could not even muster any enthusiasm when Emmy and Sasha tried to make her a small birthday party. Nothing they did could keep her from wandering off into her fantasies. She tried to find solace in letters to Frank:

Imagine, last Thursday, the 27th of June, I was sixty-six years of age. Never before did I feel my years so much. Never before was it borne in on me how utterly incongruous is my mad infatuation for you, a man thirty years younger than I. And with all the numerous odds against such a love. But not only that. Something even more vital is the ever-present thought of America. The fact staring me in the face that I am useless in Europe and that America is closed to me forever. All these disheartening thoughts swept over me on my sixty-sixth birthday like an avalanche. I could not even write you a post card on that day. And yet you were so much in my blood and on my mind I could almost touch you. A crazy state, isn't it?

Heiner wrote that love was ageless. He had had a relationship with a woman of fifty-two when he was twenty-nine, and many renowned people followed this pattern:

Ambrose Bierce was with a woman of seventy. In France in the eighteenth century, love between a younger man and an older woman was thought best, and these unions often lasted for years. Benjamin Franklin advises the choice of an older woman as conducive to happiness. Mary Shelley was, if I remember rightly, several years older than her husband. The wife of Stephen Crane was ten years older than he. Mrs. Browning was twenty years older than her husband and in these cases, there was certainly permanence. . . . Oh, I almost forgot the first wife of Mehemet who should be included for good measure. She was a widow of forty and he in his early twenties. After her death, he rebuked his young wife, Aisha, for supposing that he could forget her.

When Emma felt the force of Heiner's appeal to her, it "rekindled . . . youth long dead and buried"; when she allowed herself to enter into the fantasy of his love for her, her longing to be with him was agonizing. She wrote to her "tender but also violent lover":

> The yearning for you, and the plans and schemes of how to have you near or get within reach of you, has been so intense it just unfitted me for human association. I try devilishly hard to eliminate you from my mind if only to find some peace. But the more I try the more restless I grow.
>
> Some days I feel as if I must take the next steamer back to Canada. It's insanity, of course.
>
> But what will you when the longing has become an idea fixe, an ever-present thought, an emotion that leaves no room for anything else and defies all reason? Many are the years I have been in such a maddening state. . . . I am [in] constant conflict with myself, with you, with our love.
>
> Frank, my Frank, I long for you with every fiber of my being.

The love letters gave Emma an escape from her increasingly intolerable relationship with Emmy. Their rapprochement, built out of hopes nurtured over almost two years of separation, turned out to be fragile. Some days the air was so thick with tension that, in desperation, Emmy and Emma would go to their rooms and write out their complaints, in an effort to tame their fury. Emmy lashed out first, after months of having kept to herself the disappointment of Emma's lack of appreciation for her efforts to refurbish Bon Esprit. Emma, never one to accept criticism with grace, replied angrily that Emmy's lack of trust in

Emma was at the root of their misunderstandings. The basic issue, Emma felt, ignoring her own fierce jealousy, was what she called Emmy's "inordinate, almost pathological sense of possessiveness of Sasha."

It is this which colors your every thought and action. It is this which simply cannot bear that anyone, especially I, should have any part in Sasha's life, his thoughts, his work, in fact in anything pertaining to Sasha. Of course, I know how bravely you tried to emancipate yourself from that feeling of complete ownership, that monopoly of, not only a human body, but what is more deadly, the human spirit. Every one of your letters breathed your brave effort. . . . You were determined to be free and big about me and what I can bring Sasha. But when I arrived and you were face to face with the need for my part in Sasha's life and work, it was too much for you. . . . It was too much for you that in any important issue related to our social attitude we should speak the same language. Of course you were not ever aware of the dominant cause of your irritations. Hence you ascribe all our trouble to my tactlessness, or to the lack of capacity in me to be gay or joyous. Forgive me, Emmy, my dear, I really have no desire to hurt you, but I must say these ideas are childish, childish and, what is more, they are not true. I admit that I see a worldwide difference between gaiety and childishness. . . . Not only do I understand and love childlikeness in others but I have a lot of it myself. How else would I have attracted youth all my life, how else would they flock to me and be able to let themselves go in my presence even now at sixty-six? . . . But I cheerfully admit that childishness in a grown person does get on my nerves. Especially the childishness which expresses itself in silly baby talk with one's lover. I hope nothing human is alien to me. I know only too well how very childish the wisest of us are in the privacy of our love relation. That is all right. But when it becomes demonstrative, in the presence of outsiders, it does not sound true or convincing, and it makes us appear foolish in the eyes of those who have to witness or listen to it. . . . Unconsciously you try to distract Sasha's interest or absorption from whatever he may do or with whom he is by your "baby talk." The tragedy to me is that you are completely unaware that men of Sasha's intellectual caliber grow tired of such demonstrations of love. . . . No, dearest Emmy, it is not that I failed to appreciate gaiety when I called your attention to the fact that you were after all no longer five years old. Not that I should consider that such a heinous offense, important enough to stand in the way of our friendship. You of course took it in the wrong light. You felt that I was trying to dampen your gay spirit. Therefore you were quick in assuring me that you mean to remain young and a child to the end of your days. If you had thought for a moment you would not have done so because you would have trusted me enough to know that nothing was further from my intention than to check your laughter, laughter that springs from you, and not childish giggling, which is a sort of exhibitionism of the very thing we try to hide. In your case your sense of owning Sasha.

Emma continued her spiteful outpouring by complaining that Emmy was insensitive to her lonely situation, in the process exposing her own feelings of insecurity, her fear of having her every move judged by Emmy and Sasha, and her dread that they might reject her:

As to tactlessness, my dear girl, have you any idea how very tactless you have been? I am sure you do not, nor do I intend to enumerate all the things you say to me or try to make me smart under. I only wish to point out your violent objection to my energy, your constant complaint that I fill the house with gloom, your reiteration that Sasha is more wonderful to you than he had ever been to anyone else, this to a woman who had shared forty-five years of hell itself with the man.

What do you call all this, dear Emmy, if not tactlessness. What did you do in your recent attack of mood when for days you ran in and out of your room brushing by me, never saying a word, as if I were nonexistent. Didn't you fill the house with gloom, did you not say bitter things, only in a much louder and harsher way than you ever heard me use. Yet you know that I had infinitely more reasons for my mood than you. Yours is of course your poor stomach, I appreciate that. Mine is my loneliness, the fact that I put three thousand miles between me and the man who meant the last greatest experience in my life. . . . Tactless, my dear, are you aware of the fact that since I came back I [have] felt as if I were walking on glass. I, who am used to freedom of expression—my feelings for those precious to me stifled everything in order not to hurt you. How ridiculous, therefore, to charge me with tactlessness? But . . . you are blinded by your sense of possessiveness to see anything pertaining to me in the right light.

Unfortunately I was already in Sasha's life when you came. Nothing can change that or the place I have in his life, whether he shows it or not. During my stay in Canada I had begun to hope that you had actually come to reconcile yourself to that and accept me as your friend as well as Sasha's companion, comrade and friend. I evidently expected the impossible. So let's make the best of the situation, Emmy dear. The summer is nearly over. In the Fall you will go back to your own little apartment and have Sasha again all to yourself. You can rest assured I will not intrude on your idyll. . . . I really am out of place in domesticity. So let's hold together as long as we can and must, economically speaking.

Once Emma had expressed her venomous and hurt feelings, she denied that she had ever been angry:

I was not angry. I was only grieved and unspeakably sad that you continue to see in me, if not an enemy, at least one whom you have to fear, in regard to Sasha. . . .

I myself feel more of the "ebiger Jude" than ever before. So I mean to go my way when the time comes. As you say yourself, you like me so much better from the far.

Thank you, my dear, for all you have again done for Bon Esprit. Never think I fail to appreciate everything, even if I do not express it all the time. . . . I will again try hard not to impress you as tactless and bitter.

Affectionately

Whether Emma intended kindness to Emmy or not, her resentment was so deep and her hostility so great that she could not help expressing them. Sasha, in his own fashion, had tried to make a truce. He wrote to Emma at the end of August, when he and Emmy returned to Nice:

Dearest Em,

I am very sorry you feel so disappointed with your homecoming this time. I am surely not given to emotional expressions, particularly not orally. There is no change whatever in my feelings for you, and they cannot change. But the atmosphere in St.-Tropez was rather heavy, mainly due to your state of mind, your longing for Frank, etc. . . .

But all that is not the important part of the bad atmosphere at Bon Esprit. I think the real situation is due to your general dissatisfaction with things, which is part of your nature, and to the fact that a "ménage à trois," as the French call it, is never a success.

You have tried it for years now, and surely it does not work. My experience is that it never works properly. Every person, especially such three very definite natures as we three, must have his or her own atmosphere.

I know that your explanation will probably be that Emmy is jealous of you and that that is the cause of the trouble. But nothing is further from the truth in this matter. In the past Emmy may have been jealous of you, in a certain way, but that is long past. Nothing is more certain [than] that all last winter she was dreaming of nothing else than of your return and planning to make life beautiful for all three [of us] in St.-Tropez. That was the reason she went down to St.-Tropez two weeks before you came, to prepare a surprise for you, renovate the house, etc. And she was determined to make YOUR stay there happy, as happy as possible.

Well, it proved a failure. Now, my dear, I surely know that Emmy has many faults. But I prefer to see the good sides in people. And since I was in St.-Tropez all summer and I could observe how things were working, I must tell you that she exerted herself to the utmost to make things pleasant for you. Well, as I have said, it did

455

not work. It's probably nobody's fault, but the fact must be recognized.

You will admit, I hope, my dear, that you are not a very easy person to live with. I think your very best friends will tell you that, if they are frank with you. And a person cannot always permit himself to be suppressed and not break out now and then. By suppressed I mean more the atmosphere you create than any words you utter. Do you realize that it [went] so far that Emmy was afraid even to laugh or to express her native joy of life because it disturbed you and even was resented by you, as I myself noticed on several occasions. Well, surely people cannot live together under such conditions.

And I must tell you, my dear, that I myself was often oppressed by the atmosphere you created. Now, I am not high-strung like Emmy. I can stand a good deal, in every sense. And yet your frequent heavy moods and bad humor were oppressive to me and often I could not even work because of it. You can imagine, then, how such conditions must affect a woman of a nervous and over-sensitive nature like Emmy. No wonder she exploded several times.

All this simply shows that a ménage à trois does not work. At least not in this case, though I believe it works in no case. It is unfortunate, but a fact.

Sasha was the only one of Emma's close friends who could criticize her without fear of reproach. And though some of Emma's friends thought he had abandoned her for Emmy in his old age, Emma rejected such an interpretation. It was easier to blame Emmy. In the fall, when Emma had her place to herself once again, she wrote more philosophically to Sasha about Emmy. At this point in her life, she vowed not to let anything or anybody interfere with her relationship to Sasha, the only man she could depend on for abiding friendship. Emma and Sasha were briefly able to visit alone at Bon Esprit in peace that autumn:

I wish I could give her the certainty that I never mean to be unkind or impatient with her. I want her to feel more at ease with me for her own sake of course. But mainly for your and my sake. For I have convinced myself that in that way alone can I bring you peace and in return also have an occasional visit with you in peace and lovely camaraderie, as the last two weeks brought me. That I need [this] now more than ever should not be so puzzling to you. For I have nothing from the past, neither man, child, nor the activity for our ideas. And after all, that had always filled my life more than any lover or friend with the exception of yourself. Now that we are both getting on in age we should cling to the precious thing our friendship has been and will be to our last breath.

In this spirit, Emma brought herself to write Emmy an affectionate letter, and they were able to return for a while to a cessation of hostilities. As was often the case for Emma, it was easier to be close to Emmy in letters than in person. While Emmy genuinely yearned for Emma's approval and love, Emma only needed Emmy's friendship as a means of maintaining her ties to Sasha. On occasion the two women felt close to each other again, but they knew that suspicion and anger could burst through any ordinary interactions. For the next few months, Emmy and Emma kept up an unspoken truce, no doubt also the result of Sasha's precarious health and their fear of final separation. With Emma in St.-Tropez planning to tour England, and Emmy and Sasha in Nice, there was enough distance to maintain the peace.

As early as November 21, 1935, on Sasha's sixty-fifth birthday, Emma began to include in her letters, among the accounts of her daily life, formal farewells and statements of appreciation.

My dear, old Dush,

As a greeting to your sixty-fifth birthday it is fitting that I should tell you the secret of my life. It is that the one treasure I have rescued from my long and bitter struggle is my friendship for you. Believe it or not, dear Sash. But I know of no other value, whether in people or achievements, than your presence in my life and the love and affection you have roused. True, I loved other men. I love Frank with a silly but none the less intense emotion. But it is not an exaggeration when I say that no one ever was so rooted in my being, so ingrained in every fiber, as you have been and are to

457

this day. Men have come and gone in my long life. But you, my dearest, will remain forever. I do not know why this should be so. Our common struggle and all it has brought us in travail and disappointment hardly explains what I feel for you. Indeed, I know that the only loss that would matter would be the loss of you or your friendship.

Such an abiding feeling could be better explained if you had always been all kindness or understanding. but you were not that. On the contrary, you were and are still often harsh and lacking in comprehension of the inner motivations of my acts. But all that is as nothing compared with the force you have been from the moment I first heard your voice and met you in Sach's Café and all through the forty-five years of our comradeship. I seem to have been born then as woman, mother, comrade, and friend. Yes, I believe my strongest and most compelling feeling for you is that of the mother. You have often resented that, saying you are no mollycoddle. Of course, you failed to understand that it was not my desire to impose my mother authority on you. It was the everpresent concern in your welfare and the equally present fear that something may befall you that would tear you away from me. Terribly selfish feeling, isn't it, dear heart? Or is it that you had bound me by a thousand threads? I don't know and don't care. I only know that I always wanted to give you more than I expected from you. Indeed I know that there is nothing I can think of that I would not joyfully give out of fullness of my being to enrich your life.

Sasha appreciated Emma's tacit understanding of the precarious state of his physical and, consequently, emotional health, even enjoying her arguments with him about aging. Emma and Sasha had long acknowledged that they thrived in "a fighting atmosphere," but Sasha pointed out, "one gets old, my dear—though You do NOT." Emma protested against Sasha's preoccupation with aging.

About old age, I don't believe a word of it. I insist as I always have that your old-age fixation would leave you in a second were you

in a position to take part in activities of interest. Haven't I seen it
on the *Buford*? You were sick as a dog and even a little meshuge
[crazy] before we sailed away. And then behold, you worked like
a beaver for ten people. Not merely physical labor but also mental.
And was it not the same in Russia? . . . Of course you will say
that was fifteen years ago. Nonsense. I am willing to bet my last
shirt that you would no longer speak of "old" age if something
required your complete absorption in an important issue and you
had the freedom to grab it. . . . However, regardless of your *idée
fixe* that you are old, you are still good for some years. I hope and
pray that you are, for Emmy's sake and my own. After all, my
Sash, I too need you, more desperately perhaps. Forty-five years
are no joke. Every phase of my life has been interlocked with
yours. Just being away from you for a year is pain enough. I
cannot visualize what it would be without you altogether. My one
hope is that I will go before you. You will still have our sweet
Emmy, who loves you deeply. I would have no one, hence my loss
would be infinitely harder to bear.

Despite optimistic letters, there was frank negotiation about their
wills. Emma had decided to leave Bon Esprit to Sasha, or to Emmy
should Sasha, who was Emma's heir, predecease Emma. Emma saw
Emmy as a child for whom she must provide, even more than for her
niece, Stella. Less able to face the prospect of Sasha's death than her own,
she wrote to their mutual friend Fedya (Modest Stein) that she did not
believe Sasha had prostate problems so much as a "weak heart from
material insecurity and intellectual stress." Emma denied a grim reality,
the possibility that Sasha had cancer and that his health (as well as
Emmy's, who had pyloric gastritis and recurrent diverticulitis) would
continue to decline. Alone in St.-Tropez, Emma could not shake the
gloom of Sasha's illness, nor did she feel sufficiently at ease with Emmy
to be by his side.

Heiner's letters were no longer enough to sustain her, either.
Though he maintained the same devotional tone, the frequency of his
letters decreased, signaling his gradual withdrawal from Emma. Her

resolve to break off her relationship with Heiner came in part because she could sense his reticence, and knew that her hopes of his coming to Europe were misguided. Mary wrote promising that Frank might come to France to see Emma next spring, with the patently absurd explanation that it might be good for his career. But it was too late, and Emma could tell that something fundamental had changed.

By the end of 1935, Emma felt that she could no longer bear the frustration of this relationship and vowed to break the spell; her economic difficulties and the long gaps between letters from Heiner had broken her spirits. "I do not know whether it is a virtue or a vice to prefer almost any suffering except futility," she wrote to Heiner. Her hope was to refocus her energies by leaving St.-Tropez and moving to London, where she could do useful political work. In England, having the advantage of speaking the language and the benefits of citizenship, she could begin to lecture, do research, and write again. Although the British had never appreciated her fully, Emma was now propelled by her inner needs to make an attempt to settle there.

I cannot continue on the rack. More than ever do I need every bit of energy and power of concentration to establish myself in England. . . . It will require superhuman strength and determination to clear the ground from all the debris that has accumulated for so long. And unless I put behind me all personal emotions and craving and give myself utterly to the task I will not succeed. AND I MUST SUCCEED, OR MAKE AN END. I CANNOT FACE THE YEARS LEFT ME GAGGED AND BOUND hand and foot. So, you see, my dearest, it is really a question of life and death with me.

The summer has convinced me that my feeling for you completely unfits me for anything else. I am determined, therefore, not to be as obsessed by that any more. I know myself enough to know that while I will not forget you, or cease to care profoundly, the effort to make Anarchism heard in England and to create a basis for systematic propaganda will fill the void our separation and the long and excruciating intervals of work from you has created. After all, our ideal has always meant more to me than all else. I do not say that I found it easy to choose. But there is no help. . . . It had to be done.

Emma moved to London in December, and began to put together a life of work and friendship there. Acutely aware that she could never recapture the success of her early years in America, she braced herself for the cold, physically and emotionally.

Sasha looked forward to the letters of his "dear little fighter and faithful soul," and Emma never let a week go by without writing to him. He was amazed by her hectic life in London, as his own dwindled: "The things you manage to do, the numbers of people to see, parties to attend, and at the same time read and prepare lectures—and not to forget, to write long letters! It's astounding." Emma insisted that her activity gave her life: "Dear heart, what would I do if my vitality and energy would leave me? I simply could not go on. I have so little of a personal nature in my life that I must be active to fill the void. I am grateful that I still have my health and that my energy grows with my activity."

But although Emma had written within the last year that she seemed "to thrive on tzores [troubles]," she felt at times that her efforts were futile, and "More and more I am coming to believe it matters little what any one of us do[es] or leave[s] undone. Life goes on its stupid old way."

Sasha understood how it felt to bear the burden of political consciousness on one's shoulders and at the same time to fear that no amount of effort would make enough difference to justify the pain. Even before Emma settled in London, he tried to counter her despair: "One must not carry Weltschmerz into his daily life, for in that manner, existence becomes impossible."

But Emma had always believed that the strength of her message was in direct proportion to how deeply she was willing to feel, to identify with, and to articulate the pains of the world. She believed that her dramatic emotional swings were the price she paid for her ability to see and feel. It did not occur to her that she might have a part in creating her anguish. Rather, she believed it would be a betrayal not to stay in touch with the "terrible agony of the human family." How could she experience joy while others suffered?

Frank tried to comfort Emma with love letters. No long absence, or "drought" as he called it, could make him forget "my Brunhilde. . . . Sweetheart, in my imaginings there is no inch of your body that I have not pressed with ardent kisses." He marveled at what he felt for her, a "reverence amounting to idolatry."

Her doubts were confirmed, however, when Heiner explained why he had become a less faithful correspondent:

> It must have seemed to you that I had simply forgotten you in the midst of gaiety and other interests. You also felt that I was completely absorbed in my struggle for economic independence, which is not the case, as I am used to that by this time, like the man hanging. What really happened is that the past year was a terrible one for me. I was bled white with suffering. Things are better now, though, and at a stage of calm and understanding. I gave you a hint of the storm which I saw approaching when I was in Canada.
>
> Before I met you, Mary made a discovery which gave her infinite pain. I did not clearly know this about myself, but she discovered it and pointed it out to me. This discovery was, due to some primary fixation of early life, I had a craving, amounting to a physical necessity, for women who were physically above the average weight and who could give me definitely maternal responses.

Heiner's admission of his attraction to women "physically above the average weight" was guaranteed to wound Emma, never mind whether he had set out deliberately to hurt her. No longer could she idealize her love with Heiner or escape the truth of her age and physical condition. She now felt herself to be merely a cipher in Frank's obsessions. He went on to confide in Emma about an affair he had had immediately before he met her, not knowing that Mary had already told her about it. Although he had given up Minnie for Mary's sake, he wrote,

> the loss . . . brought me to the verge of insanity or at least a nervous breakdown. It was a sudden wrench.
>
> Then, shortly after, in time to save me, came the Goddess whom

I had loved without knowing her and in whom I discovered response to those fundamental physical needs as well as the intellectual bond. Mary was glad of my resurrection but later, that same personal torment began to beset her, not jealousy of you but the feeling that I did not love her.

The rest of his letter was an old refrain—he could not leave his wife and family, because they needed him and he owed them too much. Since Emma seemed by comparison stronger, less dependent, and a true believer in the freedom of love, she could withstand being left. Feebly he tried to deflect the question of why, if he knew of his weakness for maternal types long before he met Emma, he had not been fully honest with her up to now.

Question, why did I not tell you all this as it happened, since I knew you loved me and would feel with me. Partly for that very reason. Why add the burden of my misfortunes to one who had more than a reasonable share of her own. Again, you might blame yourself and feel that you were the cause of our difficulties, which was not, decidedly not, the case. I felt that I could tell you all that in conversation but not on paper. Then I just felt it hopeless to make the whole situation, the strange psychological dilemma, clear in a letter. It would take a book. I think that as it is, I have made botch of the whole business. I fully intended to tell you about it when we met. But my reticence often prevented me from writing you. I wanted my letters to you to be free from any pain or vexation or personal trouble, and frequently, when I was in the midst of depression, I knew I could not keep them that way. So I waited until I could, then, when you misunderstood my motives, how could you have thought otherwise, I knew that I would have to tell you about it all or try to tell you. Ever since Christmas, I have been trying to frame a way of telling you and finally decided to give you the story hit or miss.

Clearly wishing to end the relationship, he wrote to Emma as if to a good friend, not a woman who was passionately in love with him. Only at the end did he address her feelings as a lover:

Now, as to your feelings expressed in recent letters, so beautifully and tenderly in your last letter, your missing me but feeling that you must not think so much about it, I understand those feelings thoroughly, my darling, I would be the first to help you and the last to hinder you in them. You must let me be a bit ardent with you, though. I cannot write to you on a merely friendly plane. I would not, though, try to set up barriers against your happiness. I love you as I always have and always will but we have to bow to circumstances to a certain extent. I know you love me, and do not feel that I have lost you. Sometimes, in the midst of last year's difficulties, I used to dream of living with you permanently, but a second's reflection showed me that such an arrangement was completely out of the question. The life we are compelled to lead, you on account of your work, I because of my financial difficulties, would make it impossible. Looking at the situation as objectively as I can, I also cannot help advising strenuously against your return to Canada. I could be with you there only for short spaces of time at long intervals. . . . In the meantime, I do not see why things should not be much as they have between us. We may take it a bit more calmly but just as deeply. . . . It will be easier for me to write to you now. There is nothing to hold back.

You are always the Goddess, and for me, to know you, to think of you, is, always, always, to love you

Frank

Once Frank had confessed his obsessions, he admitted that his relationship with Emma had contributed to other problems between himself and Mary during the previous year. They had temporarily separated, ostensibly for Mary to take higher-paid work in another town, leaving him with his mother and their child in Chicago—and forcing him to recognize the pre-eminence of his allegiance to Mary. However, he still wanted to continue to write and dream of Emma, without pressure from her to try someday to revive the passion that they had awakened in each other in Canada.

With the illusion gone, Heiner's overweight goddess was surprisingly willing to curtail their relationship without lashing back at him.

Emma must have felt anger and disappointment, but she complied with the idealized image Heiner had painted of her generosity in such situations. Refusing to acknowledge the real reasons for his decision to end the affair, she claimed that she had suspected his economic distress and even the presence of some disturbing element in his relationship with Mary (not with herself). She wrote to him, in fact, as if she already had decided to make the break, saying that she could no longer manage the intense conflicts and uncertainties he had brought into her life. She claimed that their relationship had so disrupted her life that she could not function well politically—and that she would always choose devotion to her ideal over a relationship with a man. In her letter to him from London—never once mentioning his reference to her as overweight—she strove to assert that the fact that Heiner had chosen Mary over herself had nothing to do with her own decision.

> But all that had no bearing on my condition, which decided me to make the break. You took me by storm, my dear, and you left me in a mad whirl which took me months to overcome. I had plenty of time last summer to analyze the madness that had taken hold of both of us. And the more I thought of the event, the more fantastic and hopeless it became. I realized that if I do not cut the Gordian knot I will become utterly useless to my purpose in life, the continuation of my work for our ideas. I had never permitted anything to stand in the way of this, my only raison d'être. . . . So there was nothing else to do but suggest the change in our relation. I am frank enough to tell you that it has brought me considerable relief and peace.

Emma went on to assure Mary that Frank was completely hers now, that Emma had only been his fancy. She was glad to be "on the firing line again, to plead for our ideal, to make people see its justice and beauty has put new energy into me. It is frightful uphill work, more than once I have felt lacerated, my spirit bleeding from a hundred wounds." Once again Emma's sense of suffering fueled her idealism.

Despite the opposition of the communist groups in England—who called her "liar, Hitler, Fascist . . . [with] oozing hatred in their young

maddened eyes" when she spoke against the evils of Stalinism—
Emma felt most herself when she was in the thick of a political fight. Her
relationship with Heiner had blocked that part of her life. Now, without
the possibility of fulfilling her reawakened longings for love, Emma's
devotion to a political life came to the fore. The power she felt in
articulating her vision of the world and her feelings of connectedness
with something universal and greater than herself served as an antidote
to the cycles of excitement and disappointment she experienced in her
intimate relationships with men. And so, with a renewed sense of
political involvement, Emma was able to bid farewell to the obsessive
aspect of her relationship with Heiner and yet retain the confidence she
had gained: "Goodby, my dear Frank. Nothing can take away from me or
my memory the wonderful two weeks in T. I shall always cherish them
and everlastingly thank my good star that has brought you to me. We
have deeper ties than the emotional and they will never be broken. I
embrace you, my dear, in deepest comradeship."

Getting back into politics inevitably stirred up feelings about her
old comrade Ben Reitman, who continued to write to her almost every
year to commemorate their first meeting. Now that her relationship with
Frank was essentially over, Emma appreciated Ben's insistence on reminding her of their "rich past," although sometimes it made "the
present seem doubly poor." Certainly Emma could have used a talented
advance man in England to win her the public reception she felt she
deserved. Although she had criticized Ben at great length to Frank—
who had envied the role Ben had played in Emma's early life—no doubt
she, like Ben, still drew some of her self-confidence from what they had
achieved together.

In Chicago, Ben had been trying to reform himself. When he
visited New York in 1935 to attend the meeting of the American
Sociological Congress, he was interviewed by the newspapers and given a
chance to reflect on his past.

Doc Reitman will be 57 on Tuesday. He has a head of shagging hair,
a heavy physique, and unbounding energy. Last night at the
banquet of sociologists in the Commodore he kept pacing up and
down. His restless roving temperament was confined by the ban-

quet hall. A bottle of rum stuck out of his overcoat pocket which he folded up underneath his chair at the table. Whenever his foot itched to be moving, he told his mealmates:

"Hold my seat and watch my liquor."

He wore his hair like Senator Borah, a large black mustache, and huge Windsor tie of cream colored silk. He was one of the leading anarchists of his day; a traveling companion of Emma Goldman, an IWW and one of the original sponsors of birth control literature. He was tarred and feathered in California. He was jailed in Cleveland and points west for spreading contraceptive propaganda; he was house physician for Al Capone and in recent years a Bible teacher and reformer in Chicago. . . . He established the first Hobo College in Chicago. . . .

"My present work," he said, "is to encourage citizens of the underworld to reform. I'm also trying to reform sociologists. I'm trying to teach them to concentrate less on research work and more on the application [of] their studies to the people I know." He spoke in a soft, cultured fluent way. How did he do it?

"Life tames one," he said. . . . "But, most of all, I guess the reason for it is that to succeed in any walk of life you must be a gentleman. You'll never see a big-time crook who is a tough guy. Tough guys are the small fry. Everybody knows that, even crooks."

Ben did not want to play the tough guy anymore: he wanted to rewrite that part of his history. His newest scheme was to go to Europe and live once more near Emma and Sasha, to write an autobiography that would include a history of anarchist theory. By the spring of 1936 he had narrowed his scope to an earlier plan, to write a book about Emma, Sasha, and himself entitled "The Great Decade."

The whole idea was abhorrent to Emma. She was already enmeshed in an uncomfortable triangle with Sasha and Emmy, made still more uncomfortable lately by the fact that Sasha and Emmy were both ailing and in need of hospitalization. When Ben wrote her to wish her cheer during the month that marked twenty-nine years since their first tour together, she let him know how she felt:

Dear Ben.

If only I had your gift to see life through magic glasses, I should be a more contented woman. But you know of yore that I see reality as it is. Life to me is pretty serious business, especially since I am in exile. That accounts for my silence. The struggle of months in England to gain a footing, Sasha's grave illness and the general chaotic state of affairs in Europe have absorbed me to the exclusion of nearly everything else. Besides, your life is full with your own affairs and successes. Why burden you with mine?

She agreed to help him with his abbreviated autobiography and cautioned him to take his time and write "vividly and as near life as one can make it," but she could not assure him that Sasha would be well enough to help him also.

For myself, it hardly needs assurance that I will be glad to read your MSS and give you my frank and sympathetic opinion, if you will be willing to accept it in the spirit [in which] it will be given. Do you think you will be able to rise to that without any of your old suspicion that I want to hurt you in any way? Meanwhile you certainly have my blessing, largely because YOU believe in blessings. And you have my friendship because I believe in it.

By the spring of 1936, Emma could focus only on her friendship with Sasha. She was preoccupied with mortality, particularly since Sasha's prostate trouble was not cured by an operation, and she felt weary in England and alone now that her relationship with Heiner had ended. Assorted ailments—varicose veins, foot problems, fluid reten-tion—kept getting worse. A deep depression crept into much of their correspondence. Only a year earlier, Emma had written that she was still as "strong as a bull. . . . But one survives everything except death, fortunately. For how could one go on forever and ever and go through purgatory every day? So I feel relieved to know there will be an end someday." But this year, with Sasha's body deteriorating, she could not feel any relief in the knowledge that death would come to everyone. It was difficult for Sasha, too, to admit how much he needed

Emma, particularly before he faced his second prostate operation and when he knew that Emmy would soon need an operation for her pyloric gastritis. He decided not to tell Emma, and instead tried to reassure her that he was "as ever the same, even if non-pissing." After his first operation, Emma had acknowledged the seriousness of his condition, fearing that he would have to face the ordeal again, without her, because she could not leave England yet. They both fantasized that they would spend their last minutes together. She herself had just narrowly escaped asphyxiation when she fell asleep in a room with an unlit gas heater. "Talk about Dutch luck. . . . Frankly, I am not keen for such an end to happen just when you and Emmy need me so much. Otherwise it might have been an easy escape from life with all its rotten conditions. Evidently it was not to be. I suppose the struggle must go on."

Still, the two comrades managed to balance each other's despair with hope and mutual appreciation. Sasha, who was confined to bed after his first operation, vicariously lived through the joys and sorrows of Emma's political victories and defeats. He lovingly praised her ability to struggle "single-handed" against all odds in England, "with the absence of active comrades, disillusionment, war clouds, and the great poverty of the crisis," and still to "accomplish wonders"—large meetings and the reawakening of social conscience.

Emma's reply expressed her need for Sasha's affection as well as her own affection for him as the anchor of her life.

> Then, too, one begins to value [more] the few most precious friends of a lifetime when one goes on in age than one does in one's youth. Youth has all of life to live and is so callous and indifferent to time and relationships. But when one gets to my age, one clings more hungrily to the few unchangeable friends. That's why your letter gave me such a lot of joy. I felt it was almost worthwhile to go through the pain and the misery of four months to have you say such lovely things about me. I hope to give you a special hug when I come back.

The special effort Sasha took to praise Emma's work and to show her affection was spurred by his fear that his imminent operation might mean he would never speak to her again. Although he asked Emmy to wire Emma on March 23, 1936, "No operation at present," he was scheduled to have a second operation the next day. Also on the 23rd, he wrote to his "Dearest Sailor Mine, staunchest chum of a lifetime" from his hospital bed in Nice. In the letter, which was to be mailed only in case of his death, he wrote that he hoped that she would forgive him for not calling her back to him, for not taking her away from her political meetings: he did not want to alarm her in the midst of her trip to South Wales. He tried to assure her and himself that all would be well, but just in case he wanted to be sure to say good-bye.

Well, dearest, I think everything will be OK and I don't feel anxious at all. But there is never any telling and so, in case anything happens, don't grieve too much, dearest. I have lived my life and I am really of the opinion that when one has neither health nor means and cannot work for his ideas, it is time to clear out.

But it is not of this I want to speak now. I just want you to know that my thoughts are with you and I consider our life of work and comradeship and friendship, covering a period of 45 years, one of the most beautiful and dearest things in the world.

In this spirit I greet you now, dear immutable Sailor Girl, and may your work continue to bring light and understanding in this topsy-turvy world of ours. I embrace you with all my heart, you bravest, strongest, and truest woman and comrade I have known in my life.

Your old chum, friend, and comrade,

Sasha

P.S. I am happy that you and Emmy have grown to understand each other better. She has been wonderful to me and her devotion limitless. I hope that you will both prove solace to each other.

S

. . . Tell our comrades I send them all my fraternal greetings. May they keep up energetically the work for a brighter and better day and a future of liberty, sanity, and human cooperation.

S

The letter was never mailed, and Emma was informed about the operation after it was over. It seemed to have been successful, though the recuperation period was long and tedious: May Day came and Sasha was still hospitalized. After spending only four months in England, Emma rushed back to his side, visiting him in the hospital daily. Then, when he seemed stabilized, she made the nearby St.-Tropez her base of activity once again, to be near her "chum of a lifetime."

At Bon Esprit, Emma had to clean out the disorder and dirt that had invaded her quiet retreat by the sea while she was gone. Everything bothered her, down to her feet. News of a year's extension of Sasha's visa was not enough to lighten her mood. She wrote to Emmy, with whom she had established a temporary truce because of Sasha's illness, to find out the truth about his condition, certain that Sasha would hide his pain to protect her from worry.

The two old friends still maintained a semblance of their former contentiousness in their correspondence. Emma took offense that Sasha generalized about her lack of attention to detail just because she was a miserably inaccurate typist. And Emma criticized Sasha's recent insistence on the need for an anarchist society, arguing that he focused too narrowly on the oppressive nature of the state and did not pay enough attention to cultural issues and the broader manifestations of the capitalist system's ills. Their bickering was reassurance that everything was as it had been.

They sought to delude themselves that by sheer force of will they could stave off the inevitable. But Sasha had cancer; daily his body was overtaken by disease. Emmy's ailments made their situation even more woeful. In June, just as Emma's birthday was approaching, Sasha's surgical incision opened internally, and for the next several days he could hardly move.

Sasha had planned to surprise Emma on her birthday by coming to see her by boat with Emmy and several friends. Two weeks before the date, it was clear that no party would take place and that Sasha could only send Emma his good wishes. "May you have a pleasant birthday and pass it in good company. . . . I embrace you heartily and hope that this birthday may bring you some joy and brighten the days that will follow. Affectionately, my dear old chum and *copain*, Sasha."

Emma wrote back, disappointed. "Yes, that would have been a grand surprise for you and Emmy to have come. Poor dear, it is awful how long it takes to recover from a serious illness." She thought of what a sad birthday it would be, with her brother Moe now seriously ill, her niece, Stella, with terrible bursitis pains in her arm, and Sasha's setback.

But as you say, what is there in birthdays, especially when the years begin to mount. I wish I knew why one goes on?
—About my birthday . . . I remain like the poor girl who sang "ich sitz auf a Stein und wein und wein. Alle Maidlach Kales weren nour ich bleib allein" [I sit on a rock and cry and cry. All the other young girls have married, and only I am left alone]. "Bleiben allein" is reasonably certain for my old age.

Emma's birthday had always been a time for her to assess her friendships and her position in the world. Knowing this, Sasha kept writing to her steadily before her birthday. On the day itself he wired:

Dear,
This is your birthday. Sorry I can't be with you. Some other time, I hope.
Nothing new here. Both feeling some better. Will call you up later in the day—it's only 7 A.M. No autobuses yet. . . .
Got yours of the 25th. Will answer your points by and by.
I hope you have a nice day there (the weather uncertain here today) and enjoy the day.

Affectionately,
S

Emma passed the day lunching with some friends, finding "relief in housework and cooking," and missing Sasha and Emmy terribly. She had prepared a room for them, and now it looked so sad. But, she wrote, "if you feel better and are gaining strength, I do not mind the disappointment."
Sasha was not feeling better. His condition worsened during the day. By evening he was in such agony that Emmy raced hysterically into

the streets looking aimlessly for a doctor. While she was gone, Sasha took the gun that he always kept in a drawer, aimed at his heart, and pulled the trigger. But his attempt failed: as he had so many years before in his attempt to kill Frick, he missed his heart and instead perforated his stomach and the lower part of his lungs, paralyzing his legs as well.

He pulled the sheet up to cover his entire body, so that Emmy would not see the blood. When she returned, having failed to find a doctor, she managed to rush Sasha to the hospital and call Emma before collapsing in shock. When the police discovered a revolver under the sheets, Emmy looked like the likely suspect in a murder attempt, and she was dragged to the police station. Fortunately, a neighbor who had witnessed Emmy pacing the streets waiting for a doctor told the police that she had not been in the apartment when the shot was heard, and Emmy was released.

Sasha lived for sixteen agonizing hours after his suicide attempt, long enough for Emma to make her way to his side, a journey she recalled as "the most torturous hours" of her life. He was in such agony that he could not speak. Even so, he became aware that the police, his friends, and possibly even Emma suspected that Emmy might have shot him. With what little strength he had, he scrawled on a piece of paper, "Emmy didn't do it! Emmy didn't do it." Soon he lapsed into a coma. Seeing that he no longer recognized those by his side, Emma left the room for a short while. He died at 10:00 P.M. on June 28, 1936, before she returned. She followed his body to the morgue and sat with him, alone, in silence, feeling grief but also some hostility that his desperate act had been executed on her birthday. Later, a note was found: "I don't want to live a sick man, dependent. Forgive me, Emmie Darling, and you too, Emma. Love to all. Help Emmie."

Grieving, Emma and Emmy dealt somehow with the burial arrangements, lacking the money to pay for the cremation they both knew Sasha would have preferred. The two women were left with their loss, their guilt, their long resentment of each other. Emmy felt dependent, remorseful, angry, and in terror now that her companion, her "saint," was no longer with her. Emma sublimated much of her grief and anger at Sasha into blaming Emmy, implying in every letter she wrote to others about the suicide that Emmy's insensitivity to his despair had allowed her to leave him in his hour of greatest need—thus implicating Emmy in his death. Emmy believed that Emma had spoken to the police about her suspicions. But Sasha had thrown them together, and for better or worse, Emmy was now Emma's dependent. Emma was true to her word about providing material aid, but, angry, accusatory, and sorrowful after this nightmarish birthday, she could not bring herself to give emotional support.

In a letter to their mutual friends and comrades, she was able to restore her dignity:

As for myself—the largest part of my life followed our comrade to his grave. Death had robbed me of the chance to be with my lifelong friend until he breathed his last. But it could not prevent me from a few precious moments with him alone in the Death House—moments of serene peace and silence in contemplation of our friendship that had never wavered, our struggles and work for the ideal for which Sasha had suffered so much, and to which he had dedicated his whole life.

These moments will remain for me until I myself will breathe the last. And those moments in the House of the Dead will spur me on to continue the work Sasha and I had begun on August 15, 1889.

I have a double task to perform, I must help Emmy, not only because that was Sasha's last request, but because she has been in his life for fourteen years and has given her all to him. And I have Sasha's memory to hold high, that it may continue to live in the hearts and minds of those who loved him. That it may inspire the young generation to heroic deeds, even as his own life had been heroic. For had not Sasha died as he had lived? Consistently to the end? I hope fervently I may be as strong as he, if ever I should be stricken beyond endurance. . . .

Our sorrow is all-embracing; our loss beyond mere words. Let us gather strength to remain true to the flaming spirit of Alexander Berkman. Let us continue the struggle for a new and beautiful world, but let us work for the ultimate triumph of anarchism, the ideal Sasha loved passionately and in which he believed with every fiber of his being. In this way alone can we honor the memory of one of the grandest and bravest comrades in our ranks, ALEX-ANDER BERKMAN

Emma collected herself sufficiently to respond with a similar call to action to the hundreds of friends and comrades around the world who had honored Sasha's death with their letters and telegrams, but privately acknowledged that the blow of Sasha's untimely death had left her "completely shattered." When she returned to Bon Esprit, her friends Mollie Steimer and Senya Fleshine came and stayed with her to ease the shock of her bereavement. The loss of her friend and comrade of nearly half a century haunted Emma. At night, unable to sleep, she took a candle and walked through her garden crying, "Sashenka, my Sashenka, where are you?" In the next several weeks, Emma was obsessed with the idea of following Sasha. Friends feared for the woman who had only recently urged Sasha's comrades to make his death a source of commitment to the cause.

She wrote friends about her grief, but no words could fill the emptiness, nothing could lift her spirits. To Stella she wrote, "Sasha's end has been the most devastating blow life has dealt me. Especially as it was unnecessary." She blamed herself for not staying with him until he was completely well, and wrote to her friend Netha Roe, who, with her late husband, Gilbert, had long ago been part of a campaign against Emma and Sasha's deportation:

And yet I cannot get rid of the thought that if Sasha had not remained alone he would have overcome his agony as he had the other times when overtaken by it. Oh, my dear, life is so cruel. It plays one such senseless tricks. Last year while in Canada I refused to remain there permanently because I would not stay away too far from my old pal. I said, if anything happened to him and I were not near I would never forgive myself. Yet, on June 27th I was only two hours from Nice, and I could not get to him in time to prevent his act. The irony of it, the bitter irony has been haunting me day and night. I do not think it will ever leave me. . . .

And so I suppose I MUST go on, though I really do not know for what, for whom? I am not fool enough to blind myself to the fact that my years in exile as well as Berkman's have been utterly useless. Except perhaps the writing we have done. And even that reached but the few. For the rest, we were too cut off from our past and too far removed from our former field, transplanted into alien and barren soil, to be of any help to any living creature. While our own lives became a void.

Frank Heiner wrote to Emma to express his sympathy, but it only depressed her further to hear from another person she had loved and could not be near. She lamented, "Ah, if only you could be here, if only for a short time. But it is all so helpless, so futile." Emma's attitude toward Ben revealed that her despair had a vein of anger. She wrote to Stella when, after receiving no word from him, she heard through others that he had sent a cable. "Ben said he'd cabled—the damned fool— he was always insanely jealous of Sasha, and envious of his gifts and of his place in my life. He never forgot that or forgave that."

Sasha's death marked his apotheosis for Emma and reactivated her ire against anyone who had ever spoken critically of him. Still scarred by Ben, Emma took not hearing from him immediately after Sasha's death as another slight. Her loss of Sasha made her feel angrier than ever with Ben for what now seemed like ten years she had spent demeaning her-self in loving someone who was not so worthy of her attention as Sasha had been.

. . . forty-seven years of ordinary lives make it hard to continue when one of the two departs. . . . Lives of dreams, of ideals, of struggle. Lives of friendship that had never wavered, that gave without stint and always understood? In the Romantic age poets sang of such friendship. In our own, few can boast of it, nor does it enrich the lives of many.

I once thought I would always find strength to overcome the greatest shocks. I confess I find myself lacking in the very quality my friend admired most, courage and fortitude. He had both in abundance. And he credited me with the same. But the bolt from the sky so clear for his recovery is taxing my will beyond anything I thought possible.

And yet I shall and must go on. If only to articulate to the world the personality and spirit that was Alexander Berkman. To do what he had been too reticent and too shy to do for himself. That is my innermost desire for the years still left for me, on this callous and cruel earth. Just now I am far from detached enough for anything that would do justice to my friend. Perhaps later, when the wound has left but a deep scar, I pray I may have the ability and the objectivity to give Alexander Berkman to posterity. . . .

Well, Alexander Berkman remained consistent to the last. He ended his life when he could no longer give it for his ideal. I hope I may do no less when my moment of usefulness has ceased.

With a second world war looming ominously and her great "chum of a lifetime" dead, Emma could not muster her usual optimism about the future. In fact, she envied Sasha, who no longer had to cope with the pain of existence.

18

AGAINST AN AVALANCHE

Fearing that Emma's depression might overwhelm her, Mollie Steimer and Senya Fleshine agonized for over a month to devise a plan that would revive the spirits of their political mother. They knew that the only way to awaken Emma's will to live would be through a call to action to serve her ideal.

The main center of anarchist activity in the world during that summer of 1936 was Spain. In April 1931, the Spanish monarchy had been overpowered by a popular vote for a Spanish republic. Emma had written to her friend Max Nettlau, "my whole heart is with the Spanish people, though my mind calls out a warning not to be carried away by it." The leaders within the republic, primarily socialists, had succeeded in implementing many progressive changes, including the granting of autonomy to the predominantly anarchist Catalonia. By 1933, the moderates and the Catholics had managed to defeat the republican-socialist coalition, and temporarily gained control of the republic.

Emma had been following these events and admired the courage of the Spanish anarchists, who had a stronghold in Catalonia. On July 17,

1936, while Emma was still grieving over Sasha's death, General Francisco Franco led a rebellion of nationalist anti–left-wing forces within the army. His goal was to defeat the republic and to establish a fascist government in Spain led by the Falangist Party, of which he was a member. The country was immediately divided into a republican zone and a Nationalist zone, and civil war broke out in Spain. With the threat of losing their stronghold in Catalonia as well as the advances that had been made over the past several years, many anarchists, who were generally opposed to centralized governmental control, and had even boycotted the elections, reluctantly joined with the unionists, socialists, communists, and liberals to form the Popular Front, which had gained a plurality—by one percent—in the February 1936 elections. On July 19, 1936, the organized anarchist movement came into its own, seizing factories, communalizing farms, and making self-government a reality, particularly in Barcelona.

Franco was able to get military supplies from Hitler and Mussolini, whereas the Popular Front government was gradually isolated militarily because of an official nonintervention policy adopted by Britain, France, and the United States, which left only the Soviet Union to aid the popularly elected Loyalist forces. Their urgent need was answered by ordinary people from progressive movements of every gradation all over the world, who came in brigades to fight beside the Popular Front in battle against Franco and fascism.

Nothing short of an actual war could bring Emma out of the depths of mourning. Mollie and Senya secretly wrote to Augustine Souchy, whom Emma had met in the Soviet Union years before. Souchy, a German anarchosyndicalist and founder of the German Anarchist International, was now the secretary of the Comité Anarco-Sindicalista in Barcelona. He had been publishing a bulletin in German representing the Confederación Nacional del Trabajo (CNT), the largest trade union in Spain, trying to attract international attention to the significance of the events in Spain. Mollie and Senya offered Emma's talents and energy to the Spanish anarchists, who were a large and influential contingent of the CNT, on the condition that Souchy would formally solicit Emma's assistance without giving her a hint that his request was not spontaneous.

On August 18, Souchy, representing the CNT, sent Emma a formal letter (backed up on August 21 by one from a representative of the Federación Anarquista Ibérica, FAI, the anarchist political wing of the CNT), emphasizing that her talents were urgently needed in Spain. They wanted her to witness the brave and inspiring battle against fascism, and then return to England to act as their propagandist to the English-speaking world. Surprised and flattered, Emma, who had not been actively engaged with the Spanish anarchists before, rose to the occasion and accepted their offer.

Her future seemed so empty that she confided in Stella that the danger involved in her new mission attracted her. Faced with the prospect of never returning, she wrote that it would be "a worthy end" to her life. As she prepared to leave for Spain, her misery over Sasha's death turned to an affirmation of the ideals that he and she had shared. Her letters about Sasha were still sorrowful—she lamented that he had not lived long enough to join her in Spain—but no longer despairing. Meanwhile, she rid herself of all prior commitments, including another book that some of her friends had encouraged her to write.

In September 1936, Emma arrived in Barcelona, full of revolution-ary fervor. She wrote with great anticipation to her friends around the world that Sasha's "spirit will renew my own and give me strength for whatever task is awaiting me." In Catalonia, Emma was so inspired by what seemed to be the first example of anarchist principles in action—collective farms, industry, even military units—that she wrote, "I am walking on air. I feel so inspired and so aroused that I am fortunate enough to be here and to be able to render service to our brave and beautiful comrades."

Once Emma met individual anarchists in Spain, heard their tales of heroism, and saw that they were living out her dream, she felt that she had finally found her home, after years of exile. She wanted to stay in Spain permanently, as she wrote Fitzi: "I would rather go down with the revolution if it should come to that than return to Europe, England or Canada." Departing from her lifelong pattern of setting herself up for disappointment, Emma confided that she was not optimistic about the outcome of the struggle, and that she had reservations about the ultimate worth of the coalition of anarchist and communist forces, particularly in the context of a joint government. But she thought of it as a coalition to defend an eventual revolution, not just a democratic government. What she saw—the idealism, the cooperation, the willingness to take risks for freedom—renewed her faith. "I have faith in humanity. I have infinite faith. I know th[at] governments come and go. But the intrinsic quality of human feeling and the sense of justice remains forever," she wrote. No formal defeat could take that away from her. She was "fairly drunk with the sights, the impressions and the spirit of our comrades."

In October, only a month after her arrival, Emma addressed a rally of sixteen thousand people organized by the youth section of the FAI. She jubilantly asserted that the Spanish anarchists were an example to the world, proving that anarchism is "the most constructive social philosophy worth living, fighting and if need be, dying for."

Emma's unmitigated enthusiasm shattered against the realities of war, "the blood of Spain." She wished she could fight on the front lines with the brave soldiers, instead of supporting them from afar: "It is hard to see great spirits fall in battle. One feels so small and useless doing small jobs in safety. I never felt my age as I do now."

At the same time, Emma remained more optimistic and fulfilled than she had been in years. As the wrenching year of 1936 drew to a close, she sent her friends a holiday card whose greeting reflected her new outlook: "Remembrance of Yesterday, Bright Hopes of Tomorrow."

By January 1937, Emma was back in London, filled with a sense of purpose, hoping to elicit support for the Civil War in Spain as a deterrent to fascism and as a means for giving the Spanish anarchists the best chance to triumph. Emma contacted old friends and influential liberals from all parts of her past life to stir up some support for Spain. She even wrote to John Dewey, seconding his opposition to political persecution in the Soviet Union (and reminding him that she had spoken out sixteen years before), and urging him to register similar opposition for Spain.

The brutality of the war, in which the bombing of civilian populations and other atrocities of modern warfare were first employed, led Auden to call it "the second crucifixion." The horror of the air raids over Guérnica, which aroused the indignation and sympathy of people around the world with the Republican side, was immortalized by Picasso's magnificent painting.

Although there had always been rumblings of disapproval within the anarchist ranks about uniting with the communists to fight fascism, now, as the Popular Front relied more heavily on the Soviet Union for supplies, it seemed that the communists held an uncomfortable edge, and the old split among the anarchists was revived. Emma, as a formal representative of the CNT-FAI, editing an English version of their bulletin in London, refrained from publicly commenting about these issues. She felt free to criticize the feudal attitudes toward women in Spain, but not yet the anarchists who were fighting beside the communists on the front lines, albeit in separate brigades. No doubt Emma's experience in the Soviet Union influenced her to distrust too close a collaboration with the communists, but, ironically, she was criticized by an anarchist group, the AIT (Association Internationale des Travailleurs), which was more militantly opposed to any cooperation with hierarchical institutions than the CNT, for supporting the CNT-FAI in light of their collaboration with the communists. Believing that the collaboration was a necessary evil for the survival of the Spanish anarchists in the fight against Franco and fascism, Emma continued to organize support for them in the form of fund-raising benefits for various British-based groups whose support was not exclusively anarchist, like "Spanish Democracy," and the Spanish Medical Aid Society in London.

Privately, Emma counseled the Spanish anarchists to be more cautious in their dealings with the communists, but to hold firm with the Popular Front, which already seemed to be "hanging on a straw." She feared that it was just a matter of time before the political splintering would lead to the disintegration of the Popular Front; this intense factionalism, along with the daily bloodshed of the war-torn country, left Emma with a pessimistic view of the future of Spain.

By May 1937, news reached her in London that the Catalan government "had sent assault guards [a national urban police force created by the first republican government] led by the communists, to take over the Telephone Exchange Building" in Barcelona, "which the Anarchists had seized from the fascists in the previous July...." A seemingly insignificant struggle turned into an uprising. Outnumbered, the anarchists put down their arms but never expected the greater losses that followed. The anarchists were abruptly ousted from the Popular Front government. The communists were not satisfied with this measure and formally withdrew from the Cabinet when Prime Minister Largo Caballero refused to prosecute the Trotskyites for their alleged part in the crisis. Dr. Juan Negrín, a socialist allied with the more centrist republican forces, replaced Caballero, making new alliances with the communists and continuing to exclude the CNT. Some anarchist factions of the CNT that had been opposed to cooperation with this government felt vindicated, but, no doubt, the anarchists as a whole felt defeated by the truce they made in Barcelona. The anarchists remembered the slaughter and imprisonment of their comrades who had helped win the Russian Revolution.

Privately, Emma wrote to her friends Millie and Rudolf Rocker, about the aftershock of the recent developments: "Spain has paralyzed my will and killed my hopes. . . . No saying where it will end."

Emma shared her painful disappointment over the events in Spain with her friend Ethel Mannin: "It's as though you had wanted a child all your life, and at last, when you had almost given up hoping, it had been given to you—only to die soon after it was born!"

Emma applied to the Popular Front to re-enter Spain, to see for herself what had happened to the anarchists, hoping against hope that their split with the government would enable them to retain their idealism and survive as an example for the world. But when she returned, on September 16, it was to find her fears, not her hopes, confirmed. The prisons now housed her comrades from the CNT and FAI forces. And the other anarchists' previous enthusiasm for battle had dissipated with these internal rifts. Emma began to speak out against what seemed like communist injustice, even against the judgment of the remaining CNT leadership, who she felt had compromised the anarchists in the fight against fascism. Her right to represent the CNT was rescinded, and her vocal opposition to the communists—and to Juan Negrín, whom she called a Stalinist—only isolated her further from the struggle.

Alone, without Sasha, no lover at her side, confronted with the failure of the anarchist movement in Spain, Emma at last began to shed her illusions, though she still held on firmly to her ideals. Mollie Steimer, the most staunchly doctrinaire of the anarchists close to Emma, had written to her that the Spanish anarchists' mistaken compromise was the key to the failure of their efforts. As Emma defended her Spanish comrades, she articulated her new sense that it would take more than one revolution for anarchism to take root. She assessed the failure of the anarchists in Spain, but without giving up hope:

Anarchism in Spain, far from having failed, has actually proven consistent and realizable . . . not only [as] a theory, a wild irresponsible fancy, a destructive force. But that it applies to life and the inmost needs of the people. . . .

[Since the May events in Spain, Emma had been wondering] whether we Anarchists have not taken the wish for the thought. Whether we have not been too optimistic in our belief that Anarchism had taken root in the masses? The war, the Revolution in Russia and Spain and the utter failure of the masses to stand up against the annihilation of all countries of every vestige of liberty have convinced me that Anarchism even less than any other social idea has penetrated the minds and hearts of a substantial minority, let alone the compact mass. Actually there is no Anarchist movement anywhere in the world. What we have got is so insignificant, so piffling it is ridiculous to speak of an Anarchist organized movement. In other words, everywhere the soil for our ideas has proven sterile. In Spain alone has the ground proven fertile . . . and the harvest promising. In our enthusiasm we forgot the natural forces the young, tender plants will be subjected to, the storm and stress, the drought and winds. We admit this in nature. But we were not willing to admit the forces that beset social growth. . . .

It was our mistake and we are now paying for it in *the agony of our bitter disappointment*. . . . It will take more than one revolution before our ideals will come to full growth. Until then the steps will be feeble, our ideas no doubt fall from the heights many times and many will be the mistakes our comrades are bound to make. . . . I will die as I lived, with my burning faith in the ultimate triumph of our ideal.

Emma countered the disillusionment over how cheap human life and how dulled human sensibilities had become in the terrible slaughter, with elation at the heroism, "the optimism," and "the sublime faith" of the people under attack. "One completely forgets one's self and everything of a personal character amidst the life of the collective spirit of the masses. There is no power to destroy that, it is ingrained in the very texture of the Spanish masses."

Emma wrote to her friends all over the world about the struggle of the Spanish anarchists, the living embodiment of the ideals by which she had tried to live her life.

They are fighting on because they are the only people in the world who still love liberty passionately enough to be willing to die for it. I should not have believed such a thing possible had I not seen with my own eyes the epic greatness of the Spanish people. Their defense of Madrid, their superhuman struggle now to defend Catalonia against all odds. Whatever the outcome of the unequal struggle, the contribution they have already made to the greatness of the human spirit that will not be daunted can never die and never be lost.

My work for my Spanish comrades, while bringing but meager results for them, has meant the greatest experience of my public life. It has given me the opportunity to come in contact with men and women of the rarest type, and it has helped me to overcome the great loss I have sustained in the end of my lifelong friend.

The Spanish anarchists, in fact, had inspired the whole world, and their heroism gave Emma some sense of humility about her own life and work. Their noble failure allowed her to see her own limitations more clearly, without obliterating her sense of worth.

She was drawn back to Spain as much to renew her spirit as to aid the Spanish people. From Barcelona she wrote friends, "Spain is too fascinating even if terrible in some respects, one cannot escape its sway. Like a grand passion it holds one tightly clasped in her arms."

But, of course, she could not shield herself completely with such thoughts. The situation in Spain, and throughout the world, was growing worse. It was a dismal period in Western history, with the specter of war and atrocity haunting everyone. Emma's own prospects for happiness diminished accordingly, and her old sadness took hold of her again: "The world is in such a frightful condition that one can hardly expect anything in one's own life. For myself, I have lost all consciousness of my individual tragedies and comedies. The sorrow, suffering and sacrifice of the people in Spain and the awful harrowing misery in Germany have quite obliterated on my part any personal hopes."

Now that Emma had dared to speak out against the CNT-FAI cooperation with the communists, the more militant AIT in Paris allowed her presence at a December 1917 international conference, in an attempt to make peace between the factions that had developed among the anarchists. Emma was glad to leave Spain to do something that might ultimately prove constructive. Emma came as an observer at the request of the CNT. Although at first there was some opposition to her participation, because of her past involvement with the CNT-FAI, Emma was allowed to speak. In a moment of political wisdom, she did not express her most extreme position against the policies of the anarchists in Spain. Instead, she spoke out against the forces behind the impending second world war, which made the fight against fascism ultimately most critical. Even if the Spanish anarchists had made mistakes, she asserted that theirs was the only significant arena for anarchist ideas in the modern world and that now they needed support more than criticism.

Doing political work alone, as she had long ago, during Sasha's fourteen years in jail, Emma found herself departing from what she thought Sasha would have done in her place. As she confided to Fitzi, she believed that Sasha would have found her defense of the CNT-FAI inconsistent with her basic anarchist stand against any form of government centralism. "If I have continued the work it was only because the Anarchists are hated and maligned by all the rotten Socialist and Communist gang and because the CNT-FAI is engaged in a life-and-death battle with the whole world, Fascist, Imperialist and the so-called

Republics. But it has not been easy, I can tell you." She felt certain that Sasha would have been too uncompromising to share her public position, yet she felt confident in it. She had defended the CNT-FAI "as a mother would defend a condemned son." But while the conference was in session, Emma was offended by the suggestion by the leadership of the CNT that the AIT elicit the support of the Second and Third Internationals against fascism.

Despite the relatively moderate stand she took at the conference, Emma began touring around London and Scotland likening fascism to communism, even implying that the doctrinaire anarchists were just as bad as Stalinists. Her meetings were sparsely attended and often broken up by militant fascists. She began to keep a flask of whiskey under her corset, to fortify herself against the hostility of the audience. Emma sensed the diminishing support for the anarchists, and now believed that the whole world had betrayed Spain.

Emma articulated her analysis of the deterioration of the anarchist cause in Spain:

Unfortunately the evil hour began when Soviet Russia after three and a half months, the most critical months indeed, finally decided to help Spain with arms. It was indeed an evil hour, it was the beginning of the end. From the moment Russian arms and Stalin's satraps arrived, the process of boring from within began, until Stalin's power spread like a contagious disease over revolutionary Spain infecting everybody, even some of my own comrades. . . . During my last visit I succeeded in sending out documentary evidence of the crimes committed by the Spanish Russian Cheka, the number of men in the army killed, the frightful destruction of the collectives and the demoralization the insidious propaganda from Russia succeeded in spreading. All this reached the pinnacle in the May events, but even as late as May 1937, it was still time to check the frightfulness of Stalin's agents. Alas, the leading men in the CNT and some of my FAI comrades were naïve enough to believe that the Communists as a party could not possibly be responsible for the frightfulness created by them. Then, too, they were the first and last to make concession after concession so as to keep the anti-Fascist front intact. They are now paying dearly for it, paying in blood, ideals and in life. The most heartbreaking thing about the collapse of everything is the fact that the CNT and the FAI had built up a powerful movement over a period of many years, a movement for which they had been hounded and persecuted, imprisoned and checked a thousand times. Then to come into its own on the glorious 19th of July, to see the first beginning of the dream realized, to have every opportunity and every chance which they had in the palm of their hands torn from them and gradually robbed of strength and fervour—that is the tragedy of tragedies.

As to the horrible condition of the refugees, for myself I should have preferred death at Franco's hand rather than to be exposed to the horrors of tramping the road from Barcelona to the French border, cold, starved and under constant bombardment, and then to be placed in a perfect hellhole of concentration camps and treated like criminals—that is the hardest thing to bear for me, and I know for many of the comrades the insult and the humiliation they are subjected to must be greater agony than even the hunger and the cold.

... This, my dear, is all I can tell you about the collapse of a great beginning, the greatest in history, and of a struggle that does not know its equal in any centuries.

Given her alienation from the tactical and political direction taken by the Popular Front, all she could do in loyalty to the cause was to set up a Committee to Aid Homeless Spanish Women and Children. Emma planned to solicit support in Canada and the United States, where she thought she would be more effective than in England.

Emma knew that she would be most persuasive in North America if she had recent impressions to bring to audiences there. Yet although she wanted to return to Spain, most of her friends and comrades were afraid that at sixty-nine she would not be able to withstand the shortages of food, the strenuous walking (the use of vehicles was restricted), and the danger of bombardment. Emma, however, was convinced she could manage for a few weeks. She asserted to Fitzi, "As to danger, if I survived

Russia, I will survive Spain. I simply must go back for new impressions. Besides, it will help me greatly if on my arrival in Canada I will be able to say I come directly from Spain. So wish me luck."

Emma visited Spain for the third and last time in September 1938, although it was difficult to scrape together the necessary money, and her health had gradually declined. Renewed contact with the Spanish anarchists always inspired Emma. She wrote friends that she would have given anything to stay; the heroic spirit of nationalist confederation of labor and the anarchist Federation of Iberia confirmed Emma's sense that the Spanish anarchists were the only people willing to live and die for liberty. She continued to do support work in England for the Spanish refugees, despite her weakening condition and the undeniable fact that she could no longer command the audiences she once had, in the United States; she could not rest. Untiringly she spoke out against the injustices she saw wherever she could find a hall or a platform. Her brother Moe, who was a doctor, wrote to her with some humor about her compulsion to right the wrongs of the world: "Why don't you sit down awhile and take it easy—don't be a monopolist . . . they may indict you for the Sherman Anti-Trust Act."

But Emma was impatient at this interim period before she could leave for Canada. As much as ever, she missed the United States: "I have tried desperately to acclimatize myself in other countries. . . . I am ashamed to say that I have not been able to be a great success. I suppose it is more difficult to take root in alien soil, when one [gets] on in years, than it might be in one's youth. I have not ceased to be an Internationalist."

She had sold Bon Esprit the year before and given most of the money from the sale to Emmy, who had already undergone so many surgical operations for her intestinal ailments that the $25 a month that Emma sent her could barely support her.

Whenever Emma thought about Sasha and St.-Tropez, she felt that the "agony of the dead past come to life [was] too hard to bear." To put her life in Europe and her relationship with Sasha to rest, and to obtain money to help Emmy, Emma decided to go to the International Institute for Social History, in Amsterdam, to organize Sasha's and her political papers so that the archive could preserve them for history. Organizing

Sasha's papers as well as donating some of her own was a way of reckoning with her own mortality and feeling close to her old friend again. The more creative and idealistic side of Sasha had written plays, biographical sketches, screen treatments, articles, stray thoughts. Yet, in the process of culling through his personal papers, Emma shed her illusions about him, as she had shed her hope for the Spanish anarchists. She could see the smaller side of him, the aspects that she had chosen not to focus on when he was alive. "Our own dear Sash," she wrote Fitzi, "as time goes on I miss him more terribly although I have come across among his writings some things that hurt like hell and showed me how very naïve and blind Sasha was in many respects. But with all that he looms higher than ever as a truly great personality and my love for him is deeper than ever."

In part, she was angry with him for burdening her with Emmy, whose letters to Sasha about Emma, which Emma had read among his papers, were full of jealous invective. Finishing the work of arranging the archival collections helped Emma put the intensity of what she had lived through with Sasha and Emmy behind her.

By the time Emma was on her way to Canada, Franco had succeeded finally in crushing all opposition; when Barcelona fell on January 16, 1939, after being bombarded by land, sea, and air, the civil war was essentially over. Emma decided to follow through on her commitment to the people of Spain by raising money for the war refugees, but she admitted to Fitzi that in a perverse way she wished she had perished with her anarchist comrades in Spain. "I wish I had remained in Spain—I have lived long enough, the agony over the debacle of the Russian Revolution was enough for one life. Now the Spanish revolution is also to be crushed. Life holds nothing else. I feel like one drowning grabbing the air."

She reached out for Fitzi, in part because Stella had recently suffered a nervous breakdown, and was still not emotionally available to Emma. Fitzi, who had been close to Stella, could provide a connection to Emma's past and still function as a staunch supporter in the present to pull her ashore: "No matter our present void, yours and mine, the years we were together and did our work were rich and colorful as that of few lives. So I am selfish enough to be exceedingly glad that you are in the world, one human being one can turn to for understanding and love." Soon she would be closer to Fitzi, and to Stella. She knew that it might take a year for Stella to revive from her "black depression" and hoped to witness her recovery. Emma believed that Stella had been too isolated in Bearsville, New York, emotionally abandoned by her husband who was absorbed in his own theater career, while Stella worried about the cost of her son, Ian's, college education, went through menopause, and, most of all, had no "outlet for her vivid spirit."

Emma sailed for Canada on April 8, 1939. There was no fanfare on her arrival; the Canadian anarchists, she declared, were "living corpses." Because of her new realism, perhaps for the first time in her life, she was not disappointed. As she wrote to Fitzi, "If I did not know the appalling condition of the Spanish refugees in the dreadful French camps, I shouldn't care if I never again faced an audience. As it is I must move the heavens to raise some money for those I left behind in France and 50 Spanish comrades in London."

In light of the worldwide depression, the prospects for raising money for the Spanish refugees seemed dim; Emma herself had come to Canada almost penniless. To add to her financial stress, Emmy had written her asking for money for a sixth stomach operation and a stay in a convalescent clinic. Emma believed that Emmy was killing herself by having multiple operations but remained dutiful, if unsympathetic. In fact, Emmy died within the year. Emma emptied her pockets to bury the younger woman, though emotionally the two of them had long since given up any semblance of closeness.

Faced with the question of her own financial survival, Emma asked Fitzi to organize a Seventieth Birthday Fund for her. Fitzi rallied to the idea, as did Emma's oldest friends in the United States, including Roger Baldwin, Leonard Abbott, and Harry Weinberger. The birthday tribute was organized by Fitzi, who sent fliers to as many friends and comrades as she could remember. Ben, of course, was among the recipients and offered to distribute information about the birthday event—once again hoping to take over as Emma's manager. He mused to Fitzi, his "Lioness," about the passing years: Emma nearing seventy, himself at sixty, and his mother still thriving at eighty. Three years had passed since he and Emma had been in contact, and although Ben was living with a young woman named Medina Oliver and had had another child, Mecca, he welcomed Emma's birthday tribute as a way to renew their friendship. He wrote to Fitzi:

> EG had a great life before she met me and we had almost ten years together.
>
> And then she had had another twenty exciting years. I think that her decade with me was her happiest and most productive.
>
> America gave her a wonderful opportunity for expression and she accomplished much in the Labor movement, Drama, Birth Control. Russia, Spain, Germany and England have been such a disappointment to her.
>
> Dear "Mommy," she ain't never written none for three years. She became provoked at me for something I was supposed to have said. . . . Medina, my Mate, is all gold and we have a delightful life together. Is it luck, or my just deserts, or is it due to the fact that you and EG and Anna trained me?
>
> EG ought to have a successful lecture in Canada, I hope she can come to America. I am going to Canada to see her, she may not want to see me. But I need to see her for many reasons, I would like to have her go over some of my manuscript, I am writing a book about our ten years [of] propaganda. My other books continue to sell and I have several orders for books and articles. With most of the Doctors in Chicago, I am not making a living.

Fitzi sent Ben's letter on to Emma, hoping to reopen the door to their relationship. But Emma was offended that Ben thought the reason she had not written in three years was that she had been angry with him.

> . . . it was something much deeper, my dear. It was the blow of Sasha's untimely death which had knocked the bottom from under me and during the previous year his illness and our poverty. Then came the Spanish Revolution, its glorious rise and its heartbreaking fall through the dastardly betrayal of the Spanish people by your friends, the Communists. All this completely wiped out the past,

not only with you, but all the years lost their meaning. That, and not anger with you over something you had written or had said, made writing you utterly impossible. . . . Truth is, nothing else matters, public or personal, except my passionate desire to expose the perfidy and black crime committed in Spain by Stalin's henchmen. I hope I am big enough to forgive and forget an injury done me. But I could neither forgive nor forget the betrayal of Spain. The rest of my years will be devoted to the exposure of the scourge that has been imposed on the world by Soviet Russia. Now, I know that you would not understand this feeling, or share it, and there is really nothing else that interests me.

Emma volunteered to help Ben with his manuscript and said she wanted to learn more about his recent life and his family, but she did not want him to come to see her on her birthday, which, the Emma Goldman Seventieth Birthday Fund aside, would never again be a time for genuine celebration, with Sasha's agonizing death marking the event. Besides, a few friends had already reserved her company that day, and Emma much preferred to meet Ben alone. She sent him her "old friendship."

Ben welcomed the idea of spending the Fourth of July with Emma, recalling that they had spent the day together on Catalina Island many years ago. He wrote that he could not understand Emma's sadness about Sasha, who, in his opinion, had "lived a good life . . . was a truly great man . . . had a fine brain and much courage . . . did his work well . . . served liberty and mankind." He countered Emma's sadness about the Spanish rebels, too, affirming that they had bequeathed an inspiration to the world, as had America's Abraham Lincoln Brigade, who had fought with them. As for Emma's assertion that he had had an affiliation with the communists, he denied any such thing, citing as proof his being banned from their meetings because of his connection to Emma.

What he really wanted to tell her was that she should not focus on the misery of the world. She had to learn about positive "faith" in the future. "I have faith in the God of the Cosmos*** It is all right, yes, everything is all right. Please, I know about Poverty, Disease, Prisons, War, Alcohol and Despair. But I am fairly content and the future is bright. Brutus and Mecca are such joys. You see, Blue Eyed Mommy, I have Anarchism, Revolution, Jesus and Religion to comfort me."

Emma was strangely receptive to Ben's message, which meant so much to him that he felt as though the circle of their relationship had been completed.

My dear EG Mommy:

Your beautiful, soul-warming letter came to me. It's the letter I've been waiting for for years—to know that you feel kindly and somewhat appreciative of our work together and that you are sharing your troubles and your confidences and our defeat and your victories with me is all that I ever asked for. . . . You see, Mommy, I have disappointed so many women and great is my sin and great is my punishment. . . . Of course, dear old friend, I'm not disappointed or vexed that you can't give me any more than you can give. I understand the sands of seventy flow slowly, and with a Franco and a Hitler and a Mussolini and war and hatred in the world, you at most having so few years left to work, wanting to devote yourself to what is most important. So when I come to you, give me what you can of your love and your time. I hope we will have a few days to get some things down on paper. I have a market for an article on TEN YEARS WITH EMMA GOLDMAN. I wanted so much to write something that you would be proud of, that would tell the story of how you took a hobo and made a crusader out of him. I wanted to tell the power of anarchism, the glory of freedom. . . . The past week my diabetes and nephritis have caught up with me. And I broke out with a painful boil on the spot where I sit down so much. . . . And, as I lay at home suffering and my mother and Brutus putting hot cloths on my boil, instead of thinking about our joys and victories together, I think about Alexander Berkman, and the pain that drove him to despair. . . .

Of course, it's very selfish and cheap to be consumed by your own pain, with 10,000,000 unemployed and millions of refugees and hundreds of tyrants. But that's life. I hope for us, dear Mommy, that our faith and our love will never desert us as it did Berkman. I hope we can—that's the terror of self-destruction. It's a bad example for those who remain. I hold your hand, I look into your lovely blue eyes. I would weep.

With love,
Ben

Both Ben and Emma were susceptible to depression around the anniversary of Sasha's suicide. In Emma's affectionate response to Ben was an acceptance of the ups and downs of their relationship, a tolerance she did not always have.

Dear Ben.

I received your very nice letter for my 70th anniversary, and also a short scrib arrived yesterday. For a man who swears by Jesus, you are of faint heart to doubt my feeling about the ten years we spent together. I admit they were for the most part very painful years for me, and no doubt also for you. But I would not have missed knowing such an exotic and primitive creature as you. And I have always told everybody what a worker you were, in fact, the only man of all the men I had known who had completely dedicated himself to the work and aims that were the strongest raison d'être in my life. . . . You must remember my saying that there is no sinner who is not also often a saint, or vice versa. You certainly were both.

Emma went on to tell him of the tributes she had received on her birthday. Rather than listing people who had forgotten her, as she might have in the past, she felt at peace with the love that had been expressed for her. And like the Anarchist Queen she once was, she held court in Canada.

. . . my comrades have not forgotten me, in fact, they gave of their love and their admiration more profusely than at any time since I entered the Anarchist ranks. When you [are] here I will let you read all the cables, wires and letters that came from Europe, the

States and Canada. . . . Naturally I was moved most deeply by the tribute paid me by my Spanish comrades. It is the most beautiful tribute I have ever received. All in all, I was tremendously enriched this year.

The high point for her was a letter in broken English from her comrade Mariano Vázquez—the exiled leader of the CNT, now representing an amalgam of libertarian groups founded in 1938, the MLE, Movimiento Libertario Español — which captured the mutual admiration between Emma and the Spanish anarchists. It also sealed her personal bond to Vázquez and the CNT, though they had disagreed politically at the end of the civil war.

Dear and admired comrade Emma:
. . . Seventy Years! A whole life consecrated to the service and liberation of the people!
These seventy years truly represent incessant labor and sacrifice which shall never be forgotten by us.
You represent living and vibrant experience! You are the incarnation of the eternal flame of the ideal which you have demonstrated in your own life. The Spanish Militants admire and revere you, as Anarchists should know how to admire and value those of a great heart and abiding collective humanism. . . .
We express our fervent hope and desire that you may continue to dwell in our midst for many years to come.
SALUTE MOTHER EMMA!
We declare you our spiritual mother and in proof of our admiration we promise you once more that we will follow your example of sacrifice, austerity and unswerving constancy you have shown all through the years in the face of social injustice, inequality, cruelty and lack of appreciation of your grand aim.
We pledge ourselves before you to remain at our posts as the advance-guard in the battle for the liberation of the masses and the emancipation of the proletariat.
Dear and revered comrade Emma, accept our must cordial and sincere salutation on this your seventieth anniversary.

Emma's initial contact with the Spanish anarchists may have been arranged by Mollie Steimer and Senya Fleshine, but it was a fated love match from the beginning. This tribute brought her back in touch with the warmth and vitality of her first impressions of the Spanish anarchists. She felt compelled to return their kindness.

In response to all her birthday wishes, Emma sent out a general letter of appreciation and a request for a celebration of her next anniversary, the day she had left Rochester, August 15, which would mark the fifty years since her arrival in New York, a kind of political birthday for her. The purpose of this celebration would be to raise money for the Spanish refugees. She ended her letter:

> Today I wish to close with overflowing thanks and appreciation for all you have given me for my 70th anniversary. You can rest assured that as long as life will last me it will be devoted to the realization of our ideals and to the service of our Spanish comrades, who have set us such glowing examples of revolutionary zeal and determination to conquer fascism and to establish real freedom and well-being in their beautiful country.
>
> To save my comrades and friends the trouble of putting up a monument on my grave, I intend to ask them to help create a permanent Emma Goldman Spanish Repatriation Testimonial on August 15.

Emma confided in her old friends the Rockers that if it were not for Spain, "I shouldn't continue." Even though she was given abundant personal and political recognition on her birthday in June, and on the fiftieth anniversary of the first day of her political blossoming in New York City in August, the autumn in Canada was a period of relative isolation and her spirits sank even lower. "I am so terribly cut off from all intellectual contact. I grow so depressed and unhappy at times it seems I could not stand it another day."

Supporting herself after all these years felt like drudgery, and she resented that despite all the work she did for the anarchist movement, she could not rely on the comrades to provide for her. There had always been several people who intermittently gave her money, but her finances were unpredictable. Emma was generally able to displace her insecurity about her own financial predicament by focusing on those less fortunate than she. The homeless women and children of the Spanish Civil War preoccupied her now.

Amid her work for the Spanish refugees, she continued a busy schedule of heartfelt reunions across the border with friends and family who had not seen her since Sasha's death. She had to postpone Ben's visit because of other commitments, but he, uncharacteristically, showed none of the old defensiveness, and whimsically signed his reply,

> Keep sweet, get passionate
> Until I see you Friday
>> Love
>> HO BO

But just before he was to see Emma, Ben remembered the emotional distance between them, and quite possibly the lingering anger he felt as well. He wrote Emma a note saying that he had been trying to work himself into a creative mood, so that he would be able to take copious notes when he visited her, and instead was feeling "dull and uninspired." He added, perhaps with unconscious hostility, that although he and Emma had done more for the birth-control movement than Margaret Sanger, who "demanded the credit and took the glory," he had been encouraging women in Chicago for years since to have children despite poverty, depression, or the threat of war. He was convinced that "babies were essential for a completed life for many women."

The aging Ben was still breathtakingly erratic in his judgments. Although he had written to Emma about the horrors of Hitler, he wrote to another friend in 1939 about his fascination with Hitler as a "skilled propagandist" who "tamed the Jews." With a self-hating anti-Semitism Ben wrote:

> I think Hitler has made a more important contribution to society than has any Jew that ever lived with the exception of Jesus. All irritants, all tyrants, are more important than creative artists,

slaves, or industrialists. . . . Hitler stripped the Jew of his commercialism, vulgarity and egotism. He made the Jew prove that he can
fight and organize and be loyal to his own people—that is important. Please don't worry about the Jews. They have survival
qualities, capacity to suffer and faith that will enable them to
surmount every kind of persecution.

He continued this letter with his own form of American optimism,
asserting that since in America the Constitution guarantees that all
people are created equal and entitled to the same pursuit of liberty and
happiness, the United States was not fertile ground for anti-Semitism.

On the day Ben was due to arrive at Emma's for their grand
reunion, she wrote to Fitzi to help pass the time, since he was late, and to
share her feelings with someone who had known both Ben and her in
the old days:

Ben R. was to arrive this morning. So I got up at six o'clock and
cleaned my apartment. It is about 3 P.M., he is not here. I suppose
he will come. What tricks fate plays us. There was a time when
Ben's arrival made me tremble in every nerve and count the
seconds, though I knew that each reunion broadened the breach.
Now it is so immaterial, as if I had never been bound by him, or
rather my passion for him. Naturally I will entertain him the best I
know how, though I hope he can afford a hotel for a few days. I
really would rather not have Ben in close proximity. The dead is
buried and no one can resurrect it. Well, I will see. One thing is
certain, he has not changed in the least, as the copies of his letters
he writes will show you. A strange mixture, this Ben.

While Ben stayed with Emma, she helped him to recall their past
together for his book. In the process, she soon remembered the aspects
of Ben that had repelled her. They talked over old times, acquaintances,
and the political significance of the events of those years. In almost every
instance, Ben fell short of seeing what was of value in Emma's eyes.
Rather than directly discouraging him from publishing anything about
their relationship, Emma asked Fitzi to do the dissuading:

About Ben R. and his book on ten years with me. I realize it will be a mess, as everything published under his name. The man never learned to write or to take his time doing it. But the only one who can prevail upon him not to do anything on his new obsession is you. Ben always had a great regard for you and I am sure he still has it. If you would write him to say that my name should not be dragged into the limelight until the matter of my re-entry is decided one way or another, I am sure Ben will postpone his masterpiece. Please do it, darling. You see, my dear, I myself being involved in Ben's new mania, it is impossible for me to ask him to leave off publicity for the present. But you can easily do it. Please write him.

Ben felt wounded by the suggestion that anything he might write about his relationship with Emma could jeopardize her chances of obtaining a visa. It touched a sore spot for him—Emma's account of him in her own autobiography. He protested to Fitzi that "Emma's *Living My Life* hurt me, branded my soul much more than the vigilante's scar did my buttocks in San Diego." He went on to explain that something far more damaging was about to be published about the two of them—a book "conceived in malice," which Ben was trying to counteract by publishing something of his own.

Excerpts of what Emma agreed was a vulgar book were sent to her, for her legal approval, in manuscript form by the prospective publisher. At first, she assumed that Ben had commissioned it, as part of his craving for publicity. She read eleven chapters about Ben's relationship with her, which vulgarized the story presented in her own autobiography without giving the source. The biographers, Elmer Gertz and Bruce Milton, in *Clown of Glory: The Reitman Tale*, attempted to psychoanalyze Emma's every thought when she was with Ben. "It made me want to vomit," she wrote to Fitzi. ". . . as I have always fought for the right of free expression I could not very well hold up the rotten stuff about my affair with Ben. I really don't much care anyhow. It is so far removed from me as if it had never happened. But is it not just like Ben to choose . . . such an exhibitionist . . . to write his life?"

What Emma did not know was that Ben also was upset by the

biography, especially a chapter about him called "The Most Vulgar Man in America": Emma had seen drafts of only a portion of its chapters. Although she agreed that her affair with Ben merited a book, she did not want it to be vulgar or sensationalized. And, too, at this point in Emma's life she saw herself more as a political heroine than a lover.

Ben's somewhat farfetched account of how the book came to be written included his own indirect attack on Emma:

> I quarreled with one of the authors and he said "I'll fix you, you bastard. I'll expose you. I'll write a book about you." And the book is a vindictive, amateurish, spiteful biography. In an introduction of mine which will appear in the book I said, "If Emma Goldman could live and work with me for 10 intense years and then label me a thief, because, out of the tens of thousands of dollars we earned together, I sent a few dollars to my mother, while Emma sent thousands of dollars to Berkman and other comrades and then the authors could take up the cry 'Thief, thief,' I have no objection. 'Go on, you hyenas; feed on my blood. It is your funeral feast.' I deny nothing, I do not ask the publishers to change 'one jot or one tittle.' To those who choose to believe it, everything said about me is true, only it is worse."

Fitzi, the go-between, sent Ben's letter on to Emma, who was unsympathetic to his plight although in agreement that the book was a vicious attack on Ben. Emma then responded to Ben's thinly veiled hostility in the introduction:

> Poor, martyred Ben, I made him out a thief. I did nothing of the kind. I described Ben's character, seeing himself in every book he ever read and becoming obsessed by it, as he did with Boyer's work *Confession*, and by Lawrence's *Sons and Lovers* and so many others. As if I cared what he did for his mother, or how much he gave her. It was the underhand way he used, the lies he told when the receipts proved short. As he did with the hundred or more women he confronted me with. I thought it was all dead and buried. But there is no escaping Ben. He clings like a leech. . . . But as I said, I

cannot invoke the court against the book. . . . Besides, the tragedy of Spain and the suffering of our comrades shove everything else in the background. Ben and his affairs pale into nothingness in the face of this overwhelming calamity.

Eventually, Ben was persuaded by Fitzi to write to the publisher and the authors of the forthcoming *Clown of Glory: The Reitman Tale*, stressing that anything sensationalistic about Emma could damage her chance of ever entering the United States again. Eventually, the project was canceled, and Ben even slowed work on his own book, in deference to Emma's wish to return to the States.

Emma and Ben's relationship remained at a stalemate, however, for several months, until Emma received word that Ben had had a stroke in October. Then she overlooked their squabble and wrote to him as an old lover, with kindness and a trace of humor:

> I am frightfully sorry, dear Ben, that you were stricken. I cannot say I am surprised, with the pace you kept all your life. I hope you will lay off for a while. I mean rest as much as possible. I know you still attract the ladies. But the heart is not so young any more, hence cannot respond to your affairs d'amour. Seriously speaking, dear Ben, you should make up your mind and sit back and invite your soul in wisdom and contemplation. . . . Your old friend.
>
> Emma

At first, Ben despaired over the limitations of his weakened body; all he felt he had left to him was the possibility of writing his account of the time when he was politically active with Emma. He could hardly tie his own shoes or button his clothes, and had to stay on a rigid diet coupled with insulin injections. True to his character, however, he came to see this illness as a time to start over, writing to Emma:

> At 62, I have to begin life anew. I'm somewhat in the same position that I was when we separated and I came back to Chicago to start life anew. . . . The ten years with Anna and Brutus were blessed. I made a great deal of money. Incidentally, I haven't made a living

since she died ten years ago. This last illness of mine and being forced to give up my office and practice and be cut off from making a living was quite a shock to me, and my ego is considerably punctured, although the deflation is not complete. I never realized my limitations and poverty so much before in my life. In the 15 years I have been in my office, I've had over 6,000 patients. In two months they all disappeared, and not one account was collectible. My publishers, the Vanguard Press and Macaulay Company [who published *The Second Oldest Profession* and *Sister of the Road*], both sent me a check when they learned I was ill. A few friends saw my needs and tried to help but "my public" deserted me. . . .

I realize for the first time in my life that I didn't belong to the anarchists and the radicals, nor did I belong to the sociologists and criminologists, the groups that I have devoted so much of my time to in the last 20 years. You have so often quoted Ibsen, "That man is strongest who stands alone." I have been with the mobs and the crowds and the groups and the meetings so long that I had forgotten how to stand alone. . . . I'm not frightened, or fearful. I'm only shocked to find out how little use or value I have been to the multitudes I have worked with. I always felt that, if ever an emergency arose, some University or Foundation would give me a scholarship, or make me a grant that would enable me to do a sociological treatise covering my experiences with the unemployed and the hobo and the birth controllers and the anarchists. I have thousands of letters, pamphlets and documents which might easily be incorporated into a sociological treatise. I've applied to the Social Science Research Group, the Guggenheim Foundation, University of Chicago and a number of other groups and they have all turned me down. I'm either too old or too unreliable, or too limited—at least too unsatisfactory—for their use.

This, of course, is not surprising. It's only disconcerting—to realize that you're not acceptable to God or the Devil. You always said I'd go back to the church—well, the joke of it is, the church don't want me. . . . My one ace in the hole is to go back to the practice of medicine. . . . We had worked out a simple technique for the prevention of syphilis and gonorrhea, and had developed a satisfactory method of propaganda in teaching venereal-disease prevention to the public . . . so successful . . . the Chicago Board of Health and the U.S. Public Health Service kicked me out.

No, I'm not discouraged. I have a home, a delightful big son, a beautiful 3-year-old daughter and a comrade, and I have a feeble will to go on. I'd like to do [an auto]biographical novel and tell about the wonderful moments and propaganda that I've been associated with. I hope this message finds you well and cheerful, and that you are doing things you want to do.

With love,
Ben

Emma stopped trying to dissuade Ben from his by now obsessive desire to tell his side of their story and thereby guarantee his immortality; instead she tried to give him back some of the confidence he had lost, but she could not console him without belittling him at the same time:

I received your letter of the 13th. Coming from you it was a very depressed and sad letter. . . . I hope that your mood was only temporary. I realize what your physical shock and even more so the moral shock you received must have been when you found out that the world goes on without us. It will not leave a scar. I cannot imagine it in you. . . . I felt all along since I have known you that you are entirely too optimistic about the effect of your work and the so-called appreciation, applause and flattery you received. I was afraid that some day you might wake up and find everything so superficial. However, I know that you will regain your old happy-go-lucky spirit. But first of all you must get well. . . . I rather think that with all your disappointments you still have reasons to be exceedingly glad. According to your own account, you have a great son, a lovely girl-child, a companion and a lot more. So you are still rich, my dear, much more so than tens of thousands of people who have nobody and who are wanted nowhere. I am glad that you are not among them. . . . One lives from day to day now. . . .

Ben began to think that if he never lived to complete his own autobiography, perhaps he could influence others to write well of him. To Herbert Blumer, then a professor of sociology at the University of Chicago and a former "dean" of the Hobo College, he wrote, "If you ever write about me say that my greatest value was not my nuisance value. Just say, he lived and died like an anarchist, he had no grievances, not even against the sociologists."

Ben had spent the last month of his recuperation reading Hutch Hapgood's autobiography. Although he considered it more honest than Emma's, he was again dismayed to find that he was remembered most for his vulgarity. He wrote Hapgood: "I've been practicing medicine and writing and lecturing and am just as much of an anarchist (or just as little) as I ever was. And just as vulgar. It's rather interesting to note that the only thing you could remember about me in your book was my vulgarity. That's the thing that struck a great many people."

Hapgood responded with a declaration of his appreciation for Ben:

> I liked you in the old days, in spite of what was to me a needless aggression and what is called "vulgarity." I would not have minded that so much if you had not seemed possessed with the desire to hurt people with it—but yet I felt friendly, as many articles I wrote show—notably "Ben the Bum" and about the San Diego tarring and feathering—I felt something in you was "life enhancing." . . .
>
> I remember how wonderful a salesman you were when working with EG and how you could collect crowds to hear her speak.

Ben acknowledged Hutch's accusations:

> There's nothing else to do but to plead guilty to aggression and vulgarity, and gross stupidity. You see, Hutch, when I came to 210 and was permitted to associate with the anarchists and the genuine intellectuals, I was a hobo, an intellectual ragamuffin. I knew nothing about literature or culture or movements. The only way that I could attract attention was to talk about sex and be vulgar, or shocking.

It seems likely that Ben retained his old habits, if one can judge from his letters (in 1939) to "State Street Blondie," "Blue Eyes," a prostitute named Gretchen in New York, and another woman who referred to him as "Daddy Reitman."

Full of contradictions, the same man who reveled in vulgarity and praised and practiced promiscuity all his life, who wrote "that all men and women should have all the sweethearts they want in freedom and decency," in a treatise on his beliefs, warned his son in a letter:

Your glands seem to be the most dominant force in your life, and you need to be told that all men and women who get more pleasure out of sex than anything else are billetted for serious trouble. You must be warned that there is no free jazzing, and you pay for all love favors. The more women, the more trouble, son. There's not only the danger of syphilis and gonorrhea and pregnancy, but there is the probability that you will make your lady friends unhappy and you may do irreparable harm.

Such advice confirmed that an earlier judgment of Emma's was at least partly true: "Ben's trouble was, and is, that with all his boasted freedom, he is a puritan at heart. He did things he considered wrong. He did not have the courage to do them openly: like all puritans."

Ben actually attributed his physical ailments at this time of his life to his guilty conscience about the women he had left, the child, Helen, from his first marriage to May, both of whom he had deserted, the by now four young children he had fathered with Medina who would no doubt grow up without him, and in general, the trouble he had caused to those closely associated with him.

But in general Ben kept these guilt feelings to himself, and, on the surface, tried to assert his self-worth through action. Imagining that he was still at liberty to "manage" her, he attempted to exploit his new rapport with Emma by taking the liberty of arranging an interview for her with the *Chicago Times* about her current activities. Emma was outraged. The only publicity she would accept was in connection with her meetings. Penniless as she was, Emma was no longer willing to give anything to a newspaper for nothing. She could not even afford to buy Hutch Hapgood's new book.

With this final rebuke, Ben ceased his efforts to be part of Emma's public life. The most he could do for her was to get Hapgood to send her a free copy of his book. Despite the temporary revival of their friendship, Ben had become smaller in Emma's eyes since Sasha's death. She had no patience for him anymore. Emma had no greater patience for the course her political life had taken.

Lecturing in Canada in the fall of 1939 was no way to survive financially or spiritually, given the worsening political situation in Europe and the limitations by the Canadian government on what she could speak about publicly. She could not directly address the political situation in Canada, or lecture against conscription. Although eight hundred people came to one lecture, it was now a rare occasion for Emma to attract such an audience. She could still write what she wanted, but, in the Depression, was unable to find a publisher willing to give her an advance for an unwritten book. Emma felt gagged and lonely. Periodically, waves of mourning for Sasha overtook her. She longed to speak out as she had done in the old days with him, and most of all she longed for the camaraderie they had shared.

A few months over 29 years since Sasha and I began a large anti-war campaign. It only lasted six weeks and all we had labored for through the years was swept away as by a tornado. Now, when I have nothing to lose and would willingly take a stand against the new horrors, I have no Sasha at my side or anyone else. No movement and no comrade willing to risk anything except an Italian chap, and in his case it would mean deportation to Italy. I cannot take that responsibility. In my case it would probably also mean deportation, to England. The very thought makes me shiver. I have suffered misunderstanding and accusations of the most fantastic manner in that shopkeeper country. I cannot face it again. In other words, it means to be condemned to silence when one wants to cry out against THE MADNESS, the hypocrisy, the awful sham.

It was "the Italian chap" who stayed by her side until the end, as she stood by him. Emma's dedication to saving this young man typified her pattern of escaping an unpleasant personal situation through ennobling work. Her efforts to save *his* life, in fact, saved her own as well. She had met Arthur Bortolotti in 1934, when she came to Canada en route to the United States. They had spoken on the platform together on the anniversary of the deaths of Sacco and Vanzetti. Arthur even urged her not to go on her 1934 tour, not to submit to the United States government's restrictions during the three-month term of her visa. Anxious to return to the United States, she had become angry with her purist comrade. By 1939 he had been in Canada for twenty years, but he, like Berkman before, refused on principle to take out citizenship papers. He devoted himself to anarchist activities, notably to a fight against fascism. After a new War Measures Act was passed, he and three other anarchists were arrested for possession of subversive literature. It was alleged by *The Nation* that the prosecution of the Italian anarchists was a test case to see how much censorship could be enforced during the coming war without eliciting mass protest.

Emma began to organize a support committee in Canada and in the United States, to exert pressure for the release of the four anarchists and to pay for the legal battle that was being waged for them.

Suddenly, Emma found herself "at my old job—trying to help someone out of the clutches of the police." And in being "busy as a bee" looking after the four Italian anarchists, she stopped pining for the public limelight. Concerning a dinner Fitzi was organizing in her honor, she wrote, "Never mind about any dinner for me. I have lost the desire for it when I realize the difficulties, especially now, when all my thoughts are centered on how to save Arthur and the other comrades. So don't bother anymore. One cannot stand out against an avalanche."

The situation was urgent: Bortolotti faced additional charges of possessing two revolvers and of having violated his residency rights as an alien in Canada, which would be cause for his deportation to Mussolini's Italy. Since it was difficult to do support work in Canada, "with no movement of any kind," Emma asked Fitzi, in New York, to organize further help in the United States:

They were arrested October 4, their house raided and literature confiscated just five days after the new War Ruling has been passed. It's a very drastic law. . . . If it succeeds, our comrades are likely to be locked away for a number of years. Besides that, their conviction and sentence would establish a precedent and would strengthen the Law in grabbing anyone who happens to look askance at the powers that be. . . .

You see, Arthur is the most outstanding comrade among the Italians, very intelligent, well-informed and an idealist if ever there was one. You would love Arthur if you knew him. . . . If he were sent to Italy—the very thought makes me shiver. We simply cannot permit such a thing. So far I have carried the whole brunt of raising money for the defense almost alone. . . . But it is not only the money, it is also some moral backing for Arthur. A sort of SAVE BORTOLOTTI COMMITTEE, or something.

Fitzi refused at first, but Emma insisted, maintaining that few others in the movement were as well known or as well liked as she was—or as capable. Emma feared that any delay might mean that Arthur would soon be in "some concentration camp in Italy or dead." By the end of November 1939, Fitzi reported that she had "been on the go all week on the Bortolotti case." She wrote: "Well, Emma darling, I don't know what to say to you in your anxiety for Bortolotti—you know, with all the protest and publicity and money for Sacco and Vanzetti they were finally executed—and the work we did for Mooney and Billings, after twenty-two or -three years they are now what is called 'free.' I will do what I can. I can't say more."

Emma had not formally abandoned her Spanish comrades, but the immediacy of Arthur's case swept her up. Bortolotti was a man toward whom she felt personally and politically attracted, and, unlike Spaniards, he was part of her everyday existence. She wanted to see the effect of her work and to save this one individual—a young man who had enhanced her life in Canada. She enlisted the help of a young woman named Dorothy Rogers, a kindhearted anarchist, to act as her secretary on the Bortolotti case in Canada, while she toured Winnipeg to give lectures on drama, the war, and "Stalin—the Judas of Spain," and to attend meetings that had been arranged long before the case arose. Even though Emma had not "seen a penny from lectures in I don't know how many years," she kept lecturing. Her last tours in the United States had not been financially successful, yet she clung to the belief that if she were ever able to re-enter the United States, she could make herself financially independent by lecturing. But for the moment, Emma realistically assessed her situation and gave up hope of any immediate return. She was content to work from Canada to save Arthur Bortolotti. Every request to allow her to return had been turned down, and to petition Roosevelt "would feel like spitting in my own face." Twenty years after her deportation, there was too much public resistance to Emma's re-patriation, and Emma herself was still too angry either to compromise or to scheme, no matter how much she wanted to get back.

When she returned to Toronto from her Canadian lecture tour, she found that her mail had been held up for six weeks, after one of the Windsor papers labeled her "the most dangerous woman in the world." But this did not dishearten her: it was renewed proof that Emma had not lost her power to inspire and persuade audiences, which was her most deadly weapon against the state.

She continued to work hard to raise money and increase public support for Bortolotti, while claiming to see in him similarities to Sasha, even down to their initials. He began to fill in for Sasha, as the last platonic love of her life, and she was possessed with the drive to save him. Emma wrote to Fitzi:

> He too is a strange mixture. He is very big in his attitude toward human motivations, he is generosity personified, he spends next to nothing on himself, gives away his earnings as a very skilled mechanic but he hates to accept anything, especially from someone who is not of sterling quality in his ideologic professions.... You and I know how Sasha used to be in some cases. His namesake A.B. in this city is sort of a younger Sasha, ... of the same fine nature and large spirit.

When Arthur was finally released on bail, he had a high fever, so Emma tried to put him to bed in her apartment to nurse him back to health. But neither Arthur nor the other Italian comrades could stop themselves from returning to political activity. His friends, Emma wrote, "are really lovely people and most devoted to him, but they are oblivious to such a thing as illness, or mental stress—a man so sensitive as Arthur must have suffered in jail." Emma thought Arthur "frightfully run-down" after fourteen weeks in jail. She was worried that he would have no time to recuperate before being imprisoned again.

Whenever they took some time to relax in the midst of their work, Emma always asked Arthur to drive her to the Canadian border; there she would sit and stare at the America that she loved, tears streaming from her eyes.

Bortolotti, too, wanted to take care of the woman who had been so devoted to him. As soon as he regained his balance and some steady work, Arthur began to search for a house to buy for Emma, Dorothy Rogers, and himself. His mother in Italy had just died, and Emma's vibrant and somewhat motherly presence comforted him. These were wrenching times, and the image of some stability was attractive to all of them.

On February 13, the immigration board ordered him deported for an illegal-entry offense committed ten years previously. Emma, who had been feeling tired and run-down herself, quickly forgot her own aches and pains, even warnings to watch her diet. She ate as she liked, and worked at the quick pace she preferred. In a letter to Ben, she complained about the general lack of willingness in the anarchist movement, in both Canada and the United States, to do the hard work necessary to free Bortolotti. "There is no spirit of helpfulness or interest in the fate of human beings, so most of the work has fallen on my old shoulders. I do not regret it, because I would rather be kept busy than mope about my own future. One lives from day to day now."

There was still more work to be done in arousing public sentiment, since an appeal on the Bortolotti deportation decision was to be heard by the Minister of Ottawa. Emma was so busy that she quickly turned down a chance to return to the States for a family visit, rationalizing that it would be intolerable to accede to the government's condition of silence.

The very thought of having to watch every step and count every word while on a visit in America gives me shivers. It is painful enough here to be compelled to keep silent while my whole being is convulsed with indignation against the frightfulness in the world. Oh, I realize that nothing I might do would have the slightest effect on the world situation. It's not that. It is that I feel all bottled up and stifled in the atmosphere of cowardly silence. At least, I am not known here, and there is no public opinion of any sort to which to appeal. It is different in America. My whole life is centered there. I know if I could speak out I would be heard by the few at least, if not by the many. Also I could raise some money to save Arthur Bortolotti and for my unfortunate Spanish friends. What sense would it have to come on a visit if that implies inactivity and silence? I just could not face it.

On a snowy Saturday night, February 17, 1940, Emma waited for Bortolotti, who had gone to pick up some comrades in his car and bring them to her flat for a meeting of the Toronto Libertarian Society. To pass the time, she played cards with Dorothy Rogers and two young Dutch comrades from the floor below. She could do nothing halfheartedly. After one of the cardplayers took his turn Emma exclaimed, "God damn it, why did you lead that?" They were her last words. She fell over; at first, the comrades thought she had leaned down to look for a dropped card.

Emma suffered a stroke that left her speechless, one side of her body completely paralyzed. Bortolotti was alerted, drove back in a panic, and arrived with the other comrades to find her lying on her bed, eyes full of fear, trying to get up. An ambulance had been called, and within minutes, Emma was on a stretcher. Amid all the confusion, Emma noticed that her long dress had rolled up. In a moment of modesty, and in an effort to maintain her dignity in sickness, Emma used what strength she had to pull down the hem of the dress to cover her naked knee. She was rushed to Toronto General Hospital, where a neurologist determined that diabetes had contributed to the collapse of her cardiovascular system.

The stroke came as a shock to those who had believed Emma's energy was ceaseless. She had not been seeing a doctor regularly, nor had she complained much about her health, except for minor aches and pains. Now she remained in the hospital for six weeks, until the doctors determined that they could do nothing more for her and sent her home under a nurse's supervision. Her first intelligible words were "Stella," and "Sasha." Emma never regained her speech or her ability to move.

On the day of Emma's stroke, Ben had written her a letter that she was never to read, in which he used Emma's inability to lecture as a metaphor for censorship, not yet knowing that she was literally mute:

Poor dear EG, with such great talents, isolated in bleak Canada, unable to talk, write and do such great things, so many things the world needs. Why? Yes, why so many in the trenches, concentration camps. Why?

As I sat in the comfortable hall, listening to Rocker, I wondered why you couldn't be doing the same thing. But why lecture? What lectures or books will stop the war or exploitation? What will do good? What will help? I do not know. How are we going to stop men and women from drinking so much, using dope? Why? How are we going to stop lovers and families from making each other unhappy? You see the horrors of War and Poverty; I see the misery of gambling and drinking, petty quarrelling and jealousy, the desire for revenge, foolish ambition. And the pathos is that nothing can be done to help. We can't even help ourselves. . . .

But you have lived your "Three score and ten." I hope you will have many more healthy, happy, useful years. . . .

Yes, birth and death—up and down we go. Hope springing eternal. It is all worthwhile. None of us know what it is all about. . . .

Keep sweet. Write me when the spirit moves.

With love and devotion,

Your old Hobo,

Ben

This letter was held up along with the rest of Emma's mail until March. Stella, who had rushed to her side despite her own precarious mental health, wrote to Ben about Emma's condition:

> She is still unable to read, so I have put it in her desk, to be given her when she is better, together with the many wires that keep coming for her from friends whom she hasn't heard from in years. . . .
>
> Emma is unable to speak as yet and cannot move her right side. She weeps a great deal and seems fully aware of her helpless condition. She responds by pressing my hand and patting my cheek. . . .
>
> I need not tell you how dreadful it is to watch her helplessness—Emma of all people. . . . I shall stay by her side till she improves and I will make an attempt to bring her back to the States with me. . . .
>
> How I wish she could read the enclosed editorial. This is entirely due to her Herculean efforts in behalf of Arthur Bortolotti.

The widely read editorial Stella sent to Ben was a strong statement in favor of the appeal of Bortolotti's deportation. The writer noted that Bortolotti's anti-fascist activities in Canada had already prompted the ransacking of his home in Italy, so that his deportation would amount to an indirect death sentence from the Canadian government. This editorial, along with other signs of popular opposition to Bortolotti's deportation, was generated by Emma's efforts. The reversal of the decision was her last victory.

Emma lived for three months after her stroke. She could communicate only with grunts and by moving her eyes from one direction to another, in an effort to give expression to her inner feelings. In this physical state, she was visited by one of the other Italian comrades who had been released on bail, who had secured papers from the Mexican Consulate to travel to Mexico. This man came to pay tribute to Emma. When Emma became agitated and motioned with her head to her study,

Dorothy Rogers brought boxes of correspondence to her bedside until she hit upon one that was met by a grunt of approval from Emma. It contained the address of a comrade in Mexico with whom the young Italian man could stay.

On May 12, Emma lapsed into a coma, with Stella, Moe, and Arthur by her side. After thirty hours of unconsciousness, on May 14, 1940, the great orator was silenced forever.

Her body was taken to the Labor Lyceum in Toronto, the Jewish labor headquarters, so that friends and comrades could pay their last respects. Reverend Salem Bland of the United Church of Canada was the sole person to deliver a eulogy. Only now was the United States government willing to allow Emma to return to her chosen home. Her body was shipped to Chicago, to be laid to rest, next to the monument marking the graves of the Haymarket martyrs, at the Waldheim Cemetery, not far from Voltairine de Cleyre. This cemetery was to become populated with many from her old political circles, including Bill Haywood and Harry Kelly.

Less than a dozen friends gathered for the funeral on Friday, May 17, one day before the anniversary of Sasha's release from his fourteen years in the Western Penitentiary. Harry Weinberger, Emma's lawyer and friend of more than thirty years, delivered one of several eulogies. Emma Goldman, he said, was a "tireless, fearless, uncompromising battler for freedom and justice."

> Liberty was always her theme; liberty was always her dream; liberty was always her goal. . . . Emma Goldman in her lifetime had been ostracized, jailed, mobbed and deported from these shores for advocating that which all the world now admits should be brought about—a world without war, a world without poverty, a world with hope and the brotherhood of man. . . .
>
> Courage in Emma Goldman was as natural to her as it was for her to breathe.

He paused, with tears in his eyes and a lump in his throat, then continued to speak as if directly to Emma herself:

Emma Goldman, we welcome you back to America, where you wanted to end your days with friends and comrades. We had hoped to welcome you back in life—but we welcome you back in death. You will live forever in the hearts of your friends and the story of your life will live as long as stories are told of women and men of courage and idealism.

The tearful orations continued, though, as the next speaker remarked, Emma's "eloquence [was] second to none yet uttered by any lips."

Ben is said to have cried, in his melodramatic style, as the last shovel of dirt was thrown on her coffin, "They have taken away my savior and I know not where they have laid her."

Her old friend Ethel Mannin memorialized Emma in her book *Women and the Revolution*:

Red Emma! A four-square, thick-set, domineering little woman, square-jawed, disconcertingly forthright, irascible, and as relentless in her demands on herself as on others where the revolutionary cause is concerned, and behind that forbidding exterior, a martyr burnt up with the flame of her passion for human liberty, a soldier who will die fighting; a warm and gentle woman who has known the love of men, who loves children, who has known many and enriching friendships, warmly and quickly responsive to love and affection, sympathetic to the troubles of her friends, loving beauty and peace, though there has been so little time for either in her crowded life; a truly great woman, a great Person, judged by any standard. Her heart might break; over Berkman, the martyrdom of his fourteen years' imprisonment, the tragedy of his death; over Russia; over Spain; but whose spirit, never! Her whole life is an example of unfaltering courage and unswerving faith, in the face of persecution and bitter disappointment.

The New Republic maintained, "The example of courage that she set during a lifetime should stiffen the backbone of the present generation in the fight which daily grows sharper against hysteria and hate."

Even the *Chicago Daily News* paid tribute to her magnetism, reporting that "Emma Goldman had a powerful seductive voice and 100,000 persons used to hear her every year. . . . She [even] turned a lot of newspaper men into anarchists."

The *Daily Worker*, however, mocked Emma for dying "with the laurels of the capitalist press on her brow. She was the kind of 'radical' they like. . . . Anarchism, a form of petty bourgeois 'radicalism' has always been fertile soil for police spies, provocateurs, and stool pigeons . . . so that when newspapers soaked with capitalist interests . . . welcome her to their bosoms as a 'lover of freedom' they are welcoming back one who never left it."

There was also a memorial service for Emma in New York. Leonard Abbott, who had written for *Mother Earth* as early as 1907, worked with Emma at the Ferrer Center, and had been her loyal friend, described it to Ben: "I felt that I was presiding at the *end* of an era rather than the rebirth of something vital. Anarchism will never really be a vital force unless it can be applied to life (as Emma Goldman applied it) in a compelling way."

Emma's death was the occasion for many from the old *Mother Earth* circle to get back in touch and reminisce about what Emma had given them. To Hutchins Hapgood, for instance, Ben wrote, "my ten years with her was the most important decade in my life and justifies my existence."

Sadakichi Hartmann, the writer-photographer of the early *Mother Earth* group, wrote to Ben, giving him partial credit for Emma's fame and even giving him credit for Emma's immortality because of his promotional efforts, as well as the emotional ingredient he supplied to her own tempestuous nature. "Emma was an exceptional character, a brave woman, a fighter who could deliver a message with flaming enthusiasm and keep it up for many years. Whether her teachings have any economic value, I cannot say, but I know she educated MANY. Half of her success she owed to you, who were so loyal and owned the brutal ability to assist her materially through thick and thin."

By the summer of 1942, Ben was part of a committee to raise money for a monument that was to be erected on Emma's gravesite.

Because the committee had been organized after the fifty-fourth anniversary of the hanging of the Haymarket anarchists, on November 11, 1941, Ben wrote to his comrades about that solemn event, harking back to his days with Emma:

> As I stood there in Waldheim . . . I thought "about the things that were and the things that is." I recalled those ten glorious years with Emma Goldman and wondered where the thousands of people that had applauded Emma in Chicago during her many lectures were. . . . I thought of Emma's beloved comrade Alexander Berkman, buried in Nice, France. I recalled the thousands of meetings at which Emma spoke, the time we were in jail in Portland and San Francisco and Bellingham, Wash., and in New York. . . . The Chicago Anarchists did succeed in giving America the 8-hour day; Emma Goldman's birth-control propaganda was a success. Proletarian literature and poetry and a revolutionary drama was one of the effects of her propaganda. No, Emma, and the Chicago comrades and Berkman, did not work in vain. . . . Emma's grave is unmarked and unknown. . . . I have urged that a small stone be placed at her grave, and later if we can build a real monument, it will be well. Emma Goldman found me an ignorant, hobo reformer. She gave me a soul and a vision. Although her comrades have denied and belittled me, I have never had an occasion to regret that I am an anarchist, and at the close of a long and happy life, I say that Kropotkin, Tolstoy, Proudhon, the Chicago Martyrs, Emma Goldman, Voltairine de Cleyre have given the world a vision of freedom and beauty that is incomparable.

The next year, the fifty-fifth anniversary of the Haymarket executions, Ben visited the Waldheim Cemetery with a reporter from the *Chicago Daily News*. They read the words uttered by August Spies on the gallows, now inscribed in bronze: "The day will come when our silence will be more powerful than the voices you are throttling today." Ben complained to the reporter that he missed his old anarchist comrades— "Now, all we have is Communists—and I don't like them!"

A monument for Emma was finally erected, but so long after she had been buried that it listed the date of her birth and year of her death inaccurately. It displayed a bas relief of Emma's face, by the sculptor Jo Davidson, with her own proclamation: "Liberty will not descend to a people. A people must raise themselves to liberty."

On November 17, 1942, less than a week after he had visited Waldheim Cemetery to commemorate the death of the Haymarket martyrs, the sixty-three-year-old Ben Reitman suffered a fatal heart attack. Chicago's most dignified and least respectable citizens gathered to mourn his passing. It was widely known that he had become the Chicago Mafia doctor to treat and prevent venereal disease in houses of prostitution, that he had opened the first municipal venereal-disease clinic in Chicago, and that, as a sociologist, he had published two books and written close to one hundred articles, studies, and character sketches of the people and conditions that touched his life—not the least of which was a study on techniques for attracting women. Ben had written an unpublished essay on "The Curse of Wanderlust," and in it complained that his money bothered him: "I don't know what to buy." He was nostalgic for the times when he had to "beg or hustle up a few cents to make a purchase of something I needed. Oh, the misery of traveling first class!" He wanted to beg for his meals—"they taste better. I want to get hungry."

> . . . a full thousand hobos and friends of this friend of the denizens of the underworld lined the street as his body was borne to its final resting place beside the Haymarket riot martyrs in Waldheim Cemetery. . . .
>
> . . . he stipulated in his unique will that $250 shall be spent for food and drink for hobos and unemployed who will be invited . . . to a funeral dinner. . . .
>
> He lived with the city's outcast.
>
> He chose his intimates from the radicals and the social uplifters.
>
> He made his bed with the queer and the underworld type.
>
> In his death he bequeathed almost his all to the hungry and the unemployed. He was proud to be buried with those he always regarded as martyrs for the good life.

Ben's gravestone read "Liberty was his life, Liberty in thought, word, and deed." Many anarchists objected, and even threatened in jest to dig him up one day, asserting that since he never belonged in the movement during his life, he should not have such a privilege in death. His gravesite was near, but not adjacent to, Emma's.

Ben's mother, the one woman to whom he had been true his whole life, outlived him. To calm her worries after both he and his brother suffered strokes, he had written, "I hope you don't get excited and rush in—just keep your black dress pressed and your heart pure. [For] both Lew and me, living and loving was easy and a pleasure and so will dying and returning to the elements be."

Ben's son, Brutus, who had become an aviator, died shortly after his father, in a plane crash. Apart from his first child, Helen, Ben and Medina Oliver had four daughters, Mecca, Medina, Victoria, and Olive, all of whom were under six years of age at the time of his death.

Ben repeatedly asserted that his ten years with Emma were his most rewarding—a sentiment Emma echoed throughout her life. It was during those years that love and work, the two needs perhaps most basic to human happiness, were inextricably connected for both Ben and Emma. Often the connection was satisfying, but frequently the conflicts between Ben and Emma, the pulls exerted from public and private spheres, made for a tempestuous relationship—the significance of which overshadowed the many others in Emma's life. The relationship resonates for us through Emma's efforts to make of her life a consistent whole.

Like Emma and Ben, most people seek the shelter of a loving relationship to cushion them from the blows of the outside world and accommodate their needs for both security and independence. Not many, however, try to make the world itself a haven, risking personal comfort in the belief that their voices will be heeded, that their efforts will affect history. Emma tried to do just that; Ben could not. Emma remains a revolutionary figure, Ben a minor, though colorful, reformer.

Emma gave her politics a heart by bringing her longings for love into the public sphere. In so doing, she articulated commonly held, but rarely voiced, yearnings. In a sexually repressive era, Emma dared to speak about intimacy in a political context, to posit the ecstatic experience of romantic love as the ideal state of everyday existence. The hope that fueled Emma's vision inspired thousands of people throughout the world to feel powerful in their personal lives and, in the larger world, to believe in decency as a standard for human behavior.

Although, in part, Emma's ability to recognize and respond to the pain of others was motivated by the sadness and lovelessness of her early life, she had survived her own pain by superimposing upon it a vision of total harmony. No public speech was written without a messianic finale, no anguished love letter was complete without a reiteration of her fixed ideal of what true love could be.

Emma's dream for society and for herself was seductive in its promise of the perfectability of the human spirit. Emma, who feared her own deficiencies, offered an extreme interpretation of the anarchist doctrine that all that was negative in society could be attributed to government and institutional forces, while human nature was inherently benign. She embraced a theory that exorcised feelings of jealousy, personal anger, and aggression, because the thought that such frailties might be part of the human condition was terrifying to her. She often experienced the manifestations of these undesirable aspects of life as a personal affront and countered her chronic disappointment by giving voice to a dream of a world more consistent with her expectations. Often she would say that given a choice she would rather do without reality than give up her beautiful ideal.

Perhaps her very need to protect herself from the darker side of human nature and of herself helps to explain her formidable energy and dedication to the cause. Undeniably, Emma did succeed in moving beyond her particular emotional limitations by giving the world a vision of unlimited freedom. Although the conflicts between what Emma experienced and what she wished for have meaning for anyone who aspires to live honestly and generously—and her disappointments are not alien to anyone who cherishes ideals—the intensity of disappointment she suffered, the depth of her sadness, the compulsion to reproduce patterns of behavior that forced her to confront the same issues again and again, indicate that her reactions were often more rooted in her past than in her present dilemmas.

No doubt, a vision of the world that did not excuse injustice, but still acknowledged human weakness, that aspired to universal harmony without the illusion that antisocial instincts can be banished at will, might have left Emma with a better perspective on her accomplishments. A vision of love relationships that sought to preserve the joy of intimacy without discounting the stresses of daily life, in which one could acknowledge the weaknesses of the other and even of oneself without renouncing either hope or love, might have been more sustaining for Emma, but clearly less exalting.

Emma herself was not entirely unaware of the emotional pitfalls of the road she chose. In her book on modern drama published in 1914, she wrote of Edmond Rostand's allegorical play *Chantecler* in which she identified with the heroic rooster, an "intense idealist ... aglow with deep human sympathies [whose] great purpose in life is to dispel the night. . . . [L]ike all great visionaries, Chantecler is human, 'all too human'; therefore subject to agonizing soul depressions and doubts."

One morning, distracted from his daily task of signaling the change from night to day, Chantecler is dismayed to discover that he is not responsible for causing the sun to rise. The realization leaves Chantecler feeling inadequate and dejected, but he comes to accept that he can do no more than herald the bright promise of each new day. Later in the play, when the nightingale, the friendly rival from whom he reclaims the dawn, is killed, a grieving Chantecler is amazed to hear another, more liquid-voiced nightingale singing in the distance.

Emma applied Chantecler's insights to herself when she counseled her readers to "learn this sorrowful and reassuring fact, that no one Cock of the morning or evening nightingale, has quite the song of his dreams . . . for there must always be in the soul a faith that it comes back even after it has been slain. . . . It is vital to understand that . . . though we cannot wake the dawn, we must prepare the people to greet the rising sun."

NOTES

GUIDE TO THE NOTES

The story of Emma Goldman's inner life as it related to her public life took shape from letters in archive collections throughout the world and published works by and about Emma Goldman. Abbreviations for major individuals referred to in the notes, as well as frequently used books, periodicals, government sources, and archive collections, precede the notes and selected bibliography. When no date could be determined on a letter, "n.d." appears in the notes. For those letters that had no date but for which a date could be determined with some certainty, the date appears in parentheses. A date that appears in brackets is as close an approximation as possible, given the available information. For the full text of the letters, the reader can request copies from the specific repositories. Within the next few years, a complete microfilm of Emma Goldman's letters, government documents, and selected news clippings will be compiled by the Emma Goldman Papers Project under the auspices of the National Historical Publications and Records Commission of the National Archives. A selected letters and government documents letterpress will follow.

ABBREVIATIONS USED IN THE NOTES

Archive Collections

CtY-B	Yale University, Connecticut, Beinecke Library
CtY-SM	Yale University, Sterling Memorial Library, Harry Weinberger Collection, Beinecke Library
CU-BANC	University of California, Berkeley, Bancroft Library
DLC	Library of Congress, Washington, D.C.
IISH	International Institute for Social History, Amsterdam, Emma Goldman Collection
MBU-SC	Boston University Libraries, Special Collections
MCR-S	Radcliffe College, Cambridge, Mass., Schlesinger Library
MiU-L	University of Michigan, Ann Arbor, Labadie Collection
MNS-S	Sophia Smith Collection, Smith College
NARG	National Archives Record Group
NNU-T	New York University, Tamiment Library
NYPL	New York Public Library
WH	State Historical Society of Wisconsin, Manuscript Division
UI-CC	University of Illinois, Circle Campus
YIVO	YIVO Institute

Books, Periodicals, and Government Sources

AAA	*An American Anarchist: The Life of Voltairine de Cleyre* by Paul Avrich
AOE	*Anarchism and Other Essays* by Emma Goldman
FTM	"Following the Monkey" by Ben Reitman
GS	General Services
LML	*Living My Life* by Emma Goldman
MDR	*My Disillusionment in Russia* by Emma Goldman
ME	*Mother Earth*
MEB	*Mother Earth Bulletin*
MID	Military Intelligence Division
NAH	*Nowhere at Home: Letters from Exile of Emma Goldman and Alexander Berkman* edited by Richard and Anna Maria Drinnon
NARG	National Archives Record Group
NYT	*The New York Times*
PMA	*Prison Memoirs of an Anarchist* by Alexander Berkman
RES	*Red Emma Speaks: Selected Writings and Speeches by Emma Goldman* compiled and edited by Alix Kates Shulman
RG	Record Group
RIP	*Rebel in Paradise* by Richard Drinnon

SSMD   *The Social Significance of the Modern Drama* by Emma Goldman
TPA   *The People's Almanac*

Names of Individuals

AB	Alexander Berkman
AI	Agnes Inglis
AS	Agnes Smedley
BR	Ben Reitman
EG	Emma Goldman
EK	Ellen Kennan
FH	Frank Heiner
HH	Hutchins Hapgood
HW	Harry Weinberger
KROH	Kate Richards O'Hare
LM	Leon Malmed
MEF	M. Eleanor Fitzgerald (also referred to as Fitzi and Lioness)
MN	Max Nettlau
MR	Millie Rocker
RR	Rudolf Rocker
SB	Stella Ballantine (also referred to in text as Stella Comminsky and Stella Comyn)
VV	Van Valkenburgh

PREFACE

Page

xiv   a guitar shop: the Fret Shop in Harper Court, Hyde Park, Chicago.

xv   "It is like tearing off my clothes . . .": EG to BR, January 11, 1928. (UI-CC)

xv   the owner of the guitar shop: John Leibundgunth.

xv   Herbert Marcuse: In the spring of 1976, Marcuse taught a graduate seminar for the History of Consciousness Board of Studies at the University of California, Santa Cruz, in which I participated.

xvi   "In letters happily, though tip top . . .": MN to EG, February 16, 1929. (IISH; RIP, 266–67)

xvii "Now, to the point . . .": MS to Candace Falk, January 5, 1978. (Now included in the Emma Goldman Papers Project.)

xvii "look for a Ph.D. student": 1941. (UI-CC)

xviii   Arthur Bortolotti: an Italian anarchist who is still living in Canada. Goldman organized a Save Bortolotti Committee in 1939. See Chapter 18 for more details.

1: SOMETHING TO HIDE

Page

1   "the philosophy of a new social order . . .": EG, "Anarchism, What It Really Stands For," *AUL*, 56.

1   "I want freedom . . .": *LML*, 56.

2   "I know they will not be published . . .": EG to Evelyn Scott, July 5, 1934. (IISH)

2-3   "woven of many skeins . . .": *LML*.

3   "be torn between the yearning . . .": ibid.

3   "I am writing . . .": EG to AB, December 23, 1927. (IISH)

3   "with the sweep of a cyclone . . .": EG to BR, February 14, 1928.

3   "When you read these over . . .": BR to EG, November 28, 1927. (UI-CC)

3-4   "If ever our correspondence . . .": EG to BR, July 29, [1911]. (UI-CC)

4   "I'd rather do without reality . . .": EG to BR, June 22, n.d. (UI-CC)

4   "Do you know, lover mine . . .": EG to BR, September 30, 1908. (UI-CC)

4-5   "You have opened up . . .": EG to BR, September 27, 1908. (UI-CC)

5   "tear at my very vitals . . .": EG to BR, July 28, n.d. (UI-CC)

5   "All is blank . . .": EG to BR, June 1908 (Wed. 4:00 A.M.). (UI-CC)

5-6   "Ben dear . . .": EG to BR, September 28, 1908. (UI-CC)

6   "Mary Wollstonecraft, the most daring woman . . .": EG to BR, July 1911. (UI-CC)

6   "for America like a woman for a man": EG to AB, December 23, 1927. (IISH)

6-7   "About my proposed memoirs . . .": EG to HH, October 26, 1927. (IISH)

7   "Besides, in my case . . .": EG to Frank Harris, October 26, 1927. (IISH)

7   "Letters should only be published . . .": EG to BR, December 30, 1927. (UI-CC)

7   "The worst I would do . . .": BR to EG, January 2, 1928. (UI-CC)

7-8 "Again, let me hold your hand . . .": BR to EG, July 20, 1928. (UI-CC)

8 "primitive": *LML,* 694.

8 "like a narcotic," ibid., 523.

9 "It was very painful . . .": EG to Gwyneth Roe, January 5, 1932. (WH, Roe papers)

10 "We all have something to hide . . .": EG to AB, December 1927. (IISH)

2: THE DAUGHTER OF A DREAM

Page

12 "I was 25 years old . . .": Roger Baldwin, "Recollections of a Life in Civil Liberties," *Civil Liberties Review* 2, no. 2 (1975): 43–45.

12 "an ignorant, vulgar, shrieking harridan . . .": William Marion Reedy, "The Daughter of a Dream," *St. Louis Mirror,* November 5, 1908.

12 "Where there is no vision . . .": Proverbs 29:18.

12-13 "She's a little woman . . .": Reedy, "Daughter of a Dream."

13ff Description of Emma Goldman's early life is pieced together from intermittent references throughout *LML.*

15 For the effects of the death of Emma's brother I am relying on Alice Wexler's discovery, which is treated psychoanalytically in her article, "The Early Life of Emma Goldman," *Psychohistory Review,* 8: no. 4, 1–21.

15 "Stricken with . . .": *LML,* 59.

18 . . . Yiddish stories of Sholem Aleichem: for example, "Tevya."

21 "This is necessary for a girl . . .": *LML,* 21.

22 ". . . between two fires . . .": *LML,* 23.

23 "If you think that by hanging us . . .": article in *The People's Almanac* quoting from August Spies, 42.

25 "Rochester, N.Y. . . .": EG, *ME* V, no. 1 (March 1910): 22.

26 "If we eat grass . . .": "And Tomorrow Will Be Even Nicer," Larry Bush, *Jewish Socialist Critique,* Winter 1980, 2: 15–29.

26 Johann Most: Yvonne Kapp, *Eleanor Marx* (New York: Pantheon Books, 1976), II: 152, 159.

29 "Also your intimacy with F. . . .": AB to EG, December 1928. (IISH)

30 endometriosis: a disease of the uterine lining; characteristic symptoms include the onset of painful or difficult menstruation,

painful intercourse, premenstrual spotting or increased bleeding and menstruation, painful bowel movement or urination, and infertility. This diagnosis is based on physical symptoms described by Emma Goldman in her autobiography in 1931 and checked by C. Falk in 1982 with Dr. Sadja Greenwood of the Min An Health Center in San Francisco.

30 "overcome the strongest . . .": *LML*, 48.

30 ". . . to dedicate themselves to the cause . . .": *LML*, 62.

35 "children should not play with fire"; "All right, grandmother . . .": *LML*, 115.

36 "demonstrate before the palaces of the rich . . .": ibid., 123.

37 "There is no doubt . . .": Voltairine de Cleyre, *In Defense of Emma Goldman and the Right of Expropriation,* published Philadelphia, 1894; lecture delivered in New York on December 16, 1893.

37 ". . . a Judas . . .": *LML*, 60.

38 Ambrose Bierce: 1842–1914, writer and participant in Ferrer School. James Gibbons Huneker: 1860–1921, writer, journalist, American art and music critic. Sadakichi Hartmann: writer, artist, photographer, on the fringe of the anarchist ranks and a participant in the Ferrer School. John Swinton: editor-in-chief of the *New York Sun.*

39 "In our opinion . . .": Len Dehors, August 17, 1892, as cited in Vernon Richard's book, *Malatesta: Life and Idea,* London: Freedom Press, 1961, 69.

40 "anybody or anything": *LML*, 183.

41 "could find expression . . .": ibid.

42 "mania for meetings"; "meetings"; "separations": *LML*, 236.

42 "Havel had once . . .": Paul Avrich, *The Modern School Movement,* 122.

44 . . . WOMAN ANARCHIST WANTED: *LML*, 296.

44 "We stand by you to the last": *LML*, 301.

45 "Acts of violence . . .": *NAH*, 95.

45 "The Psychology of Political Violence": *AOE*, 79–108.

45 "modern martyrs . . .": Björnstjerne Björnson, *Beyond Human Power,* translated by Lee M. Hollander in T. H. Diekenson, chief contemporary dramatist, 1915, 573–97.

45 "the guilt . . .": *AOE*, 86.

45-46 "High-strung . . .": *AOE*, 107–08.

47 "Tante Emma": Yiddish for "Aunt Emma." Emma's real Yiddish name was Charele, given her for her mother's mother, who had died a few months before her birth.

50   "mirrors the complex . . ."; "at once the reflex . . ."; "the dynamite which undermines . . .": *SSMD*, 6.

50   . . . Orleneff to return to Russia: Nazimova decided to stay in America to prepare for the English-speaking stage.

51   "a child born of love": *ME* I, no. 1 (March 1906).

51   *The Masses:* a socialist literary and political magazine published between 1911 and 1917. See Leslie Fishbein, *Rebels in Bohemia,* for a fascinating history of this group.

53   Criminal Anarchy Act: New York Law, 1909 (Consolidated Laws, Ch. 40) Sec: 160 pl. seq, then from 1917–1920 criminal syndicalism statutes were effected in 20 states.

54   "My greatness adds nothing . . .": EG to AB, March 19, 1907. (IISH)

3: LOVE, LIKE A MIGHTY SPECTRE

Page

57   "Yes, I am a woman . . .": EG to MN, October 17, 1907. (IISH)

58   "High Priestess of Anarchism": *Chicago Daily Tribune,* March 6, 1908; this was one among many variants on the royal title that appeared in the press.

59   "all alien anarchists . . .": *Chicago Daily Tribune,* March 4, 1908.

60   newspaper accounts of the beating: *LML,* 415; *Chicago Inter-Ocean,* January 22, 23, 24, 25, 1908; *Chicago Daily News,* January 22, 23, 24, 28, 1908; *Chicago Daily Tribune,* January 24, 1908; *Chicago Record Herald,* January 24, 1908.

60   "He arrived in the afternoon . . .": *LML,* 415–16.

61   "From the moment . . .": ibid., 417.

61   "Prior to meeting Emma Goldman . . .": FTM, 257.

61   "an American by birth . . .": BR, unpublished essay, 1907. (UI-CC)

61   *Sister of the Road: The Autobiography of Box Car Bertha,* as told to Dr. Ben L. Reitman.

62   many "husbands": BR to Theodore Schroeder, October 24, 1942. (UI-CC)

62   stopped his mopping: taped 1982 interview with Herbert Blumer, professor emeritus at the University of California, Berkeley; Blumer got to know Ben Reitman when, as a professor at the University of Chicago, he was asked to be a "dean" at Reitman's Hobo College.

63   "the county jail . . ."; "Hobo banquet"; "Although Reitman declared . . .": Roger Bruns, *Knights of the Road: A Hobo History,* 173–74.

64   "Nearly 200 anarchists . . .": *Chicago Daily Tribune,* March 14, 1908.

64   more genteel . . . more brazen: taped interview between Mr. and Mrs. Bernard Shain and R. Malmed, Leon Malmed's grandson.

64   "Miss Goldman with pinkish cheeks . . .": *Chicago Daily Tribune,* March 16, 1908.

64   "There's plenty of room . . .": ibid.

65   "Anarchism as It Really Is": this lecture evolved into the essay "Anarchism: What It Really Stands For," which is in *RES* and *AOE.*

65   "Captain Mahoney . . .": *ME,* III, no. 2 (April 1918): 74.

65   "The police are here to cause . . .": *LML,* 418.

66   "Ben Reitman, dressed as a tramp . . .": *Chicago Daily Tribune,* March 17, 1908.

66   "clinging to [her] faith . . .": *LML,* 418.

67   "Whatever doubts . . .": *LML,* 419.

67   EMMA GOLDMAN SUFFERS RELAPSE: *San Jose Herald,* March 20, 1908.

67   "a great longing possessed me . . .": ibid., 420.

68   "This is Emma Goldman" . . . "we heard you were back": *Chicago Daily Tribune,* March 24, 1908.

68   "I craved life and love . . .": *LML,* 420.

68   ". . . chumming with detectives! . . .": ibid., 421.

68-69   "I love you, I want you" . . . "I dreamed that Ben . . .": ibid., 421–23.

69   "this primitive creature": ibid., 417.

70   "I want you to rent . . .": EG to BR, October 1, 1908. (UI-CC)

71   "Meetings were veritable encampments . . .": *LML,* 426–27.

71   "flitted hither and thither . . .": *San Francisco Examiner,* March 8, 1908.

72   "Patriotism": *AOE,* 126–44.

72   Emma's version of the Buwalda story can be found in *LML,* 429–30.

73   "How do you do, Miss Goldman?": Judge Advocate General George B. Davis to the Honorable Secretary of War, June 19, 1908. (NARG 60, Records of Adjutant General's Office, #1389930)

73   Theodore Roosevelt wrote a personal letter: Theodore Roosevelt to the Judge Advocate General of the Army, Oyster Bay, New York, June 24, 1908. Ibid.

73 "affairs in the Harbor of San Francisco . . .": ibid.

73 "lawyers, judges, doctors . . .": *LML,* 431.

73 ". . . for LIBERTY": *The Labor World,* April 25, 1908.

73 "The Relationship of Anarchism to Trade-Unionism": the preface to her essay "Syndicalism: Its Theory and Practice"; in *RES,* 64–77.

73 The conservative press . . .: *The Oregonian* (Portland), May 26, 1908.

73 "Do not be alarmed . . .": ibid., May 24, 1908.

74 "it is a mistake . . .": ibid., May 26, 1908.

74 "his blue-eyed Mommy": *LML,* 425.

74 "Mummy Reitman": EG to BR, n.d. (UI-CC)

75 "I have a great deep mother instinct for you . . .": EG to BR, n.d. (UI-CC)

75 "whether love last . . .": "Marriage and Love," *AOE,* 227–39.

75 "Hobo, I am raving . . .": EG to BR, n.d., 1908. (UI-CC)

76 "Have I ever told you the legend . . .": EG to BR, June 1908 (Wednesday, 4:00 A.M.). (UI-CC)

76-77 "Darling, darling . . .": EG to BR, July 3, [c. 1908]. (UI-CC)

77 "intellectually crude"; "socially naive"; ". . . liberal Americans . . ." *LML,* 432.

78 "Good night, or, rather, good morning, dear . . .": EG to BR, n.d. (UI-CC)

78 "obscenity in the mails": Title 18, United States Code, Section 334; currently, Title 18, United States Code, Section 1461.

78 "fountain of life": EG to BR, n.d. (UI-CC)

78 "like a mighty spectre": EG to BR, September 30, 1908. (UI-CC)

79 "would devour you . . .": EG to BR, n.d. (1908). (UI-CC)

79 "take a bath": EG to BR, June 22, 1909. (UI-CC)

79-80 "The day seems unbearable . . .": EG to BR, n.d. (UI-CC)

80 *The Power of a Lie:* see *LML,* 439, for reference.

81 ". . . to understand a thing . . .": EG to BR, n.d. [c. 1909]. (UI-CC)

81 "promiscuity tears my very vitals . . .": EG to BR, July 28, n.d. (UI-CC)

82-83 "The moon standing witness . . .": EG to BR, n.d. (UI-CC)

83 "home of lost dogs": *LML,* 517.

83-84 "But 210 always makes me rational . . .": EG to BR, July 3, [1908]. (UI-CC)

84 "no rebel spirit"; "didn't belong in our movement": AB, quoted in *LML,* 435.

84-85 "a terrible man . . .": interview with Roger Baldwin, May 5, 1982, Oakland, N.J.

85 Senya Fleshine . . . disliked him intensely: interview, November 1977, Cuernavaca, Mexico.

85-86 "Also, dearest, you . . . failed . . .": EG to BR, October 1, 1908. (UI-CC)

86-87 "I have tried hard . . .": EG to BR, September 28, 1908. (UI-CC)

88 "I know the ecstasy . . .": EG to BR, September 28, 1908. (UI-CC)

88-89 "My own, my very own . . .": EG to BR, September 30, 1908. (UI-CC)

89 "Yes, Alex has wonderful qualities . . .": EG to BR, September 26, 1908. (UI-CC)

89 "Just think of it . . .": EG to BR, October 1, 1908. (UI-CC)

90 "Poor forsaken M——— . . .": EG to BR, October 1, 1908. (UI-CC)

90 "If I were religious . . .": EG to Meyer and Sophie Shapiro (friends), December 10, 1908. (UI CC)

90-91 "After ten weeks . . .": EG to [Meyer and Sophie Shapiro], January 4, 1909. (UI-CC)

91 "So you have read of Reitman's . . .": EG to "Dear, dear friend," January 4, 1909. (UI-CC)

91 "putting his weight . . ."; "protesting his arrest": LML, 442.

91 two lawyers offered bail: "Mr. Schamel and Mr. Lynch," according to ibid., 443.

92 "dangerous criminals": ibid., 446.

92 prompted a re-evaluation: William Buwalda to President Roosevelt, January 8, 1909. (NARG 60)

92 "Personally, I do not care . . .": EG to "Dear Friends," January 20, (1909). (UI-CC)

92 "unlawful assemblage . . ."; "preaching anarchist doctrines": LML, 447.

93 "Every gleam of hope is covered . . .": EG to "My dear, dear Friend" (Meyer Shapiro), February 20, (1909). (UI-CC)

93 ". . . your best friends": AB to BR, January 15, 1909. (UI-CC)

94 WASHINGTON REVOKED . . .: LML, 449.

94 Kershner's fraudulent naturalization: John Grunberg, Immigrant Inspector to F. P. Sargent, Commissioner General of Labor, Immigration and Naturalization Service (USINS), D.C. (via S.F.) #51692.

94 "great care not to put the government . . .": (NARG 60, 1909).

4: PROMISCUITY AND FREE LOVE

106   "I love you, dearest . . .": EG to BR, June 17, 1909. (UI-CC)

106-107   "in work, ironing, cleaning . . ."; "Hobo! Hobo! cried my soul . . .": EG to BR, June 19, 1909. (UI-CC)

107   a grand scheme: ibid., and referred to in EG to BR, June 25, 1909. (UI-CC)

108   "Unfortunately I am but human . . ."; ". . . Now, that force has come into your life . . .": EG to BR, June 21, 1909. (UI-CC)

109   "My love has indeed changed my psychology . . .": ibid.

109-110   "Your method of eating . . ."; ". . . Do you think I am less sexed?": ibid.

110   ". . . required no sacrifice on your part . . .": ibid.

110   "There is but one thing . . ."; "followed up his habits . . ."; "a complete slave . . .": ibid.

110-111   "Many people go through life . . ."; "If you could only see . . .": EG to BR, June 23, 1909. (UI-CC)

111   ". . . so generously . . .": EG to BR, June 22, 1909. (UI-CC)

111   Ben's generosity with "his Mommy's body"; . . . "the kind of love . . ."; "If you only knew . . .": EG to BR, June 25, 1909. (UI-CC)

112   "you are light and air . . ."; "wayward and impulsive": EG to BR, August 29, 1909. (UI-CC)

112   "You are just the manager I want . . .": EG to BR, [before August 29] 1909. (UI-CC)

112   ". . . to give you delight . . .": EG to BR, August 29, 1909. (UI-CC)

112   Francisco Ferrer: See Paul Avrich, *The Modern School Movement,* for an in-depth discussion of Ferrer, the Modern School, and its significance.

113   "Through the terrible shock . . .": EG to BR, October 13, 1909. (UI-CC)

113   "ill at ease in the presence of children": interview between Mr. and Mrs. Bernard Shain and R. Malmed, Leon Malmed's grandson.

113   "I have no right to speak . . .": EG to BR, December 13, 1909. (UI-CC)

113   "Marriage and Love": *AOE,* 227-39. "False Fundamentals of Free Love," unpublished.

114   "Your love is all sex . . .": EG to BR, December 1909. (UI-CC)

114   Discussion on the historical significance of Emma's ability to bring private issues into the public sphere informed by conversations with Barbara Epstein, history and women's studies professor at University of California, Santa Cruz; see bibliography.

115-116   "an insurance pact"; "that other paternal arrangement . . ."; "Free love? . . .": "Marriage and Love," *AOE,* 228, 235, 236.

117 "bruised from all the wounds . . .": EG to BR, December [14 or 15,] 1909. (UI-CC)

117 "'Marriage and Love' is hateful to me . . .": EG to BR, December 18, 1909. (UI-CC)

117 "self-respect . . . It's too bad we did not meet . . .": EG to BR, December 13, 1909. (UI-CC)

118 "Perhaps, if my love for you . . ."; "Work? success? . . .": EG to BR, December [14 or 15,] 1909. (UI-CC)

119 "We will keep apart . . .": ibid.

119 "Life is a hideous nightmare . . .": EG to BR, December 12, 1909. (UI-CC)

119 "I shall probably never again . . .": EG to BR, December 16, 1909. (UI-CC)

119-120 "my love for you . . .": EG to BR, December 29, 1909. (UI-CC)

5: ADDICTION TO LOVE

Page

121 "After all, I am right . . .": EG to BR, December 23, 1909. (UI-CC)

122 "I have a horror . . .": EG to BR, December 21, 1909. (UI-CC)

122 "before the mob . . .": EG to BR, December 22, 1909. (UI-CC)

122 "I may be all wrong . . ."; "Do you know the phantoms . . .": EG to BR, December 29, 1909. (UI-CC)

122 "hoped to give . . .": EG to BR, December 30, 1909. (UI-CC)

122 ". . . never so miserable in my life . . .": EG to BR, January 1, 1910. (UI-CC)

122 "How could you think . . .": BR to EG, January 23, 1910. (UI-CC)

123 "burying the magazine . . .": ME IV, no. 11 (January 1910): 343.

123 "White Slave Traffic": ME IV, no. 11 (January 1910): 344–51; reissued as "The Traffic in Women," which appeared in AOE.

125 She told one audience: from NYT article, December 13, 1909.

125 "Yes I may be considered . . .": "The Tragedy of Women's Suffrage," reissued as "Woman Suffrage," in AOE, 210-11.

126 "in American women and not men . . .": ME V, no. 5 (July 1910): 160.

126 "Life as Art": ME V, no. 1 (March 1910): 18.

126 "was never more discouraged . . . paralyzed me": EG to BR, June 20, 1910. (UI-CC)

127 ". . . why make an effort for the new? . . .": EG to BR, June 22, 1910. (UI-CC)

127   "I'd rather do without reality . . .": ibid.

127-128   "I think I am not exaggerating . . .": *ME* V, no. 5 (July, 1910): 163.

128   "If Ferral can give you a better nose . . ."; ". . . all men love to be dictators . . .": EG to BR, June 24, 1910. (UI-CC)

128   "the only being . . .": EG to BR, n.d. (UI-CC); similar references in *LML*, 528.

128-129   "So you think . . .": EG to BR, June 29, 1910. (UI-CC)

129   "on the unfortunate day of my birth"; "of what avail is reason . . .": EG to BR, June 27, 1910. (UI-CC)

129   ". . . a poor puny little scrap of paper . . .": ibid.

129   "Alex, for whom I worked 22 years . . .": ibid.

130   "My love for you . . .": EG to BR, August 12, 1910. (UI-CC)

130   "a trembling leaf . . .": ibid.

130   "You said 210 is in my bones . . .": EG to BR, June 29, 1910. (UI-CC)

130   "bring no joy": BR to EG, n.d. (UI-CC)

130-131   "I am daily knifed . . ."; "I must live . . .": EG to BR, June 29, 1910. (UI-CC)

131   "You foolish boy . . ."; "angry cruel voice": ibid.

131   "sorrow beyond tears . . .": EG to BR, July 21, 1910. (UI-CC)

131-132   "that the light has gone out . . ."; "Lover, my only one . . .": ibid.

132   ". . . You cruel, cruel man . . . impossible . . . it's mine!" ibid.

132   "what's the use of grieving . . .": ibid.

132   "the most forlorn human derelict . . . outrageously, unforgivably weak . . .": EG to BR, July 22, 1910. (UI-CC)

133   "changing elements of life": ibid.

133   "Fate has been kind to you . . .": ibid.

133   "I think, if you loved me as much . . .": EG to BR, July 24, 1910. (UI-CC)

133   "You say in your soul sketch . . .": EG to BR, August 9, 1910. (UI-CC)

134   "I knew you are the savage . . .": ibid.

134-135   "Civilization . . . Little black devils . . .": Ben Reitman, M.D., Paris, September 15, 1910. (UI-CC)

136   ". . . love is beginning to be a mockery . . .": EG to BR, July 28, 1910. (UI-CC)

136   "The essay on Marriage and Love . . . A nice mess . . .": EG to BR, August 1, 1910. (UI-CC)

136   "Boy, boy, you have hypnotized me . . .": EG to BR, July 26, 1910. (UI-CC)

136   "No man on Earth . . .": EG to BR, August 15, 1910. (UI-CC)

136   "I miss you more than food . . . You were angry . . .": ibid.

137 For general background reading on Kropotkin and Malatesta, see bibliography.

137 "You must not misjudge Kropotkin . . .": EG to BR, August 12, 1910. (UI-CC)

137 "One thing more about K . . .": ibid.

137 Kropotkin's wife: interview with Roger Baldwin, May 5, 1981.

138-139 "Hobo my darling . . .": EG to BR, August 26, 1910. (UI-CC)

140 "Of course, dear, I realize your right . . .": ibid.

140 "thoughtless irresponsibility . . . a broken Patella . . .": EG to BR, August 30, 1910. (UI-CC)

140-141 "Human nature is such a foolish thing . . .": ibid.

141 "Dearest, I am so glad you want . . .": EG to BR, August 25, 1910. (UI-CC)

142 "baby"; ". . . strong and fine": EG to BR, November 30, 1910. (UI-CC)

142 "First, I must tell you something . . .": EG to BR, October 22, 1910. (UI-CC)

142 This account of "An Evening for Outcasts" comes from the Ben Reitman Collection in UI-CC, which also contains a huge map depicting the symbols of the inner life of the hobos; the program for the event in NYPL's Manuscript and Archive Collection.

142-143 "Hobo, dear, you are a wonder . . .": EG to BR, November 22, 1910. (UI-CC)

143 "like the rising of the Sun . . .": EG to BR, December 13, 1910. (UI-CC)

143 "with all the love a mother can feel . . .": ibid.

143 "Baby arrived . . .": EG to BR, December 17, 1910. (UI-CC)

143 "see what a father you make . . .": EG to BR, December 18, 1910. (UI-CC)

143 "Dr. Denjiro Kotoku . . .": *ME* V, no. 10 (December 1910): 306–07.

144 "hoarse as a drunken sailor"; "crushing . . . from all sides": EG to BR, December 9, 1910. (UI-CC)

144 "excruciating pain . . ."; "Oh, hobo, hobo . . .": EG to BR, December 11, 1910. (UI-CC)

144 "just in the age of passion's highest expression"; "suspend all meeting . . .": EG to BR, December 21, 1910. (UI-CC)

144 "Do you really think my passion . . .": EG to BR, December 28, 1910. (UI-CC)

144 "But dear, they have never added . . ."; "The one I can well forgo . . .": EG to BR, December 23, 1910. (UI-CC)

144-145   "Dearest, have I ever tried . . .": ibid.

145   ". . . craving for companionship . . .": EG to BR, January 2, 1911. (UI-CC)

145   "What are all hopes of tomorrow . . . pain, and soul agony": EG to BR, December 31, 1910. (UI-CC)

145-146   "My dearest Mommy . . .": BR to EG, January 2, 1911. (UI-CC)

146-147   "You hold up the Home . . .": EG to BR, January 4, 1911. (UI-CC)

147   even to buy underwear: interview with Senya Fleshine, October 1911.

147   ". . . your Hobo is having the first experience . . .": BR to EG, January 12, 1911. (UI-CC)

147-148   "I've been in jail with her . . .": BR, on "Emma Goldman." (UI-CC)

148   "on the good will and bad taste of police officials": ME V, no. 10 (December 1910): 335.

148   On the United Mine Workers in Columbus, Ohio, see ME V, no. 12 (February 1911): 388.

149   "mesmeric methods": ME VI, no. 1 (March 1911): 19.

149   "the drudge work . . .": ME II, no. 5 (July 1911): 157.

149   "Our Lady of Sorrow . . .": ME VI, no. 3 (May 1911): 84–89.

149   "Mommy is in her bed, but no Hobo . . .": EG to BR, June 29, 1911. (UI-CC)

150-151   "It is insanity to continue . . .": EG to BR, July 7, 1911. (UI-CC)

151   "stranger everywhere . . . Miracles do not happen": EG to BR, July 9, 1911. (UI-CC)

151   "After all, I am like Ibsen . . .": EG to BR, July 18, 1911. (UI-CC)

151   "out loud when the dagger is thrust . . .": EG to BR, July 23, 1911. (UI-CC)

151   "Oh, if you only knew how I feel . . .": ibid.

152   "salvation"; "Perhaps, if Mary could have found . . ."; "You are such a wonderful worker . . .": EG to BR, July 26, 1911. (UI-CC)

152   "As to my lover . . .": ibid.

153   Firebrand: anarchist newspaper first published in San Francisco, January 29, 1895, to September 5, 1897; superseded by Free Society (1898–1904), with an expanded base, in San Francisco, Chicago, and New York.

153   "The whole thing is very terrible to me . . .": EG to BR, July 23, 1911. (UI-CC)

153   "Why are you not here . . .": EG to BR, July 27, 1911. (UI-CC)

153   "I have absolutely no one . . .": EG to BR, July 28, 1911. (UI-CC)

153   "You speak of being dependent . . .": EG to BR, July 28, 1911. (UI-CC)

154   "For three years, Ben dear . . .": ibid.

154   "Chicago, indeed . . .": EG to BR, July 29, 1911. (UI-CC)

154.   "kiss and massage . . .": BR to EG, July 30, 1911. (UI-CC)

155   ". . . propaganda to be mixed with love . . . You are like Anarchism to me . . .": EG to BR, July 31, 1911. (UI-CC)

155   "Why do I do them? . . .": EG to BR, August 1, 1911. (UI-CC)

155-156 "Listen, my precious boy . . .": EG to BR, August 2, 1911. (UI-CC)

156   "Human nature is a queer thing . . .": EG to BR, August 7, 1911. (UI-CC)

156   "a prisoner of America": ibid.

157   "What a terrible force love is . . .": EG to BR, August 31, 1911. (UI-CC)

6: TAR AND SAGEBRUSH

Page

159   "Oh, lover, I am so glad . . .": BR to EG, January 23, 1912. (UI-CC)

159-160 Lecture titles are from *ME* VI, no. 12 (February 1912): 354.

160   "Sex the Great Element for Creative Work": manuscript folder XXIX-A, IISH.

160   "Bread and Roses": Milton, Meltzer, *Bread—and Roses: The Struggle of American Labor, 1865–1915.*

161   "If, then, my work had accomplished nothing else . . .": *ME* VII, no. 1 (March 1912): 27.

161   "I wish I were in Lawrence . . .": EG to BR, Tuesday, n.d., 1912. (UI-CC)

161   "We want the anarchist murderess": *LML,* 496.

161   "I charge all of you men . . .": ibid., 497.

162-163 "'If you utter a sound . . .'": BR, "The Respectable Mob," *ME* VII, no. 4 (June 1912): 109.

163   "bound and gagged . . .": *LML,* 498.

163   "Emma was carried . . .": *San Diego News,* May 18, 1912.

163-164 "Ben lay in a rear car . . .": *LML,* 500.

164   "some of him lived . . .": BR to EG, July 25, 1912. (UI-CC)

164-165 "I hope, Hobo dear . . .": EG to BR, Wednesday, n.d., 1912. (UI-CC)

165   Voltairine de Cleyre: see *An American Anarchist: The Life of Voltairine de Cleyre (AAA),* a wonderful biography written by Paul Avrich, giving Voltairine the treatment and space she deserves.

165   "After every public appearance . . .": EG, *Voltairine de Cleyre* (manuscript in IISH; later published as book [see bibliography]).

165   "I do not believe . . .": *LML,* 56.

165   "poor, the ignorant, the brutal . . .": EG, *Voltairine de Cleyre.*

166   "Emma was jealous . . .": interview between Paul Avrich and Jeanne Levey, Miami, Florida, December 1972, in *AAA,* 92.

166   "But the famished soul of Voltairine . . .": EG, *Voltairine de Cleyre.*

166-167   "Voltairine's emotional defeat . . .": ibid.

167   "peace and rest . . .": EG to BR, January 16, 1912. (UI-CC)

167   Ben in turn began to fear: BR to EG, July 18, 1912. (UI-CC)

167   "But you are very strange . . .": EG to BR, July 22, 1912. (UI-CC)

167   "Your tender life-giving treasure box . . .": BR to EG, July 24, 1912. (UI-CC)

167-168   "God—In a few months to learn . . .": BR to EG, July 27, 1912. (UI-CC)

168-169   "I want no one but you . . .": ibid.

169   "the wound that never heals": EG to BR, July 19, 1912. (UI-CC)

169   "Hobo mine, the pain you suffered . . .": EG to BR, July 25, 1912. (UI-CC)

169   "I hold you close . . .": BR to EG, August 1912. (UI-CC)

169   "It is pathetic . . .": BR to EG, July 31, 1912. (UI-CC)

169-170   The information on Almeda Sperry comes from Jonathan Katz, *Gay American History,* and the repository at MBU-SC.

170   "hunk of humanity . . .": Almeda Sperry to EG, July 27, 1912. (MBU-MM)

170   "How much like our relations . . .": EG to BR, August 29, 1912. (UI-CC)

171   "You sweet dear . . .": Almeda Sperry to EG, August 8, 1912. (MBU-SC)

171-172   "lovely bruised purple grape . . .": Almeda Sperry to EG, n.d. (MBU-MM)

172   "Never mind not feeling as I do . . .": Almeda Sperry to EG, [handwritten, 2 pages] n.d. (MBU-SC)

172   "O, rock of indifference . . .": Almeda Sperry to EG, n.d. (MBU-SC)

172   "I never *saw* a man . . .": Almeda Sperry to EG, March 4, 1912. (MBU-SC)

172   ". . . Sash Berkman's baby . . .": Almeda Sperry to EG, October 21, 1912. (MBU-SC)

173   "not to make her realize you know . . .": EG to BR, Friday, n.d., 1912. (MBU-SC)

173-174 "I don't think I used any worse language . . .": Almeda Sperry to EG, n.d., 1912. (MBU-SC)

174 "I wish I had a mother like you . . .": Almeda Sperry to EG, December 23, 1912. (MBU-SC)

174 ". . . Perhaps she is just studying me . . .": Almeda Sperry to EG, October 22, 1912. (MBU-SC)

174 "cruel side . . .": ibid.

174 "God, how I dream of you . . .": Almeda Sperry to EG, n.d. (MBU-SC)

174-175 "Dearest: It is a good thing . . .": Almeda Sperry to EG, n.d. (MBU-SC)

176 "Well, I'll smoke a few more cigarettes . . .": Almeda Sperry to EG, April 20, 1912. (MBU-SC)

176 "I have read *Mary Wollstonecraft* . . .": Almeda Sperry to EG, September 21, 1912. (MBU-SC)

176 ". . . Modern woman is no longer satisfied . . .": EG, in Jonathan Katz, *Gay American History,* 380.

177 "the man with the magic touch": anonymous ex-lover to BR, 1907. (UI-CC)

177 "'Will' shrinking": BR to EG, n.d., (1912) ("My dear Mommy," 11:45 A.M.). (UI-CC)

177 "denied his Willie": BR to EG, referred to in phone conversation, Tuesday, n.d., 1912. (UI-CC)

177 "How dare you say I denied W . . .": EG to BR, Tuesday after phoning Hobo, 1912. (UI-CC)

177 "Do not torture W . . .": EG to BR, August 14, [1912]. (UI-CC)

178 "You need not worry . . .": EG to BR, August 12, 1912. (UI-CC)

178 "I really think that if . . .": BR to EG, September 27, 1912. (UI-CC)

179 "We are some direct actionists . . .": ibid.

179 "To live and to love . . .": BR to EG, October 1, 1912. (UI-CC)

179 "Hurrah, Hobo is coming . . .": EG to BR, October 2, 1912. (UI-CC)

180 "I need not tell you how often . . .": EG to EK, December 9, [1912]. (IISH)

180-181 "Yes, dear, it was love that made me return . . .": EG to BR, July 11, (1912). (UI-CC)

181 ". . . a revolutionist first and human afterwards": *PMA,* 8.

181 Jack London refused to write an introduction: *LML,* 506.

181 ". . . Sasha's real resurrection . . .": ibid.

182 "Ben would not be freed . . .": ibid., 511.

183 "Reitman! We want Reitman!": ibid., 694–95.

183-184 "No play was ever staged . . .": ibid., 513.

184 "He was impulsive, but he lacked stamina . . .": ibid., 514.

185 "Could anything be nobler . . .": *PMA,* 8.

185 "dedicate [herself] . . .": *LML,* 62.

185 ". . . draw [his] inspiration from [his] precious T.B.": BR to EG, "My Best Lover," n.d. (Wednesday). (UI-CC)

186 "The workers no longer believe . . .": BR, in *ME* VIII, no. 3 (May 1913): 85.

186-187 "I know you are sensible . . .": AB to BR, April 7, 1913. (UI-CC)

187-188 "On July 13, 1913, Maynard took part . . .": Miriam Alan de Ford, *Uphill All the Way,* 143–44, 147–48.

189 "My lover, my wife, my all . . .": BR to EG, n.d. (the 26th; "At Home near to Mommy"). (UI-CC)

7: SONS AND MOTHERS

Page

192 "But, then, Jewish families . . .": EG to BR, September 4, (1913). (UI-CC)

192-193 ". . . tasted the invigorating breeze . . .": EG to BR, June 29, n.d. (UI-CC)

193 "remain separate personalities": Voltairine de Cleyre, "They Who Marry Do Ill," *ME* II, no. 11 (January 1908): 511.

193 "My mother is my home": EG to BR, September 3, n.d. (Rochester). (UI-CC)

193 "when we have a decent home . . .": EG to BR, September 13, 1913. (UI-CC)

194 "I assure you, Hobo mine . . .": EG to BR, September 12, (1913). (UI-CC)

194 "However, we have a great work . . .": ibid.

195 "I want you with me . . .": EG to BR, September 21, 1913. (UI-CC)

195-196 "Now, as to the arrangement of the house . . .": EG to BR, September 20, 1913. (UI-CC)

196 "I have a peach of a room . . .": EG to BR, September 21, 1913. (UI-CC)

197 "I have left out one thing . . .": EG to BR, September, n.d., 1913. (UI-CC)

197 "There were no facilities for heating . . .": *LML,* 516–17.

198 "Ben and Miss Fitzgerald . . .": ibid., 518.

198   "lived among her pots and kettles . . .": ibid.

198   "he had dropped his practice . . .": ibid.

198   ". . . given the best room in the house . . .": ibid., 519.

199-200   "She exults—she exults . . .": D. H. Lawrence, *Sons and Lovers,* 203–04.

200   "The office, our work, and our life . . .": EG to BR, September 13, [1913]. (UI-CC)

200   "free himself from the office": *LML,* 519.

201-203   ". . . I have had no drink . . .": EG to BR, October 29, [1913]. (UI-CC)

203   "The break came . . .": *LML,* 520.

8: DENYING FINALITIES

Page

205   "kick out the Old . . .": *LML,* 520–21.

205   "poets, writers, rebels . . .": ibid., 521.

206   "an American swagger": ibid., 433.

206   "radiate gloom constantly"; "accuse me of superficiality . . .": BR to EG, February 1914. (UI-CC)

206-208   ". . . You always write me long letters . . .": BR to EG, January 1914. (UI-CC)

208   "This much I want . . .": EG to BR, n.d., 1914. (UI-CC)

209   "I fear, dearest heart . . .": EG to BR, February 17, 1914. (UI-CC)

209-210   "Your dear letter . . .": BR to EG, February n.d., 1914. (UI-CC)

210   "I shall always remain wedded to you": ibid.

210   "Ten days in Chicago effected the *cure* . . .": BR to EG, n.d., 1914 (Friday, 4:00 P.M.). (UI-CC)

210-211   "a dead inertia . . .": EG to BR, Sunday n.d., 1914. (UI-CC)

211-212   "I have no explanation to offer . . .": BR to EG, Sunday n.d., February 1914. (UI-CC)

212   "Today I put the finishing touches . . .": EG to BR, February 26, 1914. (UI-CC)

212-213   "Work, work, and no end . . .": EG to BR, n.d., 1914 "Sunday, midnight, after the meeting." (UI-CC)

213   ". . . Seems strange that I should be pleading . . .": BR to EG, Sunday n.d., February 1914. (UI-CC)

214   "It's the realization of how utterly alone . . .": EG to BR, March 3, 1914. (UI-CC)

214   "someone like Ben": EG to BR, March 1914. (UI-CC)

215 "Hobo, my hobo . . .": EG to BR, March 4, 1914. (UI-CC)

216 "74, chilled to the bones . . .": EG to BR, March 7, 1914. (UI-CC)

216 "Alex is so slow and so pedantic . . .": EG to BR, March 18, 1914. (UI-CC)

216 "I want nothing to interfere . . .": EG to BR, March 21, n.d. (1 A.M.). (UI-CC)

216 "a coward or a dreamer . . . follow your natural impulses": BR to EG, March 28, 1914. (UI-CC)

216 "It is really true . . .": EG to BR, March 27, 1914. (UI-CC)

217 "Soon I will see the beautiful face . . .": EG to BR, Sunday, March 1914. (UI-CC)

217 "If you drink, you'll die . . . To be away from Ben nights . . .": *LML*, 527.

217 "alive to new art forms . . .": ibid., 530.

217-218 "She answered, thanking me . . .": Margaret Anderson, *My Thirty Years* (Connecticut: Greenwood Press, 1971; originally published 1930), 69–71.

218 "I went to the Lexington [Hotel] . . .": ibid., 72–73.

218 "the shackles of their middle-class homes": ibid., 531.

219 "The exasperating thing about Emma Goldman . . .": Margaret Anderson, "Emma Goldman in Chicago," *ME* IX, no. 10 (December 1909): 320–24.

9: BIRTH CONTROL AND "BLOOD AND IRON MILITARISM"

Page

222 "that only perfect freedom . . .": *SSMD*, 18–25.

222 ". . . to prevent conception of undesired and unloved children . . .": ibid., 174.

222 "Not one of my lectures . . .": EG to Margaret Sanger, May 26, 1914. (DLC)

222 "I know you will be amused . . .": EG to Margaret Sanger, April 9, 1914. (DLC)

223 "We are certainly living in wonderful times . . .": EG to Margaret Sanger, May 1, (1914). (DLC)

223 "In a depressed state of mind"; "About myself . . .": EG to Margaret Sanger, June 22, (1914). (DLC)

224-225 ". . . if I can't have a home with you . . .": BR to EG, September 3, 1914. (MBU-MM)

225-226   "driving [her] to distraction . . .": EG to BR, September 13, 1913. (UI-CC)

226   "temperamental creature . . .": BR to EG, September 10, 1914. (UI-CC)

226-227   "And so Hobo wants me to give up *Mother Earth* . . .": EG to BR, September 13, 1914. (UI-CC)

227   "My suggestion is . . .": BR to EG, September 12, 1914. (UI-CC)

228   "Dearest. To ask questions . . .": EG to BR, September 14, 1914. (UI-CC)

228   "I am tired of feeding leeches . . .": EG to BR, September 16, 1914. (UI-CC)

229   "Emma's wife": interview with Meridel LeSueur, March 1983.

229-230   "About myself, I hold this position . . .": EG to BR, September 16, 1914. (UI-CC)

230   "because it is unpardonable . . .": ibid.

230   "In re Violence . . .": BR to EG, October 1914. (UI-CC)

231   "and the Rest could go to hell . . .": BR to EG, n.d., 1914 (Tuesday morning). (UI-CC)

231   "Hobo, you are quite an anti-Semite . . .": EG to BR, September 24, 1914. (UI-CC)

231   "Owing to a lack of country . . .": EG, *ME* I, no. 1 (March 1906).

232   "wedded to [her] and to *Mother Earth*": BR to EG, n.d. (1914). (MBU-SC)

232   "to nurse his soul . . . religion": BR to EG, October 7, 1914. (MBU-SC)

232-233   "My Ben, my Ben, there are days . . .": EG to BR, October 1, 1914. (UI-CC)

233   "Life is an eternal merry-go-around . . .": EG to BR, September 25, 1914. (UI-CC)

233   ". . . TECHNIQUE . . .": BR to EG, September 3, 1914. (UI-CC)

233   "Yes, Margaret is coming . . .": EG to BR, October 1914 (Pelham Manor, late Sunday night). (UI-CC)

234   "invaluable organizing and managing force . . .": EG, *ME* IX, no. 11 (January 1915): 368.

234   ". . . despair in the radical ranks": EG to BR, December 25, 1914. (UI-CC)

235   "I can't say I minded . . .": EG to BR, December 26, 1914. (UI-CC)

235   "Indeed, dearest, I will not say . . .": EG to BR, December 30, 1914. (UI-CC)

235-236   "You speak of being old . . .": EG to BR, December 30, 1914. (UI-CC)

236 "replaced wife, kiddies and home": EG to BR, December 30, 1914. (UI-CC)

236 "After the meetings I would ride home . . .": FTM, 362.

237 Margaret and William Sanger: see *Signs* article for an interesting and informative study of the progression of strategic changes in the Sanger birth control campaign. Joan Jensen, *The Evolution of Margaret Sanger,* "Family Limitation," 1914–1921.

237 "I will frankly say . . .": Margaret Sanger to *ME* X, no. 2 (April 1915): 77-78.

238 "During all of that time we pushed *The Woman Rebel* . . .": EG, *ME* X, no. 2 (April 1915): 78.

239 "although normal people love and want children . . .": BR, "How and Why the Poor Should Not Have Many Children." (MI-CC)

239-240 "Four wonderful months in New York . . .": BR, "The Tour," *ME* X, no. 7 (September 1915): 245.

240 "the free speech fight . . .": BR, *ME* X, no. 7 (September 1915): 246.

240 "thereby breaking the nervous tension . . .": EG, *ME* X, no. 6, (August 1915): 222.

240 "triumph was due . . .": *LML,* 559.

240-241 "My dear Hobo . . .": EG to BR, September 25, 1915. (UI-CC)

241 "to not discuss last month": EG to BR, October 15, 1915. (UI-CC)

242 "I feel deeply with your loss . . .": EG to Margaret Sanger, December 7, 1915. (DLC)

242 "That would be too awful . . .": EG to Margaret Sanger, December 8, [1915]. (DLC)

242 "We'd both gain much . . .": ibid.

242 "How I wish I were rich enough . . .": EG to Margaret Sanger, December 7, 1915. (DLC)

243 "I know that it is not . . .": ibid.

243 "to enter a plea of not guilty . . .": Margaret Sanger, "Not Guilty," postscript by EG, *ME* X, no. 11 (January 1916): 363–65.

243 ". . . what our readers do not know . . .": ibid., 365 (postscript by EG).

244 "in the most vulgar manner . . .": EG, *ME* XI, no. 1 (March 1916): 430.

244 "for the right of the masses . . .": ibid., 426–30.

244 Sanger defended herself: *ME* XI, no. 2 (April 1916): 492–93.

244 "started out on birth control agitation . . .": EG to EK, April 6, 1916. (IISH)

245 "But getting back to the original proposition . . .": William Sanger to EG, March 14, 1916. (DLC)

245 "I may be arrested, I may be tried . . .": EG, *ME* XI, no. 2 (April 1916): 468–75.

245 ". . . their mouths shut, and their wombs open": "Emma Goldman," *The Little Review Anthology,* ed. Margaret Anderson.

245 "her blue prison uniform . . .": BR, "EG in Jail by The Manager," *ME* XI, no. 3 (May 1916): 523.

245 "I took your loving contribution . . .": BR to EK, April 25, 1916. (IISH)

245 "Oh, I am not sorry I was sentenced . . .": EG to Margaret Anderson, "Letters from Prison, Queens County Jail, Long Island City, N.Y., April 1916," *The Little Review,* May 1916.

246 "If the authorities think . . .": BR, *ME* XI, no. 3 (May 1916): 507–08.

246 "white fleshed, waxy-looking doctor . . .": Max Eastman, *The Enjoyment of Living;* see also Linda Gordon, ed., *Women's Body, Women's Right,* for a discussion of Ben and Emma's role in the birth-control movement.

246 "a sort of advance agent for social revolution": "BR Before the Bar," *ME* XI, no. 5 (June 1916): 512.

247 "a physician and a poet": FTM, 333.

247 "No, don't bother about getting me a pardon . . . I gave the pie a very chaste kiss": FTM, 333–40.

248 "without his elemental activity": *LML,* 574.

248 ". . . Mommy getting up at seven all by myself . . .": EG to BR, July 13, [1916]. (UI-CC)

249 "The atmosphere was very tense . . .": *LML,* 577–78.

249 "to tabulate [his] ideas . . .": ibid., 581.

250 "At the time I developed . . .": FTM, 361, 363.

251 "absurd and grotesque . . .": *LML,* 582.

252 "The family, the home, even at best . . .": EG to VV, April 14, 1915. (MiU-L)

252 "The hardest and most trying life . . .": EG to VV, August 29, 1916. (MiU-L)

254 "It is tragic but yet true . . .": EG to AI, May 10, 1916. (MiU-L)

254 *The Masses* published a tribute to EG: June 1916, 27.

254 "an Anarchist, who comes to our fair city . . .": FTM, 341.

254 "no matter what he or any jury should say . . .": ibid., 343.

254-255 "given the limit of the law . . .": ibid.

255 "The jury was out long enough to smoke . . .": ibid., 344.

255   "a little paler than he left . . .": EG to AI, January 26, 1917. (MiU-L)

255   "blood and iron militarism": EG to AI, March 1917. (MiU-L)

10: "1917—EXCRUCIATING EVEN NOW TO WRITE ABOUT IT"

Page

257   "Excruciating even now to write about it": EG to AI, January 6, 1930. (MiU-L)

257   "everything [was] so uncertain": EG to AI, March 20, 1917. (MiU-L)

258   "Why You Shouldn't Go to War": BR, *ME* XII, no. 2 (April 1917): 41.

258   "as if possessed by divine fire": EG to AI, May 23, 1918. (MiU-L)

259   "In 1916 and '17 . . ." FTM, 364-65.

259   "If my brother, my fellow citizen . . .": ibid., 358.

259   "The Anarchist movement had become . . .": ibid., 366.

260   "On June 5th the Moloch militarism . . .": EG, *ME* XII, no. 4 (June 1917): 97.

260   "the political clap-trap": EG, *ME* IV, no. 1 (March 1909): 5.

260   Emma estimated: EG to AI, June 4, 1917. (MiU-L)

260   "'Are you advising men . . .'": *New York Times,* May 30, 1917.

261   "Then came Emma Goldman . . .": ibid., June 5, 1917.

261   "I will arrest this Goldman woman . . .": ibid., June 12, 1917.

261   "a disgusting old age": *LML,* 609.

262   "You see, dear, the upholders of law . . .": EG to AI, June 17, 1917. (MiU-L)

263   "We believe in Violence": Rebecca Edelsohn speech, *ME* IX, no. 5 (July 1914): 145–46. Exact quotation was: "Yes, we believe in Violence. We will use violence whenever it is necessary to use it. We are not afraid of what your kept press says; . . . when you train your machine guns on us, we will retaliate with dynamite."

264   "Whatever liberties you have . . .": EG's speech in court, printed in *ME* XII, no. 5 (July 1917): 157.

264   "The real Emma Goldman . . .": *LML,* 620.

265   ". . . All else is immaterial": EG to AI, July 10, 1917. (MiU-L)

265   "Friedrich Nietzsche was right . . .": EG, *ME* XII, no. 6 (August 1917): 210.

265   Emma's mail from prison . . .: evidence of transcribed correspondence. [EG to Lillian Kisliak (anarchist from Washington, D.C.), July 11, 1917, NARG 165, Folder #173]

266   . . . the extradition could cause problems . . .: U.S. Attorney to Hon. C. M. Fickert, District Attorney, San Francisco. (NARG 60, Central File #186233)

267   "Another situation might arise . . .": U.S. Attorney Caffey to Hon. C. M. Fickert, District Attorney, San Francisco, October 24–November 2, 1917. (NARG 60, Central File #186233-13, sect. 1)

267   "Indistinguishable of Dreamer"; "Indistinguishable of Overdoer": U.S. N.V. Attorney General Caffey to Attorney General, October 4, 1970. (NARG 60, DoJ, Central File #186233-13, sect. 1)

268   "Now you get only two years . . .": *LML*, 631.

268   correspondence with Washington's Committee on Public Information: Harry Weinberger to Hon. George Creel, October 25, 1917. (RG 63, Records of the Committee on Public Information, Correspondence of the Chairman, OP I 1-A1)

268   "I now instruct you in writing . . .": T. W. Gregory, Attorney General, to Thomas D. McCarthy, Esq., U.S. Marshal, November 2, 1917. (NARG 60, Central File #186233-13, sect. 1) in response to Thomas McCarthy, Marshal of District of N.Y., to Thomas W. Gregory, Attorney General, October 28, 1918. (NARG 60, DoJ, Central File #186233-13, sect. 1)

268   dissension within the government: ibid.

269   ". . . rather go to jail or die . . .": BR to Herman Schuettler, October 6, 1917. (NARG 165-GS, MID 9884-19)

270   ". . . ill-smelling Mother Earth people . . .": NARG, agent report (1917).

270   "Not a word has been said about the . . .": *MEB,* I, no. 3 (December 1917): 4. NARG 28, Records of the Post Office Department, ser. 40, records relating to the Espionage Act, WWI file #46647.

270   "to destroy everything . . .": Edmund Leigh, Plant Protection Division, Military Intelligence Section, to the Chief of Military Intelligence, November 16, 1917. (NARG 165, GS, MID, 10110-476)

270   "the best known system of anti-draft organization . . .": ibid.

271   "a committee of five . . .": January 1918. (NARG) 165, GS, MID, 10110-524 8)

271   "Step high, stoop low . . .": *Chicago Daily News,* Slim Brundage (n.d.).

271-272 "Ben Reitman now acts as chairman . . .": Agent P. J. Barry to Capt. Hayes, December 13, 1917. (NARG 165, GS, MID 10110-551).

272 ". . . no use for sickly sentimentality . . .": AB to BR, September 20, [1917]. (UI-CC)

272 "Our strained relations could not last . . .": *LML*, 643.

273 "big blow out of the year . . .": *LML*, 650.

273 "Wishes for any personal joy . . .": EG to AI, December 27, 1917. (MiU-L)

11: THE LAST PAGE OF A STORMY CHAPTER— 1918-1919

Page

275 "take care of my love child . . .": *MEBI*, no. 5 (February 1918): 1.

276 "Joy and sorrow mingled . . .": FTM, 659.

276-277 "The grief he had caused me . . .": *LML*, 659.

277 "It was strange to see my little blue-eyed . . .": FTM, 368.

278 "My boy, I am glad you are on earth . . .": BR to Brutus Reitman, May 6, 1918. (UI-CC)

278 "How about Ben . . .": EG to AI, August 11, (1918). (Mi-U-L)

279 "I suppose you think I am sentimental . . .": EG to SB, August 25, 1918.

279 "All his interest centered around himself . . .": SB to AB, August 15, 1918. (IISH)

279 ". . . why fear pain? . . .": EG to SB, July 25, 1918. (IISH)

279-280 "Nothing new about myself . . .": EG to AI, July 13, 1918. (MiU-L)

280 ". . . my request for so many feminine things . . .": EG to AI, August 11, (1918). (MiU-L)

280 "dope friends . . .": FTM, 388–92.

281 "emotional bondage to Ben"; *LML*, 660.

281 "You are by nature a reformer . . ."; EG to BR, October 17, 1918. (UI-CC)

281 "fifty years of anarchist revolutionary work . . .": *LML*, 661-62.

282 "dwelling in such utopias . . .": Louis How, Office of the Postmaster, N.Y., to Hon. William H. Lamar, Solicitor, Post Office Department, Washington, D.C., April 12, 1918. (NARG 28, Records Relating to Espionage Act—WWI, 1917, #46445)

282 "while colored soldiers were being obligated . . .": *Justice for the Negro—How He Can Get It*. IWW recruiting pamphlet. (NARG 165, GS, MID 1011-1460)

282 "To her Emma Goldman was a prophetess ...": Robert A. Bowen, Postmaster, to William H. Lamar, Solicitor, Post Office Department, Washington, D.C., April 10, 1918. Enclosure to letter from William H. Lamar to Alfred Bruce Bielaski, Chief, Bureau of Investigation, Department of Justice, Washington, D.C., April 30, 1918. (NARG 28, Records of the Post Office Department, Records Relating to the Espionage Act World War I, 1917–18, File #46647)

283 "to use her as bait ...": Agent Report #101, #102, re: Los Angeles Anarchists, January 2, 1918. (NARG 165, GS, MID 10110-564 6)

283 "name-drops": Report, January 14, 1918. (NARG 165, GS, MID 10110-555 13)

284 "A trustee brought her in ...": S. Comminsky, *Instead of a Magazine,* June 29, 1918.

284 "on account of a change of period in her life": HW to C. H. McGlosson, Assistant Superintendent of Prisons, Department of Justice, Washington, D.C., April 6, 1918. (NARG 60, #186233-13 sect. 2)

284 "The prison authorities show the parcel to him ...": Stella Comyn [Comminsky], in *Instead of a Magazine,* June 29, 1918.

285 "above the stomach": ibid.

285 "something should be done and done quick": President of the Missouri State Prison Board to Attorney General Gregory, January 27, 1919. (NARG 60, #186233-12, sect. 2)

286 "Don't think we compete in 'isms.' ...": EG to BR, May 19, 1919. (UI-CC)

286 "loyal comrade and cosmic mother ...": *KROH, Selected Writings and Speeches,* 268.

286 "a child of the open ..."; "I can truthfully say I am here ...": EG to VV, May 24, 1919. (MiU-L)

286 "live[d] the events now changing ...": EG to AI, April 14, 1919. (MiU-L)

286 "ON THIS YOUR BIRTHDAY ...": BR, Walter Merchant, and others, to EG, June 27, 1919. (NYPL)

287 "have all but killed me ...": EG to BR, May 19, 1919. (UI-CC)

287 "I have set my face toward the red glow ...": EG to EK, July 24, 1919. (IISH)

287 "Dearest boy, what greater love is there ...": EG to LM [after July 19, 1919] (Thursday night). (MCR-S)

287 "... it has brought me much pain and little joy ...": ibid.

288 "The ultimate goal is 6 feet of clay . . .": AB to MEF, September 7, 1919, in *NAH*, 10.

288 "attitude of mind": "Statement by Alexander Berkman in re Deportation," September 18, 1919. Records of INS, DoJ (via S.F.).

289 "Spanish Inquisition . . ."; "Today, so-called . . ."; ". . . five years of bloodshed": "Statement by EG at the Federal Hearing in re Deportation," New York, October 27, 1919.

289 "those damned kikes": Marion Barling, reporting to Mr. Finch, her superior, October 28, 1919. (New York State Archives, Lusk Committee Records, Box 3, Folder 14)

289-290 "The tragic part is Ben does not realize . . .": EG to AI, October 22, 1919. (MiU-L)

290 "Anarchist Queen": *Chicago Tribune,* December 2, 1919.

290 "with prohibition coming in . . .": George Dlizell to HW, December 5, 1919. (CtY-SM, Harry Weinberger Collection)

291 "Emma Goldman and Alexander Berkman are, beyond doubt . . .": J. Edgar Hoover to Creighton, August 23, 1919. (NARG 60, DoJ, Central File #186233-13, sect. 3)

291 "Emma came into my life . . .": *Chicago Tribune,* December 2, 1919.

292-293 "One does not live in a country . . .": EG to BR, December 12, 1919. (UI-CC)

294 "the worst dump I have ever stayed in": EG to VV, December 16, 1919. (MiU-L)

294 "I never felt more peaceful . . .": EG to VV, December 16, 1919. (MiU-L)

294 "made every effort to get deported with them": J. Edgar Hoover to A. S. Suter, March 18, 1920. (NARG 65, Records of the FBI, OG 216033)

294-295 "My dearest Fitzi, I too feel the pain . . .": EG to MEF, December 18, 1919. (IISH)

296 "Bolshevik Ambassador . . ."; "Worker's Republic . . .": *New York Post,* December 15, 1919. (NARG 165, GS, MID 10110-1194-321)

296-297 "We have been told this afternoon . . .": EG and AB to "Dear Friends," December 19, 1919. (IISH)

298 "We shouldn't expect from any person . . .": Congressional Record, January 5, 1920. Congressman William N. Vaile, House of Representatives Remarks, December 20, 1919.

12: *MOTHER RUSSIA*

Page
299   "I could only blurt . . .": *MDR,* 4.

300   "PREMET AT SOVIET BORDER . . .": EG and AB to SB, January 29, 1920, intercepted. (General Records of the Dept. of State, Office of the Counselor, file #861. 0-668)

300   "the same old persistent pest": Bill Shatoff, quoted in *LML,* 729.

301-302   "a few dull grey spots": *LML,* 757.

302   "the most salient contradictions in Soviet life": ibid., 763.

302   "to regain their revolutionary balance": ibid., 766.

307   "tools of former tsarist . . .": *LML,* 878.

307   "To remain silent . . .": *MDR,* 197–98; *LML,* 882–83.

307   . . . although the next day, March 6, the Petrograd Soviet . . .: Paul Avrich, *The Kronstadt Rebellion,* 148.

308-309   "In the spring of 1921 . . .": "The New Economic Policy—1921," *Collected Works of V. I. Lenin,* IX: 202.

309   "city drenched in blood": *LML,* 886.

310   "I would return . . .": *MDR,* 24.

310-311   "In the Russian cataclysm . . .": *LML,* 829.

311   "I wish I had a tongue of fire . . .": *New York World,* July 1, 1920.

311   "The only difference . . .": EG to HW, December 19, 1921. (CtY-SM)

311-312   "It was excruciating . . .": EG to SB, November 21, 1921. (IISH)

312   "a matter of fact": EG to SB, October 17, 1921. (IISH)

312   "often when I feel I can . . .": ibid.

312   "Ah, dearest girl . . .": EG to AI, August 17, 1921. (MiU-L)

312   "absence seem like many years": EG to BR, March 8, 1920. (UI-CC)

312   "floating prison . . .": ibid.

313   "The one great delight . . .": ibid.

313   "I think of you often . . .": EG to BR, May 1, 1920. (UI-CC)

313-314   "Dear little Mommy . . .": BR to EG, June 27, 1920. (IISH, carbon at UI-CC)

314-315   "A successful Dr. business . . .": ibid.

315   "was formerly a close associate . . .": (BR file number 202600-246) J. Edgar Hoover, Special Assistant to the Attorney General, to William L. Hurley, Secretary of State, August 31, 1921. (NARG 59, 811.01-129)

315   "a tragic end of a great love . . .": *MDR,* 239.

315   "radiant dream"; "burning faith": ibid.

316   "[Revolution] is the herald of NEW VALUES . . .": *MDR,* 261–63.

13: BLOWN TO THE WINDS

328   "I myself have for 30 years . . .": EG to MN, August 21, 1924. (IISH)

328   "when I get settled somewhere . . .": EG to BR, August 2, 1924. (UI-CC)

328   "To be sure . . .": EG to Minna Lowensohn, May 12, 1925. (IISH)

328   "My trouble is not that I am poor myself . . .": EG to VV, April 5, 1925. (MiU-L)

328   "a man's woman . . .": EG to Arthur Leonard Ross, January 23, 1934. (NNU-T)

328-329   ". . . the opponents of woman . . .": EG to MN, March 24, 1924. (IISH)

329   "Already the new American youth . . .": EG, "America by Comparison." (IISH, Nettlau archive, filed with 1925-26 correspondence)

330   "the curse": EG to LM, December 11, 1923. (MCR-S)

330   "In my childhood . . .": EG, "America by Comparison."

331   "the function of the strong . . ."; "the time and energy . . .": EG, "On the Equality of the Sexes," manuscript. (IISH)

331   "one of the truly great saints . . .": EG to Havelock Ellis, December 27, 1924. (IISH)

331   "We all need love and affection . . .": EG to AB, May 28, 1925. (IISH)

332   "I only wish . . .": EG to EK, November 16, 1923. (IISH)

332   "Peter Kropotkin . . .": EG to Frank Harris, April 30, 1924. (IISH)

333   "I wish I could say . . .": EG to KROH, February 24, 1925. (IISH)

333   "nowhere at home": EG to AB, "Introduction," *NAH.*

333   "Dear old Ben": EG to BR, May 22, 1925. (IISH)

333-334   "It is because . . .": ibid.

334   "respectable": ibid.

334   "You are of the Jewish race . . .": ibid.

334-335   "As I have often told you . . .": ibid.

335   "Forgive me if I seem aloof . . .": ibid.

335   "there is no Calif. . . .": ibid.

336   "to see or to feel . . .": BR to EG, June 3, 1925. (IISH)

336   "It will be almost six years . . .": EG to BR, n.d. [after June 27, before July 7, 1925]. (UI-CC)

336   "always [be] knocking, kicking . . .": BR to EG, July 10, 1925. (IISH; UI-CC)

336-337   "It is good, it is wonderful . . .": ibid.

338   "So you are trying to write a better book . . .": EG to BR, July 17, 1925. (UI-CC)

338-339   "You must have thought . . .": EG to BR, August 4, 1925. (UI-CC)

339 "Baby dear, I have seen you argue . . .": BR to EG, August 14, 1925. (IISH)

339 "Now that the old Mommy is dead . . .": EG to BR, April 29, 1926. (UI-CC)

340 "Of course the price . . .": EG to AB, September 10, 1925. (IISH)

340-341 "The one intrinsic cause is the tragedy . . .": EG to AB, September 6, 1925. (IISH)

341-342 "The only interesting person . . .": EG to AB, November 9, 1925. (IISH)

342 "unable to earn something by my pen . . .": EG to Frank Harris, n.d. (MiU-L)

342 "When she rose to speak . . .": *Autobiography of Bertrand Russell,* vol. 2, *1914-1944,* 180-81.

342 "the glowing dream [of Russia] was dead now . . .": *LML,* 982.

343 "I did not have many more years . . .": ibid.

344 "I don't want to have started something . . .": Kathleen Millay to VV, December 7, 1927. (NYPL)

345 "Isadora Duncan's life . . .": EG to Nellie Harris, November 29, 1927. (IISH)

345 "I just got your letter . . .": EG to LM, September 5, 1926. (MCR-S)

14: BORDER CROSSINGS

347 "Border Crossings": title inspired by novel, *Border Crossings,* by Dan Peters, about Canada and the United States during the Vietnam era.

347 "HOPE YOU CAN COME SOON": EG to LM, October 15, 1926. (MCR-S)

348 ". . . how cold it feels in this city . . .": EG to LM, November 2, 1926. (MCR-S)

349 "sublime festival of love"; "a stranger among strangers"; "a mad longing for all . . .": EG to LM, November 4, 1926. (MCR-S)

349 "I got so worked up, I am shaking . . .": EG to LM, November 5, 1926. (MCR-S)

350 "the one star on the dark horizon": EG to LM, November 11, 1926. (MCR-S)

350 ". . . if that too should fail me . . .": ibid.

350 "only extravagant and crazy people . . .": EG to LM, November 8, 1926. (MCR-S)

350   "Your maidale, who is your mother . . .": EG to LM, December 13, 1926. (MCR-S)

350-351   "My darling boy, how wonderful . . .": EG to LM, November 18, 1926. (MCR-S)

351   "give a damn who knows about it": EG to LM, November 19, 1926. (MCR-S)

351-352   "I am afraid I cannot ask you . . .": EG to BR, October 28, 1926. (MCR-S)

352   "Thanks, dear, for wanting to do something . . .": EG to BR, November 20, 1926. (IISH)

352-353   "What I really want the letters for . . .": EG to BR, November 20, 1926. (IISH)

353-354   "Dearest Mommy, Where did we used to be . . .": BR to EG, December 7, 1926. (MCR-S)

354-355   "Dear Ben. I shall not need the letters . . .": EG to BR, December 11, 1926. (UI-CC)

355   "Just like Ben not to consider . . .": EG to LM, November 24, (1926). (MCR-S)

355   "But it is good to know . . .": EG to BR, December 30, 1926. (UI-CC)

355   "love of my comrades": EG to BR, January 24, 1927. (UI-CC)

355-356   "If only you were here tonight . . .": EG to LM, November 26, 1926. (MCR-S)

356   "is one of the few truly big souls . . .": EG to LM, December 11, 1926. (MCR-S)

356   "the platform"; "rival": EG to LM, December 1, 1926. (MCR-S)

356   "Once I had to choose between . . .": *Toronto Weekly Star,* December n.d., 1926.

356   "Present day schools turn out automatons": *Toronto Daily Star,* December 4, 1926.

356   "the spirit of youth against outworn traditions": *Toronto Daily Star,* December 18, 1926.

357-358   "In fact my longing for you . . .": EG to LM, December 23, 1926. (MCR-S)

358   "My darling, how marvelous life would be . . .": EG to LM, January 1, 1927. (MCR-S)

358-359   "In 1915 the gap between Ben and myself . . .": EG to LM, January 1, 1927. (MCR-S)

359   "Everything was empty in me . . .": EG to LM, January 7, 1927. (MCR-S)

359   "You do not know the depths . . .": EG to LM, January 7, 1927. (MCR-S)

359-360   "Oh, my darling, how wonderful it is . . .": EG to LM, January 24, 1927. (MCR-S)

360   "Or has my Leon loved me 25 years . . .": ibid.

361   "But to sit around to wait for snatches . . .": EG to LM, February 4, [1927]. (MCR-S)

361   "there is no use hiding our heads . . .": ibid.

361   "Leon mine, you seem to think . . .": EG to LM, February 17, 1927. (MCR-S)

361-362   "You see, lover mine, the abyss . . .": EG to LM, February 14, 1927. (MCR-S)

362   "But you must not think I was so naïve . . .": EG to LM, February 20, 1927. (MCR-S)

362   "There are only the chains . . .": ibid.

362   "One would think Queen Mary arrived . . .": EG to LM, March 4, 1927. (MCR-S)

363   "I am leading such a crazy hectic life . . .": EG to LM, March 10, 1927. (MCR S)

363-364   "That you could consider [the letters] . . .": EG to LM, May 10, 1927. (MCR-S)

364-365   "If you think I enjoy being harsh . . .": EG to LM, May 14, 1927. (MCR-S)

365   "The very reasons why you don't want . . .": VV to LM, May 22, 1927. (MCR-S)

365   "Whatever makes you think . . .": EG to BR, April 28, 1927. (UI-CC)

366   "It is awful to think that so strong a man . . .": EG to LM, June 5, 1927. (MCR-S)

366   "No girl of eighteen waits . . .": EG to LM, July 10, 1927. (MCR-S)

367   "How can you say to *me* . . .": EG to LM, June 2, 1927. (MCR-S)

367   "It is something you are unwilling to face . . .": EG to LM, September 1, 1927. (MCR-S)

367   "I am not able to be content . . .": EG to LM, September 21, 1927. (MCR-S)

367   "a small income and the boy were willing": EG to AB, January 1932. (IISH)

368   "caught in the chariot wheel of commercialism . . .": EG to LM, n.d. [c. August 1927]. (MCR-S)

368   "Oh, dear Leon, both our lives . . .": ibid.

368   "I am absolutely determined to sail . . .": EG to LM, October 2, 1927. (MCR-S)

368   "not as a publicity hound . . .": BR to EG, n.d. [September/ October 1927]. (UI-CC)

369   "What happened, did you have a monkey gland . . .": EG to BR, October 14, 1927. (UI-CC)

369   "I am sure when you read over . . .": BR to EG, November 28, 1927. (UI-CC)

370-371   "For eight years . . .": EG to BR, December 17, 1927. (UI-CC, NAH, 142)

371-372   "I hope in your autobiography . . .": BR to EG, December 26, 1927. (IISH)

372   "I hope, Ben, you will never use my letters . . .": EG to BR, December 30, 1928. (UI-CC)

373   "fear no evil"; "in a way that would hurt . . ."; "The worst I would do . . .": BR to EG, January 2, 1928. (UI-CC)

373   "the living documents of my dead past sins": EG to BR, January 11, 1928. (UI-CC)

373   "I came to the conclusion . . .": ibid.

373   "letters which contain reference . . .": EG to BR, January 11, 1928. (UI-CC)

373   "no medicine could heal": EG to BR, December 17, 1927. (UI-CC)

373   "sacrifice and the bitterness . . .": EG to BR, January 11, 1928. (UI-CC)

373-374   "If I would believe in such nonsense . . .": ibid.

374   "It is a long time since I had . . .": EG to BR, February 1, 1928. (IISH)

374   "absolutely no intellectual inspiration": ibid.

374   "friendship is often more enduring . . .": ibid.

374   "After 15 months, I feel like a desert wanderer . . .": EG to LM, January 27, 1928. (MCR-S)

374   "only in a worse form": EG to LM, February 3, 1928. (MCR-S)

374-375   "It is to laugh . . .": ibid.

375   "bought for a song": ibid.

375   "Life is full of bitter disappointments . . .": EG to LM, February 18, 1928. (MCR-S)

375   "It was beautiful while it lasted . . .": EG to LM, July 7, 1928. (MCR-S)

15: RELIVING HER LIFE

Page

378   "between two fires"; "squelching effect . . ."; "You are too strong . . .": AB to EG, January 30, 1928. (IISH)

379   "an economic prostitute": *Victorian in the Modern World,* 205.

379   "alternately despairing and bewitched": Ethel Mannin, *The Red Rose,* 204.

379   "Will not the poor girl feel lonesome . . .": EG to AB, December 23, 1927. (IISH)

380   "Darling, you are a funny member . . .": EG to AB, December 1927. (IISH)

380   "I want passionately . . .": ibid.

381   "Well, Frank dear . . .": EG to Frank Harris, August 7, 1925. (IISH)

381   "To me one of the great delusions . . .": EG to Evelyn Scott, June 26, 1928. (IISH)

382   "was the most cheerful in years": BR to EG, July 10, 1928. (UI-CC)

382   "danced the kazatzka": AB to EG, July 10, 1928. (IISH)

382   "a mad American girl . . . knock her manuscript . . .": Peggy Guggenheim, *Out of This Century,* 79.

382   Lawrence remarked . . .: ibid.

382   "It is agony . . .": EG to BR, June 19, 1929. (UI-CC)

383   "if the separation would mean . . .": EG to AB, February 20, 1929. (IISH)

383   "So far Sasha . . .": EG to BR, May 7, 1929. (UI-CC)

384   "Not even when I thought . . .": EG to AB, February 20, 1929. (IISH)

384   "To do our work lightly . . .": EG to AB, June 29, 1928. (IISH)

384-385   "Lover, and friend and teacher . . .": BR to EG, July 10, 1928. (IISH; carbon at UI-CC)

385   "such cases, whether of love . . .": EG to AB, February 20, 1929. (IISH)

385   "I am not asking you . . .": EG to BR, November 25, 1928. (UI-CC)

386   "his MANNER of activity . . .": AB to EG, May 11, 1929. (IISH)

386-387   "Ben during ten years . . .": EG to AB, May 14, 1929. (IISH)

387   "Of course it is nonsense . . .": ibid.

387   "Ben was a Christian . . .": AB to EG, May 20, 1929. (IISH)

387-388   "The most important decade . . .": BR to EG, May 22, 1929. (UI-CC)

388   "Yet, my obsession . . .": BR to EG, May 30, 1929. (IISH)

388   "Yes, Emma, you are a great woman . . .": ibid.

388   "My god, what a romancer . . .": EG to BR, June 19, 1929. (UI-CC)

389   "I loved your last letter . . .": BR to EG, July 17, 1929. (IISH)

389   "is nothing now but a God-damned fool . . .": EG to AB, May 24, 1929. (IISH)

389   "I must write as I felt . . .": EG to BR, June 19, 1929. (UI-CC)

389   "old, fat and ill": BR to EG, August 8, 1929. (IISH)

389   "It is extremely difficult . . .": EG to BR, March 11, 1930. (IISH)

390   "the Ben Reitman relationship beautifully": Henry Alsberg to EG, April 3, 1930. (IISH)

390   "whole being was suffused . . .": *LML,* 425.

390   "lived away from the disturbing presence of Ben . . .": ibid., 695.

390   "Emotionalism had guided his passion . . .": ibid., 694–95.

391   "The dead had buried the dead . . .": ibid., 695.

391   "I suppose you know the tragedy . . .": EG to AI, May 21, 1930. (MiU-L)

391   "I used to weary you . . ."; "Now only the memory of my denial . . .": BR to EG, June 9, 1930. (IISH)

392   "Dearest Mommy. Into these crowded days . . .": BR to EG, August 23, 1930. (IISH)

392   "a thick-built woman . . ."; "the fat nincompoop . . . such a weakling . . .": Harry Kemp, *Tramping on Life,* 285–86.

393   "Did they all hate Ben . . .": AI to EG, January 6, 1931. (MiU-L)

393   "I SHALL D[ED]ICATE TO YOU . . .": BR to EG, December [24] 1930. (IISH)

393-394   "I dedicate this book . . .": BR, *The Second Oldest Profession.*

394   "Hurrah! The baby is born . . .": EG to AI, February 22, 1931. (MiU-L)

394   ". . . I have told the story of the people . . .": BR to EG, February 25, 1931. (IISH)

395   "I would just like to lay my head . . .": BR to EG, April 10, 1931. (IISH)

395   "Author, *Second Oldest Profession* ": BR to EG, April 10, 1931. (IISH)

395   "purely negative, pimp evil": "What is a Pimp?" Industrial [News], March 28, 1931. (NNU-T)

395   "I do not think any part . . .": EG to AI, January 26, 1930. (MiU-L)

396   "I went over old trunks . . .": BR to EG, June 15, 1931. (IISH)

396   "You are unfair to me . . .": ibid.

396-397   "*Living My Life* will be a powerful book . . .": BR to EG, November 14, 1931. (IISH)

397   "There were other forces at work . . .": *LML,* 343.

397   "an exotic picturesque figure . . .": ibid., 45.

398   "weakness of the body . . ."; "no Mommy, no Anna . . .": BR to EG, June 15, 1931. (IISH)

398-399   "In the Postscript George Bernard Shaw wrote . . .": EG to BR, December 14, 1931. (UI-CC)

398   "'. . . No man is a good judge . . .'": *Frank Harris on George Bernard Shaw*: an unauthorized biography based on first-hand information, with a postscript by Mr. Shaw (London: V. Gollancz, 1931).

399   "he tells me I have taken . . .": EG to AI, December 8, 1931. (MiU-L)

399-400   "My Dear Mommy. For a month I have been ill . . .": BR to EG, December 6, 1931. (IISH)

399-400   "She was not only America's . . ."; ". . . she interested the multitudes in Good literature . . .": BR to Louis Adamic, December 29, 1931. (UI-CC)

400   "Emma certainly had it in for you . . .": BR to EG, June 22, 1932. (IISH; carbon at UI-CC)

400   "Your page in history depends on Ben Reitman": BR to EG, August 7, 1932. (IISH, with carbon at UI-CC)

400   "the whole world is a prison . . .": EG to MR, March 6, 1930. (IISH)

401   "The events since 1914 . . .": EG to MN, February 21, 1931. (IISH)

401   "the most real thing in any sane society": EG to MR, March 6, 1930. (IISH)

401   "a grouchy old thing": EG to Saxe Commins, July 14, 1931. (IISH)

401   "It seems to have been sung . . .": EG to AI, May 21, 1930. (MiU-L)

401   Stallings review: *New York Sun,* November 20, 1931.

401   "Herein lies her undeniable power . . .": untitled review of *Living My Life,* by Freda Kirchwey, *The Nation,* December 2, 1931.

401-402   "I feel that you are wrong in emphasizing . . .": EG to John Haynes Holmes, n.d. [Fall 1931 or Winter 1932]. (NYPL)

402   "that no life is worth anything . . .": EG to Netha Roe, January 5, 1932. (WH)

403   "Young active person (female) . . .": Harry Alsberg to EG, May 25, 1930. (IISH)

16: BLIND FAITH

Page

405 "never felt so beaten": EG to Michael Cohn, (December 1931). (IISH)

405 "I feel completely torn out . . .": EG to EK, September 19, 1932. (IISH)

406 ". . . as regards myself . . .": EG to AB, January 1932. (IISH)

406 "the only place where he could go . . .": author's telephone interview with Kay Boyle, 1982.

407 ". . . our episode which began at Naperville . . .": EG to LM, [1932]. (MCR-S)

407 "flirting with Communism"; "fortunately the communists dislike me": BR to EG, March 26, 1932. (IISH)

408 "You didn't want capitalism destroyed . . .": BR to EG, June 22, 1932. (IISH)

408 "I have never considered you particularly profound . . .": EG to BR, October 1, 1932. (UI-CC)

408 "Kansas grasshoppers in August . . .": BR to EG, June 22, 1932. (IISH)

409 "Although Living My Life paralyzed me . . .": ibid.

409 "I AM SAVED . . .": BR to EG, May 13, 1932. (IISH)

409-410 "I shall feel the same towards Emma Goldman . . .": BR to EG, June 22, 1932. (IISH)

410 "You begin, 'As you know . . .'": AB to BR, December 11, 1932. (UI-CC)

410 A 1932 critique . . .: Marcus Graham, "Nothing to Be Proud of . . ."; L'Adunata Dei Refrattari, May 21, 1932.

410-411 ". . . that rotten putrid attack . . .": EG to AB, December 9, 1932. (IISH)

411 "A man can knock about . . .": ibid.

411 "(And, strictly between me and you . . .)": AB to MEF, November 11, 1932. (IISH)

412 "so tired of chasing windmills . . .": EG to AB, March 6, 1933. (IISH)

412 "They hug their chains . . .": EG to RR and MR, March 13, 1933. (IISH)

412 "It is disheartening . . .": EG to MR, May 31, 1933. (IISH)

413 "Perhaps it would be the wisest . . .": EG to MR, August 20, 1933. (IISH)

413 "Yesterday was the sixth anniversary . . .": EG to AB, August 23, 1933. (IISH)

413   "vegetated the summer": EG to MN, November 22, 1933. (IISH)

413   "I hate America now ...": AB to EG, December 31, 1933. (IISH)

414   "it is really my last resort ...": EG to AB, November 26, 1933. (IISH)

414   "It enabled me to get the grievance ...": BR to EG, March 23, 1933. (IISH)

414-415   "I think you'll be very happy ...": ibid.

415   "EG was a wonderful woman ...": BR, sketch in "Outcasts." (UI CC)

415   "the Irish Queen, half-mad Sarah ...": BR to EG, April 6, 1933. (IISH)

416   "If all the friends ...": BR to EG, November 8, 1933. (UI-CC)

417   "You certainly have not changed ...": EG to BR, December 23, 1933. (UI-CC)

418   "buoyant"; "... conqueror of their hearts and all else": EG to BR, January 13, 1934. (UI-CC)

418   "Is there a greater drama in the world ...": EG, notes for lecture at the Brooklyn Academy of Music, February 15, 1934. (IISH)

418   "Only liberty is worth fighting for ...": Ann Lord scrapbook, 1934 lecture tour. (NYPL)

418-419   "I don't know him ...", "I am delighted to be back ..."; "a hungry man ...": Interview with film news crew, 1934, featured in the film, *Anarchism in America,* Pacific Street Film Collective, New York.

419   "I'll certainly be blamed ...": Joseph Mitchel, "'Was I Bad? I'm Worse Now,' Says Emma Goldman Here," *New York World-Telegram,* February 1934.

419   "calmly delivered eulogy on the Russian anarchist ...": "Emma Goldman Extols Anarchist," *NYT,* February 12, 1934.

420   "mild, gray-haired woman ...": ibid.

420   "Please don't feel ...": *Democrat and Chronicle* (Rochester, N.Y.), March 18, 1934.

420   "a she Peter Pan ...": *Chicago Daily News,* March 24, 1934.

420   "The intelligence and vitality ...": Ernest L. Mayer, "Making Light of the Times," *The Capital Times,* March 29, 1934. Ann Lord scrapbook. (NYPL)

421   "There is nothing more excruciating ...": EG to Henrietta Posner, n.d. (Sophia Smith Collection)

421   "The moment Ben Reitman learned ...": EG to Benny Capes, January 11, 1934. (IISH)

421   "And so my Mommy will ...": BR to EG, January 20, 1934. (IISH)

421-422   "A handsome young lady as a traveling companion . . .": EG to Arthur Ross, January 23, 1934. (NNU-T)

422   "Dear Mommy: I shall follow you . . .": BR to EG, January 31, 1934. (IISH)

423   "triumphant tour; daily meetings with the unemployed . . .": BR to EG, March 11, 1934. (IISH)

423   "Another thing that I have thought . . .": ibid.

423   "wandering women"; "because they make up . . ."; "We have no men in the Anarchist movement . . .": ibid.

424   Emma had sent Ben a copy . . .: EG to James Pond, March 3, 1934; and EG to BR, March 11, 1934. (UI-CC)

424   "a passionate word . . .": BR to EG, April 7, 1934. (IISH)

424   "the best . . . letter . . .": BR to EG, April 14, 1934. (IISH)

425-426   "My dearest I have indeed found . . .": EG to Emmy Eckstein, July 3, 1934. (IISH)

426-427   "But I know the vulgarity . . .": EG to FH, [between May and August 1934]. (IISH)

427-428   "Dearest, you say you know me . . .": EG to FH, May 6, 1934. (IISH)

428   "Mary may not ever have admitted . . .": EG to FH, May 6, 1934. (IISH)

429   "Only, please, please do not come . . .": ibid.

429   "Your letters are like a brook . . .": EG to FH, April 20, 1934. (IISH)

429   "hungry for love"; "the miracle of miracles . . ."; "wildly beating heart": ibid.

429   "One does not offer fragrance . . .": FH to EG, n.d. (IISH)

430   "Not very complimentary to the men . . .": FH to EG, May 22, 1934. (IISH)

430   "He seems to me wholly emotional . . .": ibid.

430   "the rest were attracted to Ben . . .": EG to FH, May 23, 1934. (IISH)

430   "understanding and grace"; "The tragic fact . . .": EG to Mary Heiner, June 23, 1934. (IISH)

430   "play the game fairly . . .": Mary Heiner to EG, June 1934. (IISH)

431-432   "Well, hearing you . . .": Mary Heiner to EG, August 10, 1934. (IISH)

432   "my life is so uncertain . . .": EG to Mary Heiner, August 14, 1934. (IISH)

432-433   "the grove, the grotto of bliss"; "[his] Goddess, [his] darling"; "more than the world": FH to EG, n.d., 1935. (IISH)

433 "Oh, my mother who put water and cigarettes . . .": FH to EG, September 1934. (IISH)

433 "to sublime heights . . ."; "doubt, despair and fear": EG to FH, September 14, 1934. (IISH)

433 "My past with Ben . . .": ibid.

433 "Oh, imagine my tongue . . .": FH to EG, n.d., 1934. (IISH)

433-434 "in a general way . . ."; "I really feel embarrassed . . .": EG to FH, June 23, 1934. (IISH)

434 "bereft of all its meaning . . .": EG to FH, September 22, 1934. (IISH)

434 "did you ever dream . . .": EG to SB, August 11, 1934. (IISH)

434 "Your shameless sister . . .": EG to Morris Goldman, August 23, 1934. (IISH)

434 "it has been a great experience . . .": EG to Evelyn Scott, September 9, 1934. (IISH)

434-435 "Can you imagine, dearest . . .": EG to Emmy Eckstein, August 28, 1934. (IISH)

435 "the first American Anarchist . . .": EG to RR and MR, September 4, 1934. (IISH)

435 "But I have been too battered by life . . .": EG to AB, September 13, 1934. (IISH)

436 "It is strange, isn't it . . .": EG to SB, September 9, 1934. (IISH)

437-438 "You said that my page in history . . ."; "crush, sink and degrade"; "prevent . . ."; "standard of loyalty and love . . .": BR to EG, August 7, 1934. (IISH)

438 "live through it", "admire and rave", "I think you're worth raving over . . ."; "'You know nothing about art.' Right again.": BR to EG, August 7, 1934. (IISH)

438 "I only wonder why you should be . . .": EG to BR, September 15, 1934. (UI-CC)

439 "I need a new woman to whom . . .": BR to EG, November 14, 1934. (IISH)

439 "You are much younger, dear Ben . . .": EG to BR, December 5, 1934. (UI-CC)

440 "I see that age and experience . . .": EG to BR, December 12, 1934. (UI-CC)

440-441 "Canada is all right to be buried in . . .": ibid.

442 "Well, dearest girl, do come soon . . .": AB to EG, n.d., 1935. (IISH)

443 "Dear, neither S. nor you have ever guessed . . .": EG to Emmy Eckstein, [1935]. (IISH)

443   "in spite of your wonderful success abroad . . .": Emmy Eckstein to EG, [1935]. (IISH)

444   "I tell you that now . . ."; "be free towards him . . .": ibid.

444   "a much sadder Emma . . .": EG to AB and Emmy Eckstein, February 25, 1935. (IISH)

445   "it is so difficult to write . . .": EG to FH, March 27, 1935. (IISH)

445   "I refuse to expect too much . . .": EG to MR, May 2, 1935. (IISH)

17: FATAL ENDINGS

Page

447-448   "Your letters . . . are like a fresh brook . . .": EG to FH, June 12, 1935. (IISH)

448   "First, before I let you go . . .": FH to EG, n.d., (1935). (IISH)

449   "there [was] no greater fool . . .": EG to FH, September 30, 1934. (IISH)

449   "Such are the vagaries . . .": EG to FH, May 21, 1935. (IISH)

449-450   "EG arrived from Canada pretty much exhausted . . .": AB to SB, August 14, 1935. (IISH)

450   "Imagine, last Thursday . . .": EG to FH, July 1, 1935. (IISH)

450-451   "Ambrose Bierce was with . . .": FH to EG, n.d., 1935. (IISH)

451   "rekindled . . . youth long dead and buried": EG to FH, August 12, 1935. (IISH)

451   "tender but also violent lover": ibid.

451   "The yearning for you . . .": EG to FH, July 7, 1935. (IISH)

452   "inordinate, almost pathological sense of possessiveness . . .": EG to Emmy Eckstein, August 1, 1935. (IISH)

452-453   "It is this which colors . . .": ibid.

453-454   "As to tactlessness, my dear girl . . .": ibid.

454   "I was not angry . . .": ibid.

455-456   "Dearest Em, I am very sorry . . .": AB to EG, August 20, 1935. (IISH)

456-457   "I wish I could give her the certainty . . .": EG to AB, October 21, 1935. (IISH)

457-458   "My dear, old Dush . . .": EG to AB, November 19, 1935. (IISH)

458   "a fighting atmosphere"; "one gets old, my dear . . .": AB to EG, June 3, 1934. (IISH)

458-459   "About old age, I don't believe . . .": EG to AB, September 23, 1934. (IISH)

459   "weak heart from material insecurity . . .": EG to Fedya Modest Stein, September 28, 1935. (IISH)

460   "I do not know whether it is a virtue . . .": EG to FH, December 5, 1935. (IISH)

460-461   "I cannot continue on the rack . . .": EG to FH, December 26, 1935. (IISH)

461   "dear little fighter and faithful soul": AB to EG, November 4, 1934. (IISH)

461   "The things you manage to do . . .": AB to EG, January 9, 1936. (IISH)

461   "Dear heart, what would I do . . .": EG to AB, January 12, 1936. (IISH)

461   "to thrive on tzores": EG to AB, January 24, 1935. (IISH)

461   "More and more I am coming to believe . . .": EG to AB, January 5, 1935. (IISH)

461   "One must not carry Weltschmerz . . .": AB to EG, September 1, 1935. (IISH)

461   "terrible agony of the human family": EG to BR, n.d. (UI-CC)

462   "draught"; "my Brunhilde . . ."; "reverence amounting to idolatry": FH to EG, n.d., 1935. (IISH)

462-464   "It must have seemed to you . . ."; "the loss . . . brought me . . ."; "Question, why did I not tell you . . ."; "Now, as to your feelings . . .": FH to EG, n.d., 1936. (IISH)

465   "But all that had no bearing . . ."; "on the firing line again . . .": EG to FH, March 2, 1936. (IISH)

465-466   "liar, Hitler, Fascist . . .": ibid.

466   "Goodby, my dear Frank": ibid.

466   "rich past"; "the present seem doubly poor": EG to BR, June 13, 1935. (UI-CC)

466-467   "Doc Reitman will be 57 on Tuesday": New York Sun, December 30, 1935.

468   "Dear Ben. If only I had your gift . . ."; "vividly and as near life . . ."; "For myself . . .": EG to BR, April 27, 1936. (UI-CC)

468   "strong as a bull . . .": EG to AB, April 17, 1935. (IISH)

469   "as ever the same, even if non-pissing": AB to EG, March 5, 1936. (IISH)

469   "Talk about Dutch luck . . .": EG to AB and Emmy Eckstein, March 9, 1936. (IISH)

469   "single-handed"; "with the absence of active comrades . . ."; "accomplish wonders": AB to EG, March 18, 1936. (IISH)

469   "Then, too, one begins to value . . .": EG to AB, March 22, 1936. (IISH)

470 "No operation at present": AB to EG, via Emmy Eckstein, March 23, 1936. (IISH)

470 "Dearest Sailor Mine . . .": AB to EG, March 23, 1936 (unmailed). (IISH)

470 "Well, dearest, I think everything will be OK . . .": ibid.

471 "May you have a pleasant birthday . . .": AB to EG, June 14, 1936. (IISH)

472 "Yes, that would have been a grand surprise . . ."; "But as you say . . ."; EG to AB, June 25, 1936. (IISH)

472 "Dear, This is your birthday . . .": AB to EG, June 27, 1936. (IISH)

472 "relief in housework and cooking"; "if you feel better . . .": EG to AB, June 27, 1936. (IISH)

473 "the most torturous hours": EG to "Friends," July 1936. (IISH)

473 "Emmy didn't do it . . .": interview with Kay Boyle, June 25, 1982.

473 "I don't want to live a sick man . . .": AB to Emmy Eckstein and EG, June 27, 1936. (IISH)

473 "saint": Emmy Eckstein to EG, November 18, 1935. (IISH)

474-475 "As for myself—the largest part . . .": EG to "Dear Comrades," July 12, 1936. (IISH)

475 the blow . . . "completely shattered": EG to SB, July 6, 1936. (NYPL)

475 "Sashenka, my Sashenka, where are you?": interview with Molly Steimer. 1977.

475 "Sasha's end has been the most devastating blow . . .": EG to SB, July 6, 1936. (NYPL)

475-476 "And yet I cannot get rid of the thought . . .": EG to Netha Roe, August 12, 1936. (MiU-L)

476 "Ah, if only you could be here . . .": EG to Frank Heiner, July 16, 1936. (IISH)

476 "Ben said he'd cabled . . .": EG to SB, August 6, 1936. (NYPL)

476-477 ". . . forty-seven years of ordinary lives . . .": EG to John Cowper Powys, July 31, 1936. (IISH)

18: AGAINST AN AVALANCHE

Page

479 "my whole heart is with the Spanish people . . .": EG to MN, n.d., 1931. (IISH)

481   "a worthy end": EG to SB, August 22, 1936. (NYPL)

481   "spirit will renew my own . . .": EG to "Comrades," September 9, 1936. (IISH)

481   "I am walking on air . . .": EG to AI, September 23, 1936. (MiU-L)

481   "I would rather go down with the revolution . . .": EG to MEF, September 25, 1936. (NNU-T)

482   "I have faith in humanity . . ."; "fairly drunk with the sights . . .": EG to RR and MR, October 1, 1936. (IISH)

482   "the most constructive social philosophy . . .": draft of speech, October 8, 1936. (RR collection, IISH)

482   "the blood of Spain": from the title of Ronald Fraser's book; see bibliography.

482   "It is hard to see great spirits fall . . .": EG to SB, November 22, 1936. (NYPL)

483   "had sent assault guards . . .": Ethel Mannin, *Women and the Revolution,* 183.

484   "Spain has paralyzed my will . . .": EG to MR and RR, July 13, 1937. (IISH)

484   "It's as though you had wanted a child . . .": EG to Ethel Mannin, October 4, 1937. (IISH)

485-486   "Anarchism in Spain . . .": EG to Mollie Steimer and Senya Fleshine, September 12, 1937. (IISH)

486   "the optimism"; "the sublime faith"; "One completely forgets one's self . . .": EG to Ethel Mannin, October 4, 1937. (IISH)

486   "They are fighting on because . . .": EG to Arthur Ross, June 17, 1938. (NNU-T)

486-487   "Spain is too fascinating . . .": EG to BR, September 27, 1938. (UI-CC)

487   "The world is in such a frightful condition . . .": EG to Marjorie Goldstein, December 13, 1938. (IISH)

487-488   "If I have continued the work . . ."; "as a mother would defend a condemned son": EG to MEF, August 5, 1938. (NNU-T)

488-489   "Unfortunately the evil hour . . .": EG to Lillian Mendelsohn, February 17, 1939. (MCR-S, Lillian Mendelsohn Collection)

489-490   "As to danger, if I survived Russia . . .": EG to MEF, August 5, 1938. (NNU-T)

490   "Why don't you sit down . . .": Morris Goldman to EG, (late 1938). (IISH)

490   "I have tried desperately to acclimatize myself . . .": EG to Dr. Eliot White, February 19, 1937. (IISH)

490   "the agony of the dead past . . .": EG to MR, September 11, 1937. (IISH)

491   "Our own dear Sash . . .": EG to MEF, August 5, 1938. (NNU-T)

491   "I wish I had remained in Spain . . .": EG to MEF, January 28, 1939. (NNU-T)

491-492   "No matter our present void . . .": EG to MEF, March 7, 1939. (NNU-T)

492   "outlet for her vivid spirit": EG to MEF, January 12, 1939. (NNU-T)

492   "living corpses": EG to MEF, April 18, 1939. (NNU-T)

492   "If I did not know the appalling . . .": ibid.

493   "EG had a great life . . .": BR to MEF, May 22, 1939. (NNU-T)

493-494   ". . . it was something much deeper . . .": EG to BR, June 6, 1939. (UI-CC)

494   "lived a good life . . .": BR to EG, June 9, 1939. (IISH)

494-495   "I have faith . . .": ibid.

495-496   "My dear EG Mommy . . .": BR to EG, June 23, 1939. (IISH)

496   "Dear Ben. I received . . .": EG to BR, June 29, 1939. (UI-CC)

496-497   ". . . my comrades have not forgotten me . . .": ibid.

497   "Dear and admired comrade Emma . . .": Mariano R. Vazquez to EG, June 12, 1939. (UI-CC)

498   "Today I wish to close . . .": EG to "Dear Comrades and Friends," June 28, 1939. (IISH)

498   "I shouldn't continue": EG to RR and MR, August 4, 1939. (IISH)

498   "I am so terribly cut off . . .": EG to RR, October 7, 1939. (IISH)

499   "Keep sweet, get passionate . . .": BR to EG, June 30, 1939. (UI-CC)

499   "dull and uninspired": BR and EG and C.V. Cook, July 3, 1939. (UI-CC)

499   "demanded the credit and took the glory": ibid.

499   "babies were essential": ibid.

499-500   "I think Hitler has made . . .": BR to Heinrich Hauser, June 3, 1939. (UI-CC)

500   "Ben R. was to arrive . . .": EG to MEF, July 7, 1939. (NNU-T)

501   "About Ben R. and his book . . .": EG to MEF, July 24, 1939. (NNU-T)

501   "Emma's *Living My Life* hurt me . . .": BR to MEF, August 7, 1939. (NNU-T)

501   "It made me want to vomit . . .": EG to MEF, [Summer] 1939. (NNU-T)

502 "I quarreled with one of the authors . . .": BR to MEF, August 7, 1939. (NNU-T)

502-503 "Poor, martyred Ben . . .": EG to MEF, August 10, 1939. (NNU-T)

503 "I am frightfully sorry, dear Ben . . .": EG to BR, October 6, 1939. (UI-CC)

503-505 "At 62, I have to begin life anew . . .": BR to EG, November 13, 1939. (IISH)

505 "I received your letter of the 13th . . .": EG to BR, November 22, 1939. (UI-CC)

506 "If you ever write about me . . .": BR to Herbert Blumer, October 7, 1939. (UI-CC)

506 "I've been practicing medicine and writing . . .": BR to HH, December 30, 1939. (UI-CC)

506 "I liked you in the old days . . .": HH to BR, January 3, 1940. (UI-CC)

506 "There's nothing else to do . . .": BR to HH, January 6, 1940. (CtY-SM)

507 "that all men and women . . .": from Ben Reitman's late life sketches of his beliefs. (UI-CC)

507 "Your glands seem to be the most dominant force . . .": BR to Brutus Reitman, February 22, 1940. (UI-CC)

507 "Ben's trouble was . . .": EG to Fremont Older, December 29, 1931. (University of California, Berkeley, Bancroft Library)

508 "A few months over 29 years . . .": EG to MR, September 7, 1939. (IISH)

509 "at my old job . . ."; "busy as a bee": EG to MEF, October 24, 1939. (NNU-T)

509 "Never mind about any dinner for me . . .": ibid.

509 "with no movement of any kind": ibid.

510 "They were arrested October 4 . . .": ibid.

510 "some concentration camp in Italy or dead": EG to MEF and Pauline Turkel, October 17, 1939. (NNU-T)

510 "been on the go all week . . .": MEF TO EG, November 25, 1939. (NNU-T)

510 "Well, Emma darling . . .": ibid.

511 "seen a penny from lectures . . .": EG to MEF, December 2, 1939. (NNU-T)

511 ". . . spitting in my own face": EG to MEF, April 24, 1939. (NNU-T)

511 "He too is a strange mixture . . .": EG to MEF, January 12, 1940. (NNU-T)

512 "are really lovely people . . .": ibid.

512 "There is no spirit of helpfulness . . .": EG to BR, November 22, 1939. (UI-CC)

513 "The very thought of having to watch . . .": EG to MEF, February 11, 1940. (NNU-T)

513 . . . cover her naked knee: Ahrne Thorne, former editor of the *Freie Arbeiter Stimme,* radio interview, on Emma Goldman, produced by Paul Kennedy, Canadian Broadcasting Company.

514 "Poor dear EG, with such great talents . . .": BR to EG, February 17, 1940. (IISH)

515 "She is still unable to read . . .": SB to BR, March 1940. (UI-CC)

516-517 "tireless, fearless, uncompromising . . ."; "Liberty was always her theme . . ."; "Emma Goldman, we welcome you back . . .": speech delivered by HW at EG's funeral, Chicago, May 17, 1940.

517 "eloquence [was] second to none . . .": speech by Curtis Reese at EG's funeral, May 17, 1940.

517 "They have taken away my savior . . .": BR at EG's funeral, Chicago, May 17, 1940.

517 "Red Emma! a four-square, thick-set . . .": Ethel Mannin, *Women and the Revolution,* 140.

517-518 "The example of courage . . .": *New Republic,* June 3, 1940, 747.

518 "Emma Goldman had a powerful seductive voice . . .": *Chicago Daily News,* May 14, 1940.

518 "with the laurels of the capitalist press . . .": *Daily Worker,* May 17, 1940.

518 "I felt that I was presiding . . .": Leonard Abbott to BR, June 19, 1940. (UI-CC)

518 "my ten years with her . . .": BR to HH, March 9, 1940. (NYPL)

518 "Emma was an exceptional character . . .": Sadakichi Hartmann to BR, June 2, 1940. (UI-CC)

519 "As I stood there in Waldheim . . .": BR to "My dear Comrades," November 11, 1941. (UI-CC)

519 "The day will come when our silence . . ."; "Now, all we have is Communists": *Chicago Daily News,* November 11, 1942.

520 "a full thousand hoboes and friends . . .": Frank O. Beck, "Ben Reitman: A Superb Showman," in *Hobohemia.*

521 "I hope you don't get excited . . .": BR to Ida Reitman, August 21, 1940. (UI-CC)

523 "intense idealist . . .": *SSMD,* 138.

523 "learn this sorrowful and reassuring fact . . .": ibid.

SELECTED
BIBLIOGRAPHY

BOOKS

(Includes dissertations and other book-length unpublished works.)

Anderson, Margaret, ed. *The Little Review Anthology.* New York: Hermitage House, 1953.

————. *My Thirty Years' War.* New York: Covici, Friede, 1930.

Anderson, Nels. *The Hobo.* Chicago: University of Chicago Press, 1923.

Apter, David E., and Joll, James. *Anarchism Today.* New York: Doubleday, 1971.

Atherton, Gertrude. *Journal of Contemporary History.* Beverly Hills, Calif.: Sage Publications, 1926.

Avrich, Paul. *An American Anarchist: The Life of Voltairine de Cleyre.* Princeton: Princeton University Press, 1978.

————. *The Anarchists in the Russian Revolution.* Ithaca, N.Y.: Cornell University Press, 1973.

————. *The Kronstadt Rebellion.* Princeton: Princeton University Press, 1970.

————. *The Modern School Movement.* Princeton: Princeton University Press, 1980.

————. *The Russian Anarchists.* Princeton: Princeton University Press, 1978.

Banner, Lois W. *Women in Modern Drama.* New York: Harcourt Brace Jovanovich, 1974.

Baum, Charlotte; Paula Hyman; and Sonya Michel. *The Jewish Woman in America*. New York: New American Library, 1975.

Beck, Frank O. *Hobohemia*. New Hampshire: Richard R. Smith Pub., 1956.

Benson, Frederick R. *Writers in Arms*. New York: New York University Press, 1967.

Berkman, Alexander. *The Bolshevik Myth*. New York: Boni & Liveright, 1925.

————. *Now and After: The ABC of Communist Anarchism*. New York: Vanguard Press, 1929.

————. *Prison Memoirs of an Anarchist*. New York: Mother Earth Publishing Association, 1912.

————. *The Russian Tragedy*. Berlin: Russian Rev. Series, 1922.

Berman, Paul. *Quotations from the Anarchists*. New York: Praeger Publishers, 1972.

Berry, Elizabeth W. *Rhetoric for the Cause*. Los Angeles: University of California Press, 1969.

Bessie, Alvah. *Spain Again*. Novato, Calif.: Chandler & Sharp Publishers, 1975.

Björnson, Björnstjerne. "Beyond Human Power." *Chief Contemporary Dramatists*. T. H. Diekenson, ed. New York: Houghton Mifflin, 1915.

Blake, Fay M. *The Strike in the American Novel*. Metuchen, N.J.: Scarecrow Press, 1972.

Bolloten, Bernard. *The Grand Camouflage*. London: 1961.

Bookchin, Murray. *Post-Scarcity Anarchism*. Berkeley: Ramparts Press, 1971.

Borkenau, Franz. *The Spanish Cockpit*. Ann Arbor: University of Michigan Press, 1971.

Brenan, Gerald. *The Spanish Labyrinth*. Cambridge, England: Cambridge University Press, 1969.

Brooks, Van Wyck. *The Confident Years: 1885–1915*. New York: E. P. Dutton and Co., 1952.

————, and Otto L. Bettman. *Our Literary Heritage. A Pictorial History of the Writer in America*. New York: E. P. Dutton and Co., 1956.

Bruns, Roger. *Knights of the Road: A Hobo History*. New York: Methuen, 1980.

Carter, April. *The Political Theory of Anarchism*. New York: Harper & Row, 1971.

Cate, Curtis. *George Sand*. Boston: Houghton Mifflin Co., 1975.

Chernyshevsky, N. G. *What Is to Be Done?* New York: Random House, 1961.

Commins, Dorothy. *What Is an Editor*. Chicago: University of Chicago Press, 1978.

Cook, Blanche Wiesen. *Crystal Eastman: On Women and Revolution*. New York: Oxford University Press, 1978.

D'Agostino, Anthony. *Marxism and the Russian Anarchists*. San Francisco: Germinal Press, 1977.

Dancis, Bruce. *The Socialist Women's Movement in U. S.* Thesis-UC Santa Cruz, 1973.

Dell, Floyd. *Women as World Builders: Studies in Modern Feminism*. Chicago: Forbes, 1913.

Dolgoff, Sam. *The Anarchist Collectives*. New York: Free Life Editions, 1977.

Dreiser, Theodore. *A Gallery of Women.* New York: Horace Liveright, 1929.

Drinnon, Richard. *The Blast: An Introduction and an Appraisal.* Lewisburg, Penna.: Bucknell University Press, 1970.

————. "Emma Goldman: A Study In American Radicalism." Diss., University of Minnesota, 1957. Available through University Microfilm, Ann Arbor, Mich.

————. *Rebel in Paradise.* Chicago: University of Chicago Press, 1961.

————, and Anna Maria Drinnon, eds. *Nowhere at Home: Letters from Exile of Emma Goldman and Alexander Berkman.* New York: Schocken Books, 1975.

Dubofsky, Melvyn. *Industrialism and the American Worker.* New York: Thomas Y. Crowell Co., 1975.

————. *We Shall Be All: A History of the I.W.W.* New York: New York Times Book Co., 1969.

DuBois, Ellen Carol. *Letters: Elizabeth Stanton and Susan B. Anthony.* New York: Schocken Books, 1981.

Duncan, Isadora. *My Life.* New York: Boni & Liveright, 1927.

Durant, Will. *Transition.* New York: Simon and Schuster, 1927.

Eastman, Max. *The Enjoyment of Living.* New York: Harper, 1948.

————. *Great Companies.* New York: Farrar, Straus & Cudahy, 1942.

————. *Love and Revolution.* New York: Random House, 1964.

Ellis, Havelock. *The Dance of Life.* New York: Random House, 1929.

————. *Psychology of Sex.* New York: Emerson Books, 1933.

Epstein, Barbara. *The Politics of Domesticity: Women, Evangelism and Temperance in 19th Century America.* Middletown, Conn.: Wesleyan University Press, 1981.

Fishbein, Leslie. *Rebels in Bohemia.* Chapel Hill: University of North Carolina Press, 1982.

Fishman, William J. *Jewish Radicals: From Czarist State to London Ghetto.* New York: Pantheon Books, 1974.

Flexner, Eleanor. *Mary Wollstonecraft.* New York: Coward, McCann & Geoghegan, Inc., 1972.

Flynn, Elizabeth G. *The Rebel Girl.* New York: International Publishers, 1976.

————. *Sabotage: The Conscious Withdrawal of the Worker's Industrial Efficiency.* Cleveland: IWW Publishing Bureau, 1916.

Foner, Philip S., and Sally M. Miller. *Kate Richards O'Hare: Selected Writings and Speeches.* Baton Rouge and London: Louisiana State University Press, 1982.

de Ford, Miriam A. *Up-Hill All the Way: The Life of Maynard Shipley.* Yellow Springs, Ohio: Antioch Press, 1956.

Fraser, Ronald. *Blood of Spain.* New York: Pantheon Books, 1979.

Fried, Albert, and Ronald Sanders. *Socialist Thought.* New York: Anchor Books, 1961.

Ganguli, B. N. *Emma Goldman: Portrait of a Rebel Woman.* Bombay: Allied, 1979.

577

————. *Social Development.* New Delhi: Sterling Publishers Pvt. Ltd., 1977.

Gans, Lydia. *Glimpses of Emma Goldman.* Pasadena, California: Tabula Rasa Press, 1979.

Gelb, Barbara, and Arthur Gelb. *O'Neill.* New York: Harper & Row, 1962.

Goldman, Emma. *Anarchism and Other Essays.* New York: Mother Earth Publishing Association, 1911.

————. "Foremost Russian Dramatists." Unpublished manuscript, International Institute for Social History, folder EGIII, 1926.

————. *Living My Life.* New York: Alfred A. Knopf, 1931.

————. *My Disillusionment in Russia.* Garden City, N.Y.: Doubleday, Page and Co., 1923.

————. *My Disillusionment in Russia.* London: C. W. Daniel Co., 1925 (complete, uncut text).

————. *My Further Disillusionment in Russia.* Garden City, N.Y.: Doubleday, Page and Co., 1924.

————. *The Social Significance of the Modern Drama.* Boston: Richard G. Badger, 1914.

————. *Voltairine de Cleyre.* Berkeley Heights, N.J.: Oriole Press, 1933.

————, and Alexander Berkman. *Deportation: Its Meaning and Menace.* Introduction by Robert Minor, League for the Amnesty of Political Prisoners, 1919.

Goldsmith, Margaret. *Seven Women Against the World.* London: Methuen, 1935.

Gordon, Linda, ed. *Women's Body, Women's Right.* New York: Grossman Publishers, 1976.

Grosskurth, Phyllis. *Havelock Ellis: A Biography.* New York: Alfred A. Knopf, 1980.

Guerin, Daniel. *Anarchism.* New York: Monthly Review Press, 1970.

Guggenheim, Peggy. Confessions of an Art Addict. New York: Universe Books, 1979.

————. *Out of This Century.* New York: Universe Books, 1946.

Hapgood, Hutchins. *An Anarchist Woman.* New York: Duffield & Co., 1909.

————. *A Victorian in the Modern World.* New York: Harcourt, Brace and Co., 1939.

Harris, Frank. *Contemporary Portraits.* 4th ser. New York: Brentano's, 1923.

Hauser, Heinrich. Feldweg Nach Chicago (Bypaths of Chicago). Berlin: S. Fischer Verlag, 1931.

Hays, Samuel P. *The Response to Industrialism: 1885–1914.* Chicago: University of Chicago Press, 1959.

Homer, William. *Robert Henri and His Circle.* Ithaca, N.Y.: Cornell University Press, 1969.

Hopkins, Pryns. *Both Hands Before the Fire.* Penobscot, Maine: Traversity Press, 1962.

Howe, Irving. *World of Our Fathers.* New York: Harcourt Brace Jovanovich, 1976.

Jackson, Gabriel. *The Spanish Republic and the Civil War.* Princeton: Princeton University Press, 1965.

James, E. T. *Notable American Women: 1607–1950.* Cambridge, Mass.: Harvard University Press, 1971.

Joll, James. *The Anarchists.* New York: Grosset and Dunlap, 1971.

Joselovitz, E.A. *Splendid Rebels.* New York: Brandt and Brandt Dramatic Department, 1981.

Katz, Jonathan. *Gay American History.* New York: Thomas Y. Crowell Co., 1976.

Kemp, Harry. *Tramping on Life.* New York: Boni and Liveright, 1922.

Kennedy, David M. *Progressivism: The Critical Issues.* Little, Brown and Co., 1971.

Kolko, Gabriel. *The Triumph of Conservatism.* New York: Macmillan Publishing Co., 1963.

Kollontai, Alexandra. *The Autobiography of a Sexually Emancipated Communist Woman.* New York: Schocken Books, 1975.

Kornbluh, Joyce. *Rebel Voices: An IWW Anthology.* Ann Arbor: University of Michigan Press, 1964.

Kraditor, Aileen S. *The Ideas of the Woman Suffrage Movement: 1890–1920.* New York: Columbia University Press, 1965.

Kuhn, Reinhard C. *Dying We Live.* New York: Pantheon Books, 1956.

Lang, Lucy Robins. *Tomorrow Is Beautiful.* New York: Macmillan Publishing Co., 1948.

Lasch, Christopher. *The New Radicalism in America: 1889–1963.* New York: Random House, 1965.

Lawrence, D. H. *Sons and Lovers.* New York: The Viking Press, 1913.

Lawson, Peggy. *Roger Baldwin.* Boston: Houghton Mifflin, 1976.

Lenin, V. I. *Selected Works.* New York: International Publishers Co., 1943.

Levine, Isaac Don. *Eyewitness to History.* New York: Hawthorn, 1973.

Luhan, Mabel Dodge. *Intimate Memories, Vol. 3: Movers and Shakers.* New York: Harcourt, Brace and Co., 1936.

Luxemburg, Rosa. *Comrade and Lover.* Cambridge, Mass.: MIT Press, 1979.

Madison, Charles A. *Critics and Crusaders.* New York: Henry Holt and Company, 1947–1948.

Mannin, Ethel. *Comrade O Comrade.* London: Jarrolds Publishers, 1945.

———. *Lover Under Another Name.* London: Jarrolds Publishers, 1953.

———. *Red Rose: A Novel Based on the Life of Emma Goldman.* London: Jarrolds Publishers, 1941.

———. *Women and the Revolution.* New York: E. P. Dutton and Co., 1939.

Marsh, Margaret. *Anarchist Women: 1870–1920.* Philadelphia: Temple University Press, 1980.

McElroy, Wendy. *Freedom, Feminism and the State.* Washington, D.C.: Gato Institute, 1982.

Meltzer, Milton. *Bread—and Roses: The Struggle of American Labor, 1865–1915.* New York: Alfred A. Knopf, 1967.

Miller, Henry. *My Life and Times.* La Jolla, Calif.: Gemini Smith, 1975.

Morgenstern, Christian. *"Emma": The Gallows Songs.* Berkeley: University of California Press, 1966.

Morris, Lloyd. *Postscripts to Yesterday.* New York: Random House, 1947.

Morrow, Felix. *Revolution and Counter-Revolution in Spain.* New York: Pathfinder Press, 1974.

Nowlin, William B. "The Political Thought of Alexander Berkman." Diss., Tufts University, 1980.

O'Hare, Kate R. *In Prison.* Seattle: University of Washington Press, 1976.

O'Neill, Eugene. *Ah Wilderness,* in *The Plays of Eugene O'Neill.* New York: Random House, 1948.

O'Neill, William L. *Everyone Was Brave.* Chicago: Quadrangle Books, 1969.

Orwell, George. *Homage to Catalonia.* New York: Harcourt, Brace & World, 1952.

Ostrovoki, Nicholas. *The Making of a Hero.* E. P. Dutton and Co., 1937.

Palmer, A. Mitchell. *A Letter from the Attorney General: Investigation Activities of the Department of Justice.* Washington, D.C.: Government Printing Office, 1919.

Payne, Robert. *The Civil War in Spain.* New York: Capricorn Books, 1970.

Payne, Stanley. *The Spanish Revolution.* New York: W. W. Norton, 1970.

Peirats, Jose. *Anarchists in the Spanish Revolution.* Detroit: Black and Red, 1977.

———. *Emma Goldman: Anarquista de Ambos Mundos.* Madrid: Campo Abierto Ediciones, Pinilla del Valle, 1978.

Perlin, Terry M. "Anarchist Communism in America." Diss., Brandeis University, 1970. Available through University Microfilm, Ann Arbor, Mich.

Post, Louis F. *The Deportations Delirium of Nineteen-Twenty.* Chicago: Charles H. Kerr & Co., 1923.

Reed, James. *From Private Vice to Public Virtue.* New York: Basic Books, Inc., 1978.

Reichert, William O. *Partisans of Freedom: A Study in American Anarchism.* Bowling Green: University Popular Press, 1976.

Reitman, Ben L. "Following the Monkey." Unpublished manuscript, c. 1925. (UI-CC)

———. *The Second Oldest Profession.* New York: Vanguard Press, 1931.

———. *Sister of the Road: The Autobiography of Box Car Bertha.* New York: Macauley Co., 1937.

Renshaw, Patrick. *The Wobblies.* New York: Doubleday and Co., 1967.

Reynolds, Reginald. *My Life and Crimes.* London: Jarrolds Publishers, 1956.

Richards, Vernon. *Lessons of the Spanish Revolution.* London: Freedom Press, 1972.

———. *Malatesta: Life and Idea.* London: Freedom Press, 1961.

Rocker, Rudolf. *Anarchism and Anarcho-Syndicalism.* London: Freedom Press, 1973.

Rosenstone, Robert. *Romantic Revolutionary.* New York: Alfred A. Knopf, 1975.

Rostand, Edmond. *Chantecler.* New York: Duffield and Co., 1910.

Rowbotham, Sheila. *Hidden from History.* London: Pluto Press, 1973.

————, and Jeffrey Weeks. *Socialism and the New Life.* London: Pluto Press, 1977.

Russell, Bertrand. *Autobiography of Bertrand Russell, vol. 2, 1914–1944.* Boston: Little, Brown and Co., 1968.

Schaack, Michael J. *Anarchy and Anarchists.* Chicago: F. J. Shulte and Co., 1889.

Schmalhausen, Samuel, and V. F. Calverton, eds. *Woman's Coming of Age.* New York: Horace Liveright, 1931.

Schuster, M. Lincoln. *The World's Great Letters.* New York: Simon and Schuster, 1940.

Shatz, Marshall S. *The Essential Works of Anarchism.* New York: Bantam Books, 1971.

Sheaffer, Louis. *O'Neill: Son and Playwright.* Boston: Little, Brown and Co., 1968.

Shulman, Alix Kates. *Five Sisters: Women Against the Tsar.* New York: Schocken Books, 1977.

————. *To the Barricades: The Anarchist Life of Emma Goldman.* New York: Thomas Y. Crowell Co., 1971.

Silverman, Henry J. *The Libertarian Tradition.* Lexington, Mass.: D. C. Heath and Co., 1970.

Sochen, June. *Movers and Shakers.* New York: New York Times Book Co., 1973.

Steffens, Lincoln. *The Autobiography of Lincoln Steffens.* New York: Harcourt, Brace and Company, 1931.

Sunstein, Emily W. *A Different Face.* New York: Harper & Row, 1975.

Thomas, Hugh. *The Spanish Civil War.* New York: Harper and Brothers, 1961.

Venturi, Franco. *Roots of Revolution: A History of the Populist and Socialist Movements in Nineteenth Century Russia.* New York: Universal Library edition, Grosset and Dunlap, 1966.

Vizetelly, Ernest Edward. *The Anarchists.* New York: John Lane Co., 1911.

Wallechinsky, David, and Irving Wallace. *The People's Almanac.* New York: Doubleday & Co., 1975.

Wardle, Ralph M. *Collected Letters of Mary Wollstonecraft.* Ithaca, N.Y.: Cornell University Press, 1979.

————. *Mary Wollstonecraft.* Lawrence: University of Kansas Press, 1951.

Weinstein, James. *The Corporate Ideal in the Liberal State: 1900–1918.* Boston: Beacon Press, 1968.

Weisbard, Vera Buch. *A Radical Life.* Bloomington: Indiana University Press, 1979.

Whitehead, Don. *The FBI Story.* New York: Random House, 1956.

Wiebe, Robert H. *The Search for Order.* New York: Hill and Wang, 1967.

Woodcock, George. *Anarchism: A History of Libertarian Ideas and Movements.* Cleveland: The World Publishing Co., 1962.

PAMPHLETS

Goldman, Emma. *A Beautiful Ideal.* Chicago: J. C. Hart and Company, 1908.

————. *Patriotism: A Menace to Liberty.* New York: Mother Earth Publishing Association (1908).

————. *What I Believe.* New York: Mother Earth Publishing Association, 1908.

————. *The White Slave Traffic.* New York: Mother Earth Publishing Association, 1910.

————. *Anarchism: What It Really Stands For.* New York: Mother Earth Publishing Association, 1911.

————. *The Psychology of Political Violence.* New York: Mother Earth Publishing Association, 1911.

————. *Syndicalism: The Modern Menace to Capitalism.* New York: Mother Earth Publishing Association, 1913.

————. *Marriage and Love.* 2nd ed. New York: Mother Earth Publishing Association, 1914.

————. *La Tragédie de L'Emancipation Féminine,* trans. E. Armand. St.-Joseph, Orléans, France: La Laborlease [1914].

————. *Philosophy of Atheism and the Failure of Christianity.* New York: Mother Earth Publishing Association, 1916.

————. *Preparedness: The Road to Universal Slaughter.* New York: Mother Earth Publishing Association, 1916.

————. *Trial and Speech of Alexander Berkman and Emma Goldman in the United States District Court, in the City of New York, July, 1917.* New York: Mother Earth Publishing Association, 1917.

————. *The Truth About the Bolsheviki.* New York: Mother Earth Publishing Association, 1918.

————. *A Fragment of the Prison Experiences of Emma Goldman and Alexander Berkman.* New York: Stella Comyn, 1919.

————. *The Crushing of the Russian Revolution.* London: Freedom Press, 1922.

————. *Russia and the British Labour Delegation's Report.* London: British Committee for the Defense of Political Prisoners in Russia, 1925.

————. *Dos Años in Russia.* New York: Aurora, 1923.

————. *War Against War.* The Hague: International Anti-Militarist Bureau, ca. 1925.

————. *Trotsky Protests Too Much.* Glasgow: Anarchist Communist Federation, 1938.

————. *The Place of the Individual in Society.* Chicago: Free Society Forum, undated, ca. 1940.

ARTICLES

Articles by Emma Goldman are to be found in the following publications:
Mother Earth, published from March 1906 through August 1917 (vol. 1 can be
  bought from Greenwood Reprint Corporation, ser. 1, vol. 1, 1906).
Mother Earth Bulletin, published from October 1917 through April 1918.
During the 1930s, many of Emma Goldman's articles appeared in the *CNT-
  AIT-FAI, Spain and the World,* and *Spanish Revolution.*

Abbott, Leonard D. "Emma Goldman, 'Daughter of the Dream.'" *The Road to
  Freedom* VIII, no. 9 (April 1932): 7.
Baldwin, Roger. "A Challenging Rebel Spirit." *New York Herald Tribune Books*
  (October 25, 1931).
Basen, Neil. "Kate Richards O'Hare," forthcoming biography.
"Birth Control and Emma Goldman" *The Masses* (8). May 1916.
Bly, Nellie, "Emma Goldman." *New York World* (September 22, 1893).
Bossin, Hye. "A Rebel Speaks." *Jewish Standard* (June 29, 1934).
Cook, Blanche Weisen. "Female Support Networks and Political Activism:
  Lillian Wald, Crystal Eastman, Emma Goldman." *Chrysalis* 3 (1977): 43–61.
Creel, George. "Free Love." *The Independent* [Kansas City] (November 14, 1908).
"Emma Goldman." *American Magazine* LXIX (March 1910): 605, 608.
"Emma Goldman." *The Nation* CXXXVIII (March 21, 1934): 320.
"Emma Goldman's Defense." *The Masses* (8) (June 16): 27.
"Emma Goldman's Faith." *Current Literature* (February 1911): 176–78.
Frank, Waldo. "Elegy for Anarchism." *The New Republic* LXIX (December 30,
  1931): 193–94.
Goldberg, Harold J. "Goldman and Berkman View of the Bolshevik Regime."
  Slavonic and East European Review 53, no. 131 (1975): 272-76.
Goldman, Emma. "Anarchy." *Labor Leader* XXI (June 5, 1897): 19.
———. "What I Believe." *New York World* (July 19, 1908).
———. "Die Masse." *Der Sozialist* (Berlin) (August 1, 1911).
———. "Bolsheviks Shooting Anarchists." *Freedom* (London) (January 1922).
———. "Russia." *New York World* (March 26 through April 4, 1922).
———. "Persecution of Russian Anarchists." *Freedom* (London) (August 1922).
———. "The Bolshevik Government and the Anarchists." *Freedom* (London)
  (October 1922).
———. "Appeal by Alexander Berkman, Emma Goldman, and others." In
  Letters from Russian Prisons, ed. Roger Baldwin. New York: Albert and
  Charles Boni, 1925.
———. "Russian Trade Unionism." *Westminster Gazette* (England) (April 7,
  1925).

————. "Women of the Russian Revolution." *Time and Tide* (England) I (May 8, 1925): 452.

————. "Johann Most." *American Mercury* VIII (June 1926): 158–66.

————. "Reflections on the General Strike." *Freedom* (London) (August-September 1926).

————. "The Voyage of the *Buford.*" *American Mercury* XXIII (July 1931): 276–86.

————. "The Assassination of McKinley." *American Mercury* XXIV (September 1931): 53–67.

————. "Emma Goldman Defends Her Attack on Henry George." *The Road to Freedom* VIII, no. 3 (November 1931).

————. "America by Comparison." In *Americans Abroad, 1918–1931,* ed. Peter Neagoe. The Hague: Servire Press, 1932.

————. "Most Dangerous Woman in the World Views U.S.A. from Europe," *British Guiana New Day Chronicle* (February 21, 1932).

————. The Observer (pseudonym for Toronto-based journalist and preacher Salem Bland). "Emma Goldman on Hitlerism." *Toronto Daily Star* (January 12, 1934).

————. "The Tragedy of the Political Exiles." *The Nation* CXXXIX (October 10, 1934): 401–02.

————. "Was My Life Worth Living?" *Harper's Monthly Magazine* CLXX (December 1934): 52–58.

————. "There Is No Communism in Russia." *American Mercury* XXXIV (April 1935): 393–401.

————. "Anarchists and Elections." *Vanguard* III (August–September 1936): 19–20.

————. "Berkman's Last Days." *Vanguard* III (August–September 1936): 12–13.

————. "Emma Goldman's First Address to the Spanish Comrades at a Mass-Meeting Attended by Ten-Thousand People." *CNT-AIT-FAI* (September 25, 1936).

————. "Enlarged Text of Emma Goldman's Radio Talk in Barcelona, 23 September 1936." *CNT-AIT-FAI* (September 25, 1936).

————. "Whom the Gods Wish to Destroy They First Strike Mad." *CNT-AIT-FAI* (October 6, 1936).

————. "The Soviet Executions." *Vanguard* III (October–November 1936): 10.

————. "The Soviet Political Machine." *Spain and the World* I (June 4, 1937): 3.

————. "Naive Anarchists" (letter). *New York Times* (July 4, 1937).

————. "Madrid Is the Wonder of the World." *Spain and the World* I (October 13, 1937).

————. "Reports on Spain." *Spanish Revolution* (December 6, 1937).

————. "Preface." In *Pensieri e battaglie,* by Camillo Berneri. Paris: Edito a cura dei Comitato Camillo Berneri, 1938.

————. "On Spain." *Spanish Revolution* (March 21, 1938).

————. "Letters from Prison." In *The Little Review Anthology,* ed. Margaret Anderson. New York: Hermitage Press, 1953.

Griffin, Frederic. "Toronto's Anarchist Guest." Toronto *Star Weekly* (December 31, 1926).

Hansen, Harry. "Once a Dangerous Woman." Brooklyn *Eagle* (October 30, 1931).

Hapgood, Hutchins. "Emma Goldman's Anarchism." *The Bookman* XXXII (February 1911): 639–40.

————. *Review of Anarchism and Other Essays,* by Emma Goldman. In *Bookman* 32, no. 6 (February 1911): 639.

Havel, Hippolyte. Introduction to *Anarchism and Other Essays,* by Emma Goldman. New York: Mother Earth Publishing Association, 1911.

Jensen, Joan M. "The Evolution of Margaret Sanger's 'Family Limitation Pamphlet, 1914–1921," *Signs* 6, no. 3 (Spring 1981): 548–67.

Kern, Robert. *Anarchist Principles and Spanish Reality: Emma Goldman as a Participant in the Civil War.* Journal of Contemporary History II (1976): 2–3.

Kirchwey, Freida. Review of *Living My Life,* by Emma Goldman. *The Labor World* (Paper of Socialist Party), 1908.

————. "Emma Goldman." *The Nation* CXXXIII (December 2, 1931): 612–14.

Mencken, H. L. "Two Views of Russia." *American Mercury* II (May 1924): 122–23.

————. "The United States Sustains a Loss in Berkman and Emma Goldman." *Baltimore Sun,* April 26, 1925 (syndicated column).

Merman, Cynthia. "Rebel in Print." *Harper's Magazine,* October 1975.

Meyer, Ernest L. "Making Light of the Times." *Madison Capital Times* (March 29, 1934).

Pachter, Henry M. "The Private Lives of Rebels." *Harper's Magazine* (August 1975): 83.

Pawel, Ernst. "Alexander Berkman—The Assassin as Saint." *Midstream* 17, no. 5 (1971): 67–72.

Reedy, William Marion. "The Daughter of the Dream." *St. Louis Mirror* (November 5, 1908).

Shulman, Alix Kates. "Dancing in the Revolution." *Socialist Review,* no. 62 (March–April 1982).

Stillman, Clara Guening. "Two Worlds." *Hound and Horn* VI (October–December 1932): 143–57.

Tattler, "Notes from the Capital: Emma Goldman." *The Nation* CIV (June 28, 1917): 766–67.

Tead, Ordway. "Emma Goldman Speaks." *Yale Review* XXI (June 1932): 851–52.

"Uncle Sam's Obstreperous Niece." *Literary Digest* LV (August 18, 1917): 54–57.

Wexler, Alice. "The Early Life of Emma Goldman." *Psychohistory Review* 8, no. 4 (1980): 7–21.

Zinn, Howard. *Emma.* (Script.) Boston: Boston University, 1976.

ACKNOWLEDGMENTS

It has been eight years since I first discovered Emma Goldman's letters to Ben Reitman. In that time, bolstered by the general enthusiasm for Emma Goldman and all she stands for, I have received the intellectual, material, and emotional support of many people whose encouragement and hard work made it possible for me to research and write this book.

I owe special thanks to John Bowen, who first unearthed the letters from the back of the Fret Shop in Hyde Park, Chicago; to Merlin and Ruth Bowen, who fostered my enthusiasm for their son's discovery; and to my friends and advisers at the University of California, Santa Cruz, History of Consciousness Board of Studies, including the late Herbert Marcuse, Robert Alford, Billy Harris, Hayden White, Julianne Burton, Marge Frantz, Eleanor Engstrand, Doug Foster, Madeleine Moore, Richard Gordon, Jens Christiensen, and Brigette Kahnert.

Richard Drinnon, the author of *Rebel in Paradise,* a biography of Emma Goldman, and the editor, with Anna Maria Drinnon, of a collection of Emma Goldman and Alexander Berkman's letters, not only encouraged my work, but also shared his own research materials with me, wrote several grant recommendations, and read early stages of the first part of the book. His books have been a major resource for my bibliographic research. They have established the historical context of Emma Goldman's life and are an invaluable source for future scholars. It was the Drinnons who warned me early on that "When Emma Goldman steps into your life, she really takes over!" Alix Kates Shulman, who has also published two books on Emma Goldman, was equally gracious and supportive of my work. My initial conversations with Alice Wexler, who at the time was planning to write on Emma Goldman's early family life, were helpful as well. Paul Avrich's generosity and well-researched books provided a basic resource for this book and made Emma Goldman's anarchist comrades come alive. Roger Bruns, who is working on a biography of Ben Reitman, never failed to share his keen insights and material, and read through a very long draft of my book.

David Plotke applied his talent and political and historical acuity to the writing of each page of the book.

Sarah Crome not only read and criticized the manuscript, but did a tremendous amount of the archival and bibliographic research as well. My co-worker on the Emma Goldman Papers Project, she also served as my primary assistant in the writing of this book.

Conversations with Richard Lichtman, Deirdre English, Eli Zaretsky, Bruce Dancis, Lorraine Kahn, and Eli Katz helped me in the early stages of research and writing. Camaraderie and constructive criticism from Barbara Epstein, Harriet Skibbins, Kristine Pfleiderer, and Robert Meyer helped me enormously in preparing the final draft; their reading of the original fifteen-hundred-page manuscript was a great act of friendship. Consultations with Temma Kaplan on the Spanish Civil War and with Harry Chotiner on the Russian revolution were critical to the historical integrity of the book.

The National Historical Publications and Records Commission of the National Archives hired me midway through the writing of the book to collect, edit, and publish a complete collection of Emma Goldman's papers in microfilm and a selected papers book edition. The opportunity to support myself and my family on a closely related project, while working on the book, was an unexpected gift. The staff of the NHPRC, including Roger Bruns, in their work on the Emma Goldman Papers Project have been enormously helpful to the research for my book; Mary Giunta, Sara Jackson, Anne Harris-Henry, and their archival assistants found government surveillance documents from the National Archives and correspondence from the Library of Congress, which added an important dimension to my understanding of Emma Goldman's public life.

Mary Ann Bamberger and her assistant, Terry Littmann, of the University of Illinois at Chicago Archive and Manuscript Library, have been generous with their time and supportive of my work in supplying me with reprints of the Goldman-Reitman correspondence. Thea Duijker and Rudolf de Jong of the International Institute for Social History in Amsterdam, which houses perhaps the largest collection of Emma Goldman's letters, offered their kind services and genuine enthusiasm about my book. Patricia King of the Schlesinger Library at Radcliffe College generously provided me with a full array of letters from the Malmed Collection. Edward Weber of the Labadie Collection, based at the University of Michigan, offered special assistance as well. The staffs of the State Historical Society of Wisconsin, the New York Public Library Manuscript and Archive Collections, the Yale University Archives, YIVO, Boston University Archives, and many other smaller collections referred to in the source notes, cooperated in making their material available.

Among the people who knew Emma Goldman whom I was fortunate enough to interview, I am indebted to Arthur Bortolotti, the late Mollie Steimer and Senya Fleshine, the late Roger Baldwin, Meridel Le Sueur, Dan and Bertha Malmed, Ahrne Thorne, Johanna Boetz, and Ian Ballantine, Emma Goldman's grandnephew, who generously gave me permission to publish her letters.

I did my writing in an office for over five years in the company of an extraordinarily supportive and creative community of independent documentary filmmakers. Shirley Kessler's compassion and respect for the creative process gave me the courage to believe in the book. Vivian Kleiman's daring and persistence nurtured me, as did my contact with Bill Jersey, Howard Dratch, Gene Rosow, Veronica Selver, Richard Bermack, Jane Scantlebury, Deborah Hoffmann, Alice Erber, Marilyn Mulford, Barry Spinello, Charles West, and my other filmmaker friends, Lorraine Kahn and Connie Field, who did some photo-archival research for the book, as well. While working in Chicago, I had the support of Ken and Julie Dunn, David Moberg, Jo Patton, and the members of the Blackstone house. At the University of California, Berkeley, the Institute for the Study of Social Change, an organized research unit that houses the Emma Goldman Papers Project, offered a stimulating academic setting, the support and encouragement of Arlie Hochschild, and the presence of a fellow writer, Herb Mills. Even my mailman, Bill Trampleasure, has added his daily encouragement.

Initial help with the organization and layout of photographs was provided by Lorraine Kahn. Some preliminary photographic research from the International Institute for Social History was provided by David Schickele. Newspaper research was done primarily by Sarah Crome, Nancy MacKay, and Bruce Boylen. The bibliography and footnotes were refined and organized by Caroline Pincus, with the help of Jonel Larson, Frances Christie, Nancy MacKay, and Pearl Raz. Last minute fact-finding and checking was done with unusual gusto by Howard Besser, Khojesta Beverleigh, Sarah Crome, and Caroline Pincus.

My dear friend, Joanne Sterricker, worked tirelessly on the typing and word processing of the many versions of the manuscript. Others whose word processing skills were critical were Brian Kane, Lavinia Meadows, Carol Straus, Margo Meierbachtel, Pam Blair, and Rupali Bose.

Carol Nusinow's deep understanding of young children, and of their parents, made my work on the book possible. Others who provided significant childcare for my daughter, Mara, were Leslie De Neveu, Anat Meyers, Pearl Raz, Ann Pusina, and Duff Munson.

The emotional support, encouragement, and intuitive talents of Susan Posner carried me through my worst anxieties in the writing of the book. Thelma Elkin's sense of irony and conviction eased the burdens of balancing my home and work life. Marion Rosen, Eileen Poole, Wing-Tong Ho, Jennifer and Hanmin Liu, Sadja Greenwood, Natasha Heifetz, Tom Condon, W. Joe Weick, Linda Robrecht, Henry Wong, and Cathe Sierra were vital to my physical well-being. The friendship of Susan Wengraf, Tina Jencks, Alan Bern, Erica Rosenfeld and Jim Wilson, Janet Kranzberg, and Deborah Hirtz-Waterman smoothed the day-to-day ups and downs of writing and being a parent.

Material support from the Woodrow Wilson Women's Studies Foundation, the Mabel MacLeod Lewis Foundation, the Memorial Foundation for Jewish Culture, the Hebrew Free Loan Society, the History of Consciousness Board of Studies Patent Award and Graduate Studies Grant, Glenda and Stewart Pawsey, Jack and Louise Manley, Sam Blight and Norma Manley, Linda and Byron Harris, and Peter Rose made it possible for me to work on the book when financial pressures became intense. Peter Franck provided legal counsel.

My editor at Holt, Rinehart and Winston, Jennifer Josephy, bore with my many unrealistic completion dates and wildly inaccurate book-length projections, and contributed countless hours to the editing of the original fifteen-hundred-page manuscript. For her talent and judgment and empathy with the issues of the book, I am grateful. Anne Borchardt, my agent, cheered me on, acted on my behalf, and tolerated my naïveté in the ways of book publishing with intelligence and understanding.

My mother and father, Mildred and Nathaniel Falk, and my maternal grandparents, who raised me, Teme and Hyman Rosen, never lived to read this book, but, no doubt, they contributed to my ability to empathize with the pain and joys of Emma Goldman's life. My aunts and uncles, cousins, and family friends, and my sister's enthusiasm and curiosity about my work have given me an important sense of family continuity, and I thank them: Lydia and George Aronowitz, Irma and Julius Sherman, Steven Aronowitz, Merrill and Andrew Stone, Valerie, Amy, James, and Cornelia Sherman, Suzie Moody, Faye and Terry Levy, Sadie Falk, Judith and Neil Bergman, Linda and Matthew Creager, Paul and Sandra Gruskoff, Donald and Shelly Gruskoff, and Jane Falk.

My husband, Lowel Finley, worked tirelessly with me on the initial and final stages of writing, listened to endless details and interpretations of Emma Goldman's life, traveled with me and did archival research in Amsterdam, tolerated going deeply in debt in order for me to finish the book, and lovingly endured being blamed for Ben Reitman's transgressions as I chronicled them each day. The continuity of our bond with each other fortifies me still, and I thank him for it with all my heart.

My daughter, Mara Falk-Finley, shared the first years of her life with the mythical presence of Emma Goldman, even came to see her as a fixture in our family constellation. Mara's very immediate life energy kept me from losing myself in the past, and grounded me in the daily issues of human development, so inextricably tied to love.

I extend my general appreciation to all those who worked on the book formally and informally and to those whose belief in the value of the continuity between personal and political commitment gave me the certainty that the time had come for the story of Emma Goldman's inner life to be told.

— CANDACE FALK
Berkeley, California
August 1983

INDEX